HORROR MOVIE A DAY: THE BOOK

by Brian W. Collins

Edited by
Jace Anderson
Meredith Borders
Kolleen Carney

Foreword by
Todd Farmer

©2016 Fright Club Publishing. All Rights Reserved.

TABLE OF CONTENTS

Special Thanks	5
Foreword by Todd Farmer	7
Introduction by the Asshole	11
Entry Guide	15
Genre Glossary	17
Why Did You Buy This Book?	19
P.S.	23
JANUARY (Asian Horror)	25
FEBRUARY (Slasher Movies)	75
MARCH (Killer Kids!)	117
APRIL ("Quiet" Horror)	159
MAY (Batshit Crazy Horror)	201
JUNE (Monsters & "Monsters")	251
JULY (Indie Horror)	293
AUGUST ("Junk Food" Horror)	347
SEPTEMBER (Vampire Movies)	395
OCTOBER ("Alt" Horror)	441
NOVEMBER (Zombies & Cannibals)	487
DECEMBER (Horror Around The World)	537
The End	585
Index	587

SPECIAL THANKS

Horror Movie A Day would be a pretty threadbare site if not for the inadvertent contributions of Blockbuster Video (both the store and online rental service), Netflix, The New Beverly Cinema, Moviepass, Shriekfest, Fantastic Fest, Frightfest UK, and Hollywood itself. Anchor Bay, Image Entertainment, and Scream/Shout Factory also deserve props for being the only companies to regularly supply me with review copies without my having to beg. Personal friends Mike Williamson (backyard screening king), Rob Galluzzo and his giant DVD collection, and especially Phil Blankenship and Jacqueline Greed and their seemingly infinite number of screeners (and screenings!) also played a huge role in keeping me with stuff to watch every day.

I'd also like to thank Devin Faraci for asking me to join the Birth.Movies.Death. (which was then Badass Digest) team as "Horror Movie A Day's Brian Collins", validating the site more than I ever could on my own. I couldn't be more honored to be part of the writing crew there, or more grateful to have Meredith Borders as my editor for the weekly Collins' Crypt articles. She also edited this very book, along with Kolleen Carney and Jace Anderson, because clearly my grammar abilities are too ungood for just 1 people.

Likewise, thanks to Brad Miska (aka "Mr. Disgusting") for giving me my first regular writing gig at Bloody-Disgusting, and Rachel Belofsky of Screamfest LA for being the first to acknowledge HMAD as a real site when it came time for press-y type stuff. For the first year I lived in LA I didn't have a lot of friends or a social life to speak of, but volunteering at Screamfest in 2006 (and attending every year since as press) changed all that for the better.

HUGE thanks to JB Sapienza for not only designing the cover, but also roping in several of the other artists who contributed those terrific images you see at the top of each chapter (and he did one of those, too). Props again to those artists: Nathan Chesshir, Eric Shonborn, Patt Kelley, Joe Badon, Cole Rothacker, Sean Kasper, Daniel XIII, and Jeff O'Brien, with additional recognition to longtime HMAD artist Jacopo Tenani who has done terrific artwork for HMAD over the years – I wouldn't have done images at all if he couldn't be involved.

Additional thanks to BJ Colangelo, Alex DiVincenzo, Siddhant Adlakha, James McCormick, C. Puffer, and Kolleen Carney for assisting with the boring data compiling (director names, distributors, review dates, etc.) that allowed me to focus on the actual writing.

Obviously I couldn't neglect to thank my mom, who took me to see *Poltergeist II* when I was six, rented *The Texas Chain Saw Massacre* for me when I was seven, and (most fortuitously) vetoed my pick of *The Great Outdoors* and instead rented *Halloween 4* when I was nine, introducing me to my beloved Michael Myers. I'm not saying I wouldn't have discovered my love of horror movies eventually – but I have her and her alone to thank for my terrific head start.

And finally I'd like to thank my wife Theresa for putting up with this crap for over half of her married life, watching a lot of terrible movies with me (a witness!) and never once complaining that I'd take over the TV to watch a movie I didn't even want to see in the first place. A saint, she is. Though I think she's still mad at me for the time she wanted to watch something festive on Christmas Eve and I put on *Inside*. It didn't go well.

FOREWORD
by Todd Farmer

My name is Todd Farmer. I went from being that one guy sitting around the campfire in Kentucky telling ghost stories, to being one of the many sitting around Hollywood writing screenplays. Although I had some raw talent (and by 'raw' I mean unpolished, unstructured and ungood at spelling), I was extremely lucky to find myself working as a writer within a month of my 1996 arrival. I started out in horror working for Sean S. Cunningham, the director of the first *Friday the 13th*. Back then, most writers started in horror; low budgets, low pay, low risk. Horror was a stepping stone. A rite of passage. And while there wasn't the competition you find today, it was still tough to get your foot in the door because only a few places (like New Line and Dimension) were unafraid to make horror. You see, back then "horror" embarrassed most executives. Most producers were "above" it. Then *Scream* came out and shoved 100 million up Hollywood's keister. Before you knew it, every studio and production arm had a "genre" branch. "Genre", because the word "horror" still embarrassed. As a result of this newfound financial interest in horror, I found myself with pretty steady work. Craven, Carpenter, Raimi — I have even been lucky enough to work with horror royalty! Yeah. Horror has been good to me and with the exception of one challenging year, I have paid my bills as a writer since 1996. I accomplished this with some talent, knowing the right people, a whole lot of luck, a reliable computer, a love of life experience (both good and bad), and since 2007, Brian Collins.

I met Brian in January of 2009 when he hosted a Q&A for the release of *My Bloody Valentine 3D* (a movie he only supported to get an uncut release of the original). But I'd been aware of him because he had been watching a horror movie a day for nearly two years. In fact, according to a link I found in an old outline, my first run-in with his website was likely August of '07. A meeting had been set with producers who wanted to remake *Stigmata*. So, while I waited for the Netflix DVD to arrive I ran across Brian's review. Not only did it refresh my movie memory, it made me laugh. Brian referenced *Starship Troopers* without being so boring as to actually mention *Starship Troopers*. He referred to a sequence in the movie as a music video edited on a broken Avid. He referred to actor Rade Šerbedžija as "the archenemy of spellcheck". More importantly, he gave me his opinion of pros and cons in a uniquely entertaining way. In a completely outside-the-box-thinking kind of way.

In 2003 I wrote a screenplay for Revolution Studios called *Scarecrow*. After eleven writers, two directors (one being future friend and partner, Patrick Lussier) and a studio shift, the movie was released in February of 2007 as *The Messengers*. A month later I was contacted by Ghost House Pictures. One of the execs there had read my original draft and thought it might make a great prequel. One script enters, two movies leave. Since the original concept was, in fact, a scarecrow movie and since Raimi actually loved scarecrows, by the end of the year I was reading every review Brian had written that contained a scarecrow. Because as Brian wrote in one such review "Like just about every other killer scarecrow movie, it's just fucking stupid." In the end, that movie wasn't perfect, but I think we were able to avoid stupid.

Around the same time, I was pursuing the *Bedlam* remake at RKO pictures. So once again, I checked out Brian's site. And sure enough, of those 900 or so current reviews, the 1946 *Bedlam* was one of them. In fact, he even commented on how ripe it was for a remake. I don't think I realized it at the time but Brian's site had become a real resource for me. I wasn't just going there for work; it had become a part of my morning routine. Of course, he wasn't perfect. For instance, he didn't bother to review 1981's *My Bloody Valentine* until we were in preproduction on the remake. And it isn't like we always agreed. In fact, we rarely do. I mean, I get that *Jason X* has its flaws but ranking it behind *Jason Takes Manhattan*? Dipshit.

After *MBV3D's* success, Lussier and I were suddenly bombarded with remake and reboot options and would be for years to come. *The Funhouse, The Fly, The Exorcist, Halloween, The Tingler, Scanners, I Saw What You Did and I Know Who You Are, Prince of Darkness, Fright Night...* and that's just a fraction off the top of my head of the movies Lussier and I either pitched or in some cases wrote. I visited Brian's site for each one and rarely was I unable to find the review. That said, the greatest gift he gave me was his willingness to point out flaws in movies that had reached a do-no-wrong cult status. Because, like it or not, the original *Fright Night* has some flaws. When you are pitching a remake or a reboot, it's not a bad idea to be aware of said flaws. Sometimes, I was already aware, but most of the time his outside-the-box thinking would open my eyes to something I had not seen. For instance, he asked me once, since we had introduced Jason Voorhees' regenerative power in *Jason X*, then why wasn't the regenerative technology used in the future a result of the testing done on Jason in the past? I recall sitting there in a daze. I mean, what a great idea. So... obvious. Yet, I hadn't thought of it. And no one else in over ten years had either. Later, he commented that *Drive Angry*'s trailer made it sound like Cage's escape from hell was the plot, as opposed to a twist. That was the problem exactly. But I'd never thought of it that way. In the end, I just like the way the kid thinks.

When Brian sent me *Horror Movie A Day: The Book*, I honestly didn't think I'd read the whole thing. I would read his opening comments. Browse the middle. Read the close. Then write the foreword. I mean, I'd already read most of his reviews... even the ones he's added since March of 2013. But that's where his outside-the-box thinking comes into play again. He didn't just regurgitate old reviews. He added this brilliant little section called "Reflection", where he... reflects on, adds to, and even argues with his former review. I ended up reading the whole stinking book and I realized what really drew me to the reviews all those years ago. It wasn't the research. It's wasn't the size of the library. It wasn't the horror knowledge that I could steal and then sell to an executive as my own.

It was the writing.

It was always the writing. Always strong. Always witty. Always outside the box. But as Stephen King said, "There's no shortcut to getting better at writing other than writing every. single. day." Brian did that. For over 2,000 days in a row. And continues to do so. And it shows. This isn't just a book with a collection of movie opinions. This is a book written by a gifted writer.

A gifted writer who moronically thinks *Jason Takes Manhattan* is better than *Jason X*. Dipshit.

INTRODUCTION BY THE ASSHOLE

Welcome! Thank you for purchasing this book, or at least downloading it illegally (on one hand I'd like to say it's the thought that counts, but on the other... you're still a thieving piece of shit). If this has made it into your hands, you likely fall into one of three categories:

1. You are my mother. Hi, mom! No, I still haven't watched *The Blacklist*.
2. You are one of my friends that I guilted into buying a copy, and you won't get much further than this intro. That's OK. I probably haven't listened to your podcast past the first episode, so it evens out.
3. You're a horror fan that is looking for something new to watch. With all due respect to my friends and mother, you're the target audience for this book, so thanks again for being here.

But maybe you don't know who I am or what Horror Movie A Day (frequently abbreviated to HMAD in the pages ahead) is/was, so let me quickly sum up (as quickly as I sum up anything – longtime readers can attest that my idea of short is often dangerously close to their idea of "way too goddamn long"):

Let's get me out of the way. I'm a lifelong horror fan who has had the pleasure of being able to channel that love and admiration into something of a profession. I have a regular boring day job that pays my bills, but my true joy comes from writing for several online outlets (including Birth.Movies.Death., obviously) and getting to moderate Q&As, host screenings, join panels, etc. I've even been on TV a few times for it, which is surreal to me. Somewhere along the line I went from a kid begging his mom to drive him to see *In The Mouth of Madness* to standing in front of a room full of people, hosting a screening of the same movie and talking to its producer. That's cool, and it's something I still get giddy about and never take for granted.

More personally, I'm a dad/husband who enjoys video games (RPGs and open world/sandbox types for the most part), Chevy Chase movies, and the sort of foods that singlehandedly exceed the recommended daily allowance of calories. I also have a tendency to fall asleep almost at random; it's not quite narcolepsy but it's close, and it seems to particularly affect me during movies (even when I'm loving them), so you'll see a lot of references to me falling asleep or dozing off in the pages ahead. I fell asleep a few times writing this book, in fact.

Ah yes, the book. The creatively titled Horror Movie A Day: The Book. What is Horror Movie A Day, (I hope most of) you (don't have to) ask (but I'll answer for the maybe one guy that doesn't know)?

In February of 2007 I noticed that I had the same three unwatched disc rentals from Netflix for the past four months or so, which at 15 bucks a month for the subscription (this was before Instant) meant I could have just bought those three movies for less money. This seemed ridiculous to me, and I got to thinking about my day and how much time of it I was wasting online or merely staring off into space. I had also recently begun writing for Bloody-Disgusting.com, and was trying to think of what I could bring to the table beyond a few lists and reviews.

One or two trains of thought later, I got the idea – I would watch a horror movie every single day. I figured 8 hours of sleep and 8 hours of work left 8 hours of the day to do SOMETHING, and thus there was no reason I couldn't fit in a 90-minute movie during that time. And so, on February 7, 2007, I popped one of those disc rentals – 1987's *Return to Horror High* – into my DVD player, and never looked back. At first I was just watching the movies, but eventually I realized that writing at least a few thoughts down on each one would keep me on track, and also make it more fun. I figured I'd do it for a year, tops.

You see, I've always loved talking about horror movies with folks. I'd go to a convention, or on a message board, and spend hours debating nonsense like the continuity in the *Friday the 13th* series or unanswered questions from *Halloween 6*. And with blogging all the rage at this time, I thought updating a daily blog with a few thoughts on the movie I watched that day would be a fun way to open up a dialogue on the more obscure films I was seeing – maybe my close circle of genre pals wouldn't have seen these oddities, but posting something online would almost certainly attract attention from one of its fans. I pitched the idea to my boss at Bloody D, but it was turned down as a site feature for reasons I never understood, so I used all of my web design knowledge (read: none whatsoever) and launched HorrorMovieADay.com on my own, sometime in March of 2007.

Well a year came and went, and not only was I still having a lot of fun with the site (and improving as a writer), but there were still a lot of movies I hadn't seen, so I figured I'd just keep going until I got sick of it or I could no longer remember anything about the movies I had watched when I started. By now it was so ingrained into my daily routine that it actually seemed as unlikely to miss another as it did that I'd forget to go to work one day. And while I was certainly getting fatigued toward the end, I never really DID get sick of doing it – I just realized that as I got older (slower?) and other opportunities presented themselves, I would have to cut this anchor. Barring a lottery win that would allow me to quit my day job, I knew I'd never have time for other things I wanted to do as long as I had to dedicate 3+ hours of my day to watching/writing up horror movies, especially after I DID run out of ones I wanted to see and was spending more and more time with nonsense no one besides me was watching anyway. If the site was originally created to talk horror movies, and I was watching horror movies no one else had seen, then what was the point? Also, my day job used to be less intensive, but two rounds of layoffs (one in 2010, another in 2012) resulted in my absorbing more duties – which made me want to relax when I went home, not suffer through another bad found footage movie and write about it.

Thus, on March 31st, 2013, I fulfilled the promise I made to myself over five years earlier. I popped a DVD of *Return to Horror High* into my player, having no strong memories of my first viewing, sat down and watched it... and then I called it a day. I didn't stop just like that, of course – I had announced the site's looming "demise" over a year in advance, having decided on 2,500 movies to be the end point. As fans of the site can attest I always enjoyed playing April Fools' pranks (one year I claimed that the site actually had six writers working under one name – it was almost too successful a joke as some people got really angry I wasn't giving credit to the others!), and so the timing was a bit ironic as it seemed almost like a too-perfect (and long) setup for the best prank yet. But no – April 1st, 2013, was the first day in over six years (SIX YEARS!) that I didn't sit down to watch a horror movie. It was beautiful. I took the day off of work, slept a bit later, wasted an inordinate amount of time online, and (at around 2:00 in the afternoon) finally cracked open my copy of *Mass Effect 2,* which I had bought not long after its release but could never give the attention I understood it deserved.

It took some adjusting – much like when you start wearing contacts but keep habitually trying to push up your glasses, I had this constant nagging feeling that I was missing or forgetting something. I even momentarily panicked one day when I got home late from work and saw that there were only a few minutes left in the day to watch something. But it eventually wore off, and after some time "away" (I still updated the site a couple of times a week with the films I would see theatrically, or for discs I was sent for review), I finally got cracking on this book you hold in your hands at this second.

I had some surprising reactions to the site's end – I was interviewed by Matt Singer of Indiewire, got to be on the *Harmontown* podcast, and my wife even organized a "wake" complete with cake and "HMAD 2007-2013" shirts and the like. Some folks even wrote eulogies – BMD's Devin actually made me choke up with his! But the existence of this book is the real reward for doing it for as long as I did. It's something tangible, something organized.... and (thankfully) it's something that can be useful to horror fans without having to wade through all the generic tripe that I watched.

I watched 2,500 horror movies so you wouldn't have to... these are 365 of the films you should.

BC, 2015

ENTRY GUIDE

Title, director, etc. – basic info so you can find the movie. Horror titles tend to get reused a lot (there are something like 20 movies named *Uninvited*), even two or three times in a single year, so this should ensure you're renting/buying the right one if you've put that trust in me. Also, the most current studio to put the disc out is included – these may (almost certainly WILL) change over time, due to the films (particularly independently produced ones) changing hands. Not much I can do about that, but it should at least give you a place to start if you're having a hard time finding a particular film.

"Synopsis Based on Fading Memory" – I saw the vast majority of these movies without knowing much, if anything, about them, and I'd like to offer you the same experience as much as possible. But I know some folks just downright hate certain plot devices or sub-genres, so I've given you a bit of context, to keep you from wasting time with a movie you'll know you'll hate. But my memory is poor, so in some cases they're about as detailed as the *TV Guide* description.

Review excerpt – A quick bit of the original review, albeit with some minor alterations to improve bad grammar or remove references to other parts of the review that were not included in the excerpt. I'd never reprint the reviews in full, as chances are a number of you have already read them (and it'd take up a lot of space, adding hundreds of pages to the book for no reason), but it's fun to go back and read a bit of my thoughts at the time, and many of them tie into...

Reflection – the meat of this book, and what you paid for! They differ from movie to movie; some of these are sort of like sequels to the original review, as sometimes my thoughts have changed (at least two movies in this book got negative reviews at the time, now I'm telling you to watch them!). Others just use the movie as a jumping off point for a larger point I want to make or something I want to rant about. And then other times I just talk about myself, like an asshole. I've tried to mix it up, because even if you're jumping around, 365 entries that boil down to nothing more than "You should watch this movie because..." would get just as boring to write as it would be to read.

GENRE GLOSSARY

Most of my sub-genre tags are self-explanatory, but some are not or might not mean to me what they do to you, so here's a quick glossary.

Alien: A movie where the threat is alien in nature. *Attack the Block* is a good example. *Species* is not. Sil was a lab creation, not an alien.

Blank From Hell: A sort of horror/thriller blend where the antagonist is primarily characterized by their occupation. They were real big in the 90s (*Hand That Rocks The Cradle, Unlawful Entry*, etc.), but not so much anymore.

Breakdown: A movie that wouldn't happen if the car didn't break down. Cars break down in a LOT of horror movies, but a lot of them occur at inopportune moments during situations that had nothing to do with a faulty automobile (i.e. Ginny's car in *Friday the 13th Part 2*). These are the movies where the car/van/bus breaking down is what puts them into danger in the first place.

Cannibal: Movies featuring cannibalism as a primary story element.

Comedic: Horror movies with a hefty dose of humor, or flat out comedies that require an appreciation of horror to work (i.e. the *Scary Movie* films). Satire, such as *Dawn of the Dead*, does not count – this is something where you are actively laughing (or at least, should be) for most of the runtime.

Cult: Not a "cult horror movie", like *Rocky Horror* or whatever – these are movies about actual cults.

Ghost: Movies with paranormal entities that have a significant presence. *Witchboard*, for example, is NOT a ghost movie even though it's about a dead kid, because you never see him as a specter. Also different than...

Haunted House: Movies where the presence is tied to a specific location, i.e. if the characters leave they'll be OK.

Hero Killer: These are movies where the person killing everyone is also kind of the hero. I don't mean when you start rooting for Jason Voorhees – I mean films like *The Devil's Rejects* where you want the trio of murderers to come out of the movie victorious in some way.

Horror?: These movies were labeled as horror by IMDb or even their own filmmakers, but didn't really fit in my opinion. The line between horror and thriller is often blurred, but in these cases I'd usually prefer to call them "weird dramas" or something.

Killer Kid: A movie where the villain (or villains) is 18 or under (preferably way under).

Mad Scientist: A movie where there might be a monster of some sort, but the scientist who created it is just as much (or even more) of a villain.

Mockumentary: Basically, found footage. Some horror movies do take on the form of a legitimate documentary, like *The Last Broadcast*, but most are just *Blair Witch/Paranormal Activity* rip-offs. I just never bothered making a distinction with my tagging.

Mutant: Movies where the villain is basically human, but for whatever reason is really messed up (toxic waste, birth defect, etc.).

Monster: A movie with a giant (usually created) monster. Not to be confused with...

Predator: These are movies where the "monster" is actually a regular animal. Perhaps it's a bit larger than average (like *Jaws*), but it's not a lab experiment or something like *Deep Blue Sea* (which would be a monster movie).

Possession: Movies where a good person gets turned into a bad person due to supernatural powers, a ghost, witchcraft, etc. The key idea is that these people can be cured and return to normal.

Post-Apocalyptic: Movies where the world (or at least, the part of it that the film concerns) has gone to shit and civilization is no longer possible. To use the Romero *Dead* series as a guide, I'd put *Day of the Dead* as the first fully post-apocalyptic entry; the apocalypse was just beginning to encroach in *Night* and in *Dawn*, and they still had TV broadcasts and such.

Psychological: Movies where the horror is all in someone's mind, or is springing forth from it. OR movies where they're really messing with your head.

Revenge: Movies where the villain is a bit more sympathetic and has a legitimate reason to want to kill/harm the individuals he/she kills or harms during the movie.

Serial Killer: Movies about a reality based serial killer (meaning: not Jason Voorhees or Freddy Krueger). Your Hannibal Lecters and the like, or true story ones.

Slasher: Movies that are AWESOME. No, OK – movies that involve a killer (usually masked) offing a group of friends, preferably in one location (a school, the woods, etc.).

Supernatural: All-purpose tag for films involving demons, witches, strange presences (not ghosts), voodoo, etc.

Survival: Movies where the protagonists are subjected to extreme distress and/or have to battle the elements along with whatever killer or monster is after them. Being trapped is a common occurrence.

Technology: Movies where the villain is a robot or a computer or a video game, etc.

Teen: A movie specifically targeted at teens, usually PG-13 and focused more on typical adolescent problems (dating, school, etc.) than the horror elements. A movie where an adult viewer kind of has to accept that they're not the target audience, but if it's in this book that means they should still find enough to enjoy.

Thriller: Movies that are more grounded in reality, less jump-scare driven, and would probably be OK to show your grandmother. Racking up a body count or breaking records for fake blood used isn't important – getting you on the proverbial edge of your seat is.

Weird: Movies that are bizarre, feature wonky dialogue or characters that act like aliens impersonating humans... that sort of thing. These aren't movies that would have played on 3000 screens.

Vampire/Werewolf/Zombie: OK, I don't REALLY need to explain them all.

WHY DID I WRITE THIS BOOK?
(AND FURTHERMORE, WHY DID YOU BUY IT?)

As of this writing, HMAD hasn't been regularly updated for almost three years, yet the site still gets a healthy number of readers per day. I assumed it was just robots and my own clicking (I often have to re-read my own review to remember anything about certain movies), but there are still comments and Twitter replies and the like to prove that human beings still head there almost as often as they did when the site was running strong. It took me a while to figure out why that was, and I finally deciphered it a few months ago – the site is like a mini encyclopedia of lesser known horror. As the main rule for the site was to watch a NEW movie (or one I had seen years ago and completely forgotten about) every day, as opposed to whatever *Halloween* or *Nightmare on Elm Street* sequel I felt like watching, the site proved to be a fine resource for folks to find a couple of gems that they had missed, or newer independent films that stuck out from the others for one reason or another. Just because there aren't as many new updates doesn't mean the site has no value – there are six years' worth of entries to wade through! A review from February of 2007 is of no less value than one from February of this year (though the writing will be a lot worse).

In other words, you bastards were letting me do all of the work, sifting through dozens of awful movies to find that one good one that I could recommend you add to your Netflix queue. Well now it's time for payback! I just made you fork over a couple of bucks for a digest of that process! Suckers!

In all seriousness, folks had been asking for a book almost as soon as the site began. Many even suggested simply arranging a years' worth of reviews and releasing it as is – but I knew I couldn't do that in good conscience. While I encouraged donations to help pay for Netflix and Blockbuster and such, I never seriously considered locking the site behind a paywall or adding obtrusive ads – I even turned down the latter on more than one occasion. Sure, it probably didn't help my finances any, but I liked doing the site and liked that people enjoyed its simplicity, and the same mentality carried over to the book. Even if it was curated and organized, there was no way I could ever charge you all for something you already read for free.

But I DID want to do some sort of compilation book, and after the site wrapped up its daily run, I started brainstorming ideas. The 100 best (or worst) movies I saw were obvious ideas, but they seemed a bit dull to me, and I wanted to emphasize the "A DAY" part of something that would almost certainly be called "Horror Movie A Day: The Book". And then it hit me – I could give you guys 365 titles, grouped by themes for each of the 12 months, providing a great place to start if you, like me when I started, hadn't really begun to dig deep and watch the indie/ DTV/ foreign/ forgotten stuff that gets overlooked in favor of the traditional "Fifty Horror Movies You Have To See!" selections like *The Exorcist* and *Halloween*. You've seen those. Now see more.

That said, I should get something out of the way right now – these are not the "best" or most perfect movies. I was mixed on several, in fact. But think about it – if they were all amazing you probably would have seen them by now, because they'd have been championed by everyone writing about horror and thus become the sort of ever-present movies I'm avoiding here. There's been a plague infecting the online world for the past couple years, where movies are categorized as either "AMAZING!" or "GARBAGE!". The in-between titles, the ones that commit the sin of being "pretty good", seem to be forgotten. I still recall having a few minor complaints about a much loved (read: good but slightly glorified in my eyes) movie and being accused of "hating" it a few days later. It's one thing to nitpick about a continuity error or something just to be negative, but if an otherwise solid film has a gaping plot hole or a weak performance, why not point it out? To me, it makes those other nice things you say all the more trustworthy. When someone walks out of a movie and says it's their new favorite film, I will not put much stock in what they have to say about it. If someone walks out of that same movie and says that it had a few noticeable flaws but ultimately was a must-see, I'll be much more excited. Few movies are flawless – even my favorite movies aren't (why doesn't Dr. Loomis notice Michael Myers' car across the damn street until he's been there for hours?), and there's nothing wrong with letting your reader know that you aren't blind to its blemishes.

So a lot of these are what I call "B+ movies". The term "B-movie" is kind of a dismissive one, suggesting bad acting, cheap FX, etc. A B+ movie is something in between those titles and the *Exorcists/ Rosemary's Babies/ Halloweens/ Shinings* of the world, where it might miss the mark to become a bona fide classic that every horror fan worth his or her salt has already seen, but is certainly a step or two (or ten) above the forgettable junk that clogs the virtual shelves of the horror section in today's rental outlets.

Ideally, all of the movies would be available on Netflix Instant or something similar, i.e. just sitting there waiting to be watched on a service you already pay for, but alas, that would be pointless – those titles come and go all of the time due to rights and clearance issues. I really wanted to make a game out of the book, challenging you to watch all of these movies in a year, but that would just be impossible unless you had a surplus of disposable income. See, when I was doing the site, the most common question I got was "Are you really watching a movie every day?" and the answer, I swear on my father's grave, is YES. I didn't always FINISH them on the day, but every single day, for 6+ years (minus one day, less than two weeks after I began), at some point between 12:01 am and 11:59 pm, I would sit down with a new horror movie and begin to watch. Family vacations, Comic-Con, even the occasional romantic getaway with my wife, all had to be partially interrupted to watch whatever killer scarecrow or found footage movie I happened to bring along with me. I did this for six goddamn years, and I really wanted to see if anyone out there could do it for one, boosted with the knowledge that unlike me, you'd never be stuck watching anything truly worthless or forgettable.

Once I came to my senses I more or less removed the challenge aspect of the book (I mean, you're welcome to try, but I'm not expecting anyone to actually do it), but I want to keep the theme of daily viewing alive. So instead, I want you to think of the book as a way not to have to rely on asking the internet when you're in the mood to watch a horror movie you've never seen or even heard of before. Rather than tweet "What should I watch?" to me or one of my colleagues (Scott Weinberg gets these requests a lot), just grab the book and flip to that day! That's my answer! If you've seen it already, just move on to the next day, and the next, until you find one you haven't seen yet that is readily available. I mean, if you've already seen *every* movie in this book... you should have had your own Horror Movie A Day site.

This brings me to my next point – the reason I can almost GUARANTEE you haven't seen every movie in this book is that I mostly left out big hits and well-known titles. I assume you, dear reader, are more than a casual horror fan, and I don't want to insult you by suggesting you check out something like *Re-Animator*. You've all seen the horror hero franchises of the '70s and '80s (Leatherface, Jason, Michael Myers, etc.), and you've seen all the major titles from the past decade, possibly in theaters. The Universal and Hammer monster franchises I also skipped; even if the younger fans probably haven't seen them all yet, singling one or two out would be tough. But I'm not a monster, so I've peppered the book with semi-popular films that you'll probably recognize. Foreign titles that made a bigger than usual splash in the US, indie gems that probably made a bunch of top 10 lists on the horror sites... there are even some movies that were wide releases and maybe even made a decent amount of money, but are fading from memory in my eyes and thus included. In short - if you are completely new to the genre, this might not be the book for you (I recommend Alan Jones' *The Rough Guide to Horror Movies* for newcomers), but if you flip around a bit there will be a few familiar titles to make you feel at home.

There are also some bad movies in there. Twelve of them, in fact: one per month. Horror fans know perfectly well that if there's a pile of 100 random horror movies, 2/3s of them (at least) are probably going to be lousy. Scary movies, on average, are cheaper to make than any other genre, and there's rarely any serious need for big stars to appear in them. In short, it's "easy" to make one, which means the genre is flooded with more soulless cash-ins and knockoffs than all other genres put together. You'd be in for a false experience if all 365 of the following titles would be deserving of Siskel or Ebert's upraised thumb, so for each month I've thrown in a piece of crap that will just make you appreciate the next good one that much more.

However, even those films offered something to my tired eyes. I didn't single out a bad movie merely for the sake of cleansing your palate; if it's here it was something that was bad in a way that stood out – including what I eventually considered to be the worst film I watched out of the 2,500. Maybe it was a well-intentioned film that just couldn't get its act together, or it was seemingly made by aliens that were doing their best impression of what they thought was a motion picture – there are a lot of reasons one could label a movie as bad. Trust me – I saw plenty of films that left no impression on me at all, making it insanely hard to write a review later. The bad movies folded into the mix here at least gave me something to work with, which in my opinion is preferable to a technically well-made but bland and forgettable slasher or ghost movie that I can't remember a single thing about the next day.

Similarly, some (not all) months have a theme of a certain sub-genre, but I wouldn't want you to get burned out on a certain type, watching 30 *Saw* rip-offs in a row or something. So on those months I have tried to ensure that I am covering as much of the spectrum within that sub-genre as possible. The great thing about horror is how much variety there is to it (unlike, say, the romantic comedy, which works from a strict template), and I wanted to cram as many different kinds of movies I could in here without just offering up a random bunch of titles for you to see for whatever reason. Plus, having a theme for each month made it a lot easier to narrow the recommendations down – something that took me months as it is!

And one final note – while I hope this book can be just as useful in London, Japan, Antarctica... I just didn't have the time/manpower to research each of these titles' availability throughout the world. I made sure to avoid films that have never been released on DVD or any of the major streaming services here in the United States, because I want you to be able to see them all with relative ease, but that effort only extends to Region 1, unfortunately. I know I had a lot of UK readers (seriously, when I went to London I met more HMAD readers in a week than I'd meet in a year here in the US), so I hope they and the other countries can find these movies without too much trouble. At least I can assure you that they're all worth it!

So without further ado...

P.S.

OK, I lied, I have one more ado! I'm a sucker for traditions and the like, but I also wanted to have some structure within the month, so you could kind of know what to expect. So certain days of the month are always gonna be a certain kind of selection. Thus, so you know what's what, here's a handy guide to the "traditions" for each month:

1st movie of the month: My favorite, or at least one that perfectly encapsulates the theme for me.

7th, 14th, 21st, and 28th: Movies that are probably a bit more well-known than the others. You're welcome.

15th: A bad movie for the halfway point. As I explained above, part of being a horror fan is watching some really bad crap. For each month's theme, I have selected a memorably terrible movie that fits with the others in every way except quality.

23rd: A "dumb but I love it anyway" movie. I'm not a fan of the phrase "guilty pleasure", because fun is fun and you shouldn't have to apologize for it with any feelings of remorse, but that's the sort of thing I'm going for – movies that lack conventional critical merits, but are in no way less entertaining and (to my eyes) are made by people who knew exactly what kind of film they were making. As opposed to the "bad movies" on the 15th, where it seems they thought they were making something good.

And then the last movie of the month will always be one that bridges that month's theme with the next. To avoid movie whiplash, you see. So the last movie of September (vampire movies) will also be a sort of horror-lite entry (October's theme). And yes, the last movie of December ties back to January, so you can start anywhere and it will all loop nicely. Like Pink Floyd's *"The Wall"*! Speaking of Floyd, if you read this book while listening to *"Dark Side of the Moon"* you'll... probably get distracted.

Again, you obviously don't have to follow this book to the letter, but if you DO (and even more miraculously, actually watch every single movie I've recommended) you'll hopefully never get that "Didn't I just watch a movie like this yesterday?" feeling I often did, as I've done my best to mix it up as often as possible. Think of this book like a mixtape, except instead of songs it's populated with 365 movies, and also you have to procure them yourself instead of just listening to a cassette I've handed you. And I'm not dropping hints that I'm in love with you. And it's not suitable entertainment for when you're driving.

JANUARY - ASIAN HORROR

ARTIST: NATHAN CHESSHIR

In one of the site's earliest reviews, I commented that I wasn't crazy about Asian horror, and that I hoped my tune could be changed by the time I was finished with Horror Movie A Day. Thankfully it didn't take that long; while I still don't care much for a lot of the Japanese ghost stuff, I truly loved many of the Korean and Thai films I was able to find, and I found more variety from Japan as well. So let's kick this beast off by making amends! Right off the bat I'm gonna tell you about 31 Asian horror films that you should watch, with a minimum of long-haired ghosts coming out of televisions or phones among them!

Note - and this goes for the book as a whole - some (especially these) movies will be in another language besides English. Personally, I don't mind dubbing as long as it's done well, and I found something kind of interesting over the years – dub tracks were often more accurate than the subtitles. I don't know why that is the case, but there were several times where I'd turn on BOTH (the dub audio with the subs turned on) and the dialogue would be noticeably dumbed down on the subtitles. For example, a line like "Hello mother, what are we having for dinner tonight?" on the dub track would be subtitled as "Hey what's for dinner?" Sure, there's no information being lost, but the character sounds less polite/intelligent as a result. Such laziness was called out for the (non-Asian) *Let The Right One In* when it first came out on Blu-ray (look around online for some examples), resulting in Magnolia re-issuing the film with proper subtitles, but that might be the only time where such a travesty was corrected.

So for these and all the other foreign language films, I urge you to try both language options and make sure the one you're getting is truer to the writer's original text (I don't think I ever ran into the opposite, where the dub track was dumbed down while the subs were accurate). The original language is always preferable to listen to, sure, but if it's being translated into moron-speak, the benefit is reduced to almost nothing. Why strain your eyes for gibberish?

But I don't care if it's been inexplicably translated into Klingon, you absolutely must see...

MOVIE #1 – JANUARY 1st

BEDEVILLED (2010)
Dir: Cheol-soo Jang
HMAD Review Date: August 30, 2010 (Festival screening)
Genre: Revenge
Available from Well Go USA

Synopsis Based on Fading Memory: A woman gets tired of being demeaned by her husband and co-workers, so she starts killing them all.

Review excerpt:
"...it's a testament to how engaging both the characters and story are that, despite being what was I think the longest movie in the entire festival (just under two hours) and not in English, I stayed awake through the whole thing. I was never operating on more than 4-5 hours' sleep each day at the festival, coupled with jet lag and a lot of walking around (keep in mind I spend most of my day on my ass whether there's a film festival or not), so dozing off was pretty common. One nice thing about slow burns is that you are determined to know when/where the traditional horror action comes into play (as long as the story and characters are interesting, anyway), and in this particular film's case, this stuff is quite good and fairly fast paced, as she makes her way around the island, killing just about everyone. So my fear of missing something exciting kept me alert, and then the action itself kept me wide-eyed."

Reflection: It's fitting that this book begins with a movie for which I wrote an obnoxiously vague "review", spending more time rambling about things like my bladder and the festival's lineup than the film itself. Since I never took any writing classes or anything of that sort, I'm always the first to denounce the idea that I'm a "critic", because a critic writes reviews and I write a bunch of nonsense (with way too many parenthetical asides). And when it was a film I saw at a festival (this one was at London's Frightfest), the "review" would be even less useful to anyone, because I'd write it a few days later, after seeing who knows how many films since, and barely sleeping.

So if you're for some reason picking up this book without having ever read any of my "reviews" before, fair warning – they're not always particularly helpful in deciding whether or not you should watch the movie, and I never included much of a synopsis unless I had good reason. Part of the goal of this book was to trim the fat of the site with regards to the movies (choosing 365 out of 2,500), but also present slightly more useful "reviews" for each one. That's why I've opted to only offer excerpts of the original posts, usually highlighting something that actually works as a review (this is an exception, obviously) while excising the other nonsense, and adding an actual synopsis (to the best of my memory) of the movie. However, vagueness will still be the order of the day for a lot of these, as I went in blind to a great deal of them and would like to preserve that "virgin" feeling for you as well.

Anyway, this is a great movie, the sort of title where I've never talked to anyone who disliked it (among the few who have seen it). Welcome to our little club!

MOVIE #2 – JANUARY 2nd

CINDERELLA [SIN-DE-REL-LA] (2006)
Dir: Man-dae Bong
HMAD Review Date: June 2, 2012 (Streaming)
Genre: Ghost
Available from Tartan Asia Extreme

Synopsis Based on Fading Memory: A very dark and scary version of the basic *Cinderella* story, at least the part involving evil stepsisters and the like.

Review excerpt:
"...closer to a tragic drama than a horror film; I was surprised to find it actually somewhat moving at times, which is very rare for an Asian horror flick (usually because I can't figure out what the hell is going on for long enough to get invested into anyone's personal drama). The plot involves a spoiled girl whose mother is a plastic surgeon, and after a few somewhat generic scare scenes (though the one with the ghost crawling under the hospital bed is quite good) and a friend seemingly killing herself by cutting off the part of her face that she just had surgery on, the back-story starts filling in, and the scares take a back-seat."

Reflection: Like I said in the intro, I wasn't a big fan of most of the Asian horror films I had seen before starting the site, and I chalk that up to just watching the ones I had heard about or that had been remade, which meant a lot of them were similar – long-haired ghost girls using electronic devices to get at their victims, basically. So over the site's run I not only saw more of those (and found a few that elevated the concept), but I started to really appreciate movies like this, which starts off in line with the *Grudge/Ring*-types only to forge its own unique and far more interesting path.

Also, I came to discover that of all the Asian countries that were producing horror films, I tended to like Korean ones the most. They had some duds and some truly impenetrable movies, sure, but on average I found them to be more grounded and even more technically impressive. They also didn't use their own culture as explicitly, making them a bit more accessible as well (Thai films, for example, often played on their own unique customs and traditions, of which I know very little). This one is actually a bit of an exception since it tackles a plastic surgery obsession that is apparently worse in Korea than it is here in Los Angeles, but that's hardly a difficult concept to grasp. Plus, Korean films would often deliver the scares just as well as anyone else, making them all around solid entries, which is why I started the month off with two of theirs in a row.

MOVIE #3 – JANUARY 3rd

INFECTION [KANSEN] (2004)
Dir: Masayuki Ochiai
HMAD Review Date: July 16, 2007 (Cable)
Genre: Psychological
Available from Lionsgate

Synopsis Based on Fading Memory: A virus spreads at a hospital that seems like it already had enough problems on its hands.

Review excerpt:
"The concept of a virus that spreads with guilt is an intriguing one, and one almost wishes the film had gotten remade, as the American version would likely explore the this notion in greater detail. Some of the back story relies a bit too much on coincidence, but that's easily forgivable. More importantly, it's actually pretty unnerving. Of course, hospitals are naturally terrifying, what with the knowledge that you're probably in the same room where someone has died, not to mention the possibility that Michael Moore may be nearby, ready to film you and then re-edit it to fit his purposes. But Ochiai one ups the inherent terror by proving himself to be a master of misdirection, with creepy goings on appearing in the corners of the frame (despite a 1.85:1 ratio, this film would definitely suffer on a pan and scan version), and editing away from a scene before the "corner monsters" do something cheesy (or get discovered by the protagonists)."

Reflection: I saw this one pretty early in HMAD's run (it was only the fourth Asian horror film I watched for the site), so I didn't have much to compare it to – I hope it's as good as I remember and not benefiting from my then-ignorance. However, I *had* seen a few Asian horror films BEFORE I started the site, and the very first one was I saw was called *Parasite Eve*, which I bought because I saw the title and thought it was a Japanese film adaptation of the video game (indeed, I bought it at a video game store). Two funny things about that: one is that this is actually from the same director (and a much better film), and two: I never finished that game because someone broke into my room at college and stole a bunch of my PS1 games, including *Parasite Eve* and a game called *Theme Hospital*, which tasks you with running a hospital just as strange as the one in this movie.

However I may feel about the film's merit should I ever get around to seeing it again, I certainly still wish that there was an American update. The wave of Asian horror remakes in the US was kind of destroyed by redoing movies that were fine in the first place (*The Eye, Shutter*, etc.), and often without any real justification for the update beyond "Now it's in English". But with a theme like guilt? Hell, you could remake this movie for EVERY major nation and come away with fresh takes, because of our differing sensibilities. Japanese men might feel guilty about something we never do here in the US, and vice versa. Plus our hospitals are terrifying for different reasons. Alas, the likes of *One Missed Call* ensured that the Asian horror remake trend had to die, for better and for worse.

HMAD Fun Fact: Despite my initial dislike of the "sub-genre", I ultimately watched 114 Asian horror films for HMAD - more than my preferred "foreign" Italian or British films.

MOVIE #4 – JANUARY 4th

DEATH TUBE (aka X GAME) (2010)
Dir: Yôhei Fukuda
HMAD Review Date: July 3, 2012 (DVD)
Genre: Survival
Available from Cinema Epoch

Synopsis Based on Fading Memory: A guy in a teddy bear costume (or an actual anthropomorphic bear?) makes a bunch of folks compete in silly games to stay alive.

Review excerpt:
"...a really goofy version of a Saw/Cube *type movie, in which a bunch of strangers are forced to solve puzzles in order to proceed closer to freedom. But unlike those films' inventive traps and (in* Cube's *case) advanced mathematically based puzzles, the games our folks have to solve are just silly kids' games: hopscotch, "hot potato", Rubik's cube, etc. It'd probably be more fun if they were presented with riddles like in* Die Hard With A Vengeance, *because part of the fun of that film was laughing at the silliness of Simon's games but also trying to figure it out and thus feel superior to John McClane (if only for a moment...)."*

Reflection: Keep the fast forward button handy for this one, because it's too damn long, but there really is nothing else like it that I've ever seen. It's basically a *Saw* rip-off (specifically *Saw V*, oddly) but instead of Jigsaw/Billy you get this goofy Chuck E. Cheese reject with a shrill voice, and rather than put the contestants through death traps he makes them play musical chairs or whatever. There aren't a lot of Asian horror films that I'd comfortably describe as "goofy", but of those few this is definitely the silliest, and the success of the game *Five Nights At Freddy's* and its sequels has proven that there is inherent scare value in these fluffy mascots.

A sequel exists, but I have yet to see it. It's shorter (and from the same director), so it's certainly an enticing proposition, but as I quickly learned after "quitting" – once I stopped watching these things every day, it was suddenly "impossible" to find the time for such fare. I can barely manage to get three or four reviews a month up at HMAD (though the writing of this book certainly had an impact on that), so unnecessary sequels to "one and done" movies like this don't land particularly high on my to-do list. Even if I had time, the reviews suggest it's basically the same movie but with different deaths, so that's not really helping matters. But I'll get to it, I swear. I gotta hear that goofy voice again.

MOVIE #5 – JANUARY 5th

RE-CYCLE [GWAI WIK] (2006)
Dir: The Pang Brothers
HMAD Review Date: November 29, 2008 (Blu-ray)
Genre: Ghost, Supernatural
Available from Image Entertainment

Synopsis Based on Fading Memory: A woman gets trapped in a terrifying fantasy world that may be of her own design.

Review excerpt:
"The best thing about Re-Cycle *is how it manages to blend horror and fantasy so seamlessly. I was reminded of* What Dreams May Come, *which is a fantasy drama for 99% of the time, but then wastes a perfectly awesome concept of Hell in a should-be-scary scene that feels totally out of place with the rest of the movie. But here, it starts off like a straight up Asian horror movie (complete with an elevator scene), and then suddenly (but not jarringly) shifts into a fantasy world that seems like Terry Gilliam's live-action version of a Miyazaki film. But even then, the horror aspect is never absent; there are like 3 scenes that can't be described as anything but zombie attack sequences, and the Pangs manage to out-"gah!" Takeshi Miike's* Imprint *with their ideas concerning aborted fetuses."*

Reflection: The Pang brothers fascinate me, because when they're on, they're REALLY on, making some of the most memorable films of that year (not just Asian films – ALL genre films), but they're just as likely to churn out something that barely qualifies as watchable. This is my favorite of their work by far, but unfortunately it's SO good that it's going to give them a lifetime pass from me... which means seeing more of their dreck like *Child's Eye*. I mean, no director knocks it out of the park every time, but usually they're dependable for a while and then just go into a slump that they never manage to pull themselves out of (Tobe Hooper is a good example). The Pangs, on the other hand, go back and forth with alarming regularity, and I just can't put my finger on why.

As the excerpt notes, there's a scene involving aborted fetuses, so if the A-word is a trigger for you, you might not be able to enjoy this one as much as I did. But pro-life viewers should take solace in that the would-be mother doesn't get off so easy with her decision. It's a major plot point and dealt with intelligently, as opposed to something like the original *Dawn of the Dead*'s weirdo "Do you want to abort it? I know how to do it!" conversation (I always hated that scene). But back on point, this topic seems to be a very strange good luck charm for the Pangs, as *The Eye 2* (the best in the franchise by a mile) also concerns an unwanted pregnancy. Perhaps they can do another and have a makeshift trilogy?

MOVIE #6 – JANUARY 6th

NIGHTMARE DETECTIVE [AKUMU TANTEI] (2006)
Dir: Shin'ya Tsukamoto
HMAD Review Date: March 8, 2008 (DVD)
Genre: Serial Killer
Available from Dimension Extreme

Synopsis Based on Fading Memory: A suicidal guy who can enter dreams helps the police find a serial killer.

Review excerpt:
"...the dream sequences actually resemble real dreams. For example, one guy is killed in a room that is jam-packed with bicycles. There are at least a thousand of the damn things all around him, piled together. THAT'S a dream image! And then he's killed by a lightning quick monster straight out of Clive Barker's *Tortured Souls* toy line. The kill is one of the many gore/makeup highlights in the film, all of which are highly impressive and more than make up for the fact that the movie doesn't make a lick of sense, even by J-horror standards. Couldn't tell you what was going on at any point during the last half hour, but I was still highly entertained and impressed by the technical side of things."

Reflection: This movie is hard to follow even by Asian horror standards, but that kind of fits since it was released stateside by Dimension, who had a knack for releasing incoherent films (usually thanks to the re-editing they themselves imposed). There's a sequel that isn't as good, but is easier to follow and thus more accessible (it's not a direct sequel so it's not crucial to watch them in order). I assume the similarity to Freddy (or *The Cell*) prevented anyone from doing a remake, which is oddly kind of a shame – the concept and imagery are very cool, but the hard-to-follow narrative (and Tsukamoto's too close camerawork making some of the climactic action as impenetrable as the storyline) will likely frustrate some viewers. A smoother script could have created a rarity in horror: a franchise where the hero, not the villain, was the marquee star.

Tsukamoto also directed *Tetsuo the Iron Man*, a much more recognizable title here in the US. But as with many of those, I haven't seen it yet. I had a fun tendency to miss the movies "everyone" had seen from certain filmmakers, which turned out to be a blessing in some cases as their previous work had elevated expectations for these follow-ups. Perhaps someone who came into this movie seeing it as "the new Tsukamoto film" would be let down, but I was just watching a movie about a nightmare detective. Same thing for Ryûhei Kitamura's *Midnight Meat Train* - people were disappointed because it wasn't as good as *Versus*, or so I understand. I've never seen it! But I sure liked *Meat Train* as a Clive Barker adaptation. Throughout this book you'll see me refer to "going in blind" to a movie, and it applies to the credits just as much as the content – ALWAYS try to keep your expectations on ground level. You'll probably like a lot more stuff, or at least not get disappointed as often.

MOVIE #7 – JANUARY 7th

I SAW THE DEVIL [ANG-MA-REUL BO-AT-DA] (2010)
Dir: Jee-Woon Kim
HMAD Review Date: March 4, 2011 (Theatrical)
Genre: Revenge, Serial Killer
Available from Magnolia Home Entertainment

Synopsis Based on Fading Memory: A cop vows revenge on a serial killer that has gone free.

Review excerpt:
"It's a remarkably colorful film, almost like old-school Argento at times, and there's a nice balance of dark and light scenes. Red obviously comes up a lot (this movie has to have some sort of record on showing fast-forming pools of fresh blood), but the palette is very wide-ranging, another unexpected surprise (I heard it was "like a Korean Seven" and immediately pictured a movie filled with browns and grays). There's also a wonderful energy to the action scenes, particularly the big finale where Lee "kidnaps" Choi in the middle of a police capture, as well as their first fight in a greenhouse. I wouldn't be surprised if Jee-woon Kim was the next director to be courted by Hollywood (assuming he hasn't been already) – I think he could make a kick-ass Bourne type action film. The rape and often quite disturbing violence might put some off, but if you could handle Oldboy then you should be fine with this. The length doesn't really hurt and the two leads are endlessly watchable, plus even the weak spot of the film has its moments. A terrific film."

Reflection: Chances are you've seen or at least queued this one, but if not... man, you are missing out. It was my favorite genre film of 2011 (would have been favorite overall if not for *Fast Five* –I am a total sucker for those movies), and I've even grown to love the part of the movie that left me cold the first time around, though I still think it stalls the pace a bit more than necessary (you'll know it when you see it). I also love that I accurately predicted Kim's transition to Hollywood, as he followed this up with *The Last Stand*, the first big Arnold Schwarzenegger action movie in a decade. It unfortunately didn't do too well (it was at the time Arnold's lowest grosser ever), and Kim quickly returned to Korea. All for the best, probably – *Last Stand* was fun but hardly deserving of his talents, and was just another example of an Asian filmmaker not being able to deliver their particular brand of magic when working in the Hollywood system (though *Oldboy* genius Chan-Wook Park made the incredible *Stoker*, and John Woo managed a few pretty good English movies before returning to China).

The great thing about *I Saw the Devil* is that it offers two equally compelling leads, the sort of guys that could easily star in their own solo vehicles and you'd love it just as much (sort of like Woo's *Face/Off*, incidentally – who wouldn't want a full on Castor Troy movie?). It's one of those stories where the line between hero and villain becomes increasingly murky as the film proceeds, and it is nothing short of breathtaking watching that unfold. Kim and screenwriter Hoon-jung Park create a wonderfully strange world, too, one where serial killers are kind of all pals and help each other out when in need. Like *John Wick*, you feel like you're only seeing a small slice of a fully fleshed-out universe, and I wish that was something I saw more often in genre films. Most modern horror movies can't even convincingly sell the part of the world that directly affects the plot, let alone hint that there's anything else going on beyond the camera range. Movies like this prove it can be done, and the beauty of it is that Kim and Park didn't risk ruining it with a sequel.

(*John Wick 2* is coming in 2017.)

MOVIE #8 – JANUARY 8th

SILK [GUI SI] (2006)
Dir: Chao-Bin Su
HMAD Review Date: January 13, 2008 (DVD)
Genre: Ghost
Available from Tartan Asia Extreme

Synopsis Based on Fading Memory: A group of scientists are convinced the ghost of a young boy will help them solve the problem of anti-gravity.

Review excerpt:
"This film contains the best use of beef noodles in a movie ever. One of the team says "I want beef noodles," and later in the movie he repeats this desire, and leaves to get them. Then, a few minutes later, an unrelated scene is interrupted by him walking up to a clerk and ordering beef noodles, and once again a few scenes later they cut to him receiving his beef noodles (the waiter refers to them by name). At this point, we have heard the term BEEF NOODLES four times in about 10 minutes. So it comes as no surprise that the ghost climbs out of his bowl of beef noodles and chokes him to death. This results in the cook seeing the guy die (not the ghost), and then yelling "Who ever heard of dying from beef noodles!" It's fucking delightful, and makes me want to eat beef noodles."

Reflection: I haven't read any of them as an adult, but during my teen years I gobbled up a lot of Michael Crichton novels, and I noticed how often he returned to a plot where a group of experts in various fields would come together to solve a problem (or check out a theme park), and most of them would die. They made most of them into movies (none as good as *Jurassic Park*, though I think *Sphere* isn't as bad as its reputation suggests), but I've always wondered why this scenario wasn't ripped off more often, especially for SyFy type movies. They often had scientists and monsters, but they wouldn't ape Crichton much (and usually it'd be like two scientists and twelve SWAT or commando types, instead of half a dozen scientists and maybe one hardass). This is actually one of the very few I've ever seen that had that vibe (*Prince of Darkness* is another, although a bunch of the scientists never get to show off their specific skill), so it shouldn't be much of a surprise that it's one of my favorite Asian ghost films.

It's also one of the few I saw from Taiwan, which I regret. But following director Su's career wouldn't have helped much; he wrote one of the stories in *Three Extremes II*, but hasn't done too much else. His lone film since *Silk* is a period action movie, making him one of several directors in this chapter who made a horror movie I really liked and then moved on to other genres. Why can't they be pigeonholed like our filmmakers?!?

MOVIE #9 – JANUARY 9th

THE VICTIM [PHII KHON PEN] (2006)
Dir: Monthon Arayangkoon
HMAD Review Date: August 28, 2008 (DVD)
Genre: Ghost, Possession
Available from Kino Lorber Films

Synopsis Based on Fading Memory: A professional murder scene re-enactor (this is a real profession in Thailand) tries to solve one of the murders herself... but there's a twist!

Review excerpt:
"Some of the early scares are effectively creepy (ghosts appear to us, but not to her, so their appearances are subtle), and the cast is great, especially Pitchanart Sakakorn, who is essentially playing three roles. I also really love the score, the piece that plays over the flashback that sort of explains that we have been watching a movie so far is fantastic. Also, I love that the editing system they use in the traditional "look, I have footage of a ghost" scene is a legit program (Final Cut, in fact) instead of some made up movie shit that usually gets used."

Reflection: A few entries back I noted that Thai movies often used their traditions as a plot point, which might be hard for foreign audiences to grasp – and here is a terrific example. Apparently, when someone is murdered there, the forensic and police folk have suspects restage their crime (and in murder cases, hire actors to play the victims). And it's, like, a big draw for fans, too! Like people gather to watch these things the way fans crowd around a premiere or whatever. In fact the practice was in the news just a few months ago, with a bomb suspect being paraded around the places he terrorized. It's so bizarre to me.

Anyway, this movie isn't the only one that I saw that included this practice as part of its narrative, but it's certainly the most confusing. For those of you who like your horror to be a bit impenetrable as well, you'll have a field day with this, which offers more layers of reality than that goddamn *Bewitched* movie with Nicole Kidman. I admit I couldn't tell you what was going on for most of its back half, but it's stylish and compelling all the same, and the lead actress was pretty terrific. If you can clearly explain what was going on (and the killer's motive), please email me.

MOVIE #10 – JANUARY 10th

X-CROSS [XX (EKUSU KUROSU): MAKYÔ DENSETSU] (2007)
Dir: Kenta Fukasaku
HMAD Review Date: June 25, 2008 (Festival screening)
Genre: Cult, Survival
Available from Tokyo Shock

Synopsis Based on Fading Memory: Two girls are separated in the woods and go on unique but equally scary adventures.

Review excerpt:
"We start off with suspense (suspense that actually works for that matter), then go into some light survival/"torture" elements, and finally just the gonzo type of stuff that director Kenta Fukasaku is known for (he did Battle Royale 2, *for example). It works much better than you might think, and the way the film keeps elevating is admirable to say the least. Plus I always like these sort of 'two sides to a story' movie setups. You see a broken light swinging around in one story, and the second story explains how it got that way. It's not an easy thing to pull off – you run the risk of making the first part of the story incomprehensible because there are too many pieces that won't be filled in until the next part, but Fukasaku and screenwriter Tetsuya Oishi do a good job of providing a lot of these type of "ohhhh.... that's how that happened" moments without sacrificing story coherence."*

Reflection: As an avowed fan of *Pulp Fiction, Memento,* the *Saw*s, etc., I clearly have a thing for jumbled chronologies. It probably stems from my equal love/obsession for jigsaw puzzles (I recently bought a 9,000 piece one. Not a typo), seeing how parts that make no sense on their own eventually come together to form a fuller picture. Like I said in the excerpt, this can be tricky to pull off in films, which is why you don't see it all that often – there's only so much you can do before the audience is just sitting there completely confused. And this is even trickier/ rarer in horror, because if the audience is trying to sort out the narrative, their brain will be too busy piecing things together to get lulled into a scare (which is probably why the *Saw* films largely stayed away from anything traditionally scary).

This is why I think the movie deserves a much bigger following than it ever got here. It took a long time to come out on DVD in the US (2011, over three years after I saw it at a festival) and wasn't given much of a push, which probably didn't help its fortunes any. A pity, as it's by far one of the most accessible Japanese horror films out there, and it dipped into the waters of the then-popular "torture" horror sub-genre, so it stands to reason that it would have been a breakout hit if given a chance or a more timely release. Oh well. Hopefully some of you take the plunge.

MOVIE #11 – JANUARY 11th

CHAWZ (2009)
Dir: Jeong-won Shin
HMAD Review Date: June 30, 2011 (Streaming)
Genre: Comedic, Predator
Available from Magnolia Home Entertainment

Synopsis Based on Fading Memory: *Jaws* but with a boar. And on land, obviously.

Review excerpt:
"...what made it work for me were the likable characters. In another reference of a sort, it's kind of like the Lake Placid team, with a hunter, a cop, a state official, a wildlife expert, and a badass ultimately joining up to hunt down the monster, each with their own motives ("Study it!" "A hunting challenge!" "Protect the town!", etc.), But unlike most films with this setup, all of them are likable and get along. One of the better joke scenes involves the wildlife expert wanting to film everything for a documentary, and she doesn't catch a crucial discovery on camera, so she asks them to "do it again". You'd expect one of them to be like "I don't have time for this nonsense", but they all happily oblige, ridiculously overacting for the camera and seemingly have a grand ol' time. And this has another perk – it's actually kind of hard to tell which of them will die.

Reflection: It's been said that the reason the *Fast & Furious* films went from mid-level hits to gigantic blockbusters (the last one is the sixth highest grossing movie of all time! IT'S A PART 7!) is because we grew to fall in love with the characters, a bunch of hardass criminals who goof off and truly love each other like a family. The stunts and action are great, of course, but they're nothing without those bonds at their center, and that's what makes the movies increasingly more appealing (and profitable, I guess).

Well, *Chawz* is like *Fast Five* in a way, because you get the crew coming from all over and they're all really loving of each other instead of at each other's throats like 99% of movies of this sort. Hell, even *Jaws* has everyone pissed at each other more than once during the Orca segment of the film, but the scene everyone loves is the part where they sing "Show Me the Way to Go Home". We like seeing people get along, in other words, and *Chawz* offers a lot of that. And I mean a LOT – the movie is definitely a touch too long (almost as long as the actual *Jaws*, in fact) but the camaraderie between the heroes makes up for it – and PLEASE watch the end credits as they are just as delightfully endearing. The humor may not be for everyone, but as I very rarely came across any "funny" Asian horror films I found it to be a welcome diversion. Likewise, I didn't see too many movies where they showed off their love of other films – *Jaws* is obvious, but director Shin clearly has an affinity for *Hot Fuzz* as well, as the hero's arc is very similar (but not a total lift). A lot of this month's selections are kind of grim, so I wanted to put something in to lighten the mood.

MOVIE #12 – JANUARY 12th

YOGA [YOGA HAKWON] (2009)
Dir: Jae-yeon Yun
HMAD Review Date: March 1, 2011 (DVD)
Genre: Supernatural
Available from Well Go USA

Synopsis Based on Fading Memory: A nearly incomprehensible story centers on the creepy goings-on at a yoga studio.

Review excerpt:
"...it appealed to my "fear" of yoga. Back in 2004, my girlfriend convinced me to join her for "couple's yoga", which, as you might expect, wasn't exactly my cup of tea. I was too out of shape to do much anyway (plus our height difference didn't help – we made one lopsided "yoga tree", that's for sure), but some of their maneuvers legitimately frightened me – I was convinced someone was going to break their neck or back or something. So in the movie, when a girl twisted her legs around in a 360 degree turn, or another began moving like a snake, I was genuinely unnerved, because it wasn't too far from what I expect to happen in yoga studios NOT run by immortal witches. Oh yeah, I got a *Suspiria* vibe at times, particularly in the 3rd act when coherency sort of goes by the wayside. It's not as gory or colorful as Argento's film, but the influence is still apparent, and it was a nice surprise."

Reflection: The Asian horror films I tended to enjoy more were usually the ones I could follow, but this one left me baffled and yet here we are, with the film beating out 83 other potential Asian horror films for a slot in this month's chapter. Like *Nightmare Detective*, the accurate depiction of dream sequences was something I really appreciated, having grown up on the *Nightmare on Elm Street* series (and countless wannabes) where 99% of dream scenes were intended to make you think they were real for their majority. Here they dive into a regular dream scenario, i.e. one that makes little sense and jumps around a lot. That, plus the aforementioned *Suspiria* vibe (finally! After years of the Italians ripping the US off, and the US ripping off the Asian horror, we have an Asian horror ripping off an Italian one), more than make up for all the head-scratching you'll endure. And maybe you'll learn a few new yoga poses, if you're the active sort.

Oh, for those who might be concerned about my lack of exercise - I've since gotten more in shape, albeit in a very offbeat way. Last year, I bought a used

Xbox from Gamestop that had the *Biggest Loser* game for the Kinect still inside the console's disc tray, and as my doctor had told me that very week that I needed to make some lifestyle changes (my good cholesterol was low and I had high triglycerides – in addition to a better diet, exercise is the way to improve those), I took it as a sign. So I started playing the game on a rigid 12 week, 7 days a week program (HMAD fans will appreciate that I once again only missed one day) and lost like 10 lbs. without even really changing my diet. And I no longer huff and puff after taking the stairs at work! I still play it a few times a week and have dropped a pants size, thank you very much. And I can even do the tree pose now!

MOVIE #13 – JANUARY 13th

CARVED (aka A SLIT-MOUTHED WOMAN) [KUCHISAKE-ONNA] (2007)
Dir: Kôji Shiraishi
HMAD Review Date: September 17, 2008 (DVD)
Genre: Possession, Serial Killer
Available from Tartan Asia Extreme

Synopsis Based on Fading Memory: Well, it's in the review excerpt, so just read that.

Review excerpt:
"...one of the most coherent and straightforward Asian horror films I have ever seen. At no point during the film did I need to rewind it, check an IMDb synopsis, or consult a friend to understand just what the hell was going on. Women get possessed by an urban legend known as The Slit-Mouthed Woman (not "Carved", so the new title doesn't make much sense), and kill their kids. Some get a bit of control over the possession and ask their children to kill them instead. Either way, the father's gonna be pretty depressed when he comes home."

Reflection: I was obviously in a peculiar mood when I wrote this review (I mention *Rock Band*, so maybe I just wanted to get back to playing that), because even though I liked the movie I'm kind of flippant and sarcastic about it. I know my older write-ups (2007) were almost always like that, which is why you won't see too many entries from that year in this book (they were largely unusable!), but by this point I had largely shed myself of that attitude. And I find it kind of appalling now that I'm a dad, because I am a giant baby when it comes to kids being killed (especially by their own parents), and here it almost seems like I'm amused by the notion that I might come home one day to something unthinkable. So watch this movie for a disturbing (and, as I say, very straightforward) Japanese horror film, but don't read any more of my jerkish review!

As for the title, I still don't know why it was changed at the time I saw the film, since the other one made more sense. It was re-released in 2011 under the *Slit-Mouthed Woman* title, but that one seems to be out of print now. So look for either title, I guess – thankfully the covers are the same (a spooky woman with scissors over her face) so it shouldn't be too hard to track down. As far as I can tell, there are no differences with regard to the cut of the film – it should be 90 minutes either way.

MOVIE #14 – JANUARY 14th

RETRIBUTION [SAKEBI] (2006)
Dir: Kiyoshi Kurosawa
HMAD Review Date: March 20, 2011 (Streaming)
Genre: Ghost
Available from Lionsgate

Synopsis Based on Fading Memory: A cop is looking for a killer where all the evidence suggests he himself is the murderer. It's not a movie from the online Giallo Generator, I assure you.

Review excerpt:
"Kiyoshi Kurosawa doesn't "announce" his scares with musical stings, or cut to a wide shot of our hero so that something can scurry past in the foreground. Instead, he frequently uses long takes, with characters moving back and forth in the foreground, and careful viewers will spot our ghost suddenly appearing unnoticed in the background. Sort of like the scene in Halloween *when Annie is on the phone and Michael suddenly appears in the doorway (and then vanishes again), but again, without the sting to help us. He also uses mirrors in a very creative way, allowing us to see things the hero does not, but again, not cutting to it to hammer the point home. I wouldn't be surprised if I were to watch the film again and see the ghost in a shot or two that I had missed before."*

Reflection: I saw this movie not long after the devastating Japanese earthquake/tsunami of 2011 (literally, like, a week after it), which made this a curious choice – it had been on my radar for a while, but I just then got around to it... and it happened to be the only Japanese horror film I saw where earthquakes played such a major role. It wasn't until that disaster happened that I became fully aware of how bad Japan's earthquake problem was (worse than California's, which I thought was bad enough since I live here), a fact a commenter on this review chastised me for. Hey, it's better I learned late than never at all, right?

Anyway, they're an unusual backdrop to this intriguing murder mystery/ghost hybrid, and I found it to be superior to Kurosawa's more famous *Pulse (Kairo)*. Unfortunately, he hasn't made a horror film since; he's still making movies but they're in the fantasy and sci-fi genre instead of terror. Hopefully he hasn't retired from the genre – I'd probably put Japan as my least favorite supplier of Asian horror (compared to Korea, Thailand, etc.), but the Kurosawa films that I saw were among the exceptions. Plus I like that his IMDb trivia has to stress that he's not related to that "other" Kurosawa, because presumably someone got sick of being asked.

Oh, and if the Giallo Generator reference confused you, please Google it. You'll have a blast.

MOVIE #15 – JANUARY 15th

ZOMBIE STRIPPER APOCALYPSE (aka BIG TITS ZOMBIE) (2010)
Dir: Takao Nakano
HMAD Review Date: January 20, 2013 (DVD)
Genre: Comedic, Zombie
Available from Entertainment One

Synopsis Based on Fading Memory: Some escorts are sent to a spa where they face off against a zombie horde in this bizarre would-be *What's Up Tiger Lily* update, where a bad Japanese film is redubbed for comedic effect.

Review excerpt:
"...when it works, it's actually pretty hilarious if you're in the right mood. Making fun of even the best of these movies is akin to shooting fish in a barrel, but this one is particularly dreadful (apparently on purpose), with visible wires during the FX scenes, terrible acting across the board, and (my favorite) plastic covering on nearly every surface and piece of furniture despite the fact that nearly all of the blood is CGI and thus wouldn't be able to wreck anything. If I'm understanding correctly, there are a group of strippers who are sent to a spa in order to make a little more money (unknowingly being prostituted; not sure if this is an invention of the redub or part of the original), where they find a Necronomicon and unleash an army of colorful zombies. There's actually not a lot of action (even less if you consider a big chunk of it is a repeat), and most of the movie finds the girls standing around bickering, which provides plenty of fodder for the redub folks."

Reflection: So here's the fun thing with this entry – you can watch *Big Tits Zombie*, which is a totally awful/hilarious zombie movie with porn actors (who rarely disrobe, so if that's a selling point you will be disappointed), OR you can watch the version called *Zombie Stripper Apocalypse*, which was *BTZ* but redubbed, making it a LEGITIMATELY hilarious version of what is still an awful movie. That version might be harder to find, since it was seemingly only released at Blockbuster (?), which of course is no longer a thing. Ideally, there would be a release with both audio tracks so you can enjoy the joke to its full extent (by suffering through the original version and then going back with the redub, which occasionally references the original), but to the best of my knowledge no such version exists.

Either way you're covered for this month's (and the book's inaugural) bad movie entry! Each month, on the 15th (right in the middle, more or less), I'll be recommending an UNUSUALLY bad movie for you to watch instead of the usual just plain good ones. As explained in the intro, but repeated here for those of you who skipped ahead to the regular content, the sad/fun fact about horror, and being a horror fan, is that most of the movies you'll see are probably bad. Some REALLY bad. And some... well, if you're a horror fan that still enjoys other genres of film, there's a good chance that the absolute worst movie you've ever seen is probably a horror movie. It's just how it is. So it'd be dishonest – in a strange way – to give you 365 horror movies in which none of them are lousy. Watching junk horror movies is an important part of being a horror fan! Rest assured, the ones I've picked will be memorable – no anonymous found footage *Paranormal Activity* rip-offs or anything like that. The average shitty movie *wishes* it could be as entertaining as these!

P.S. Adding to the confusion, this movie is apparently also known as *Big Tits Dragon*. I give up.

MOVIE #16 – JANUARY 16th

BLACK HOUSE [GEOMEUN JIP] (2007)
Dir: Terra Shin
HMAD Review Date: April 16, 2008 (DVD)
Genre: Revenge
Available from CJ Entertainment

Synopsis Based on Fading Memory: An insurance investigator is drawn into a terribly disturbing case.

Review excerpt:
"If I had known the twist that occurs halfway through, the film probably wouldn't have been as enjoyable. Not that it's terribly surprising, but the film is carefully constructed, constantly building on what you know (or think you know). It's also well-paced, and for a change, fairly short for an Asian film (100 minutes, as opposed to the usual "thisclose to two hours" ones I usually watch). In fact, it could even be a bit longer; the deleted scenes are almost all worthwhile and could only be cut from the film for length (there is no commentary or any sort of marker that explains where the scenes would be in the film, though it's not too difficult to figure out for the most part)."

Reflection: Initially, I wanted to revisit every film in this book (at least, the ones I had only seen that one time), but realized that would be impossible because I'd basically be doing Horror Movie A Day again, plus many of the films were no longer readily available to me (screeners I had since chucked, Netflix Instant titles that were no longer streaming, etc.). However, this is one of the few I managed to find time to watch again, and I'm happy to say it held up. It wasn't quite as eye-opening as my first time, because that was 2008 and I had only seen a handful of other non-ghost Asian horror films (this one has zero supernatural elements; it's almost not even horror), but damned if it wasn't just as effective where it counts, in that it's disturbing and original.

It's a shame that director Shin hasn't made another genre film since; his two follow-ups were both rom-coms, of all goddamn things (and please, don't tweet me any jokes about how rom-coms are scarier – that's hack). Not a lot of these movies truly disturbed me, but this one has not one but two scenes that legitimately left me unsettled, and the plot as a whole is kind of sickening to me as a dad (I won't elaborate, because spoilers). I tend to get more freaked out once ghosts and zombies and other things I don't believe in are taken out of the equation, and when you add my ever-increasing roster of parental fears into the mix... well let's just say maybe I SHOULDN'T have watched *Black House* again post-kid. But I'd love to see Shin work this sort of magic again, if he's up to the task. Maybe he just genuinely wants to make rom-coms, I dunno.

MOVIE #17 – JANUARY 17th

FACE [PEISEU] (2004)
Dir: Sang-Gon Yoo
HMAD Review Date: February 5, 2011 (Streaming)
Genre: Ghost, Serial Killer
Available from Tartan Asia Extreme

Synopsis Based on Fading Memory: A police officer and a facial reconstruction expert work to solve a murder. But unlike the show *Bones*, it's good.

Review excerpt:
"The final scene is a bit too melodramatic for my tastes, but it's so rare for these Asian horror films to be more concerned with the drama and character development than spooky jump scares, I easily forgave it. It also makes up for the film's sort of main problem, which is that the killer turns out to be someone we only saw once (another Bone Collector *connection). But when you factor in the twist, you realize that it would be impossible to include the character more often without giving it away (unless they cheated, which would be worse). Thus, I no longer minded the issue – I'll take that "problem" over yet another vengeful ghost tale, or a twist that simply makes no sense, OR a movie that you can tell how it ends after the first reel."*

Reflection: I hate repeating myself. Let me repeat: I LOATHE SAYING SOMETHING A SECOND TIME. Like, to a nearly obnoxious degree – if the kid at the drive-thru doesn't hear me the first time and I have to say "a hamburger and a chocolate shake" again, I get infuriated. If I do it without grimacing, it's probably because I've forgotten saying it the first time, or I was pretty sure whoever I am talking to in the present couldn't have heard it in the past (and even then, I usually preface it with "I was telling so and so a while back..."). As it turns out, that hatred meant it didn't take long before I found it hard to write about a movie without saying stuff I already said, since a lot of horror movies tend to resemble other horror movies. So by the halfway point, I had to start dipping back into spoiler territory* in order to say something new. All of that is my explanation for why this review is almost entirely spoilers and the pros/cons of the movie's twists and finale – the above excerpt is actually re-edited from three paragraphs so I wouldn't spoil it here. But hell, we're seventeen movies into this thing, and I'm not changing my format now! You'll get review excerpts even if they're of little use.

Regarding the *Bone Collector* reference – I frequently cited that movie as a (bad) example of how *not* to do a whodunit film, because the guy who turned out to be the killer was a recognizable actor who only appeared in one, somewhat pointless scene in the first 90 minutes. He's a great actor, but he's not the sort of guy they'd hire for a cameo (as opposed to, say, George Clooney – if HE shows up in one scene early in a whodunit movie, he's not the killer, he's just George Clooney stopping by), so you inadvertently figure out the movie after an hour or so just by wondering why they'd hire a familiar face to be a random technician or whatever he was. So to any screenwriters reading this, free advice: give your eventual killer TWO scenes in the movie before his reveal unless you want jaded assholes like me comparing you to a shitty Denzel Washington thriller down the road.

*Early HMAD reviews were spoiler-heavy and not marked as such, since the idea was that you wouldn't read my "reactions" unless you also saw the movie. But when the site became more traditionally review-oriented I backed off from it, or would at least be selective and give plenty of advance warning, and confine such material to a paragraph or two.

MOVIE #18 – JANUARY 18th

THE BUTCHER (2007)
Dir: Kim Jin-Won
HMAD Review Date: April 29, 2010 (DVD)
Genre: Mockumentary, Survival
Available from Palisades Tartan Asia Extreme

Synopsis Based on Fading Memory: A found footage film about a crazed director who is kidnapping people and forcing them to star in his snuff films.

Review excerpt:
"...a disturbing movie, and should be only viewed by the strong-stomached among you. The POV gives the "this is happening to YOU" feeling more often than not, the sound effects easily take the place of the visual impact, and there isn't a frame in the film that doesn't have some sort of bodily fluid (puke, blood, pee, and possibly excrement) strewn about. And the "director" of the film is so casual about everything, it makes it all the more disturbing. If it was just the pighead guy doing this shit, it would just be repulsive and boring, but having a very normal looking guy in control gives it that unsettling edge. Regardless, if Hostel and its ilk disgust you, then this won't change your mind. But if you, I hate to say ENJOY, but I guess, can stomach these movies, then this one is at least one of the more interesting on a technical level."

Reflection: The found footage craze that soured the American independent horror scene for much of the late '00s/early '10s never really caught on in Japan, Korea, etc., as best as I can tell – this is one of the very few of its type that I came across during HMAD's run. I couldn't avoid the damn things if I TRIED if picking from US and UK films, but whenever I saw a new Asian horror film, it would thankfully be a traditionally shot one. That means experiments like *The Butcher* – while tough to watch and not without flaws – stuck out as interesting and thus worth a look for those among you who enjoy the *Hostel/Saw* type hardcore horror films, especially since those are few and far between these days.

And for what it's worth, except for the moments when they switch to the killer's POV, it's one of the better examples of how to properly execute this kind of movie. Far too many of these things are shot by professional cameramen instead of the actors, and/or offer multiple angles on a moment when it's impossible for a single camera to be capturing those moments, and this one gets it right, something I always champion. I think the POV approach can be a wonderful thing when it's done right, but unfortunately most filmmakers botch it entirely, sinking the rest of their film along with it. It's unfortunate that one of the best examples is in a film that may be too difficult for some to watch in order to appreciate it, however.

MOVIE #19 – JANUARY 19th

GOKE, BODY SNATCHER FROM HELL [KYUKETSUKI GOKEMIDORO] (1968)
Dir: Hajime Satô
HMAD Review Date: February 17, 2013 (Streaming)
Genre: Alien, Possession
Available from Criterion

Synopsis Based on Fading Memory: A jetliner with more problems than the one in *Airplane!* crashes in the middle of nowhere, where an alien parasite gets on board.

Review excerpt:
"*Goke* is a Tarantino favorite (the ridiculous red lighting in the Bride's flight to Japan in Kill Bill was inspired from this film), but I have to wonder if it's an influence on Carpenter as well, as it follows one of his favorite scenarios - a bunch of folks trapped somewhere and facing off against a common enemy. In this case they are the passengers on a commercial airliner that has the absolute worst luck in the world: there's a hijacker, a terrorist with a bomb, and birds keep hitting the windows, smearing blood on the windows and rightfully freaking everyone out. It's basically a relief when the aliens show up and cause the plane to crash (quite safely! A few people die as a result but as depicted via miniature, it's very smooth and efficient, all things considered), because I suspect another 5 minutes in the air would have produced 2-3 MORE problems for the flight crew to deal with; maybe they were out of coffee too."

Reflection: Like *The Butcher* (yesterday's movie, for you skip around-ers), *Goke* fascinated me because it was another country's take on a trope that I'm familiar with from US films, in this case the "Group of people trapped somewhere fight with each other rather than uniting against their common enemy" movie. In fact it came out the same year as the most famous of the lot (*Night of the Living Dead*), so it's even more interesting because it's certainly not inspired by that. Every single "infection" or "the real enemy is each other" movie that has been made since is consciously or subconsciously cribbing from Romero, so it's nice to enjoy one of the few that couldn't possibly be influenced by his film. It's also got a touch of *The Flight of the Phoenix*, with the movie taking place in/around the crashed plane rather than the usual plot including the survivors' attempt to make their way back to civilization on foot.

It also allowed me a rare glimpse at older Japanese horror. I'm not overly jazzed about giant monster (i.e. *Godzilla*) films, and their ghost films like *Kuroneko* are often too drawn out to grab me like they should, so there aren't too many pre-'80s films that speak to my sensibilities. Thus, I rarely made the effort to seek out older Japanese movies I hadn't seen yet, and while I'm sure I was doing myself a disservice (it's why I repeatedly encouraged recommendations for the sub-genres I was not familiar with, rather than blind-rent titles that might be terrible examples), it made me all the more excited to find a film like this that was right up my alley.

MOVIE #20 – JANUARY 20th

DREAM HOME [WAI DOR LEI AH YUT HO] (2010)
Dir: Ho-Cheung Pang
HMAD Review Date: August 28, 2010 (Festival screening)
Genre: Hero Killer
Available from MPI Home Video

Synopsis Based on Fading Memory: A woman will stop at nothing to obtain her dream home.

Review excerpt:
"Most of the kills remain in the realm of good fun (like a Friday the 13th movie), and the film offers an unusual fragmented narrative in which we gradually learn what has pushed her this far in order to obtain the titular dream home. It doesn't build toward a twist or anything, but it allows it to fill in the story without having to save all the kills (which all occur in a single night; the movie spans two decades) until the end of the film. And some of them are fairly touching - I particularly liked the ones involving when her family was forced out of their apartment home, which costs her her friendship with a kid who lived across the way. They communicate through a two cans and a string device, and at one point manage to turn the word "asshole" into an endearing part of their normal conversation (which has a pretty great payoff at the end of the film). Most of the other flashbacks are just about her getting screwed over by bank loans and the then-current housing market problems, but these give the film an unexpected heart."

Reflection: The least common kind of film you'll find this month is anything that reminds you of a *Friday the 13th* movie, but that's what *Dream Home* did on several occasions with its gory, crowd-pleasing kills and plot about how far family members will go for one another. Unfortunately, it also shares another thing in common with Jason Voorhees – *Part 3* in particular – in that the killer murders a pregnant woman (and unlike *Friday*'s victim, this lady is showing, making it hard to forget). Even before I considered having a child of my own this scene upset me, and it didn't fit with the rest of the film's tone (or even the plot – the victim wasn't one of the killer's targets). So that's a warning for anyone who might take offense to seeing what is technically a baby being killed. Otherwise, fun stuff!

You'll notice the genre is "Hero Killer". Most of my genre descriptions should be self-explanatory (slasher, ghost, etc.) but this one might require a bit of clarification, though it's exactly what it says – it's a movie where the hero is the killer. I don't mean in a twisty way, I mean we're sympathetic to and seeing everything through the lens of our protagonist, as always, but the protagonist is the one killing everyone. It's a tough film to pull off, because it's hard to feel bad for or even care about someone who's butchering innocent people, but sometimes – like in this movie – the ingredients are all there and it works. I mentioned the one exception, but otherwise, even though no one she kills specifically did anything to harm her, the audience is always on her side. That's what separates a "hero killer" movie from something like *Halloween: Resurrection*, where you might be inclined to root for Michael Myers because everyone around him is so awful, but he is still the villain, technically. Make sense? I probably should have thought of a better name for this kind of film, but it's too late for that.

P.S. Please make sure you haven't rented/bought *Dream HOUSE*, the American movie with Daniel Craig. That movie is garbage.

MOVIE #21 – JANUARY 21st

SHUTTER (2004)
Dir: Banjong Pisanthanakun, Parkpoom Wongpoom
HMAD Review Date: January 26, 2008 (DVD)
Genre: Ghost
Available from Tartan Asia Extreme

Synopsis Based on Fading Memory: An asshole runs over someone and leaves her for dead, and then her ghost starts haunting him and his friends... but not for the reason you think!

Review excerpt:
"Does the Asian world make any horror movies about vampires, werewolves, devil worshipping cults, killer dolls, etc.? Why are so many of these movies about vengeful ghosts using some sort of ordinary device to haunt their victims? Shutter of course fits right in, what with a ghost appearing in some guy's photographs and driving his pals to suicide. Come on, guys, cars breaking down in the vicinity of cannibalistic rednecks must be a global problem. But this one's got a couple of things going for it. One, it's short, clocking in at 90 minutes or so (most of them hover near 2 hours). Also, the story isn't quite as fragmented as Ju-On *or whatever; relatively speaking, it's actually pretty logical and doesn't leave you entirely clueless for an hour and then suddenly give you 10 straight minutes of exposition. So that's a plus."*

Reflection: Again, I largely shied away from well-known titles for this book, but since this film's obligatory remake didn't exactly make *Grudge/Ring* money, I can safely assume not as many people went back to watch the original – though they should, because it's one of the better films of this type. It's fun to see a group of guys go through these motions, and for once (spoiler, sorta) the people being haunted deserve their torment. So many haunting stories kick off when our heroine moves into a new home or sees something she shouldn't have, but these guys? The ghost is kind of the hero here.

Fun thing about the remake: it was the English language debut (and, to date, swan song) of Masayuki Ochiai, whose *Infection* was previously recommended this month, from a review where I sort of wished for a remake. Instead, he got to make an inferior remake of someone else's movie. Now he makes *Ju-On* sequels, natch.

MOVIE #22 – JANUARY 22nd

MAREBITO (2004)
Dir: Takashi Shimizu
HMAD Review Date: March 8, 2009 (DVD)
Genre: Psychological
Available from Kino Lorber films

Synopsis Based on Fading Memory: A guy who likes to videotape everything finds - and then takes home - a very strange girl.

Review excerpt:
"What's cool about the movie, however, is that for the first time I can recall in one of the J-horror films from the past 10 years or so, there is evidence that they are aware of other cultures. I can't be certain, but the "underground city" that the guy investigates seems dropped in from a Lovecraft story, and that's BEFORE he refers to it as "The Mountains of Madness". He also refers to Deros, a reference to the work of Richard Shaver. Usually, for better or for worse, the only sort of literary (or pop culture in general) references I see in Eastern films are from their own country, so it was interesting to see it tackled in a rather subtle way. Since the US is so adaptation-oriented, I wonder how a Stephen King story or something would translate if done by someone like Shimizu or the Pang Brothers."

Reflection: I was going to edit the excerpt so I sound less ignorant, but elected to maintain it for posterity. I'm sure this is not the *only* J-horror movie that dropped in references to Lovecraft or what have you, but it's the first one that I saw, which is what I meant. And I still never ran into it much in the years that followed; I don't know if it's just a cultural thing, but nearly all of the Asian horror films I saw were free of the sort of referential/homage inclusions you see in probably half of American horror. The only other referential Asian horror films I can recall are *Reincarnation (Rinne)*, which referenced *The Shining* quite a bit, and *Chawz*, which I recommended last week. Three movies in over six years; in the US you're bound to find six movies like that in three days.

In another part of the review I mention that I planned to re-watch it soon and see if a second viewing resulted in more clarity on some of its plot details. Well, it took me six damn years to finally do that, which of course meant it was basically like watching it for the first time since my memories had been eroded by all of the movies I saw in between. But some things came back while I was watching it, and I think it's safe to assume that this is not a movie that will spell everything out, no matter how many times you watch it. I've grown to enjoy vague or ambiguous horror conclusions more than I did back then (I still don't *love* them, but they don't get me angry like they used to), so it doesn't bother me as much that the film ends without answering everything. But just so you know: if you're the type that demands complete coherency and explanation from your films, this one won't provide it even on a second viewing. Sorry!

MOVIE #23 – JANUARY 23rd

ESCAPE FROM VAMPIRE ISLAND [HIGANJIMA] (2009)
Dir: Tae-gyun Kim
HMAD Review Date: October 3, 2011 (DVD)
Genre: Vampire
Available from Funimation

Synopsis Based on Fading Memory: Some folks are stuck on Vampire Island and decide to escape, probably?

Review excerpt:
"I'd love to see more non-ghost films from Japan, but I'm also not a big fan of what my Twitter pal Evan Husney refers to as "Robo fart ninja" movies (i.e. Frankenstein Girl) – those things tend to wear out their welcome long before they're finished even when they're technically short. I was afraid this would be like one of those, but instead I was more often reminded of the '80s Hong Kong comedy-horror films that Brian Quinn programs on occasion for the Grindhouse nights at the New Bev, where the tone sort of veers between slapstick-y comedy and melodrama at the drop of a hat, and the plots tend to be loose at best, but everyone involved seems to be working hard to ensure that the audience is never really bored. The action isn't particularly great – director Tae-gyun Kim loves close-ups and shaky-cam, unfortunately – but there's plenty of it. And there's some variety to it; big brawls, one on one sword fights, even a big monster rampage/scramble not unlike in Fellowship of the Ring *when they take on that giant troll in the mines (except this is some spider-vampire beast)."*

Reflection: The length here is a bit punishing: 122 minutes was tough for me even before I had a baby, so the fact that it would take two, maybe even three sittings to re-watch this movie today is kind of ridiculous, considering the thin plot. But it's just so damn hell-bent on trying to entertain you, like those '80s films I mention, that I had to include it here. And I know you're probably thinking "Why not just recommend one of those?" Well, for starters, shut up – it's my book and I'll do what I want. But mostly it's because those films are extremely hard to find here in the US; almost every single movie Quinn showed barely even had an IMDb page, let alone a Blu-ray release that you could grab from Amazon. And the ones that are available are often poorly dubbed (the subtitle errors were a big part of the fun) and taken from VHS transfers. I'd rather you just watched a fun homage than suffer through a subpar presentation of the real thing.

(If you do want recommendations of older titles, *Eternal Evil of Asia* and *Blood Call* were my favorites of those. The latter can be bought on used VHS tape for the low cost of $1,591.36 right now on Amazon. It's really only worth $1,327.67, but you can splurge.)

MOVIE #24 – JANUARY 24th

ROOT OF EVIL [AKASIA] (2003)
Dir: Ki-hyeong Park
HMAD Review Date: October 13, 2011 (DVD)
Genre: Supernatural
Available from Kino Lorber films

Synopsis Based on Fading Memory: A couple adopts a boy, who seems obsessed with a tree in the backyard. Then he disappears, and things get... unsettling.

Review excerpt:
"...starts off a lot like Orphan, *and even seems to be heading into similar killer kid territory (yay!) but switches gears midway through and becomes more of a tragic supernatural/ghost-type story, which might be a "lesser" genre in my eyes (look, I like seeing kids kill people) but was no less compelling. See, that's what can happen when you base a horror film around characters, not a particular subgenre. This isn't so much a ghost movie as it is about a couple dealing with what is obviously an unhappy marriage, and how the things they do to repair it only end up making it worse. If you strip away any supernatural/horror elements, you're still left with that rather sad story; maybe not as interesting a tale, but there would be SOMETHING there to latch on to. Take the killer out of a slasher movie and what are you left with, 99% of the time? Nothing. A bunch of kids hanging out in the woods and then going home, I guess."*

Reflection: I really wish more horror movies took a cue from this one (which is also called *Acacia*), because we could have far more surprises in our genre films if they trusted the audience to follow a character instead of a sub-genre. My example of the slasher film is flippant (believe me, it stung a bit to take such a shot at my beloved slashers!), but it's true – far too many horror films revolve around their established type (monster, slasher, ghost, etc.) instead of a character. If we love a character, we'll follow him or her anywhere – case in point (apologies for the non-horror example): James Bond, who dialed things down for *Skyfall* and was rewarded with record box office (even more impressive considering it was following up one of the worst-ever Bond films in *Quantum of Solace*). It didn't matter that it wasn't the usual "save the world" scenario - James Bond could go fight aliens and we'd still probably go see it, because he's James Bond. On the other hand, Bond-*esque* movies (like the recent *The Man from UNCLE*) tend to flop, because they're doing that silly stuff without the benefit of a lead character we've grown to love over fifty years/twenty-something films.

Here, the movie goes to some weird places that you'd never expect from the earlier, more grounded scenes, but you'll never mind because the characters are strong enough to follow them there. And that's within one film! Look at the *Scream* sequels – they can't bring themselves to kill off any of the core trio of Sidney, Dewey and Gale, because they know we love those characters... but the films also never have the guts to do anything different with them, to the extent that even the killers' motives are always the same ("Sidney ruined my life!", basically). It might have been frustrating for tagging purposes (especially when it came time to put together this book), but believe me – feeling like I had to hide a surprise "sub-genre" in a movie because it was presented as a sort of twist (think *From Dusk Till Dawn* with the vampire stuff being an out-of-nowhere turn to someone going in blind) was always appreciated. It's a shame it so rarely happened.

MOVIE #25 – JANUARY 25th

DUMPLINGS [JIAO ZI] (2004)
Dir: Fruit Chan
HMAD Review Date: November 23, 2009 (DVD)
Genre: Cannibal
Available from Lionsgate

Synopsis Based on Fading Memory: What's the secret ingredient for these delicious dumplings?

Review excerpt:
"...it's a strange and entertaining little movie. The _____ is treated so casually that you almost never really find it as sickening as it really is, which is impressive in a terrible sort of way. And it's nice to see Bai Ling playing someone with a little more depth and realism to her. If I were to judge from her performances in The Crow and Crank 2 and such, I'd guess she was just some weird Asian woman with a penchant for scenery chewing, not an actual actress. Hell, I didn't even recognize her at first. Also, she keeps a poodle on her counter nearly at all times. You'd think that the weirdest part of a movie with _____ would be _____, but no - I was continually weirded out by this little pooch sitting on a counter for no reason."

Reflection: Leave it to Lionsgate to release a part 2 as a part 1, and then release the original as its sequel, but that's what they did to us in America with the two *Three Extremes* anthologies. The one we think of as the original is actually the second film, presumably because two of its filmmakers had made bigger waves in the US (Takashi Miike and Chan Wook Park), whereas the first *Three Extremes* only had one name to sell it on (Jee-Woon Kim, who had not yet reached his level of fame here). Regardless, the other filmmaker from this film is Fruit Chan, from whom I still haven't seen anything else, but his entry sticks out the most because he turned his short into this feature version. To this day I'm not sure if he recut a feature down to short length for *Three Extremes*, or if he painstakingly made a longer version out of an existing short without any of the usual telltale signs of such a process, but it doesn't matter. It's a fascinating exercise to watch both, so if there's one movie in this chapter you should buy instead of renting or watching online, it's *Three Extremes*, as the disc release gives you the anthology film (in which *Dumplings* takes the silver; Chan Wook Park's segment is unsurprisingly the best) and the *Dumplings* feature. I made the "this would be better as an anthology segment" complaint a hundred times on the site, and saw many anthology segments that I wish could have been standalone features – this is the only time that I got to see both sides of that coin.

Oh, the "____" s above are a spoiler I originally included because I was writing assuming anyone who saw *Dumplings* had already seen the shorter version in *Three Extremes* (especially in the US, where I don't believe you can buy *Dumplings* on its own). For the purposes of this book, I'd like you to watch *Dumplings* first if possible!

HMAD Fun Fact: The shortest review, comprised of only 15 words (not counting the "What say you?" that ended all reviews), was for Jee-Woon Kim's film A Tale of Two Sisters. *The longest, at a whopping 3,243 words (not counting the "What say you" OR two P.S.s!) is Rob Zombie's* Halloween II.

MOVIE #26 – JANUARY 26th

EPITAPH [GIDAM] (2007)
Dir: Beom-sik Jeong, Sik Jung
HMAD Review Date: May 20, 2012 (Streaming)
Genre: Ghost, Psychological
Available from TLA Releasing

Synopsis Based on Fading Memory: A very confusing but very scary movie concerning a loose trilogy of intertwined stories set around a hospital.

Review excerpt:
"...it's actually kind of sad; all of the stories deal with someone who lost a loved one and how they deal with their grief – one guy becomes obsessed with a corpse, another becomes catatonic, etc. It's the mental anguish stemming from these losses that usually results in the horror-centric things that follow, so throughout the movie you can't help but feel sorry for pretty much everyone. There are no real "villains" per se, just a lot of broken hearts (and minds), unusual for a horror film in any genre."

Reflection: I admit in the review and here again that I had trouble following this one, but it was also one of the few Asian horror films that I found pretty scary. I can put aside my opposition to repeating myself for a few things, and the fact that I don't scare easily is one such example – I think it's important every single person reading this book understands that either due to my exposure to fright fare at an early age, or just my adult *over*-exposure leaving me numb, I just don't get startled when I watch most horror films. When I see something theatrically, I gauge a film's scariness by how much the crowd is being affected, but when I'm at home alone I really have no idea if a film is hitting those marks.

Because of this, as dumb as it sounds, a film's scare factor is never anything I consider when writing my review; I'll note if it was one of those rare films that did scare me, but otherwise it's off the hook; if I didn't like it it's because of poor writing, bad performances, or something else entirely. This might be part of why it took a while for me to warm up to a lot of Asian horror, because they tend to care more about freaking out the viewer than telling coherent stories, so I'm just not the target audience. But this one grabbed me thanks to its emphasis on grief and the always fun crisscrossing of a narrative (even if I didn't always follow it), and then had some scares to boot! Perfect! If I understood more of it, it'd probably be my favorite film this month.

MOVIE #27 – JANUARY 27th

VOICES [DU SARAM-YIDA] (2007)
Dir: Ki-hwan Oh
HMAD Review Date: April 28, 2009 (DVD)
Genre: Supernatural
Available from Lionsgate

Synopsis Based on Fading Memory: A girl is terrorized by a curse that turns people into extremely angry/violent attackers.

Review excerpt:
"...a unique take on the curse/weird things happening type of Eastern horror film that we've seen so many times. It's similar to Ju-On/The Grudge in a few ways, namely a curse that is seemingly born from intense anger and how it seems to focus on a few school girls (like Ju-On 2). But to its credit, that's more or less where the similarities end. There are no ghostly children making noises, nor do any ghosts with long hair covering their faces make an appearance. Hell, I don't even think water factors in to any of the scare scenes, which may be a first."

Reflection: It's funny - I almost scrapped this selection from the book. See, the process of writing this thing was a lengthy one, and it started with re-reading the entire site and picking every good/interesting title that wasn't too famous. I had too many, and couldn't decide on the themes for every month (some I knew I'd have, like slashers; others, like vampire movies, are here because I happened to have 30 vampire movies), so it took a while just to get the 365 titles down. And that's why this film almost got axed, because the generic, ghost-y sounding title made me think it was probably another haunting/ghost movie and I've already had enough of those this month (I was also probably thinking of *Voice*, the *Whispering Corridors* entry that is indeed along those lines). But then I re-read my review and "discovered" (hey it's been almost seven years since I wrote it) that the original title was *Someone Behind You*, which makes sense - unlike *Voices*, which does not, since no one hears voices or anything. Also, it's incredibly violent, which isn't unusual for a Korean horror film but that usually only applies to their reality-based entries like *I Saw the Devil*. For a supernatural movie like this, I'm not sure you'll see anything else with so much carnage in its first 45 minutes or so, making it one of the faster-paced Korean horror films I've seen. The third act isn't as effective, as it leaves a few questions unanswered, and some other answers create plot holes, but getting there is worth the relative disappointment.

It's also another winner for the ~~now defunct~~ recently revived After Dark series, which I'll get into more later in the book. Their first wave of titles offered *Reincarnation*, which I didn't like all that much, and their second wave didn't have any Asian horror at all, so this was a pretty solid way to make up for it. Alas, their fourth wave again lacked an Asian title, which bummed me out; US distributors tended to stick to proven commodities (i.e. *Ring* wannabes) when it came to selecting titles to import, so things like After Dark were our best chance of seeing things off the beaten path from Korea, Japan, etc. They had OTHER foreign titles (the Norwegian *Skjult*, for example, was in the fourth wave), but out of four collections they only had two Asian horror flicks, and one was kind of weak. Not a great batting average for a "franchise" that was allegedly devoted to showing us things that we wouldn't get to see otherwise.

MOVIE #28 – JANUARY 28th

THE EYE 2 [GIN GWAI 2] (2004)
Dir: The Pang Brothers
HMAD Review Date: July 17, 2008 (DVD)
Genre: Ghost
Available from Lionsgate

Synopsis Based on Fading Memory: A woman survives a suicide attempt and gains the power to see ghosts. Win-win! (or lose-lose, depending on your POV I guess)

Review excerpt:
"The story is pretty powerful and even melancholy. The incredible score (other than "ghosts", this is about all the two films have in common; the original's was great too) aids a lot of the more emotional scenes, particularly the big reveal which is when the movie turns from decent to simply GOOD. If anything, the movie becomes even SMALLER at this point, and it's a gamble that pays off. There are still some horror elements (including the only real gore in the film), but it's still completely focused on the character and story, not spectacle. Very admirable."

Reflection: I wrestled with whether or not to include this one; with very few exceptions I shied away from sequels (explained in the intro), and the original is one of the better known Asian horror titles here in the US, so it's likely a number of you have seen this one. But I DID want to throw in a few better known titles each month, and in that regard I can't think of a better one to include – since it's superior to the original (and any that followed) and just a solid movie to boot. You don't even need to see the original since they're not connected in any way, so if you missed the original (or the largely terrible remake with Jessica Alba), you can just start here if you like. The only thing you'll miss out on is the feeling of "Wow, this is a lot better!"

I wonder if they would have remade this story had the first remake been a big enough success to warrant a follow-up, or if they'd just go off on their own path like the *Quarantine* sequel (which was not a *[Rec] 2* remake). As I mention in the full review, THIS story would probably be a better fit for Alba's limited range, and it'd be interesting to see if the US versions could follow the original series' pattern and improve from part 1 to 2. But, alas, while Alba's version was technically successful, no one really liked it either, and it was near the end of the Asian remake craze, so any chance it had of getting a sequel was somewhat less than slim.

MOVIE #29 – JANUARY 29th

THE GUARD POST [GP506] (2008)
Dir: Su-chang Kong
HMAD Review Date: February 14, 2013 (Streaming)
Genre: Psychological
Available from Asian Crush

Synopsis Based on Fading Memory: A bunch of soldiers are dead, and our hero is questioning a survivor to find out what happened.

Review excerpt:
"Kong strikes a fine balance between past and present, and keeps both stories about equal in terms of excitement and intrigue. Sure, we know that just about everyone from the past is dead, so there's not a lot of reason to get invested in any of the characters in those scenes, but since they contain the bulk of the answers they retain their worth. And there are some fun minor mysteries that carry throughout the film, like a tape that Noh finds with one of the dead soldier's confession. It's mysteriously missing a chunk of what he is saying, so not only do we have to find out the missing information, we also want to know who erased it in the present day. There's a nice symbiotic relationship between the two storylines, making it a lot more interesting than a guy telling a story about how he survived this awful thing. Also, of course he has to be interrupted from time to time so that Noh (and the audience) doesn't have all the information too soon, and these all work well as they tend to be urgent matters."

Reflection: Kong made an earlier film called *R-Point*, which was similar, but this is the superior of the two, so it's like he had a do-over or something. It's not often Asian horror films used the war (any war) as a backdrop, and while they have more male heroes on the average than American films, I think this is the only one I ever saw that took a page from *The Thing* and had an entirely male cast. Another great quality is that it blends horror and action nicely – the climax is actually kind of taken from *The Rock*, of all things, and it actually works! The (spoiler?) lack of a supernatural element also works in its favor, at least for me. Ghosts don't scare me much, but give a guy some kind of brain-attacking illness when he's around a lot of weaponry? Terrifying.

If you're just reading this chapter along like a regular book, I hope you've realized by now that I tended to gravitate toward the sort of Asian horror films that *didn't* get routinely remade throughout the '00s. Those are all well and good, and serve their purpose as scare machines, but they never really interested me much, and I'd have trouble remembering anything specific about them down the road (or even seeing them; I was recently surprised to discover there were more than three Japanese *Ringu* films, which is sad since I watched four of them). This one isn't the best example since it's only been a little over two years, but some of the other films in this chapter I only saw once, five or six years ago, and still remember specifics. But on the other hand, I would have trouble recalling the basic plots of the "ghost in the machine" types a few weeks after viewing them. It's a shame they don't generate enough revenue over here for distributors to scour Japan, China, Korea, etc. for more titles to acquire – if there's a new *Ju-On* film you can bet it'll be picked up here rather quickly, but movies like this were probably always slipping through the cracks. I'm glad I got to see at least a few of them.

MOVIE #30 – JANUARY 30th

JU-REI: THE UNCANNY [JU-REI: GEKIJÔ-BAN - KURO-JU-REI] (2004)
Dir: Kôji Shiraishi
HMAD Review Date: May 22, 2012 (DVD)
Genre: Ghost
Available from Pathfinder Home Entertainment

Synopsis Based on Fading Memory: We track a *Grudge*-y curse in reverse!

Review excerpt:
"...it's well written, with little tidbits being dropped into the narrative that won't be important until "later". Like Memento, *watching the film in sequence wouldn't work at all (ever try that feature on the DVD? It becomes the boringest movie ever), because halfway through you'd be hearing the vague news report about a killing that you already saw, and it would basically be an aimless movie about a bunch of people dying due to their Kevin Bacon-y connections to the person who dies in Chapter 1. It might be an interesting experiment to watch it in order, but it would ruin the fun and suspense of the film."*

Reflection: The "gimmick" of *Memento* is so singular and awesome that it's rarely attempted by anyone else, because the film is automatically dubbed a *Memento* rip-off and would have thousands of misguided Batman fans who think Christopher Nolan shits gold coming after it. But that's not to say he's got the exclusive rights to telling a story backwards, and for the most part the concept serves this otherwise routine ghost/curse J-horror entry quite well. The lack of a central character is a bit of a hurdle (the climax – which is also the beginning of the narrative – isn't particularly exciting since it revolves around someone the audience is just meeting), but it's a fine way to mix up this sort of story, and it's fun how the director builds suspense, not around *if* someone will die (they always do), but *when* – the chapters all run around the same length, making it a wonderful surprise when there's an exception to that rule, offing the new chapter's protagonist within seconds.

I should note that this is not a particularly great-looking movie, shot with what appears to be a consumer grade camera. I mellowed out some on this unfortunate development in modern low-budget filmmaking over the years; at first seeing images I could literally produce myself would be enough to make me hate a movie. But after a while I realized this trend wasn't ever going to go away and so I might as well work with it. In this case, the unique hook was enough to overcome the sub-par imagery, coupled with the fact that even a few of the genre's classics, like *Ju-On*, look no better. I still won't forgive bad color timing or sound editing, though. No excuse for that shit.

MOVIE #31 – JANUARY 31st

BLOODY REUNION (aka TO SIR WITH LOVE) [SEUSEUNG-UI EUNHYE] (2006)
Dir: Dae-wung Lim
HMAD Review Date: August 25, 2007 (DVD)
Genre: Slasher
Available from Tartan Asia Extreme

Synopsis Based on Fading Memory: A reunion is disrupted by a slasher in a bunny mask.

Review excerpt:
"For a slasher, it delivered what I expect – one or two kills I don't see coming (at least not at the time they do), some decent splatter, an interesting killer disguise (a giant bunny mask! Gah!!), non-ignorance of basic suspense, and a good back story. The back story is what impressed me the most. Sort of like LOST, *we learn mainly through quick flashbacks what led the characters to be the way they are today. And I admit I was pretty surprised at what was revealed along the way."*

Reflection: I really wish I saw more slasher films from Korea, Japan, etc., because those countries tend to produce... let's say "offbeat" movies, and if there's one thing the slasher sub-genre isn't known for, it's originality. Don't get me wrong, I love the damn things more than any other kind of horror movie (turn the page for a month's worth of evidence!), but I'll also be the first to admit that they tend to stick to a basic template – if you watch a hundred slasher movies at random, I bet fewer than ten will leave you surprised with any reveals that unfold in the plot. Of course, sometimes said surprises don't sit well with folks, and this is no exception – *Bloody Reunion* has a twist that I won't spoil, but it's one that also happened in a more famous horror import and resulted in a lot of folks hating that movie. The surprise has a better execution here, for what it's worth – the one in the other film really didn't work as well because it wasn't set up properly, but here it was, so when we get to the reveal, it doesn't feel completely out of nowhere. There's a certain Oscar-winning movie from the mid-'90s that more or less pulled the same trick and no one really got mad at that - it's all in the execution, folks!

Anyway, this is the end of Asian horror month. I tried to mix it up as best as I could, among not only sub-genres but also the different countries. They each have their strengths and weaknesses, and again, since I wasn't a fan when I started the site, one of my favorite things about that six-year journey was not only acquiring more of an affinity for them, but also getting into tune with their varied sensibilities. Now I know that I'm more likely to get into a Korean horror film than a Japanese one, or that if I want something a bit goofier I should look at Hong Kong titles from the '80s. Thanks, HMAD!

FEBRUARY – SLASHER MOVIES

ARTIST: ERIC SHONBORN

February is known as "Women in horror" month in some circles, so why not pay tribute to the noble slasher film, which has allowed many a virginal (or at least, somewhat shy) young woman to survive the mass murder happening all around her, and in many cases symbolically castrate the evil man who means to do her harm?

It's also the shortest month, which is ironic because I had more potential titles for this month than any other – almost enough to cover half the book on its own (which is why you'll see a lot of slashers in the more generally themed months ahead). I consider it my favorite sub-genre of horror, so I would seek out more slasher movies than say, werewolf or haunted house films, and thus it shouldn't be a surprise that I had a lot more of these to choose from. Suffice to say, it was pretty hard narrowing this crop of titles down, so for this month in particular I hope you enjoy many of the titles I've selected, as they made it in over something that might have become your favorite movie!

On that note, I realized something not long after starting this experiment – a lot of slashers, even the universally acknowledged "great" ones, coast a bit on our nostalgia of seeing them at a young age. Many men in my generation saw their first pair of breasts in a slasher movie, and their simplistic plots made them more readily digestible to a young mind, as you wouldn't find them "boring" at eight years old like you might with *Rosemary's Baby* or *Silence of the Lambs*. So as much as I love these things, I have to accept that my favorites now are likely to be my favorites forever – which is why a newer slasher that impresses me stands out all that much more. So for the first selection this month, I could think of only one movie that deserved the honor...

MOVIE #32 – FEBRUARY 1st

COLD PREY (2006)
Dir: Roar Uthaug
HMAD Review Date: January 15, 2009 (DVD)
Genre: Slasher
Available from Anchor Bay Entertainment

Synopsis Based on Fading Memory: A group of snowboarders take refuge in an abandoned hotel, and a killer shows up.

Review excerpt:
"The back of the DVD says that this is more than a typical 'body count' movie, but I'm really not sure why. Its greatest strength is that it's EXACTLY a body count movie, with no supernatural or twisty nonsense to sink it down. There's a guy in a mask (actually he's covered head to toe), brandishing a weapon, and one by one he stalks and kills four of our five kids, leaving one girl to fight back. What the hell isn't slasher about that?"

Reflection: Two of the worst slashers I've ever seen took place at ski resorts (*Iced* and *Shredder*), so I had low expectations for this – but it's pretty goddamn great! I've even re-watched it a couple times and found that it holds up (as does its first sequel, which is basically *Halloween II*-ing this one by picking up right where it leaves off and taking place in a hospital). Someone once said that doing a straightforward slasher would be impossible post-*Scream*, but this movie deftly proves them wrong. There's also a third film, but as this writing it has yet to be distributed in the US. I understand it's a prequel, and not a very good one at that, however.

Back on point - what's funny is that the film works so well by just doing things the way they should be done. It's not reinventing the wheel, it's not really trying to be the next icon of horror, or whatever – it's just *done right*. The kids are likeable, the suspense scenes play like gangbusters, and the killer is imposing without being cartoonish. There's a small twist that you might be able to see coming right away (pay close attention to the opening scene, more specifically what you *don't* see, if you're the type that likes to be ahead of the movie for such things), but even though I figured it out it didn't hamper my enjoyment one bit.

P.S. Uthaug followed this up with a pretty great action/adventure movie called *Escape* that I also recommend, starring this film's ass-kicking Ingrid Bolsø Berdal.

MOVIE #33 – FEBRUARY 2nd

ALONE IN THE DARK (1982)
Dir: Jack Sholder
HMAD Review Date: March 20, 2007 (DVD)
Genre: Slasher
Available from Image Entertainment

Synopsis Based on Fading Memory: A group of mental patients who have escaped from an institution run by Donald Pleasence (!) terrorize their new doctor and his family during a blackout.

Review excerpt:
"THIS movie titled Alone in the Dark *is actually quite good, but it's fairly obscure, so if you bring it up, you always have to say, "No, not the one where Tara Reid plays a scientist." Thanks Uwe Boll. So just to be clear, THIS film has Donald Pleasence, Martin Landau, Jack Palance, and some other dudes no one has seen since. Pleasence is the head of the institution and is just as loony as the patients. I particularly enjoy when he gives Landau a match, knowing perfectly well Landau's character is a known arsonist. Immediately, Landau sets his shirt on fire and begins waving it around while Pleasence comforts a patient who believes she is being turned into porcelain."*

Reflection: This underrated gem was near the top of my "wishlist" for my (mostly) monthly HMAD Presents screening series at the New Beverly. Sadly, a 35mm print could never be located, and it's certainly not a title for which a studio will have a DCP (and I'd rather slice my own dick off than charge people to watch a DVD), so I never got the chance. But the home invasion plot means it'll work just as well at home, so I hope you aren't holding out for a chance to see it theatrically anyway. I actually saw this as a kid (at least 95% of HMAD entries were of movies I never saw before, but for the others I made exceptions for movies I watched when I was younger and couldn't remember very well) and was happy to see it held up, though I felt a bit dumb as an adult that the film's "twist" shocked me so much when I was a younger lad. Did it fool you, too?

Fun fact about this one – it's the first film for Jack Sholder, who went on to direct *Nightmare on Elm Street 2: Freddy's Revenge*, aka "the gay Freddy movie". I actually considered putting that film in the book somewhere, because it gets a bum rap (it was even skipped over in *Nightmare* series' continuity; its events and characters are never mentioned in the following sequels) and is such a uniquely odd movie for a franchise entry. Not *Halloween III* odd, mind you, but still – what a strange direction to take when the series was just getting started (even if you ignore the homoerotic element, Sholder disregards a number of the rules the first film established). I didn't like it as a kid, but as an adult that can appreciate that sort of risk (I'm also a champion of the *Blair Witch* sequel for similar reasons), I'm in its corner. If you're among the few that HAS seen this movie already, give *Freddy's Revenge* another look. If you're being honest with yourself, it's probably better than you remember.

MOVIE #34 – FEBRUARY 3rd

NIGHTMARE (1981)
Dir: Romano Scavolini
HMAD Review Date: October 26, 2012 (Revival screening)
Genre: Slasher
Available from Code Red

Synopsis Based on Fading Memory: An escaped mental patient makes his way back to his childhood home, as flashbacks reveal the source of his murderous rage.

Review excerpt:
"The cop in particular is a delight; he has this really whiny voice (it sounded like a guy doing a Richard Dreyfuss impression) and a computer that is incredibly advanced for 1981. At one point he finds out about a stolen car in South Carolina that is also the site of a possible homicide, and rather than consult the file or even click "more info" or something, he types in "WHY POSSIBLE HOMICIDE?" and the computer explains it to him! He also uses it to project where the guy is going (and it's right), so it's a wonder he didn't just put legs on the damn thing and let it go out and find the guy itself."

Reflection: In 2012, the awesome Phil Blankenship (if you read the special thanks, you'd know his importance to HMAD) was one of the brains behind the marathon of Video Nasties at the Cinefamily repertory theater, a mini-fest that included this very entry. If you're unfamiliar, the Nasties were a group of seventy or so mostly horror movies that were banned in the UK for one reason or another (I'm *really* simplifying for the sake of brevity – look it up, it's pretty fascinating), and seeing them all is kind of like a rite of passage for hardcore horror fans. So Phil and his partners picked 31 of them and ran a different one every night at midnight in October, programmed in order of how hardcore they were (as one of the Cinefamily programmers explained, you'll go from asking "Why was *this* banned?" on the first night to "Why isn't this STILL banned?!?" on the last). As you can tell from the review date, this would be one of the more legitimately "nasty" ones, but the weirdo stuff kept it feeling lighter than it probably was. Also: not too many horror movies are set in Florida for whatever reason, so that's kind of novel.

Seriously though, look up the Nasties. Do a checklist and try to see them all (if you watch every movie in this book, you'll have a decent head start), though even though it's only around seventy movies it's tougher than it seems. I intended to see them all before finishing HMAD, but fell short because I kept forgetting to queue them up. There was even a reader who'd always remind me that I was forgetting to mark them - he probably knows better than I do which ones I still need to see. The list was pretty random; there are movies that you'd expect would most certainly be on there that aren't, and yet it includes such relatively tame fare as *Evil Dead*. There's even a documentary or two on the subject if you want a full history, though no books as far as I know. Hmm...

MOVIE #35 – FEBRUARY 4th

AMER (2009)
Dir: Hélène Cattet, Bruno Forzani
HMAD Review Date: October 29, 2011 (DVD)
Genre: Giallo, Weird
Available from Olive Films

Synopsis Based on Fading Memory: A *giallo* homage where we see the freaky things that happen to a woman at three different periods in her life... right?

Review excerpt:
"...it's an artsy horror film, something that usually turns me off, but there was something quite compelling about *Amer*. It was almost like the world's longest experimental short film; every shot was striking but short, it was very flashy and stylish, and I often wasn't sure where it was going at any point. It was also remarkably short on dialogue – I'm not exaggerating when I say that there were probably only 30 lines in the entire movie, most of them in the first act and almost none of them delivered directly on camera. However, it did not lack for sound FX – EVERYTHING in this movie had exaggerated sound work, from the whrrrp of a tight leather glove to the bouncing of a soccer ball. If someone was watching *Amer* in an adjacent room, you might suspect they were just listening to some sort of "Foley 101" CD."

Reflection: This is one of the few films in the book I've actually had time to revisit during the writing process, and as a result I actually moved it from May (batshit crazy horror movies) to here, slasher/*giallo* month. It's a strange film, don't get me wrong, but as I revisited I realized it wasn't as gonzo as the other May movies, and since I was short on *giallo* entries, I decided it would make a better fit here. Plus, slasher movies are kind of good date movie options, and *Amer* has a peculiar effect on me and other fans I've talked to, in that it... well, it kind of works as an aphrodisiac. The heightened sound FX, odd close-ups, breathy characters... even though there isn't much actual sex, it definitely taps into that part of your brain. Maybe I should have put it in on Valentine's Day, now that I think of it.

If you're a fan, I highly encourage you to check out the pair's follow-up film, *The Strange Colour of Your Body's Tears*, which has a more traditional narrative but otherwise dives headfirst into the same stuff that makes this one great. And by that I mean it might turn you on, too. Don't watch on an airplane or whatever!

MOVIE #36 – FEBRUARY 5th

FRAYED (2007)
Dir: Norbert Caoili, Rob Portmann
HMAD Review Date: August 25, 2009 (DVD)
Genre: Slasher
Available from Lionsgate

Synopsis Based on Fading Memory: A killer clown stalks some teens in the woods – but there's a twist!

Review excerpt:
"The opening scene is one of the best horror openers in recent memory, and the film as a whole favors suspense and atmosphere over a body count. I do not make kind comparisons to Halloween *easily (i.e. usually it's "Screw you for ripping off* Halloween!*"), but for the most part I'd be comfortable with making that association here. Had I spent another half hour or so completely buying into the ruse (I figured it out 15 minutes in), I'd probably have liked it even more. But in a way that's even more of a compliment to the film - I wasn't buying half of what they were showing me, but I was still engaged by it."*

Reflection: The average review would get a few comments within a week or so after being published and then kind of die off, but *Frayed* is one of the exceptions – for FOUR YEARS after I posted the review I'd continue getting new comments on it, mostly from people asking to clarify the film's twist ending – or thanking previous commenters for explaining it. And that's funny, because not only do I spell it out in the review (not in the excerpt), but specifically discuss how it was a bit too easy for me to spot. So why are so many folks having trouble? My guess? The film's (admittedly overlong) 110 minute length meant more distracted viewings, or full-blown fast forwarding over "boring" stuff, causing them to miss important details. Because it really isn't that hard to figure out, and the movie has one of those *Saw*-style "let's cut back and show how it all worked" things at the end, so I don't know why anyone would be confused if they were paying attention. But since HMAD was started as a way for folks to discuss a horror movie, I like that the comment section helped others piece it together. It's actually one of the rare instances where the comment section lived up to the site's original intention.

When putting this book together I was dismayed to see its directors had yet to make another feature, and sadly it wasn't the only time. There were also a depressing number of filmmakers who had seemingly left the genre behind after knocking one out of the park, which is in some ways worse. This generation lacks the number of titans we had growing up (Carpenter, Romero, Dante, Cronenberg), and when I'd see something as near-great as this I'd have hopes that we were seeing the birth of a new major player in the genre. I still hold out hope, but it seems to me that with very few exceptions (James Wan and Neil Marshall are safe bets), those '70s/'80s guys will still be the go-to names for "Masters of Horror" for my son's generation.

HMAD Fun Fact: My favorite sub-genre is the slasher film, and it shows - I reviewed 367 such films for the site. Yes, this is almost exactly the number of movies I would need to fill a book on its own, and don't think it didn't cross my mind. (If you're wondering, the one movie I'd leave out would be Halloween: Resurrection, *probably.)*

MOVIE #37 – FEBRUARY 6th

MASK MAKER (2010)
Dir: Griff Furst
HMAD Review Date: November 20, 2011 (Streaming)
Genre: Slasher
Available from Screen Media

Synopsis Based on Fading Memory: A group of young adults are fixing up a house that one of them just purchased, and a killer shows up.

Review excerpt:
"...it's shot incredibly well, which is all the more surprising considering Furst's background in Asylum productions like I Am Omega, though he also helmed Lake Placid 3, which was a vast improvement on its predecessor. Thus, I think this guy might deserve a shot at a real production. He clearly knows how to put a movie together, and make even the most generic stories entertaining – imagine what he might be able to pull off with some dough and a good script."

Reflection: As I got further and further along with this "experiment", I ran out of older stuff I wanted to see and found myself watching more and more DTV filler, which was part of the reason that I eventually quit. But within that realm, a few names would give me hope – Griff Furst was one of them. Sure, it may have been a "in the land of the blind, the man with one eye is king" kind of deal, but still – he knew how to engage even a jaded/bored viewer (me), which is more than I can say about far too many others. This was, I THINK, the only non-Syfy/Asylum movie I saw from him, and I hope for his sake he has continued to move beyond that kind of rubbish.

I also found that sequels were becoming rarer in the slasher sub-genre; even when the film would end with a clear indication of a follow-up, the odds were a lot slimmer than they were during the early '80s or late '90s slasher cycles. It's surprising, because these movies often had the same (or even lower) budgets as their '80s predecessors, but more avenues to generate income – if a $10,000 slasher from 1981 didn't land a theatrical release, it was dead – there was no DVD, VOD, or Netflix Instant to sell it to and earn a nice little profit and get the ball rolling on part 2, like nowadays. More often than not, the sequels we're getting now are the same ones we got back then – another *Scream*, more *Halloween* and *Friday the 13ths* in development... hell, they even made a third *I Know What You Did Last Summer*! But no *Mask Maker 2*. Boo.

MOVIE #38 – FEBRUARY 7th

TOURIST TRAP (1979)
Dir: David Schmoeller
HMAD Review Date: October 2, 2007 (DVD)
Genre: Slasher, Supernatural
Available from Full Moon Pictures

Synopsis Based on Fading Memory: A group of friends break down in an out-of-the-way town and stumble across a creepy tourist spot and its seemingly kindly owner. And then a killer shows up.

Review excerpt:
"There's a scene about halfway through the film that ranks as one of the creepiest and yet most hilarious scenes in slasher history. Tanya Roberts finds herself in a room full of mannequins, and then, one by one, the mannequins let out a choir note ("La!") and fall onto her. Eventually there's like 10 mannequins on top of her. It's one of my favorite set-pieces in any horror film ever, and now, anytime I pass a mannequin at the mall or whatever, I usually let out a "La!" before throwing one on top of Tanya Roberts."

Reflection: I love this damn movie so much. In 2007 (the first year) I decided to double up my entries for October – the day's traditional "new to me" movie and one of my favorites. It was basically a way to combat all of the other sites that had their own "horror movie for every day in October!" features with more popular movies than the ones I was watching for my "new movie every day" rule. As you can see from the review date, I wasted little time taking the opportunity to show this movie some love. I tried repeatedly to make it one of my HMAD screenings at the New Beverly, but alas it never worked out (though I did get to see it on 35mm at a different theater). I've often said that the *House of Wax* remake from 2005 was more of a remake of this film than the Vincent Price movie, and I hope more and more people can catch on to that so that we can be spared an official, unnecessary remake. It's the best movie that you'll ever see Charles Band's name in the credits, that's for damn sure.

Don't let Band's presence scare you away, however – it's nothing like anything else he ever made. That the villain is a full-sized human being - instead of a puppet or Gremlin rip-off - automatically sets it apart from 90% of his filmography, and while Schmoeller's later output would unfortunately include some of that crap (including the original *Puppetmaster*), in some ways it just makes this one all the more impressive – it's really well-made! The scares work, it's kind of intense at times, and he manages all that without resorting to gratuitous violence – the film is actually rated PG (it was before the PG-13 existed; obviously it would get that today, but still not an R). A lot of the films here are unrated because they were independent releases that didn't need to bother going to the MPAA, but if they DID they'd get R ratings – this is one of only two (I think?) PG films in the book, and yet it's one of the scarier ones you'll find within it.

MOVIE #39 – FEBRUARY 8th

CARVER (2008)
Dir: Franklin Guerrero Jr.
HMAD Review Date: March 22, 2008 (DVD)
Genre: Slasher, Survival
Available from Allumination

Synopsis Based on Fading Memory: Two brothers get stuck in an isolated town, and a killer shows up.

Review excerpt:
"Our hero enters a stall, and the toilet is kind of dirty. He makes a disgusted sigh and opens the adjacent stall, which is ten times WORSE. He retches, and then notices a large pile of poop on the wall. "How do you shit on the wall?!" he asks no one in particular. It's hilarious. I should note at this time that the film has a particular fascination with bodily functions, particularly poop. After this sequence, another guy walks into another outhouse that is even MORE disgusting than the previous one. The guy shrugs and sits down on the toilet anyway, and then the disgusting bowl is used as a weapon against him a bit later. We are also treated to the sight of a girl puking, and in the film's most memorable kill, a testicle being plied, which results in blood and whatever else is inside a testicle to explode over the camera lens. Christ."

Reflection: I honestly think the only reason this one worked for me (besides the repetitive use of "Turkey in the Straw") is the fact that the male hero shared my penchant for yelling at inanimate objects. I almost never raise my voice to another human being, but if you're a thing I stub my toe on, or a cell phone/computer that's taking too long to load, or (especially) a screw for a piece of furniture I have to assemble, you best invest in some earplugs, because I will unleash a torrent of angry profanity at you if you don't cooperate! So I felt endeared to the movie when the hero yells at some wine glasses, because that's ridiculous even by my standards.

But I also enjoyed the brother dynamic, as it's not something you see in this kind of movie. Male protagonists are rare enough in this sub-genre, so brothers? This might be the only one, in fact. I mean, sure, there's a female along for the ride, but the focus is on the brothers, and she... well, let's just say she doesn't become the Final Girl and leave it at that. I'm sure some rabble rouser will try to say the movie is misogynist, ignoring the testicle squishing described above and focusing only on whatever misfortune is directed at the female characters, but that's just what such people do: ignore the things that conflict with their pointless argument. Take it from a guy who barely remembers it beyond what he wrote in his review: it's not a misogynist movie - it hates everyone equally!

MOVIE #40 – FEBRUARY 9th

BLOODY MOON (1981)
Dir: Jess Franco
HMAD Review Date: September 9, 2011 (DVD)
Genre: Slasher
Available from Severin

Synopsis Based on Fading Memory: A group of girls are attending a language school, and a killer shows up.

Review excerpt:
"I was kind of impressed with the mystery. It's almost like there are two plots going on and then at the end they tie together, Johnny Gossamer-style. And I also like that it ultimately had nothing to do with the main girl – by this point in the slasher cycle we had gotten to the point where the Final Girls were often directly targeted by the killer (even if he usually killed everyone but her), but this goes back to something like Friday the 13th *where the motive was more general and she just happened to be the last one left alive."*

Reflection: This is the only Jess Franco title in the book, which statistically should be impossible since he seemingly directed 50% of all movies ever made (an exaggeration, yes, but IMDb lists over 200 – and given his many, MANY aliases, it's very likely that number is low compared to the real count). It's got some lulls, and the murders aren't that inventive, but there are several weirdo highlights (including a Mickey Mouse mask for the killer), making it stick out.

Plus it was interesting to see a European take on the then-popular (and mostly US-based) slasher craze. As a slasher aficionado, I'd go out of my way to see foreign takes on the sub-genre, but they were relatively few and far between (at least, as best as I could find). Take out the Italian stuff and there were almost NONE while they were coming out every week in the US, and the 2nd cycle of the late '90s seemed all but exclusive to us silly Americans. Where are the Mexican slashers? Or the Thai ones? Even the UK didn't produce as many as I would expect, given that they had a pretty consistent output of genre fare that made its way to the US. For Christmas I would like a slasher from every nation. Thanks in advance.

MOVIE #41 – FEBRUARY 10th

MY SUPER PSYCHO SWEET 16 (2009)
Dir: Jacob Gentry
HMAD Review Date: August 5, 2010 (Cable)
Genre: Slasher, Teen
Available from MTV Networks

Synopsis Based on Fading Memory: A spoiled brat is throwing a huge party for her birthday, and a killer shows up.

Review excerpt:
"It's an effective slasher, with a unique setting (a roller rink!) and a pretty creepy looking killer. But I guess that's what happens when you get a real filmmaker to helm a throwaway movie. The Signal's Jacob Gentry could have phoned it in, but instead he made an effective slasher, which is even more impressive when you consider the film's basic cable requirements don't allow for several slasher movie traits (nudity, excessive gore, and even smoking pot). The unfortunate commercial breaks are the only real TV movie thing about it – even the gore is decent (love the fire extinguisher kill, and any movie featuring a corpse, sans head, smashing into a cake while on roller skates, is automatically worth a look)."

Reflection: MTV eventually made two sequels to this; the first sequel was disappointing but the third entry made a minor comeback in quality. But they lacked a key ingredient: the element of surprise that made this one so enjoyable. When I sat down for the sequels, I KNEW that a movie called *My Super Psycho Sweet 16* from MTV could be pretty good – I had no such expectation when I watched the original. But since it's attempting to be *Scream* for the kids who were only a couple years old when that film came out, I kind of like that it's not a whodunit – we know who our killer is right off the bat (another reason *Part 2* paled, as they brought him back despite having less of a motive – the third film changes things up a bit), so we can just get on with it rather than deal with a lot of backstory (probably a necessity since it's a TV movie – gotta keep it exciting or the kids will change the channel!).

And props to whoever designed the mask (yes, there's a mask even though we know the identity), because it kinda looks like the "King" from the Burger King ads (or the game *Sneak King*, if you will), but for the bulk of the movie our killer's half burnt and wearing ratty clothes, not unlike the same year's polarizing *Halloween II* (the Rob Zombie variant). The films obviously did well for them, or else they wouldn't have dove into the slasher well again with their (not bad!) *Scream* series. Funnily enough, I used to watch MTV for hours on end when I was a younger lad, but angrily jumped ship when they stopped showing videos in favor of scripted/reality programming. Now that I will likely hate any music videos they DO show, they pull me back in (temporarily) with slasher stuff.

MOVIE #42 – FEBRUARY 11th

HORRIBLE (1981)
Dir: Joe D'Amato
HMAD Review Date: December 3, 2009 (DVD)
Genre: Slasher
Available from Mya Communication/ Ryko

Synopsis Based on Fading Memory: In this sorta sequel to *Anthropophagus* but definite knockoff of *Halloween*, a killer with regenerative properties hacks his way through a town and sets his sights on a particular household as a cop and a priest try to bring him down.

Review excerpt:
"The *Anthropophagus* tie stems from the fact that the killer is played by the same guy (George Eastman), and his name is similar. They also say he's from a Greek island (there's a lot of racism levied at the Greek people early on in the film), which puts this pretty much at the top of the pack when it comes to unrelated sequels actually having some semblance to the "original" film. Then again, it has the same director (Joe D'Amato, who also has a number of pseudonyms; he uses Peter Newton here), so I guess it's fitting that it would have more similarities than usual."

Reflection: Since watching *Horrible* (also known as *Absurd, Anthropophagus 2, Rosso Sangue,* and even *Zombie 6* for some goddamn reason), I revisited *Anthropophagus* and discovered that when sober and watching without a crowd of horror fans, it's a pretty boring movie. So this one – which also has its share of lulls in between the nutty highlights - might actually be better, and certainly shouldn't be piggybacking on the other when it doesn't even have to. That said, I'd be curious to watch them as a double feature, provided I had some caffeine beforehand (and during).

Also this is probably the tenth or so mention of *Halloween*, so if you're new to me it's probably a good time to mention that *Halloween* is not just my favorite film of all time, it's my favorite THING, period (tied with the Meat Loaf album "*Bat out of Hell*", and if you think I'm kidding, ask my wife – per my will I am to be buried with copies of both). Because it has inspired so many slasher films, I see rip-offs of it a lot, and I go back and forth with whether or not it annoys me. There's no real rhyme or reason to it; sometimes I find it quite insulting, but other times I actually find it kind of "cute", like a little kid imitating his older brother or something. If it's in this book it's probably one of the latter, at any rate. And also, since I've seen it so many times it has been kind of ingrained into every part of my brain, which means I find it easy to compare it to just about anything. In short: if you read this entire book, you're gonna see it mentioned a lot. Hope that's OK. I also hope you're not John Carpenter, because then it'd be kind of embarrassing. Though I guess he can take solace knowing that all of his movies are too popular to be included in this book.

MOVIE #43 – FEBRUARY 12th

BLOOD RAGE (1987)
Dir: John Grissmer
HMAD Review Date: November 22, 2012 (VHS)
Genre: Slasher
Available from Arrow Video

Synopsis Based on Fading Memory: It's Thanksgiving, and a man breaks out of an institution to clear his name for a murder caused by his twin brother. Upon hearing of the escape, the actual evil twin realizes he has license to kill more people and blame his poor brother again.

Review excerpt:
"...the body count is more than sufficient, and I enjoy that Terry has a Voorhees-ian opposition to sex, killing most people during sex or some sort of romantic encounter. One such bit is incredible enough to rewind (on a 25-year-old VHS tape being played on a 20-year-old VCR, this is dangerous territory); two of the teens are making rather tender love on a diving board, with the male lightly kissing his lover's lips in a very sweet way. Then we hear Terry casually say "Hey, stop that!" like one would scold a furniture scratching cat, and then Grismmer cuts to a wide shot just in time to see Terry nearly take the guy's head off with his machete and then throw him into the pool.."

Reflection: This one almost didn't make the book, as it was unavailable for so long and the only DVD version was severely cut. And that bummed me out, because there aren't many late '80s slashers that I enjoy beyond a handful of the franchise ones *(Halloween 4, Dream Warriors*, and yes, Mr. Farmer, *Jason Takes Manhattan*), and this is legitimately good stuff, with some great kills, a dash of black humor, and a grim ending I didn't see coming. Thankfully, Arrow and my own laziness came to the rescue - by the time I actually got the book finished, two years after sadly excising *Blood Rage* from consideration, the movie was "found", remastered for Blu-ray, and finally released. Perhaps *London After Midnight* can be found in time for a second edition of the book?

This is one of only two Thanksgiving-set slasher movies that I know of, and the other (*Home Sweet Home*) is as hard to find as *Blood Rage* was up until recently (I've listed it for February 29th, since it's a made-up day). But they share another similarity - both of them do almost nothing with the namesake holiday. It's just the excuse for everyone to be together, with nary a decoration in sight or turkey-driven kill scene. Eli Roth's *Thanksgiving* trailer had all that stuff and it's not even a real movie! I realized long ago that Thanksgiving is skipped over when it comes to holiday-based slasher movies because it's more of a strictly family celebration on the average, and it's too much of a bummer to see a family wiped out in a movie as opposed to a bunch of friends (and if a slasher movie doesn't kill off a bunch of its cast, it's not a slasher movie!). However, this film actually does have a group of friends, and yet they still basically just name-check the day a few times and mention food every now and then (there's a great cranberry sauce gag), so maybe I'm wrong. Maybe everyone's just lazy.

MOVIE #44 – FEBRUARY 13th

TORSO [I CORPI PRESENTANO TRACCE DI VIOLENZA CARNALE] (1973)
Dir: Sergio Martino
HMAD Review Date: February 17, 2008 (Revival screening)
Genre: Giallo
Available from Blue Underground

Synopsis Based on Fading Memory: A group of female pals head out to a villa someone's family owns... and a killer shows up.

Review excerpt:
"...most of the movie is simply people leering at each other. Literally every 30 seconds there is a shot of someone looking at someone who is looking at them with a sinister face. Some are reasonable, but at one point a woman somehow senses a guy watching her from down a hill, seemingly a mile away. If you cut all of the looking out, the movie would be about 12 minutes long."

Reflection: I don't recall much of this one, to be honest – I saw it back to back with *Pieces*, the most insane slasher movie of all time, so that has dominated most of my memories of the evening. I've always meant to go back and watch it again on its own, but as of yet I haven't found the time. I do vividly recall the "key in the door" scene, which is worth the price of admission alone (and will make you appreciate a moment in last week's *giallo* tribute *Amer* all the more). I also recall that it had a funny plot thread about the design of someone's scarf, which I must respect.

So why include it, if I can barely remember it? Well I remember *liking* it, so it qualifies in terms of me saying "Hey, watch these movies!" And Mondo, who for a lengthy period could probably sell out a poster of my cat in less than two seconds*, had a pretty nice print honoring this movie that remained available for months, so I guess it's not as widely loved/known as other '70s *gialli*. But really, I wanted more Italian films this month as is, so I certainly didn't want to take one out and replace it with a traditional American slasher.

*And per tradition it'd sell out before I could snag one, and then I'd have to pay some asshole on eBay five times the original price for it. "But it's MY cat on the poster, dude, come on..."

MOVIE #45 – FEBRUARY 14th

VALENTINE (2001)
Dir: Jamie Blanks
HMAD Review Date: February 13, 2009 (DVD)
Genre: Holiday, Slasher
Available from Warner Home Video

Synopsis Based on Fading Memory: It's Valentine's Day, and our four beautiful heroines find themselves targeted by a guy in a Cherub mask. Could it be the nerdy kid they rebuffed 20 years ago?

Review excerpt:
"Cupid was one of the best looking slasher getups in ages (certainly better than the I Know... fisherman or either version of the Urban Legend *killer), and the design got the two issues of making a good slasher costume down perfectly. You can't just have a guy who looks like he bought the mask at Wal-Mart, but you can't have anything too elaborate either. It got it just right, and it's a shame that the movie tanked, because I would have loved to have seen the mask (complete with bloody nose - an overused gag) on the shelves at Halloween time."*

Reflection: Fans of the site will probably remember "Non Canon" reviews – these would be the HMAD version of hit-bait – popular titles that I already saw before starting the site. To post one meant re-watching it *plus* watch/review the official movie for that day, so as time went on they became pretty scarce, since I barely had time for the new movies let alone revisits. Anyway, I didn't include too many of these entries in this book, and for good reason – most of them were of very popular horror films and I am keeping such fare to a minimum. But it's Valentine's Day, dammit, and also "more well-known" day, something that the *My Bloody Valentine* films are too famous for while *X-Ray* (aka *Hospital Massacre*) isn't famous *enough*. And *Lover's Lane* (the only v-day slasher I know of) stinks anyway.

This one gets a bum rap and was pretty much the last gasp in the post-*Scream* slasher revival due to its poor box office performance, but I think it's worth a reevaluation. Blanks is a solid director with a great eye, and he does his best with a plot derived from a book that wouldn't work on film (as the killer in the novel was known to all of its characters under different names – in a film we'd obviously know it was the same guy). And you get to see Katherine Heigl get killed, so it probably has the endorsement of the *Grey's Anatomy* crew, as well. Sure, it's undeniably more "studio" than slasher fans probably want, and Denise Richards already used up our tolerance of her in *Starship Troopers*, but I'd take it over *Scream 3* or *4*, and the *I Know What You Did Last Summer* trilogy. Give it another look if you've dismissed it in the past. Harry Warden will still be there after.

MOVIE #46 – FEBRUARY 15th

SHADOWS RUN BLACK (1984)
Dir: Howard Heard
HMAD Review Date: March 31, 2010 (DVD)
Genre: Slasher
Available from Artisan Entertainment

Synopsis Based on Fading Memory: A serial killer stalks a college campus… and Kevin Costner shows up.

Review excerpt:
"*Shadows Run Black* is indeed a terrible movie, but it's got that je ne sais quoi that makes it inherently watchable, not unlike *Disconnected*, or most car crashes. It seems to be a student film at times, due to the laughably stiff camerawork and careless storytelling (the non-slasher scenes mostly play out like the stream-of-conscious joint screenwriting of a beat cop and a racist). But there's something entertaining, even delightful, about a "slasher" film where most of the kills are off-screen, victims are introduced only moments before their demise (whereas others are introduced and simply never mentioned again), and nearly every red herring suspect (and half-assed motive, including one that's racially charged) is vastly more interesting than the identity/motive of the actual killer."

Reflection: If you, like me, are a Kevin Costner apologist, then your loyalty will be tested with this one. Or it will just reassure you of how much Costner rules, because there's almost nothing to like here except for the novelty of seeing him show up in a couple of scenes. Warning: the film has got more than a touch of casual racism and homophobia, making it even harder to recommend for any reason beyond extreme curiosity. Really, the only reason I'm including it is because it reminded me of *Disconnected* at times, and that's a movie I wish I could be recommending, but alas it's long out of print and the director (who owns the distribution rights) informed me personally he has no intentions of releasing it again. So I'm telling you to watch this instead of, I dunno, loading up a very popular video sharing website and checking to see if *Disconnected* (1983, 84-minute runtime) has been shared in its entirety.

But this thing also kept sticking out as THE title I should use for February's "bad movie" option. Not just for the Kevin Costner factor (I love that you can find slashers with so many of our top '90s leading men – Costner here, Tom Hanks in *He Knows You're Alone*, George Clooney in *Return to Horror High*, etc.), but the ugliness of it and the fact that it was like four years too late to the slasher party (it wasn't released until 1986) made it almost a must-see on peculiarity alone. It's like everything you *shouldn't* do in a slasher movie all at once. Except putting Costner in it. That's the only thing they got right.

MOVIE #47 – FEBRUARY 16th

FORGET ME NOT (2009)
Dir: Tyler Oliver
HMAD Review Date: November 13, 2011 (Streaming)
Genre: Slasher, Supernatural
Available from Phase 4 Films

Synopsis Based on Fading Memory: A bunch of high school graduates begin disappearing, and it seems to have something to do with a girl they wronged in the past.

Review excerpt:
"I dug the variety in the death scenes – a pretty spectacular car crash, a gory workshop "accident", someone is buried alive... when one happens off-screen later in the movie, I was actually kind of mad. Not because I was spared some visual carnage (which is never a good thing), but because I was enjoying the effort that they were putting into each one. So many modern body count type movies (especially low budget ones) don't bother doing anything creative with the kills anymore, so again, I walked away quite impressed and wondering why the movie wasn't given a bigger release."

Reflection: There's a twist to this movie that Netflix's description spoiled, so I hope you see it blind and enjoy it even more than I did. Insult to injury, I could have seen it at Screamfest two years before, but opted to do something else. Had I watched it (I tend to watch just about everything at Screamfest, at least I did back then) I would have been unspoiled as well, since I don't look at anything about the movies at the festival – I just go in totally ignorant as often as possible. The third act drags a little (once you know everything about what's happening, it loses some luster), but otherwise this one impressively started off like a typical generic slasher and turned into something fairly inventive and unique.

And that's something I wish I could say more often, especially about the slasher film. I love them, but there weren't too many occasions where I could say "I don't want to spoil the twist" unless I was referring to the killer's identity. I would think that the same-ness of so many in the sub-genre (and the accompanying dismissal from critics) would encourage filmmakers to try a little harder, even if for no other reason than to stick out a bit and get singled out in some asshole's book five or six years later.

HMAD Fun Fact: February 16th, 2007, is the only day I ever missed a movie. I was on a trip and didn't have time. It was also a week after I started so I hadn't really gotten used to it being part of the daily routine yet. Still: one day in six years - not too shabby.

MOVIE #48 – FEBRUARY 17th

RED VELVET (2008)
Dir: Bruce Dickson
HMAD Review Date: December 4, 2009 (DVD)
Genre: Slasher
Available from 3Mac Studios

Synopsis Based on Fading Memory: A would-be couple goes on a date that seems disastrous, as flashbacks reveal that the male may or may not have killed all of her friends in a typical slasher movie scenario.

Review excerpt:
"...it's obvious that the writers know their slasher movies. In addition to the *Friday the 13th* homages, there's a bit of *Happy Birthday To Me* thrown in at the end, and one could even consider the killer's final trick to be an homage to *Valentine* (this might be wishful thinking on my part). I also dug a POV shot from the heroine's perspective - pretty rare, might even be the first instance. Imagine if there was a shot in *Halloween* where we would be literally watching through Laurie's eyes as we had been watching through Michael's for key scenes in the film."

Reflection: Given the rather limited template they work from, any slasher movie that attempts to deconstruct their scenarios, or at least put them in a different perspective, is fine by me. I've often wondered about what a slasher would do if his plan worked (the ones where they kill all of a girl's friends so they could be together, I mean), so seeing something sort of like that in action is enough to win me over. There's another movie that came a bit too late for inclusion in this book, called *No One Lives*, which kind of does the same thing (except it plays out like a full-blown sequel to a slasher film no one's seen). In both cases, the movies had some issues, but I am happy to forgive them based on the fact that they were trying to think outside the slasher film box without resorting to *Scream*-like humor.

It's also one of the very few slasher movies where you can praise not one but two performances – Henry Thomas (yes, that one) and Kelli Garner, who recently appeared in the underrated *Horns*. They have tough roles since Thomas is playing kind of an asshole and she has to believably still be drawn to him, and it actually works really well, since the movie is also kind of playing with the conventions of romantic comedies for good measure. It's not going to be for everyone, but it's one of those movies you'll keep thinking about it either way – it's really trying to do something unique with the slasher movie, and that alone earns my respect.

MOVIE #49 – FEBRUARY 18th

THE BOOGEY MAN (1980)
Dir: Ulli Lommel
HMAD Review Date: May 3, 2007 (DVD)
Genre: Slasher, Supernatural
Available from Synergy Entertainment

Synopsis Based on Fading Memory: A supernatural killer stalks a family through their mirrors.

Review excerpt:
"...as the saying goes, "No film about broken pieces of a mirror that contains the ghost of a guy who wears a stocking on his head can be altogether bad." Though it would have been nice if he was a bit more consistent with how he went about his business. Sometimes he apparently just possesses the victims into killing themselves, other times he uses telekinesis, and then he possesses people into attacking others. Hey, whatever works."

Reflection: This is not a great movie, BUT it's the best Ulli Lommel ever got. Throughout HMAD's run I'd often try to give Lommel another chance, mostly based on the strength of this film – he got it (kinda) right once, why couldn't he do it again? All of the other films of his that I watched – including sequels to this one - are among the worst I saw that year, so the fact that this one was kind of entertaining, in hindsight, is miraculous.

In fact, among repeat offenders on HMAD, he's probably the worst, because I know he was at one point capable of making a decent film. Some of the other frequent targets on the site (Mike Feifer, various Asylum cohorts), I'd at least see a glimmer of improvement when placing their films in chronological order (even if I didn't watch them that way), so there's hope for them yet. But Lommel just got worse, going from a rather entertaining movie in 1980 to nearly unwatchable and wholly amateurish garbage like *Curse of the Zodiac* in 2007, with over 25 years' worth of experience seemingly being forgotten. I actually dare you to watch that one, or perhaps *Zombie Nation*. Within minutes you'll take back every mean thing you've ever said about Uwe Boll or whoever.

Oh, the sequels are typical Lommel affairs, so don't assume he remembered how to be competent when returning to his moneymaker. Just watch this one.

MOVIE #50 – FEBRUARY 19th

KILLER MOVIE (2008)
Dir: Jeff Fisher
HMAD Review Date: March 29, 2010 (Cable)
Genre: Slasher
Available from Peace Arch Home Entertainment

Synopsis Based on Fading Memory: A crew descends on a small town to make a reality show, and a killer shows up.

Review excerpt:
*"The thing I liked most about Fisher's script was that it kept me off-guard and misdirected, something I can't say about too many slashers at all, let alone modern ones. Early on, we learn about two warring hockey coaches, and that the town is prone for people getting into "accidents", and that the director (*Vampire Diaries' *Paul Wesley) was specifically requested for the gig by the lead actress (Kaley Cuoco), who was recently under investigation for assault, etc. It's a lot of red herrings, but it's ultimately pretty simple - which I loved. So many slasher movies (hell, movies in general) exist in this sort of bubble, where we only learn about things/people that are directly important to the plot, so I liked the idea of presenting this* Twin Peaks-*y town but having the killer's motive basically come down to simple jealousy."*

Reflection: I lost count of how many "film crew is killed by a slasher" movies I watched for HMAD, but I can assure you that most of them were bad. This one worked because that aspect of the plot was more or less backgrounded once firmly established – it provided an excuse for talking head shots that were sprinkled throughout the film, but that was pretty much it. Few scenes involved them filming their show, and it was shot like a traditional film (if made today it was almost assuredly be found footage), so it all worked. Plus, I find Kaley Cuoco to be a very lovely presence, but unfortunately the easiest way to see her work is on one of the lousiest (yet most inexplicably popular) TV shows of all time, so I was grateful to see her in something a little more to my liking.

And I didn't guess who the killer was, which at this point in my life means an automatic thumbs up from me. I've seen so many slashers that I can often skip over simply picking the killer (easy) right into also picking the character *we're supposed to think is the killer* within seconds of their introduction, so it's rare that the unmasking scene can come along and surprise me. I never got around to watching the film again to see if they ever "cheat" like some others do (*Hospital Massacre* is one of the worst offenders, with the guy ultimately revealed to be the killer HIDING FROM THE KILLER at one point), but I suspect it holds up as well as *Scream*, where it surprised you the first time but you'd feel silly for missing the telltale signs on your second viewing (that look between Stu and Billy at the door – was I BLIND?!?).

MOVIE #51 – FEBRUARY 20th

WRECKAGE (2010)
Dir: John Asher
HMAD Review Date: May 10, 2012 (DVD)
Genre: Slasher
Available from Phase 4 Films

Synopsis Based on Fading Memory: Some young folks' car breaks down, so they head into a junkyard to find the parts they need... and a killer shows up.

Review excerpt:
"...it's surprisingly enjoyable in a *Final Destination*-y way, like when a girl is rescued from a compactor only to be crushed by a falling car a few seconds later. And Scoot McNairy is simply brilliant as the redneck junkyard employee who is petrified of both heroes and villains alike, but not above making a few oddball remarks at their expense (I particularly liked his answer to how hard it can be to screw in a light bulb). I should note that if you like his performance, make sure you stick around for all of the credits, as we get more of his craziness (and a firework show!) in what must be the longest post-credits bit I've ever seen in a slasher."

Reflection: At least once a week someone posts that video of actor Aaron Paul losing his shit on *The Price is Right*, but to me this is the far more interesting find – a horror movie he shot right around the time *Breaking Bad* premiered. The production suffered some financial problems that left it unfinished for a while, so *Bad* had already become a cultural sensation by the time it saw the light of day – allowing them to center its marketing around him even though he's a supporting player. His performance isn't that far removed from his most famous character, so if you ever wanted to know what Jesse Pinkman might do in a slasher scenario, look no further. Bonus: Scoot McNairy (who is always great) was seemingly aping Billy Bob Thornton in *U-Turn* for his performance – that's an inspired, er, inspiration.

It also more or less satisfied my desire to see a good horror movie set in a junkyard. There are junkyard SCENES in many horror flicks, but despite their inherent creepiness, vast supply of killing implements, and the fact that a location shouldn't be that hard to secure (day or night, how much could shutting down a junkyard disrupt the public? They shut down major roads to film car chases – THAT's an inconvenience), I've seen very few. Two others are actually a would-be franchise; a terrible slasher named *Machined* and its supernaturally-tinged, *slightly* better sequel *Reborn*, both of which failed to utilize their rarely used setting. Maybe the danger involved with running around rusty cars and scrap metal is too much for the insurance folks? I dunno. All I know is, until this movie came along the champ was probably *Nothing But Trouble*, which sets a chunk of its third act in one. Mr. Bonestripper forever.

MOVIE #52 – FEBRUARY 21st

FINAL EXAM (1981)
Dir: Jimmy Huston
HMAD Review Date: March 14, 2008 (Revival screening)
Genre: Slasher
Available from Scream Factory

Synopsis Based on Fading Memory: It's final exam week, and the students are off alone in their rooms studying… and a killer shows up.

Review excerpt:
"On a surface level, it's a boring movie (in Halloween, *they constantly had Michael watching from the shadows; but here it's like the killer is an after-thought), but there are so many "what the HELL?" moments of absurdity that it seems a lot better than it actually is (or would be if you were watching it alone). For example, one of the girls is nailing her professor. That's fine, but she has a FRAMED PHOTO of the guy on her desk! Discretion? Why bother? There's also a fraternity initiation scene (lifted almost verbatim in* Scream 2*), except with the added "bonus" of a cop pouring whiskey into the kid's underwear."*

Reflection: Okay, by now you've probably noticed the "and a killer shows up" running gag for a lot of these synopses, but in this case that's pretty much exactly right – the killer is named Killer, he doesn't have a costume, and no backstory of any sort is offered. The trailer claims "He came BACK!" which I guess suggests he's a former student, but since nothing in the actual film backs that up we can't accept it as canon. Why he targets these people is none of our business, and there's never been a sequel to explain it all away with Druid nonsense or whatever.

But what it DOES have is Radish, quite possibly the most memorable male character in slasher history, and almost assuredly a major influence on the creation of Randy in *Scream* (Kevin Williamson definitely saw the film, as explained above). He's kind of an unusual blend between the usual nerd character and the male hero – unlike Randy Meeks, the heroine actually kind of seems to be into him. However, his true slasher movie soulmate is Brenda from *Friday the 13th*, as he offers an awkward, already dated reference to Watergate that tops her "Worst run of luck since Richard Nixon!" in that film. You might forget the kills and killer (and bland campus setting), but Radish will remain in your heart forever.

MOVIE #53 – FEBRUARY 22nd

THE HOUSE THAT SCREAMED [LA RESIDENCIA] (1969)
Dir: Narciso Ibáñez Serrador
HMAD Review Date: December 17, 2011 (DVD)
Genre: Slasher
Public domain title, available through several DVD companies

Synopsis Based on Fading Memory: A disturbed young man and his domineering mother do the *Psycho* thing but in a girl's school.

Review excerpt:
"A bit slow at times (you'll feel its 99 minutes), but being that it's basically a slasher film from 1969, you can't really expect a Friday the 13th*-style pace. On the contrary, I was quite surprised to see a few on-screen murders, including a decent throat slashing – such things were certainly not in vogue at this time, especially not in a fairly classy-looking production. Most of the movie takes place inside the school, but the scope imagery, above average acting, and slow burn,* Psycho*-tinged storyline puts it well above the HGL-type low budget films of the day (where such gore shots wouldn't be a surprise)."*

Reflection: I wanted to include this one because it's from 1969 and yet has several elements that one would recognize from the typical slasher film – something that movies of the '70s (*Black Christmas, Halloween*) are often credited with creating. I find the evolution of the slasher film to be pretty fascinating, as the sub-genre was more or less created by people looking to top the film that came before theirs, first in body counts, then creative murders, and finally how far out of reality they could take things. I mean, *Scream* was considered a spoof of sorts and then it had at least two legit spoofs of it – there's something nutty about a sub-genre that can allow for that sort of thing. So any "proto-slasher" like this is definitely worth your time.

Serrador went on to direct one of the all-time great killer kid movies, the awesomely named *Who Can Kill A Child? (*answer: the hero of the movie, who guns down several – you'll hear more about this next month). Oddly enough, despite this solid track record, those are pretty much his only feature films – everything else I could find was a television project. Nothing wrong with that, but given how much he embraced what features allowed over television, I wish he had stuck around longer. He was still working steadily until 2006, when he did one of the "6 Films To Keep You Awake" (you'll also read more about those soon), but hasn't done anything since – I assume he retired (he's now 80 years old), leaving behind a wealth of TV material and a pretty great double feature for anyone who wants to watch his two films back to back.

MOVIE #54 – FEBRUARY 23rd

SWEET INSANITY (2006)
Dir: Daniel Hess
HMAD Review Date: April 27, 2011 (DVD)
Genre: Slasher
Available from MTI Home Video

Synopsis Based on Fading Memory: Basically *Slumber Party Massacre* but with a couple of twists, one I caught right away, one I missed entirely.

Review excerpt:
"In addition to *Slumber, the writer and/or director clearly knew his* Halloween. *There's a scene of our two leads walking home after school (which would take about 14 hours if one of them didn't get picked up by a friend with a car, since they are literally walking about 1 mph – guessing they didn't have dolly track and the camera operator was too afraid to walk backwards), and even though you're probably focused on them, if you look you'll see "the killer" following them in the background, out of focus and unaccompanied by any sort of stings or anything like that to draw our attention to him. Too many horror movies make sure you see each and every scare; it's nice to have some that you might not even notice until a second viewing."*

Reflection: Every now and then a writer friend will tell me he named a character in his script after me, and I always want to tell them not to do it, because so far none of those movies have been made and I suspect my name is cursed. But at least I can take comfort in knowing that there is indeed one movie out there with a character named Brian Collins –this one, in fact.

Admittedly it's not the best movie this month (the ending kind of derails it), but even if it were a rom-com I'd be tickled to see a "Brian Collins" in a movie – that I found one for the first time in a slasher movie was just wonderful, and even better (spoiler) – he survives! I rule! Here's the rub, though – he's also kind of a loser. If memory serves he only survives because he pissed his pants and left the party where everyone else is getting killed. If this movie came out in 2013 I would be convinced that the writer or producer was someone I pissed off with an earlier review and this was their petty revenge. But in 2006 I wasn't even part of this silly world yet, so that couldn't be it. It's just a hilarious, slightly disappointing coincidence.

P.S. At a pitiful 2.2, this movie has the lowest IMDb score of any movie in the book, I think. Just fair warning! I saw it in 2011 so I was four years deep at this point – I knew total garbage and this wasn't it, but apparently I'm in the minority. I assume the weak ending is to blame for all those 1 and 2 votes. I'd give it like a 6 or 7, for the record.

MOVIE #55 – FEBRUARY 24th

MADHOUSE (aka AND WHEN SHE WAS BAD) (1981)
Dir: Ovidio G. Assonitis
HMAD Review Date: December 6, 2009 (DVD)
Genre: Slasher
Available from Dark Sky Films

Synopsis Based on Fading Memory: A schoolteacher is about to celebrate her birthday, and a killer shows up.

Review excerpt:
"This movie is ripe for a midnight crowd, especially during the kill scenes with the dog. See, the movie actually has THREE killers: the dog, our heroine's crazy sister, and a third surprise killer (and it's COMPLETELY out of nowhere; the reveal that this character is a killer is delivered in the most casual manner possible). Unsurprisingly, the dog kills are the highlight, particularly his attack on the heroine's friend near the end of the second act. And the scene where he gets his comeuppance is equally wonderful, since the puppet dog is so hilariously Muppet-like and the kill is so needlessly violent (a power drill through the head)."

Reflection: They were produced around the same time, so I won't call shenanigans, but if you're a fan of the (more popular) *Happy Birthday To Me*, this one might give you a lot of déjà vu. But as it is an Italian co-production, you're treated to a lot of the silliness that *Happy Birthday* lacked, like an out of nowhere Japanese stereotype and a kid going "HEEEEEEEEEEEEEEEE'S DEAD!" about a fellow classmate as if it was something to boast about. And as a bonus: an ill-fitting but still wonderful Riz Ortolani score.

Of the three films I watched called *Madhouse*, this one is my favorite (and since one of the others had Vincent Price, you should take this as a firm endorsement), which is funny because that title isn't as common as some. The IMDb has it listed under one of its original titles (*And When She Was Bad*), but it's also been named *There Was A Little Girl*, and was apparently originally released in the US as *Scared to Death*. The *Madhouse* title is seemingly prominent only in European countries, so I'm not sure why my (region 1) DVD was under that title instead of one of the others (perhaps to cash in on the notoriety of the "*Madhouse*" title, since that was what it was listed under on the Video Nasties list). Title changes are obnoxious enough now, so I can't imagine how frustrating it must have been in the '80s and early '90s before the internet was there to help us sort through this nonsense.

MOVIE #56 – FEBRUARY 25th

SHATTERED LIVES (2009)
Dir: Carl Lindbergh
HMAD Review Date: January 16, 2010 (DVD)
Genre: Psychological, Slasher
Available from Lionsgate

Synopsis Based on Fading Memory: A girl with severe issues imagines that her clown dolls become human and encourage her to kill her awful mother.

Review excerpt:
"I admire the balls of Carl Lindbergh to start the film off with his biggest set-piece and then more or less present a character-based psychological drama for the next 75 minutes. In fact, I wouldn't be surprised if the overlong and rather pointless hyper-edit replay of the opening massacre that comes near the end of the film was the result of a producer or distributor demanding more "action" in the finale. Rather than focus on more kills, the film slowly reveals the true nature of the killings, which adds another layer of tragedy to it."

Reflection: If I could, I'd do a double feature of this and *Frayed*, the slasher from earlier this month that also incorporates subtle touches to *Halloween* alongside a psychologically-charged killer clown movie. This one isn't as successful as *Frayed*, but it's also got a tougher job, considering the slow pace and front-loaded body count. It isn't easy to pull off a psychological, character-driven story using the language and traditions of a slasher film, because you can narrow that description down to "hide a smart movie inside a silly one", which takes discipline and skill you won't often see in a relatively new filmmaker. And it's even less common when the filmmaker's previous movie was terrible - Lindbergh's debut, *Shadows of the Dead*, is nearly unwatchable. This was his follow-up, and rarely did I see such an improvement on a filmmaker's second film.

This is why I tend to give more leeway to genre mashups that "mostly" work. It's tough, because not only are they often exploring new-ish territory, but they have to make sure that they are meeting expectations for two kinds of horror films while keeping the audience from experiencing tonal whiplash (which is why really great horror-comedies are so rare). On the independent scene, such challenges are a surefire way to scare off investors who just want to copy what's popular so they can get their film sold, so off the beaten path fare like this earns my respect, and I'll eventually forget about whatever nitpicks I had when watching it.

MOVIE #57 – FEBRUARY 26th

MURDER OBSESSION (aka MURDER SYNDROME) [FOLLIA OMICIDA] (1981)
Dir: Riccardo Freda
HMAD Review Date: January 13, 2012 (DVD)
Genre: Giallo
Available from Kino Lorber Films

Synopsis Based on Fading Memory: A guy who killed his dad when he was younger returns to the family estate with some colleagues, and the bodies start piling up.

Review excerpt:
"...it's never dull; even with pretty much all the kills confined to the final 35 minutes, it's still peppered with "action". And that includes some wonderfully goofy attempts at keeping everyone as a suspect – it's remarkable how many characters own black gloves, and how they act sneaky with regards to wearing them. I like to think that because this was 1981, the characters had all seen a bunch of gialli by now and realized that owning black gloves might make you look suspicious to anyone else. I was also charmed by a ten minute "dream sequence" that includes a giant spider and a bunch of bats on strings - and since it was a dream sequence, the strings don't even matter! We're told it's a dream right off the, er, bat (sorry), and parts of it really do resemble dreams (instantly changing locations and such), so it's nice that Freda gets to go for broke, without the usual crutch of having to try to fool the audience into believing that what they are seeing is actually happening."

Reflection: I came home one day to find FOUR *gialli* that were sent for review, and this was the best of the lot in my opinion. The others were *Body Puzzle*, which I also enjoyed, *The Perfume of the Lady in Black* (eh), and *Ubaldo Terzani Horror Show* (great concept, muddled execution) – a perfectly good "starter" set for anyone looking to see some non-Argento entries in the genre. I'm no expert on *gialli* (I only saw about thirty or so of them – compared to over 350 slashers), but I saw enough to know that you really have to keep an open mind with these things. Along with the usually rampant misogyny and woozy plotting, many of them rip one another off, making it hard to remember specifics months later (let alone years, as is the case here). I consider myself a fan, but I'd fail miserably at any sort of trivia quiz about the ones I saw, because I tend to get them mixed up later. I reread this review three times and very little jogged my memory, though as one of the last films I reviewed for the site I can say with some certainty that by then I knew what I was talking about. So if you don't trust 2016 me, at least trust 2012 me.

Sadly, this is the last *giallo* entry for the month, which really bums me out as there are only three. I originally planned for an all Italian month, but came up too short for titles that I thought were different enough that also weren't likely to have already been seen by the average reader. As I said in the intro, I'm sure you've seen *Deep Red* or whatever by now (or at least, are aware that you haven't, and don't need me reminding you), so once I weeded that stuff out I only had a dozen or so solid titles with a few maybes – certainly not enough for a month. So I spread them around (you'll find a couple more in later chapters) and tried to include as many as I could here in slasher month, but again – I love slashers and had enough of those to cover three months! It wasn't easy making these decisions, I assure you – more than once I considered dropping the "one theme per month" thing and just offering the 365 best movies. But I realized the variety of suggestions was more important, so the theme stayed, and a number of perfectly good Italian films were left orphaned. Book #2!

MOVIE #58 – FEBRUARY 27th

SEVERANCE (2006)
Dir: Christopher Smith
HMAD Review Date: October 22, 2007 (DVD)
Genre: Comedic, Slasher, Survival
Available from Magnolia Entertainment

Synopsis Based on Fading Memory: Office workers on a corporate retreat find themselves under attack from a killer or killers.

Review excerpt:
"This movie had a lot of laugh out loud moments for me, though the horror scenes are done just as well. I wasn't a huge fan of Christopher Smith's previous film, Creep, but I could see he had talent as a director. Which is probably why this one, which was written by James Moran (with additional writing from Smith), turned out so much better. I don't know who wrote the funniest lines ("You found a pie?") but whoever it was deserves an award for some of this stuff. There's a scene where everyone is understandably panicked due to seeing a masked man outside their window, and one character says "Okay, you and Jill go up the hill...", at which point he stops and giggles to himself about his unintentional reference. Stuff like that kills me, and there are plenty of similar dry jokes throughout the film."

Reflection: This isn't the only Christopher Smith entry in this book, and I believe screenwriter James Moran is accounted for elsewhere as well. But this remains my favorite of their work, and I hope they work together again as they prove to complement each other nicely. The comedy works just as well as the horror, which is the problem with roughly 99% of all horror-comedies, so any time a team can get it right, we horror fans kind of demand they do it again someday.

Now, before anyone nitpicks, no, this is not traditional slasher – more survival horror and also a comedy to boot. But it uses the language of slasher films to tell its story, and that's an important distinction to make when labeling these things. I remember getting into a debate with one of my colleagues concerning a certain film (one that pops up later in this book) because he said it wasn't a horror movie. He's technically right, but the movie is specifically engineered to make you THINK it is one in order for its twists to work, so saying "it's not horror" is basically a spoiler. Same thing here, though far less likely to hamper your enjoyment – the way things are introduced, and the way the first few characters are killed, will very much have you thinking about slasher films, and thus for that it "counts" – by the time you can mount an argument, you should just be having a blast with the movie and not caring that you went in expecting something else.

MOVIE #59 – FEBRUARY 28th

BEREAVEMENT (2010)
Dir: Stevan Mena
HMAD Review Date: August 21, 2011 (Blu-ray)
Genre: Slasher
Available from Anchor Bay Entertainment

Synopsis Based on Fading Memory: In this prequel to the indie slasher *Malevolence*, we see how Martin (*Malevolence*'s killer) was formed into the brutal murderer we met in the other film.

Review excerpt:
"I commend Mena for presenting a story that doesn't seem reverse engineered from the start point of the next chapter the way that Star Wars *and other prequels have felt. He clearly had this trilogy all worked out in his head (at least in general), and never stooped to total nonsense, like showing the younger versions of the characters from* Malevolence *standing in front of a bank or something stupid like that (i.e. what Lucas did in his movies)."*

Reflection: If you haven't seen *Malevolence* yet, I actually recommend starting with *Bereavement* – there are one or two things that won't land as well, but so many more that will work infinitely better if you're going in without knowing the fate of one of its major characters. Unlike most prequels, it really does feel like he wrote them in order and just happened to start in the middle (the scope of *Malevolence* is smaller, so I assume it fit within his budget range and that's why it was made first), and it's cool that they each have their own flavor – *Bereavement* is kind of a character-based, suspense-driven thriller with slasher elements, whereas the second is more traditional "A group of folks are in a house and a killer picks them off" type. Plus, as a *Halloween* fan, I love the weird little things he chooses to reference in both films (less so here than in *Malevolence*), like framing two characters the same way Michael and that one bully kid are after they smash Tommy's pumpkin.

And if you're a *True Detective* fan (S1, specifically) you might want to enjoy an early performance by Alexandra Daddario, as the film's heroine (it's because of her presence that I'm putting this as this week's "famous" movie; knowing how, er, enticing she is I'm assuming a number of folks rented every movie on her resume after her *True Detective* appearance). The *Malevolence* cast, for the most part, hasn't exactly seen their career skyrocket (a number of them have never appeared in a film again), but it's obvious from her work here that Daddario wouldn't have the same fate – the camera loves her and she's an engaging presence on it. It also features a solid performance from Michael Biehn, in a rare turn as a nice, normal guy. The third film was mostly shot, but the production hit some heavy setbacks, including the death of a lead actor with still lots of his footage to shoot, so it may never see the light of day, which is a travesty. I don't know if it will ultimately help, but if there's one movie this month to blind buy for a good cause, it's this one. Perhaps if enough copies are sold, Mena can prove to someone that funding the necessary reshoots for his final chapter will be a worth investment.

This concludes slasher month! Well, the real part of it – the next page is a bonus for leap year. Anyway, I hope the lack of *Friday the 13th*-y types wasn't a problem; like I said, this is a sub-genre with a LOT of repetition, but it doesn't need to be. Sure, we always need another group of kids going into the woods for some reason – it just doesn't have to be the case every other time. So even if some of these aren't exactly great, they're a pretty varied lot, I think, and cover a span of over 40 years. That should make up for the minimal number of people being killed in or around a tent.

FEBRUARY BONUS MOVIE (FOR LEAP YEAR)

HOME SWEET HOME (1981)
Dir: Nettie Peña
HMAD Review Date: March 4, 2009 (DVD)
Genre: Slasher
Available from Hollywood Entertainment

Synopsis Based on Fading Memory: It's Thanksgiving, the family has gotten together... and a killer shows up.

Review excerpt:
"I swear the movie was produced by Pep Boys. No less than 20 minutes of the film revolves around cars breaking down or people talking about said cars breaking down. And it's not even in the traditional "she's running from the killer and the car doesn't start" way. No, someone will ask to take a car to go to the store, and the owner will explain that the battery is on the fritz, so someone else lets them take HIS car, which has a faulty fuel gauge. Then there's a lengthy scene where the family's patriarch steals gas from an abandoned station wagon, then his battery gives out (again) so he tries to steal the wagon's battery as well. And of course, the made up dialogue never lets us forget each car's problems and what the drivers could be doing about it ("well he said the battery is dying, so maybe he went to the gas station to get a new one."). It's actually kind of charming in a peculiar way"

Reflection: Eli Roth's *Thanksgiving* is never going to happen. If it does, I swear I'll do HMAD again for a full month, and I can offer that bet with complete confidence that I'll never have to follow through. But thankfully, he was wrong when he said there was never a Thanksgiving slasher – there's *Blood Rage*, which I recommended earlier in the month, and this one. Granted, both are obscure so you can forgive him for not knowing about them, and neither of them really make much use of the holiday beyond people having a dinner, but, you know, at least THEY ACTUALLY GOT MADE.

(Sorry, I'm just really bummed that we never got the full movie.)

I lucked out when I got this one from Netflix – it must have been one of the last copies they had, as it's no longer available to rent. I assume they're out there somewhere, and I don't want to say it's worth spending a lot of time or money tracking down (even if the movie was great, the disc was lousy – clearly taken from a VHS), but I assure you – there is nothing else quite like it. The giggling, nameless killer, the confusing family dynamic (I've seen it twice and I still can't figure out how most of the characters are related to one another), the guitar-playing mime who likes to watch his parents have sex… there's just something so goddamn OFF about this movie that I had to love it, even though it was fairly boring and wasted its potential as the first Thanksgiving slasher movie. I really wanted to include it in the regular lineup for the month, but since it's out of print I realized it'd be too hard to find, and thus gave it this "February 29th" slot. It's too late to get one for 2016, but on the flipside that means you have four years to track down a copy for 2020. It's… sort of worth the effort?

MARCH – KILLER KIDS!

ARTIST: JACOPO TENANI

Ah, March. Not only is it the month of my own birth, but it's when spring begins. New life blooms! Everyone is happy about the new things in the world... so let's ruin it by focusing on movies about murderous children (or just basic parental horrors – pregnancy via medical experiment, losing a child, etc. I didn't have enough killer kid movies for the whole month so I had to stretch it a bit.)

Real world tragedies (the types involving guns and schools) have resulted in these movies becoming a harder sell than usual – it's almost never been easy to get a *Bad Seed*-type flick going unless it's so watered down that it fails to resonate (see: *The Good Son*), but nowadays? A screenwriter probably wouldn't get through the front door of even a smaller studio trying to pitch one of these, let alone one of the majors. Movies ABOUT dead kids are probably a bit easier to get funding for, which is weird if you think about it. What's more likely to happen: the first act of *Pet Sematary*, or the third? Shouldn't the movies that are less likely to traumatize someone by reminding them of a real tragedy be the ones that get made?

As I am now a father myself, some of these no longer amuse me as much as they once did – *Pet Sematary* is now a movie I can barely even *think* about without getting hysterical (the little shoe on the road, nope nope nope). But I'm guessing there are younger readers who don't have to worry about that just yet, or even parents that simply aren't as cripplingly paranoid as I am and thus can watch poor little Gage Creed get creamed by a truck without becoming convinced it's going to happen to their child, as well.

Besides, parental fears or not, I'd be damned if I was going to write an entire book without pimping...

MOVIE #60 – MARCH 1st

CATHY'S CURSE (1977)
Dir: Eddy Matalon
HMAD Review Date: April 10, 2007 (DVD)
Genre: Ghost, Killer Kid, Possession
Public domain title, available through several DVD companies

Synopsis Based on Fading Memory: A little girl is possessed by the spirit of her aunt and becomes a foul-mouthed demon.

Review excerpt:
"...the writers' use of profanity is simply unparalleled. The words (primarily "bitch" and "shit") come spewing with such venom and hatred (mostly out of the mouth of the eponymous Cathy, a 7-year-old girl) that nearly every line becomes a 'memorable quotes'-worthy classic. My personal favorite comes about halfway through the film, when a medium is attempting to rid Cathy of her curse. The understandably angry Cathy responds "Medium?!? I'd say EXTRA RARE PIECE OF SHIT!" Whether you're a 7-year-old girl possessed by the ghost of your dead aunt or not, what the hell kind of thing is that to say to someone? I have no idea, but I love these guys for writing it."

Reflection: I really hate the "___ is my spirit animal" meme, but if I had to name my own, it would be *Cathy's Curse*. There is something about this (admittedly bad) movie that taps into my sensibilities like few others, and even though I saw it relatively early in HMAD's run I never managed to find anything quite like it. The nonsensical dialogue, borderline impenetrable editing (key example: quite late in the film, it cuts to some random guy leaving his house and getting into a car, never to be seen again), and narrative populated with mostly terrible people combine to make a uniquely wonderful/awful cinematic stew. Seeing it so soon after I started (a mere two months in) unfortunately set the bar for such fare quite high – I kept hoping it was just scratching the surface of... whatever you'd call this kind of movie, but by the end of the run I was still looking for anything that even measured up. This is the sort of movie that, had I seen it on the planned final day of the site, I would have been inspired to keep going for another year, searching for another one like it. But in the six years that followed, nothing ever scratched that particular itch quite like this one (the closest runner-up was a movie you'll be reading about in May – you'll know it).

I recently finally had the pleasure of seeing this on 35mm (thanks Phil Blankenship/Cinefamily!), as the (I think?) lone audience member out of 150 or whatever that had seen it before, but I'm pretty sure some fans were made. Indeed, it was part of an all-secret horror marathon (meaning: you buy a ticket and trust you get some good stuff out of six movies), and *Cathy's Curse* was the title I saw namechecked most often the next morning on Facebook and the like. But even if everyone hated it, it still would have been the highlight of the night for me; as no good home video version exists, it was nice to finally see it clearly and at its proper aspect ratio (the DVD has some narrative text that is cropped out). And I got to see it with a crowd of bewildered horror fans, ultimately enjoying all these wonderfully terrible lines as much as I have for the past eight years, so bonus! When you see it, you'll hopefully understand why I used my milestone 100,000th tweet to once again remind people to watch this thing. Bless you, *Cathy's Curse*.

MOVIE #61 – MARCH 2nd

HOME MOVIE (2008)
Dir: Christopher Denham
HMAD Review Date: February 27, 2009 (DVD)
Genre: Killer Kid, Mockumentary
Available from MPI Home Video

Synopsis Based on Fading Memory: A father making typical home movies starts to realize his kids are insane.

Review excerpt:
"...unlike *The Good Son* or *Godsend*, these kids are legit terrifying. The Poe family unfortunately seems to own every kind of house pet there is, and they are all offed in order of small (goldfish) to large (the dog). Of course, then they move on to humans, resulting in a surprisingly chilling denouement. Near the end of the movie, there's a shot of the kids wearing paper bag masks and holding forks in the air which gave me real chills."

Reflection: When you remove the 90% or so of found footage movies that are just about assholes investigating a haunted asylum or something, you're left with a pretty varied collection of films that, more often than not, actually do have a real justification for being shot POV-style. So this is not only an above average killer kid movie, but it's also one that I can say is a solid use of the format. It has a few "Why is he still filming?" moments, but most of the shots have real motivation, and Denham makes up for it with some pretty chilling reveals. The dad is a bit slow to accept the reality that his kids are evil, but it's a forgivable stretch, and the climax is so chilling that you'll likely forget any minor issues you may have had along the way anyway.

It's also worth noting that the movie is one of the very few found footage entries where casting a recognizable actor (Adrian Pasdar in this case) actually works to its advantage. Pasdar is usually cast as a bad guy (or at least, one that exists in a very gray area), so you're probably expecting him to be the real villain while the kids turn out to be innocent (like *Hide and Seek*). I know we never actually believe that what we are seeing is real found footage (though there was a brief period, long before release, that I thought *Blair Witch Project* was real), but having recognizable folks in the movie just shines a light on its phoniness, rendering the whole doc approach kind of pointless unless there's a good reason for the casting. This is one such exception.

MOVIE #62 – MARCH 3rd

THE CLINIC (2010)
Dir: James Rabbitts
HMAD Review Date: October 10, 2010 (Festival screening)
Genre: Survival
Available from Image Entertainment

Synopsis Based on Fading Memory: A woman is kidnapped by a mysterious medical clinic, and her husband races to find her in time.

Review excerpt:
"Just when I thought I'd had enough of "let's tie a woman up and do stuff to her" movies, along comes The Clinic, *which gives the sub-genre a breath of fresh air, thanks to a unique scenario, a decent twist, and way above average technical and acting qualities. And the period setting (1979) also keeps the movie from having the standard "no signal" cell phone scene, or explaining away other modern elements that ruin the plotting of horror movies – I'm actually surprised we don't see more period horror films because of this."*

Reflection: I got really bummed when I re-read my review (which is somewhat mixed? I like the movie a lot more than the full review seems to suggest), because I mention that co-star Andy Whitfield was currently battling cancer and that I looked forward to his recovery. Sadly, that didn't happen – he passed away not long after the film got released in the US, about a year after I saw it. This remains the only thing I've seen him in, but he had the charm and charisma that his Australian peers (Sam Worthington, or Jai Courtney, who was a close friend of his) often lack on screen, and I really think he could have been as big or an even bigger star than those two had his life not been cut short by the menace that is cancer. He also reminded me of Paul Walker a bit, so watching it now is just a big bummer all around.

But don't let that stop you from checking out this above average entry in the "torture + medical experiment" sub-genre, which has a pretty nifty twist and some great little scare moments (including one involving a turnstile counter), plus a pretty horrific nightmare involving a drowning baby. My son HATES baths so this sort of thing didn't make me feel any better about terrifying him every time we just want to clean him up. Also, with all due respect to the *Friday the 13th* franchise, the movie uses roman numerals better than any horror film in history.

MOVIE #63 – MARCH 4th

THE CHILDREN (1980)
Dir: Max Kalmanowicz
HMAD Review Date: May 29, 2009 (Streaming)
Genre: Killer Kid
Available from Troma Entertainment Inc.

Synopsis Based on Fading Memory: Zombie-like children terrorize a town by hugging people to death. Naturally, the only way to stop them is to chop off their hands.

Review excerpt:
"...it's essentially a Moebius strip film, where the same two scenes more or less repeat in succession for the bulk of the running time. We have the sheriff investigating the disappearance of about a half dozen kids from a school bus alternating with scenes of those children, who have been turned into zombies of a sort, killing people by hugging them. Eventually though, the sheriff does his job and figures out what is going on, and then the film kicks it up a notch. And by that I mean we see kids getting shot. But since they are zombies, shooting them in the chest does little besides make me laugh. No, the only way to stop them is to cut their hands off (!!!). There's a hilarious shot during the epilogue of a bunch of their bodies lying on the ground with disembodied hands laying around. In short, the movie's kind of awesome."

Reflection: This is the first of two movies named *The Children* in this month, and it's the inferior but infinitely more ridiculous entry, If you're more of a "get drunk and laugh at a silly horror movie" type, this is the one you'll probably prefer – the other one is a more serious-minded take on a similar story. Like many of the movies in this month, I question how amusing I'll find it now that I have a kid of my own; the other one wasn't schlocky so it wouldn't be an issue, but I tend to get more repulsed when levity is added to the idea of dead kids, now that I know what it's like to be a parent. But either way: the "cut off their hands" thing is pretty inspired.

Fun fact: watching this movie, you might have the thought "Man, this score was ripped off *from Friday the 13th*!" But as it turns out, both films were scored by Harry Manfredini, whom I gave more shit to on the site than any actual filmmaker or actor, due to his rampant laziness. I mean, it wouldn't be much of a surprise that he started lifting from himself in the later part of his career, since every composer does that – but he was doing so right from the start! He began composing for features only a few years prior to these two films, which were released a month apart. And the melody is kind of a lift from *Psycho* to begin with, making it twice as shameless. Of course, when he tried mixing it up the results were horrendous; he didn't use many of his usual themes for *Jason X*, and the score is nearly unlistenable (I heard a rumor that the film actually tested better with a temp score than with his actual music). Hack.

MOVIE #64 – MARCH 5th

THE PIT (1981)
Dir: Lew Lehman
HMAD Review Date: April 25, 2008 (DVD)
Genre: Killer Kid, Weird
Available from Starz/Anchor Bay

Synopsis Based on Fading Memory: An odd little kid throws people into a pit in his backyard.

Review excerpt:
"One hilarious thing about the movie is that you can't really blame Jamie for tossing folks into a pit. As the film begins, he simply goes to talk to an older kid, and the dude punches him right in the face. A neighbor girl is so mean to him it makes Lucy pulling the football away from Charlie Brown look sort of sweet, and an old lady calls him a freak for no reason whatsoever. Sure, the kid is a bit off, but these people are downright vicious. Kick their ass, Jamie! Also, it has a really odd sense of what women can or can't do. In one scene the babysitter picks up a knife after Jamie offers to get it. When he gets mad, she explains "Women are capable of a lot more these days." Later, when someone claims that they can't spell very well, she replies "Who can?"

Reflection: A lot of horror movies from the early '80s really only work if you saw them back then. This can be true about any era, I suppose, but that's my demographic so it comes up more often than say, 1930's horror. So when I found a gem from that period that I had missed 20 years or so ago, I got REALLY excited, as many of those '80s movies that I never got to see until the HMAD era ended up disappointing me. *The Burning* is a pretty solid example; I just do not get the love for that movie, but I assume I would have been a big fan if I saw it in my formative years instead of when I was 28. Luckily, *The Pit* delivered on every level I could ask for: a murderous kid, some uncomfortable weirdness (the bathtub scene... yikes), and a laughably mean-spirited ending that would have been reshot on the spot if this movie were made today. And it never could be.

A bit later, I saw a movie called *Freaky Farley* that was basically a full-length homage to this movie and *Silent Night Deadly Night Part 2*, and it was then I realized that the two films share a unique passion for being just plain WRONG, but in a very (drunken) crowd-pleasing manner. If you are a fan of *SNDN2*'s warped sense of what passes for entertainment, then *The Pit* should be right up your alley. Due to the DVD being out of print (it was only ever released alongside the not-good *Hellgate*, at least in the US), it might be harder to find than some of the others in this chapter, but I assure you it's worth the effort and money.

MOVIE #65 – MARCH 6th

JULIE DARLING (1983)
Dir: Paul Nicholas
HMAD Review Date: April 16, 2009 (Revival screening)
Genre: Killer Kid, Weird
Available from Code Red

Synopsis Based on Fading Memory: A disturbed teen fixates on her father and kills anyone who might come between them.

Review excerpt:
"Some might be reading all of this and wondering if this is even a horror movie. Well, had I known nothing about it beforehand, I wouldn't have considered it one. It does have some elements of a Killer Kid movie, obviously, but it's not played for scares or even thrills, really. It's just a weird little movie. But, it played the festival under the "Psychosexual Maniacs" banner, and IMDb lists it as horror, so it qualifies for my purposes. I wouldn't have minded a bit more bloodshed (they set up Julie killing her little stepbrother, but they pussy out and save the kid before writing him out of the movie all together), but the lack of violence pays off with the surprising and somewhat mean-spirited ending."

Reflection: I saw this when the Alamo Drafthouse did a "roadshow", coming to theaters in towns not blessed with their own Alamos (they're primarily based in Texas, but they have a few locations around the country) and giving them a sense of their programming. This was before I was associated with them (they own Birth.Movies.Death.) and obviously they couldn't provide the FULL Alamo experience since a big part of it is the ability to order alcoholic beverages and full meals for the movie, but it made me a fan all the same. I wish they had done this sort of thing more often, but they're making up for it – in the near future we're finally getting an Alamo here in LA (well, downtown LA, which from where I live in the Valley is just as far away as Texas, I think).

Anyway, this is a weird movie and only counts as horror in the barest sense, but given my love of *Orphan* I felt I should include it since it's kind of a predecessor. They'd make for a great double feature! In fact...

MOVIE #66 – MARCH 7th

ORPHAN (2009)
Dir: Jaume Collet-Serra
HMAD Review Date: July 17, 2009 (Theatrical)
Genre: Killer Kid
Available from Warner Home Video

Synopsis Based on Fading Memory: A family adopts a child, but she's...

Review excerpt:
"Even without Esther the film packs a punch. The opening nightmare scene is more horrifying and disturbing than anything in the Nightmare on Elm St. *films ever presented for a nightmare (the fact that it actually RESEMBLES a dream, with unexplained character/location changes and such, doesn't hurt). And then later there is a terrific bit that plays on our understanding of cinema. Vera Farmiga pulls up to a red light and begins daydreaming as she spies a pregnant woman walking across the street. She keeps watching for a while, and then we hear a car honk. We all know this means that she's daydreamed past the light turning to green again, so she starts driving toward. And then BAM! she narrowly misses getting side-swiped. It is then that we see the light, which is still red - the honking was unrelated. Great misdirection."*

Reflection: This is one of the more famous movies in the book, and I'm fine with that. Sometimes I see it described as a dud because it was a summer movie that didn't gross over $100m, so I'll use that (erroneous) thinking to my advantage and consider it under the radar enough for inclusion here. Because really, I don't get to pimp this movie nearly enough; I would have hosted at the New Beverly if someone hadn't beaten me to it. It's a shame director Jaume Collet-Serra (who also gave us the above average *House of Wax* "remake") has since resigned himself to making Liam Neeson thrillers; they're not bad movies but he was shaping up to be a dependable source of quality studio horror. He's got an *Open Water*-esque movie called *The Shallows* coming this year, but after that he's jumping back in bed with Neeson for another action flick. Maybe if *Shallows* is a hit he can at least go back and forth between action and horror? Or combine his two passions and get Neeson back in a genre movie?

Fun anecdote – the day after I wrote my review I had to interview the cast and the producers (not Collet-Serra, sadly), something I barely tolerated doing. The only time I had fun was when I talked to Kate Beckinsale for *Whiteout*, because the camera crew had a glitch and while they worked on fixing it I got to make casual chit-chat with this impossibly beautiful woman, mostly about nonsense like how she saw her husband (Len Wiseman) looking at our site in the middle of the night and thought it was porn. Anyway, the *Orphan* interviews with the producers and the two main actors (Vera Farmiga and Peter Sarsgaard) were typically generic affairs, but the one with the little girl who played Esther was funny because it was the only time ever that I ran out of questions before the publicist told me my time was up. You only get four minutes for these things, and usually I'd have to ignore their warnings in order to get a third question in, but the little girl answered my questions so fast that after about two minutes I had nothing left to ask. So I went with the always awful "What are you doing next?" hoping to fill up the time, but she even raced through THAT, so I had no choice but to say "OK, well, that's it!" and stand up, surprising her and the publicist. I quit doing junkets for good a couple years later; my last one was *Final Destination 5* and I got into an accident on the way home, so I took it as a sign that I should retire my career as a hard-hitting junketeer. I haven't had a fancy breakfast since.

MOVIE #67 – MARCH 8th

VINYAN (2008)
Dir: Fabrice Du Welz
HMAD Review Date: March 19, 2009 (DVD)
Genre: Horror?, Survival
Available from Sony Pictures Home Entertainment

Synopsis Based on Fading Memory: A couple travels to the Burmese jungle in order to find their son.

Review excerpt:
"It's like Terrence Malick's version of a jungle/survival movie. If you like looking at trees and people gazing in awe at lush landscapes and such, you'll love this movie, and maybe I would too - had I not been told it was a horror movie, or if I hadn't already seen 90 versions of the same movie. The Thin Red Line is a great film, and I don't mind that it's "slow", because at its heart is another WWII movie. I've seen plenty of those, so I enjoyed the change of pace. But you don't see a lot of jungle-set movies (horror or otherwise) that aren't about cannibals, and I was genuinely interested in whether or not they would find their son."

Reflection: This one almost ended up in October (the "not full blown horror" month), as the majority of its (nearly non-existent) horror elements are confined to the final ten minutes. But I saw it as a non-parent, and now I will probably find it a lot scarier, because I'm a worry-wart and now this sort of thing chills me to the bone. Plus, since then we've had to endure another two or three movies where Rufus Sewell plays a villain in some period action film, so now I can appreciate his heroic, present day turn even more. My review is mostly negative, but it grew on me over time (even before I had a kid), and I think as long as you go in knowing how minimal the horror aspect is (despite Sony's terrible marketing for it trying to convince you otherwise), I think you'll find it to be a worthy addition to the "Parents grieve" sub-genre in the vein of *Don't Look Now* and another movie I'll be recommending later.

While we're talking about misleading marketing, it's pretty weak when a major studio does it. Well, it's weak when ANYONE does it, but at least for independent stuff I get why they feel the need to fib a bit – they're on the shelf right next to major studio releases and they have to stand out. But this is a Sony release, and while he's not exactly an A-lister, Rufus Sewell is certainly a recognizable actor. They had enough to go on to sell it honestly, and it's a shame that they didn't as I'm sure I wasn't the only viewer who was disappointed on my first viewing. However, I may be the only one who was willing to give it another chance. I'm almost certainly the only one putting it in *Horror Movie A Day: The Book*.

MOVIE #68 – MARCH 9th

JOSHUA (2007)
Dir: George Ratliff
HMAD Review Date: July 8, 2007 (Theatrical)
Genre: Comedic, Killer Kid, Psychological
Available from 20th Century Fox

Synopsis Based on Fading Memory: It's like *The Good Son,* except something happens.

Review excerpt:
"Despite the unexpected humor, the movie is still pretty creepy. I still wonder if it was only toys inside Joshua's giant bag of stuff for Goodwill. And the scene of him pretending to mourn the loss of the family dog is definitely one of the most unsettling scenes in a horror movie all year. Hell, even the normally upbeat Dave Matthews contributes a depressing and, again, creepy song for the end credits. Come on man, eat, drink and be merry!"

Reflection: Between this, *Orphan*, and *Bates Motel*, I have to wonder what kind of mom Vera Farmiga is. Maybe it's how she works out her own fears about being a parent or something? I mean she's a great actress who takes on a variety of roles across all genres, so it's weird that she's been the mom to THREE murderous children (don't correct me if you know that's not technically accurate, you know what I mean, nitpickers). But what's interesting is that they're all different; here she's the mom who doesn't suspect that her child could be a monster, whereas in *Orphan* she's the proactive parent while her husband remains clueless. And on *Bates* she knows he's a killer and covers for him, like a good mom. Anyway, of the three roles, this one seems to have the smallest following and it's likely you haven't seen it, so fix that.

It's also a fine showcase for Dallas Roberts, whom many folks probably remember as the right hand man to the Governor on *Walking Dead*. I believe this was the first thing I saw him in, and he left quite an impression as Joshua's uncle. He's probably the only person in the movie Joshua seems to genuinely like, giving Roberts a fun, uncomfortable role to play as he knows the kid is messed up but at the same time, as a gay man he knows a thing or two about feeling different from the folks around him. Outside of the titles you've all heard of (*The Omen, The Exorcist*, etc.), evil kid movies aren't exactly famous for their good performances, so the fact that this modern entry offers several (I haven't even mentioned Sam Rockwell as the dad!) should count for something.

Did you catch the Dave Matthews lyrical reference in the excerpt? I assure you, I'll never inflict a music recommendation book on you.

MOVIE #69 – MARCH 10th

BABY BLUES (2008)
Dir: Lars Jacobson, Amardeep Kaleka
HMAD Review Date: September 9, 2008 (DVD)
Genre: Slasher
Available from Allumination Filmworks

Synopsis Based on Fading Memory: While her husband is away on a work trip, a stay-at-home mom has a psychotic break and begins murdering her kids.

Review excerpt:
"On the IMDb, some folks are complaining that the movie should be banned and whatnot because it's so disturbing and tries to make entertainment out of a real life problem (postpartum depression, which is what sets the mom off). Of course, that means we should also ban Candyman *(inner city people being ignored),* Stir Of Echoes 2 *(the Iraq War),* Texas Chain Saw *(the economy), etc. And the idea of banning a horror movie for being disturbing is both hilarious and sad; it's so rare anymore that a horror film even TRIES to disturb the audience; when one does it's considered a crime?"*

Reflection: This one might be the most disturbing entry for the month, since it's basically a slasher movie where all of the victims are kids. Not teens, KIDS. Even with the premise known, you'd probably expect that there might be one off-screen kill of the oldest kid and the others would be safe, with random adults filling in for the rest of the carnage, but no. It's pretty grim stuff, and it weighed heavily on my mind after our baby was born, because someone suggested that our little guy came early (37 weeks, which is full term - so he wasn't *premature*, just "early") because my wife was overstressed, which could be a trigger for the same awful affliction the mom here is suffering. And like the dad in the movie, I had to go to work and we don't have any family around, so it was really tough for me to leave her alone the first time I had to – memories of this particular film certainly didn't help. Luckily/obviously both she and the baby are fine, and the only threat to his wellbeing comes from the possibility of my giant DVD collection of movies like this falling on him during one of California's monthly earthquakes.

Please note that there's another movie called *Baby Blues* that's actually about a killer doll, a type of movie that the US box art for this film resembles. So make sure you got the right one; the other one is from China so a mere glance at the credits should tip you off (it's also bad, which is why you didn't see it in the Asian horror chapter). This one keeps going in and out of print, so keep checking back – it's worth the effort (and also the price hike if it is out of print but available through third parties).

MOVIE #70 – MARCH 11th

THE BLOOD ON SATAN'S CLAW (1971)
Dir: Piers Haggard
HMAD Review Date: April 20, 2008 (Revival screening)
Genre: Cult, Killer Kid, Supernatural
Available from Odeon

Synopsis Based on Fading Memory: Some kids try to resurrect Satan.

Review excerpt:
"The storytelling is very loose, something that was a bit strange but eventually won me over. For example, the film begins with a dude visiting his uncle to introduce him to his fiancée. The film follows the young couple for the first 15 minutes or so, and then once we have met a few other folks, they have seemingly served their purpose. The girl is never heard from again, and the guy just sort of gets phased out, to the point where the last time we see him he's basically an extra in a scene. Later, five of the townsfolk are chasing one of the suspected cult members, a scene that comes out of nowhere. You might occasionally get a bit confused, but in the end it all more or less makes sense (at least in an interior logic sort of way – we ARE talking about a movie in which people begin growing parts of the devil on their person)."

Reflection: Despite its limited availability in the US, I got a chance to see this again recently and was dismayed to discover how many of my pals disliked it. True, it's a bit slower than some might hope, but it's just such a WEIRD goddamn movie that I think it more than makes up for it. And it's one of the very few that combine killer children (they're mostly teens, I should mention) with occult stuff, so the novelty alone should make up for the occasionally lax pace. I mean, it's basically *Wicker Man* mixed with *Children of the Corn* – how can you not at least kind of love that? You'll have to import it if you're in the US, but I think it's worth the hassle.

When I saw the film it was titled *Satan's Skin*, which is a pretty generic title and one I never remember. I'm glad that, because of the internet and growing reliance on global box office, running into title changes like this is mostly a thing of the past. I mean, sure, there's stuff like *Harry Potter* being named *Sorcerer's Stone* in the US and *Philosopher's Stone* in the UK, because the words mean different things, but for weirdo horror like this they usually just go with the one title. Makes things a lot easier for folks like me; I love this movie but if you ask me about a movie called *Satan's Skin*, I'll probably forget that I even saw it, let alone like it quite a bit. *The Blood on Satan's Claw* is a much easier title to remember (and if you change "Satan" to "A Rat" or something, you have a fine *giallo* title as well).

MOVIE #71 – MARCH 12th

DEVIL TIMES FIVE (1974)
Dir: Sean MacGregor, David Sheldon
HMAD Review Date: April 12, 2007 (DVD)
Genre: Killer Kid, Weird
Available from Synergy Entertainment

Synopsis Based on Fading Memory: Some kids (presumably, five of them) kill some folks.

Review excerpt:
"Fans of the film are well aware that the film had a troubled production (the first cut ran less than 40 minutes, so another director was brought in months later to pad the film to an acceptable running time), and enough has been written (mocked) about the resulting problems, so I won't bother. Who cares if different actors appear to play characters we have barely seen thus far, or if entire scenes are played in slow motion (4 frames per second) to pad the time, or if it's easier to just point out continuity non-errors? Why should we be confused when a character is woken up by a persistent "dumb car horn", only to get dressed, go downstairs and watch the car pull up to the house?"

Reflection: At this point, all I really remember about this movie is that it had ridiculous production issues that resulted in a total, but entertaining mess. Like most of my 2007 reviews, re-reading it in preparation for this book doesn't really help much, because I was so desperately holding on to the idea that people would read the review only after they watched the movie and thus would know what I was referring to with minimal context. With my memory shot to shit by now, I have no idea what I'm talking about in most of those older write-ups, so I don't know why I expected anyone else to. Oh well. Luckily it's a public domain-type title, so you can watch it on pretty much any streaming service and thus not have to risk paying for a poor-quality DVD.

One thing I DO distinctly remember is that it features a woman seducing a mentally challenged guy in order to get him to do her bidding, which is not only a weird plot point for a killer kid movie, but the movie I watched the following day (a not-good slasher called *Funeral Home*) had the same damn thing happen! These sort of coincidences would happen more often than you'd think over the six years I did HMAD, and on occasion I considered doing it on purpose, though I realized it'd be impossible due to availability (and also because I didn't like to know much about a movie before watching it). Still, if I could have pulled it off

AND timed it so that I could circle back to *Return to Horror High* on the last day? That would be pretty goddamn impressive.

Oh, Leif Garrett is in it. There's a bizarre thing on the internet where if someone famous is in a junky movie, you have to mention it, or someone will comment "No mention of ___?" I find it to be one of the most obnoxious things about writing online, and you should know that if you've ever written a similar comment or tweet, you're a bad person.

MOVIE #72 – MARCH 13th

GHOST SON (2007)
Dir: Lamberto Bava
HMAD Review Date: August 3, 2007 (Theatrical)
Genre: Ghost, Possession
Available from Xenon

Synopsis Based on Fading Memory: A woman's infant son seems to be possessed by her dead husband.

Review excerpt:
"It sounds sillier than it is. Granted, you got to employ some suspension of disbelief, especially in the final act, where the baby begins talking and getting aroused, but since this IS a Bava film, you should have checked logic at the door anyway. At least the mother isn't saved by a random helicopter crashing through the ceiling."

Reflection: Somewhere in my original review, I said "Recommended!" and apparently it was the only memorable part to the publicity team, because without ever asking me they used it on the DVD box (credited to Bloody Disgusting, however, as my review ran both there and on HMAD). It's kind of sad that *that* was one of the best blurbs they could find for this perfectly enjoyable little oddity, which is basically Lamberto Bava updating *Shock* (aka *Beyond The Door II*). *Shock* was the elder Bava's final film, but apparently Lamberto co-directed it unbilled (he's listed as an assistant director, as well as its screenwriter), so maybe he just wanted to finally get the top credit for a movie about a dead guy possessing his son.

Admittedly, *Shock* is a better film, but being a *Mario* Bava entry you probably saw it if you're up on your Italian masters, whereas this probably went way off your radar. And *Ghost Son* gives you a chance to enjoy a rare horror film performance from the late, great Pete Postlethwaite, who sadly died a few years ago. He went out on top, however, with performances in *The Town* and *Inception* being among his final ones. But then again, *Shock* features the most hilariously fake crash sequence ever committed to film (and one of the all-time great jump scares, sadly spoiled in most of its trailers), so it's just as vital to see. If you haven't seen it, consider this an entry for *Shock* – everyone else give this loose remake a look. You win either way!

P.S. You like how I refer to *Lamberto* as "Bava" in the excerpt? That's the kind of balls you only get at HMAD. You're welcome.

HMAD Fun Fact: As far as I know, HMAD was only ever quoted on one trailer - but it was for Trick 'r Treat, *so it's not like I could ask for a better film anyway. Fittingly, the quote is too long to actually read before it cuts to the next one.*

MOVIE #73 – MARCH 14th

IT'S ALIVE (1974)
Dir: Larry Cohen
HMAD Review Date: June 15, 2008 (DVD)
Genre: Killer Kid, Monster
Available from Warner Home Video

Synopsis Based on Fading Memory: An expecting couple discovers their baby is actually a mutant.

Review excerpt:
"...that's not to say it's all frowns and melodrama. I got quite a few laughs out of it, mainly because everyone in the movie is so blunt. At one point, the dad's boss tells him "Hey you know Ted in accounting? He's got a retarded kid!" in an attempt to cheer him up. There's also some nice black humor – a (non-monstrous) baby is at one point surrounded by gun-toting cops who are hunting the monster baby. Cohen is brilliant here, as you fully believe that these cops will actually shoot the tyke (aided by a sudden cut to black that lasts 10 seconds – as if we might just hear the shot). Great stuff."

Reflection: In addition to the finest teaser trailer in history, *It's Alive* boasts a pretty impressive pedigree: two sequels and a remake. And yet I still feel it's one of those movies that people know the title but actually haven't seen (I myself have only watched it the one time). The sequels are decent (I prefer the second film to the third, even though the latter has Michael Moriarty and thus *should* be the best of the lot), and I actually kind of liked the remake for the most part, but none top the original for me.

I think it's because I was surprised at how serious it was – you hear the plot and see that it's directed by Larry Cohen and you wouldn't be crazy to assume that it was kind of schlocky, but it's played fairly straight, which works in its favor more often than not. In fact, if you've never seen any Cohen movies, I'd suggest starting here before diving into his more famous works (*The Stuff, Q*). Don't spoil yourself on prime Michael Moriarty efforts right off the bat, like I did! Just be sure to skip his 1984 film *Special Effects* – I don't know what went wrong there, but until then I was sure if nothing else a Larry Cohen film couldn't be BORING. However, there is no other way to describe that chore.

MOVIE #74 – MARCH 15th

666: THE CHILD (2006)
Dir: Jack Perez
HMAD Review Date: December 22, 2011 (Streaming)
Genre: Killer Kid, Supernatural
Available from Asylum Home Entertainment

Synopsis Based on Fading Memory: *The Omen*, but cheap.

Review excerpt:
"...the deaths really help keep this one going. They're all pretty splatter-y, and there's a lot of variety - a falling pipe, a trip through a glass door, a doctor's drill... even a good ol' fashioned old lady (a nun!) getting hit by a car. The movie is only 79 minutes long (a whopping 10 of which are just the hilariously slow end credits), but director Jack Perez seems to know how to balance the "talk" to "ridiculous death" ratio so that it feels even shorter."

Reflection: If you've somehow picked up this book without ever being exposed to an Asylum mockbuster, let me get you up to speed. This production company primarily makes generic rip-offs of big budget Hollywood films, making them very quickly and dumping them on DVD right around the time the real title hits theaters. The idea is either A. they can dupe people into thinking that big movie they saw a trailer for is already on DVD (hence movies like *Transmorphers* and *Paranormal Entity*), or B. they can inspire curiosity among idiots like myself. Anyway, of the many I watched, this may be the best. They were cashing in on the *Omen* remake of 2006, so if anything it might actually be the only Asylum entry that's BETTER than the movie they were aping. They ramp up the ridiculous kills (an element that exists even in the real *Omen*) and keep things under 80 minutes. I mean, it's still a bad movie in the traditional sense, but among Asylum films it's their *Citizen Kane* or whatever. Take it from a guy who watched at least a dozen.

Fun anecdote: they made a sequel called *666: The Beast*, and on Twitter one of its crew warned me against watching it. I didn't listen to him. Turns out he was right.

MOVIE #75 – MARCH 16th

RISE OF THE DEAD (2007)
Dir: William Wedig
HMAD Review Date: November 18, 2007 (DVD)
Genre: Possession, Weird
Available from Lionsgate

Synopsis Based on Fading Memory: A ghost possesses people and kills other people. It's not a zombie movie.

Review excerpt:
"It's almost like writers Joshua & Jeffrey Crook and Kris Scotto wanted to make a film that served as a metaphor for living up to your responsibilities as a parent, but somehow got forced to make it into a horror movie. The horror elements seem fairly shoehorned in (and the music is just a straight up rip-off of the Halloween *score, for good measure), and hell, the movie doesn't even end on a "scary" note, which makes the DVD's excessive attempts to sell it as a zombie movie all the more puzzling."*

Reflection: Over the years I probably gave Lionsgate more shit than any other studio, due to their rampant "crimes" that include but are not limited to: retitling movies to something that didn't fit, giving them box art that sold a different movie entirely, and forcing people to watch their 20 minutes of trailers at the top of each and every disc they put out. But I can almost forgive all of them for releasing this batshit indie. Hell, the misleading title/cover might have even been a good thing - if just *one* person watched this thinking it'd be a generic zombie movie but walked away delighted as to what it actually was, it'd be worth it.

That said, I don't want to spoil much about the actual plot (though the fact that it's included in this month's selections gives part of it away), only to reiterate that it's NOT a zombie movie. It's something much more inspired. Stick with it. Trust me. Even the A.V. Club sung its praises (and hosted a screening I desperately wish I could have attended), so that should be your first inkling that this isn't some run of the mill piece of junk. I remember going to a bar after I saw it and trying to describe it to my friends over the usual (loud) noise – I probably sounded more like a lunatic than I usually do. Putting it in this book will presumably be more effective.

MOVIE #76 – MARCH 17th

EDEN LAKE (2008)
Dir: James Watkins
HMAD Review Date: October 17, 2008 (Festival screening)
Genre: Survival
Available from Dimension Extreme

Synopsis Based on Fading Memory: A couple runs afoul of some very unsettling youths.

Review excerpt:
"It's not wall to wall gore and violence; in fact nothing "bad" happens until 45 minutes in or so. That means we get some goddamn character development (remember that stuff?) for our two heroes, and our villains are actually set up, as is the conflict (which IS somewhat original, actually) that ultimately elevates their antagonism to full blown terror. Also, as there are only two "good guys", we are spared excessive violence -no nosy cops, no random folks in the woods, etc... the focus is kept on our two protagonists throughout the film."

Reflection: It's funny, Dimension is responsible for some of the blandest and lousiest big screen horror movies of the past 20 years, but their Dimension Extreme label (now defunct, I believe) allowed US audiences easy access to a number of imported gems. Through them we were blessed with *Inside, Black Sheep, Dead in 3 Days* (all movies you'll find in the pages ahead!)... and this, which is surprisingly still kind of under the radar despite the fact that it stars Michael Fassbender (plus Kelly Reilly, who SHOULD be a bigger star but as of this writing is not. I still hold out hope that'll change). Another thing that should have elevated its visibility – it was directed by James Watkins, who was at the helm of *The Woman In Black*, one of the better big screen ghost films of recent memory (and a huge hit).

Granted, it's not the most original evil kid movie, and unlike *The Strangers* it's probably fair to make comparisons to *Them (Ils)*, but the solid performances and unexpected ending (which offers a reverse of the ending of one of horror's most notorious movies, though to say which one would effectively spoil it) elevate it a few notches. I assume Dimension's less than stellar marketing (the movies would be dumped unceremoniously on DVD, with little press coverage) was part of why the movie remains kind of obscure, but since they're the ones who took a chance on it it's hard to get too mad at them. They've got a lot on their plate, what with ruining the *Halloween* and *Hellraiser* series and what not.

MOVIE #77 – MARCH 18th

WHISPER (2007)
Dir: Stewart Hendler
HMAD Review Date: February 11, 2008 (DVD)
Genre: Killer Kid, Supernatural
Available from Universal Studios

Synopsis Based on Fading Memory: A kidnapping goes wrong when the kid turns out to be... you'll see.

Review excerpt:
"Even though the movie was shot entirely in Canada, I give the production team an A+ for really putting in the effort to sell it as Massachusetts and Maine. While I wasn't entirely fooled (the roads are a dead giveaway – no highway in Massachusetts has more than ¼ mile without a sign for a Dunkins!), they have the right newspapers, police cars, license plates, even a nice local microbrewery (Wachusett Ale) that any native New Englander such as myself will appreciate. And since they don't have anyone do the accent, it actually makes it even more believable, since it's always exaggerated beyond any reasonable belief."

Reflection: Now that *LOST* is off the air and kind of fading from popular memory (a lousy ending will do that), maybe it'll be easier to watch this movie without thinking about Sawyer the whole time. Josh Holloway is a good actor, but his role here is so close to his *LOST* character that it was a major distraction for me at the time, and overshadowed the more intriguing elements of this low-key but fairly original take on the evil kid movie.

It's also got Joel Edgerton in an early role, so like yesterday's *Eden Lake*, it's something that folks might want to check out just to enjoy fresh performances by future alpha male actors. And unlike *LOST*, it doesn't end with the hero trying to protect a urine cave. *Walking Dead* fans (that never watched *Prison Break*) can also enjoy a look at what Sarah Wayne Callies is like when she's not playing the worst written character in major television history. Spoiler: she's engaging and lovely! Callies and Holloway are currently reteaming for a show called *Colony* – I am going to watch and pretend it's a sequel to this film (and judge it accordingly).

MOVIE #78 – MARCH 19th

THE PLAGUE (2006)
Dir: Hal Masonberg
HMAD Review Date: July 4, 2008 (DVD)
Genre: Killer Kid, Zombie
Available from Sony Pictures Home Entertainment

Synopsis Based on Fading Memory: James Van Der Beek returns to his (seemingly Creek-less) hometown, where A. everyone hates him and B. a bunch of comatose teens have become zombies.

Review excerpt:
"Whoever's vision the released version of The Plague *is, it's a pretty good one for the first hour. We essentially have a sort of traditional zombie movie setup/execution, except the zombies are not actually undead. Ten years prior to the film's events, every child under the age of 9 suddenly went into a comatose state. New children were stillborn, and the kids just old enough to avoid the plague have seemingly all become delinquents. Anyway, all of a sudden they wake up, and begin killing everyone, naturally. Like the best zombie movies, eventually we get all of our characters trapped in one location, and the movie truly shines here (though the slower stuff at the beginning is also pretty good – I always like the "hometown boy returns and everyone now hates him" scenario)."*

Reflection: Regarding the "whoever's vision" comment above – the director has gone on record to say that the film was taken away from him and what we saw was compromised. When I reviewed the movie I linked to a page that had a petition to get his original director's cut of the film released on DVD. It currently has 411 likes on Facebook, so my guess is that there isn't enough interest for it to come out any time soon, since I could probably get twice as many likes for a fan-page about one of my cats (Butters, not Meeko). If you'd like to be the 412th, it's worth it just to read the director's comments about the Beek – he is not a fan, to say the least. Have to say - publicly trashing the film's (much more famous) star probably won't help his situation any, right?

BUT, on the other hand, the movie was produced by Clive Barker, and I thought I'd see angels flying out of my ass before I ever saw a proper release of the longer cut of his film *Nightbreed* – which not only exists but has a special thanks for yours truly in the credits (presumably for watching a cut and offering a few notes). So it COULD happen for *The Plague*, and if so I'll be sure to check it out. However, like the theatrical cut of *Nightbreed*, it may be a bit messy but it's still an enjoyable movie – and it was shot by Bill Butler, a name you might recognize from a film called *Jaws*. The pedigree alone demands a viewing! And Van Der Beek is good in it, for what it's worth.

MOVIE #79 – MARCH 20th

GRACE (2009)
Dir: Paul Solet
HMAD Review Date: May 18, 2009 (Theatrical)
Genre: Thriller
Available from Starz/Anchor Bay

Synopsis Based on Fading Memory: A pregnant woman goes through some traumatic shit.

Review excerpt:
"Unlike most horror films, this is the type of movie that demands a "the less you know the better" approach. Furthermore, I urge you NOT to watch the trailer that is currently online, as it gives away more than I would have liked even for a regular movie. I can understand why they would want to entice viewers by showing them some "highlights", but this is not a slasher movie. Its success stems from the subtle storytelling, the realistic approach, and the unnerving tone that the film conveys almost from the start, with occasional jolts of surprising violence that should be as shocking to the audience as they are to the characters. The trailer, in my opinion, severely dulls the effectiveness of those moments."

Reflection: I assume by now most people know what this one is about if they haven't already seen it, but just in case I'm gonna keep it vague. Not that it's a game-changer like knowing about the Bradley Whitford/Richard Jenkins characters before you see *Cabin in the Woods*, but it's a slow-paced movie that has a very pulpy-sounding plot, so if you say "It's about ___" you're going to go in expecting something a lot more ridiculous and fun, and that's not what this is. It's a serious, very grim take on what COULD be one of those movies, and I think that's what makes it work so well. Also, this is over five years old and Solet only recently released a second film – this is unacceptable, Hollywood.

Full disclosure: the film was produced by Adam Green, who made a slasher movie I quite loved called *Hatchet*. Thanks to mutual friends we became pals a year or so after I saw the movie, and later I actually did end credits on the *Hatchet* sequels. Because of social media it'd be pointless to deny I became friendly with other genre filmmakers over the years, including a few who have films in this book, but I also find it irrelevant. Most of them have thick skin and thus I've been able to be honest with how I feel about their movies while remaining on good terms with them (more than once I've pointed out that the only *Hatchet* I really love is the one that DOESN'T have my name on it), so if I'm saying one of their movies is worth your time, you can be assured I'm not just saying so because I'm their pal.

MOVIE #80 – MARCH 21st

CHILDREN OF THE CORN (2009)
Dir: Donald P. Borchers
HMAD Review Date: October 5, 2009 (DVD)
Genre: Cult, Killer Kid
Available from Starz/Anchor Bay

Synopsis Based on Fading Memory: A bickering couple gets lost in the Midwest and come across some children. And some corn.

Review excerpt:
"If you haven't read King's original story, I hate to spoil it, but it's far grimmer than the 1984 film was. Those less commercial elements are retained for this new version, something I quite appreciated. However, based on reactions from friends who watched the film's premiere on Syfy, the bitter characters were too hard to swallow, and they all hated it. Maybe because I was prepared for this, I didn't mind it as much. Again, they were like this in the source material, so it's not some random decision on the part of Borcher's, and who are we to argue with Stephen King? Perhaps it goes a bit overboard (the Vicki character has not one sympathetic moment in the film), but I'll take it over the original's annoying singing/dancing version of the character."

Reflection: I still haven't gone back and re-watched this one like I said I would in the review, but my memory of it is still fairly positive (this isn't always the case; without re-watching *Final Destination 4* I can tell you right now my glowing review is perhaps a bit over-exaggerated re: its quality). The characters may be hateful assholes, but they're played by actors I quite like (David Anders and Kandyse McClure), and since it premiered as a cable movie I am charmed by the fact that it's got more balls than the theatrical one. Plus, let's keep in mind that there isn't exactly a high bar to clear when it comes to *Children of the Corn* movies. Some of them can't even get the elements that are right there in the title correct (at least one of them doesn't have any corn), so let's give credit where credit is due.

I am curious which version Stephen King prefers. Not many of his stories have been adapted twice without his direct involvement in one of them (I think *Carrie* is the only other title where he was left out all *three* times – but there's no contest there), so free of the bias he'd obviously have for the TV *The Shining* over Kubrick's, or to a lesser extent *Maximum Overdrive* over the cable remake *Trucks*, how does he feel about one *Corn* over the other? I don't know if I've ever heard him say much about either version, now that I think about it; while he's famous for the "my books are still there on the shelf" line, he has occasionally damned or praised his adaptations. Depends on his mood, I guess. I hope he shares my affinity for *Dreamcatcher*, at any rate. That's the sort of bonkers nonsense Hollywood doesn't make nearly often enough for my tastes.

MOVIE #81 – MARCH 22nd

PLAGUE TOWN (2008)
Dir: David Gregory
HMAD Review Date: June 9, 2009 (Theatrical)
Genre: Killer Kid, Survival
Available from Dark Sky Films

Synopsis Based on Fading Memory: A dysfunctional family breaks down in a town populated by murderous children.

Review excerpt:
"Like Eden Lake, *we once again have tourists being menaced by a mob of the town's children, but in this case they are mutated freaks, with some truly freaky designs on a few of them (I love the main girl, Rosemary, who has a bandage and doll eyes covering where her real eyes would be). And instead of a couple, we have a dysfunctional family (father, two daughters, new stepmom, and one of the daughters' boyfriend), which allows for more kills and more suspense."*

Reflection: Director David Gregory read my review on HMAD, then emailed to thank me and said he'd send me the Blu-ray (which I had said I wanted to see because the audio at this screening wasn't the best). Well guess what, HE NEVER DID. But I don't hold a grudge, so I'm going to include it in my book six years later. Gregory usually makes DVD bonus features and behind-the-scenes documentaries, but I believe this is his only narrative feature. Sadly it's kind of hard to tell because his IMDb has every single featurette listed alongside it in his filmography and I'll be damned if I'm gonna go through them all to double check.

I have proof that my one viewing struck a chord though – for the monthly horror trivia game here in LA, the host occasionally posts screenshots from movies on the game's official Facebook page, and first team to identify what movie it is gets an extra point. Last year she put up a shot from this film, and I was the only one to get it! Usually there are about five people answering (correctly) almost simultaneously (the Facebook equivalent of a photo finish), but I alone recognized it, despite nearly six years having passed since I saw a single frame of it, let alone that particular one. So that should be enough endorsement, and as the saying goes, the only thing better than one killer kid is a whole town full of them.

MOVIE #82 – MARCH 23rd

BLOODY BIRTHDAY (1981)
Dir: Ed Hunt
HMAD Review Date: March 18, 2007 (DVD)
Genre: Killer Kid, Slasher
Available from Severin Films

Synopsis Based on Fading Memory: Three kids who were born during an eclipse wreak havoc in a southern California town.

Review excerpt:
"Killer kid movies are at their best when they don't try to make any point or include any symbolism. These kids just kill for the hell of it. Since they were born during an eclipse, they have no souls (possibly the most ridiculous exposition in a film up until 1989, when Jason Takes Manhattan *had us believe that the sewers of New York were flushed out with toxic waste every night), so they go about killing their parents, a teacher, and a seemingly endless supply of horny teens. Also, I must note that the kid with the glasses is the most terrifying killer kid I've ever seen in a film."*

Reflection: The aforementioned kid with glasses would be Curtis, played by actor Billy Jayne, who also popped up as the killer's younger version in *Hospital Massacre* (as did the female *Bloody Birthday* killer). He also appeared in *Cujo* and the immortal *Demonwarp*, so he could probably net some coin signing autographs at a convention (I'd lose my shit if there was a panel with all three of the killer kids). I saw this movie as a kid and mostly forgot about it until revisiting for HMAD, at which point I was kind of astonished that my mom let me watch it as an 8- or 9-year-old, though I do recall she vetoed it a couple times before relenting. It's got a higher body count than most killer kid movies, and the way they make some of the deaths look like accidents could have given me some ideas! I guess she knew I'd turn out okay-ish.

Unfortunately, director Ed Hunt kind of disappeared from making horror films – I dunno what it is about making great killer kid flicks, but so many of their directors sort of bail on the genre after. Again, look at Jaume Collet-Serra, following the amazing Orphan with a string of Liam Neeson action movies. And the guy who directed *The Pit* never directed another feature, period! But Hunt *is* still working, at least; tellingly, his filmography is mostly sci-fi movies about UFOs and the like, so that explains the random eclipse subplot – the dude just loves looking up at the sky and wondering what strange powers the stars and planets have over us. Also it beat *Halloween 6*'s silly Thorn constellation explanation by fourteen years. Good on you, Ed.

MOVIE #83 – MARCH 24th

THE CHILDREN (2008)
Dir: Tom Shankland
HMAD Review Date: November 6, 2009 (DVD)
Genre: Killer Kid
Available from Ghost House Underground

Synopsis Based on Fading Memory: While on vacation, some children snap and go after their parents... and the parents eventually fight back.

Review excerpt:
"I enjoyed the occasional creepy bits, such as one kid banging endlessly on his xylophone (this has an amazing payoff in the toy's final appearance), and another speaking in some sort of robot tongue. Shankland also gets a lot of mileage about the family cat, who is pretty obviously dead but we never really see what happened to it (a deleted scene explains a bit more, so it's the rare deletion that resulted in a more interesting subplot). And you gotta be some sort of sick genius to come up with the 'surgery' scene that serves as the film's goriest highlight."

Reflection: The first thing I mention in my review is that I should re-watch the movie (and a few others I've already covered in this chapter) after I have kids and see how I feel about them then, which I haven't done because, as readers with their own children can probably attest, you simply don't have time to be revisiting movies all that often. And I don't remember much about it in detail, but I do recall that unlike the other film with this title (March 4th's entry), it's much more serious and atmospheric, with a much smaller cast (only nine people: four adults and five kids) and a plot decidedly less schlocky than "radioactive gas turns kids into zombies that kill by hugging". There's some *Good Son*-style "Do I save my own kid who is evil or save an innocent that's not related to me?" action in the climax that I found fairly nerve-wracking then, so now that I can fully sympathize as a parent I'm curious how I'll take it.

I should note that this is a rarity in the evil child sub-genre, as it's a British film. For some reason they don't often dip into this well, which is a shame because they're pretty dang good at it. I assume it has something to do with their stricter "decency" guidelines over there, as well as the tragic case of two young boys who murdered a toddler in England (the press erroneously claimed they were inspired by *Child's Play 3*), making getting funding and/or distribution for such fare more trouble than it would be worth. Rereading the details of that case made me sick, almost to the point of deleting this and the entire chapter from the book, but I'm pretty sure every single horror movie ever made will trigger such reactions if the circumstances are right. If I omitted "dead kid" movies out of sensitivity to those who may have lost a child, it would be insulting to anyone who lost an adult loved one to a senseless murder for me to include... well, nearly every other movie in this book. I assume anyone looking for horror movie recommendations is more or less prepared to be inadvertently reminded of something terrible that happened to them. Ideally, it might even help you cope in some way – I know some folks who find these things to be very therapeutic in dealing with their own tragedies. But man, do NOT read up on that England case unless you want your day/week/life ruined. No movie can ever chill you as much as those details, I assure you.

MOVIE #84 – MARCH 25th

WHO CAN KILL A CHILD? (1976)
Dir: Narciso Ibáñez Serrador
HMAD Review Date: June 28, 2009 (DVD)
Genre: Killer Kid
Available from Dark Sky Films

Synopsis Based on Fading Memory: A pregnant couple gets trapped on an island where only killer children remain.

Review excerpt:
"The great thing about this movie is how goddamn unnerving it is. They never really explain why all of the kids snapped and killed the adults (the answer seems to be supernaturally-based though; there's a scene where an evil kid stares down one who seems to be normal, and then the normal one is crazy too), but that's what makes it scary. Plus, the kids seem to be having a grand old time, which makes it even scarier. The turning point comes when a really small child crawls into a duct in order to shoot our heroes, who have trapped themselves in a room. The kid smiles a big shit-eating grin before cocking the hammer, only to be gunned down by the hero, much to his wife's horror."

Reflection: It's funny; my review of this gem repeatedly suggests a remake – I fan-cast Tom Jane as the hero, mention its technical snafus as a good enough reason to do it, and also claim it'll never happen due to the subject matter, as '70s filmmakers were cooler about the on-screen death of children than their modern day counterparts. As it turns out, I was wrong, as it was indeed remade (under the title *Come Out And Play*), and ironically it's a pretty terrible movie, the sort of remake I usually rally AGAINST, not practically ask for. Maybe they fixed the technical issues I had, but they didn't change a damn thing about the narrative, offering a practically shot for shot piece that had no reason to exist. Please avoid it, and seek this one out instead.

Of course (broken record alert!), I haven't seen it since I had my own child, so my mileage may vary nowadays (especially the bit where… well, I won't spoil that, but pregnant women may be particularly unnerved). But unlike yesterday's movie, I think this one will pass my test; the fact that it's ALL the children as opposed to a select few (or just one) puts it into more *Village of the Damned* territory than *The Bad Seed* – I may have to someday worry about my son trying to murder me (he's had to listen to enough Meat Loaf already to warrant justification), but I can't really see myself being the target of a whole army of murderous kids. So it's harder to relate to even in my overactive imagination.

MOVIE #85 – MARCH 26th

CITADEL (2012)
Dir: Ciarán Foy
HMAD Review Date: November 17, 2012 (Theatrical)
Genre: Supernatural
Available from Flatiron Film Company

Synopsis Based on Fading Memory: A single dad struggling to care for his infant son runs afoul of some creepy ass feral children.

Review excerpt:
"It's rare to have a male as the lead in a horror film (especially one about parenting), and it's even rarer that one is as sympathetic as Tommy is here. Foy wastes no time in setting up his plight; the mother is attacked in the opening moments, and quickly establishes the fallout - in addition to now having to raise the child alone, Tommy has become agoraphobic as a result, and (in a plot point that was slightly muddled) he now lives in an isolated part of town as the result of some urban redevelopment program, one where the bus doesn't stop after a certain time of day and the cops don't come at all. In short, his life is shit and kind of scary even without the little demons terrorizing him."

Reflection: If I haven't already, I apologize for how much I talk about my son in this book (and on HMAD's newer reviews, and on Twitter, and...). They say to "write what you know" and since May of 2014 all I really know beyond caring about/for my baby boy is my day job, and that's not even interesting to talk to myself about let alone write about for strangers. That said, I saw this long before he was even conceived, and I suspect if I watched it again I would have chickened out of deciding to have a baby, ever. Even with my wife around it can be pretty tough, so I can't even fathom the idea of going through what the father does in this film – I have enough trouble getting my baby fed/dressed/cleaned up on my own when my wife has to go to work early. Doing it every day, and everything else too, with no one to ever tag in so you can get a break? HORRIFYING!

Interestingly, this and *Attack the Block* were my among my favorite genre films of 2012, and both of them involve tenement structures "on the wrong side of the tracks" (they're also both from European countries, for what it's worth). Even more interesting: also on that list was *Sinister*, and Foy followed this up with that film's sequel. That one didn't turn out so great (it's fine, just not nearly as memorable as the original *Sinister* or this film), but he's already lined up another film that will see him returning to Ireland, and I can't wait to see it. Anyone who makes a debut this strong deserves the benefit of the doubt if their follow-up (and first US production) disappoints.

MOVIE #86 – MARCH 27th

IT'S ALIVE 2: IT LIVES AGAIN (1978)
Dir: Larry Cohen
HMAD Review Date: April 6, 2009 (DVD)
Genre: Killer Kid, Monster
Available from Warner Home Video

Synopsis Based on Fading Memory: Look, even if I had a picture clear memory of the film, and I don't, the title tells you everything.

Review excerpt:
"Cohen takes the best approach to a sequel I can imagine. He brings back the hero of the first film (the Frank Davis character) while introducing a new couple on the verge of having their own monster baby. So if you liked Davis, you get to see him do something new (he now works for a company that aims to help - or so they claim - those who are about to have a mutant child), and if you just liked the idea of a couple having a monster baby, you get that too. It's familiar and yet different in nearly perfectly equal helpings (Davis kind of disappears for most of the second act). It may not be a perfect movie, but in terms of successfully "following" the first film, it's definitely one of the better examples I can think of in the horror genre."

Reflection: I feel I'm kind of cheating here by including this one when I have the original listed, as well, but it's a worthy follow-up, something that's not always guaranteed in the horror genre. I really love Cohen's approach to doing a sequel, which is to split the time between his original hero doing something new and showing a couple going through the same thing that happened last time – imagine if a *Friday the 13th* sequel did the same thing? Like if *Part 3* still had Jason stalking Higgins' Haven, but also kept cutting away to what *Part 2*'s Amy Steel was up to after her ordeal? That'd be awesome! So I spotlight the film in the hopes that more franchises take a cue from Cohen here.

Don't worry, I have NOT included the third film, which, despite Michael Moriarty's presence (I truly love that man, especially in Cohen's films), is my least favorite of the series. The subtitle was *Island of the Alive*, suggesting a whole world full of these delightful mutant babies, but they spend less time there than Jason spent in Manhattan, and there isn't nearly enough action (though it has a pretty fun climax). As for the remake, I didn't think it was too bad, even though people who actually *worked* on it claimed otherwise. The new creative team stripped out the humor, which I thought was an inspired choice – you'd expect them to double down on the schlock factor since that's what the movie is kind of known for. Unfortunate CGI and some not-great acting were the real problems – their intent was actually solid! Since it was part of the late '00s remake craze, any update I saw where the filmmakers seemingly actually had a goal beyond cashing in was enough to earn a little bit of my respect.

MOVIE #87 – MARCH 28th

WE NEED TO TALK ABOUT KEVIN (2011)
Dir: Lynne Ramsay
HMAD Review Date: January 21, 2012 (Theatrical)
Genre: Killer Kid, Thriller
Available from Oscilloscope Pictures

Synopsis Based on Fading Memory: A mom (Tilda Swinton) has to deal with her day to day life after her son goes on a killing spree at his school.

Review excerpt:
"And yes, it's scary. Not in the jumpy sense (though there IS one of those, oddly enough), but in the unnerving, getting under your skin kind of way, it's one of the most terrifying movies in years. Right off the bat director Lynne Ramsay makes the audience feel uncomfortable, with off-kilter close-ups, heightened audio editing (you'll hear every crunch as Kevin mashes some Fruity Pebbles into dust), and just an overall sense that something awful has happened - just in the first five minutes! The non-chronological structure also allows for some terrific "when is it going to happen?" plot threads - I don't want to spoil things, but one character sports a horrific injury in the first few minutes, but it's about 90 minutes into the movie by the time we know how it occurred. So every object that COULD cause such an injury gets a bit of a murmur whenever it shows up on-screen, which is even more fun when it turns out to be misdirection. "Ohhhh, that's how - oh wait, nope..." It's like the serious, upsetting version of the running gag from Hot Tub Time Machine *regarding Crispin Glover's missing arm."*

Reflection: This is one of those movies that I had to query Twitter if it counted as horror before I went to see it, and I'm glad most people said "yes". I might have seen it eventually otherwise, but who knows how long that might have been, and it ended up being one of my favorite films (not just horror) of 2012. Sure, it's not pulpy like most movies dealing with murderous children/teens, but it's no less terrifying than any of them, and it gets under your skin better than most legit horror films (any sub-genre), so who cares if it's also more of a drama? Plus, there's a movie called *Beautiful Boy* that tackled this sort of thing, and that's not scary/thrilling in the slightest, so there's definitely a way to do this story without invoking the "H" word. *Kevin* doesn't go that way.

Also it's the only opportunity I'd have in this book to sing the praises of John C. Reilly, who is quite simply one of the greatest character actors of all time (and a damn hilarious man to boot). He first caught my attention in, of all goddamn things, *The River Wild*, a 1994 attempt to make Meryl Streep an action star. He was playing (main bad guy) Kevin Bacon's partner, one of those thankless roles that an actor like Reilly can turn into something memorable. It's the sort of movie that you'd otherwise forget everything about as soon as it was over, but even though I was only fifteen, I remember thinking, "This guy deserves better". Luckily, it wasn't long before Paul Thomas Anderson came along and his Q rating skyrocketed, but the great thing about Reilly is that he'll STILL take on these sort of nothing parts and make them great. I doubt in 2005 he needed the money/exposure to appear in junk like *Dark Water*, but there he was, elevating one of the decade's umpteen unnecessary Asian horror remakes.

MOVIE #88 – MARCH 29th

WAKE WOOD (2011)
Dir: David Keating
HMAD Review Date: June 28, 2011 (Blu-ray)
Genre: Killer Kid, Supernatural
Available from Dark Sky

Synopsis Based on Fading Memory: Hammer does *Pet Sematary*!

Review excerpt:
"...the movie plays better as a sad drama than a horror flick, which is fine by me. The movie wastes no time in setting the grieving parent plot in motion, and that could have caused a problem if the actors weren't up to the task, but Aiden Gillen and Eva Birthistle sell their grief fairly well even though we never got to see much of them in "happier times". I also liked that they didn't waste too much time explaining how the townsfolk came across this dead-raising ability, or what their little abacus thing was for, or any of that stuff that doesn't really matter. The more you explain a somewhat ridiculous plot like this, the harder it will be to focus on the characters, so by keeping it simple they end up with a far more effective tale, with a tragedy at its core that actually works."

Reflection: I got a bad introduction to actor Aiden Gillen. I never saw *The Wire* and I'm just now catching up on *Game of Thrones*, so before this I only knew him from two things. One was the not-terrible but hardly great *12 Rounds*, a *Die Hard With A Vengeance* rip-off where he was the villain, and the other was *Blackout*, a horrendous movie about three people trapped in an elevator. In both he was doing this weird Edward Norton thing with his delivery, sneering his way through everything like he got ready for his role by watching *Fight Club* on a loop. So this, in addition to being a pretty good movie (certainly one of the rare bright spots in Hammer's new incarnation), can be credited with how I started to appreciate the actor more. He's actually one of my favorites on *Thrones*! I hope his character is still alive. I assume by the time this sees print I'll know, and if not someone will assuredly spoil for it me.

Speaking of Hammer... well, you won't see any of their other new movies in this book. I liked *Woman in Black* too, but per the "no hits!" rule it's out. Otherwise it's been pretty dire, and while I'm all for new ideas and such I can't help but think that maybe they'd have better luck dusting off a few of their old originals. I don't mean the *Dracula* and *Frankenstein* movies, as we've had enough of those, but certainly something like *Plague of the Zombies* or the *Quatermass* series would be well-served by an update. Something like that could get this attempt at a revival really cooking; they kind of blew their momentum with *Woman in Black* by taking three years to release a (not-great) sequel, so if they want to stick around they need their next movie to make a big splash.

HMAD Fun Fact: Despite my love of the sub-genre, I only watched a mere 46 Killer Kid movies for the site. However, I chalk that up to the sub-genre's limited numbers in general more than my own ignorance.

MOVIE #89 – MARCH 30th

THE DEVIL WITHIN HER (aka SHARON'S BABY) (1975)
Dir: Peter Sasdy
HMAD Review Date: January 10, 2013 (Streaming)
Genre: Killer Kid (Baby!), Possession
Available from Scorpion

Synopsis Based on Fading Memory: Joan Collins gives birth to an evil baby that is possessed by a dwarf.

Review excerpt:
"Pleasence gets in one great line (I might be a little off, but it's basically "I thought today would be boring, but here I am talking about mysticism with an Italian nun."), but otherwise this is one of his unfortunate "normal" roles, and he's not in it all that much to boot. Most of the upfront silliness is given to the villain, a pervy dwarf who curses Joan Collins after she spurns his advances, which is why she has an evil baby. If I'm not mistaken, he's actually possessing the tyke - they cut in shots of his face over the baby's on occasion in order to hammer home what is happening, but being a 1970s Exorcist *wannabe you can be assured that the specifics are a little vague."*

Reflection: If you've seen the trailer for this, you might be thinking it's one of the nuttiest '70s horror movies ever, which would be a tall order for that particular, glorious post-*Exorcist* time. But actually it's a bit tame compared to many of them; even Donald Pleasence is kind of normal for a change. I mean, it's not exactly cookie cutter fare by any means, but if you're expecting nonstop batshittery, you'll be disappointed. Then again, 1975 was rather early for this trend; *Exorcist* was released late into 1973, which means it made a good chunk of its enormous pile of money in 1974. So it makes sense that the first non-Italian rip-offs, factoring in their production and all that, would be coming along in late 1974, into 1975 (the Italians waste no time, so they had a few gems in that immediate post-*Exorcist* period). It really wouldn't be until later in the decade that the bigger budgeted stuff started getting really goddamn weird (see, well, *The Exorcist II*), so I can't fault one of the first ones for being low-key any more than I can knock *Friday the 13th* for only giving us five or six onscreen kills.

Long story short: ignore the trailer's claims; there's some kookiness here but it's not a main focus. Come for the relatively high body count, a fetching Collins (I doubt she's related to me, so I can say that without it being weird), and lots of (perhaps too many) establishing shots of '70s London, and it will leave you very satisfied. Bonus: you'll sorta see a baby kill some folks!

MOVIE #90 – MARCH 31st

THE OTHER (1972)
Dir: Robert Mulligan
HMAD Review Date: September 20, 2008 (DVD)
Genre: Killer Kid, Psychological
Available from Twentieth Century Fox

Synopsis Based on Fading Memory: A little kid and his twin brother cause deadly mischief.

Review excerpt:
"One peculiar thing about the movie is that the twins are played by real life twins (Chris and Martin Udvarnoky) but you never see them both in the same shot. Why bother hiring twins when everything is shot as if there were only one actor? I'm sure there's some sort of creative reason for this, but it's still kind of odd. Both actors are pretty good though, as is the rest of the cast. Other than a brief turn by John Ritter (I miss that dude), I don't recognize a single name in the credits, except for Jerry Goldsmith, whose score here will definitely appeal to fans of his work on Poltergeist."

Reflection: This movie employs a twist that I grew rather tired of over the years, but I have to keep in mind that it was released in 1972, a long time before those other films. In fact this might even be one of the first to use it, so: respect. It's a bit too slow at times, but Mulligan makes up for it in the final reel, with a surprise death and a real bummer ending. The film is often overlooked when discussing the killer kid sub-genre, so even if I had some issues with its pacing (and a few unresolved story points) I wanted to make sure it was given its due.

And this is the last selection for the month, so as you should know by now that means it leads into next month's theme. It was a pretty easy choice to make; April is centered around slower, "moodier" horror films, and that's something you don't often see in anything that can be considered a killer kid movie. Not that they're all trashy fun like *The Pit*, but they're usually somewhere in-between – there's a level of exploitation that usually can't help but creep into even the classier entries (even *The Bad Seed* has that gonzo finale), but *The Other* is one of those rare exceptions. The recent *Goodnight Mommy*, which had many similarities to this film, would also qualify.

Anyway, I hope you've enjoyed the time you've spent with all these murderous tykes this month! I also hope I haven't inadvertently caused you to decide not to have children of your own! As a parent I can tell you it's pretty awesome and also the odds of anything you've seen in the above films actually happening to you are, like, 1 in 5.

APRIL – "QUIET" HORROR

ARTIST: PATT KELLEY

After all of last month's crazy-ass killer kids, and next month's movies which are just plain crazy, I figure you could use a little break in the middle. Plus it's April, which is a traditionally rainy month in a lot of the country, so you might be home a bit more often than usual. So here is a month's worth of low-key, (mostly) subtle horror movies that are perfect for a quiet evening on the couch. I see everything I can theatrically, because I prefer that method of seeing a movie (as long as the crowd is respectable), but I'll be the first to tell you that some horror movies actually work better at home than they do on a giant movie screen – these are some of the more memorable examples I found over those six years.

The irony is that these are the sort of movies that also demand your total attention to really work, something that they might not receive at home what with your smartphones and laptops and such. At an occasional glance when you're more focused on Twitter or *Candy Crush*, these movies will strike you as "boring" and not much else, which is a pity. So I implore you – turn off your devices and give these movies your undivided attention. I think they all make that modern-day Herculean effort worthwhile. I got the chance to see some of these theatrically, but I can practically guarantee the majority of the following entries are suited better for home, and will get under your skin that much more if you let yourself be immersed by them on your standard television screen, same as you would in a big dark theater.

That said, it was at a theatrical screening that I was witness (victim?) to pure terror, which is why I'm going to start with...

MOVIE #91 – APRIL 1st

THE ECLIPSE (2009)
Dir: Conor McPherson
HMAD Review Date: March 12, 2010 (Theatrical)
Genre: Ghost
Available from Magnolia Home Entertainment

Synopsis Based on Fading Memory: A widower working at a book fair starts seeing ghosts as he falls in love with a lady who writes books about ghosts. Aidan Quinn mucks things up.

Review excerpt:
"The movie doesn't exactly scream horror, but that's actually what makes it work. There are only five attempts at scares in the entire movie, two of which made me jump and another just plain creeped me out. And the reason they work so well is that the love triangle plot was compelling enough for me to keep forgetting that there was a horror element to the proceedings, catching me off guard."

Reflection: I wrestled for quite a while with the movie to kick off this theme, but as I looked over the list of qualifying entries, this one kept catching my eye. It's one of the least straight-horror titles I picked for this month (and it unfortunately shares a title with a *Twilight* sequel), but five years later I still get a chill thinking about one of the jolts in the movie. In fact, of all the hundreds of times I've watched a horror movie in the theater, it remains the only one that prompted a total stranger to grab my arm, so that's got to count for something.

It's also a horror movie focusing on adults – apart from maybe a few random people at the book fair, every character in this movie is in their forties or above, something that is fairly rare nowadays for genre films. Back in the day it was more common, but after the studios learned that kids preferred horror with teens and 20-year-olds, horror films with all adults became more or less a thing of the past, with the rare entries like this shuttled off to limited release, if not straight to VOD. Which sucks, because as I get older I'd rather see movies like this than, well, the other one named *Eclipse*. No mopey vampires here, just a legitimately solid drama with well-rounded characters – one that just happens to have two of the best jump scares I've ever seen.

MOVIE #92 – APRIL 2nd

BABY'S ROOM (2006)
Dir: Álex de la Iglesia, James Phillips
HMAD Review Date: January 14, 2009 (DVD)
Genre: Supernatural
Available in the "6 Films To Keep You Awake" set from Lionsgate

Synopsis Based on Fading Memory: A couple with a newborn moves into a new house and start seeing/hearing strange things on the baby monitor.

Review excerpt:
"I enjoyed the better than average character development. Usually these sort of "newborn baby = trouble" movies focus on the mother, but the dad (Javier Gutiérrez) is front and center here. We quickly learn that he's struggling with the 'trappings' of being married and having a newborn child (at one point, he's trying to seduce his wife and she suddenly begins talking about the baby's poop), but he's always sympathetic. At one point he hits on the girl who sells the baby monitors, which could have put him in the "this guy's a douche" category, but the idea is dropped as quickly as it's introduced. Plus it helped throw me off - I started suspecting the supernatural stuff was just a manifestation of the guy's cold feet about being a family man or something, but it's something else entirely."

Reflection: Two thousand and five hundred movies is *a lot*, and the brain cannot possibly store the specifics for all of them – which is why I'm not even sure what I'm referring to in my own review when I say to skip this film's first chapter (on the DVD; five minutes or so if using a streaming service) to make the film's mystery harder to solve. For the life of me I cannot recall the specifics, so if I ever find the time to watch this again I'll take my own advice and see if I'm right!

This film served as my introduction to the work of Alex de la Iglesia, by the way – I have since become a big fan and encourage you to check out his stuff if you haven't already. I wasn't as enamored by *The Last Circus* as some of my pals (probably because I saw it after their angry insistence, instead of something I just happened to discover, like many of them did), but his most recent genre film *Witching & Bitching* was a highlight of Fantastic Fest 2013. Some of its later plot developments didn't totally work for me, but I swear, it has the best opening sequence of any horror film in years, and an admirably gonzo finale that one couldn't possibly predict from the movie's first half. Somehow I still haven't seen *Day of the Beast* though; I gotta fix that. Preferably before I finish this book so I can edit this paragraph and be all "And you GOTTA see *Day of the Beast* if you haven't yet, what's wrong with you?" (PRINT EDITION UPDATE: Sigh, still haven't seen it.)

MOVIE #93 – APRIL 3rd

100 FEET (2008)
Dir: Eric Red
HMAD Review Date: October 11, 2008 (Festival screening)
Genre: Ghost
Available from The Asylum

Synopsis Based on Fading Memory: Famke Janssen kills her abusive husband and is sentenced to house arrest for it. Unfortunately, that's where the jerk's ghost is!

Review excerpt:
"The film is played 100% serious, and it works. There are at least four great jump scares in the film, plus one of the all-time best "hand in the garbage disposal" scenes. Lots of horror films have this gag, and sometimes it fails to deliver the intended effect (i.e. scaring me out of ever putting my own hand in one again - I'm always losing bottle caps down there!), but this one nails it. I also like how Red chose to not beat us over the head with some of the details. Early on the ghost begins tossing plates at Famke at breakneck speed. Later on, we see that she has replaced all her kitchenware with plastic or Styrofoam, but we don't have a cutesy scene of her buying bulk Dixie stock."

Reflection: I was pretty upset to learn that this movie couldn't get a better distribution deal than from The Asylum, and was thus lumped in with the likes of *Transmorphers* and *Snakes On A Train*. But then again, maybe that'll help the movie look even better by comparison, inadvertently leading people to believe that The Asylum is capable of legitimate horror movies. I'm not sure why Janssen never really became a major leading lady – she should be toplining more films or at least starring in her own show by now (she was top billed on *Hemlock Grove*, yes, but that was an ensemble and the two younger guys were clearly the focus).

However, that just makes me appreciate those rare Famke Janssen vehicles like this all the more – it's great to have her front and center for the whole film instead of playing second fiddle to Wolverine or whoever. And she has to play a giant chunk of the movie against nothing; there IS a recognizable actor as her husband (someone who worked with Red before; I can't recall if he was credited so I don't want to "spoil" it), but he only makes a brief appearance. Most of the time it's just an invisible force, and she gives it 100%. That said, those rare on-screen ghost FX are pretty great, another thing that makes this an unusual entry in the Asylum library. Those guys usually can't even get the backgrounds on driving scenes to look halfway good.

MOVIE #94 – APRIL 4th

THE TORTURE CHAMBER OF DR. SADISM (1967)
Dir: Harald Reinl
HMAD Review Date: March 5, 2013 (DVD)
Genre: Revenge, Supernatural
Public domain title, available through several DVD companies

Synopsis Based on Fading Memory: After being executed for the murder of twelve virgins, Count Regula (Christopher Lee) returns seeking revenge and the completion of his ritual.

Review excerpt:
"The sets are terrific; it takes a bit for our heroes to arrive at the castle, but it's worth the wait - Universal should track down the production designer's original notes and build the thing for their Halloween Horror Nights attraction, as it's much more exciting than the Van Helsing or whatever inspired ones I've seen. Skulls! Pits! Passageways! It's got everything and more! Plus Christopher Lee, who I honestly thought was just doing a cameo when he died in the opening scene."

Reflection: Despite the title, this is actually a pretty low-key, even kind of fun hodgepodge of several horror movie archetypes – it's basically an Old Dark House movie but with a villain that is one half Dracula and one half Poe villain, as there's a "Pit and the Pendulum" thing going on along with everything else. The title (one of many, *Castle of the Walking Dead* is another) had me thinking this would be a depressing and grim movie, like most German films, but if anything it could actually use a bit more genuine terror. Still, a fine late period attempt at making the sort of horror movie you couldn't escape in the '30s and '40s.

This isn't the first public domain entry in the book, nor is it the last – when it comes to this sort of stuff, you might as well just watch it on YouTube or whatever. Unless you want to do some research and pay extra for a version that's restored or "official", chances are whatever copy you get will be in a budget pack of some sort, with a piss-poor transfer and possibly even a truncated version (always check the runtimes, at the very least). I mean, it's not like Harald Reinl's estate will see a penny of the version you buy in a cheap box boasting "50 horrific horror movies on 12 DVDs!", so you might as well just settle for what's probably the same transfer on your favorite streaming site. Just make sure you're only doing that for these public domain titles! I'm watching you!

(Not really. I mean, I WAS, but I'm too busy now.)

MOVIE #95 - APRIL 5th

LAKE MUNGO (2008)
Dir: Joel Anderson
HMAD Review Date: January 31, 2010 (Theatrical)
Genre: Ghost, Mockumentary
Available from Lionsgate

Synopsis Based on Fading Memory: A family deals with the loss of their daughter and learns some troubling secrets about her as they take part in a documentary about her disappearance.

Review excerpt:
"The faux news footage is so good I began questioning whether or not the story WAS based in reality. The actors are good, another thing that can sink this type of movie (they say "Uh...." a lot and sometimes trip over their words - like real people do and actors playing real people always forget to do). And even with its multiple plot branches keeping the movie from having a focus, the basic story (family coping with their loss) resonates in a way few faux docs manage."

Reflection: Part of the problem with writing a review every day is that I often had to put my thoughts down without having a lot of time to digest the film, so I'd end up changing my tune on many films but stuck with a review that sounded more negative (and, on the flipside, I'd end up with excited reviews for a movie that didn't really hold up on a second view). This is one of them; I still don't think the film is perfect by any means, but another dozen or so lesser mock docs after it gave me more appreciation for what it did right – and even then I recognized the power of one of its jump scares, which remains one of the best I've seen. To this day I see people bringing it up fairly regularly, which is pretty good for a movie that was, for most of the country, a direct to video release. The first two After Dark Horrorfests opened on a few hundred screens, but the later installments - including the one that had *Mungo* in its lineup - were only released on a handful of screens, with even less promotion.

It's a shame that Anderson hasn't made another film yet; I think he's got a full-blown classic in him. He can even try again with the mock doc sub-genre; I think traditional found footage is played out for the time being, but creative approaches to what seems like a genuine documentary will always be in vogue, as far as I'm concerned. I recently caught one called *The Atticus Institute* that was so well fleshed out I legitimately thought it might be based on a real case for a while – and that's with recognizable actors in the cast! I was like "Oh I wonder what the real people looked like" and then Googled the name of the place, discovering it was all made up. It's still possible to pull the wool over the audience's eyes (albeit temporarily) with that approach, unlike the umpteen millionth "a group of ghost hunters with cameras go into an abandoned asylum" type.

MOVIE #96 - APRIL 6th

THE THAW (2009)
Dir: Mark A. Lewis
HMAD Review Date: November 16, 2009 (DVD)
Genre: Monster
Available from Lionsgate

Synopsis Based on Fading Memory: A group of scientists are besieged by some regular-sized insects that have thawed from the ice. It's icky.

Review excerpt:
"I like that the insects were normal-sized insects, instead of oversized mutant things that are never as terrifying as the type of bugs I might find near my car (or, in a super creepy moment, on my couch - it was a house spider, but still - gah! Bad timing, little now-dead spider!). The film's queasiest gag is given away on the trailer (a bug pokes its head out of a hole on a girl's forehead, only to retreat when someone attempts to pull it out), but there are a few other choice moments that will make Entomophobics run out of the room crying."

Reflection: I really shouldn't have a Val Kilmer movie in this book. Not that he should stay away from horror; on the contrary, he was a welcome appearance in this and a few others I saw over the years. No, it's that his movies should be too successful to be included in this book of "B-sides", though I will say the same about anyone involved in *MacGruber*, because it's truly one of the best comedies ever made. Anyway, I assume it's because of his legendary dickishness that his career went downhill, but it's still a shame that a guy with that much talent pissed it away so quickly. I mean, he was on fire in 1995 thanks to *Batman Forever* and Heat, and then the following year's *Dr. Moreau* was the beginning of the "Val Kilmer's an asshole!" stories that he never really recovered from.

Anyway, he's not the main star of this movie – a group of young budding scientists are, and the Crichton-y scenario made this *Sphere/Jurassic Park/Prey* fan very happy (I also like *The Terminal Man* a lot, though that one strayed from his trademark "bunch of scientists fight off a monster" plot). And if you're an older fan who doesn't want to watch a bunch of kids, fear not – this is no teeny bopper fare, and it contains one of the most nauseating and squirm-worthy moments in the site's history (without spoiling, I'll just say male viewers will find it more repulsive than females).

I had other movies that could fit in this chapter, but ultimately I chose this one because in the past few months I've had more than my fair share of bug problems at the house, so it kept coming to mind. First we had ants coming in from a crack near the door, then flies attracted to a gas leak (and getting into the house via a vent), then it was crickets, which were in the walls at one point. Now it's... I don't even know what they are. I thought they were cockroaches but they're too tiny and don't have antennae, so who the hell knows. All I know is they appear near the sink and freak me out, and reminded me of this "creepy because they're not giant" bug movie. So now you can share my squirminess.

MOVIE #97 - APRIL 7th

DEAD SILENCE (2007)
Dir: James Wan
HMAD Review Date: March 15, 2007 (Theatrical)
Genre: Ghost, Puppet
Available from Universal Studios.

Synopsis Based on Fading Memory: A guy's wife is killed by a puppet, but naturally the cops don't believe him, so he goes to the town where the puppet was made to get proof and solve the mystery of her murder.

Review excerpt:
"Of course, the comparisons Dead Silence *will get to* Saw *are unavoidable, since it's the same director, writer, and producers. Yet it's entirely different, and in a good way. I dunno about you, but I am more creeped out by puppets looking at me than I am by the hitman from* The Firm *lying on the floor."*

Reflection: James Wan and Leigh Whannell attempted to make an old school Hammer-type horror film here, and mostly succeeded – Universal's meddling throws off their vintage approach with some unnecessary gore bits, so try to get the R-rated cut (as opposed to the unrated one) to minimize their presence. A box office dud at the time, Wan's genre resurgence thanks to *Insidious* and *The Conjuring* has given this one a new lease on life (it pops up on cable a lot), but I won't rest until everyone has given it a shot!

Of course, my review probably won't help the film's fortunes any. By the time I finish this paragraph, the entry in this book will be longer and more fleshed out than the "review". This was an early post on HMAD (I think I only actually started the site a week before) and I wasn't really writing much for any of them then, but even by the standards of that time period, this post was terrible. Look at the above excerpt – I barely explain what I mean (that *Dead Silence* is a legit scary movie, unlike *Saw*) and that's probably the most useful thing I wrote in the entire review. But I suspect part of that was due to how I saw the film; Universal had a contest for folks to host the "premiere" in their hometown, and the guy who won was from Boston. Uni wanted to fly out a few of the horror writer guys there, and normally I never got to do anything cool like that, but since it was Boston (i.e. MY hometown) Mr. Disgusting told them to have me go instead of him. Alas, I could only get one day out of work with such short notice, so I had to fly in to Boston late afternoon and fly back to LA early enough the next morning to get to work. So even though I went for a free trip "home", I didn't even tell my family I was coming because the trip was too short to see them anyway! I didn't sleep much that night (we all went out; by the time we got back to the hotel it was almost time for me to go to the airport), and then of course watched another movie for the following day before I had time to write anything. Long story short, the lack of sleep, delay in writing, a newer movie taking up that part of my brain, and copious amounts of alcohol that I consumed after the movie resulted in my memory being pretty useless by the time I sat down to write anything. But I've watched the movie several times since (and written a much more thorough defense on Birth.Movies.Death.), so at least I know I was right when I said it was good.

MOVIE #98 - APRIL 8th

OUTPOST (2007)
Dir: Steve Barker
HMAD Review Date: October 26, 2010 (DVD)
Genre: Supernatural
Available from Sony Home Entertainment

Synopsis Based on Fading Memory: Ray Stevenson and his fellow soldiers are hired to escort a businessman through war-ravaged Eastern Europe to a Nazi bunker from WWII that houses a mysterious device. However, when the device is activated, it unleashes a terrifying supernatural force (read: Nazi zombies!).

Review excerpt:
"...it's quite well-directed. Some might disapprove of director Steve Barker's decision to leave a key death off-screen, but I liked it, it was sort of tasteful – and really, what's the "best" way to depict the horrible death of a major hero? Either way, the film is great to look at throughout – the scope imagery fits well, and like The Descent, it's dark but filled with enough contrast to keep it from being an ugly mess. The early, pre-explanation scenes are quite eerie and drenched with atmosphere, and the big action scenes are as exciting as they should be. And the script by Rae Brunton never lags, nor does it make it obvious who will live or die first – always a plus."

Reflection: A HMAD reader bugged me for years to watch this one, and I wish I hadn't waited so long - it's a solid action/horror hybrid, the sort of thing I wish I saw more often (there aren't many such films, and most tend to suck). Stevenson is always a welcome presence, and director Steve Barker puts every cent of his relatively meager budget onscreen. It's also one of the better examples of this sub-sub-genre, of soldiers investigating a bunker or something like that and facing off against a supernatural presence. I guess they're all inspired by *The Keep*, which isn't a great movie so you gotta wonder why so many horror movies seemed to have sprung from it. I saw what must have been a dozen like this during HMAD, and while they were mostly okay, they also tend to blend together in my memory. This one was an exception.

Maybe that's why it has, to date, spawned two sequels. The first is worth checking out if you liked this one, but the third left me disappointed as it was a prequel that told us what we already know, instead of going forward and further developing the intriguing mythology laid out by the first two films (plus the second one ends on a cliffhanger that is now ignored). Here's hoping part 4 sees the light of day – in the meantime, check this one out if you haven't already (if you have, sub in the first sequel, *Black Sun*).

And yes, it's not really as "quiet" as the other movies this month, but the feeling of dread it offers (and the largely underground setting) gives it that sort of claustrophobic feel that a lot of these other, less action-driven titles deliver. Plus it didn't really fit anywhere else and I promised that reader it'd be in here, so nyeah. It's my book, I can do what I want!

HMAD Fun Fact: The most popular talkback in the site's history is for Open Water 2, *with an incredible 98 comments (the average is probably around 5). Most of them are questions about the film's baffling ending.*

MOVIE #99 - APRIL 9th

HOLLOW (2011)
Dir: Michael Axelgaard
HMAD Review Date: February 26, 2013 (Streaming)
Genre: Mockumentary, Supernatural
Available from Tribeca

Synopsis Based on Fading Memory: In this found footage flick, two couples set out to do a piece an abandoned English village – marked by a striking, gnarled tree - that allegedly drives people to suicide.

Review excerpt:
"It's got some legitimately creepy bits, mostly focused on Jimmy's increasingly unhinged behavior and how that affects his camerawork. There are a number of quick bursts of random close-ups and the like, as if he was just recording things at random, and also a running "theme" of insects that I never quite understood but enjoyed all the same - army ants are freaky, man. The climax is also a pretty good nail-biter; the two girls are trapped in the car with a slowly dying camera, limiting the amount of time they can turn it on (and thus see - again, the only way to keep the light on) and having no idea where their attacker was. Also, they're pissed at each other because of the "love quadrangle" thing, adding more tension to the sequence."

Reflection: Thanks to the success of *Paranormal Activity* and its sequels, I found myself positively deluged by found footage movies in the last two years or so of daily HMAD-ing – it got to the point where I swore them off entirely for a while. As they were so "easy" to make (and even cheaper than the average low horror budget), they'd in turn be easier to sell, and so the virtual rental shelves would be flooded with the damn things, most of them so bad they'd have you taking back every bad thing you ever said about *Blair Witch*'s camerawork. So when one stuck out to me, you can be all but totally assured that it's one that put some effort into the proceedings. This one starts off a bit stock, but the surprisingly dark second half, aided by better characterization than these things usually offer, makes it a minor gem in a "sub-genre" that shouldn't be nearly as populated as it is.

On that note, the main issue I have with found footage isn't even its omnipresence –it's the fact that so many of them are made by people who have no idea how to properly wield the tool they have at their disposal. Impossible cutaways, people filming things for no reason (in addition to a flimsy reason for filming in the first place), and a bizarre insistence on making them more "movie-like" (adding scores and recognizable actors) mutes their inherent appeal – they're constantly reminding us that we're watching a traditional movie. *Blair Witch* and some others we love work because they never once tipped their hand or cheated to make something more cinematic – a scene even begins with Josh describing creepy sounds he heard the night before, because logically no one would have been filming that! Nowadays not only would he film it, but he'd even have 30 seconds of pointless jibber jabber before it, with no explanation for why the character turned on his camera to film something so inane. It's why I was never bothered by the excess number of slasher films that popped up in the '80s – a lot of them sucked, sure, but at least their filmmakers knew how to get the basics right.

MOVIE #100 - APRIL 10th

THE PRESENCE (2010)
Dir: Tom Provost
HMAD Review Date: February 14, 2012 (DVD)
Genre: Ghost
Available from Lionsgate

Synopsis Based on Fading Memory: A lonely ghost's existence is made more tolerable by the arrival of an author (Mira Sorvino) that hopes the isolated cabin is the best place to write her book. But does he have her best interests at heart? (Serious question, as I forget.)

Review excerpt:
"Some may lose patience with it, and I couldn't exactly argue with them. I am a sucker for slower-paced, small cast movies like this, especially when the emphasis is on visuals over dialogue (if it was paced the same but was just a non-stop series of conversations, I'd probably be bored out of my mind). Director Tom Provost has given us a wonderful scope image, and uses the frame very effectively – Sorvino on one side, West standing motionless on the other. A cropped version of this movie wouldn't work at all, which is not a very common thing I can say – Halloween is one of the few others. And after 5 years, anytime I compare something favorably to Halloween you should perk your ears up!"

Reflection: I rented this one on Valentine's Day assuming it'd be more like *Ghost* or something, but it was actually fairly scary – Shane West is spooky as all hell as the ghost, and the long dialogue-free stretches made me uneasy. It might be TOO sluggish for some, even those who like slow-paced horror films, but if you can handle it, you're in for a good treat. Worth noting – one of the producers is *Blair Witch Project* co-director Dan Myrick, faring better in that capacity than he did as a solo director (*Solstice*, anyone?).

Fun fact: someone on Twitter (I think? It was a while ago) asked what the plot of *Horror Movie A Day: The Movie* would be if one was ever made, and I said it'd be about BC (played by someone far more handsome, maybe from a CW show) going off to a cabin to write a book about all of the movies about people who go off to isolated cabins to write their books. I'm not sure what happens next. Maybe Shane West shows up. But jokes aside, this basic plot setup was used almost as many times as a group of college kids going off to spring break and running afoul of backwoods types, making the few that struck a chord with me all the more impressive.

MOVIE #101 - APRIL 11th

SOLITARY (2009)
Dir: Greg Derochie
HMAD Review Date: October 3, 2010 (Festival screening)
Genre: Psychological
Available from Osiris Entertainment

Synopsis Based on Fading Memory: An agoraphobic woman is trapped in her house due to her affliction – it doesn't help matters any when she starts to believe her shrink is plotting against her.

Review excerpt:
"It reminded me a bit of Premonition *(the Sandra Bullock one), in that it's ultimately a sort of sad movie about someone letting go of their spouse (when are they going to do one from the guy's point of view? We have feelings, too, dammit!). They sort of cheat us in the way that things are presented, but I don't think it's spoiling much to say that a major traumatic event was the cause of her agoraphobia. They tip some things off a bit unnecessarily and awkwardly (the locked room is introduced way too early), and some things are never satisfyingly explained, but overall it works, and you'll go home and give your spouse an extra big hug."*

Reflection: I saw this one at a festival practically back to back with *Fugue*, which also concerned a mentally unstable woman who spends the entire movie in her house. But this is the one that I remember more five years later, and considering that Derochie's main gig is doing FX for bloated Hollywood blockbusters (like *The Great and Powerful Oz*, which threatened to end my admiration for Sam Raimi), I love how restrained it is. And even if you don't love the movie, it'll be worth your time simply to appreciate the lead performance of Amber Jaeger, who is in nearly every frame of the film and deftly carries it despite it being her first ever lead role.

Interestingly, I thought about this movie recently, as I watched a movie called *The Drownsman* that centered entirely on a woman's fear of water, and realized how rare it is that a horror film revolves around any one specific phobia. Most fear-driven horror movies focus on a group of people, allowing the filmmakers to work in a variety of phobias (spiders, the dark, clowns, etc.) with a narrative driven by distinct set pieces. But those things never quite work unless you happen to fear all of the same things. When a screenplay focuses on just one thing (agoraphobia, in this case), there is time to flesh out the affliction and let the audience understand it (and in turn, feel scared by it), which makes it far more unsettling than a basic two minute spider scene in a movie if you yourself aren't afraid of spiders.

MOVIE #102 - APRIL 12th

TO LET (2006)
Dir: Jaume Balagueró
HMAD Review Date: January 21, 2009 (DVD)
Genre: "Blank" From Hell
Available in the "6 Films To Keep You Awake" set from Lionsgate

Synopsis Based on Fading Memory: A down on their luck couple find what they think is the perfect apartment, only to discover the very disturbing catch.

Review excerpt:
"What I really dug is how it seemed like it was going off into supernatural territory every now and then, only to quickly reveal the very ordinary (and chilling) reasons for these things. It starts off like a typical haunted house movie; at one point the couple sees a photo of themselves on the shelf of the apartment they just entered for the first time, so you might think it's a riff on The Shining *or whatever, but then the brain-beatings begin and you forget all about it."*

Reflection: Almost all of the "6 Films To Keep You Awake" are recommended in this book, and for good reason – they're admirably short and thus free from the padding that weighed down far too many movies I watched over the course of six years. Each disc had two features united by some common thread; *To Let*'s "disc-mate" is *Baby's Room* and while they're both about people moving into new apartments, they otherwise couldn't be less alike . And I truly love the idea of starting a movie off like every other haunted house movie ever, only to turn the tables and turn it into a very grounded survival horror effort.

Also if you don't already know the name Jaume Balagueró, you should fix that. He's probably best known for his involvement in the *[Rec]* series (co-directing the first two, going solo for the fourth), but this and another film you'll see pop up later in this book are the real gems. Don't get me wrong, I really liked the first two *[Rec]* films (his fourth is... let's just say underwhelming and leave it at that), but his others are much more interesting to me, and cemented him as someone to always keep up with – even if he leaves the genre, I'm sure it'll be for something that's worth our time to watch.

MOVIE #103 - APRIL 13th

THE BROKEN (2008)
Dir: Sean Ellis
HMAD Review Date: April 9, 2009 (DVD)
Genre: Psychological, Supernatural
Available from Lionsgate

Synopsis Based on Fading Memory: Lena Headey starts seeing her double around town. Normally having a second Ms. Headey would be a good thing, but in this case it starts to unravel her sanity. Also: mirror people!

Review excerpt:
"It's all about the impressively quiet scares, and the fact that the mirror people are actually kind of creepy. I also liked how Ellis avoided the usual clichés as much as possible. Of course there's a scene where a reflection suddenly diverges from its owner and does something scary, but it turns out to be a nightmare. Otherwise, reflections are surprisingly AVOIDED at times. There's a part where Headey is trapped in the bathroom, and there's not a single shot of the mirror reflecting her or anything else of importance. That's unprecedented!"

Reflection (heh): The After Dark Horrorfest was, at best, a mixed bag, but the sad thing is that they started getting it right once everyone had written it off. The first two years had heavy promotion and even a halfway decent theatrical release, but with lackluster lineups the label looked more like a warning sign for future installments – despite the fact that on the whole they got more interesting and diverse. Oh well. Anyway, this was one of the better entries from the third installment, featuring an impressive cast (Headey, Richard Jenkins, the always awesome Ulrich Thomsen) and a much better script than the same year's *Mirrors*. And by that I mean no one in this movie explains that water can also cast a reflection.

It's also a rare example of a good haunted mirror movie. Most of them are bad, some downright terrible, but this one works (probably because it deals more with the supernatural presence of the reflections, rather than the mirror itself). The only other one that's any good is *Oculus*, which I didn't love theatrically but when it gave me a horrific nightmare on a second viewing (I got the Blu-ray to review), I changed my tune. Otherwise... oof. *Mirrors* was laughable, and the requisite *Amityville* sequel focusing on reflections (subtitled *A New Generation*) is particularly bad even for the very low bar of *Amityville* sequels. I don't know why filmmakers keep returning to this particular well; I can only assume that there are so many bad ones because everyone thinks that they'll be the one to get it right.

MOVIE #104 - APRIL 14th

THE PACT (2012)
Dir: Nicholas McCarthy
HMAD Review Date: July 15, 2012 (Theatrical)
Genre: Ghost, Serial Killer
Available from MPI Home Video

Synopsis Based on Fading Memory: A woman's sister goes missing shortly after the death of her mother, and she fears she may be in danger as well. Casper Van Dien is a cop who wants to solve the mystery, too.

Review excerpt:
"...there are serial killer elements, which are mostly confined to the third act, but if you go back and watch the film a second time (or just think about it real hard, like I have to) you'll realize that there was actually a lot to it that you were probably attributing to the ghost. It's a tough balancing act, and it might not completely hold up to scrutiny, but writer/director Nicholas McCarthy (expanding from a short film version) should be commended on holding back until the best possible moment. Without spoiling anything, the moment you realize that there's a flesh and blood presence to contend with is one of the best shock scares in recent memory."

Reflection: I was lucky enough to see this one theatrically, but I think it'll play just as well, if not better, at home - pretty much the entire movie takes place in very average suburban homes. Even more interesting: McCarthy sets 90% of it in the daytime, giving you a false sense of security and making the scares work all the more. It's also got a nice little homage to *Halloween* (one that didn't involve ripping off the score or the POV opener), so I walked away quite happy with this little gem. The sequel (from the guys behind *Entrance*, another of this book's selections) is more of the same, but not necessarily in a bad way - if you liked this as much as I did it's worth seeking out to get some more backstory and closure for one of this film's survivors.

McCarthy himself followed it up with *At the Devil's Door*, which was fairly similar to *The Pact* (mostly interior/daytime-set, moody) but not quite as effective, as it kept jumping forward in time and focusing on new characters, making it rather difficult to really latch onto anything. But the term "sophomore slump" exists for a reason, so it's not a real surprise it didn't measure up, and I'm sure he'll rebound with his next feature (right now he's working on a segment for a Kevin Smith anthology, so I question his (or his agent's) judgment but won't use it to gauge his talent). Even though *Devil's Door* wasn't as good as *The Pact*, I can tell that he's a guy that shares my own sensibilities, and so I will continue to look forward to his new films. As should you.

MOVIE #105 - APRIL 15th

WIND CHILL (2007)
Dir: Gregory Jacobs
HMAD Review Date: October 26, 2009 (DVD)
Genre: Survival, Breakdown, Ghost
Available from Sony Pictures Home Entertainment

Synopsis Based on Fading Memory: Two unpleasant college kids are driving home for the holiday break and get stuck in the middle of a snowy nowhere.

Review excerpt:
"Having driven through Pennsylvania/Delaware backroads in the middle of winter myself, I am astounded at how well they fake Canada for them, and they match that gloomy coldness perfectly (I love how all of the daylight scenes seem to have been shot at 4 pm). And while the 2.35 aspect ratio is a bit surprising due to the confined setting, Jacobs fills it well all the same. Carpenter would be proud."

Reflection: I didn't like this one in theaters, but I kept thinking about it. So I rented it a while later for a short-lived column on HMAD called "Second Chances", and liked it a bit more, but not as much as I'd like. And now, years later, I STILL find myself wanting to love this movie, but I'm sure if I watched it again I'd only like it a tiny bit more than last time (it'd take like 100 views, I guess). It's the abrasive characters that kept me at bay – but it takes a LOT to make Emily Blunt seem unlikable, so they had to be intentionally making her so shrill, right? I'm just missing something?

At any rate, I love the concept (it's like *The Sure Thing* mixed with *The Shining*, which is weird since those titles are kind of similar) and always appreciate attempts at such claustrophobic thrillers, making its flaws more forgivable. Therefore, I'm giving it a slot in the book (albeit this month's "bad movie" slot, because I didn't really have a truly bad movie to put in here) in the hopes that you, dear reader, find Blunt and Ashton Holmes slightly more likable and enjoy this one without any of the reservations I have. It's possible you might be checking it out of curiosity now that Jacobs has helmed the far more successful *Magic Mike XXL* (Steven Soderbergh is a producer here; Jacobs has worked in some capacity on nearly all of his films for the past 20 years). *XXL* is his first time in the director's chair since *Wind Chill*, actually, and the films couldn't be less alike; I like to imagine there's some die-hard *Wind Chill* fan out there that has been waiting for this would-be horror icon to make another feature, and went into *XXL* completely unware of what he was in for.

MOVIE #106 - APRIL 16th

THE YELLOW WALLPAPER (2012)
Dir: Logan Thomas
HMAD Review Date: July 27, 2012 (Streaming)
Genre: Haunted House
Available from Ascent Releasing

Synopsis Based on Fading Memory: A family moves into a new house and scary things start happening, but what seems like a typically generic haunted house flick becomes something more admirably weird and unhinged, plus surprisingly kind of sad.

Review excerpt:
"The main thing I liked was that all of the characters were a bit off, so it avoided the usual pratfall of turning the family members against one another. While they have their spats, there's no clear "villain" like Jack in The Shining *or George in* Amityville - *it seems any one of them could snap. The husband is the most likely suspect due to years of haunted house movies setting the precedent, and he's on edge throughout most of the movie as he blames his wife (and himself to a degree) for the death of their child, with the added issue of their now being completely broke as a result. And the wife is seeing things and spends most of the movie in a daze (plus the original short story is about her descent into madness), which is where the psychological element comes into play - it's possible that everything we're seeing is just her imagination. Then there's her sister, a woman who feels that she's never accomplished anything in life and is now too old to find a husband. So basically they all got baggage, and it's not hard to think that we're watching a domestic tragedy unfold via the imagery and structure of a haunted house/ghost movie."*

Reflection: Now that I'm no longer updating HMAD on a daily basis, I can say this with certainty: this is the only horror movie that I've ever seen where Thor showed up (you'll have to see for yourself), and since this book is mainly comprised of the movies that stuck out for one reason or another, I knew I had to include it. It's probably a bit too slow for many viewers, but it's still one of the more memorable haunted house flicks I watched, with some fun supporting turns (Michael Moriarty is always a plus) and a good variety to the scares instead of the usual tropes like faucets dripping blood or cupboards opening on their own.

What it does have in common with many other films is the fact that it's based on a story or novel that I wanted to read after seeing the movie, and never got around to actually doing that. Some of the books I ended up buying, and they're all just sitting there waiting to be opened. Not that I'm not a reader; I always keep a book in my car, and another by my desk, but the time I actually get to crack them open these days is far more limited than my bookshelves would suggest. Sometimes I actually kind of hope for an EMP to come wipe out all the tech so I have nothing else to distract me away from all of those written treasures. Until then... *listens to 20 minutes of the Stephen King audiobook that's been on the iPod for months*

HMAD Fun Fact: The first movie I watched on Netflix Instant (in 2008) was Graduation Day, a slasher that's not that great and was given a rather awful transfer. It didn't make me think much of the service, but by the end of the site's daily run I was using it for roughly half of the entries.

MOVIE #107 - APRIL 17th

THE AWAKENING (2011)
Dir: Nick Murphy
HMAD Review Date: August 18, 2012 (Theatrical)
Genre: Ghost
Available from Universal Studios

Synopsis Based on Fading Memory: A woman (Rebecca Hall) who specializes in exposing fake "hauntings" is called to a school so she can help them rule out supernatural activity as the cause of recent disturbances. Needless to say, the place is really haunted.

Review excerpt:
"...the mystery is a pretty good one, and thankfully not too complicated. I think that the more you have to think about how the plot works, the less likely it is that you'll be scared - you're not able to "settle" enough for the boo moments to have their full effect. The Halloween *series is the best example - the more we knew about Michael and why he did things, the less scary it became. Same sort of idea applies here, as thankfully the back-story isn't too intricate, and its clues are doled out at a nice pace that emphasizes character (and scares) for most of its runtime."*

Reflection: My favorite Guillermo Del Toro film is *The Devil's Backbone*, so while I've given up hope that he'll go back to making something that small and chilling again (*Crimson Peak* came close, at least - a pity no one saw it), I'm happy to have movies like this that explore similar territory. The film's final twist will likely burn a few bridges, but Rebecca Hall is so wonderful (and has great chemistry with Dominic West) that it's easy enough to forgive. Also: from the dawn of time horror movies have been using dollhouses for scare scenes, and you should know that, of the ones I've seen (a lot), this movie's is the best.

I saw the film right around the same time as *Red Lights*, a similar "skeptic investigates supernatural phenomenon" story that took place in modern times and offered a bigger cast (Robert DeNiro, Sigourney Weaver, etc.). But it was also more of a drama with some horror built into it, and thus didn't get as much love in my circle. *Awakening* is the better film (horror or not), but give that one a look, too, if you're into the whole "skeptic becomes a believer" angle. I'd also recommend a great book called *Will Storr vs The Supernatural*, where a (you guessed it, skeptical) reporter goes around and investigates different hauntings. Some he walks away with a plausible/scientific explanation, others he doesn't. It's pretty fun, and unlike *Ghost Hunters*, he doesn't blame plumbing for everything.

MOVIE #108 - APRIL 18th

SECONDS APART (2011)
Dir: Antonio Negret
HMAD Review Date: January 29, 2011 (Streaming)
Genre: Psychological, Supernatural
Available from Lionsgate

Synopsis Based on Fading Memory: Twins with some unusual abilities are suspected of a string of murders.

Review excerpt:
"...one nice surprise was Orlando Jones' turn as the cop who is investigating the initial murders and quickly zeroes in on the twins. He is known mainly for comedic roles (or as the friggin 7UP pitchman), so I was a bit puzzled by his casting at first, but he really did some great dramatic work with minimal humor (his fondness for Bazooka Joe comics is pretty much the extent of his levity). His character has a past tragedy, and he sells the obligatory flashbacks to this event as well as any traditional choice for this sort of thing, even when saddled with some rather silly hallucination/ dream sequences, such as when he has visions of being trapped in a snow globe."

Reflection: I've actually seen a few genre films with Orlando Jones, including a buddy action movie with him and Tom Everett Scott (you know, the action icon from *That Thing You Do*), to the point where I no longer really think of him from his comedic work. It's odd that I haven't seen the twins in anything else since, though – they're pretty great actors, I think, and were popping up with some frequency for a while there (they were in the terrible *Rest Stop* movies, and also played the creatures in a movie called *The New Daughter* that you will find in a later chapter). However, I think the writers of *The Following* saw this movie as they had creepy twins that seemed a bit too similar to these (sans the abilities).

Anyway, there's a really great twist in this movie. I will say no more about it, but I WILL say that there weren't a lot of twists that really got me over the six years I did this site. Part of it was just seeing so many movies that I got attuned to the tricks that are employed to pull it off (like when a character is around but no one is actually addressing him or her because they're not really there), but also because, frankly, a lot of them don't even try. But that's good in a weird way, because it makes these unexpected successes work that much better. The pacing isn't perfect in this movie, but if you are fooled as I was, you won't care much by the time the credits roll.

MOVIE #109 - APRIL 19th

THE DEPRAVED (aka URBAN EXPLORER) (2011)
Dir: Andy Fetscher
HMAD Review Date: October 18, 2011 (Festival screening)
Genre: Survival
Available from Phase 4 Films

Synopsis Based on Fading Memory: A group of urban explorers checking out a subterranean section of Berlin find themselves trapped, and then hunted by a "resident" of the maze of tunnels underneath the city.

Review excerpt:
"...it has one up on The Descent *in one respect – the location offers a lot of variety. Submerged pathways, bunkers, fully functioning emergency stations, pipe/ladder filled passages, the actual subway tunnel... the layout may never be clear (intentionally so, I assume), you can tell one room from the next, unlike* Descent *where it was mostly just the same sort of caverns with stalagmites everywhere. Minor light sources also provide a variety of lighting schemes – green hallways, red rooms, etc. It's definitely one of the more visually interesting films of this type, and that is because Fetscher and his crew got the most out of the numerous "sets" at their disposal."*

Reflection: For the past several years I've been privileged with the opportunity to moderate Q&As at a variety of screenings here in LA. Usually they're for the movies I myself programmed at the New Beverly, but I often get called up to do them at Screamfest – sometimes just before I head into the theater to watch it. This tends to be a trickier endeavor; not only is there a chance I hate the movie and have to hide my contempt from its makers, but I may also fall asleep if it's a later screening (some don't start until around 10:30pm) and have no idea what happened in it! This was one of those last minute "hires", but luckily I stayed awake for the whole thing AND liked the movie, and found Fetscher to be a fun guy to talk to.

The movie was originally called *Urban Explorer*; not sure why they changed the title to something that sounds like a generic *Saw* rip-off, but no matter what the title is I consider this to be one of the most memorable films from that year's festival. In addition to being my favorite horror film of the '00s, *The Descent* is one of the most highly respected horror films in recent memory, and was a pretty sizable hit here in the States, so I'm surprised that I haven't seen more films that invite comparisons to it. This carries on its "claustrophobia + humanoid threat" tradition with ease, where you feel like the movie would be scary enough with just the one thing and then they add the other. Also, claustrophobic folks can get an extra bit of uneasiness, since they're not likely to go into the caves you see in *Descent*, but will certainly go into a building. This could happen to you!

MOVIE #110 - APRIL 20th

THE SHUTTERED ROOM (1967)
Dir: David Greene
HMAD Review Date: September 24, 2009 (DVD)
Genre: Thriller
Available from Warner Home video.

Synopsis Based on Fading Memory: An allegedly cursed woman and her husband return to a mill owned by her family, only to be threatened by a gang of thugs, as well as an alleged creature that has been racking up kills on the island.

Review excerpt:
"...a pretty good little British chiller. I never figured out the twist, which is always a plus with me, and the gothic mansion is a great setting. It's also largely set during the day, something that I find eerie. And Oliver Reed is in it, so you know there are some wonderfully batshit moments (the best of which, naturally, revolves around his finding a bottle of some sort of alcohol on the floor, and then sort of sneaking up on it to drink it)."

Reflection: The only way to get this movie in the US seems to be on the flipside of *It!* (note the exclamation point; this is NOT the Stephen King movie), which is a good movie as well – but still, this deserves better than to be any film's B-side. Reed is in fine form, and there are a number of fine set-pieces, particularly one involving the rarest thing in all of horror: a car malfunction that is actually set up earlier in the film! A million horror movies and maybe four of them bother to ever hint that the hero's car is a piece of junk before the inevitable moment where it breaks down.

On the subject: I think it'd be fun for someone (certainly not me) to track down the very first instances of all of these various horror movie clichés that we have come to expect/ love/ begrudge. I'm sure the first "I can't get a signal" wouldn't be too hard, but the car breaking down at the worst time, or the creepy gas station clerk, or the person backing into something harmless and getting scared... how far back do these things go? Since folks can't even agree on what the first slasher movie was, I assume that something that specific would be even harder to pin down, but it'd probably be fun to try if you had the time.

MOVIE #111 - APRIL 21st

DARK SKIES (2013)
Dir: Scott Stewart
HMAD Review Date: February 23, 2013 (Theatrical)
Genre: Alien, Haunted House
Available from Anchor Bay

Synopsis Based on Fading Memory: It's a haunted house movie... but instead of a ghost, it's an alien!

Review excerpt:
"...it takes a page from Insidious - *no fake scares! The first time we see an alien is a pretty great jolt, and even what appears to have been a nightmare (booo!) turns out to be a reality (oh, cool!). No people standing behind family members in the mirror, no spooky noises chalked up to a mischievous cat, etc. There aren't a lot of scares in the film, but at least those that are there are genuine and related to the alien. It's a relief."*

Reflection: Jason Blum and his Blumhouse productions have a pretty rigid model: they cost 3-5 million bucks and usually make at least 10x as much back. This one is one of the rare box office "duds" (it still made around five times its production budget, but when you count marketing and all that...), but hopefully it found an audience on video. I quite liked the idea of making an alien invasion film so personal, and while his appearance is too brief, JK Simmons' conspiracy theorist ranks as one of the all-time best incarnations of this sort of character.

It's also a "third time's the charm" effort from Stewart, who made *Legion* and *Priest* – two films with intriguing concepts but sadly suffered from bungled executions (possibly/probably the studio's fault in those cases, to be fair). Working with a smaller budget and less ambitious scope, he pulled out a winner – hopefully he'll continue to work within this range, though first up he's oddly the second director this month (after Nicholas McCarthy) to be working on that Kevin Smith anthology called *Holidays*. But he also somehow managed to adapt *Legion* into a TV series for Syfy (called *Dominion*), which ran for two seasons - twice as many as fellow movie-to-TV series efforts like *Minority Report* or *Tremors*, so congrats!

MOVIE #112 - APRIL 22nd

THE HAUNTING (2009)
Dir: Elio Quiroga
HMAD Review Date: August 24, 2010 (DVD)
Genre: Haunted House, Religious
Available from Phase 4 Films

Synopsis Based on Fading Memory: A couple with a newborn baby rent a house that belongs to the Catholic Church, where they discover a long-buried secret. Plus ghosts, of course.

Review excerpt:
"Once the characters we've met start interacting, the film picks up considerably, mainly because the film's most interesting character (Héctor Colomé) takes on a more prominent role. He's a priest/shrink that investigates claims of supernatural occurrences, and he is neither a complete skeptic nor unshakable believer. And that's good, because the mom, who's the only one seeing the ghostly apparitions and such, might just be crazy, so it helps prolong the answer a bit. And, without spoiling much, the movie sort of has it both ways, so skeptics/believers alike can enjoy the film's revelations!"

Reflection: I watched this on a plane en route to London for Frightfest UK, my first and so far last trip overseas (I got a passport for the occasion and it'll probably expire before being used again). So my positive comments about the FX in the full review might be erroneous, as I watched it on a tiny screen that might have hidden such blemishes. Also I was partially distracted, as my longtime actress crush Danielle Harris was not only on the same plane (attending the same festival for the *Hatchet II* premiere), but sitting directly across the aisle from me. So I might have been sneaking a few glances instead of paying full attention. But of the three movies called *The Haunting* it's a lot better than one of them, so it's at least got that much going for it. Also, it was nice to see a movie using Catholicism without dipping into *Exorcist* territory for a change.

Like too many other filmmakers this month, Quiroga seemingly departed the horror genre after making this one, focusing on documentaries and short (non-horror) films. It's interesting that so many of them are also foreign (to US) filmmakers; I wonder if it's simply easier to switch gears than it is here? When our genre guys want to branch out they have to jump through hoops, usually having to agree to provide that studio with more horror. For example, Wes Craven only got to make *Music of the Heart* if he agreed to do *Scream 3*, but I guess it's a win he got to make it - Romero can't get funding for anything unless it has zombies in it. But Quiroga and many others seemed to be able to just jump into another genre without any of that stuff holding them back. It'd be great if guys like John Carpenter could jump around in different genres when they wanted to without everyone making a big deal about it. Some have been able to find success outside of horror – David Cronenberg is obviously a fine example, and a couple of the current Marvel directors (like James Gunn and Scott Derrickson) got their start in low budget genre films. But such cases are the exception; it'd be nice if it was the rule… as long as they come back!

MOVIE #113 - APRIL 23rd

THE ECHO (2008)
Dir: Yam Laranas
HMAD Review Date: December 18, 2009 (DVD)
Genre: Ghost
Available from Image Entertainment

Synopsis Based on Fading Memory: In this remake of 2004's *Sigaw*, a young man (Jesse Bradford) moves into his late mother's old apartment and hears what sounds like a man beating his wife in the adjacent apartment. He calls the cops, only to discover that the apartment has been empty for quite some time…

Review excerpt:
"*Like* The Grudge, *we actually have a couple ghosts, and part of the fun of the film is figuring out which ones mean us harm and which ones are trying to warn us (if any). Since one of them is played by the great Kevin Durand, you know he's bad, but the little girl and the mother are a bit less obvious, and I must say I was surprised by the end, where we finally learn what the ghosts were after, making the film a bit of a morality tale in the process.*"

Reflection: Released long after the Asian-horror remake boom had dried up, this one felt like putting on a comfy old sweater – and it was nice to see a male going through the motions for a change. Laranas was remaking his own movie here, and if memory serves he actually improved on his original (he provides a better reason for the guy to stay in the apartment here than he did with his first attempt, for starters). Doesn't reinvent the wheel, but now that it's been even longer since the *Rings* and *Grudges* terrorized us, it should fit the bill if you're in the mood for that sort of thing again.

Director Laranas made two films after this, one I didn't see called *Patient X*, and another called *The Road* which had a terrific first act and a pretty great concept, but overall didn't work for me. As of this writing he's got another one called *Abomination* that's coming soon – the trailer is creepy, so hopefully the full film is just as successful. I think he's got a distinctive way of tackling what seem like typical horror movies on the surface, offering a good blend of the familiar and the unique. I can't get into something that's way out there (if a movie is described as "David Lynch-esque", chances are I will not like it), and I certainly don't want something I've seen a million times, but I do like the feeling of being lulled and comforted by the familiar, and then get the rug pulled out from under me.

MOVIE #114 - APRIL 24th

BABYSITTER WANTED (2008)
Dir: Jonas Barnes, Michael Manasseri
HMAD Review Date: September 26, 2010 (DVD)
Genre: Cannibal, Religious
Available from Big Screen Entertainment Group

Synopsis Based on Fading Memory: A girl agrees to babysit a kid at an isolated house, and things get weird.

Review excerpt:
"It's somewhat spoiled by the mere existence of another film: House of the Devil*. This one was shot first, but unfortunately released later, so there is a sense of déjà vu to the proceedings that would have affected the other film had they been released "in order". Both films concern a girl (one with roommate issues no less) who takes on a babysitter job in a remote part of the area, and ends up fighting for her life against Satanic types. The key difference, of course, is that something happens before the 70 minute mark in this one. Even if the twists were obvious, the film admirably shifts gears several times without ever feeling jarring. The pacing can be a little awkward, and there's a little too much of our heroine being tied up and threatened with death, but it's rarely boring."*

Reflection: I had a different movie here originally, having somehow passed this one over when finalizing my title choices, but it was saved by Bill Moseley! Someone had asked me about movies where Moseley played a hero, and when re-reading my review after sending a link to it to that person, I realized it deserved a place in this month's lineup, partially on the strength of being a faster-paced *House of the Devil*. Now, I'm not going to say this is a BETTER movie, as it's got a few issues (described above) and lacks Ti West's keen eye for detail, but the most common complaint about that film is that "nothing happens" – this movie has a similar setup and *lots* of things happen! Some you may see coming, but that's OK.

As for Moseley, it's like an anti-spoiler to say he's not a villain here. Astute horror fans will probably THINK he's a bad guy because he's Bill Moseley, but if this is somehow your first horror movie (or at least, your first one with Moseley) there's nothing to indicate that he might be up to no good. So it's a "spoiler" only to jaded viewers who think they're ahead of the script. I am a big fan of the actor and love seeing him in rare "normal" roles like this, so it's a shame that this movie is more commonly known as "that *House of the Devil* rip-off" or whatever.

MOVIE #115 - APRIL 25th

THE DEVIL'S ROCK (2011)
Dir: Paul Campion
HMAD Review Date: May 4, 2012 (DVD)
Genre: Supernatural
Available from Entertainment One

Synopsis Based on Fading Memory: A pair of soldiers sent to disarm a German anti-aircraft gun during WWII uncover, you guessed it, Nazi occult stuff.

Review excerpt:
"It's impressively detailed, with many of the Nazi's comments referencing things that really happened, while set against the backdrop of a real WWII event that's not often covered in films (horror or not). The film is takes place in the Channel Islands, which were occupied by the Nazis throughout most of the war and ultimately cut off (the search for food is what led the soldiers to discover the Grimoire that raised the demon), and occurs the day before D-Day. And they have a little fun with the historical touches; amidst all the real actions mentioned, the Nazi mentions Hitler's near-possession of the Ark (Raiders of the Lost Ark) and attempt to raise the Old Ones (Hellboy). Pretty cool, and not distracting if you don't get the reference."

Reflection: It seems I saw like twenty movies that could be described as "Soldiers investigate a base and uncover creepy supernatural stuff" (it's the second one in this chapter!) so, like bad *Paranormal Activity* wannabes, a lot of them blended together after a while. But this one carved out a little corner of my brain permanently, because the Nazi character wasn't a cardboard villain – he actually had a human side and an intelligent point of view on the situation. There's nothing easier to hate than a Nazi, but getting an audience to kind of sympathize with one, at least as it relates to the specific situation in the film? That takes some skill.

Another thing in its corner was the impressively compact cast and limited locations. You could pretty much turn this into a stage production with minimal revising, which would be a fascinating experiment if anyone wanted to try. I'm sure there have been actual stage plays featuring two soldiers from opposing sides of a war, trading barbs and waxing poetic about the situation, but I bet none of them had a lady demon to liven up the proceedings. Someone get on this! I've seen *Donnie Darko* on stage (it was terrible, for the record), so clearly there's not much of a vetting process for whoever makes these decisions.

MOVIE #116 - APRIL 26th

SPECTRE (2006)
Dir: Mateo Gil
HMAD Review Date: December 4, 2008 (DVD)
Genre: Ghost
Available in the "6 Films To Keep You Awake" set from Lionsgate

Synopsis Based on Fading Memory: A middle-aged man goes back to his hometown and discovers that the older woman he had an affair with as a teenager (hey-o!) hasn't aged at all.

Review excerpt:
"I really dug how the movie carefully laid out the information. I was never completely confused as to what was happening, but at the same time there was always a sense of urgency and mystery to the proceedings; a difficult balance to pull off. Mateo Gil's script provides exactly as much information as you need as the scenes unfold, no more or less. And the end, which almost cancels the film out as a horror movie, is wonderfully bittersweet. It's like Nicholas Sparks writing a Twilight Zone movie."

Reflection: After *Skyfall*, it was inevitable that the next Bond film would be a disappointment, but this- wait, wrong *Spectre*.

Like many of the films on the "6 Films To Keep You Awake" set, the horror elements here are subdued, but (as I mention in the excerpt) the nostalgia-driven storyline reminds me of some *Twilight Zones* (like the classic "Walking Distance"). It also recalled *Stealing Home*, a film I absolutely loved as a kid (it also had a teenager losing his virginity to a sexy older woman, a very enticing prospect to an adolescent watching the film on HBO). So it's a movie about nostalgia that invoked my own nostalgia – might not work as well on you, but if you're watching everything I suggest you should have just bought this set by now, and thus you already own the movie anyway.

I still wish Lionsgate had done a second edition of this series, for what it's worth. I assume the timing was just bad (this was the period where they were leaning away from horror beyond their *Saw* installments), because I think the set sold pretty well for a foreign language release – and just about everyone I've ever talked to really enjoyed the majority of its six films (I think I liked all of them, personally, though they're not ALL in this book). With Spanish becoming a more common language here in the US, I think we're bound to see more and more Spanish horror becoming readily available (i.e. not on questionable import discs), which is fine by me – like the French, I tend to like more than I don't.

MOVIE #117 - APRIL 27th

THE SHADOW WITHIN (2007)
Dir: Silvana Zancolo
HMAD Review Date: June 17, 2010 (DVD)
Genre: Ghost
Available from MTI Home Video

Synopsis Based on Fading Memory: A 9-year-old boy who can communicate with the dead discovers that the spirit of his deceased twin wants his parents to join him in the afterlife.

Review excerpt:
"If you're patient, you will be rewarded with an above average little chiller, bolstered by a terrific lead performance from Laurence Belcher, the child actor making his debut performance (!). Maybe it's just because Will Smith's ego trip (aka Karate Kid*) is the #1 movie right now, but there's something really refreshing and rewarding about seeing a genuinely good performance from a young actor who is required to use his talent, not his name. And he really carries the movie - he's in pretty much every scene, reducing everyone else to supporting roles - there's no Nicole Kidman or Bruce Willis fighting for top billing with the kid. There's a heartbreaking scene where his abusive mother tears his favorite toy apart, and the kid's wordless expression of grief is award-worthy."*

Reflection: When you think of Italian horror films, you probably get mental images of gory murders (Argento) or zombies (Fulci), and those images are probably from the '70s or '80s. So even if the movie was lousy, a modern Italian horror film about a ghost definitely sticks out from the pack (the Italian film industry basically abandoned horror a while back; newer films are about as common as big budget westerns here in the States). That it's actually quite good is sort of a bonus.

In my full review, I mention that the film was rented out the first few times I looked for it at my Blockbuster, and that's a thing that simply won't happen anymore as we move into a nearly completely digital, on-demand world for watching movies. I mean there's Redbox right now, and even a few regular video stores (not the chain ones, you guys effectively killed all of those), but for the most part, having to wait to see a movie you want to rent will be a thing of the past. It's possibly the only thing about this model that I can see as a benefit, but I can even make a case that it kind of ruins the experience of discovering a movie. There's no anticipation! I tried three times to rent this movie before it was finally in, and then it turned out good, making it worth the wait. Had it been one of the hundreds of movies I just watched on Netflix Instant, the viewing experience wouldn't be as memorable, I bet. The instant gratification that folks demand nowadays kind of bums me out... there's nothing wrong with sweating it out a bit if the film is worthy.

MOVIE #118 - APRIL 28th

THEM [ILS] (2006)
Dir: David Moreau, Xavier Palud
HMAD Review Date: May 19, 2008 (Streaming)
Genre: Survival
Available from Dark Sky Films

Synopsis Based on Fading Memory: A teacher and her husband are terrorized by some hooded killers in their isolated home.

Review excerpt:
"Like High Tension, it presents the killer's identity/motive as a twist, but with two major differences. One: it doesn't damage the film in the slightest (in fact it's pretty goddamn chilling), and two: it prevents me from listing the film under a certain sub-genre. And since it's just hitting DVD and never got a real theatrical release here, I will refrain from spoiling anything concerning the killers' identity/motive (the fact that there is more than one is hardly a spoiler – it's the name of the goddamn movie)."

Reflection: A lot of folks dissed *The Strangers* at the time of its release, saying it was a rip-off of this film, but since *Strangers* actually shot in 2006 (released in May of 2008), before *Ils* had a premiere at any festival, I think it's safe to say it's just a coincidence that they share some similarities. Luckily for both, *The Strangers* was a surprise smash and thus spawned a mini-wave of home invasion thrillers, so comparing them now is about as common as coming across someone saying *When A Stranger Calls* was a *Halloween* rip-off (also inaccurate, for the record).

Anyway, it's a solid entry in the sub-genre, though I still think the climax, which leaves the house for a new locale, was ill-advised. Stay in the house - THAT's what makes it scary! The house was plenty big enough, so I don't know why they felt the need to change locales so late in the game – I can't think of one "single location" movie that benefited from going elsewhere for the finale (another movie that bungled this: the otherwise solid *Assault on Precinct 13* remake, which left the police station for the woods).

Final note - the filmmakers went on to remake *The Eye*. The experience seemingly wasn't a good one; they haven't worked together since and at least one of them considered taking his name off the movie after he was shut out of editing. Bummer.

MOVIE #119 - APRIL 29th

OUTCAST (2010)
Dir: Colm McCarthy
HMAD Review Date: October 9, 2010 (Festival screening)
Genre: Supernatural
Available from The Collective

Synopsis Based on Fading Memory: A kid who is also a monster falls in love with a girl in his apartment complex as his Van Helsing-y father tries to track him down.

Review excerpt:
"One thing I liked was how sparingly the film used the monster. It could have almost been a mystery, with us not knowing who it was, but instead they more or less tell you and then you have to wait for most of the movie to see it fully. Thus, there aren't a lot of kills in the movie, but there IS a lot of time spent developing all of the characters, making the final reel, with everyone coming together in a tragic way, a bit more resonant than these sorts of things usually manage."

Reflection: In the full review I compared this to *Let The Right One In*, a movie that I kept flip-flopping over whether to include it in the book per my "Nothing you should have seen by now" rule. I ultimately did, but for a different chapter, and put this movie in its place. And this one definitely isn't a movie I'd expect many of you to have seen already, as it barely got released and obviously hasn't been met with as much universal acclaim. I was a bit mixed on the film, but as we were besieged by the *Twilight* films and various CW shows about monster/human relationships, I think I owe it you to highlight anything that does it right. Plus: cool use of magic in a horror film – a lot better than *Warlock*, in my opinion.

It's also one of those rare Irish horror films; there are five or six in this book and I think that's more than half of those I saw over the six years of HMAD. I'd like to go for the easy joke and say that the Irish are too busy drinking Guinness or chasing leprechauns to make any horror movies, but this is no joking matter – why the hell aren't they making more horror movies? The countryside alone should inspire dozens of entries, with the rich history, abundance of water (it IS an island), big cities like Dublin and Belfast, and easy-to-recreate period locations just sweetening the appeal. You can literally make any kind of horror movie there, unlike more limited locales that get used all the time. And yet... almost nothing. Most of them, like *Stitches*, aren't even Ire-centric. Silver (shamrock) lining – those few that do get made are pretty damn good on the average (again, most of the ones I saw ended up in this book). Guess they choose quality over quantity.

MOVIE #120 - APRIL 30th

THE LEGACY (1978)
Dir: Richard Marquand
HMAD Review Date: February 3, 2010 (DVD)
Genre: Supernatural
Available from Scream Factory

Synopsis Based on Fading Memory: A bunch of folks from different walks of life are invited to an isolated estate in order to inherit... something. But then they start getting killed.

Review excerpt:
"It starts off like a lot of films of this era - very melodramatic, without any evidence that you are watching a horror film (though the opening Kiki Dee ballad about a "Sunset stained with gold" is certainly a candidate for ironic terror), and then it slowly draws you into the horrible goings-on. But the pacing is on such an even path into gonzo-ville that the silly stuff never really sticks out as such in the context of the film. For example, the finale of the movie involves Sam Elliott running around with a crossbow, while a guy on a roof shoots at him with a rifle (both men are terrible shots). Out of context, that sounds ridiculous, and it's certainly not how you'd expect the movie to end up based on the first reel. But when it comes after a woman is suddenly annihilated by shards of glass, it's almost like "Well, how else would this particular movie end?"

Reflection: I almost put this one in next month's list, which is why it's last here – I'll ease you into May's selections with a movie that starts like a lot of the others from this month but ends up being a lot goofier. This is one of many studio horror films from the late '70s that are packed with stars you wouldn't expect to see in a movie so weird – a fun byproduct of *The Exorcist* giving such fare some legitimacy, and each such film trying to top the last, which ultimately turned them into batshit crazy affairs. I never even heard of this one until shortly before I saw it, and to date it's the only other movie I've seen from *Return of the Jedi* director Richard Marquand. I like to imagine some hardcore *Star Wars* fan seeking this out and being even more bewildered than I was.

I hope you've enjoyed this slightly random collection of movies. I had trouble narrowing down the exact "theme" for this month; there's a lot of potential crossover with the films of October, and I mostly just wanted something a little quieter and more "normal" in between last month's occasionally batshit killer kid stuff and next month's CONSISTENTLY batshit other stuff. But 30 movies where almost nothing happens or that are set entirely in one location would be pretty dull back to back, so I mixed in some other stuff that I just didn't know where else to put it. Plus April as a month just kind of sucks in general. Seriously, it's got no holidays of note (Easter doesn't count since it's in March half the time), Hollywood usually doesn't deliver too many big movies since they're saving them for May, and TV is mostly in repeats. If your birthday isn't in April I defy you to tell me one good thing about it! But first, keep reading.

MAY – BATSHIT CRAZY HORROR

ARTIST: JOE BADON

The "summer blockbuster" season used to begin on Memorial Day weekend, but when *Deep Impact* of all goddamn things surprised everyone and scored a giant opening at the beginning of May back in 1998, the studios realized they could start early. Nowadays, it's common to have bigger movies throughout that month than in June/July – in fact, the summer's big Marvel movies almost always kick things off.

These movies make a ton of money because of one reason: they're safe. The quality of the *Spider-Man* series has declined, but they're still aiming to entertain every man, woman, and child on Earth . You're never going to see anything as batshit as, well, the Broadway Spider-Man musical in feature film form, at least not this month. So since you can't get anything truly interesting or dangerous in theaters for a while, I've selected some of the more unusual fare I've discovered over the years. You might hate some of these movies (I don't even love them all), but they're anything but cookie cutter, and they're part of what makes the genre the most fascinating one to explore.

That said, I hope none of them cost you too much to see – for whatever reason, this month's selections seem to be the most prone to going out of print. I took the time going over every title to ensure that everything in the book was commercially available in the US *at some point* (meaning, no festival movies I saw that never got released, or revival screenings of movies only otherwise available on long out of print VHS), but that doesn't mean they will be up for Prime shipping on Amazon. Some were in print when I started the book only to end up being incredibly rare by the time I finished. On the other hand, one of the book's selections hit DVD for the first time during the lengthy editing process, allowing me to write up a new entry literally days before the book was published. Long story short, things kept changing, so just know I did my best and hope nothing proves to be out of your reach/budget. Scour your local used shops and flea markets (not to mention your libraries) before forking over crazy amounts!

Now, obviously some of these movies are weirder than others, but I can almost guarantee that there's at least one moment in each one that will have you wondering if the DVD was broken or something. In fact, I toyed with the idea of having them run from "really not that weird" to "Holy shit what the Christing hell was anyone involved with this thinking?", but then you'd have to wait all month to experience...

MOVIE #121 - MAY 1st

THINGS (1989)
Dir: Andrew Jordan
HMAD Review Date: July 10, 2011 (DVD)
Genre: Splatter
Available from Intervision Pictures Corp.

Synopsis Based on Fading Memory: Some dudes are hanging out in their friend's cabin and weird shit happens.

Review excerpt:
"Trying to follow the plot is a fairly fruitless endeavor, so I just sort of settled for being continually amazed at what else would occur. It's actually kind of slow with regards to its horror elements, but that's actually a good thing as the main "villains" are moderately "giant" (like 1-2 feet long) ants and other insects, which is one of the few things that gross me out. Like a 50-foot ant wouldn't bother me much, because it was just a matter of staying the hell away from the damn thing. But one that was as big as my foot, that could crawl in through an open window or something? I'd be mortified (I'm not a bug guy), and seeing the things attack our characters (or even get squished/dismembered) made me kind of queasy; I actually had to stop eating for a bit. However, for every "money shot" there's 5 minutes of them just sitting around making odd comments about the art hanging on the walls or shouting "The lights went out!" even though the lighting looks exactly the same."

Reflection: Even though it's only been a few years, my strongest memory of this movie isn't of the film itself, but of how I forced it upon my friend ____, whom you may know as FilmCritHULK. As he is an actual genius who dedicates much of his intelligence to breaking down stories and narrative in feature films (and then writes those thoughts down for our entertainment/ enlightenment!), I thought it'd be fun to melt his brain by trying to apply his usual thought process to a movie that is, by any reasonable measure, completely batshit insane. But, alas, it didn't work. He was bewildered, of course, but I guess he turned off the "HULK" part of his brain and just enjoyed the wackiness like anyone else would, instead of writing a 30,000 word ALL-CAPS essay about it. I'm still disappointed.

Again, this might be one of the nuttiest movies of the month, so I hope you don't expect things to get *as* crazy from here on out. Think of it more like a Bond movie that gives you a mega action scene to whet your appetite before settling down a bit. But also, I thought it'd be good to get it in early because it's the kind of movie that you, too, will likely recommend to friends in that "you HAVE to see this thing!" way, so that they can be experiencing its majesty while you work through the other gonzo slices of cinema I have selected for you. After slashers this is probably the month I'm most excited about; it makes me happy when someone actually watches any movie I recommend, but these in particular speak to my sensibilities and joys, so if you enjoy any or all them I'll know you're a kindred spirit.

MOVIE #122 - MAY 2nd

THE MANITOU (1978)
Dir: William Girdler
HMAD Review Date: March 31, 2007 (Revival screening)
Genre: Monster, Weird
Available from Anchor Bay

Synopsis Based on Fading Memory: A woman gets a weird growth on her shoulder. As is often the case, it turns out to be a fetus.

Review excerpt:
"Much like Killer Shrews, *the dialogue in* The Manitou *has that little special something that makes almost every line a howler. For example: "Normally I wait three risings of the sun before I take on a job." Me too. Tony Curtis in particular is worth the price of admission alone (I got in for free but that's neither here nor there). There's also off-kilter little touches throughout, such as when Burgess Meredith, looking for a spell book or something, picks up and considers a wig for a few moments for no real reason."*

Reflection: If you hang out with me for an extended period of time you'll probably hear me shout MANITOU! for no discernible reason, and in the same tone of voice as the voiceover guy for the film's trailer. I can't quite explain it (maybe it's some form of Tourette's?), but it's the perfect movie for such an odd tic. If I just shouted like, JURASSIC WORLD! out of nowhere, you'd probably wonder what was wrong with me. But as long as you've seen how insane this movie is, your brain will be just as fried and you'd probably develop some weird tic, too. Such is the power of THE MANITOU! Or at least, the power of the guy saying the title in the trailer.

Speaking of the trailer, it barely even hints at the nuttiness the film offers. For example, it hardly shows Burgess Meredith at all, and if you know your '70s horror, you know that if Burgess Meredith is around things are going to get batshit. I later learned that the novel the movie was based on spawned several sequels, which is a shame since the movie itself is a standalone affair (director Girdler died before it was even released, in fact). Someday I'll get around to reading them, I hope, but at the same time I feel it might not be the best use of my time. Because I can only see two scenarios: either I'll be disappointed that they're not as crazy as the film, or I'll be REALLY disappointed that their craziness will probably never be realized on screen. Best to not know, you know? Call it Schrodinger's shoulder fetus.

MOVIE #123 - MAY 3rd

A REAL FRIEND (2006)
Dir: Enrique Urbizu, James Phillips
HMAD Review Date: December 19, 2008 (DVD)
Genre: Psychological, Weird
Available in the "6 Films To Keep You Awake" set from Lionsgate

Synopsis Based on Fading Memory: A little girl escapes from her crappy home life with her imaginary best friend: Leatherface.

Review excerpt:
"The attention to detail was truly admirable, particularly for Leatherface. They never say his name (or the name of the movie), but the costume/mask are spot on perfect, as is the performance of Aitor Mazo (credited as Bubba, another nice reference). The film clips are recreated pretty accurately (though the "Chainsaw Dance" finale is set on a beach for some reason), and Mazo actually does a better job than at least two of the actual Leatherface performers (likewise, whoever did the makeup for this should be brought on to do any future installments of the regular franchise). Writer/Director Enrique Urbizu doesn't stop there though; when Leatherface cuts down a door he makes the exact same pattern that Gunnar Hansen did in the original film. Also, the frequent news reports that we overhear echo those in the first film (i.e. they are all about the discovery of bodies, murders, etc.)."

Reflection: Copyright law is all well and good, but it's a shame that it's so strict that it prevents movies like this from being more commonplace. When I say "Leatherface", I mean the exact character – it's not some comedic approximation like Chevy Chase dressed up as 'Jason' in *Christmas Vacation*. I don't even know how they were able to pull it off (perhaps being from another country helped), but I know that character usage can get so silly that even George Romero, when making *Land of the Dead*, had to jump through hoops to use Tom Savini's biker character from *Dawn of the Dead*! They're both his movies! There should be a way to make the distinction and instantly allow someone else's character to be used in your film if it, like *A Real Friend*, not only grounds the narrative in reality (whereas using some fake version wouldn't allow), but also elevates the importance of the original in a unique way. This movie shows more respect and love for the character than some of the actual sequels!

By the way, this is the last entry in the book for the "6 Films To Keep You Awake" set. I hope you've just bought the thing by now. If you've been borrowing it from a (real) friend every time it comes up, he/she is probably getting kind of annoyed at this point.

MOVIE #124 - MAY 4th

DR. JEKYLL'S DUNGEON OF DEATH (1979)
Dir: James Wood
HMAD Review Date: June 28, 2012 (DVD)
Genre: Mad Scientist, Weird
Available from Cheezy Flicks

Synopsis Based on Fading Memory: Dr. Jekyll (sans Hyde) has some dudes fight in his basement for some reason, and he's trying to cure his sister of something...? Maybe?

Review excerpt:
"Right off the bat I knew this would be a very special movie, as Jekyll explains the history of his great grandfather, how his serum didn't work, etc. Typical stuff, but what makes it puzzling is that he says this as we watch two guys beat the crap out of each other in a dimly lit basement, as if they put the VO on the wrong movie. Later we learn what's going on, not that it makes much sense, but at least we know for sure that this is indeed the movie they were making."

Reflection: As mentioned, Twitter was a big help in getting people to stop asking me if I was really watching something every day, because I'd post "HMAD Today is..." and usually post a follow-up, like "Well that sucked. Review soon!" And I got used to certain people replying more often than not to these posts, but the "Today" tweet for this film prompted a very rare reply from none other than Jeremy Smith (aka the former Mr. Beaks from AICN), who is, for my money, one of the best writers I've had the pleasure of knowing. He's more likely to be talking about classier fare from Fincher or De Palma than obscure B-movie genre stuff, so when he replied with a few bullet points from the movie I knew it'd be something memorable. And by God, it was. It's one of those movies that if I merely picture any random, non-descript moment I will start chuckling to myself, and I truly hope you enjoy it.

And because it reminds me of Twitter, I chose it for today's slot because today is "Star Wars Day" (because May the 4th sounds like "may the force be with you", I guess), which means Twitter is currently unbearable with all the idiotic mashups and other *SW*-related bullshit. Ideally, *Force Awakens* (which I liked, making it the 3rd entry in the series I would ever want to watch again) would have tanked and maybe then this frenzy would die down, but no! Just the opposite - it became the #1 movie of all time after like three weeks or something, ushering a new wave of dumb memes and, if anything, increasing the number of people who get mad at you when you don't bow at the altar of the Force. So this is never going to go away, and the fans are always going to drive me nuts.

Long story short, I'll be off Twitter today. So if you're actually going by the book and watching films on the day I recommend them, and you love this movie, save your thanks for tomorrow. Or just tweet @MrBeaks.

MOVIE #125 - MAY 5th

OGROFF: THE MAD MUTILATOR (1983)
Dir: N.G. Mount
HMAD Review Date: March 7, 2013 (DVD)
Genre: Slasher, Weird, Zombie
Available from Artus Films

Synopsis Based on Fading Memory: I doubt even the director could provide a synopsis for this one. There's a guy killing people in the woods though!

Review excerpt:
"...early on a woman is tied up for a while by Ogroff, seemingly not wanting to kill her for whatever reason. He then goes off and kills some chess players that are just chilling in the woods, and then comes back and casually kills the girl, as well. Why would I ever want to know the logic behind any of this, and ruin what, when in the right mood, is pure bliss? Even knowing the age or biographical information about the director would ruin things. Is he a 14-year-old boy? An elderly man who had been raised by wolves? An actual psychotic? I don't want to know! Nor should you - you should let the magic that is Ogroff *just pour over you."*

Reflection: I consider it a high compliment that my good friends Phil Blankenship and Jacqueline Greed (re-read the special thanks if you need a reminder of their significance to HMAD!) started watching this thing one night only to shut it off and wait until I could join them. They were wise to do so; this is one of the most batshit goddamn things I've ever seen in my life, and I could actually feel the horror-watching part of my life change before my eyes. You know how after *Scream* there was some sentiment that we could never have regular slasher movies again? After *Ogroff* you might start to wonder if you can ever truly be baffled by a film's existence. Even the fact that they made a third *Atlas Shrugged* movie despite the first two bombing is nowhere near as puzzling as what in the hell any single person involved with this movie was ever trying to accomplish. It's a masterpiece of HUH?

Part of the allure is that it's a rare French entry in the early '80s slasher canon (if you can even call it one, since it's "inspired" by movies from several sub-genres), and to date it's the ONLY backyard indie type I've seen from Europe as a whole. I mean I've seen dozens of equally amateurish movies shot here in the US, but there's something quite intriguing about seeing the French version of it, especially when their horror films tend to be so well regarded. It's sort of like getting a watch from Switzerland that doesn't keep time properly, or finding an Italian recipe that tastes like rancid garbage.

Oh and don't worry about the language barrier - there's barely any dialogue, anyway. Even if the subtitles don't work, it will in no way affect your ability to "understand" the film.

MOVIE #126 - MAY 6th

TERROR (1978)
Dir: Norman J. Warren
HMAD Review Date: July 4, 2010 (DVD)
Genre: Revenge, Supernatural
Public domain title, available through several DVD companies

Synopsis Based on Fading Memory: A guy makes a movie about his family curse, which triggers the spirit to finish the job.

Review excerpt:
"*...it seems to be intentionally funny at times, which is unique to this film out of the four from Warren I have seen. I particularly liked early on when a guy gets blown off, so he says "What should I do, kill myself?" and everyone in earshot says "Yes" - but not in unison, which makes it funnier. And even though they kill the pace, the snafus when trying to film the movie are pretty amusing, like the guy who doesn't understand that his line is supposed to be a double entendre.*"

Reflection: If I had my own theater, I'd probably do a marathon of all of Norman J. Warren's movies. *Prey* (from the same year, and we'll get to it later) is the best of the lot, and they're all a bit slow at times, but each one is a bit different and very memorable. In fact I remain kind of puzzled why I don't hear his name more often; *Inseminoid* (aka *Horror Planet*) is a bit of an infamous title, but that's the only one – hopefully this is just US ignorance and he gets his proper due in his native UK. At any rate, I'll continue doing my best to educate folks here. Watch his movies! They're nuts!

Also, this is a pretty great idea for a movie – it could be remade as a legit scary film and probably turn out really well as long as it had a good director behind it. There is no shortage of horror movies about making movies (there are a few in this book, in fact), but usually the movie they're making is just a generic slasher or monster movie. This, as far as I can recall (which isn't very far, admittedly), is the only one about someone making something more personal, and the family angle gives it a unique flavor as well. But with its generic title and aforementioned unheralded filmmaker, it's not likely anyone is actively pursuing a remake or even a rip-off of this particular film. So you, dear reader, should get on that.

MOVIE #127 - MAY 7th

MY SOUL TO TAKE (2010)
Dir: Wes Craven
HMAD Review Date: October 8, 2010 (Theatrical)
Genre: Slasher, Supernatural
Available from Universal Home Video

Synopsis Based on Fading Memory: Seven teenagers who were born on the night a serial killer was killed find themselves targeted by another murderer... or has he returned? (Note: I actually don't know.)

Review excerpt:
"If you can look past the teen dialogue (just sort of let it be background noise; assume it's just kids being kids and that the particulars don't really matter), you will be rewarded with one of the more original concepts for a horror movie in quite some time. The press synopsis and such will probably tell you that the soul of The Riverton Ripper has been transferred to one of our seven kids, and they are trying to figure out who as they begin getting picked off one by one... but it's actually more complicated and interesting than that. Nor is it clearly explained; it takes some brainwork (and possibly a second viewing) for everything to become clear."

Reflection: My good friend Sam Zimmerman (former editor of Fangoria and Shock Till You Drop) shares my enthusiasm for this nutty flick, so I know I'm not crazy when I say it's much more interesting than almost anyone gives it credit for. I assume most folks were expecting another *Scream* or *Nightmare on Elm Street*, but thanks to studio meddling and Craven's usual handicap (fascinating ideas with not-wholly-successful execution), it's a mess, with a pace that could best be described as "off" and an occasionally crippling dependency on teen slang that Craven (nearly seventy years old at the time) seemingly devised after watching *Brick*. That said, there's something endearingly wild about the endeavor – the California Condor scene alone should be enough to keep anyone from labeling the movie as "generic".

Note – my excerpt is revised from the original review version, which hints at a theory I have about the movie that I've since backed away from, but it's a fun way to think about the narrative anyway. It'd be a disservice to watch the movie thinking about this concept, but if you're ever compelled to watch it a second time, read the full review at HMAD, or just hit me up and ask me to spell out what I originally thought the movie was implying. This is part of the problem but also the strange appeal of writing reviews on one viewing; on one hand, a second viewing would have given me enough information to know I was wrong, but on the other, it's fun to go back and see these theories (or musings, or random asides, or any of the other things that make up a HMAD review that have nothing to do with the movie), making the site kind of a diary of a sort. If you haven't figured it out by now, I've tried to retain that vibe in this book, mostly because I really like these movies and want to preserve their surprises for you. If this was a book about the 365 shittiest movies I watched, it'd be a lot different. The F-word would come up more, for starters.

Note - Wes died two days after I thought I had made the final revision to this entry. It's his only movie in the book, due to the whole "nothing popular" rule pretty much voiding everything else. And if there's a silver lining to his passing, it's that people might be more open to seeing this, which turned out to be his last original film. RIP, Wes. We'll never have another like you.

MOVIE #128 - MAY 8th

PSYCHOMANIA (1973)
Dir: Don Sharp
HMAD Review Date: July 31, 2012 (Revival screening)
Genre: Supernatural
Available from Severin Films

Synopsis Based on Fading Memory: Some bikers seek – and obtain – the secret to immortality.

Review excerpt:
"I loved the instrumental credits theme, which set a very creepy, ominous mood that the film mostly avoided. There are some minor bits of full-on terror (including an off-screen massacre that's kind of disturbing if you think about it), but mostly it comes off as a thriller with a darkly humorous touch. It also feels like a regular biker movie at times, as we're treated to three full riding scenes that are quite enjoyable. As I've mentioned in the past, there aren't too many action/horror films period, let alone ones that work, but I think this one did a fine job of balancing the action bits (including - yes! - a vehicle falling down a hill and exploding) and the horror elements. The random comedy is a very nice bonus."

Reflection: I had a lot of extra options this month, because I quite liked weirdo cinema when I saw it and, as I've said a lot, bonkers movies like this made doing the site worthwhile. I could watch slashers every day and probably be content, but this was the stuff that really energized me – the possibility that I could find something just as nutty the next day or week would give me the strength to sit through yet another found footage movie.

So how did *Psychomania* ultimately win out over the others? Well, for starters, I want you to hear the theme song I mentioned in the excerpt, as it is potentially life-changing. Plus I realized I would hate myself for missing the chance to suggest you see this utterly unique, wonderfully weird, and other alliterative descriptions movie. And it peaks kind of early, so if you don't laugh out loud or flat out APPLAUD the bit where the guy takes a bite out of a sandwich that appeared out of nowhere, you can probably just shut it off then and save yourself some time. You just aren't ready for this movie's charms. Or its frogs.

MOVIE #129 - MAY 9th

DON'T GO NEAR THE PARK (1979)
Dir: Lawrence David Foldes
HMAD Review Date: December 31, 2010 (DVD)
Genre: Cannibal, Supernatural
Available from Dark Sky Films

Synopsis Based on Fading Memory: Some cavemen are cursed with immortality as long as they disembowel someone every now and then, but... well, you'll see. Sort of.

Review excerpt:
"...it's only 82 minutes long, but we get all of the above and more - at one point, reporter Aldo Ray goes on and on about the history of Griffith Park. And there are a number of out of nowhere situations, like when some dude tries to mug the little kid, or a girl looking for her dog (curiously named "Starshine"). Plus there's a parade of some sort, and then, in a plot twist, we find out our immortal cannibals also have laser eyes! Hell, zombies even make an appearance in the final moments. It's cinematic stew - just toss in whatever you got, as long as there's some sort of center that folks can latch onto."

Reflection: You know how on *The Simpsons* there's always that opening bit that is largely unrelated but provides a way to get to the main part of the story? Okay, imagine a movie doing that for its entire runtime, and you can kind of picture what *Don't Go Near The Park* is like. The title suggests some sleazy *Last House on the Left* kind of movie, but while it does feature some icky moments (like a little kid copping a feel from our heroine and then claiming "I thought she was dead!" when he is caught), it's too goddamn silly to ever find anything offensive. Plus I like a movie in which you can skip any five minutes and come back almost positive that you're watching something else entirely, as the damn thing just keeps changing gears and introducing new would-be main characters. It's bliss.

I just wish I could remember the title when thinking about the movie. There are no fewer than eleven million movies with a title that starts with "Don't", and many of them have a very tenuous relationship to their movie. Some are retitles; *Don't Look In The Basement* (also largely unrelated to its film) was originally called *The Forgotten*, for example. This odd little trend paved the way for the funniest/best fake *Grindhouse* trailer, of course, but it's otherwise kind of frustrating because I tend to get them mixed up when recommending movies in person. And there's no real way to describe this movie, because the plot keeps changing!

MOVIE #130 - MAY 10th

DEAD SUSHI [DEDDO SUSHI] (2012)
Dir: Noboru Iguchi
HMAD Review Date: September 19, 2012 (Streaming)
Genre: Comedic, Weird
Available from Action Slate

Synopsis Based on Fading Memory: Employees and customers of a spa are menaced by killer sushi.

Review excerpt:
"The movie throws a new curveball at us every few minutes, keeping it engaging and never too repetitive, at least with regards to the antagonists, [as] the titular sushi keep changing. They fly, they form weaponry, they possess corpses, they even sing at one point ("Any sushi that sings can't be all that bad.") - it seems any nutty idea anyone had would find its way into the movie, somehow. There's even a humanoid sushi - the film's human villain injects a serum and becomes a fish-man, who uses found weapons (great use of an ax) to add to all the carnage. And I particularly liked when two of the sushi began having sex against a tree, resulting in a spawn of baby flying sushi that swarm around like insects."

Reflection: I watched a few of these "Robo Fart Ninja Zombie" movies (again, term coined by Evan Husney) during HMAD's run, and this was the last. And thus, it'll probably be the last one I ever watch; I find them amusing but without forcing myself to find something to watch every day I doubt I'll ever gravitate toward one. However, if I ever make it back to Fantastic Fest, I'd really like to watch one in its proper setting: a theater full of drunken movie fans. I enjoyed this one at home by myself, so I can't imagine how much more I'd like it with the infectious laughter of an appreciative crowd ringing in my ears. And in turn, maybe I'd be compelled to watch more movies in this vein. Win-win!

I just realized how many horror films are set around spas. There are three in this book alone (*Dead Sushi*, *X-Cross*, and a November entry called *Warlock Moon*), not to mention *Death Spa* and Craven's nutty TV movie *Invitation to Hell*. At least five spa-horror films but not a single one set in a Target-type megastore, far as I know. For shame, Hollywood.

P.S. for you gamers – I honestly forget if that quote in the excerpt is from the movie, or if I was just paraphrasing *Final Fantasy IX's* "pickles" thing. Either way I hope you enjoyed it.

MOVIE #131 - MAY 11th

THE BABY (1973)
Dir: Ted Post
HMAD Review Date: June 30, 2012 (Streaming)
Genre: Weird
Available from Severin Films

Synopsis Based on Fading Memory: A social worker is assigned to a demented family that includes a 30-year-old man who is dressed and treated as a baby.

Review excerpt:
"I was a bit sleepy while watching, and now I'm not sure – did I actually SEE a 20ish babysitter breastfeed the 30ish title character, or was my tired brain jumbling a bunch of stuff together? I assure you, that scene did happen. And it wasn't even the weirdest thing about the movie (the fact that the babysitter shows up at his birthday party later despite the fact that Baby's family beats her senseless for "molesting" him might be, however), which tells an ostensibly straight story about a social worker who wants to rescue a mentally handicapped man from his abusive family. However the script by Abe Polsky (who also produced) seemingly goes out of its way to make this as insane as possible, tossing in incest, cattle prod abuse, an intense game of darts, Michael Pataki, a school full of disabled children (the movie's ickiest moment, honestly), and a surprise ending in which we learn who the craziest person in the movie really is."

Reflection: I abhor the list-driven nature of movie sites nowadays, but if someone were to compile a list of the films that shockingly have PG ratings, I'd definitely check it out. For a while, *Tourist Trap* was my go-to example, but *The Baby* took its crown and ran pretty far away so that no one could ever catch up to it. Granted, it's not a particularly violent or profane movie, but it's just so GODDAMN DISTURBING that you'd assume it'd get an R on principle, even if the PG-13 was an option to provide a happy medium. It's a bit horror-lite in the traditional sense (it almost ended up in October's list), but few movies will make you as uncomfortable or freaked out.

As for why I was sleepy, I watched it in a hotel room in NY during an all-too-brief visit to the Big Apple for one of my best friends' weddings, where I also caught up with several college pals and even a high school friend, none of whom I had seen since I moved away seven years before. And as is always the case when I visit the east coast, jetlag keeps me awake a few hours later than everyone else, because midnight to them seems like 9pm to me, and in turn, it feels like 6 am (too early!) when it's like 9 am and probably time to get up for whatever it is I flew there for in the first place. So since getting up early to watch my movie was out of the question, I'd usually watch it after midnight, since I wouldn't be tired yet, and get a sort of jump on the day. But I was staying with some friends in their hotel, and didn't want to be a bad guest and wake them up with the blue glow of a horror movie in the middle of the night. Long story short, I didn't sleep much the night before the wedding, and had to watch the movie in between breakfast with friends and going to the ceremony itself (like I said in the intro, I never let stuff like this break my streak). It was also brutally hot that weekend which, along with my fatigue, added to the delirium the film inspired. Good times.

MOVIE #132 - MAY 12th

SATAN'S LITTLE HELPER (2004)
Dir: Jeff Lieberman
HMAD Review Date: July 12, 2008 (DVD)
Genre: Comedic, Slasher
Available from Universal Studios Home Entertainment

Synopsis Based on Fading Memory: A kid thinks he's befriended Satan and asks him to help him get rid of his sister's boyfriend, but "Satan" is actually a serial killer who humors the kid just to get more victims.

Review excerpt:
"There's a scene about halfway through Satan's Little Helper *that delighted me more than any movie I've watched since* Cathy's Curse*. The scene involves "Satan" (whether he actually is or not is never explained) and his eponymous helper running people over with a shopping basket in a parking lot. The kid thinks it's all a game, and gleefully yells "50 points! 100 points" as these poor people (including an old man, a baby, a pregnant woman...) are mowed down. I don't think any of them are actually killed, but it's still a real treat for fans of ridiculous, mean-spirited horror."*

Reflection: Most of my review is negatively charged due to the film's underwhelming ending (better to have a bad first hour and a good final half hour than the other way around), but I'd hate to allow that letdown deny you the insane charms of the film's first 60 minutes, which includes the scene described above and several others that had me cackling like a nut. That the kid thinks all these horrible events are a game lends it a deranged silliness that I haven't seen in too many other films. And believe me, I looked.

Fun fact: Last year, Jeff Lieberman hosted a bonus round at the monthly horror trivia game hosted by Rebekah McKendry (formerly of Fangoria, co-host of Killer POV) here in LA, and our team won thanks to remembering a key fact about this movie, and another one about his killer worm opus *Squirm*. We got all his other ones wrong, but our two correct answers were still enough to win the round - he asked some really tough questions! I forget what we won (not any of his movies, dammit), but it was so cool to see him show up, and we got our victory picture with him at the end of the night. And if you're wondering, yes, my team tends to often do quite well every month – as of this writing we've won more than half of the 30ish games that have been played so far. All the other players actually boo us whenever we win a round! But I'll have my revenge - when this book comes out I'm going to host a bonus round and give a copy to every member of the team with the *least* number correct. That'll teach 'em to know more pointless shit about horror movies!

MOVIE #133 - MAY 13th

THE MAFU CAGE (aka DON'T RING THE DOORBELL) (1978)
Dir: Karen Arthur
HMAD Review Date: September 25, 2012 (Revival screening)
Genre: Psychological, Weird
Available from Scorpion Releasing

Synopsis Based on Fading Memory: Character study of two sisters who had an unusual upbringing, causing one of them to exist in a somewhat feral state.

Review excerpt:
"Both actresses are so good that it never feels like camp; if I were to describe any scene in detail you might think this was one of the most ludicrous, garish movies ever made, but on-screen it always plays very real and even somewhat sad. Both women are victims of a weird upbringing and have just become broken in different ways (it reminded me a bit of *Mysterious Skin* in that regard). It's only because she's the more colorful character that the focus lands on Kane - Grant is just as solid, and without her character's turmoil the movie wouldn't work. Kane's just nuts, but Grant is forced to protect her sister and care for her while trying to have her own life. The consequences of those actions are what give the film's third act its drive; needless to say, it wasn't exactly a stand up and cheer type of ending."

Reflection: This chapter was mostly compiled in September of 2015, specifically during Fantastic Fest, which I haven't been able to attend since my son was born (my wife is shockingly not too keen on me taking off for Texas for the better part of a week to watch crazy movies while she handles the baby alone), so I've been alternating between getting jealous at friends' tweets, and reminiscing about the previous years that I was able to attend. And this remains the only repertory screening I ever watched at the fest; I can never go to the whole thing due to my day job, and so I need to cram in as many of the new movies as possible as it might be the only time I ever get to see them (*Livide* was the first movie I saw at my first Fantastic Fest in 2011 - it's still unreleased in the US). But the other movies during this slot didn't entice me, and my good friend Sam Zimmerman was excited about it, so I made an exception.

And I'm glad I did; I can't remember much about the other movies I saw that day, but this one left a fairly thorough impression on me – I can still remember the layout of the sisters' house, and how the faded 35mm print made the various Los Angeles locations look. I almost feel guilty putting it in this chapter alongside junk like *Dead Sushi* and *Ogroff*, but the fact that two classy and respected actresses (Carol Kane and Lee Grant) would star in a movie this unusual and grim deserves some sort of recognition. Ultimately, whether they're campy or serious, all of the movies in this chapter do share one common thread: they work within the framework (and, for some, limitations) of the horror genre while offering something unlike you've ever seen. I go case by case with remakes, and usually I'd rather see updates of films that were mangled in some way, but this is an exception – I really like this movie a lot and I'd love to see a modern version with two fine actresses. Not only would it give them great roles to play, but it would also remind critics that horror films can be "classy". Plus it's so obscure no one could really get bent out of shape about it and if anything, it'd help promote the original. Everyone wins!

MOVIE #134 - MAY 14th

DETENTION (2011)
Dir: Joseph Kahn
HMAD Review Date: July 28, 2012 (Blu-ray)
Genre: Comedic, Slasher, Weird
Available from Sony Pictures Home Entertainment

Synopsis Based on Fading Memory: A group of students are targeted by a time-traveling killer.

Review excerpt:
"It's got some out of nowhere genre elements, adding to the movie's kitchen sink appeal. But the surprising thing is, except for the guy who has "Fly blood", they all tie together in a satisfying way. Early on we see a Polaroid of what appears to be someone performing a sex act on the school's mascot (a grizzly bear), and through the movie's time travel plot we not only find out its origin, but also get a payoff for another gag involving a character who they meet in detention. And without spoiling the specifics, one character's obsession with the '90s has a nutty explanation that helps solve the central mystery. For a movie that can sound like it was written during an epic coke binge, I was surprised how relatively tight it was, paying off nearly everything despite how random it seemed at first."

Reflection: Director Joseph Kahn is one of those guys who speaks his mind (read: comes off like an asshole) on Twitter and such, so I didn't feel endeared enough to him to check out *Detention* during its brief theatrical run. But when I got the Blu-ray I regretted skipping my big screen chance; the man might be a bit of a dick but he's got a great eye and a firm control over his frame, and at times I was actually somewhat blown away by how well-made and fun the movie was. I'm not a big fan of the hyper-reality aesthetic (*Scott Pilgrim* is the only Edgar Wright movie I don't love), but it works here, and even if it didn't, Kahn gets a great Hoobastank joke out of the deal, which would make any of its flaws forgivable anyway.

Because of all the "stuff" in the movie it might be easy to forget that it's a slasher at all, but Kahn never betrays the folks who came in expecting a traditional body count movie. The kills are gory, with enough practical work to forgive the CG embellishments and, as I always do when this happens, I must point out that my guess as to who the killer was turned out to be incorrect. As a slasher aficionado, nothing makes me happier than actually being surprised at the reveal of who is behind the mask, since it's usually far too easy for me to spot. For that alone I'd give the film a thumbs up, but as I surprisingly enjoyed a lot of its other elements as well, I give this my full endorsement.

MOVIE #135 - MAY 15th

NIGHT TRAIN TO TERROR (1985)
Dir: John Carr, Phillip Marshak
HMAD Review Date: December 11, 2012 (DVD)
Genre: Anthology, Weird
Public domain title, available through several DVD companies

Synopsis Based on Fading Memory: Three unrelated movies get chopped up and re-edited into an anthology about God and the Devil battling over souls while riding a train and listening to a band singing "Dance With Me".

Review excerpt:
"I was on a plane while I watched this. Worse, it was an American Airlines plane, which meant my knees were jammed into the seat in front of me before its occupant even reclined and there was no in-flight progress option like on a Virgin or JetBlue plane, so I had no idea how much of the flight had passed. And since they can't even get those basics right, I had no faith in their Wi-Fi and thus didn't opt to spend 10 bucks for it. If I had done so (and if it had worked), I probably would have looked up some information on the movie and discovered its origin, which is that it's a re-edited trio of movies. In other words, I watched this thinking that its insane approach to storytelling was by design - but I assume its 1985 audience was in the same boat, and thus it was the most fitting and apt way to watch this particular film."

Reflection: If I had my own theater and unlimited access to everything, I'd program a night of the three movies that were cut down in order to fit as anthology segments in this thing. One was called *Scream Your Head Off* and was never finished, but the other two (*Death Wish Club* and *Cataclysm*) are commercially available – in fact I own a copy of the former but never got around to watching it. As I explained in the excerpt, I had no idea what I was in for when I watched this, and simply assumed all of the incoherent nonsense on screen was just how the thing was written. There really is nothing like this goddamn mess of a movie.

I also never thought I'd watch it again, but not only did I get a second go-round, it was on 35mm film! A print was located for an all-night horror fest in 2013, and while I kept dozing off (when I go to these things I let myself sleep through the movies I've seen so I have a better chance of staying awake for the ones I haven't), it was glorious to witness the reaction from unsuspecting folks. By the end of it everyone was singing "Dance With Me" along with the movie, and it was the sort of thing that reminded me of why it's so important to visit your repertory theater as often as possible. The people that frequent such theaters simply love MOVIES, and MOVIEGOING itself, making the whole "good or bad" argument irrelevant for 90 minutes.

But make no mistake, this is pretty bad.

HMAD Fun Fact: 111 movies (not this one, for the record) were deemed "crap", which means a movie with zero redeeming features, a total insult to my time and the horror genre.

MOVIE #136 - MAY 16th

BORN (2007)
Dir: Richard Friedman
HMAD Review Date: August 9, 2009 (DVD)
Genre: Religious, Supernatural
Available from Lionsgate

Synopsis Based on Fading Memory: A woman is raped (off-screen) by her demon brother and becomes impregnated with a little monster that eats people from her belly/vagina.

Review excerpt:
"...the real highlight is Alison Brie as the heroine. She comes across as a female Nic Cage (Wicker Man variant) in her "possessed" scenes, where her demon baby takes over her mind and makes her deliver horrid one-liners ("Rub a dub-dub, clean the dolly in the tub!" she shrieks as she metal scrubs a woman to death) and bug the eyes out of her head while killing people. She even borderline rapes a dude before the demon thing eats half of the guy's babymaker off (we see the head and some of the shaft lying in a pool of blood on the floor - thank you, movie), and makes out with a female friend for a bit before ripping her head off and putting it in her purse. If there is a subtle moment in this movie, it's there purely by accident."

Reflection: If you follow me on Twitter (and haven't muted me in turn), you'd know that apart from horror and busting Ryan Turek's balls, one of my favorite things to tweet about is *Community*, the Dan Harmon-created sitcom that's ostensibly about wacky folks at a community college. The show was on my radar early on thanks to my undying love and dedication to Chevy Chase, an actor I've been a fan of for literally as long as I can remember (my oldest memory is watching his film *Seems Like Old Times* with my dad). But thanks to *Born*, which I saw about a month or so before the show debuted, I had TWO reasons to be excited, because I was instantly impressed (and yes, smitten) with Alison Brie due to her astonishingly go-for-broke performance here. I never watched *Mad Men*, so this insane movie was actually my introduction to her. So being that this was all I knew of her, when you see the movie you'll appreciate how amusing it was for me to see the early *Community* episode where her character didn't know what a penis looked like.

Fun fact: I hosted a *Community* trivia game in LA in 2014, and since it happened in October I did a category on the horror/thriller movies that the cast had done (much to the chagrin of one girl, who was legit angry that I'd ask something impossible like "Which cast member once played the invisible man?" instead of a basic question like "What color shirt did Joel McHale have on in episode 221?"). Many teams did pretty well on the round (they were fairly easy questions, I thought), but not a single group knew the answer to "Alison Brie plays a woman with a demon baby in what 2007 film?" I was crushed.

MOVIE #137 - MAY 17th

THE ANTICHRIST [L'ANTICRISTO] (1974)
Dir: Alberto De Martino
HMAD Review Date: September 2, 2008 (DVD)
Genre: Possession, Religious
Available from Lionsgate

Synopsis Based on Fading Memory: An *Exorcist* rip-off, but Italian!

Review excerpt:
"...late in the film, a man tumbles down a giant flight of stairs, and you can actually see the guy making himself elongate his fall by pushing and flipping himself over when he gets "stuck" on a few steps along the way. The flashbacks (our protagonist is the reincarnation of a devil worshipping woman) are also pretty deliriously fun, as you get guys with goat heads chanting, lots of "Priest! Bastard!!!" type yelling, etc. And even though it's not laugh out loud funny, I was tickled by the fact that the title appears twice in the opening credits, just in case you forgot, I guess."

Reflection: YOU bought this book, and for that I thank you, but I hope there are 9,999 other people like you, because then there will be a follow-up tome, one that will take much more research and time but will be almost entirely new material. I don't want to give a better/faster writer the idea, but I will say it involves these kinds of movies, and this one would be one of the more prominent examples. Like, if I were to write a book about the history of '80s slasher movies, this would be the equivalent of *Friday the 13th*.

Anyway, this is a nutty, must-see movie if you like *Exorcist* rip-offs. In addition to the even filthier dialogue from our possessed girl, it's just chock-full of weird and silly moments that are par for the course with '70s Italian horror. It's just (in my experience) kind of the best example of such things; if Criterion wanted to choose a film to represent batshit '70s possession fare, they might look at this. Unfortunately, those overpriced but respectable folks opted to release the obnoxious Lars Von Trier film that shares a name with this one (minus a "The"), so that's not likely to happen as it will just make things more confusing. If you see a kid fall out of a window and Willem Dafoe's penis, you've gotten the wrong film! One that certainly wouldn't be in this book!

MOVIE #138 - MAY 18th

KILLER'S MOON (1978)
Dir: Alan Birkinshaw
HMAD Review Date: February 9, 2013 (Streaming)
Genre: Slasher, Weird
Available from Kino Lorber Films

Synopsis Based on Fading Memory: A bunch of escaped mental patients harass a group of girls.

Review excerpt:
"...this is definitely one of the most unique slasher films of the era, in that it's never particularly scary (or violent) but it always feels a bit "off", and would be a fine choice for an all-nighter horror fest, slotted toward the end when the audience is starting to get kind of loopy themselves and would thus be in the perfect mindset for the peculiarities it offers. Much like its killers, who think they're in a dream (they think the two male guys are doctors - one of them even gets a bit upset that a "doctor" tells him to go to hell), the audience can assume some of the weirder bits that you just don't see too often (usually for good reason) were part of a shared dream. And then after they could talk about it in a state of confusion: "Did we just see a three-legged dog?" "Did one of the killers just eat a raw egg for no reason?" Etc."

Reflection: I did my best to avoid too many movies that have rape scenes in this book, because I aimed for more "fun" horror and that's obviously the polar opposite of a good time, but I had to include this one because it was so peculiar. At times it almost seems to be parodying slasher movie tropes, but since it's from 1978 that'd be a pretty neat trick as most slasher movies didn't exist yet, and the ones that were around weren't plentiful enough to comment on. So my apologies for suggesting that you watch a movie with this sort of stuff (not as explicit as *Last House on The Left* or *I Spit On Your Grave*, at least) but the rest of it is right in line with the theme of this chapter.

Funny thing about that – I am forever getting this title confused with *Bloody Moon*, the 1981 Jess Franco slasher. There's an alternate title for that one that's simply "Raped College Girl", which is baffling since there isn't a rape scene in that film at all, let alone one important enough to name the film after. So that's certainly not helping my confusion, which has resulted in my owning two copies of *Bloody Moon* and zero copies of this film, which I actually prefer. And then there's *Burning Moon*, which I still haven't seen and occasionally also get mixed up. So here's my plea to young filmmakers out there: don't put "Moon" in your horror movie title unless it's the first word. Thank you.

MOVIE #139 - MAY 19th

LITTLE DEATHS (2011)
Dir: Sean Hogan, Andrew Parkinson, Simon Rumley
HMAD Review Date: December 7, 2011 (DVD)
Genre: Anthology
Available from Image Entertainment

Synopsis Based on Fading Memory: An anthology focusing on some really strange people and events – but it's surprisingly fun and even upbeat!

Review excerpt:
"What I dug the most about the film is that I had no idea where any of the stories were going when they started, which is rare for an anthology. Even the first tale, by far the most conventional, I figured would be more of a straight up survival type thriller, not anything supernatural. There's a bit of a plot hole in it (can't explain without spoiling it), but it's forgivable – better a potential oversight in a unique plot than a logically sound story that you've seen a zillion times. Even better, the film just improved as it went, with the first story being the "weakest" and the last the best. You can usually expect that one anthology segment will be much less satisfying than the others, but here the quality is fairly consistent."

Reflection: There are only two anthologies in this book, and one of them is the month's bad movie, making this the only "legit" recommend. It had been on my radar for a while before I finally saw it, and it did not disappoint in the slightest. I still smile when I think about the climax of the third segment and how strangely uplifting it is considering the storyline (which I wouldn't dare spoil here).

The lack of anthology recommendations kind of saddens me, because I've been championing their return for quite some time (if you poke around on YouTube you can even find a mini-documentary on the sub-genre featuring yours truly). And they *have* made a comeback in recent years, thanks to the *V/H/S* and *ABCs of Death* films (not to mention Mike Dougherty's *Trick 'r Treat*)... but they're all limited releases! I don't think any of them have gone wide, which is annoying, but also understandable. I might have even said this on the doc I just mentioned: anthology films have a big hurdle to clear when it comes to marketing. Audiences need something to latch on to when they see a trailer – Liam Neeson wants to find his daughter or stop a plane from blowing up or whatever, and boom. We get it. We buy our ticket. But anthologies are throwing a bunch of characters that never seem to share a scene together at you, and the narrative is hazy at best, so it's hard to get on board. Most agree that *Death Proof* and *Planet Terror* would have been hits on their own, but the confusing two movie ads for "Grindhouse" just turned folks off. And that's with Quentin Tarantino and huge stars behind it! So I may hate that I always have to see these things on DVD or in crappy little theaters by myself during their one-week release, but sadly I know perfectly well why it'll probably always be that way. It's a shame.

MOVIE #140 - MAY 20th

THE UNSEEN (1980)
Dir: Danny Steinmann
HMAD Review Date: November 12, 2009 (DVD)
Genre: Mutant
Available from Code Red/Scorpion

Synopsis Based on Fading Memory: Some girls stay at a hotel run by a weird family.

Review excerpt:
"The writers do a good job of balancing the stories of the victims (three women) and the crazy family, particularly the father, played by Cuckoo's Nest's Sydney Lassick (who has since passed away, as have two other cast members out of the eight in the film. Curse?). There's a scene just before the halfway mark where we learn that his wife is in fact his sister, information dealt to us by the "ghost" (psychologically speaking) of his father, and Lassick finds the perfect line between crazy and simply pathetic. And Stephen Furst as the titular character delivers a pretty brave performance; he's caked in fat mutant makeup and wearing a diaper, and his role primarily requires him to roll around on a dirty floor, drink from a puddle on said dirty floor, smack himself in the head, and groan/laugh in typical mentally challenged movie character fashion."

Reflection: This is actually the most normal movie in the month, but if you're an *Animal House* fan (you probably are, since everyone is) then there might be nothing more bizarre than the sight of Stephen "Flounder" Furst as a giant man-baby, something I'm almost positive influenced the design of Bobo and L'il Debbull in *Nothing But Trouble*. Plus Lassick is one of those actors that's always a bit "off", and at this point in his career he wasn't doing a lot of horror (his only previous genre credit was *Carrie*; later in his career he'd slum more often with junk like *Curse 2: The Bite*), so it was fun to watch him chew scenery as the Jim Siedow stand-in for a minor *Texas Chainsaw* wannabe.

Otherwise it's fairly grounded; the second weirdest thing about it is that it's directed by Danny Steinmann, who made the sleaziest (and most underrated!) *Friday the 13th* movie (that would be *Part V*) and the notorious *Savage Streets*. This is probably his least known work, which is funny because in some ways it's his most mainstream (yes, more so than the fifth entry in a mega popular franchise). He passed away in 2012, but before he did he offered an interview to the Stone Cold Crazy blog that explains why he vanished after *Friday V* – it's pretty damn sad, if you ask me; just bad luck followed by worse luck, over and over. He will be missed.

MOVIE #141 - MAY 21st

THE SENTINEL (1977)
Dir: Michael Winner
HMAD Review Date: September 4, 2009 (DVD)
Genre: Religious, Supernatural
Available from Scream Factory

Synopsis Based on Fading Memory: It's *The Exorcist* but with a woman in her twenties instead of a little girl, and a cast of everyone!

Review excerpt:
"A nightmare sequence is incredibly realistic, in that it actually feels (and is even presented as) a dream, not some ultra-real nonsense that is REVEALED to be a dream, something that annoys me more every time it is used. And even if the cast is too large, the novelty value of seeing so many folks looking so young keeps it feeling short; I actually thought the film was less than 80 minutes. Time goes by fast when you're being distracted by a still young and fully naked Beverly D'Angelo. And Burgess Meredith tops even his *Manitou* performance here, playing a whacked out neighbor of Christina Raines'. He is introduced with a bird on his shoulder and a cat by his side, and then begins to confuse Eisenhower and Herbert Hoover. Later he throws the cat a birthday party. And since the plot is wacky anyway, he gets to deliver some nonsensical dialogue in the climax, also a delight. He actually reminded me a bit of his *Foul Play* character (eccentric pet-loving neighbor of the heroine), something that doesn't bother me in the slightest."

Reflection: This movie almost didn't make the book, because it's not as weird as the others so it kind of stuck out. But I needed a more well-known title, and the cross section on the Venn diagram of "weird horror movies" and "well-known horror movies" is kind of small, so it slipped back in! It qualifies mainly due to the unusual (and somewhat off-putting) decision of director Michael Winner to cast people with deformities as a bunch of freaks, which gives the movie a slight whiff of taboo appeal. Or just "what the hell were they thinking?" appeal.

Also it's got what HAS to be the actual on-screen killing of a parakeet. Plus, Christopher Walken and Jeff Goldblum are in it and they're kind of the most normal characters, making it special in that unique sort of way. I'd really love to read the book that it's based on someday, because the movie is so jam-packed with characters that only appear in a scene or two – those folks *had* to have more to do in the source material. So in a way it qualifies as weird because you'll see so many recognizable people with almost nothing to do. Additionally, it's the rare post-*Exorcist* flick that seems just as influenced by the studio wannabes as the Italian ones, adding to its unique flavor.

MOVIE #142 - MAY 22nd

NIGHT OF DEATH [LA NUIT DE LA MORT!] (1980)
Dir: Raphaël Delpard
HMAD Review Date: April 1, 2010 (DVD)
Genre: Cannibal, Weird
Available from Synapse Films

Synopsis Based on Fading Memory: The residents of an old folks' home are actually cannibals, eating people to stay young.

Review excerpt:
"The residents are pretty kooky, so they're always doing odd things, laughing for no reason, etc. Delightful. And apart from the cannibalism (the old folks eat people to stay young), there is also a loose but still intriguing subplot about a serial killer who stabs his victims with gold pins through the neck, which sounds like it was stolen from some unseen Argento movie. The identity of the killer isn't too hard to figure out, and I wish it was a little more prominent in the movie (most of it plays out via newspaper headlines), but it's a welcome diversion, and adds to the film's unusual plotting."

Reflection: I really wanted to have a month of French horror, as it's my favorite foreign supplier of genre fare, but I came up a few movies short. So I just found places for nearly all of the titles elsewhere in the book, thus ensuring I could still recommend them. Everyone wins! I actually don't recall a lot about this one, which is insane when you consider the concept, but my review is chock-full of ringing endorsements. So either I made up the review for a very strange April Fool's joke (note the review date), or my memory should be checked. Probably the latter.

In all seriousness, part of why I wanted to do this book is to ward off anyone from doing what I did, which is watching/reviewing a horror movie every single day for over six years (that's over 2200 days in a row, math wizards). And believe me, it's not because I'd like to lay claim to the record, if that even qualifies as a record. No, it's because it's doing a disservice to movies like this, which is (per my review) quite good, but also the 1300th or so of 2,500, and the brain can't possibly retain anything of use when it's being overloaded like that. On top of the sheer volume, you have to consider that I watched a lot of these in the same spot (my couch) and even at the same time of the day (after work). So these memories blend together even more, and become useless. Ideally, I'd have really strong memories of these 365 movies and completely forget the ones that sucked, but that's not how the brain works. Someone once said I had an unfair advantage for horror trivia because of HMAD, but it's actually the opposite – I don't retain much at all from all this stuff, and the time I spent watching so many forgettable titles could have been spent re-watching the movies that are actually referenced at trivia! My team may win a lot but it's because we have a good team – if I was playing those games solo I doubt I'd even place, let alone win. In other words, don't watch a half dozen anonymous DTV killer scarecrow movies, because it won't do you any good. Watch the movies in this book, and then watch *The Shining* or *Dawn of the Dead* again. Then you'll be a horror trivia champ!

MOVIE #143 - MAY 23rd

DARK FLOORS (2008)
Dir: Pete Riski, Alan Smithee
HMAD Review Date: November 17, 2008 (DVD)
Genre: "Christ, fuckin... all of em"
Available from Lionsgate

Synopsis Based on Fading Memory: Some folks are trapped in a hospital and menaced by monsters, played by the members of a silly rock band named Lordi.

Review excerpt:
"Lordi's combined screentime is probably less than 10 minutes, so what do we get instead? Christ, what DON'T we get? Ghosts, zombies, monsters... and maybe it got edited or I just missed it, but since the end credits point out that no animals were harmed, I guess there were some rabid dogs or whatever in there too. Plus, it all starts when the elevator breaks down, so it's kind of a Breakdown/Survival movie too. And then there's all the supernatural stuff. None of it is ever explained, and on top of all that, the movie is ultimately in the vein of Jacob's Ladder, Silent Hill, *and most closely,* The Sickhouse."

Reflection: It's been over seven years since I saw this movie and I STILL cue up "Beast Loose In Paradise" on my iPod fairly often – it's just a delightfully cheesy song (if I was nine when I saw this movie, I'd probably consider it just as essential as *Shocker* and its soundtrack). My review spoils the film's twist, which I won't do here, but I will stress that if I did, it wouldn't matter much as the movie doesn't really make any sense anyway (note the genre listing above). But my review neglected to mention something I'll remedy here – one of the stars of the movie is William Hope, aka Gorman from *Aliens*! He mostly does voice acting these days (including different characters in *Alien* games, oddly enough), so it's always nice to see him on screen.

It was also nice to see a (short-lived) revival of the rock horror movie, of which the '80s gave us plenty with movies like *Trick or Treat, Monster Dog*, and others. You'd get a rocker looking to do something different, and he certainly wouldn't be cast in a Merchant Ivory costume drama or the like, so he'd make a horror movie. Slash is producing a few nowadays (such as the not-that-bad *Nothing Left to Fear*), but he's not appearing in them, so it's not quite the same. If you skipped the credits you wouldn't know Slash was involved in *Nothing Left to Fear*, but it's not like you can watch *Kiss Meets the Phantom of the Park* and miss the fact that Kiss is in it. Unfortunately, bands like Lordi aren't exactly in vogue these days, so there isn't a lot of potential for this sub-genre to thrive. Like anyone wants to see Imagine Dragons fighting actual dragons?

P.S. I have no idea who the actual Alan Smithee is here. If you're in the dark, Alan Smithee is the name given to a director who wishes to have his name taken off the final version for whatever reason. Usually it's known by the time a movie comes out (such as *Hellraiser: Bloodline*, attributed to Smithee but any horror fan knows it was Kevin Yagher and Joe Chappelle), but I Googled for a while and came up with nothing. Anyone know?

MOVIE #144 - MAY 24th

HOUSE [HAUSU] (1977)
Dir: Nobuhiko Ôbayashi
HMAD Review Date: March 13, 2010 (Revival screening)
Genre: Haunted House, Weird
Available from Criterion Collection

Synopsis Based on Fading Memory: "Meow, meow meow meow"

Review excerpt:
"If I had to "pitch" the movie to someone, I would probably say it was David Lynch's version of Evil Dead 2, or maybe The Grudge as written by James Joyce."

Reflection: Nothing, literally NOTHING can prepare you for this movie. I don't even want to spoil a single thing. I'll just point out that this – THIS! – is one of the only movies in the entire book that has been released via the Criterion Collection, and leave it at that.

Wait, I'll leave it at this: *House* screens somewhat frequently at revival theaters, so if you don't want to spend 40 bucks on an overpriced Criterion disc, keep an eye on your local repertory theater's schedule. It's a blast with a crowd, obviously, and since rep theaters are usually cheaper than multiplexes you can probably take your entire family for less than what Criterion will charge you. I have little love for that brand; I appreciate what they do, but their prices are ridiculous (they frequently have 50% off sales, presumably to be competitive with the normal prices of everyone else), and the lemming-like following they've amassed rubs me the wrong way. I mean, there are people who buy everything they put out and arrange them on their shelf by SPINE NUMBER. What kind of insanity is that? Like, you're in the mood for a movie in the 20s? Pretentious nonsense.

(Mostly I'm just pissed that they never ported their *Armageddon* DVD to Blu-ray.)

MOVIE #145 - MAY 25th

TERROR CIRCUS (1974)
Dir: Alan Rudolph
HMAD Review Date: December 23, 2009 (DVD)
Genre: Mutant, Survival
Available from Media Blasters, Inc.

Synopsis Based on Fading Memory: A guy kidnaps girls and chains them up in his barn for a circus.

Review excerpt:
"First and foremost on my list of things that I liked about it is Andrew Prine's performance as Andre, the crazed "ringleader" of the (occasional) titular circus. From my perspective, he was sort of the Tom Jane of his day; a solid actor who could play villains as easily as heroes, and regardless of the film's content, would always find a way to play the character as a bit "off", though not in a flamboyant way like Christopher Walken or Nic Cage. They even have a similar physical appearance, and while I don't really think casting look-alikes is the best way to go about a remake, I think the casting folks for any Prine film that gets remade should look to Jane first."

Reflection: A fun game to play whenever an actor says that "____ is the one film I regret doing" or "____ is the worst movie I've ever done!" is to look at their filmography and pick out movies that you think are worse. It's a stupid thing to do, because we don't know why actors say that (for all we know they had miserable experiences on set, or being away filming caused them to miss something important) and taste is subjective and all, but it's an amusing game, regardless. So when I heard Andrew Prine say that this was the one film he wished he'd never made, I have to wonder how *Riding With Death* or *The Evil* were somehow better experiences or films in his eyes (don't try to throw *Lords of Salem* under the bus either – if that had come out during the eligible period it would be in this book). *Terror Circus* is a solid entry in the kidnap horror sub-genre, and he's terrific in it! Take it back, Prine!

And yes, that is THE Alan Rudolph, who worked on a lot of Robert Altman films and is probably best known as the director of things like *Mrs. Parker and the Vicious Circle* and the Demi Moore/Bruce Willis thriller *Mortal Thoughts*, instead of B-horror stuff like this. In fact *Terror Circus* was Rudolph's second and last horror movie, after his debut *Premonition* (which I've never seen, but as it is a psychedelic early '70s horror I am sure I would hate it). He's had kind of a weird career where he goes through phases – in the '80s he made a lot of musical comedies, and in the '90s he was doing a lot of thrillers. Now he's seemingly retired; he averaged a film every two years from 1972 to 2002, but hasn't worked on anything since (not too surprising since just about everything he made was a flop). Oh well.

HMAD Fun Fact: Horror Movie A Day "officially" had its millionth hit in December of 2009, though that milestone was probably reached much earlier as the site was online for months before I added a traffic counter in the summer of 2007.

MOVIE #146 - MAY 26th

THE NIGHT EVELYN CAME OUT OF THE GRAVE (1971)
Dir: Emilio Miraglia
HMAD Review Date: May 5, 2011 (DVD)
Genre: Giallo, Psychological
Public domain title, available through several DVD companies

Synopsis Based on Fading Memory: A guy is being driven insane by ghosts. One of them presumably named Evelyn.

Review excerpt:
"It's pretty entertaining throughout, especially since it keeps switching gears. I'm almost tempted to watch that 82 minute version now – the movie is dangerously close to incoherent even in its complete form; without 20 minutes of footage it must seem like entirely different movies spliced together. For starters, our hero is actually a murderer; while there are a couple of kills we suspect him of that turn out to be the work of [redacted]*, there is no denying that he is the killer in the opening scene, taking home a hooker, whipping her for a bit (part of the sex), and then stabbing her. He then pays his groundskeeper (also his former brother-in-law) 30 pounds not to say anything. Our hero!"*

Reflection: My review is curiously titled *The Night Evelyn Came Out Of HER Grave*; I'm not sure why I mixed that up or (even stranger) why no one berated me for a harmless mistake. This IS the internet, is it not? Anyway, this movie isn't so much "weird" as it is "pointlessly convoluted", which is what makes it fun. Once all of the twists have been revealed, it's great fun to think about everything that happened before within that context, and realize that A. it makes zero sense and B. the villain would be able to beat you at chess with a single move, as he's just that good at planning ahead and anticipating his opponent's actions. Needless to say, it's an Italian movie.

Final note – please check your copies before renting or purchasing; find out if it's one of the good releases or not. As the movie has fallen in and out of copyright (and is foreign, which always has its own unique problems with regards to censorship or "let's cut it down for the drive-in crowd" thinking), there are any number of versions out there – you want it to be around 100 minutes and preferably at the right aspect ratio of 2.35:1. The movie is hard enough to follow as it is, so you don't need it cut down (and its image nearly sliced in half) to make it even more difficult to puzzle through. Though, then again, that might be fun. Ignore what I said. Find the most hacked-up version possible and let me know how it was.

MOVIE #147 - MAY 27th

A NIGHT TO DISMEMBER (1983)
Dir: Doris Wishman
HMAD Review Date: July 3, 2008 (DVD)
Genre: Slasher, Weird
Available from Elite Entertainment

Synopsis Based on Fading Memory: Another "inheritance scheme via scary movie tropes" thing.

Review excerpt:
"...[it peaks] at the halfway mark when the narrator describes a dream sequence thusly: "Vicky felt as though someone faceless was making love to her in bright flashing colors that were changing from one second to the next." Of course, this is precisely what we are seeing, which leads me to believe that they stuck some guy in a booth and had him narrate whatever he felt like saying as this incoherent and mute film played before his hopefully astonished eyes. And if you wonder how the narrator (a character in the film) could possibly know what she was dreaming, fear not – he even explains that. At the very end of the film, as a sort of cinematic P.S., he informs us that every single character in the film kept detailed diaries, which he presumably stole."

Reflection: Some of the movies in this book stick out in my mind due to their behind-the-scenes history (like *Devil Times Five*), but this is, I think, the only one that I remember more about the commentary track than the feature itself. If shown a frame from the film I'd never identify it in a million years, but I can STILL hear director Doris Wishman's voice in my head, yelling at the guy who joined her on the commentary. If you listened to *Serial*, she kinda sounds like that angry lawyer lady ("Did! You! STEP OUT?"), and it alone makes me want to rent the disc again just to listen to her. Normally if it's been too long I will watch the movie again before diving into its commentary, but in this case the movie is mostly narrated anyway so it's not like there's much dialogue to miss.

P.S. If you don't know anything about Wishman, look her up. She is what you might call a "character", and what I might call a "delightful loon". She made a lot of adult films, many of which she wrote herself (this is one of the very few movies in her filmography that she *didn't* write, in fact), and her filmmaking career reportedly began as a way for her to pass the time after her husband died (she didn't want to sit around and grieve). She also has more pseudonyms than the average Italian horror filmmaker, and her last film before she passed away in 2002 was called *Dildo Heaven*. That is awesome.

MOVIE #148 - MAY 28th

JOHN DIES AT THE END (2012)
Dir: Don Coscarelli
HMAD Review Date: November 3, 2012 (Festival screening)
Genre: Comedic, Monster, Weird
Available from Magnolia Home Entertainment

Synopsis Based on Fading Memory: A slacker dude gets tangled up in a pretty batshit conspiracy involving monsters, other dimensions, and Paul Giamatti.

Review excerpt:
"I can't wait to see it again. It's almost exhaustive at times, but not in a way that annoyed me like Scott Pilgrim *did. Maybe because monsters and aliens and cool character actors like Clancy Brown and Daniel Roebuck are more up my alley than whiny Canadian emo kids, but I never once felt that the constant STUFF being tossed at us was keeping me from really connecting to it. I mean, sure, the film's sarcastic, druggy tone obviously meant I wouldn't be too sad about anything (especially with a title that promises the death of its next-to-main character), but I still enjoyed going on the ride, unlike* Pilgrim *where after 40 minutes I felt I had seen enough."*

Reflection: Confession – I do not nor have I ever smoked pot. I'm allergic to cigarette smoke and even though I'm sure it's different I just always assumed I'd be allergic to pot smoke too, and just never bothered (and now I'm too old – does anyone try pot for the first time when they're 35?). Plus I figure I'm lazy and weird enough without using a drug that makes you lazy and weird. So, somewhat needless to say, I'm not a big fan of drug humor – *Cheech & Chong, Half Baked, Harold & Kumar*... these things do little for me. But throw in some monsters and all the other weird shit in this movie, and the drug jokes are less important in the long run!

That said, I can't imagine how entertaining this movie would be to a horror fan who likes to get high beforehand. From the brilliant opening scene on, this movie just constantly put a smile on my face, and I stand by my review's claim that it's Coscarelli's best film since the original *Phantasm*. I started reading the book it was based on, and it was entertaining, but I never finished it – it just kept making me want to watch the movie again. I mean, how can mere WORDS provide anything as amazing as the sight of a meat-monster? A practical one at that?

MOVIE #149 - MAY 29th

THE OTHER HELL (aka GUARDIAN OF HELL) [L'ALTRO INFERNO] (1981)
Dir: Bruno Mattei
HMAD Review Date: April 13, 2009 (DVD)
Genre: Supernatural
Available from Shriek Show

Synopsis Based on Fading Memory: Someone is killing nuns, dogs are eating a guy's hand... OK I'm not gonna lie, all I remember about this one is what I'm reading in my own excerpt below.

Review excerpt:
"Beyond the complete disregard for real world logic, it's a fun movie. Nuns are eviscerated, dogs eat a guy's hand, the devil is represented as a blinking red light, the bad nun has a full-blown mad scientist's laboratory (complete with beakers filled with bright green and red fluids), and a priest is immolated. Someone's got issues, and I enjoy seeing them try to work them out. And the ending seems to suggest that 95% of the way through the first draft, writer Claudio Fragasso took in a viewing of Zombi *and decided to work some undead elements into his script without bothering to rewrite the previous 80 pages. Again, none of this is necessarily a bad thing. The Goblin score is also terrific, though it doesn't quite fit with the film at times (I wasn't surprised to learn it was recycled from another film)."*

Reflection: If I had to do HMAD all over again, I'd definitely cut back on all the anonymous Syfy-like monster movies and zero budget indies from budget packs and try to see more films from infamous filmmakers like Bruno Mattei. This was my first Mattei film, and it wasn't really long into my tenure (a little over two years), but I neglected to catch up. I think I only saw two or three of his others before calling it a day, but he has made over fifty films. Yet I probably saw about ten Asylum mockbusters directed by the same guy I didn't like anyway. If you ever plan to copy me and do this every day for years on end, I highly encourage that you be rich and can just buy movies off of Amazon rather than leave it up to Netflix Instant and whatever's actually on the shelf at Blockbuster (or Redbox now) to supply your movies. You'll see more of what you want to see and less filler.

But even more limited than my experience with Mattei is my exposure to nunsploitation films such as this – this was the only one. Granted, it's not the most expansive sub-genre (IMDb has about 20 under horror, including *Haxan* which I wouldn't consider a qualifying entry), but I should have at least found a second one, if only to have something to compare *The Other Hell* to. This might be the worst nunsploitation movie ever made and here I am telling you it's the one to see! Ideally, HMAD would have been perfectly balanced with regards to the sub-genres (OK, I would have still watched more slashers), but due to availability, budget and, yes, my own lack of planning, it didn't work out that way. So that's why I've only seen one nunsploitation movie but at least a dozen about blood-soaked real estate scams.

MOVIE #150 - MAY 30th

THIS NIGHT I WILL POSSESS YOUR CORPSE (1967)
Dir: José Mojica Marins
HMAD Review Date: December 14, 2008 (DVD)
Genre: Hero Killer, Supernatural
Available from Fantoma

Synopsis Based on Fading Memory: Coffin Joe returns to continue his quest to produce a male heir and convince everyone within earshot that religion is terrible.

Review excerpt:
"Whereas in the first film his hatred of religion was more of a glorified character quirk than anything, it's pretty much front and center here. You can't ask this guy for the time without him ranting about how religion is for morons and how neither heaven nor hell exists. It actually gets a bit tiresome as the film goes on (it's 105 minutes long); it's as if no one told José Mojica Marins that spending so much energy putting something down is just as annoying as preaching it. [However] there's a lot more violence, mostly at the hands (legs?) of spiders and such, so there's something."

Reflection: This is actually the second film in the Coffin Joe "trilogy" (there are a couple options for the third one; my pick will show up later in this book), but you don't really need to see the first to know what's going on. This is the better of the two films – the acting is just as spotty as the original but everything else has improved, and it gets more into Joe's character, particularly his hatred of religion (which, as mentioned, can get repetitive). It's a uniquely mean-spirited series of films, and definitely one of the most out-there franchises I ever came across. I always meant to check out a couple of the other Joe films, but their availability tends to be spotty in the US.

And be sure to watch the bonus interview with Marins if you can – he explains that actors complain about getting their fingers mangled with pliers, which is why he uses amateurs. He's not being glib; it's legitimately how he feels. You know how when you get a Blu-ray or DVD from a studio and there's a warning like "The views on the bonus features are those of the participants and do not reflect those of the studio" or anyone else they're associated with? You won't find them on the first couple years' worth of DVDs, I assure you – it's interviews like this that probably inspired that warning. A hero, Marins is.

MOVIE #151 - MAY 31st

ONE-EYED MONSTER (2008)
Dir: Adam Fields
HMAD Review Date: August 30, 2012 (DVD)
Genre: Comedic, Monster, Weird
Available from Liberation Entertainment

Synopsis Based on Fading Memory: A porno film crew is menaced by Ron Jeremy's monster penis. Literally. His cock has detached and has turned into a monster.

Review excerpt:
"...the biggest laughs surround Jeremy's legacy in the genre, like when an older gentleman who appears to be a clueless movie fan admits he lost a bet with his mother about the length of Jeremy's penis. And the science guy theorizes that the reason the meteor/alien/whatever has infected Jeremy is because "50% of what we beam into space via satellite is porn, and Ron appears in 50% of them!" See, the alien wants to reproduce, and who better than the man who has had more sexual encounters than probably any other living male? And again, all of this is played completely straight, no different than the people in a slasher trying to explain why the killer is after them. It really works."

Reflection: As I mention in the full review, I've actually seen another movie about a killer penis (Frank Henenlotter's *Bad Biology*), so I'm not being a wiseass when I say this is the best killer penis movie I've seen. There actually is a spectrum on which to judge them! And this was during the final year of HMAD's run, where I was pretty burned out on stupid horror movies – the fact that I mostly enjoyed this one should count for something, I think.

Even more noteworthy: I'm not a Jeremy apologist. I usually roll my eyes when he shows up in a horror movie and makes jokes about his regular job, but I found this to be pretty amusing. As for what makes it "weird" – the fact that they play it straight gives it a strange vibe at times, as if a detached monster penis was no different or unusual a threat than a wild animal or something. If everyone was mugging and playing to the cheap seats, this movie wouldn't be offbeat – it'd just be unbearable. When it comes to stuff like this, I find the movies that play it straight to be infinitely funnier (and thus better) than those that wink at the camera and all but pause for the audience to laugh. And that's what I expected given the cast and plot, but the fact that they went about it as if this were a standard monster movie – and never lost track of that approach – is refreshing in its oddness.

So of course, that's why it's here in the last slot of the month, leading up to next month's theme of traditional monster movies. It might not be as weird as some of the others, but that's precisely why I enjoyed it – it was just weird *enough*. That said, I should point out that of all 12 months this was the only one I sought out advice from a few friends in narrowing my choices down, to make sure that nothing that WASN'T weird enough got through (as it turns out, some of my options were weirder in my head than they were in reality). This one stayed in more for the bizarre premise than its execution, and for those who have been watching everything, this should be a good way to readjust you back to traditional storytelling.

Anyway, I hope your mind has been properly melted by this month's picks! Good or bad, they all gave me something to write about, and that was the whole point of the site – more movies like this and I might have gone to 3000 reviews before quitting!

JUNE – MONSTERS & "MONSTERS"

ARTIST: ERIC SHONBORN

In June of 1975, the world was blessed with the arrival of *Jaws*, one of the greatest films of all time (and considered to be the first summer blockbuster). It spawned a million imitators, many of them bad, but it just so happens that I found a month's worth of monster/giant ___ movies that – while not as great as *Jaws* – rise above the level of your average Syfy flick. Plus it's funny to see how many different animals and things got tossed into the same basic template (*Jaws* but with a dog, *Jaws* but with a bear, *Jaws* but with a car...).

In case you skipped over the genre glossary at the top of this book, I want to make sure you all know how/why I differentiate between "monster" and "predator" movies. *Jaws* is often considered a monster movie, but it's not one, as far as I'm concerned. To me a monster implies something that probably won't exist in the real world – a mutated science experiment gone awry, an alien beast of some kind – those are MONSTERS. Otherwise, as in the case of *Jaws*, it's just a fish – perhaps a bit bigger than what you or I might see, but unless there's a toxic waste spill or something to explain it, they're not monsters. "Animal" seemed too basic (and wouldn't count for things like fish or insects), so I called these movies "Predator" movies. Make sense? No? Eh.

Since so many of the following films are basically doing *Jaws*, I wanted to reduce the repetitiveness, and therefore all 30 movies have a different predator/monster as the villain. As a result, this has increased the number of "movies you probably heard of" for this month, because there isn't a good obscure killer whale movie that I know of, for one example, so it was either use more common movies or repeat monsters. But, still, they're not exactly even *Jaws 2* level famous, so there should still be plenty of discoveries for you. And unless you've taken my personal advice sometime over the past six years, I can almost guarantee you haven't seen...

MOVIE #152 - JUNE 1st

OF UNKNOWN ORIGIN (1983)
Dir: George P. Cosmatos
HMAD Review Date: March 29, 2009 (DVD)
Genre: Predator
Available from Warner Home Video

Synopsis Based on Fading Memory: Fading memory my ass! I can remember every frame of this gem (it's about Peter Weller fighting a rat).

Review excerpt:
"It's always down to Weller and the rat, which is giant enough to be threatening but not giant enough to make the movie feel silly. That's not to say that the movie isn't humorous - on the contrary, it's pretty damn funny... but intentionally so. Weller more or less spends the entire movie alone, talking to himself, and he's got some great lines throughout (when the rat chews out the electricity about an hour or so into the film, he mutters "I was wondering when you were gonna get around to that..."), and there are some terrific sight gags as well. It's never set up or foreshadowed, so when Weller is chased by the rat into his bedroom and he dives onto a newly installed hammock, I laughed out loud. And even though it's slightly obvious, I couldn't help but grin when he grabs a copy of Moby Dick *to pound the ceiling where the rat is chewing away."*

Reflection: If not for the birth of my beloved son a few months earlier, my favorite moment of 2014, by far, would have been when I not only finally got to see this movie on the big screen (and on 35mm!) but actually HOST it for a crowd of people who didn't know what they were seeing. I was hosting a horror marathon at the Alamo Drafthouse in Lubbock, TX, and all of the titles were secret. I had to show *Night of the Creeps* (no complaints), but the other three films were of my own choice, and while I knew that a secret lineup had to include at least one guaranteed crowd pleaser (I went with *Friday the 13th Part VI: Jason Lives*), I put this at the top of my wish list, assuming the Alamo programmers couldn't find it anyway. But they did, and I didn't care if everyone there hated it, this was a bucket list moment for me.

Happily, when I asked the crowd after if they liked it (and, as expected, not a single one of them had ever seen it before), it got one of the biggest cheers of the night. Nothing against the people there, but they didn't seem to be die-hard horror fans (I asked some trivia questions for prizes and I had to give hints for ones I thought were super easy, like "Who directed *Child's Play*?"), so I was real nervous that this off-kilter, not particularly action-packed movie would turn them against me. But those who stayed (it was the third movie of the night) loved it, and for that I was incredibly pleased. If you see only one movie in this book... it should be *Cathy's Curse*. But if you see two movies, make this the other one.

MOVIE #153 - JUNE 2nd

THE NEW DAUGHTER (2009)
Dir: Luiso Berdejo
HMAD Review Date: December 22, 2009 (Theatrical)
Genre: Monster, Supernatural
Available from Anchor Bay

Synopsis Based on Fading Memory: Kevin Costner (Kevin Costner) and his children move into a new house and one of the kids starts acting strange. But by placing it in this particular chapter I guess you should know what the real threat is.

Review excerpt:
"...that it's a monster movie in disguise made me happy; I was actually weary of seeing another killer kid movie (in fact, the vagueness of it made me momentarily suspect we were in for a Hide and Seek retread, and that she was being weird because she knew her dad was a murderer). You go in expecting a little kid knocking her grandmother down the stairs or maybe slashing her father's Achilles tendon, and instead you get a scene where an Oscar-winning former Sexiest Man Alive is chased by a cave monster. Not a bad deal at all."

Reflection: Some of my reviews end up being the first match when people Google "(title of movie) ending", and thus the comment section gets littered with anonymous posters debating or arguing with one another about what that ending meant. The funny thing about it to me is that these arguments keep going long after I've completely forgotten the details, so I have no idea who to side with, or how to answer any direct questions. This is one such review, but unless I drastically misinterpreted something in the film I don't recall it being particularly ambiguous, so I'm not sure what all the fuss is about.

However, unless it's just two anonymous accounts going back and forth, it seems a number of people eventually did find this poor little orphaned movie (it bounced around a few bigger studios before being dumped to/by Anchor Bay), so there's a silver lining. I mean, I will be in his corner for life, but I know Kevin Costner isn't exactly the draw he was during the early '90s (don't blame *Waterworld* – it was actually *A Perfect World* that began his commercial decline – *Waterworld* was actually a sort of comeback), so seeing his face alone on the DVD wasn't going to move units, especially if it wasn't a film that anyone remembered being in theaters. Folks are finding it because of good ol' word of mouth, I suspect. I've even seen it pop up on articles about "DTV Treasures", which is inaccurate (it *did* play theatrically; I have the stub to prove it!), but if that's what it takes for people to give it a look, so be it. Still, I'll feel good about myself as a Costner fan to know this book inspired someone to watch it, so please let me know if this is what convinced you to check it out.

MOVIE #154 - JUNE 3rd

JAWS OF SATAN (1981)
Dir: Bob Claver
HMAD Review Date: May 17, 2012 (Streaming)
Genre: Predator, Religious
Available from Scream Factory

Synopsis Based on Fading Memory: The title is actually almost the pitch – it's *Jaws*, but with a snake that's actually Satan in disguise.

Review excerpt:
"...the whole thing is clearly ripped from the *Jaws* mold, but I like that it's kind of a laid back rip-off. "It's *Jaws* with snakes! But only a couple," the pitch undoubtedly went, likely delivered by a guy wearing sandals. Even the "close the beaches" subplot is charmingly low-key and without any major stakes – the Mayor doesn't want to do anything that might delay the opening of a new dog track. What a fun, wholesome activity! I sure hope the snakes don't harm any of the fat guys chomping cigars while betting on dogs that are being psychologically tormented with a fake rabbit!"

Reflection: If you know your *Jaws: The Revenge* lore, and you shouldn't, you'd recall that original drafts of the screenplay (and the resulting novelization) include a little tidbit that explains that the shark wasn't just acting on its own accord, but sort of working for a voodoo witch doctor that had a beef with the Brody family. Since the final version is STILL the stupidest movie of all time (but better than *Jaws 3*), you can only imagine how silly/nuts it might have been – OR you can just track down a copy of this, which preceded it by six years and had a similarly baffling concept where Satan is disguised as a snake and has a specific beef with a priest (Fritz Weaver).

But even though that plot could be used for an *Exorcist* sequel, it's otherwise a typical *Jaws* rip-off, right down to the hero trying to get the mayor to stop an impending celebration that could cost lives. Plus it looks terrific, thanks to cinematography by Dean Cundey himself, who would later shoot genuine Spielberg movies. And the snake scenes are shot with the actors right there, making them look pretty dangerous and far more terrifying than, say, *Empire of the Ants*, the Bert I. Gordon movie contained on the same Blu-ray. That was all split-screen and compositing FX, so this is far more exciting and believable. Bonus: it's got Christina Applegate as a little girl (her first role, I believe) who sneaks into the dog track, as young children are wont to do.

MOVIE #155 - JUNE 4th

DAY OF THE ANIMALS (1977)
Dir: William Girdler
HMAD Review Date: March 16, 2010 (DVD)
Genre: Predator, Survival
Available from Scorpion Entertainment

Synopsis Based on Fading Memory: Animals (but mostly dogs) vs Leslie Nielsen and Christopher George and a whole bunch of other awesome folks.

Review excerpt:
"Like Frogs *or* Long Weekend, *the film is about animals taking revenge on the humans that have ruined their habitat, but it's far more entertainment-minded than those films. And by that I mean I laughed at pretty much every death scene. The key one is when Jon Cedar's character is killed by snakes AND a dog (odd team-up) as he tries to get into a car that will allow him to rescue a little girl. Stupidly backing into his snake-filled car, he is first bitten a few times by the rattlers and such, and then the dog leaps on him and tears him apart. Not only is his death a bit of a surprise (since he was a pretty decent guy and had been more or less set up as a hero), but it's also a bit of a hilarious "bummer", since it seems likely that the little girl isn't going to get rescued either."*

Reflection: A shirtless Leslie Nielsen (ladies...) remains my most vivid memory of this flick, but what I like about it as a whole is that it often resembled a 1970s disaster movie instead of a *Jaws* rip-off (which is what Girdler's previous film *Grizzly* was). There's a huge cast of familiar faces, and they're from all walks of life, and you're not sure from the start who will live or die. So it's like *Airport* or *Black Sunday* or whatever, but with killer dogs and snakes and mountain lions and whatnot.

If you've never seen a Girdler film (if you went through last month's movies you have, of course – because he blessed us with *The Manitou*), this is a great place to start, as it's more fun than his earlier stuff but not really an "acquired taste" like the later *Manitou*. Girdler was only 30 when he died; it's a damn shame that we were robbed of what he could have done during the glorious '80s. The advancement in creature FX, the bigger budgets, and the emphasis on fun over genuine terror... Girdler was clearly well-equipped to deliver on these fronts at a time they'd be more appreciated.

MOVIE #156 - JUNE 5th

Q: THE WINGED SERPENT (1982)
Dir: Larry Cohen
HMAD Review Date: March 28, 2009 (DVD)
Genre: Cult, Monster
Available from Scream Factory

Synopsis Based On Fading Memory: A cult resurrects a giant flying monster in Manhattan, and Michael Moriarty is on hand to try to profit off its existence.

Review excerpt:
"One cool thing about the movie is how high the body count is, as Cohen stages another random attack every 5-10 minutes. The effects are terrible, but that doesn't matter - I'd rather poor effects than simply HEARING about such attacks or doing everything off-screen. And they all have their little humorous charms, like the guy who is convinced his co-workers are stealing his lunch. Again, it's all about making up for the film's weaknesses (i.e. bad effects) by maintaining a high level of "alternate" entertainment."

Reflection: Scream Factory re-released this on Blu-ray, which means the dodgy effects look even worse, but it's no matter – over time this actually became my favorite Larry Cohen movie, because it just combined so many different elements and somehow didn't get too jumbled or convoluted. Everything tracks, more or less, and Moriarty is just as good here as he is in *The Stuff* (a movie that ultimately doesn't come together as well as this), so the weak effects are really of no concern in the long run. Also, I ran the site for four more years after this and I never once saw another teaser with a line as good as "Just call it Q, that's all you'll have time to say before it tears you apart!" This movie is a classic.

Speaking of Cohen, he just about always provides a commentary track, and he's really not that great at it – he is constantly retelling stories about his other movies and getting his memories mixed up, but this is the rare one that you should listen to. He's moderated by the legendary Bill Lustig, who asks great questions and keeps him on track. He still gets things wrong (claiming that *Q*'s test screening was a disaster because people were expecting to see *Close Encounters of the Third Kind* – why would anyone expect a test screening of a five year old movie?), but of all the ones I listened to it's the only one I'd want to listen to again, so that should count for something.

HMAD Fun Fact: There are 257 Monster movie reviews on the site - picking just 30 wasn't easy.

MOVIE #157 - JUNE 6th

HYPOTHERMIA (2010)
Dir: James Felix McKenney
HMAD Review Date: September 30, 2012 (DVD)
Genre: Monster
Available from MPI Home Video

Synopsis Based on Fading Memory: A family that is ice fishing is menaced by a fish monster.

Review excerpt:
"Yay, practical FX! One of the characters gets a pretty nasty wound on his arm early on, and the other assorted injuries and deaths are given the ol' pre-CGI treatment that I always prefer. Hell, I can even appreciate that they tried to do a practical monster rather than a CGI one; it would probably look bad either way on this budget, so at least the actors have something to react to and interact with instead of staring at ping pong balls and green screens. I can also appreciate any movie that takes place almost exclusively on the ice - there's a cabin we see briefly in the first act and a little trailer that they use every now and then (which we learn is a set on the making-of featurette), but the rest of the time they're really out there on the ice, falling through holes into the freezing water when applicable and probably not having too much sensation in their fingers and toes throughout the bulk of their scenes."

Reflection: OK, let's just get this out of the way now – the monster suit in this movie looks VERY cheesy, and I don't think it's intentional. While they definitely were going for a '70s late night monster movie vibe (it's even under 80 minutes, the exact time a 1970s movie of the week would be without commercials), I don't think anyone would have cried foul if their villain looked slightly more terrifying than he does. It's a shame, because some folks can't look past the goofy design and they miss out on what's a pretty good movie.

See, for the most part, this is a solid attempt at recreating one of those older films. I've often lamented the death of made-for-TV horror, as several of them are just as good/better than their big-screen counterparts of the day *(Don't Go To Sleep* comes to mind as a prominent example, and I'm not personally in love with *Dark Night of the Scarecrow*, but enough are to warrant a mention), so it's nice that McKenney appears to feel the same way. I was mixed on this one when I saw it, but like quite a few others in this book, it stuck with me for whatever reason, and when it came time to pick movies for this chapter I honestly didn't even recall that I wasn't totally on board with it – in my mind now, it's a solid win. And even if I'm wrong and it's garbage, seeing Michael Rooker as a nice, normal guy still makes it worth a look.

MOVIE #158 - JUNE 7th

THE RUINS (2008)
Dir: Carter Smith
HMAD Review Date: March 26, 2008 (Theatrical)
Genre: Supernatural, Survival
Available from Warner Bros.

Synopsis Based on Fading Memory: A group of tourists are trapped on a pyramid with killer vines.

Review excerpt:
"It's the rare survival horror film in which actual survival elements are implemented. 30 Days Of Night completely botched this part up, with a 30-day time window seeming more like 30 hours, partially due to the fact that getting food/water was never once an issue in the film. Not the case here; we see them rationing their limited food, crafting stretchers and such out of what they have on hand, etc. The main character, Jeff (well played by Jonathan Tucker) is the most practical of the four, and watching him use his head and think things through was very refreshing. The other three are good too; Jena Malone starts off as an annoying and whiny drunk, but comes into her own as things get worse for the group. Shawn Ashmore (Iceman!) and Laura Ramsey are the other two, also impressively more than just attractive kids in a horror movie. There are no stereotypes – they are all intelligent (and about equally "famous"), which makes it far more difficult than usual to peg which ones are going to be goners."

Reflection: In a perfect, or at least better, world, *The Ruins* made a zillion dollars and Carter Smith has actually gotten to the "Maybe he should take some time off" stage of his career because he's made so many movies since. In reality, no one saw this movie and Smith has only recently shot a follow-up feature, a mystery drama titled *Jamie Marks Is Dead* which, at this time, has only played in some festivals. Hopefully I can see it for myself soon, but I hope even more that the promise he showed here wasn't just a fluke – this is a movie that features singing vines and it's actually pretty goddamn scary. He could be a "Master of Horror" candidate and we'll never know if he doesn't make some more movies!

And re: the singing vines – I guess the book (which I bought and never read, due to a lack of time. I really miss having a long commute on a subway like I did in Boston) has way more of this potentially fatal plot element, so I like that he included it to appease fans of the text, but kept it to a minimum so as not to turn it into "the singing vine movie". Well played.

MOVIE #159 - JUNE 8th

UNINVITED (1988)
Dir: Greydon Clark
HMAD Review Date: July 27, 2011 (DVD)
Genre: Monster
Available from Cheezy Flicks Entertainment

Synopsis Based on Fading Memory: A mutant cat terrorizes the yuppies on a yacht in one of the many movies with this particular title.

Review excerpt:
"*THIS* Uninvited *is the one with Clu Gulager and a mutant cat, which instantly makes it more memorable than the 40 or so others. It's also possibly the most coked out movie ever made, as the movie starts in a lab (where the mutant cat is "born") but races through the whys and hows in order to get to where the producers and* Without Warning *writer/director Greydon Clark clearly wanted to be – a party yacht! What could exemplify '80s yuppies better than a yacht decked out with plenty of floor space for aerobics exercises, endless champagne, and guys in pink shirts? Oh and embezzlers, for that added Trump'd up 1988 flavor.*"

Reflection: Let me explain the "40 or so others" line and my frustration with it. Back in the '90s, Sony tried suing Dimension over naming their movie *Scream*, because it was too similar to their movie *Screamers*, released a year earlier. The fact that neither title was original probably escaped them both, and so it always comes to mind whenever I encounter yet another movie named *Uninvited* (or *THE Uninvited*), because talking about them is far more confusing than any *Scream/Screamers* mix-up could ever be (have you ever once said "I love *Scream*" and had someone reply by referring to a Peter Weller movie?). I myself reviewed no less than four movies with that title, and IMDb lists another dozen or so – and that's not even counting shorts or TV shows. Long story short: studios shouldn't sue each other over titles, and filmmakers should try to make more use out of the million-plus words in the English language when titling their films.

And it's particularly obnoxious here because it doesn't have much to do with anything, and in no way suggests that the film is about a killer cat. Here are a few better, more accurate titles: *Meow of Death. Cat Scratch Fever. Whiskers. Nine Lives Of Terror.* Any one of those, and you could talk about this movie with ease, even with its relative obscurity in place. But *Uninvited*? Get ready for "No, not the one with Elizabeth Banks." Then again, any time Clu Gulager stars in a movie and they don't name the movie after his character, they've already done themselves a disservice, far as I'm concerned.

The director is Greydon Clark, who made a movie called *Without Warning* that features a young David Caruso and a *Predator*-y plot/monster (the guy playing the monster is the same one who played Predator, actually), but really, those two factoids are the only interesting thing about the movie. It's a plodding flick that saves its best moments for the very end, and yet it has some very vocal defenders. For the life of me I can't understand why - THIS should be the Greydon Clark monster movie everyone champions.

MOVIE #160 - JUNE 9th

YETI: CURSE OF THE SNOW DEMON (2008)
Dir: Paul Ziller
HMAD Review Date: August 17, 2012 (Cable)
Genre: Monster, Survival
Available from RHI Entertainment
Synopsis Based on Fading Memory: *Alive*, but with a Yeti!

Review excerpt:
"One thing I appreciated was that they spent a lot of time on the basic survival aspect of their plight. I think I'd prefer something more like The Grey *where they were picked off one by one as they tried to trek their way back to safety, instead of just sitting around the fuselage, but the need for food, fire, etc. made up more of the movie than the Yeti. And that is probably why they were able to go with a guy in a suit - he was probably only needed for 2-3 days, as they use him sparingly. Plus, there's some creativity to this stuff - at one point a guy uses a disembodied arm to splint his own."*

Reflection: I probably could have filled up a month just with the forgettable Syfy monster movies I watched over the years, so believe me when I tell you that this is one of the few that actually entertained me. Most seemed to be working off a template (and often involved water monsters instead of land dwellers), and so even if I went over a year in between watching them (i.e. when 365 other movies had taken up space in my brain) I'd still feel like I was watching a repeat. But this one? It's been a few years, but I can still remember certain beats, what the Yeti looked like, etc. For a Syfy original, that's the equivalent of being your favorite movie of all time or something.

The funny thing is, now we have the Chiller channel, which is owned by the same folks who own Syfy. They should be the ones airing these monster movies so Syfy can produce titles that are, you know, actual sci-fi films. They do air some sci-fi movies occasionally (usually wacky disaster films, though they did a pretty decent *Philadelphia Experiment* remake as well), but by and large they stick to monsters. Meanwhile, Chiller's original movies are consistently solid and take on a variety of topics – they did a fine *Monkey's Paw* update, a zombie flick, a cult and, yes, a monster movie or two. They don't pop up as frequently as Syfy, so I guess they're going with quality over quantity. Still, as I enjoy sci-fi almost as much as horror, it's a shame to me that Syfy doesn't take advantage of their position to offer more intriguing fare, especially when there's another channel more suited for what they're making instead.

MOVIE #161 - JUNE 10th

THE BARRENS (2012)
Dir: Darren Lynn Bousman
HMAD Review Date: October 1, 2012 (Theatrical)
Genre: Monster, Psychological
Available from Anchor Bay

Synopsis Based on Fading Memory: A family vacationing in the Pine Barrens may be the targets of the Jersey Devil... or maybe the husband is just going all Jack Torrance on them.

Review excerpt:
"I'm always down for a "is he crazy or is there a monster" plot, as long as the ambiguity is handled well and they give you plenty of evidence to support either theory, and I'm happy to report that is the case here. There's an unexplained bit with a knife, but otherwise the ultimate answer works without betraying the film's logic, or (worse) cheating by showing us things that couldn't have been happened. I might argue that it would have been fun to have the answer revealed a few minutes earlier just so there could be a bigger finale, but on the other hand I admired Darren Bousman's ability to string us along until the very last second - most films would have collapsed by now."

Reflection: Since leaving Jigsaw behind after *Saw IV*, Darren Bousman has been steadily making new features, but unfortunately they tend to fly under the radar due to limited releases and poor distribution. This and *Mother's Day* were my favorites, but his main projects post-*Saw* are his crazy music-driven films, namely *Repo: The Genetic Opera* and *The Devil's Carnival*, both of which enjoy *Rocky Horror*-esque success via traveling roadshows and "shadowcast" screenings where people dress up as the characters and act out the film in the theater. It was the poor distribution of his other features that inspired him to handle *Devil's Carnival* himself, booking the theaters and touring it around (not unlike what was done with *Repo* after Lionsgate basically abandoned it), where it plays to sold out crowds. Take that, studios!

But I know those movies aren't everyone's cup of tea, so I want to assure you that *Barrens* has no songs, best as I can recall. No, it's just a fun little variation on both *The Shining* and an urban legend-driven monster movie, with a solid performance by *True Blood's* Stephen Moyer as the dad. It makes good use of the actor's imposing presence – he's a handsome guy that is born to play shady characters, which is ideal for someone you need to be believable as a family man but also someone you're not sure if you can trust (without swinging too far in one direction or the other). And it finally uses the Jersey Devil as the backdrop for a good movie after several bad ones (like that *Last Broadcast* snoozer).

MOVIE #162 - JUNE 11th

SWAMP DEVIL (2008)
Dir: David Winning
HMAD Review Date: February 13, 2012 (Streaming)
Genre: Monster, Revenge
Available from RHI Entertainment

Synopsis Based on Fading Memory: A murderer is reincarnated as a tree and seeks revenge on the guys who put him away.

Review excerpt:
"What makes this one work is an emphasis on characters (there's only like ten people in the movie) and an actual motive for the monster. Usually these things are unleashed and just kill whoever they come across; not that there's anything wrong with that, but such movies all start to blur together after a while. However, I'll never forget that Swamp Devil *involved a giant tree monster (think an Ent from* LOTR *crossed with a skeletal demon) who is actually the reincarnation of a guy who was executed by five locals back in the day. Bonus: the guy was a murderer, so it's not a "wronged man seeks justice" thing. See, our victims don't exactly deserve their punishment like in* Dark Night Of The Scarecrow *or whatever, which gives it some added suspense. A big issue for me in a lot of these movies is I find myself rooting for the monster since the "victims" are all scumbags, so I like that this guy (tree) is more like Freddy, seeking revenge for the death that he actually deserved."*

Reflection: I bet every single "Movies you should watch" book ever published includes at least one Bruce Dern film, so I love that even though I'm specifically writing about offbeat/rare/under-appreciated horror movies, I still get to include one with this terrific legend. There actually would be a second Dern entry if I saw *Twixt* before the site's daily run ended; it's a bad film but it'd be a perfect fit for May's theme, as it was batshit nuts as is and has even wackier stories behind it (like a *Choose Your Own Adventure*-type gimmick for a theatrical release that never happened). Back to Dern, though; if you ever get the chance to listen to the man speak, either for a specific film's Q&A or just a general chat, do not pass it by – he's one of the best storytellers I've had the pleasure of listening to since I moved to LA, and believe me I've been to hundreds of such things.

Anyway, he's great in this movie about a killer tree. It's a bit of a departure from most of RHI's "Maneater" series, which usually focused on regular animals/insects (bears, snakes, spiders, etc.) instead of supernatural or "giant" ones, but it's also one of their best. In fact, most of their better movies were those that broke tradition and dove into more science-fiction territory, as opposed to the dull entries where a regular tiger menaces Gary Busey (yep, even with THAT plot, it's a dull flick). So saying it's one of the best "Maneater" films isn't saying much, but at least I'm an actual authority on the matter, having seen at least half of their output.

MOVIE #163 - JUNE 12th

ISOLATION (2005)
Dir: Billy O'Brien
HMAD Review Date: July 20, 2007 (DVD)
Genre: Mad Scientist, Monster
Available from Millennium

Synopsis Based on Fading Memory: A cow births some little monsters on an Irish farm.

Review excerpt:
"I was beginning to wonder if the film was in fact just a farm training video, as we see pretty much the entire process of checking a cow for diseases and then birthing a calf. Luckily, soon after the calf is born, the horror begins. Seems the calf itself is pregnant with some little bony monster things as the result of botched experimental drugs, and soon enough the little bastards are slithering about and killing folks. Nothing wrong with that. It's nice to see a monster movie that forgoes "big action and thrills!" and instead focuses on atmosphere and a sense of impending dread. Just be patient with it, and you'll enjoy yourself."

Reflection: I cringe when I read the reviews from the first six or so months of the site, because I was still finding my voice as a writer (read: I was being a snarky prick to get attention), and the reviews are obnoxiously vague, as well (VERY annoying when it came time to put together this book). But also, since I was still getting used to making it part of my day, I'd be more impatient with slower films, and make them sound worse than they are. Over time I grew to appreciate these slower stories more (at least, when done right), so movies like *Isolation*, where I was more mixed when I wrote the review, eventually became winners in my mind.

Again, this is one of the very few Irish horror movies I saw, and among that rare group it's the even rarer one that doesn't really feel Irish-centric – it could just as easily take place in Wisconsin or anywhere else where people have cows. I'm all for learning about other cultures (and, when it comes to Asian horror, how they approach storytelling as opposed to the American way), but I'm just as happy to find an easily accessible film from a foreign land, as it sort of highlights the unfortunate tendency for independent horror productions in America to copy what's popular instead of using their independent freedom for something a little more unique. When I see films like this, I get the impression other countries (and their distributors) aren't as risk-averse.

MOVIE #164 - JUNE 13th

NATURE'S GRAVE (2008)
Dir: Jamie Blanks
HMAD Review Date: January 24, 2010 (DVD)
Genre: Predator, Survival
Available from Screen Media

Synopsis Based on Fading Memory: A couple on the brink of divorce head off to nature to mend their relationship and find themselves the targets of angry wildlife. If that plot sounds familiar, that's because this is a remake of the film *Long Weekend*.

Review excerpt:
"Obviously the original is worthy of more respect, but Blanks does bring some stylistic touches here and there that the original lacked, and Karvan is much easier to bear than Briony Behets was in the original (they have also dropped the fact that she was still cheating on Peter, so she's not unsympathetic from the start). And obviously things like the eagle attack are less goofy, so there's something. And since everything is upgraded, we get the creepy image of a GPS trying to find its bearings in the middle of a blank area, which is better than looking at a map and saying "this road's not on here" or something. So yeah, they have "modernized" the film, but I didn't feel that the original was dated, so it's hardly a good enough excuse to bother with such an exact replica."

Reflection: If there's a such thing as a "Jamie Blanks Apologist", then I am definitely one – I remain a champion of his two Hollywood films (*Urban Legend* and *Valentine*), the latter of which even Blanks doesn't seem to think much of (when I met him at a screening and told him I was a fan of that not-loved 2001 slasher, he asked "Ugh, why?"). But even I had trouble defending his curious position to remake the 1978 film *Long Weekend* and not change a single major element – it's practically the exact same script (once again by Everett De Roche) and even retains some of the original's odd decisions, like a go-nowhere bit involving a fire.

However, the minor new touches they do bring to the table (described in the excerpt) and the fact that some of the animal attacks are better executed makes this the "superior" film if you've never seen either version. I recently revisited the original and forgot how downright horrible Behets was, making the husband (John Hargreaves there – Jim Caviezel plays him here) the clearly less awful choice. Here they're a little more even, so you're not actively siding with one of them (then again I can only speak as a male here; any female readers find the husband to be way more in the wrong in the original? Tweet me!). But it and the other changes are so trivial that it's not really a new movie as much as a polished photocopy.

MOVIE #165 - JUNE 14th

THE CAR (1977)
Dir: Elliot Silverstein
HMAD Review Date: November 28, 2008 (DVD)
Genre: Monster
Available from Universal Studios

Synopsis Based on Fading Memory: *Jaws* but with a car... almost literally. It's got POV shots, a memorable musical calling card, kooky locals, a bunch of guys teaming up in the third act to stop it... it's even from Universal! Since *Jaws* was Spielberg doing his own *Duel* but with a shark, I like that it came full circle.

Review excerpt:
"I really hope this movie gets shown at the Bev someday. It's too fantastic a film to watch at home with just one or two people."

Reflection: So that was in 2008, and then in the summer of 2009 the New Bev actually DID show it, but guess who hosted it? ME! It was actually a Shock Till You Drop screening that then-editor Ryan Turek was supposed to host, but something came up and he had to cancel his introduction, asking me to do it instead (telling me to "Collins it up", which I still don't understand). This was before I had my own screening series there, making it the first time I got to stand up in front of the New Bev crowd – and it was for a screening I dreamed about happening in one of my reviews. I dunno, I thought that was cool.

Confession: I actually like this movie more than *Duel*. The awesome car horn, the ridiculous killing of the lady in her house (watch the car carefully – it drives straight into the house and straight back out onto the road – was her house located in the middle of the street?), James Brolin, James Brolin's mustache, the cyclists getting killed (live in LA for a month, you'll have the same cathartic reaction to seeing them get run down)... it's all too wonderful for me to consider it lesser than *Duel*, even if it's a crime to speak against Spielberg. There are more killer car movies than there probably should be, but this is the best one, as far as I'm concerned (yep, even as a card-carrying Carpenter nut I actually like this a bit more than *Christine*).

MOVIE #166 - JUNE 15th

GRIZZLY PARK (2008)
Dir: Tom Skull
HMAD Review Date: April 4, 2008 (Theatrical)
Genre: Predator, Serial Killer
Available from Allumination Filmworks

Synopsis Based on Fading Memory: A serial killer kills and then impersonates the cop that's taking a group of delinquents to do community service in the woods, and they all run afoul of a bear.

Review excerpt:
"90% of it seems like deleted scenes from a better, way more fun movie. Why would the killer bring the goddamn sleeping bags up the mountain? Because it takes two minutes of cheap screentime up. At one point they just cut to poor Glenn Morshower (the film's sole bright spot) putting a clipboard up on a wall. Why are we watching this? There are also about a half dozen scenes of the kids discussing their crimes, none of which matter in the long run. And when the "twist" ending comes around, it renders some of what we saw earlier even more useless."

Reflection: My most vivid memory of this crappy killer bear movie is that Ron Howard's dad was in it for a few minutes and I ended up sitting next to Ron himself at this screening. He fell asleep during a good chunk of it (his dad's scene was long gone so I guess he could have just left entirely), which was a wise decision on his part since the movie's bad. Not terrible bad; it's probably one of the better "bad movie" options I've provided for each month, but it's just so sloppy. On paper everything sounded like B-movie gold, but it just never came to life. It's D-movie bronze.

What really irked me is that they couldn't get the damn bear right. A number of the films I've listed this month that deal with real animals found a way to film their primary interactions with the actors, but that never happens here – the bear is only on-screen for a few seconds and doesn't do much interaction at all with the actors. At times it seems like the filmmakers were trying to make it a comedy, but failed miserably – even as "so bad it's good" entertainment it misses the mark by a mile. Add in the stupid plot, the appearance by mega annoyance Whitney Cummings, and the horrifyingly awful twist, and you have a movie that seems like it *wants* the audience to hate it. Have fun! Or, pull a Ron Howard and take a nap. Or better yet, imagine Ron Howard as his *Arrested Development* narrator talking over this junk to make it more entertaining.

MOVIE #167 - JUNE 16th

THALE (2012)
Dir: Aleksander Nordaas
HMAD Review Date: October 17, 2012 (Festival screening)
Genre: Monster
Available from Xlrator

Synopsis Based on Fading Memory: A woodland monster inadvertently helps two guys reconnect; kills some jerks.

Review excerpt:
"Going in blind for my festival viewing probably worked in my favor, because the trailer plays up the suspense and "monster" stuff, and thus I might have been disappointed to see that it's actually pretty tame. Like Resolution, *the core of the film is about the friendship between the two male leads, who work together at the "No Shit" cleaning service, mopping up crime scenes and the like. Each man has something they are trying to hide from the other, and while it's understated, the monster and her presence inadvertently helps them get past their issues with their personal lives, and seemingly strengthens their friendship as well. Aww, nice monster."*

Reflection: 2012's Screamfest was obnoxiously located in downtown LA (it had always been Hollywood before that, much more convenient for me and most others), which is a shame because the lineup was one of its strongest ever. So movies like this were much more sparsely attended than they would be at the Mann's where the festival was usually held, bumming me out. To this day I still don't hear much about this little offbeat gem, which is character drama first and monster movie second – I think I should be championing it more to help it out. Indeed, I originally had it in October with the other "horror-lite" options, but swapped out another monster movie late in the writing process to make room for it here, where it can stick out a little more and hopefully catch your eyeballs.

In fact, I'd go so far as to say it probably would have gotten into Fantastic Fest if it was submitted. If you've never been to Fantastic Fest or simply don't know much about it, the movies there tend to be off the beaten path and harder to categorize. In some instances this means crowd-pleasing fare that might be just a bit too crazy for Hollywood (such as *I Declare War*, in which a bunch of kids play capture the flag but the action is staged/shot like a traditional war movie), but more often than not (at least in my experience) the movies are a little slower, a little harder to pin down or label, and ultimately harder to sell. The biggest bummer about any festival is that there might be a few movies that never get bought – there are films from both FF and Screamfest that I saw years ago and still haven't been traditionally released. Don't let the ones that got a chance pass you by!

MOVIE #168 - JUNE 17th

SPLINTER (2008)
Dir: Toby Wilkins
HMAD Review Date: October 15, 2008 (Festival screening)
Genre: Breakdown, Monster
Available from Magnolia Home Entertainment

Synopsis Based on Fading Memory: A pair of crooks take a couple hostage, but then they need to work together to avoid getting killed by a porcupine monster.

Review excerpt:
"Director Toby Wilkins (who also co-wrote) knows how to play against expectations, and therein lies the secret of the film's success. For example, one of the "bad guys" is clearly not so bad; she doesn't want to hurt anyone, tells the more insane-seeming partner to calm down, etc. Clearly she will end up being an ally! Nope, she gets it first, and pretty early on to boot. And that's just the start. Nothing's Shakespeare, but I was continually surprised as to who sides with who, who plays hero, who shows his/her true colors, etc."

Reflection: One of the worst things that can happen when you're watching a horror movie is being able to peg not just who will die, but even the *order* in which they'll get offed. So when I see a movie that can surprise me on both fronts, I bow in respect to its creators, because if they've even fooled Mr. Horror Movie A Day, they will certainly shock the average viewer who expects this person to survive, that person to be the film's villain, etc.

I actually liked this movie even more when I watched it again on DVD. The camerawork and editing that I was frustrated with during my theatrical viewing is much less obnoxious at home, and the confined setting (most of it takes place in a gas station) also fits a TV screen better than a giant one. And at the time I didn't know who Shea Whigham was, but by the time of my second viewing I was a fan, making his appearance all the more enjoyable. Alas, watching again reminded me that 2008 was seemingly kick-starting a revival of the monster movie thanks to smaller efforts like this and bigger ones like *Cloverfield*. Unfortunately, one of the next out of nowhere smashes was *Paranormal Activity*, which shared *Cloverfield's* POV aesthetic, so instead of monsters we just got an endless supply of found footage movies. Oh well.

Director Toby Wilkins followed this up with the third *Grudge* film, which went direct to video despite being miles better than the second. If you, like most sane people, didn't like *Grudge 2* and thus didn't bother with the third one, fix that! It's a decent little flick! R rated, too.

MOVIE #169 - JUNE 18th

KAW (2007)
Dir: Sheldon Wilson
HMAD Review Date: November 5, 2007 (DVD)
Genre: Predator
Available from Sony Pictures Home Entertainment

Synopsis Based on Fading Memory: Killer birds attack a small town. Yes, it's been done by a rather famous director. So what? This version has Powder.

Review excerpt:
"The movie sort of goes out of its way to kill off the nicer people in the movie, but not in a mean-spirited way (other than at some of the CG birds, I didn't laugh once watching this movie, intentionally or not). Kind of like Tremors, *they don't go the usual horror movie route and kill all but two people, so it makes the attack scenes a bit more suspenseful when you know they aren't out to simply whittle the remaining cast down to nothing in order to save on SAG fees. Hell, they even give a decent enough explanation for why the birds went nuts. Whether it makes any scientific sense I have no idea, but I certainly don't care either (drop a nuke into a hole a mere 800 into something the size of Texas and it will split in two and miss the Earth? Sounds good to me!). And it's given about one minute of screen time, so even if you totally hate the 'motive', it's not like it makes up the whole movie."*

Reflection: As time went on, I saw a lot of the same names pop up under "director", and most of them would make me groan ("Not Mike Feifer again!"). In fact, I actually went back and made sure to delete all movies from one particular filmmaker out of my (wholly random, un-researched) queue after he had proven to be terrible one time too many for my liking. But *Kaw* was the first of what would be a series of "better than it had any right to be" Syfy-type movies from Sheldon Wilson, who gave us *Screamers: The Hunting* (a sequel to an inferior theatrical film), and *Snowmageddon*, which I mention because I saw it six years after I wrote the above excerpt, which directly references the film his snow-globe based disaster flick was aping. He also made *Shallow Ground*, which I wanted to put in this book but it didn't really fit any theme, so just make a note to see it. His movies aren't classics, but he seems to give a shit and put some effort into his junky B-movies, which is more than I can say for (too) many of his peers. Here's hoping he doesn't get burned out on killer scarecrow movies and the like and gets hired for something meatier – I suspect he's someone that could be relied on for quality genre fare if he'd just get the opportunity.

The irony, of course, is that whenever you're discussing a proficient but not quite master filmmaker, someone's bound to say "He ain't exactly Hitchcock, but...", and here I am talking about his killer bird movie. There aren't a lot of such films, probably because it would be too easy to invite a comparison to *The Birds* (and by extension, Alfred Hitchcock), so it's rare anyone has the stones to suffer the risk. Hell, even Platinum Dunes reconsidered their plans to remake it – it's not like Michael Bay is known for his humility. Obviously *Kaw* is not quite as chilling as that 1963 film, but it's a damn sight better than *The Birds II: Land's End*, which was directed by Rick Rosenthal (who knows a thing or two about directing sequels to horror masterpieces by legendary filmmakers), though he used the Alan Smithee credit for reasons I've either never known or forgot. And fuck *Birdemic*.

MOVIE #170 - JUNE 19th

ROGUE (2007)
Dir: Greg McLean
HMAD Review Date: August 8, 2008 (DVD)
Genre: Predator
Available from Dimension Extreme

Synopsis Based on Fading Memory: Some folks are terrorized by a giant crocodile in Australia.

Review excerpt:
"One thing I liked is how subtle a lot of the character moments are. One of the guys on the boat steals a camera from a tourist family, but not only do they not notice, it's never even mentioned. John Jarratt's character is on the boat to spread his wife's ashes on the river, and again, they don't really spell this out for you by having him explain it away to someone. I was also happy to see that the croc was merely an angry croc, a bit bigger than average but not gigantic (on the extras they say that their croc is actually half a meter smaller than the largest ever recorded). He wasn't a science experiment gone wrong or the result of toxic spilling, he's just a pissed off animal. This is not only good because it's not so generic, but also it keeps the focus on what really matters – whether he's a mutant hybrid or just a regular animal, the audience is here only to see it eat someone."

Reflection: Greg McLean took a lot of heat for his film *Wolf Creek*, partly because he (spoiler) killed off the two female characters but let the guy live. But despite that film's mild success at the box office, his more commercial sophomore effort never got a real theatrical release here – which is a shame because he is seemingly apologizing for his alleged misogyny in *Wolf Creek* by (spoiler again!) allowing all of the female characters in this movie to survive. Yep, the croc only has eyes (teeth) for the male characters; even when it attacks a woman and leaves what seems to be a fatal wound, she is ultimately fine. It actually hurts the movie a bit, because it starts getting distracting, but on the other hand, his choosiness with victims means the movie never reaches a point where everyone left standing is safe, a rarity for a movie like this.

This movie also contains one of the rare times Sam Worthington didn't annoy the hell out of me, probably because he's playing a supporting character instead of the hero. He's one of those guys that seemed forced on us – he never really had any lead roles but suddenly in 2009 he's not only starring in the new *Terminator* but also *Avatar*, the most anticipated non-sequel of all time. The latter's success gave him some clout that is only now running out (ironically, one of the other movies I enjoyed him in was *Man on a Ledge,* which tanked and seemed to prove he was only as appealing to audiences as the CGI around him), though I'm sure if the *Avatar* sequels are successful we'll be forced to deal with him as one of our primary action heroes for a while. At least he's better than Jai Courtney.

MOVIE #171 - JUNE 20th

RAZORBACK (1984)
Dir: Russell Mulcahy
HMAD Review Date: February 21, 2010 (Revival screening)
Genre: Predator
Available from Warner Archive

Synopsis Based on Fading Memory: A giant pig stalks some folks in the Australian Outback.

Review excerpt:
*"It's nice to see Gregory Harrison as a heroic lead, as I primarily only know him from his asshole roles on various TV shows (*Ed *for example) and as the villain in Mulcahy's recent (and pretty awesome)* Give Em Hell, Malone. *And the score by Iva Davies is also great (sort of Tangerine Dream-esque); it's a shame he wouldn't compose another film again until Peter Weir's* Master & Commander, *nearly twenty years later. Also, any touching moment revolving around a personal object found in a giant pig's poop is automatically a good movie."*

Reflection: I consider myself a fan of Russell Mulcahy, but it's less for his film work than for the fact that he's been a longtime associate of Jim Steinman, the genius songwriter who has been my longtime hero (and I mean LONGTIME – I singled out his Air Supply song as my favorite from my dad's oft-played 8-track greatest hits... when I was TWO YEARS OLD). Mulcahy directed the video for "Total Eclipse of the Heart" and when he made his film *The Shadow* he roped in Steinman to write the theme song (and Steinman, in his usual fashion, merely took one of his songs that had already been recorded and changed a few lyrics). The filmmaker also tells a great story about Steinman on his *Highlander* commentary, relaying a time they went to dinner together and when the wine came, the eccentric songwriter insisted on opening the bottle himself so he could breathe the air from whatever year it was.

So what I REALLY like about Mulcahy is that he's got all these Stein-tales, forever keeping him in my favor despite the fact that he makes more bad movies than good (including the worst *Resident Evil* entry, for my money). None of his films were as good as his debut, sadly, but while they're not horror, but I highly recommend 1991's *Ricochet* and the aforementioned *Give Em Hell, Malone*. And no, I don't recommend *Highlander* – I recently re-watched it and man, I think only *The Goonies* eclipses it as the prime example for "Movies You Loved As A Kid And Should Never Revisit As An Adult". Luckily for *Razorback*, and in turn you, I first saw it as an adult so I know I'm not being blinded by nostalgia.

MOVIE #172 - JUNE 21st

HARDWARE (1990)
Dir: Richard Stanley
HMAD Review Date: October 6, 2009 (Blu-ray)
Genre: Technology
Available from Severin Films

Synopsis Based on Fading Memory: A self-repairing, ever-evolving robot stalks a lady in her apartment.

Review excerpt:
"[The robot] can re-assemble itself from other metal and electronic devices, which allows for a continually changing design, a clever way to keep the single location interesting (they have a lot of appliances and such fro the robot to build itself from), and a never-ending sense of "this thing is certainly going to kill you". It's the rare film where I was never sure if anyone was safe from the thing, including Travis. I wouldn't mind a slightly more expansive sequence of events (they never get any further than the building's rooftop), but it's still an engaging movie from start to finish regardless."

Reflection: I bought Stanley's *Dust Devil* specifically for HMAD and I never got around to watching it, which is nutty when you consider how much I enjoyed this (and it stars Chelsea Field, with whom I was quite smitten in *The Last Boy Scout*). I vow to see it before this book is published! Of course, that's the only other narrative feature Stanley has made; apart from contributing to anthologies and making documentaries, he's been MIA from the director's chair ever since the debacle of *Island of Dr. Moreau* (if you're not privy to that disastrous production, there's a full length documentary titled *Lost Soul* that covers it pretty well). Perhaps he's better off doing what he's doing instead of being at the helm of multi-million dollar productions, but still – it's a bummer to see such a unique voice (and colorful character – he's a delight to listen to) removed from our modern movie-going experience.

Anyway, *Hardware*. This movie offers one of the grossest characters I've ever seen in a more or less mainstream film. His name is Lincoln, and he's a pervert who lives across the way from heroine Stacey Travis. In addition to his disgusting appearance, he mutters things that would make the killer from *Black Christmas* blush, and even though his comeuppance is satisfying you'll probably wish it was even harsher for YOUR sake, let alone the character he was tormenting. Go, bizarre killer robot, go!

MOVIE #173 - JUNE 22nd

BURNING BRIGHT (2010)
Dir: Carlos Brooks
HMAD Review Date: August 27, 2010 (Festival screening)
Genre: Predator
Available from Lionsgate

Synopsis Based on Fading Memory: Meat Loaf sells some guy his man-eating tiger, which gets loose and traps the man's children in their home during a hurricane.

Review excerpt:
"...once it finally kicks into gear, man does it work. Even though you know perfectly well that neither of them would die, it doesn't make certain scenes any less nail-biting. The aforementioned laundry chute sequence is a particular highlight, topping even the similar one in Halloween 5 *(it's also the source of the film's best jump scare). And I love how they solve the obligatory cell phone problem; it would have been easy and even somewhat logical to have the cell service interrupted from the hurricane, but instead they do something far more interesting/entertaining."*

Reflection: I talked about Jim Steinman a couple entries back, and I hope that readers know who he is already or at least took the .0012 seconds to Google him rather than remain ignorant. But just in case you're still left in the dark, he's probably best known as the writer/producer behind *Bat out of Hell* (and its first sequel), which is, as anyone who knows me can tell you, my favorite album of all time. Of course, the other half of that album's power comes from Meat Loaf, and while I usually enjoy his non-Steinman albums to a degree, there's nothing like it when the two of them work together. Luckily, Meat considers himself an actor first, and so he makes a lot of movies in between recording songs, likely reducing the number of bland ones he'd do without Steinman (who is a perfectionist, which is why it takes him a bit longer to produce new material). The big guy actually isn't in this one that much; he shows up in the first scene and basically lays down a whole bunch of exposition about the film's main attraction – a man eating tiger that he is selling. I kept hoping he'd come back at the end like the old guy in *Gremlins*, telling the characters they weren't ready to own a man-eating tiger, but no dice.

Luckily, even though I was watching the movie mainly to see my boy Meat, I was still quite engaged by this one long after he exited. It was a lot of fun to watch with a crowd, too; a shame it didn't get a theatrical release in the US. This film's screening was my sole journey to the smaller theater at Frightfest in 2010, and I remained confused why it didn't play on the much bigger main one. Not only was the smaller theater not large enough to accommodate everyone who wanted to see it, but this was a crowd-pleasing, solidly thrilling film that would have helped break up the grimmer fare that made up the bulk of the main screen's selections. Seriously, go look up that year's lineup online – it's just one unpleasant movie after another, making this rape/torture-free movie such a welcome change of pace.

MOVIE #174 - JUNE 23rd

CAVED IN: PREHISTORIC TERROR (2006)
Dir: Richard Pepin
HMAD Review Date: April 12, 2012 (DVD)
Genre: Monster
Available from Lionsgate

Synopsis Based on Fading Memory: Some robbers kidnap a guide and his family and force him to help them navigate a cave full of man-eating beetles.

Review excerpt:
"...it's entertaining enough, and again, I like when they combine horror with survival adventure ideas. And it's a hell of a lot better than The Cave, which this movie was probably designed to cash in on in the first place (and whose bloodless deaths were a major sore spot for me!). So in the realm of Syfy Original movies, this is basically Shawshank Redemption or something."

Reflection: I'm forever fascinated by junky rip-off movies that are superior to whatever Hollywood/big budget film they're piggybacking in the first place. This one didn't even bother with changing the name much; it's obviously "inspired" by the 2005 Sony release The Cave, but this Syfy junk (which also rips off Cliffhanger, of all movies) is actually a lot better. The cheesy puns give it an '80s Schwarzenegger vibe (some of these are Running Man-level howlers), and giant beetles are more inspired than the umpteenth bat/cave creature thing that The Cave offered. As I've mentioned elsewhere in this tome, mid-2000s Syfy movies were, on the average, more genuinely fun than those they make these days, so if you've enjoyed the films I've highlighted, dig for more during the same era.

And if you're a Con Air fan, and you should be, this offers not one but TWO of its actors in the cast. One is Angela Featherstone, who doesn't have a big part in that 1997 action classic (she's one of Cusack's people; I think she only has like two lines), but the other is Colm Meaney, the Irish actor who is also one of cinema's great profanity-spewers. His character here is kind of like Morgan Freeman's in Hard Rain (yet another '90s action reference – maybe I should just write a book about those?), in that he's the villain for a while but ultimately kind of sympathetic to our hero and thus you kind of want to see him survive. Does he? You'll have to watch to find out! Or read its IMDb synopsis, I guess.

MOVIE #175 - JUNE 24th

SLUGS (1988)
Dir: Juan Piquer Simon
HMAD Review Date: March 24, 2008 (DVD)
Genre: Monster
Available from Image Entertainment

Synopsis Based on Fading Memory: The director of *Pieces* returns with this tale of slugs attacking a town.

Review excerpt:
"There is a hefty dose of what I assume is a Simón tradition: hilariously odd dialogue! In the third act, our hero tells the zoning commissioner that he is declaring a state of emergency, to which the commissioner guy shouts "You ain't got the authority to declare happy birthday!" Holy shit, what? And someone else scoffs at the idea of killer slugs by wondering "What's next? Demented crickets?" (goldmine plot for a film if there ever was one). Speaking of the commissioner, this movie tops your average real estate horror movie in terms of the boring jobs everyone has. Our lead characters are public health inspectors, sewer management officials, zoning regulators, real estate barons, land developers... it's like the cast of a public access town meeting putting a gory, hilarious spin on things."

Reflection: It's a shame that the principal players behind *Pieces* never made anything that lived up to that film's perfect blend of insanity and rubbish, because it makes everything else they've done seem disappointing, even though if you haven't seen *Pieces* you'd probably think you were seeing something extraordinary. I mean, *Don't Open Til Christmas* (from the *Pieces* producers) is a movie featuring a half dozen Santa Clauses being killed and a climax that finds the hero (and presumably his poor housekeeper) being blown up, and yet to a *Pieces* fan it almost seems tame.

That said, *Slugs* comes closer to *Pieces'* highs, thanks to the nutty dialogue, crazy death scenes (one seems to have partially inspired the ones in *Final Destination*), and the inspired idea to turn one of the slowest creatures on earth into the killer for a horror film. A sequel is hinted at in the film's closing shot, but we never got one. However, if you want more of this story you're in luck – quite incredulously, it's based on a novel! If it doesn't have the "happy birthday" line it'll be a waste of time to read, but of all the times I was surprised to learn that the wacky movie I watched was actually based on a book, this has to be the most unexpected.

MOVIE #176 - JUNE 25th

THE BAY (2012)
Dir: Barry Levinson
HMAD Review Date: November 2, 2012 (Theatrical)
Genre: Mockumentary, Monster
Available from Lionsgate

Synopsis Based on Fading Memory: An evil company dumps something in the water, releasing a flesh eating virus... and it's all on video!

Review excerpt:
"The mystery elements are quite enjoyable; there's a Contagion-*esque feel to the proceedings as the CDC and a local hospital race to figure out what's going on before more people get infected and die, and we get a new piece of the puzzle every fifteen minutes or so. And since what is in between makes up the bulk of the scares, it makes for a very effective pace - learn something, get scared, learn something, get scared. Levinson doesn't shy away from the gore when applicable, and the FX (courtesy of the Strause Brothers) are incredible - the little bugs crawling around are legit terrifying. The movie offers three terrific jump scares, including one that REALLY got to me as it involves a giant fish and a guy putting his finger inside its mouth - luckily I never saw the trailer for this movie beforehand, since it spoils it (don't watch if you haven't seen it yet!). The infected also take on a bit of a zombie-ish demeanor, so even though it's not a very big element, Levinson is able to milk scares out of the film even when no one is near the water."*

Reflection: Somehow, the director of *Rain Man* and *Good Morning Vietnam* delivered one of the last really good found footage movies, and he did it by taking an approach I still don't see very often (and probably never will now that the gimmick has been played out): he makes it an ensemble instead of focusing on one character or group with a never-ending supply of batteries and tape. Think of all the questions you have when watching these things: "Why are they still filming?" "How many tapes did they bring, anyway?" "When is something going to happen?" Levinson finds a satisfying way to avoid those pitfalls, by having one sort of main character telling the story three years later, assembling her film using all of the random cell phones, surveillance cameras, and obviously traditional video shot on the day of the horrific event that provides the film with its narrative.

In other words, it's what someone would actually do with a documentary, giving it a bit of extra realism that so many of them lack (it always kills me to see pointless footage in movies that are supposed to be the edited version of a tragic trip to the woods or whatever – who edited it and why did they leave this boring shit in?). This allows Levinson to just introduce new characters and kill them off moments later; keeping the film much more action-packed than many faux docs can ever hope to be without betraying (much) of the real world logic a viewer would be applying. It really works well, and it's a shame Blumhouse and Lionsgate didn't really give it much of a chance, limiting its theatrical release and focusing more on VOD. Levinson returns to aquatic horror after *Sphere* and gets it right this time – he deserved a bigger showcase for his efforts, dammit!

MOVIE #177 - JUNE 26th

TENTACLES (1977)
Dir: Ovidio G. Assonitis
HMAD Review Date: October 6, 2010 (Streaming)
Genre: Monster, Predator
Available from Scream Factory

Synopsis Based on Fading Memory: *Jaws* but with an octopus, and in the role of Matt Hooper, some dolphins.

Review excerpt:
"A boat race is this movie's "4th of July" – we learn about it in the first two minutes of the movie, just in case we weren't sure that this was a Jaws *rip-off (and one of the first, I might add). To its credit, they don't really do a lot of "close the beaches!" (well, "cancel the boat race!") stuff, but it's the same sort of feel, and other scenes borrow directly from* Jaws *as well, including an attack that is exactly like the sequence where Robert Shaw dies, with the fish smashing the back of the boat, causing its prey to slide down into the water and thus to their death. But there are a number of unique attacks too – I particularly liked the one where a girl sees what looks like a rogue wave heading toward her (spoiler – it's the octopus), which smashes the boat and kills them all."*

Reflection: Even if this movie was total garbage, I would probably include it in the book just so I could talk about "Too Risky a Day for a Regatta", the name given to one of the music cues in the film. If I could figure out how to do it, I'd have this music streaming from my person at all times – just walking around, nodding along to its infectious rhythm 24 hours a day. There aren't a lot of score pieces I can literally listen to on a loop without getting tired of it, but this is definitely one of them, and it's the main reason I kept the Blu-ray after getting it to review when Scream Factory re-released it (alongside the terrible *Reptilicus*).

The movie itself is admirably bonkers in spots, slow in others, and never *quite* rises above its *Jaws* rip-off origins, but somehow manages to carve its own identity anyway. Assonitis is fond of bizarre freeze frames (including several during the regatta sequence), and often spends more time on pointless side stories than the damn octopus, like when we spend a good minute watching Shelley Winters argue about a registration form. But the dolphins! When Bo Hopkins stops to give them a pep talk as the film gears up to its climax, stop everything that you're doing (meaning, put away your goddamn cell phone) and focus on what he's saying. Really think about what you're watching in that moment – it's really kind of magical. And stupid. And amazing.

MOVIE #178 - JUNE 27th

WOLF TOWN (2011)
Dir: John Rebel
HMAD Review Date: April 5, 2012 (Streaming)
Genre: Predator
Available from Naedomi

Synopsis Based on Fading Memory: Some wolves get territorial and hunt a group of kids making a documentary. Relax, it's not found footage.

Review excerpt:
"If you're in the mood for this sort of thing, you can certainly do worse. It's inane at times and again, the hero deserved to be eaten, but the pace keeps up and the interplay with the wolves is solid. And if you get to the end you are treated with the credit "The Wolves – Themselves" under the cast, so that's another perk. Also it made me want to parody Live's "Shit Towne", so I'm going to go get on that."

Reflection: I should note I never did 'get on that'. But I still sing "Shit Towne" in the shower more often than any man should, so now that I've been reminded of my promise it should be easy to get started. "Gotta live, gotta live gotta live, in Wolf Town...."

Anyway, this really should be a recommendation for *Frozen*, the non-Disney 2010 film about three college kids who get trapped on a ski lift, with a pack of hungry wolves below them. But I felt weird about it because the director, Adam Green, hired me to do credits on a few of his post-*Frozen* films (including the same year's *Hatchet* sequel), so it felt bias-y to include it (I did include *Grace*, which he produced, because it was even older than *Frozen* and too unique in its sub-genre to pass over due to some perceived bias). So this is the runner-up "killer wolf" movie, because I've never even met John Rebel, let alone worked for him.

The fact that it's about kids making a documentary and it's *not* found footage makes it pretty novel. Documentarians are great horror movie protagonists, because they're smarter than the average horror character (or at least, they should be), and it makes sense for them to go off into unfamiliar areas. There's even a built-in, plausible reason to have someone sit there and rattle off exposition at us. But it's too easy to turn such a scenario into a POV film nowadays, ruining its appeal. Luckily, the movie was shot in 2009/2010, mere weeks after *Paranormal Activity* hit theaters and thus about a year or so before every other horror movie included "keep filming!" in its dialogue. Its makers probably didn't want their film to sit on the shelf for two years, but I bet they were ultimately relieved that when it did see release in the US, it wasn't getting lumped in with all the anonymous found footage movies folks were getting tired of seeing.

MOVIE #179 - JUNE 28th

ORCA (1977)
Dir: Michael Anderson
HMAD Review Date: March 8, 2012 (Streaming)
Genre: Predator
Available from Warner Bros.

Synopsis Based on Fading Memory: *Jaws* but with a whale, and where you kinda side with the damn whale.

Review excerpt:
"The serious bits are broken up by whale action, which is pretty gonzo at times. The whale eating folks on the water is fine, and even the head-butting sabotage (such as when it rams the poles holding up a waterfront house) almost seem plausible. But when the thing somehow manages to figure out how to destroy the town's fuel supply (causing an explosion several hundred feet outside of the water!) I began to wonder if the makers of that terrible GTA-esque Jaws game had actually been influenced by Orca instead of the Jaws films. It also has an uncanny ability to pinpoint attacks; at one point a character steps out of the boat's cabin and leans over the edge, and Orca instantly leaps up, snatches him, and goes back under the water. Was he just waiting for the opportunity or did he just get lucky when he came up for air?"

Reflection: I noticed a lot of post-*Jaws* movies would try to subtly or not-so-subtly suggest that they are bigger than *Jaws*; even today, forty years later, we see this sort of tribute in things like *Jurassic World*, with a Great White being a mere snack for a giant water-based dinosaur. So *Orca* must get credit for being the first, right? It came out less than two years after *Jaws* and it has the title character eat a shark in its opening scene, setting the tone nicely even though the movie proceeds to just follow *Jaws'* template pretty carefully. It's a surprisingly serious movie, not unlike *Prophecy*, but it has more action and a drunken Richard Harris in the lead, so it's the superior film in my opinion. I know it gets a bum rap, but trust me – I've seen dozens of bad *Jaws* wannabes, and you can believe me when I say that whatever you've heard about *Orca* can be applied – and then some – to several others. No need to single this one out. Plus it's got an Ennio Morricone score, so it's automatically worth watching.

I would advise skipping over the horrible whale-killing scene though, especially if you're a parent. You see, Orca is on a revenge mission, and I can't say I blame him – Harris (somewhat accidentally) kills his mate AND his baby, and the poor whale howls the entire time as they die. That shit was *incredibly* hard for me to watch, and this was pre-fatherhood. I wouldn't even try to watch the scene now. I also stopped hunting whale right then and there.

MOVIE #180 - JUNE 29th

THE BURROWERS (2008)
Dir: J.T. Petty
HMAD Review Date: October 11, 2008 (Festival screening)
Genre: Monster
Available from Lionsgate

Synopsis Based on Fading Memory: Some *Tremors*-style giant monsters attack in the old west.

Review excerpt:
"I was quite charmed by the humor, which was as dry as the landscapes. William Mapother in particular gets in a few good lines, which was surprising as he is always playing Stoneface McGees who never even crack a smile, let alone a joke. And even though it's hardly played for laughs, the cynical asshole in me almost cheered at the ending, which is like a big "fuck you" in the tradition of the original Night of the Living Dead. It's a downer, which is possibly part of why LG has no faith in the film, but kudos for going that route."

Reflection: If there was any justice in the world, JT Petty would be a name that usually came up when discussing modern horror, and he'd frequently be in the running for big studio projects. He's proven time and time again to be an interesting, but commercially-minded filmmaker – his films may be slower-paced than the average horror fan might be used to, but he's still delivering the goods and working in crowd-pleasing sub-genres, like the monster movie (he also did the solid *Mimic 3*, which was basically *Rear Window* but with one of the big ass cockroach people). *Burrowers* was one of the many victims of the late '00s turnover at Lionsgate that also saw *Midnight Meat Train* and *Blood Creek* get dumped, but unlike those it didn't have a Clive Barker or even a Joel Schumacher to draw in fans. Hell it was probably still Petty's biggest release yet (or since), even though it should have been much bigger. I'm highlighting *The Burrowers*, but really you should take it upon yourself to see all of his movies if you haven't already (he's got one in next month's group too).

You should also try to watch all of the horror-westerns, which will probably only take the better part of a day. While people successfully blend horror with comedy, sci-fi, and action all the time, the western/horror hybrid remains elusive. And I mean real westerns, not ones just set in "The Old West" but otherwise telling the same generic zombie tale that would fit just as well in a modern day college or something. The recent *Bone Tomahawk* was terrific and well-received, but most people think it went direct to VOD (it actually did have a tiny theatrical release, one I'm happy I got to support), and so it isn't likely to spawn a wave of imitators. Even traditional westerns that make a ton of dough don't really revive this once-thriving genre – *Django Unchained* and *True Grit* were huge, but it didn't inspire a wave of cash-ins. Maybe that's why horror-westerns are the rarest of hybrids; one genre is pretty much built on people copying each other, the other can't seem to get things going even when it seems audiences are ready for that kind of entertainment again.

HMAD Fun Fact: October of 2008 was the most prolific month in HMAD history, with 74 reviews (more than two a day!). That was the second and last time I combated the Halloween-driven "Horror Movie A Day" features on a lot of websites by doubling up with "October Extras", where I'd watch a new movie like usual as well as a treasured favorite (or frequent targets that I never actually reviewed for the site, like Dark Ride*). The other twelve extras were due to festivals, because I used to review everything I saw. Youth!*

MOVIE #181 - JUNE 30th

PIG HUNT (2008)
Dir: James Isaac
HMAD Review Date: September 13, 2010 (DVD)
Genre: Predator, Survival
Available from Phase 4 Films

Synopsis Based on Fading Memory: Some hunters run afoul of some rednecks, and some giant pigs try to eat both groups.

Review excerpt:
"No one can ever make a killer pig movie that's just a killer pig movie. This is I believe the third or fourth one I've watched for HMAD, and all of them turn out to have other (human) villains. Pigs are giant things that love to eat – why do they always feel that we need an explanation for them to want to eat us? Ultimately, the pigs only kill one or two folks in the film, whereas hippies/rednecks rack up about a dozen. That said, the movie is actually sort of charmingly all over the place, with hippie communes, pot farms, killer pigs, redneck priests... I can safely say that this is the least generic James Isaac movie ever."

Reflection: It's a bummer that James Isaac finally made a movie I liked, and then died before getting a chance to make another. He seemed like a guy who loved the genre and was genuinely enthusiastic about what he did, but his final films always left a lot to be desired (he gave us *Jason X* – aka the only *Friday* movie that lost money – and the abysmal *Skinwalkers*). Going back to the independent world (real independent, not Hollywood independent) seemed like it would be a good fit for him, but sadly he passed away, of goddamn cancer of course, not long after *Pig Hunt* finally saw release in the US. Incidentally, the only other *Friday* director to leave us is Danny Steinmann, who ALSO made one of the least-loved entries (*New Beginning*, which I quite like) and left behind an all too brief filmography. Be safe, Rob Hedden!

I should warn you that there isn't as much pig action in the movie as its title or DVD cover suggest. The humans kill each other more often than the pigs do, making this more of a *Deliverance*-style action-thriller than predator/monster movie. But it makes up for it, and then some, with the finale, featuring a three-ton boar nicknamed Pigzilla. And that's kind of what I like about the flick – Syfy or Asylum would put the thing front and center (and probably name the movie after him), but Isaac uses it sparingly so that it actually means something when it appears. Quality over quantity!

I still hold out hope that a monster movie revival is coming sooner than later; even if the sub-genre is revived by a remake or unnecessary sequel, it'll be worth it to have movies like the above playing in our multiplexes on the regular. They all make for fun crowd experiences, and unlike slashers and zombie films, no one minds a PG-13 monster movie, so they're good entry horror movies for the younger crowds, too. If any good can come out of *Jurassic World* (oof) making all the money that there is, it's that maybe a few smaller scale monster movies can be put in development at rival studios.

Or maybe the indie scene will explode with such fare...

JULY – INDIE HORROR

ARTIST: COLE ROTHACKER

On July 4, 1776, America officially became a country, the first step on its way to being THE GREATEST NATION IN THE WORLD. And if you're from another country and find this to be ignorant, ask yourself this – did YOUR country produce *Halloween*? I rest my case.

July is also where we see the last of the major summer blockbusters – the stuff released in August tends to be a bit smaller, maybe more risky, or just assumed to be bad. But after May and June, you're probably kind of sick of seeing all those mega-movies anyway, so I thought we could honor Independence Day (the holiday, not the very badly dated movie) and counter-program the 200 million dollar event movies by focusing on independent flicks. Not all of these are masterpieces, but they represent the SPIRIT I want to see from my indies, as far too many that I saw over the years were merely trying to cash in on trends and bled cynicism in every poorly shot frame.

Now, to be clear – when I say independent, I mean *truly* independent. These are the movies that were funded on the director's own dime (or at least, his/her credit cards), local investors, and/or crowd-sourced – in other words: movies produced well outside the Hollywood system and lacking any recognizable names. I kind of scoff at the notion that a movie like *Pulp Fiction* is considered an independent – Tarantino had 8 million dollars of company money and a cast of big stars like Bruce Willis and Sam Jackson. To me, lumping that sort of production in with movies that took three years to make because the director could only film on weekends when he wasn't working his day job just doesn't seem right. I obviously don't know the exact nature of how all of these films came together, but they're all definitely closer to the "I begged my friends for cash and slept in my car" types than the "Cameron Diaz worked for a fraction of her usual fee" ones.

As these films don't have big marketing budgets and the like, their filmmakers sometimes have to be a bit more creative when promoting their work, making sure they stick out in a giant sea of fellow indie productions all vying for your attention without the aid of billboards. This month's first selection went above and beyond to make their promotional push memorable…

MOVIE #182 - JULY 1st

EVIL THINGS (2009)
Dir: Dominic Perez
HMAD Review Date: December 29, 2009 (DVD)
Genre: Mockumentary, Slasher
Available from Inception Media Group

Synopsis Based on Fading Memory: Typical slasher movie but presented with the restrictions of a found footage movie.

Review excerpt:
"Incidentally, several aspects of this case remind me of what happened to five cheerleaders in Tennessee a couple years back, where they were chased for reasons unknown as they drove home in the darkness, and ended up getting lost and attacked. But this case is far more upsetting, due to the fact that the subjects in this case are far more likable and tolerable (between you and me, I was hoping the killer in that case would have killed them all after about ten minutes). I was also reminded of the case from 2000 in which a group of college students (also in an isolated cabin during the winter) were videotaped for a reality show that turned out to be a hoax. But again, these kids struck a chord with me that those others failed to, which resulted in my being far more engaged and interested in their story. The evidence file is short (74 minutes) but it was long enough to really care about the group and not want to see them fall under any harm, and it is a shame that they apparently have."

Reflection: I really wish I could have done more fun reviews like this one over the six years, but alas I'm simply not that creative. But also, it's not exactly possible – there needs to be something to trigger that spark, which I'm not likely to get when I just load up Netflix and look for a killer shark movie I haven't seen yet. In this case, director Perez sent his screener along with a mock letter from the FBI, explaining that the disc contained the "evidence file" for a missing person's case, and that I was being asked to take a look at it in order to provide expert insight. The movie is a pretty good attempt at doing a slasher film as a found footage entry (though its scariest bits are early on, when the stalker is merely following them in their car), but this approach is what made it stick out in my mind, and thus in turn I framed my review as my written response to the FBI. Pretty proud of how it came out!

If you're curious, the other outside the box reviews were just plain goofy; after being invited to a press screening of the *Sex And The City* movie for some reason,

I decided to review it as if it was a horror movie, claiming Carrie was a vampire and Samantha was a succubus or something. And then when Paul Thomas Anderson's L Ron Hubbard-inspired *The Master* opened on the same day as Paul WS Anderson's newest *Resident Evil* movie, I pretended I got them mixed up and reviewed Alice's newest attempt to destroy Umbrella as if it was all a Scientology metaphor. It actually kind of fit!

P.S. The "other cases" (read: other movies) I describe in the excerpt are *Five Across the Eyes* and *My Little Eye*. Neither of which are in this book, if you didn't notice.

MOVIE #183 - JULY 2nd

DIE YOU ZOMBIE BASTARDS! (2005)
Dir: Caleb Emerson
HMAD Review Date: November 2, 2008 (DVD)
Genre: Comedic, Monster
Available from Image Entertainment

Synopsis Based On Fading Memory: The kitchen sink.

Review excerpt:
"One thing I loved was the rather random map overlays (think Indiana Jones*) that provided occasional scene transitions as our hero made his way around the world. They are all completely wrong (West Virginia is apparently located in Norway), which of course is what makes them so funny. Making fun of cinematic convention is a staple throughout the film; I particularly liked whenever Emerson would obviously use the same cutaway/reaction over and over during a scene, overdoing it to the point that you know that it's a joke and not just a low budget penny pinching technique. In a way it reminded me of* Repo*, in that the movie is so OUT THERE that you need to sort of adjust your senses to get on board. The first fifteen minutes or so made me want to quit doing HMAD forever, but by the time our hero (a serial killer; no one seems to care much though) goes to a police station to try to get them to help him find his kidnapped girlfriend, I knew I made the right choice to stick with it"*

Reflection: It didn't happen often, but every now and then I'd get a comment on one of my reviews from someone involved with the film. Sometimes it was an actor who found it because I mentioned their name (everyone has a Google Alert for themselves), other times it was an angry producer who wanted to punch me in the face for slamming his movie (fun anecdote – the director of one of those movies hired me to do credits on his next film, which had different producers, obviously). But this one was a weird one; the co-writer of this movie popped in to thank me for liking the movie and then proceeded to explain how Tarantino stole the design of the car in the film for his movie *Death Proof*. Basically both of them are black Chevys (not the same model) with a crossbones on the hood, so while someone who isn't a gearhead might do a double take if they saw the two of them side by side, I'm gonna have to assume it was a coincidence (it's not like QT is shy with pointing out his influences).

For what it's worth, I'd rather watch this nutty, long in production movie (it took them three years to make, mostly on weekends) than the one even Quentin says is his weakest effort (I do not disagree). I know my synopsis suggests I don't remember much about it, but on the contrary – I still have vivid memories of particular scenes nearly seven years later. But I think part of what I liked is that I had no idea what I was in for (the title is certainly kind of misleading, as it isn't even a zombie movie), and like a few others in this book I am trying to preserve that for you, dear reader. Except for the weirdo car thing.

MOVIE #184 - JULY 3rd

KILLING SPREE (1987)
Dir: Tim Ritter
HMAD Review Date: May 20, 2011 (DVD)
Genre: Hero Killer
Available from Camp Motion Pictures

Synopsis Based on Fading Memory: A guy thinks his wife is cheating on him so he goes on, you guessed it, a killing spree.

Review excerpt:
"I think there's enough here to warrant a viewing; there are enough murders and out-of-nowhere acts of casual violence (love when he just punches a guy at the beach for no reason) to entertain a drunken crowd. The FX are pretty fake-looking, but I was charmed by the obvious enthusiasm behind them – any movie that has a ceiling fan equipped with machete blades is a winner in my book, even if the resulting "scalped" effect looks like a hat made out of play-dough (and what's with the orange blood? Y'all using Chef-Boy-Ar-Dee sauce or something?). Some of the deaths are pretty creative too; I particularly enjoyed when our killer tore out a dude's intestine and connected the end to an electric source: Intest-ocution!"

Reflection: If you scour the independent horror section of Netflix Instant, you'll see a lot of movies that are inspired by the heyday of Troma (some even got distributed BY Troma), and more often than not they're unwatchable. I don't think any Troma film is particularly great on its own, but the enthusiasm and go-for-broke attitude usually makes them pretty fun to watch, as long as you're seeing one where Lloyd Kaufman had an active hand in and didn't just make a cameo (say what you will about Kaufman, but he actually knows how to put a movie together, unlike many of the folks he inspired). It's a shame most of the would-be imitators seem to miss what makes those movies memorable, opting to just make bad movies on purpose (never a good idea), because you never get a sense of whether or not the filmmaker has any talent.

Anyway, this is one of the best Troma-ish movies, and its director, Tim Ritter, was only 20 years old at the time of its release, making it easier to forgive its lapses (like the ending, which is a tonal 180 from the rest of the film). Also, I think it's the only movie I reviewed where I had a legit beef with the film's lack of nudity, so that's something. Finally, it's a great example for the era where the booming VHS market allowed for wacky movies like this to not only get sold, but actually find a place on the shelf at the store. Nowadays, there's even MORE stuff like this being produced, but with so many avenues of distribution and almost none of them involving brick and mortar stores (which for the most part focus on the major titles – Best Buy's horror section is only about 40 movies nowadays), it all gets lost in the shuffle unless it's truly spectacular. In the 2010s, this is the sort of movie you scroll past on Netflix while looking for something to watch (and settling for something that played in wide release). But in 1987, there weren't hundreds of guys like Ritter making these things (at least, not on film), so the movie made its mark, and is still remembered nearly 30 years later. Not too shabby.

MOVIE #185 - JULY 4th

COMBAT SHOCK (1984)
Dir: Buddy Giovinazzo
HMAD Review Date: August 13, 2009 (DVD)
Genre: Psychological
Available from Troma Entertainment

Synopsis Based on Fading Memory: A Vietnam vet suffering from PTSD has the worst day of his life.

Review excerpt:
"Let's talk the mutant baby. This thing's howls will haunt your dreams for days, I can guarantee. According to the director, the sound is simply him moaning, which was then reversed and sped up on top of that. It's almost inimitable with human vocal chords, which is probably the point, but it won't stop me from trying to mimic it when I discuss the film with friends. And it's a pretty impressive little thing; the movie only cost 40 grand (and it's on film - so suck it, DV filmmakers who claim that film is too expensive for their budget) but the puppet is up there with the It's Alive *baby."*

Reflection: GAH! NO! I don't want to think about this movie! Just re-reading parts of my review made me cringe. But I guess I have to justify putting it in the book. It's one of the most depressing things I've ever seen and barely even horror (the hero has a mutant baby, and the fact that it was distributed by Troma means pretty much only horror fans will ever see it anyway), but damned if it's not an impressive piece of work from Giovinazzo. Plus I wanted something fitting for the 4th of July and it just so happens that the movie was shot on Staten Island, which is a ferry ride away from the Statue of Liberty. It was this or *Uncle Sam*, I guess.

The Troma thing is what actually makes this memorable. Sure, it's got as many amateurish moments as their usual fare, but it's mostly a real movie and kind of a sad/serious one at that, making it stick out like a sore thumb... but in a good way. It probably resulted in several angry viewers who saw "mutant baby" and the Troma logo and figured they were in for some sort of *It's Alive*-style monster movie, but if you can put aside your expectations and see it for what it is, you'll probably appreciate it, if not enjoy it. It's a shame Troma didn't go outside this box a bit more often, though I can easily see why they wouldn't.

MOVIE #186 – JULY 5th

100 TEARS (2007)
Dir: Marcus Koch
HMAD Review Date: August 29, 2011 (Streaming)
Genre: Slasher
Available from Unearthed Films

Synopsis Based on Fading Memory: A killer clown kills people.

Review excerpt:
"...our heroes, Mark and Jen, are a pair of laid-back tabloid journalists with foul mouths. Neither of them are particularly great actors (prepare for lots of fumbled lines), and it certainly didn't surprise me to discover that the guy playing Mark was also the screenwriter since he got all the best jokes, but they're certainly unconventional as heroes, which gives the movie some added charm. At one point Jennifer maps out a plan to investigate the circus, and then concludes her scene with "In the meantime, I'm going to go take a dump." You don't hear Sidney Prescott offering up that sort of bon mot. I was also delighted by the fact that Mark was seemingly more competent than the police officers who were (sort of) investigating the murders. In a movie like this it's hard to tell if off kilter acting and even story-telling decisions are intentional or the result of amateur actors and/or under-funded productions, but either way it adds to the movie's gonzo charms."

Reflection: Xbox and Netflix have both made a lot of boneheaded decisions over the years (the "always on" thing for the former, "Qwikster" for the latter), but usually they either fixed them or undid them entirely. However, they have yet to restore one of the best features they ever offered, which was the ability to use the Xbox party chat service in conjunction with Netflix's app for the Xbox 360, letting friends watch a movie together despite being miles apart. Basically, you got a little animated living room that showed your avatars sitting together on a couch watching the movie on a big TV, and you could use your controller to show off little animations like clapping or laughing – or just shut the screen off entirely and put the movie at full size, but (with the headset) still be able to converse with your faraway pal. And the movie would sync, so if you paused it it'd pause for your friend too, ensuring that you were always watching and reacting to the same thing. I used to use it to watch movies with my good friend Matt Serafini, who was 3,000 miles away in Massachusetts, and I know of another friend who used it to watch movies with his girlfriend when she was away at college. It just disappeared one day without fanfare, and I hoped they would bring it back with the Xbox One (figured there'd be some sort of Kinect feature that would trigger a revival), but alas, it seems to be gone for good.

Anyway, that's how we watched this movie, and we had a blast. My memories of that experience are so happy that I've never actually gone back and re-watched the movie by myself, though I understand there's a longer cut out there now – I might have to check that out. Is it as good as I remember? Probably not, but this wasn't our only time using this feature and it was the only time the movie held our interest and delivered the goods, so I have to assume it is, if nothing else, better than 75% of the killer clown movies I've seen.

MOVIE #187 – JULY 6th

GRAVE MISTAKE (2008)
Dir: Shawn Darling
HMAD Review Date: July 29, 2012 (DVD)
Genre: Zombie
Available from Echo Bridge (multi-pack releases) or Gryphon's Egg Productions

Synopsis Based on Fading Memory: Toxic waste turns corpses into zombies, motley group of survivors fight them off... nothing particularly inventive in the narrative department.

Review excerpt:
"The best thing about it is that it admirably kills folks "out of order"; the first two victims of note are the sort of characters you'd expect to last a lot longer. This allows for some unexpected tension that even the poor acting couldn't ruin, because I never felt that any of the (mostly likable) characters were safe. And there's another zombie attack every 15-20 minutes, so it mostly held my attention - something even the bigger budgeted zombie films of late can't manage. The zombie makeup is also impressive, considering the number. I'm sure some of the background ones got quick appliances and a single coat of blue/gray face paint, but the "hero" zombies look pretty damn good to me. And I like the quick turn style of this particular "strain" - it's done with (fairly good) CGI, but seeing someone turn zombie just moments after being bitten was pretty cool. The more advanced CGI effects aren't particularly great, but they're used sparingly and usually for things that couldn't be done practically (at least, not without an expert like Savini to help), like blowing half of a guy's head off as he keeps staggering forward."

Reflection: In the last year or so of HMAD's run, I managed to get on Echo Bridge's review copy list, which was a blessing and a curse. It was a blessing because they released a lot of multi-pack DVDs, which were great to have on hand as filler for vacations and the like (just one 2-disc/8-movie set would be enough for the whole week! More room in the suitcase for all the crap I buy whenever I go anywhere!). Also, for a while they had the license to the Dimension library, so I could fill in holes in my *Hellraiser* collection for free instead of actually paying for crap like *Hellworld*.

But on the other hand... well, Echo Bridge sucks. The movies they released were either bad or terrible, for the most part, and often with botched transfers to boot (like when they put out *H20* at the wrong aspect ratio). I mean, you're never going to like EVERYTHING a studio sends you, but usually it's 50/50 or something, so it's not always bad news when it's time to send the publicist your links. Trust me, there's nothing fun about sending someone an email with a link to a review saying that their company did a bad job. So these occasional ones they got right were such a relief, because I could happily send the Echo Bridge lady a good review and make them less hesitant to lose my info. Alas, they eventually did just that, not long before they seemingly went out of business – they lost the license for all that Dimension stuff in 2014, and shortly after that their social media presence dried up. They live on only in my memory now.

Anyway this is a pretty good little backyard zombie flick that got more right than wrong, even more impressive when you consider writer/director Shawn Darling was pretty much a one man crew, with something like thirteen credits on the film. He hasn't made a feature follow-up yet, just some shorts and TV stuff - hopefully he'll deliver a true sophomore effort sooner than later. And do so with a real crew behind him - if he can wear so many hats and make a pretty decent flick, imagine what he could do when he'd only have to focus on one or two jobs?

MOVIE #188 – JULY 7th

MULBERRY ST. (2006)
Dir: Jim Mickle
HMAD Review Date: April 1, 2008 (DVD)
Genre: Zombie
Available from Lionsgate

Synopsis Based on Fading Memory: The blue-collar residents of a rundown apartment building fend off zombies.

Review excerpt:
"Ostensibly a zombie movie, Mickle does a good job of selling the idea that New York is under quarantine. Since he's not Francis Lawrence, he can't really shut down whole areas of the city, so he sells these ideas via a near constant stream of news and TV broadcasts that mix footage from what I assume is from 9/11, the blackout, etc., along with standard "quick no one's around let's film this street" type stuff. It works well. Most of the action is confined to a single apartment building, and thus doesn't require such extravagant shots like a deserted Times Square in order to get the point across."

Reflection: Jim Mickle has gone on to make quite a name for himself in the genre; he followed this up with *Stake Land* (which I'll spotlight in a later chapter) and the excellent *We Are What We Are* remake, and then moved into revenge drama territory with his well-received *Cold In July*. And now he's making a movie for Legendary! As I re-read hundreds of reviews in preparation for this book, I found I often said things along the lines of "I am curious to see what this filmmaker does next", and it's sad to see so many of them haven't actually gotten another feature made in all that time. So it's nice to see one who has not only continued working steadily, but rose through the ranks to potentially become a name-brand director. It gives me hope that some of those other guys and gals will eventually follow suit.

Mulberry is also part of an unusual sub-sub-genre: zombie movies that evoke 9/11. Horror films have always provided a way to comment on social/global/etc. situations, and once the initial shock wore off, the fall of the Twin Towers was no exception. Sadly, many of the films that reference it do it in an almost offensive manner, like *Final Destination 3* and the *Omen* remake using photos and footage from the actual disaster for a quick shock moment (oddly that those and this film were all released in 2006, the same year *United 93* and *World Trade Center* hit). I much preferred something more subtle like this, where you can ignore it (or actually miss it) and still enjoy the film, and that seems to be a common theme among the many zombie films that drew parallels in one way or another. Romero, of course, offered his two cents with *Land of the Dead*, though his script was actually written BEFORE that horrible day, so his conscious decision to update it afterwards wasn't as successful as it probably would have been if he had started a response from scratch. *28 Weeks Later* is another, and *World War Z* is one of the most overt (and, interestingly, the biggest hit, by far), likely due to its VERY 9/11 influenced source material. We probably see this allusion a lot because zombies are the easiest movie monster to paint a canvas on, due to their anonymous nature (kind of hard to do social commentary on something of that scale with a slasher or killer shark), but I wish there was a bit more variety when it came to this particular event. How about a (scary, not action-driven) alien movie with a 9/11 allegory?

MOVIE #189 – JULY 8th

THE MOLE MAN OF BELMONT AVENUE (2013)
Dir: Mike Bradecich and John LaFlamboy
HMAD Review Date: October 1, 2011 (Festival screening)
Genre: Comedic, Monster
Available from Level 33 Entertainment

Synopsis Based on Fading Memory: Two dimwit brothers protect their building, which is on Belmont Avenue, from the Mole Man.

Review excerpt:
"The movie as a whole sort of reminded me of Bubba Ho-Tep, *and in turn the monster sort of had a mummy-esque appearance (or Darkman in bandage/crazy homeless guy mode). It doesn't really appear in full much, which I didn't quite get as it looked cool and should have been shown off more (as opposed to some horrid CGI creation that is best kept hidden as much as possible), but at least they make it count when he does. Most of the time we just see him in long shots or in close-ups of its hand/claw reaching through a vent to steal a resident's pet to eat. On that note, it's a testament to the movie's quality that it's able to get away with the (off-screen) deaths of several cute cats and dogs – not always at the hands of the monster – and still retain the goodwill of the audience."*

Reflection: It's a shame Robert Englund will probably have "Freddy" etched on his tombstone, because it makes it easy to forget that he's a pretty great actor. And it's an even bigger shame that the "funny" version of Freddy was pretty lame, because Englund is also a pretty hilarious guy, and rarely gets to show off his genuinely comic side in anything – anyone can deliver a bad pun before killing someone, but it takes true skill to pull off genuine laughs. So I was delighted to see that directors Mike Bradecich and John LaFlamboy took advantage of Englund's underutilized gift, and even better – they did it in a movie that was entertaining even when he wasn't around. *Shaun of the Dead* was an obvious inspiration here (and possibly *Bubba Ho-Tep*, as I alluded to above), but unlike many of those wannabes I think this one worked well, making me even happier to see it find distribution a year or so later, as I saw it at an indie horror festival where pickups aren't a guarantee.

But Englund is just one of many residents under attack by the Moleman – part of what made this one shine is that it had a fun ensemble at its disposal, a rarity in modern horror. Too many films give you plenty of characters, and then sets about separating them as quickly as possible. This is fine for a slasher movie, but for a monster movie like this, you want everyone together and on the move, making it more exciting and harder to tell who will live or die. *Tremors* is probably one of the best examples of this sort of scenario, and I wish I saw it more often. Obviously you want your heroic main guy or gal, but they're only as good as the people around them. This is why *Speed* ('90s action reference again! Sorry) works as well as it does – if it was just Keanu and Sandy on the bus, it'd probably only be half as fun – the motley collective of random bus passengers gives it the flavor that helped separate it (and make it more successful) than the other, solo hero *Die Hard* rip-offs of the '90s.

So this is the *Speed* of indie comedy horror movies, is what I'm saying.

MOVIE #190 – JULY 9th

ENTRANCE (2012)
Dir: Dallas Richard Hallam and Patrick Horvath
HMAD Review Date: June 24, 2011 (Festival screening)
Genre: Slasher
Available from MPI Home Video

Synopsis Based on Fading Memory: A killer targets a lonely Los Angeles girl (and her dog) in a slasher film that keeps the Final Girl on-screen for every single frame of its runtime. Not an exaggeration.

Review excerpt:
"...the main character (Suziey Block) loses her dog, which is pretty much the easiest way to earn someone's sympathy, or at least mine. There's a bit where she comes home and looks down at the floor, seeing no one to greet her, and I almost choked up (my family dog died in January of 2010, so the next time I went back home I actually had my mom take the day off of work so I wouldn't lose my shit when I walked into the house and didn't have my pal there like usual). But it's not a manipulative storytelling decision like in some other films; I already liked her character before the little guy vanished. And by vanished I mean "was taken". Again, with Block in every single frame of the film they could have botched the possibility for scares (we never even really get a good look at her stalker), but just about every major horror scene works great. The "dognapping" bit in particular was creepy as all hell, because it plays out entirely through sound design, with the guy making those ticking sounds you make when you call for an animal and the dog pattering about and then whimpering, all while we watch poor Suziey sleep."

Reflection: As a slasher enthusiast/junkie, I've seen so many that a lot them blur together – remembering anything specific about one (especially from the HMAD era) is like trying to remember the exact model of car that was in front of you for a minute during your daily commute (in Los Angeles, you can guess "Prius" and be correct, for the record). So it's kind of amusing – to me anyway – that one of the more memorable modern slashers is actually ABOUT routine and boredom, as our heroine is practically living in a *Groundhog Day*-type life, doing the same thing every day until her dog's disappearance forever alters things.

But it's also the rare slasher that I appreciate – and hereby recommend – more for its technical qualities than "it's got great kills" or "It's actually scary". To be honest it's a bit boring (part of the point) and the final scene is kind of obnoxious, but the slasher sub-genre, and I do love it so, is fairly limited by design, and is often hampered by its "rules" and traditions. This one breaks that mold in several ways, primarily the aforementioned "gimmick" of never cutting away from the heroine. Imagine a version of *Halloween* or *Friday the 13th* that never once moved the camera away from Laurie or Alice, and you can quickly appreciate how tricky an endeavor this is. Does it always work? No. But it's a damn good attempt, and the big slasher sequence makes up for pretty much any of its faults. Stick with it!

MOVIE #191 – JULY 10th

COLIN (2008)
Dir: Marc Price
HMAD Review Date: October 18, 2010 (DVD)
Genre: Zombie
Available from Walking Shadows

Synopsis Based On Fading Memory: A zombie outbreak story shown from the POV of one of the random zombies.

Review excerpt:
"Alastair Kirton as Colin is terrific, making a compelling character without speaking a word (and, you know, being a goddamn zombie). It's not until the end of the film that we really understand where he's coming from and how he got involved with the zombie invasion in the first place, so it's kind of melancholy when everything comes full circle. How many zombie movies make you say "aww..." at the end? Zombie Honeymoon *is probably the only other one I can think of."*

Reflection: It won't shock many of you to learn I am not a trained writer. I took some screenwriting classes in college, but when it comes to this particular kind of writing I just hoped for the best when I started typing. I write like I talk, which is probably a bad thing, and I'm sure I broke every grammar rule in the book every week (and also why this book required three editors). But one rule I was pretty good at following, for whatever reason, was not ending a sentence with "of". I know the actual rule is "Don't end a sentence in a preposition", but the full extent of it is not something I care about. (See?) No, it's just "of" that bothered me for whatever reason, and I would often rewrite my sentences to make sure such a thing didn't happen. Except this time I guess! It's how I ended a PARAGRAPH, actually!

I chalk it up to still being dizzy from Price's shaky-cam obsession in this otherwise solid little indie gem. And when I say indie, I REALLY mean indie – the reported budget for the film was about 75 bucks. Even *Blair Witch Project*, poster child for cheap horror, cost 35 grand or something. 75 bucks is something some of you might even have in your pocket right now. Imagine being able to make a movie, ANY movie, with nothing more than the paper bills in your pocket (and presumably a camera you already own) – Marc Price more or less did that and it's actually pretty good!

MOVIE #192 – JULY 11th

NINJAS VS. ZOMBIES (2008)
Dir: Justin Timpane
HMAD Review Date: February 14, 2011 (DVD)
Genre: Comedic, Zombie
Available from Seminal Films

Synopsis Based on Fading Memory: Movie references! Zombies!

Review excerpt:
"...the movie is surprisingly action packed, which keeps the reference overload to a minimum, particularly in the 3rd act which is comprised of nearly non-stop fighting. Some individual battles go on for too long (the main villain and hero fight in a tiny movie theater for what seems like 10 minutes), but I admired the ambition and effort on display; even big budget movies don't always offer as much carnage. The FX and stunts are a bit clunky, but that is to be expected and I don't fault it for that (again, I've seen studio films with FX that were just as amateurish; what was THEIR excuse?)."

Reflection: Pitches beginning with "It's *Shaun of the Dead* meets ___" or "It's *Clerks* meets ___" have probably been uttered some 11 million times over the past couple decades, and I usually rolled my eyes when I came across yet another would-be opus from the next Edgar Wright or Kevin Smith wannabe. But this particular one entertained me more than its innumerable peers, for whatever reason; I laughed a lot, and I was impressed with what they pulled off with their limited means. Given that this is "true indie" month, I wanted to spotlight this one even if I didn't love it all that much, because nothing annoyed me more than when I would give an honest review to a bad indie and inevitably get someone (let's be generous and assume it wasn't someone associated with the film) blasting me, saying "Hey give them a break, they only had (small budget)!" or something along those lines. Because this one had a small budget, and so did a lot of others that turned out just as good or even better – hell, yesterday's movie, *Colin*, supposedly only cost 75 bucks! I'm not an expert on film production by any means, but I'm pretty good at telling the difference between what is bad because of a low budget and what is bad because the filmmakers shouldn't quit their day job. The worst things about this movie are all the goddamn geek references, though even some of those cracked me up (the *Lost* one in particular).

There are two sequels, but I haven't seen them. Given their comedic nature, I don't expect much – you can probably count on one hand the number of comedy sequels that actually measured up to their originals, and the odds are even slimmer for horror-comedies (don't you dare defend *Ghostbusters II* to me, you bastard). Still, good on Timpane for actually getting a franchise off the ground in this day and age, when it's so hard to get your film noticed at all let alone turn a big enough profit on it that someone will back follow-ups. Hell even Hollywood has trouble doing that with millions spent on advertising – hey, how's that *Cirque du Freak* sequel coming along?

MOVIE #193 – JULY 12th

SWEATSHOP (2009)
Dir: Stacy Davidson
HMAD Review Date: September 13, 2011 (DVD)
Genre: Slasher
Available from Screen Media

Synopsis Based on Fading Memory: A big brute with a giant hammer kills a bunch of assholes.

Review excerpt:
"I admired the production team's commitment to making an intentionally repulsive slasher movie. At times I was reminded of See No Evil, *which was another "hulking brute" sleazo-slasher with unlikable protagonists, but while that film eventually went into more typical territory (back-story for the killer, anti-hero turned real hero, etc.), this one never stopped reminding us that our characters were selfish assholes. No one makes any attempt to save anyone but themselves, or even really fights back against the killer - they just want to get the hell away if they can. I know I come down hard on these sorts of characters, but in a way, I'd rather never like them than have them suddenly turn into typical hero characters out of nowhere. Plus, it's been a long time since there's been a masked killer who was also, well, fat. Nowadays, masks are primarily used for whodunit style slashers, which means everyone in the cast has to have a similar build, so it's nice to have that bit of mystery (he is never unmasked) but also allow him to be physically imposing to the rest of the cast. I don't want to say he's a slasher icon just yet, but he makes a great first impression and passes the basic test – would you want an action figure of him? (Yes.)"*

Reflection: For those who skip over the excerpts for whatever reason, in this one I mention a basic test for slashers: "Would you want an action figure of the killer?", and it's something that I sort of wrestle with when watching modern body count movies. I think there's a problem among some where their filmmakers kind of want to make their killer an icon right out of the gate, which is the wrong way to go because that's sort of OUR job to decide. I mean, look at Jason in *Friday the 13th* – the first film was a different killer entirely, and in the second he had a bag over his head. He got his trademark hockey mask about halfway through the 3rd film, but even then he was still kind of in the shadows – I recently revisited *Final Chapter* and only really noticed for the first time that the kill scenes don't actually show much of Jason at all, sticking to his arms more often than not. Then the next one hid him as much as it could because it was a whodunit. It wasn't until *Jason Lives* - when he was a zombie – that he started having this sort of iconic presence on camera as a main attraction of the film – and that was halfway through the series. Too many filmmakers today jump ahead to that point right out of the gate (some even claim their killer is the newest slasher icon in their publicity), and while I might ultimately like some of the films, I think they should hold back and build up their would-be icon. Focus on making a movie we want to see a sequel to in the first place, THEN start dreaming of merchandising potential.

So kudos to *Sweatshop*'s crew for getting this right, while also delivering something in the vein of mid/late '80s slashers like *Slaughterhouse* and *The Mutilator*, where they were unabashedly playing for the cheap seats and delivering exactly what you'd expect. There's a sort of charm in that, I think. It's tough to pull off properly – I've seen countless awful slashers that were attempting the same sort of thing, failing miserably and often making me angry to boot. The only thing this has in common with those kinds of movies is that it isn't going to end up on anyone's list of classic slasher films, but as long as you keep in mind what the filmmakers' objective was you should have fun.

MOVIE #194 – JULY 13th

SOFT FOR DIGGING (2004)
Dir: J.T. Petty
HMAD Review Date: May 14, 2011 (Streaming)
Genre: Possession
Available from Vanguard Cinema

Synopsis Based on Fading Memory: A very quiet guy sees a murder... or DID HE?

Review excerpt:
"...it's actually kind of funny how they work around the lack of dialogue. At one point a phone rings, and I thought "A-ha! Surely there will be dialogue here!", but then they cut to an angle outside and let the hero's facial expressions more or less tell you what is being said. And since a good chunk of the first half of the movie deals with the police investigating his claims about the murder he saw and later the corpse he found, it's quite a marvel that Petty was able to get all of this stuff across without dialogue, and it never gets confusing. However, he does use "Chapter" title cards that sort of provide the gist of what the next 7 or 8 minutes will be about, which sometimes spoil things (the last one in particular) but at least help give us an idea of where the story is about to go."

Reflection: I previously sung Petty's praises in the entry for *The Burrowers* last month, so I won't gush over him again. I WILL say that this one is not exactly going to be everyone's cup of tea, and I'd recommend saving it for last if you are taken with *Burrowers* and want to see Petty's other films. It's REALLY film-school-y (by which I mean arty and slightly pretentious) and snail paced, so it's best to go in with a full appreciation of Petty and a curiosity of where he started, I think. Of course, if you really like this sort of stuff in general you might be disappointed that he followed it up with a killer bug movie, but whatever.

I should mention that the movie concerns a lost pet, and (spoiler) that subplot does not have a happy ending. I actually considered marking all of the movies in which a dog or cat is killed, or leaving them out of the book entirely, because I know there are a lot of people like me who can easily watch 100 people get their heads chopped off with no problem, but lose it when a dog is run over or something. And it's not something you want to be reminded of when sitting down with a movie you're likely watching for the sole purpose of turning your brain down a bit and having a good time. But I had to abandon any sort of "marking" of such films because I might miss one and then someone would (rightfully) get upset that I seemingly gave it the OK. Plus no one warned *me* about any of them, so why should you be spared?

MOVIE #195 – JULY 14th

THE SIGNAL (2007)
Dir: David Bruckner, Dan Bush and Jacob Gentry
HMAD Review Date: October 20, 2007 (Festival screening)
Genre: Psychological, Technology
Available from Magnolia Home Entertainment

Synopsis Based on Fading Memory: A strange virus causes folks to go insane in this trio of stories set around New Year's Eve.

Review excerpt:
"Still, it's not enough to totally derail the film, and it's astounding how good the film looks considering how little it was shot for. Atlanta is a vastly underused shooting location, especially in horror, so that helped give the film a different look (rather than the umpteenth cinematic end of the world via Los Angeles). The acting is also quite good across the board, all unknowns."

Reflection: It used to be pretty rare to see more than one director on a movie, but over the years, for whatever reason, it's become more common to see pairs, often billed as "brothers" when they're not (the Vicious Brothers, the Butcher Brothers, etc.), and there's been a revival of anthology films that rope in several directors to contribute segments. But *The Signal* not only predated those trends, it also offered something that's still pretty unique – three directors helming parts of a single storyline, focusing on different characters. So it'd be like if Tarantino only directed only the first part of *Pulp Fiction*, while someone else did the Bruce Willis segment and yet another handled "The Bonnie Situation" (which, as you may know, was originally the plan). It works phenomenally well, and given the film's acclaim (it made quite a few top ten lists within the genre) I'm really surprised we don't see more movies attempting to copy Bruckner, Bush, and Gentry's work here.

The excerpt won't help you decide to watch the movie if you haven't already (the "not enough to derail the movie" comment is in regards to the film's third segment, which I didn't enjoy as much as the first two), but I wanted to pull it out for a couple reasons. First, I point out that the actors are unknowns, which is no longer the case as several of them are now familiar faces – hurrah! The other is that at the time I was happy to see a movie shot in Atlanta – I'm now sick of seeing it thanks to *The Walking Dead*. As I've worked on this book I've been amused at how many movies I changed my tune on since posting the review, but this is a rare case where I found my perspective to be "dated" in the traditional sense. Stupid, naïve BC from 2007!

MOVIE #196 – JULY 15th

BENEATH THE MISSISSIPPI (2008)
Dir: Lonnie Schuyler
HMAD Review Date: August 20, 2011 (DVD)
Genre: Ghost, Psychological
Available from Echo Bridge

Synopsis Based on Fading Memory: Some mumbling people go up a poorly photographed river to solve an uninvolving mystery.

Review excerpt:
"I am not a deaf person, but I think I know now what the world "sounds" like to those who have at least partial hearing left – it sounds like Beneath the Mississippi. *The dialogue in the film doesn't seem to be spoken, only muttered – only about 10% of the lines are clearly spoken and recorded. After the opening scene's narration, at least 10-15 minutes went by before I could pick out another wholly discernible line of dialogue; even catching the character's names took some effort. And some lines are clearly dubbed, so the filmmakers know how that process works, so I am baffled why they didn't just re-dub the entire movie once it became clear that their sound guy was clearly drunk or working with malfunctioning equipment. I can understand a radio through a wall easier than the average scene in this movie."*

Reflection: When all was said and done, I opted to answer a question that came up all the time whenever someone would ask me about watching horror movies every day: "What's the worst movie you saw?" Until April 1st, 2013, I usually offered "I can't decide" or some other evasive answer, but now that I was done, I knew for sure – it never, ever got worse than this fucking movie. At the time I wrote my review I suspected as much, but I gave myself another 500 movies (give or take) to be sure, and thankfully I never saw anything this bad again. I could tell that it was going to be a front-runner for the bottom of my list after five minutes, but I foolishly hoped maybe I'd get used to the movie's terrible technical presentation and salvage something from the narrative once it got going. But believe it or not, the movie just got worse, offering blunders that I hadn't even been privy to in the first few minutes, while also putting up with the murky plot that just got more and more incomprehensible until the film finally ended 112 goddamn minutes later.

Luckily, it's remained as obscure as it deserves to be. No one has turned it into a bad movie cult phenomenon like *Birdemic* or *The Room*, and the IMDb board still has the same three threads that it had four years ago when I last looked at it. In fact, as of this writing, if you Google the title, my review comes up 3rd, after the IMDb page and the trailer on YouTube - this is a placement I can't usually pull off even when adding "Horror Movie A Day" to the search query. I'd rather not give it this bit of exposure, but since I was putting a bad movie in the middle of every month, I didn't even have to think about which one to use for independent month, as it represents every single complaint one could ever make about low budget films and makes up a few of its own for good measure. I do not wish anyone spend money on it directly, but it has apparently found its way to a few of Echo Bridge's budget packs, so hopefully you can justify your purchase with one of the other movies on the set if you come across it (I found one that had *Grave Mistake* – movie #187 – in the same pack, as well as the cult melodrama/slasher *Curtains*). No matter how you see it, keep in mind that out of 2500+ movies, THIS is the one that nearly broke me. I dare you to get through the whole goddamn thing.

MOVIE #197 – JULY 16th

ROT: REUNION OF TERROR (2008)
Dir: Michael Hoffman Jr.
HMAD Review Date: April 22, 2011 (DVD)
Genre: Slasher
Available from Shock-O-Rama Cinema

Synopsis Based on Fading Memory: Bunch of friends, cabin, slasher...

Review excerpt:
"I was continually puzzled by the movie's strange sexual hang-ups. In addition to the lesbians, who of course feel the need to make out in front of strangers and turn nearly every line they have into a double entendre, we also have a character that is running away from home because her stepfather was molesting her. Oh, and later she gives the guy who picked her up a hand job and one of the things he says is "Who's your daddy?", which just seems odd considering why they met up in the first place. Then he goes to buy condoms and she adds tampons to the mix – ew (and then of course we find out she's not yet 18). Plus, every older male in the movie is characterized as a pervert (the forest ranger is seen sniffing panties and pleasuring himself while looking at the erotic services ads in the newspaper), and the protagonists are constantly making homoerotic jokes and such. There are three credited writers; I think one of them needs to have a healthy relationship before writing another movie."

Reflection: Slasher motives don't tend to be very original – it's usually "you pulled a prank and I got disfigured so now I'm going to come after you all!" or "your mom slept with my dad and ruined my childhood" (believe it or not, I've seen at least three like that), or they simply don't explain it at all. But this one, I am pretty sure, is the only one to play its particular card, which I won't spoil here. I WILL say it's rather depressing, and doesn't really fit with the first hour or so (a typical B-movie slasher), but points for originality. And like some others this month, I wanted to spotlight it for the independent theme, because if you listen to the commentary you'll discover that the movie was seemingly cursed. Most of the issues would be easily avoided if they were working in a studio system with more money, but they were forced to make do – and they DID, instead of giving up. So kudos to them for that!

The commentary also sort of apologized for the tonal swing, for the record, so it won me over. I listened to a lot of commentaries over the years where the filmmakers seem to be unaware that their film is junk, so when I heard one with some honesty it left an impression. So no, it's not a particularly great movie, but it's still worth a look, because how many slashers have you seen that made you SAD? Plus, if you actually watched yesterday's movie it'll seem like *Halloween* in comparison anyway. Believe it or not, I DID put some thought into how these movies were ordered, for you rich viewers (or thieves) that are actually watching them all.

MOVIE #198 – JULY 17th

TONY (2009)
Dir: Gerard Johnson
HMAD Review Date: November 16, 2010 (DVD)
Genre: Serial Killer
Available from Revolver Entertainment

Synopsis Based on Fading Memory: A serial killer goes about his day.

Review excerpt:
"I liked that Tony never seemingly went out of his way to kill someone. Instead, he just kills the folks that would disturb his life, such as the guy who threatens to take his TV away for not paying his licensing fee (this is a very foreign concept to me – I was amazed to discover that this actually happens in the UK). He goes out to clubs and such, but again it seems to be more to find someone to hang out and watch action movies with, not to kill. The best scene in the film finds him unknowingly drawing the attention of a homosexual guy in a club, who goes home with him. Tony just thinks the guy wants to hang out and maybe listen to one of his Queen tapes, and so when the guy makes a move on him... well, let's just say it's the rare occurrence in a serial killer movie where you fear for the safety of the killer."

Reflection: One of the best things I've been able to do since becoming a guy who writes about horror was travel to London in 2010 for the annual Frightfest UK, and at the time I made a vow to return. I never did, and probably never will now that I have a kid. Anyway, there's a scene in this movie where Tony, our "hero" serial killer, walks by the theater where the festival took place, and even though it had only been like three months I was already missing it. So I'd probably start weeping if I watched the movie now, knowing it will be several years before I even have the option of returning. Apparently the festival has changed a bit - due in part to the Empire Cinema getting rid of their gigantic theater - so I don't know if it will be the same if I ever DO get to go back, but assuming the general spirit and bullshit-free introductions/hosting segments by the organizers are the same, I can encourage you to check it out without question. Tell them I sent you! It won't mean a goddamn thing, but hey, might as well start a conversation somewhere.

As for the movie, it's a bit plotless, so repeat viewings aren't likely, but if you are a *Henry* fan you should appreciate its straightforward, slightly dramatic take on the life of a serial killer. And like the earlier *Colin*, the commentary is an insightful look on how to pull off making a movie guerilla style in the modern day, so that's useful for you budding filmmaker types. Much like the "the dog dies" marker I referenced a few movies ago, I wish I had the foresight to tag all the movies that had quality commentaries; I almost always listened to them, but so many are rubbish it's no wonder so many people skip them. I wish the studios would just omit a track if it turned out bad, so we'd know that if it actually made it to disc it'd be worth listening to. Alas.

HMAD Fun Fact: HMADs were watched in Massachusetts, New Hampshire, New York, Connecticut, Texas, London and (mainly/obviously since it's where I live) California. Also a few were watched on planes so you can add some of the flyover states and "over the Atlantic Ocean" to the list.

MOVIE #199 – JULY 18th

PETER ROTTENTAIL (2004)
Dir: John Polonia and Mark Polonia
HMAD Review Date: February 6, 2010 (DVD)
Genre: Comedic, Slasher
Available from Sub Rosa Studios

Synopsis Based on Fading Memory: A killer Easter Bunny kills people.

Review excerpt:
"...after like 20 minutes or so (of the 70 minute film, five of which are the slowest crawling end credits I've ever seen) I became sort of charmed by the film's good natured silliness and complete lack of pretension. The bunny has a few one-liners and kills someone with a carrot, and the characters he encounters seem to think he's just a guy in a bunny costume, so again, it's not like they are asking us to buy into any of the nonsense. Also, this killer rabbit movie has a character named Lenny. Come on, that's awesome."

Reflection: This movie has a lot of pacing issues and some glaring errors that even the low budget should have prevented (apparently they couldn't afford a cake, resulting in a cake-throwing scene where there is no cake*), but it's so laid back and goofy I kind of loved it. I got the idea that the filmmakers were basically making a movie to amuse themselves, but released it into the wild anyway. This is something that could be disastrous - I've seen commercially released films that seem to be riddled with in-jokes for the small circle of folks that made it - but it mostly works, in my opinion. And with movies like *Jack Frost* trying so hard to shock you, I also appreciated the sort of PG-13 approach to the material – it's a killer bunny movie that you can almost allow your Easter Bunny-believing child to watch. There's something endearing about that, and over the years I never saw anything else quite like it.

That said, there are a surprising number of killer Easter Bunny movies. There's *Bunnyman* and its sequel, *Bunnyman Massacre*, the weird *Easter Bunny, Kill Kill!*, and a pair of entries that hit last year that I haven't heard much about: *The Night Before Easter* and the simply titled *Easter Sunday*, both of which involve groups of teens being slaughtered by a guy in a bunny mask. The former apparently has several references to Kevin Smith, so I'll be avoiding it, but the latter sounds more up my alley as it involves a resurrected serial killer (*Shocker* style!) and features the awesome, recently departed Robert Z'Dar. As someone who tries to find new Christmas and Halloween set horror every year, it's nice to know I can extend the tradition with Easter Bunny killers, apparently. Still barely any Thanksgiving ones though.

*I COULD have made a *Portal* joke there, but I refrained. Did you?

MOVIE #200 – JULY 19th

THE DEAD NEXT DOOR (1989)
Dir: J.R. Bookwalter
HMAD Review Date: June 12, 2009 (DVD)
Genre: Zombie
Available from Anchor Bay Entertainment

Synopsis Based on Fading Memory: An anti-zombie squad battles zombies AND a cult of people who love zombies.

Review excerpt:
"...the sheer amount of zombie action is unparalleled. Even some of Romero's films didn't have as many shootings, dismemberments, and beheadings as this one does. And the effects are quite impressive, particularly the squib work. To see a zombie run over to a human, and then the human spins around and shoots the zombie, with a big ol' exit wound spraying blood everywhere - ALL IN ONE SHOT - is pretty rare in these films. Usually it's "zombie runs over" - CUT TO A DIFFERENT ANGLE - "blood sprays from a suddenly immobile zombie". The zombie design is pretty good too; it's the standard Romero look, but considering how many zombies are shown in certain scenes, it's nice to see how many of them got fully made up."

Reflection: This one's so good I should have just put it into the regular zombie month, as it could fit comfortably alongside bigger budgeted movies. But more than any other film this month I think THIS is a testament to how much you can pull off on an indie if you play your cards right (and, OK, if you know Sam Raimi, but this was the '80s; Raimi was still making indies himself, he wasn't "*Spider-Man* director Sam Raimi" yet), because it has a ton of production value at a fraction of the cost (listen to the commentary for the hows and whys, though being 25+ years old the information might not help you today). It took four years to make and the results are still impressive, without as many of the seams showing as you might expect from such a lengthy endeavor.

However, it also indulges in a tradition that drives me up a wall: naming all of the characters after horror directors and legends. I forgave them because this was the '80s and it hadn't been done too much then, but for any filmmakers reading this book, I IMPLORE you, do NOT name people "Carpenter" or "Romero" or "Savini". It's a tired gag and will likely only serve to remind your audience of a movie that they might prefer to yours. Do something a little less obvious; I saw one where the characters all had the same first names as the folks in *NOTLD* – I didn't pick up on it until halfway through the film, and smiled when

I realized the theme. The *Sleepaway Camp* sequels did things like naming everyone after Brat Packers (I didn't put that one together until they introduced "Emilio") in part 2 and TV shows (*Brady Bunch* and *Munsters*, specifically) in part 3 – this is also far less distracting than having someone named "Detective Cronenberg" showing up. So don't do it, or at least pick more obscure directors. Thanks in advance.

MOVIE #201 – JULY 20th

SLEDGEHAMMER (1983)
Dir: David A. Prior
HMAD Review Date: August 26, 2011 (DVD)
Genre: Slasher
Available from Intervision Pictures Corp.

Synopsis Based on Fading Memory: A group of pals visiting a house in the woods run afoul of Killer and his titular sledgehammer (but usually his knife).

Review excerpt:
"Then there's the killer, who is named Killer (but he's got a mask, so he's still more distinct than the Final Exam *guy). His motive is just as vague, in the prologue (and a recap 25 minutes later, in case we forgot) we see that his mother was cheating on his dad, which set him off, killing them both. So now I guess he just sort of hangs out waiting for other folks to come around to the house, even though he apparently has supernatural powers which you'd think he'd want to exploit a little. As one of the guys from Bleeding Skull points out, his costume just sort of makes him look like someone's dad when you can't see the mask, as it's just a pair of jeans and an ugly plaid shirt. But the mask is fairly creepy; it's one of those clear plastic ones like in* Alice, Sweet Alice. *And he lives up to the title, in that he does have a sledgehammer that he frequently carries around with him, though curiously most of the film's kills are committed via knife. Someone needs to make a movie called* Knife *where everyone dies by sledgehammer so we can even this thing out."*

Reflection: If you watched *Things* from May's selections, this won't strike you as particularly odd, but man oh man, if you're going in thinking this is a typical indie slasher... you're in for such a slow, odd treat. And by slow I don't just refer to the pacing – director Prior (who unfortunately passed away in 2015) had to pad the runtime, so he just slowed down a bunch of footage at random, including a shot of someone putting down a sleeping bag. In some ways this is kind of a laundry list of things NOT to do with your independent film, and to a less insightful or intelligent critic it'd just be written off as a horrible movie without fanfare. But, perhaps inadvertently, it gets something right that so many other indies (not just slashers) got so very wrong – it's MEMORABLE. Maybe not always for the right reasons, but so what? I'll take a million goofy movies like this over a single *Friday the 13th* rip-off where the characters are all assholes, the killer's wearing a big hooded coat, and all of the kills are off-screen because the director didn't know better to hire an FX guy. So that's what makes this movie relatively essential – when all else fails, just get weird.

I mentioned *Things*, so I should also mention that it and *Sledgehammer* were released on the same label. It's called Intervision, and if memory serves it was an off-shoot of Severin Films (sort of like how Scream Factory is a spinoff of Shout! Factory) that was dedicated to releasing weirdo VHS-era nonsense like these two movies, plus the very peculiar *The Secret Life: Jeffrey Dahmer* and notorious *The Burning Moon*. Not sure what's up with them, they haven't released anything in a while and never released Blu-rays for their bigger titles, so I am guessing the brand has died. A pity, as there are assuredly more batshit titles like this that they could have given a new lease on life, and the physical disc market is slowly being eroded thanks to digital/streaming, making it unlikely anyone will pick up where they left off. Sigh.

MOVIE #202 – JULY 21st

THE DEADLY SPAWN (1983)
Dir: Douglas McKeown
HMAD Review Date: May 15, 2012 (DVD)
Genre: Alien, Monster
Available from Synapse Films

Synopsis Based on Fading Memory: Some monsters are in the basement!

Review excerpt:
"One highlight was that the characters were pretty smart, another rarity. We have two heroes, essentially – an older teen who is a budding scientist and thus can make reasonable assumptions about the enemy and figure out how it lives (along with his girlfriend, who explains the ridges on its skin), and then his little brother. The brother is the main draw for horror fans, as he's basically us – he wakes up his aunt early in the morning because of the loud screams from the horror movie he's watching, he reads monster mags at breakfast, makes masks and simple FX with blast powder and such, and is generally pretty awesome. And he's not a weirdo; when his uncle asks if he realizes that Frankenstein and such aren't real, he answers "yes, that's why I like them." Hell yeah! He's also the one that figures out that the things can't see and go only by sound, which makes for a few fun moments."

Reflection: A lot of indie horror films are constantly using humor as a sort of defense mechanism for their lapses – I guess the thinking is, if the characters are having fun or winking at the audience, no one will mind the cheesy FX or lousy acting or whatever. And that's what made *Deadly Spawn* such a nice surprise for me; I saw it in the twilight era of HMAD-ing, so I certainly had my fill of that sort of thing by then. I figured it'd be a *Killer Tomatoes* kind of deal, but it was actually pretty serious, with a legit terrifying monster and lots of carnage. I don't know where I got the idea that it was more of a spoof, but I'm glad it was planted in my head, because it made this solid and enjoyable film even more of a nice surprise.

Earlier I mentioned commentaries and how some of them aren't worth listening to, so I want to stress that this is an exception. In fact, there are TWO tracks, because director McKeown (who sadly has never made another movie) and the producer, one Ted A. Bohus (writer/director/producer of the immortal *Vampire Vixens from Venus*) had a falling out during post-production and apparently still hate each other. So while McKeown offers the better track, it's worth listening to

Bohus' as he snips at shots that are out of focus and stuff like that. So deliciously petty! I mean it's not exactly up there with the infamous *Jack-O* commentary ("Shit pickle" – look it up), but considering the commentaries were recorded 20 years later it's childishly amusing that these two guys are still pissed off at one another. Forgive and forget, fellas!

MOVIE #203 – JULY 22nd

KILL HOUSE (2006)
Dir: Beth Dewey
HMAD Review Date: January 1, 2008 (DVD)
Genre: Comedic, Slasher
Available from Trinity Home Entertainment

Synopsis Based on Fading Memory: A crazed realtor is killing people... that's all I got, but this isn't so much me not being able to remember as it is the movie making very little sense.

Review excerpt:
"...in one of the film's stranger plot developments, our wannabe Janet Leigh character who gets killed a half an hour in is clearly wearing a red wig. This is sort of explained when she gets a phone call from her doctor, and she says "The results are in? Is it cancer?" And the doctor says that she can't tell her that over the phone. So the wig is to cover her bald head from chemo, right? Wrong. A. We still see her real hair under it, and B. if she didn't even definitely HAVE cancer yet, why would she already be taking chemotherapy? Doesn't matter, she gets killed moments later, and thus we never know if she has cancer or not."

Reflection: I wish I could remember where I got this low-key gonzo movie, because I want to thank them. I don't think I got it sent for review, because the review for the very first movie I got was posted only a few days before this one, and I doubt any other distributor caught on that fast. And this was long before horror trivia winnings bulked up my collection of random indie horror films that remain in dusty piles in my house until I happen to remember that they're there.

I DO know that I kept it in my collection ever since, partly for its amaza-terrible tagline ("*Escrow just closed!*"), but mainly because it's so damn peculiar. Not particularly GOOD, mind you, but endlessly watchable due to its bizarre approach to storytelling, where plot points are introduced and instantly made irrelevant (such as the "cancer" subplot described above). Or sometimes they're just completely dropped, like when the opening sequence spends a significant amount of time establishing San Francisco, and then they quickly go to Los Angeles after that, staying there for the rest of the film. It also offers a surprising amount of female nudity (full frontal included), but no actual sex - they're just naked at times for whatever reason. And it's directed by a woman! Maybe she was commenting on something, not unlike *Slumber Party Massacre*, but if so it doesn't really come across. Considering that the backdrop is real estate – the least interesting thing possible – it's kind of incredible how memorably weird this movie is. I didn't see a lot of really peculiar stuff that was also watchable in the next-to-no budget indie world, and that's a shame. You're not going to get on 3,000 screens anyway, go for broke!

MOVIE #204 – JULY 23rd

BLOODLINES (2007)
Dir: Stephen Durham and Henry Kingi, Jr
HMAD Review Date: December 1, 2007 (DVD)
Genre: Survival
Available from ThinkFilm

Synopsis Based on Fading Memory: A bunch of women are forced to fight to the death for the amusement of rednecks.

Review excerpt:
"The cover would have you believe that this one is more dark and serious, but they are 'lying'. This one is possibly one of the best "Get totally drunk while you watch it with your buddies" movies I have seen all year. The total lack of discern for human life, the rampant incest, and just general redneck tone of the whole thing is astounding (Christ, even on the commentary, the director points out how "A 6 pack can get you pretty far in the South."). It's terrible, yes, but in that special sort of way you just don't see enough of these days."

Reflection: If you ever dig deep into one of those budget packs I'm always talking about, you're bound to find something a little off-color that was produced far outside of the Hollywood system, where you can't help but wonder if the out of nowhere racism or reprehensible views toward women were the result of filmmakers who... let's just say, aren't as liberal as you might be used to. Such things are much rarer nowadays (or they just get lost in a sea of millions of movies and their millions of viewing options), so even though this is a pretty terrible movie I found it charming in its odd, unabashedly redneck-y way. The casual attitude toward incest is particularly worth noting – it's not played for laughs or as something traumatic... it just IS.

It's also got the most unnecessary kills I've seen this side of *Friday the 13th Part V*, something else I found strangely delightful. At one point the GOOD guy wipes out some random rednecks who weren't really doing anything wrong, just happened to be nearby when he was taking down all of the villains. Whenever I watch an old '80s action movie I am reminded that collateral damage used to be far more common – nowadays they always show the randoms getting out of their recently smashed cars so you know they're OK after the villain (or hero) ruined their day. As you might have guessed by now, this is sort of an action/horror blend – the survival horror elements are upsetting in their own way but there's a lot of gunfire and "save the girl" heroics. It's like *Hills Have Eyes* one minute and *Rambo* the next, basically, so don't expect to be scared as often as you're laughing and cheering at the rampant silliness.

MOVIE #205 – JULY 24th

HALLOWED (2005)
Dir: Rocky Costanzo
HMAD Review Date: January 9, 2012 (DVD)
Genre: Slasher
Available from New Light Entertainment

Synopsis Based on Fading Memory: A priest (?) picks a girl at random and wants to "save" her, and attempts to do so by killing her friends.

Review excerpt:
"I liked that it was short. As I've mentioned a couple times, I'm all about Skyrim *right now, so watching my HMADs cuts into how much time I spent crafting leather bracers and smiting the hell out of bandits with my awesome battle axe (45 dmg, 14 pts fire damage!). So I was happy to see that* Hallowed *had a Netflix envelope listed runtime of a mere 85 minutes, and even happier to see that the disc itself promised only 80. Thus, the fact that the movie was actually only 71 minutes (!) was nothing short of orgasmic.* Hallowed *filmmakers – your refusal to add a character or two or even slow down your end titles to hit the promised 80 minutes meant I was able to dick around looking for ore veins in the cave I was clearing. Bless you."*

Reflection: I chose this excerpt not because of any particular thing about the film I wanted to highlight, but because I find it amusing that now, in 2016, it's been almost four years since I touched *Skyrim*. It wasn't long after this time that my day job duties increased for the 2nd time, which reduced how much time I had for HMAD, which in turn cut back on my gaming. Other games came along, and then my kid came along... so my poor *Skyrim* character has been sitting there in limbo for much longer than I would have liked (not that I ever finish one of these open world RPGs). Based on my Achievement listing, I last played (or, at least, accomplished anything) on April 8, 2012, and I'll be honest, I can't remember if that axe I describe is actually "awesome" or if it's some entry level thing. Nor can I remember what exactly I was doing the last time I played, so if I ever pick it back up I'll probably have to start over. THESE ARE THE SACRIFICES I MADE FOR YOU!

Anyway this is a kinda goofy religious-tinged slasher with a very specific hook – it's a full length love letter to *Halloween*. The score is a rip-off, the characters walk or drive by the filming locations, they have one of those "here's all the places he was, and now he's gone" montages... if you're a *Halloween* nut like me, you should appreciate how much they want to show off their obvious love for the movie, while crafting a decent one of their own (and it has a pretty good twist at the end to boot). I mean, the plot is nothing like *Halloween's*, so it's a rare example of someone showing their love for a movie without just copying it blind – I can get behind that.

MOVIE #206 – JULY 25th

THE SLEEPER (2012)
Dir: Justin Russell
HMAD Review Date: March 2, 2013 (Festival screening)
Genre: Slasher
Available from Gamma Knife Films

Synopsis Based on Fading Memory: Sorority sisters and their boyfriends are targeted by a killer.

Review excerpt:
"Save for the digital photography (which he has tried very hard to give a 16mm look), at no point did I feel like I was watching anything but an actual 30-year-old slasher movie. Hell it's even SET in 1979, and there is only ONE very minor anachronism in the entire movie, one you might not even notice. And that's even more impressive when you consider that it has plenty of exteriors and a number of locations; the college campus where the film was shot thankfully hasn't modernized itself much over the past 30 years. But even if it took place today he still gets the little things right. The characters are a bit dim but not unlikable, and being that they're playing sorority sisters that's even more impressive. The FX are practical, and made with the correct assumption that we'd rather see a decent effort at a dummy head than some CGI enhanced effect that looks just as fake anyway."

Reflection: Look, if you've been going through a lot of the movies this month you're bound to have noticed a lot of bad performances, and this one is no exception. It actually might have some of the worst, come to think of it. But I couldn't let that diminish the film's strong suit, which is that Russell did a terrific job aping the REALLY low budget slashers of the post-*Halloween*, pre-*Nightmare on Elm Street* period. True, he's mostly drawing from 1974's *Black Christmas* (and, admittedly, flat out ripping it off at times, particularly the score), but the film, set in 1979, feels very much at home with movies like *To All A Goodnight*, *Final Exam*, and *The Dorm That Dripped Blood*. Meaning, things aren't quite as slick, and the pacing can be a bit woozy, but damned if they don't scratch that particular slasher itch if you're in the mood.

And he pulls off a pretty great "twist" late in the game that *Black Christmas* fans should get a kick out of, if they're still on board with the film. Because *Halloween* overshadowed the significance *Black Christmas* had on the evolution of the slasher film, fans of the latter tend to get really defensive about it (the folks who made the remake can certainly attest to this), and so they should appreciate this love letter to *their* movie. In fact, there's nary a *Halloween* reference in sight! *Prom Night* kinda gets some love though, for some reason - I really don't get why folks have any affinity for that one.

MOVIE #207 – JULY 26th

IT'S MY PARTY AND I'LL DIE IF I WANT TO (2007)
Dir: Tony Wash
HMAD Review Date: May 5, 2008 (DVD)
Genre: Supernatural
Available from Scotchworthy Productions

Synopsis Based On Fading Memory: Basically *Night of the Demons*, but with a touch of slasher.

Review excerpt:
"Like some of the other indies I have watched, it's kind of contradictory to the point of HMAD, since I can't imagine many (any?) of the regular readers have seen the film. But it is available through the film's official site, and I'm sure Wash will be showcasing the film at other horror conventions. It's definitely worth checking out, and the type of indie I highly recommend supporting – it may not be perfect, but it's made with genuine care and love for the genre, which is more than you can say for (at least) half of the films I've watched; movies that spent more in a single day than Wash and his crew probably had for the entire production. Kudos to them."

Reflection: Sometimes I forget that the whole point of HMAD was to just make a forum for folks to talk about horror movies, an online version of the discussion you'd have on the way out of the theater. This is why a lot of the early reviews are so vague; the idea was that you'd only read it if you just watched the movie, and thus you didn't need a synopsis or even the names of anyone involved. Eventually it became a more typical review site, but I still enjoyed (when time allowed) replying to comments and keeping the discussion going. This disconnect is addressed in the excerpt, which is kind of funny because the only comments the review ever got were mainly about an aside in the review regarding Dramarama's "Anything, Anything". Which, for the record, I'm also happy to talk about at any time.

Anyway, this movie is worth watching on the strength of a Ben Tramer reference alone. Also the week I wrote this entry, Lesley Gore (who sang the "It's My Party and I'll Cry If I Want To" song that the title is clearly referencing) passed away, so that's an odd and depressing coincidence. It's amusing how many horror films used Gore's songs over the year – I'm sure her last name put her on the genre radar, but the songs themselves are so upbeat and catchy, they always stick out (in a good way!) in horror films. And horror TV shows as well; *American Horror Story* made great use of "You Don't Own Me". RIP, Ms. Gore!

The DVD has a "choose your own adventure" element to it, so it's worth tracking down a physical copy (Amazon currently only has a streaming version) if you want to have some more fun with it. The only other movie I remember doing this for in the modern era was *Return to House on Haunted Hill*, which I don't recommend in any fashion. Personally I think such gimmicks should be limited to half hour episodic things, where you could conceivably have the time to go through it a couple times – have I ever had the time to watch a movie back to back just to make use of some tech? But still, it's admirably ambitious for an indie.

HMAD Fun Fact: The most prolific sub-genre of horror movies on the site were "Supernatural" horror movies, which was kind of a general term for anything with demons, presences (not identifiable ghosts), witchcraft, etc. As of the site's end on March 31st, 2013, 370 such films were reviewed.

MOVIE #208 – JULY 27th

BEYOND DREAM'S DOOR (1989)
Dir: Jay Woelfel
HMAD Review Date: February 10, 2011 (DVD)
Genre: Psychological
Available from Cinema Epoch

Synopsis Based on Fading Memory: Kind of cheating since this review is one of the few to include a synopsis, but a guy who can't dream finds himself menaced by the nightmares he's kept at bay.

Review excerpt:
"The plot here (best I can figure) is about a guy who hasn't been able to dream for 15 years, since his parents died when he was a kid (sort of backwards, but I'll go with it), and thus the dreams are sort of repressed and kind of pissed off about it. And so the action stems from these dreams (including a naked chick – a repressed wet dream? Gotta be a first) trying to kill him for some sort of revenge. That's a pretty nifty concept, I think, and it lends itself to a number of different dream motifs as opposed to just one Freddy Krueger-esque villain. There's the naked chick, a goofy rubber monster, random creepy folks, even some zombies at one point."

Reflection: I don't know why so many filmmakers fail to accurately depict dreams in their films, but it drives me up a wall. I assume it's because they're always trying to trick us for a scare, so they keep things very logical and normal up until the moment the heroine is suddenly killed (GASP! Cut to her sitting straight up in bed, like no one ever does in real life!). But dreams actually make little to no sense in reality, so when a film depicts them as they are, I tend to walk away impressed.

Less impressive in this one is the acting; it's actually kind of terrible across the board, making this one of the entries this month where they really WERE crippled by their low budget and independent status, as more funding and even a smaller traditional studio probably could have at least gotten them some decent leads. So prepare yourself for that, but if you're like me and found the increasingly set piece driven nightmare scenes in the *Elm Street* movies to be disappointing, you should be able to look past the clunky deliveries and just admire Woelfel's more thoughtful and accurate approach. Plus, that concept is awesome! Someone remake this!

MOVIE #209 – JULY 28th

ABSENTIA (2011)
Dir: Mike Flanagan
HMAD Review Date: October 2, 2011 (Festival screening)
Genre: Ghost, Thriller
Available from Phase 4 Films

Synopsis Based on Fading Memory: A woman is trying to put her life back together after her husband disappears... and then he mysteriously returns. BUT IS IT HIM?

Review excerpt:
"...the film was very effective at creeping me the hell out. I have long been fascinated by kidnapping/disappearance stories (thanks to watching Unsolved Mysteries *and the like since I was 9 or so), in particular when it's an adult as they don't get the same sort of public aid that a child would, which bums me out (although it's probably because it's possible that the adult merely chose to walk away from an unhappy life). And the tunnel where most of the bad stuff goes down is just plain chilling to look at, as it's tucked away a few dozen yards from a dead end street – you just KNOW it's bad news by looking at it, even before the movie tells us so. And that it's located not too far from where I live (somewhere in Silverlake or Echo Park, judging from its proximity to the Hollywood sign) makes it even creepier – and by that I mean I totally want to go find it and see if I can run through the tunnel when it's dark out."*

Reflection: 2014 was not a good year for horror at the box office, with only two movies making serious money (*Ouija* and *Annabelle*). But those had studio money (and franchise connections, in *Annabelle's* case), so the REAL big success story of the year was the fact that Mike Flanagan's *Oculus* scored around 30 million with an R rating, no major stars (just Karen Gillan from *Doctor Who*, hardly a box office sure thing), and a rather lengthy runtime for a horror flick. It out-grossed most of the other horror films released that year, and (most importantly for readers of this book) it gave me the most awful nightmare I've ever had in my life (albeit not until I saw it again on Blu-ray; read my review on HMAD for the story!).

I bring all that up because *Oculus* was Flanagan's follow-up to this criminally under-seen gem, which did well at festivals but didn't get a particularly big push on home video. Worse, the disc release was also cursed with a horrible marketing angle that opted for the "show a girl on the ground being pulled away by SOMETHING" approach that you can see on several thousand other DVD cases. And it's not even the girl from the movie! If you read the whole review you can enjoy me quite embarrassingly drooling all over the lead actress (Katie Parker), but for the key art they just got some random instead. I find that insulting and pointless. This is a great movie and thus even though it's not exactly famous I'm putting it in one of the "more well-known movies" slots this month to make sure you indie-phobes who might be skimming this chapter still give it a look.

MOVIE #210 – JULY 29th

LO (2009)
Dir: Travis Betz
HMAD Review Date: May 16, 2010 (DVD)
Genre: Supernatural, Weird
Available from Millennium Media

Synopsis Based on Fading Memory: A guy summons a demon to help him find his girlfriend.

Review excerpt:
"What I really appreciated about the movie was that it took a very supernatural and strange approach to what is ultimately a very simple story, of a guy who is afraid to let go. Instead of the usual indie "hey let's just sort of rip off Kevin Smith" approach to a guy who just had his heart broken, Betz and co. did something unique and original, and also found a bunch of capable actors (never a true indie film's strong suit). Even with minimal characterization, I got to really like Ward Roberts (Justin), and even though he's pretty much just sitting on the floor for the entire movie, he's one of the better horror movie "heroes" in recent memory."

Reflection: Some indie films really suffer from a script that was clearly dictated by the available locations. I remember seeing a cheapie vampire movie where a big showdown took place in an elementary school classroom (none of the characters were or even had children), because obviously someone worked in the building and could get them in, and that room probably just had the best light. Thankfully, *Lo* is not one of those films. Writer/director Betz just had one room to his disposal, and used this to advantage to create something truly original – it's a horror film that is also kind of like *My Dinner with Andre* or *Before Sunrise*, in that it's basically just one long conversation. And the characters barely ever even stand up from their sitting position on the floor of this one room. It doesn't always work, but I've never seen anything quite like it in a feature film (the approach to set design is particularly inspired by stage productions). And it proves that you can make an engaging and memorable movie without even leaving your bedroom, if you put your mind to it.

Fun fact: I met Betz once at a horror gathering of some sort, and was told by whoever introduced us (Mr. Disgusting, if memory serves) that he made the film *Joshua*. This was in the spring of 2007 and I thought it was the upcoming killer kid movie that I was looking forward to seeing, and told him as much. His reply was more or less "No, not that one. Mine already came out," so of course I felt pretty stupid. I have never seen him again nor have I seen HIS *Joshua*, which is (from what I gather from its IMDb page) a psychological nightmare type movie. Someday, when I get over the trauma of my *faux pas*, I'll check it out.

MOVIE #211 – JULY 30th

RETURN IN RED (2007)
Dir: Tyler Tharpe
HMAD Review Date: February 2, 2008 (DVD)
Genre: Post-Apocalyptic, Technology
Available from Image Entertainment

Synopsis Based on Fading Memory: A white van emanating a buzzing sound causes the residents of a small town to go crazy.

Review excerpt:
"Kudos to the team for pulling off the impressive effects on what couldn't have been more than a few thousand dollars budget. On one occasion, a guy is repeatedly rammed with a forklift, until his head is partially severed. Good stuff. And speaking of being impressed, this is the rare indie where you don't see all of the same names in the cast as you do in the crew. In fact there are none, other than the makeup guys playing (non-character) victims. The crew guys make the film, the actors act. Granted none of them are going to be up for a Spirit award, but then again it's an ensemble cast (hell, the guy that's sort of the hero gets killed with a half hour to go), no one is more important than anyone else."

Reflection: I've always had a strange affinity for movies where "nothing happens", though usually it tends to be in retrospect - when I'm watching I can get pretty restless. My go-to example for this sort of movie is Bryan Singer's pre-*Usual Suspects* movie *Public Access*, a good chunk of which is devoted to a guy looking through town records. There's just something that lulls me into its odd, slowly paced charms, and I walk away a fan even if it's not exactly the most exciting viewing experience. This one has some gore and even a set piece or two, making it more "action packed" than some others, but a lot of it is also devoted to people doing their household chores. Of all the movies this month this would be the one you'd probably hate the most if you don't see things my way, but I had to give it props for being so strange, and even 7+ years later I can still vividly recall certain scenes and faces, so that's gotta be worth something.

It's also got the most face-palming director reply in HMAD history; Mr. Tharpe (or someone who coincidentally shared his name) gave his own mini-review, defending the "glacial pace" and referring to the film as a "certain kind of brilliance". It's no secret that filmmakers plant reviews on IMDb and the like, but it's just funny/sad when it's a comment in reply to what is already a positive review. Even funnier, a year later he returned to thank me for my *own* praise. Weird.

MOVIE #212 – JULY 31st

POULTRYGEIST: NIGHT OF THE CHICKEN DEAD (2006)
Dir: Lloyd Kaufman
HMAD Review Date: January 4, 2009 (DVD)
Genre: Comedic, Musical
Available from Troma Entertainment

Synopsis Based on Fading Memory: A fast food joint built over a cemetery finds its meat tainted by the angry spirits. Politically incorrect humor, scenes built around bodily functions, and some surprisingly catchy songs ensue.

Review excerpt:
"Things get off to a great start: homoerotic dialogue, songs about lesbian sex, a broken finger being used as a butt plug, a reference to a pro vs anti bestiality debate in high school... everything one would want from a Troma film. And surprisingly, it more or less holds up over the course of its rather unnecessary 102 minute run time (90 should really be the max for any movie in which a guy literally shits himself out). It drags a bit in spots, and I really thought that I would get rather sick of it after 40 minutes, but I was still laughing and giggling by the time the credits rolled. Of course, the finale features a little girl running around with her mother's decapitated head and then guzzling a beer, so even if the previous 90 minutes had been terrible, it would have gone out on a high note either way."

Reflection: If you're not a Troma fan (and please note when I refer to Troma I mean their actual productions, which are often directed by Lloyd Kaufman himself. I don't count their random acquisitions as true "Troma movies"), feel free to skip watching the movie and either listen to the commentary or watch the making of, which is flooded with evidence of the real independent spirit. The crew slept on floors, barely anyone got paid, catering was questionable... and yet they not only pressed on, but made a pretty entertaining movie to boot. I'm not saying you need to forego all those niceties when making an indie, but I have infinitely more respect for films that make sure to put every dollar they have on-screen instead of on making everyone comfortable. Hell, they even shot it on 35mm, at a time when even major studio productions were pinching pennies and using digital.

So kudos to Kaufman and his crew for not stooping to everyone else's level – they might be making something where seeing someone defecate is fairly common, but at least they made sure it looked like a real movie and putting their money where their mouth is. They've since started using digital (as evidenced by the *Return to Nuke 'Em High* films), and are dipping their toes into crowdfunding like everyone else, but Lloyd and his cronies are still dedicated to doing things their own way. Not to mention showing better gratitude; when the dipshit from *Scrubs* made his fans put up the dough to make his insufferable movie, the perk for giving him $3,000 was getting to be an extra in the film (if you know nothing about filmmaking – a. extras are supposed to BE paid, not PAY to be there, and b. it's very likely you wouldn't be plainly visible in the finished product). Lloyd's perk for the same amount for his recent Kickstarter? He would *direct your short film script* for you. Yeah, I think I'd rather support Lloyd, there.

Anyway, now that the month is over, I hope you can appreciate some real independent stuff, and join me in laughing when the term is used to describe something that cost 20 million dollars and has several former Oscar nominees/winners among its cast.

AUGUST – "JUNK FOOD" HORROR

ARTIST: JEFF O'BRIEN

I moved to a place with central air last year, and it was nothing short of heavenly. For nine hellish years before that, I lived in an apartment that had one built-in AC unit (a smaller one meant to cool a single bedroom), and we were unable to put one (or two, or ten) more in the windows due to the way that they were designed. And we live in the San Fernando Valley, which is the hottest section of Los Angeles, so even with the AC on full blast all day, the apartment – especially the bedrooms, which were nowhere near the unit – would be an oven when I got home from work.

Long story short, I hated being in there, particularly during August which is the hottest of the summer months, and would often go to the movies after work just to enjoy a comfortable environment for a while before sweating myself to sleep. Unfortunately, this particular month is not exactly bursting with quality movies, traditionally. There have been a couple of exceptions (*Guardians of the Galaxy* is almost good enough to change the point entirely), but let's be honest: if it's 95 degrees out in the middle of August and you're going to your local multiplex, it's not for the great movie you might see. No, it's for the ice-cold AC and giant fountain soda, making a movie with a 3% Rotten Tomatoes score a perfect fit for your weary brain. So for this month, I figured we'd give props to… "lesser" films in the horror genre. I wouldn't go so far as to call them truly *bad*, but if anything in this month really blows you away, it's probably best you keep it to yourself.

Now, you might be asking why I'd waste 31 slots in this book on movies that aren't that good, and it's a valid concern. But trust me – I watched a LOT of true garbage over those six years, films that even the most comfortable conditions in the world couldn't save, so I've learned the difference between unwatchable shit and movies that merely fall into the "dumb fun" category; the Michael Bay equivalent of horror (he actually produced one of them, natch). Plus, if you're of a certain age, your summer vacation is almost over, which means you'll need all your brain cells soon – let them rest up for the months ahead.

Besides, for the same reason I include a legit bad movie every month, junk horror is kind of part of the fun of the genre. A bad comedy means the jokes aren't working and the movie is worthless, but a certain kind of bad horror can be just as entertaining as a legitimately great one. And some folks can recognize that a horror movie is bad, but if they're easily startled then it might still produce the desired effect (scaring you) with its jump scares and loud musical stings. I see it with my wife all the time; she'll sit down with me when I'm watching some piece of crap, ask me why I do this to myself… and then scream at the killer jumping out just as loud as she would if it were *The Exorcist* or something. I guess it's along the lines of the "bad pizza is still pretty good because it's pizza" logic? What I'm saying is, there is fun to be had with an amateurish horror movie that simply cannot be replicated in any other genre. Don't believe me? Look no further than...

MOVIE #213 – AUGUST 1st

SUBURBAN SASQUATCH (2004)
Dir: Dave Wascavage
HMAD Review Date: May 11, 2009 (DVD)
Genre: Monster
Available from Troubled Moon Films

Synopsis Based on Fading Memory: "Dave!"

Review excerpt:
"What makes this movie so amazing is how sincerely it seems to be told. I don't QUITE get the idea that the filmmakers or actors knew that they were making the least professional movie of all time. I can be sure that they know they're not going to rival King Kong *(or even* King Kong Lives*), but it's also missing that winking feeling that you get from movies like* Die You Zombie Bastards*. It's more or less played straight, limitations of budget, talent, and resources be damned."*

Reflection: Later this month I'll recommend *Frankenfish*, which is written by Simon Barrett, whom you may recognize as the screenwriter of great genre flicks like *You're Next* and *The Guest*. But before he did those, there was a period of time where he had nothing better to do than sit around with me once a month or so and do a commentary for a public domain horror movie, which we would then sync up and release on iTunes and on Bloody Disgusting. We called it "Horror People, Dear Reader" (if you know the reference, you win a cookie) and only managed to put together I think three episodes, but if there was a fourth it would have been for this masterpiece of no-budget nonsense. Unfortunately, after we recorded our commentary we discovered that the film wasn't in the public domain as we originally thought, and thus our thoughts sit somewhere on one of my voice recorders, forever unreleased.

But really, our half-drunken, wannabe *MST3k* ramblings are nowhere near as amusing as the film is on its own, and it's worth every penny (well, assuming it's less than 500 pennies) to see it for yourself. The title should clue you in to what it's about, and then you can be as amazed as we were when you discover that Suburban Sasquatch-based footage only covers about 9% of what's going on in this movie. I actually had trouble deciding if this belonged in the first position for the month, traditionally saved for my favorite, or the 15th, which is the month's obligatory "bad movie". I even considered putting it in both slots, because you'll probably want to watch it again anyway. Ultimately I put it first, because even the title continues to bring a smile to my face, and so even though I'm not a fan of the term in general, it truly is "so bad it's good".

Oh, the "synopsis" refers to an actor who couldn't even really deliver that line convincingly. It killed me; might be the only time as an adult I rewound part of a movie just to laugh at it again.

MOVIE #214 – AUGUST 2nd

PELT (2010)
Dir: Richard Swindell
HMAD Review Date: July 24, 2011 (Streaming)
Genre: Slasher, Survival
Available from Osiris Entertainment

Synopsis Based on Fading Memory: Some kids go into the woods and get killed one-by-one by a guy in overalls.

Review excerpt:
"I liked that it was set in 1991, which was a nice way around the cell phone issue, but didn't go overboard with it. Maybe they just didn't have the dough to do much else to nail down the time period, but if this was a studio movie, you can be sure that they'd be playing, I dunno, Will Smith's "Summertime" or maybe Alice Cooper's "Hey Stoopid" on the soundtrack and other obnoxious shit like that. Whenever a movie goes overboard trying to prove what time period it is, it just comes off as even more of a forgery – having just the printed date and a lack of modern devices actually worked better. I also liked that they didn't have an opening kill scene, something that is sort of standard in these sort of Wrong Turn-*esque films. We get a few close-up shots of scattered paper (foreshadowing later events) and then meet our weird, should-be-hated group. After I watched the movie I read someone complaining that "nothing happens until the 28 minute mark" (the movie is 86 minutes long) – I feel bad for that poor bastard if he ever finds himself watching* Demonic Toys 2, *which is much shorter and takes much longer to get to the first kill. 28 minutes is actually pretty fair, I think."*

Reflection: It's funny; I started the site with tons of spoilers, explaining that you shouldn't read the "reviews" until you saw the movie. And then that changed, so now I run into the other end of the spectrum, which is that I don't even spoil the movies for myself. The full review for this one mentions a twist that I quite liked, but damned if I can recall what it is, just four years later. You'd probably be surprised how many entries in this book are based on me taking my own word for it, because I really couldn't remember anything about the movie beyond what my review says. And even some of that escapes me; apparently the movie has some anal sex (indeed, it's the only review on the site where I use the word "cornholed"), but I cannot remember it. I seem to recall someone being tied to a tree in this though?

So if you rent/buy the movie and it's just "regular" bad instead of enjoyably bad I'll give you 1/366th of your money you paid for this book back, which comes out to about 6.8 cents. I'll round it up to seven whole pennies for your trouble. Just let me know your PayPal address.

MOVIE #215 – AUGUST 3rd

HOUSE OF THE DEAD II (2005)
Dir: Michael Hurst
HMAD Review Date: May 14, 2007 (DVD)
Genre: Comedic, Zombie
Available from Lionsgate

Synopsis Based on Fading Memory: Zombies attack a campus in what may be the least anticipated movie of all time… at least until someone made a sequel to Boll's *Alone in the Dark*, too.

Review excerpt:
"…what makes the movie work is the humor. There is some truly great stuff in here. A rather mean attack on the first film is one highlight ("Your boyfriend saved you with an immortality serum? That's the stupidest thing I've ever heard!"), and an A+ (and somewhat subtle) Cheney joke is another. And most of the characters are likeable, especially Ed Quinn's hero. Even Sticky Fingaz is pretty good (in his transformation scene he displays some damn impressive pantomime). There's also a hefty bit of randomness thrown in throughout the film. Why does the entrance to the football field have a huge sign reading "NO SUNFLOWER SEEDS"? Why does everyone call Ellie Cornell (who apparently survived the first film) 'Sir'? Why would a modern dorm room have a Static-X poster??? But it all adds to the movie's unexpected charm."

Reflection: I do not have the same knee-jerk reaction to the words "Uwe Boll" that many do, but I get why his stuff inspires such vitriol - he primarily made video game movies. There is no angrier group of people in the world than gamers who feel "their" beloved properties had been disrespected in some way, so Boll was an easy (and often justified) target. Luckily for them, he had nothing to do with this one, so you don't have anything to fear beyond the minor connection it has (Cornell's character). Besides, given the shots taken at the film (described above), it would appear this film's screenwriters were no fan of it, either.

Now, I admit I saw this rather early in HMAD's run, so it's possible that I saw better "intentionally dumb", fast-paced zombie movies over the following six years. But I wanted to give this fun little movie its due, because there is no worse position to be in than "DTV sequel to a theatrical film everyone hates" – I myself never would have seen it if not for just grabbing any horror movie I could find in order to meet my daily quota. In fact, I seem to recall renting it SPECIFICALLY to have fun tearing it apart, as that was how the site got attention back in the day ("funny" reviews of shitty movies), only to discover it was actually pretty fun. So to make amends, I put it here in the book; granted it's in the "dumb movie" month so it's hardly a glowing recommendation, but if even one of you actually trusts in me and has some fun watching it, it'll be worth it.

MOVIE #216 – AUGUST 4th

BIKINI GIRLS ON ICE (2009)
Dir: Geoff Klein
HMAD Review Date: May 28, 2012 (Streaming)
Genre: Slasher
Available from Well Go USA

Synopsis Based on Fading Memory: A hilariously to the point slasher movie set almost entirely at a gas station, believe it or not. The title is actually quite specific – "On Ice" isn't even a metaphor, as the killer actually puts them (them being Bikini Girls) on ice after he kills them.

Review excerpt:
"...the male character was surprisingly smart and focused. He fixes the bus, he notices something is amiss even before the Final Girl does, and he rebuffs the advances of not one but two of the hot Bikini Girls (before they were On Ice, obviously) so he can focus on the job at hand. It's like the girls are perfectly content to follow the slasher template, and he's all "No, let's actually try to get the hell out of here before anything bad happens." It's endearing, and I was kind of bummed that he got offed. Given the lack of humor and simplistic plotting, I'm guessing the filmmakers never got to the later '80s slashers when it was pretty standard to have a Final Girl AND a Final Guy at the end, so they didn't know to copy it (or if they had the idea to let him live, assumed that'd be thinking too far out of the box). Oh well. Maybe in the sequel."

Reflection: I enjoy pointing out the flaws and goofiness inherent to slasher films almost as much as I enjoy watching them, but there's something I should give them some credit for, and that's the fact that they never really settled on a hard rule as to whether or not the male lead should die. I attribute this in part to the fact that *Halloween* and *Black Christmas* inspired them all, and neither of those really HAVE a solid male lead (Keir Dullea in the latter is too much of a red herring to ever feel like a hero), so it left everyone that followed to their own devices.

So in a way I feel bad for spoiling the guy's death above; you can call the obvious Jamie Lee type the "Final Girl" and you're not really giving anything away – any viewer would be able to tell she lived. But with the males, there's no "tradition", making their fates less easy to peg. MOST of the Golden Era slashers killed them off, but there were a few exceptions, in particular *The Burning* which basically had a Final Boy, leaving the women on the sidelines for the final battle, and *My*

Bloody Valentine, which thankfully let TJ live for the sequel we never got. Once we got into the mid to late '90s it was pretty much 50/50; for every Randy in *Scream 1* there was a Randy in *Scream 2*. It's something I find kind of interesting, particularly since the slasher is often labeled a misogynist sub-genre when I find it to be quite the opposite – on the average, men get it worse and women are the heroes!

MOVIE #217 – AUGUST 5th

ALIEN RAIDERS (2008)
Dir: Ben Rock
HMAD Review Date: February 2, 2009 (DVD)
Genre: Alien
Available from Warner Home Video

Synopsis Based on Fading Memory: A team of badass alien hunters lock everyone inside of a supermarket when they discover one of the shoppers is an alien.

Review excerpt:
"It's not as unpredictable as the screenwriters would like you to believe, but it's still an exciting and fairly original take on the "pod" genre. But what's cool is that the movie is never weighed down by explanations and backstory. You know that it's some sort of alien - do you need to know the hows and whys? Likewise, the team itself - do they work for someone or have they just taken it upon themselves to be mankind's protector? Again - does it really matter? The movie's about how badly things turn out for one of their hunts - knowing that stuff wouldn't affect the end result."

Reflection: In the late '00s, Dan Myrick (half of the *Blair Witch* team) began producing a series of indie genre films that were released under a label named Raw Feed. Unfortunately, most of them kind of stunk (*Rest Stop, Sublime*, etc.), but they finally got it right with *Alien Raiders*, a pretension-free, admirably fast-paced blend of *The Thing* (an alien life form impersonates humans) and *The Mist* (it takes place in a supermarket). Alas, it was pretty much the end of the road for Raw Feed; after this movie they gave us an unnecessary sequel to *Rest Stop* that managed to be even worse than its predecessor, and that was that.

But it's not really a surprise, since *Blair* seems to have cursed most of the people who worked on it. Myrick (and *BW* partner Eduardo Sanchez) made one of the most successful and popular horror movies of our generation, but neither man has even secured another wide release, let alone anything that even came close to matching *Blair's* success. It's a damn shame, but I love that both of them continued to work on the independent circuit while giving chances to new filmmakers (or old pals, as director Rock was the production designer on *Blair* – he constructed the iconic stick figure), even if they didn't always turn out so good. This is probably the best movie Myrick's name can be found on post-*Blair* (for Sanchez, that would be *V/H/S 2*, as he contributed a segment), or at least tied with *The Presence*, which I recommended in the April chapter. I keep hoping they will reteam, either for a *Blair* sequel or something equally inspired/original – it's impossible to tell if their lone collaboration was a fluke, or if they're just at their best when working together.

MOVIE #218 – AUGUST 6th

MANSQUITO (aka MOSQUITOMAN) (2004)
Dir: Tibor Takács
HMAD Review Date: March 10, 2011 (DVD)
Genre: Monster
Available from Alchemy/Millennium

Synopsis Based on Fading Memory: Half man! Half mosquito! ALL... well, fairly enjoyable.

Review excerpt:
"Mansquito is not a CGI creature. For 95% of the movie, it's just a dude in a pretty good suit, which allows director Tibor Takács (director of The Gate*!) to make the action scenes a little more interesting than we usually get in these things. It's not until the 3rd act (when Mansquito sprouts wings and begins flying around) that they start to use CGI, but he's grounded again for the final 10-15 minutes and thus back to a practical suit. Shame they had to derail their effort (the flying scene is hardly essential), but the fact that they used the guy in a suit for as much as they did was admirable."*

Reflection: Joe Dante's underrated 1993 film *Matinee*, which centered on a William Castle type horror producer, had a great fake film called *Mant*, and I swear it inspired half of the stuff that actually came out for real in the following decades. I mean, *Mansquito* is basically the exact same joke, albeit with a different insect – but it's a real movie!

And it's actually not too bad! It's from the director of *The Gate*, who knows something about making a horror movie that's also a lot of fun. It also has a genius approach to this kind of movie – you want lots of action, but you also want a hero to care about. So they have TWO Mansquitoes; one is a criminal who provides all the mayhem, and the other is a good guy who provides the "Oh, they saw Cronenberg's *The Fly*" feeling. I wish the 2010 *Wolfman* remake had followed their lead, because a big part of the reason that movie didn't work for me (and presumably others) is that it made our hero the villain for the middle, only to turn Anthony Hopkins into a BIGGER villain so our protagonist could do something heroic for the climax. But by then who cared? Tens of millions dollars wasted on something that was done better by something called *Mansquito*. Good one, Universal.

P.S. I was given this movie by a friend who wanted me to tear it apart on the site for his amusement, but his plan backfired when I had a lot of fun with it. I always found that to be pretty hilarious.

MOVIE #219 – AUGUST 7th

THE DESCENT: PART 2 (2009)
Dir: Jon Harris
HMAD Review Date: May 6, 2009 (Theatrical)
Genre: Monster
Available from Lionsgate

Synopsis Based on Fading Memory: Hours after escaping, a traumatized Sarah is forced by police and rescue workers to return to the cave in order to locate any survivors (or collect their remains). It doesn't go well.

Review excerpt:
"A bit too much time is spent getting our team together, and it seems that even more time is spent traversing the caves until the monsters show. But the 2nd half? Hell yeah. Not only is it exciting, gory, and scary, but it genuinely feels like an extension of the first film (note the "Part 2"), and not like the cheap cash-in I was expecting. There's a terrific bit with one of the new characters trapped between some rocks, with a monster trying to get at her. Since she's trapped, he is essentially acting as her savior by digging the rocks away, allowing her to scramble loose and then... well, I won't spoil it. But it got the biggest cheer from the audience. I also loved the Sheriff character, who is one of those guys in a horror movie who inadvertently causes half of their problems (sending an ill-timed walkie talkie call to someone who is in the "being quiet so the monster right next to me doesn't discover me" mode, for example)."

Reflection: I finally got a chance to revisit this one recently, and I stand by what I said in my original review (which was from a test screening, where I think LG was trying to decide if the film warranted a theatrical release in the US. It didn't get one, so I guess my positive score card was in the minority). Like, oh, every sequel ever made (and yes, I include *Godfather II* and *Empire Strikes Back* in this list), the original is superior, but damned if this almost wholly unnecessary movie doesn't manage to touch some of those same nerves, and I loved that they found a way to include most of the entire original cast via their still fresh corpses. Come on, if you're a seasoned horror fan you had to have seen a number of sequels that took place in the same area as their predecessor – how many of them still had all the victims of the previous movie lying around? And out of that small number, how many of them got put to good use? Remember that one girl in the first film who died suspended over that chasm? The characters in this one have to use her dangling/mangled body to get across that same spot! Come on, that is just awesome.

I also enjoy how the sequel lived up to its predecessor with regards to a controversial ending. In the original, as we all know, US audiences were spared of the true final scene, where we learn Sarah was actually still trapped in the cave, nowhere near an exit and also completely insane (the sequel splits the difference; she's out, but she's nuts). This time we get a dumb little twist that seems to be setting up a third film that we never got, in a scene that absolutely no one, including me, has liked. So feel free to shut it off the second ___ escapes - I am willing to bet a lot of the movie's negative reputation is due to the fact that the audience leaves on something completely stupid. It's a common affliction I call "TheDevilInsideosis".

MOVIE #220 – AUGUST 8th

TRILOQUIST (2008)
Dir: Mark Jones
HMAD Review Date: July 2, 2008 (DVD)
Genre: Puppet, Serial Killer
Available from Dimension Extreme

Synopsis Based on Fading Memory: A killer ventriloquist's dummy hooks up with a pair of disturbed siblings, and they go on a killing spree.

Review excerpt:
"Strangely, the goofy concept kind of works, and there are two reasons why. One is the above average acting from the two leads, Paydin LoPachin as Angelica, and Rocky Marquette as her mute brother Norbert (who looks and acts like his own goddamn puppet). They are able to bring some sympathy and pathos to their roles, and while this is hardly a Shakespearean tragedy, I actually did feel sorry for them on more than one occasion (junkie mother, abused as kids, etc.). The other thing is the soundtrack, which is pretty great for a DTV killer puppet movie. There are a few alt-country style songs and a pretty good score by Geoff Levin (including, yes, "Mockingbird", but actually used effectively!), and the songs are just as melancholy as the film is at times."

Reflection: In my garage there's a rack with something like 150 DVDs and Blu-rays (it's right next to the garage door, so if I leave it open, a movie fan/thief will have a field day), acquired from several sources. Some were sent for review and I never got around to them, others were won at trivia, and some I actually bought myself (damned B2G1 sales at Blockbusters, and damn them again for closing down and selling everything for like a buck). They're all movies I'm pretty sure I won't want to keep once I watch them, and every now and then I just grab one at random and find out.

As of this writing, the last one I watched was *Scorched*, a pretty forgettable revenge thriller with Billy Zane that was directed by Mark Jones. I bring it up because it was one of the rare occasions Jones branched out of his "tiny killer" mode – he's the guy that gave us *Leprechaun* (just the first one) and he followed it up with the terrible *Rumpelstiltskin*. This is the best of those (and better than *Scorched*), so I like that the 3rd time was the charm for him, although it's sad to see that he is at his best when dealing with this particular sub-genre. Perhaps he should do a proper *Puppet Master* remake?

To explain the "Mockingbird" comment – I lost count of how many horror movies used this song for creepy purposes, and it grew quite tiresome. At this point I'd rather they dig up "Moonlight Sonata" or "Fur Elise" again than hear "And if that diamond ring turns brass..." one more goddamn time. But here they make it work, somehow, so I felt I had to show my respect after trashing so many other films and filmmakers for using it.

MOVIE #221 – AUGUST 9th

TALE OF THE MUMMY (1998)
Dir: Russell Mulcahy
HMAD Review Date: February 25, 2012 (Blu-ray)
Genre: Monster
Available from Echo Bridge Home Entertainment

Synopsis Based on Fading Memory: A mummy is reborn in modern day London, where he must track down his missing organs.

Review excerpt:
"Mulcahy gets good mileage out of the London setting, which sticks out in particular nowadays after seeing the terrible London sequence in the 2nd *Mummy* film, a scene that probably cost more than this entire film. The opening flashback sequence (featuring Christopher Lee) is also fun as it recalls the older films (desert, archaeological digs, etc.), paying homage to their predecessors before going to the modern day, something that the Brendan Fraser films lacked as those retained the 1920s period and merely shoved a bunch of (lousy) FX into it. It's kind of like *Dracula 2000* in that regard, although in some ways this is more successful since it lacks that movie's goofy "Judas" twist and excessive plugs for Virgin Megastore (also, no pop stars in this one)."

Reflection: Some movies are in development forever, and then you have to wonder how bad the other scripts were when the finished product is junk. *Freddy vs Jason* is a good example; the movie took a full ten years to make (it was set up at the end of 1993's *Jason Goes To Hell*, and was released almost 10 years to the day later), and it was even dumber than you'd expect from the title. *Resident Evil* is another; the resulting film may have spawned a franchise of its own, but it's hardly loved, and you gotta wonder how THAT got the greenlight over all the other attempts (including one from George Romero).

So in a way it's kind of cool that we actually got two modern *Mummy* movies around the same time; this was probably considered to be THE big *Mummy* movie at one point or another, because there were a lot of failed attempts at a new Mummy movie throughout the '90s (I think Romero was involved in one of those, too). But while Universal ultimately went with Stephen Sommers and Brendan Fraser, starting a mostly bad series (I like the first one OK enough) that made a lot of money, Dimension stepped in to give us this as a sort of consolation prize. In my opinion it's the superior movie, and one of the best Dimension flicks (yeah, they cleared that hurdle!), so it's a shame it never got a theatrical release in the US. It was even finished before Sommers', so it could have stolen some of its thunder! And maybe we'd have Jet Li in *Tale of the Mummy: Tomb of the Dragon Emperor*.

MOVIE #222 – AUGUST 10th

SIDE SHO (2007)
Dir: Michael D'Anna
HMAD Review Date: August 20, 2008 (DVD)
Genre: Breakdown, Survival
Available from Lionsgate

Synopsis Based on Fading Memory: A family's car breaks down and they run afoul of mut- wait, no, carnies!

Review excerpt:
"...instead of the usual collection of jobless backwoods inbreds, they are all ex-carnies. Our hero family is doing a book on remote tourist trap attractions (they will have the market cornered since Bill Hudley's book obviously never got published), so we have a barker, a strongman, etc. It's a bit refreshing. Also, even more refreshing for one of these no-name indies, it's pretty fast paced. There are like 10 carnies, so you're never more than a couple minutes away from another action bit once it gets going (about a half hour in)."

Reflection: This is a funny review, because before I talk about the movie at all, I spend time praising Lionsgate for giving us an honest cover, the production's original title, and a decent transfer. They're the sort of things you would think would be a given, but alas I was suckered into watching many movies that didn't even belong in the same sub-genre promised by the cover art, let alone anything suggested by the title. Back in the '60s and '70s, movies would sometimes get made based around a poster that was already designed (usually to secure financing or foreign distribution), and I can't help but think that was actually preferable to what companies like Lionsgate do. At least those movies would show you what's on the cover; I once rented a movie that showed Big Ben in flames on the cover, and the movie didn't even take place in London!

Anyway, I didn't come across a lot of killer carnie folk during my six-year sentence at Horror Movie A Day prison, which I find surprising in retrospect. There's a lot of potential in the setting (and easy to franchise since the surviving circus folk are always on the move anyway – new state, new victims!), but such films are pretty rare. It's interesting because the most famous is probably Tobe Hooper's *The Funhouse*, and people have no problem ripping off *Texas Chain Saw Massacre* all the time, so why the hesitation to get compared to a movie that isn't as iconic? My only theory is that it's too hard to set up a convincing circus on the budget these things have, and using a real one would require a lot of hoops to jump through, so it's forever going to be a "special circumstances" kind of thing. What a pity.

MOVIE #223 – AUGUST 11th

SEA BEAST (2008)
Dir: Paul Ziller
HMAD Review Date: August 8, 2009 (DVD)
Genre: Monster
Available from RHI Entertainment

Synopsis Based on Fading Memory: Sea Beast and his babies attack a bunch of fishermen and the like, including a father/daughter/her boyfriend scenario stolen from *Armageddon*.

Review excerpt:
"Despite the singular title, there are actually like a dozen of the damn things in the movie; the giant one and several baby sized ones. Not only does this mean more action than usual (as the big one can be attacking at the same time as the smaller ones are somewhere else), but it also allows for some variety, a la Jurassic Park. The big one can stick to exterior locales; the tiny ones can get through an air vent and attack someone in a theoretically "safe" storage closet. Plus, it actually makes the decent FX all the more impressive, as there are more shots for the VFX guys to work on."

Reflection: Ziller directed *Yeti* (from June's selections) and I have the same sort of stuff to say about this one – it's not a great monster movie, but it's superior to the average thing Syfy would air on Saturday night. So if you're not a connoisseur of that crap like I am, you'll probably just think it's a bad movie – you'll just have to take my word for it that this *is* truly better than you'd normally get. And even if you've only seen a couple, you'll probably recognize that the FX in this one are a lot better than normal. I mean, let's face it – we're watching this stuff for the kills and the monsters, so it's nice to see one where they actually put some effort into making them look good.

But I freely admit that part of what charmed me was the recycled *Armageddon* plot. I've never hid my undying love of that (admittedly very silly) movie, so whenever I spot what I assume is a reference (and not a mocking one), I feel I've found a kindred spirit, and will champion their efforts. Anyway, this borrows the whole "Bruce Willis thinks his daughter deserves better than Ben Affleck" thing from that movie, with one difference – spoilers ahead for both! You know how at the end of *Armageddon* Bruce sacrificed himself to save Ben, now that he had finally proven himself worthy of his daughter? That doesn't happen here, instead it's RIP, boyfriend. It's kind of brutal, and thus hilarious. I would even bet that they were mimicking the *Armageddon* scenario so closely just to make this resolution all the more hilarious for people like me who can appreciate some mean-spirited slaughter every now and then. Enjoy!

MOVIE #224 – AUGUST 12th

WEREWOLF: THE BEAST AMONG US (2012)
Dir: Louis Morneau
HMAD Review Date: October 9, 2012 (Blu-ray)
Genre: Werewolf
Available from Universal Studios

Synopsis Based on Fading Memory: Some werewolf hunters hunt some werewolves.

Review excerpt:
"Its most damnable offense is that it often feels like the pilot for an enjoyable series about an area that has a werewolf problem. Unlike most werewolf movies, there's no "There's no such thing as werewolves!" discussion or complete obliviousness at how to dispatch of one - in fact the doctor's office has a little "station" of sorts where he will shoot a silver bullet into a human that's about to turn monster. And in addition to werewolves, there's a lot of "wurdaleks" running around, which are vampire/zombie type things, so basically you have this world where monsters are feared, but dealt with in a casual manner as something you just have to put up with on a regular basis. Thus, the possibilities are endless for ongoing stories of "master" villains, with the built-in allowance for a lot of action thanks to random wurdaleks that can be killed whenever the episode calls for burst of violence."

Reflection: I don't know too many people who genuinely liked the big budget *Wolfman* update with Benicio Del Toro; the film's various production issues were evident on screen and the decision to replace a lot of genuine Rick Baker FX with CGI was a terrible one. It improved a bit in its director's cut form, but it still ranks as a big disappointment. This was originally announced as a spinoff/sequel to that movie, but by the time it actually got released (on Blu-ray, as was always the intention I believe) any connection it might have had to *Wolfman* had been excised. Personally, I think it was a good move – this is actually a more satisfying movie and didn't need to be weighed down by being billed as a sequel to a movie no one likes.

I'm actually kind of bummed it DIDN'T turn into a TV series; I guarantee it'd be one of the four or five shows I have building up on my DVR right now. And I'm also kind of surprised; horror on TV is huge right now thanks to *Walking Dead* and its spinoff, *The Strain, American Horror Story*... and with *True Blood* finally over, there's room for some werewolf action. But after three years I think it's safe to say if there IS a werewolf show coming along soon, it won't have anything to do with this surprisingly enjoyable little flick.

MOVIE #225 – AUGUST 13th

SCREAMERS: THE HUNTING (2009)
Dir: Sheldon Wilson
HMAD Review Date: March 26, 2009 (DVD)
Genre: Technology
Available from Sony Pictures Home Entertainment

Synopsis Based on Fading Memory: 14 years after the original was forgotten, Sony inexplicably decided to revive the *Screamers* franchise.

Review excerpt:
"It's more or less a remake of the original, with folks going to check on a distress call and yadda yadda, but unlike the first film, this one moves things along. In the original, the first 45 minutes gave us... a mostly off-screen plane crash and a mostly off-screen opening attack. Here we get true carnage, a firefight, a couple of gory kills, etc. Unfortunately, it also retains the original's bizarre penchant of keeping important cast members to the 3rd act of the film. At least they aren't lying about Lance Henriksen's role - he is listed in the "and" role, not 2nd billed like Jennifer "I don't appear in the movie for nearly an hour" Rubin was in Screamers 1. But still, it's not until the 70-minute mark that Lance finally appears, and he dies less than 10 minutes later. I actually began to wonder if the guy making the credits just assumed Lance was in the movie ("Space? Robots? DTV? Yeah, Lance has gotta be in here...") and put his name in there just in case, as he doesn't appear on the cover either."

Reflection: I chose this particular excerpt because of the joke about Lance and the credits guy (since I make credits for a living, I probably have more critiques and jokes about titles than any other reviewer in history), because it inspired one of the several "Happy Hour Comics" that accompanied occasional reviews in 2009. The guy who did them was a fan of the site that had his regular (still going) online strip, and he would send me a new one specifically for HMAD every couple weeks, usually based around one of my random asides like that. I enjoyed them, and hoped they would continue, but I think (as with HMAD itself) real world stuff just kept getting in the way and he lost the time to do them. He emailed me in 2013 to see about resurrecting them, but by then the site was about to be wrapped up and it just didn't happen. It's a bummer, because while I never wanted to report news or anything like that, I DID always look for ways to mix the site up a little bit so it wasn't just (literally) thousands of reviews that ended in "What say you?" It's the same reason this book has artwork and factoids sprinkled throughout, so it wouldn't just be 365 half-reviews, some of which I don't even mention the movie and just talk about a comic strip or whatever.

Anyway, this is better than the first one. It may lack Peter Weller, but it's paced better, added another "win" for Wilson (see the *Kaw* entry from June), and actually had improved FX. And it was the first time I took notice of Gina Holden in something, who I continued to be smitten with in the likes of *Saw 3D* and *Sand Sharks*. Of all the movies to get random DTV sequels years later, this has to be the one I had the lowest expectations for (not to mention the most confusion to its existence), but I was happy to find it was kind of fun in its own way. Plus, there aren't enough killer robot movies in the book, so nyeah.

MOVIE #226 – AUGUST 14th

URBAN LEGENDS: FINAL CUT (2000)
Dir: John Ottman
HMAD Review Date: October 6, 2007 (DVD)
Genre: Slasher
Available from Sony Pictures Home Entertainment

Synopsis Based on Fading Memory: Nothing faded here, I can give you a DETAILED synopsis about this one... but I won't. It's about a guy in a fencing mask killing film students.

Review excerpt:
"The script is pretty dumb at times, but there are some moments of genuine wit, and John Ottman's direction is quite above average for this type of junk. Plus, and maybe this doesn't appeal to everyone, but being a former film student, I have to love a film that features, of all things, a sinister director of photography. How many times has "Find yourself another DP" been used as a borderline threat in a movie? There's also a sinister producer, sinister PA... they're all red herrings, but it's still quite amusing."

Reflection: Man, I could fill up half the chapter with good anecdotes about this one. Like the time I went to see it in theaters and had to tell the projectionist to turn it on – he didn't realize anyone had bought a ticket (it was a matinee on a weekday, so it's not TOO damning of the movie's popularity – but still). Or the time I tried to make it one of my HMAD screenings at the New Beverly and even got in touch with Jennifer Morrison about coming for a Q&A – she was actually interested! But alas it didn't happen, partly because I knew the only way anyone would show up for the screening was if she came and it was too tricky to coordinate with the schedule of her TV show. OR I could talk about how it ranked #1 on my list of hilariously stupid slasher motives I came up with for a Bloody Disgusting article, as I was so charmed by the killer explaining that he wanted to kill everyone who made a really good student film so he could pass it off as his own. See, at the time the movie came out, I was in the middle of my most intensive year of college, where I majored in communications/film (not a "film school", there's a difference!), and had certainly had my fill of awful and pretentious student films, so the idea that one would be good enough to kill its crew in order to steal was basically fantasy/sci-fi to me.

In other words, I have a peculiar affinity for all of the evidence that the movie isn't very good, so it's an ideal candidate for this month's theme. If anything I should have put it in the first slot (or, OK, #23, the "I know it's bad but I like it anyway" one) but any movie that actually opened at #1 (albeit with one of the lowest grossing takes for a #1 ever, per Box Office Mojo) by HMAD law has to go in one of the "You've heard of these" weekly positions. So it's here, perhaps not coincidentally right next to the movie that's in the month's "bad" slot. Good, bad, I don't care... I just love you, *Urban Legends: Final Cut.* Even the stupid extra 'S' in your title.

HMAD Fun Fact: My screening of the first Urban Legend *served as the debut of Jacopo Tenani's posters for HMAD shows at the New Beverly, replacing my usual terrible Photoshop ones with some really great, often abstract imagery. From that point he did posters for nearly every following screening until the series ended in 2014.*

MOVIE #227 – AUGUST 15th

THE INCREDIBLE MELTING MAN (1977)
Dir: William Sachs
HMAD Review Date: May 31, 2011 (Streaming)
Genre: Mutant
Available from Scream Factory

Synopsis Based on Fading Memory: An astronaut comes back from space and starts melting. He also starts killing people. I'm not sure what the correlation is.

Review excerpt:
"Once you get past the silly concept, it's a pretty traditional "unwitting victim on a rampage" movie, with a major downer ending that adds a touch of Romero-esque cynicism to the proceedings. As I've mentioned before, dumb plots are nothing to me. You know what a genre movie with a really realistic plot is? Boring. As long as it's doing the best job I've seen telling THAT particular story, however inane, I'm happy. I bring up the Armageddon *defense – show me a better movie about oil drillers going into space to blow up an asteroid if you think it's so bad. Same with this. I don't think I've seen a better movie about a melting man, and hell, it's even better than some of the more basic "astronaut comes back from space... but something's not right!" movies I've seen. I defy anyone to tell me that* The Astronaut's Wife *is better than this."*

Reflection: I know this is in the month's "bad movie" slot, but I genuinely enjoy it. However, this is one of those movies where even the people who made it will tell you it's terrible, so who am I to argue with them? Apparently it was actually written as a parody of monster movies, but the director didn't get that memo, which is why it taps into that part of my brain that likes something the more "off" it is. The same thing happened with *Slumber Party Massacre*, in fact (as well as the non-horror, but equally delightful Van Damme vehicle *Sudden Death*, which is just *Die Hard* at a hockey game), and while you'd think the movie would be unwatchable with that conflict of interests, it's the precise thing that makes it so special.

I'm pretty sure this is the only movie in the book that was featured on *MST3k*, but I've never seen the episode. I used to be a big fan of that show, but in the past few years I've found myself less enthralled with their brand of humor; I go to their Rifftrax events on occasion and usually find them very underwhelming, and whenever I watch an episode on Netflix to pass the time I end up losing interest. Maybe it's just a long funk I'll get over, but maybe doing HMAD made me realize the movies they were lampooning were nowhere near deserving of the scorn when there was so much worse out there. Besides, the movie is funny enough as is, and I'd be legitimately upset if Crow or Tom Servo talked over the film's key bit of dialogue: "I told you yesterday that we needed some crackers!"

MOVIE #228 – AUGUST 16th

BIG BAD WOLF (2006)
Dir: Lance W. Dreesen
HMAD Review Date: September 12, 2007 (DVD)
Genre: Comedic, Werewolf
Available from Screen Media

Synopsis Based on Fading Memory: Basically *The Stepfather*, but where he's a werewolf instead of a serial killer.

Review excerpt:
"There are some minor in-jokes and some decent gore throughout the film, adding to the enjoyment. And the end credits song is one of the best alt-rock power ballads I have heard in the end credits of a horror film since Brother Cane's 'And Fools Shine On' in *Halloween 6*. Unfortunately, the commentary is a total bore, as the director merely praises everyone (including the boom operator, and more than once) and points out filming locations and things that were shot after principal photography. Dude, you made a movie where a girl has to blow her boyfriend's step-dad to prove he's a werewolf; no one watching it gives a rat's ass that the driveway is in Griffith Park while the house is in Topanga."

Reflection: I shouldn't have spoiled that "prove he's a werewolf" scene in the excerpt, but it was how I once convinced someone in person to watch the movie, so I figure I might as well go for broke.

Anyway, this is another movie someone told me to watch specifically because they hated it and they wanted to see me tear it apart, but it backfired when it turned out that I actually kind of enjoyed it. It's got some really stupid stuff (including the worst "break into someone's office and get out before you're caught" sequence this side of Halle Berry in *Perfect Stranger*) and the transformation is an unfortunate CGI mess, but the wolf itself is a practical creature, so I approve. I should warn audiences that the werewolf rapes someone, which isn't cool and kind of goes against the "dumb fun" theme, but you can just skip over that unpleasantness and enjoy the rest of the movie, like the aforementioned example of how they prove the bad guy's a werewolf.

Plus, it's a better remake of *The Stepfather* than the actual remake of *The Stepfather*. That 2009 trainwreck might have been one of the worst ones to come out of that unfortunate trend from the back half of the '00s, and it's a shame that even though it tanked it's still probably been seen by thousands more than have ever sat down with this one. It's one of my least favorite things about remakes - the fact that there's usually a better retelling of that story out there, and yet the weaker one will get the money and eyeballs on it just because it has the familiar title.

MOVIE #229 – AUGUST 17th

ALIVE OR DEAD (2008)
Dir: Stephen Goetsch
HMAD Review Date: June 23, 2008 (DVD)
Genre: Breakdown, Survival
Available from Lionsgate

Synopsis Based on Fading Memory: A car full of- wait, there's only one woman! So ONE WOMAN runs afoul of a killer after her car breaks down in the middle of nowhere. Points for originality.

Review excerpt:
"After the cell phone charger sex we actually get a good solid 10-15 minutes of cat and mouse suspense, and the reason it works is because we still don't know if this girl is our heroine or not. It's a long standing tradition to kill off someone in the opening reel, and since the actress is a complete unknown, it's not quite clear whether she is our heroine (and safe) or our first kill (and thus a goner). Once it becomes clear she's the heroine, the movie loses some of its steam in terms of suspense, but it keeps the randomness coming at a steady clip."

Reflection: Not long after starting the site, I noticed that there would often be a very strange similarity between two movies that I watched back to back – like the time I watched *Devil Times Five* one day and *Funeral Home* the next, with both movies featuring an attractive woman seducing a mentally disabled man to get him to do something terrible for her. I certainly never planned it (how could I? I didn't know a damn thing about 90% of the movies I watched), but it came up often enough that it seemed like I was trying to link movies together from day to day. So it's kind of funny that this movie ended up after *Big Bad Wolf* in the month's lineup, because like that movie, this one sticks out in my head for its sexual kinks. That one had the "blow a werewolf for his DNA" scene, and this one has a girl using her cell phone charger as a dildo – which of course provides cinema's all-time best excuse for the cell not working later (battery dies and her charger no longer works because… well, use your imagination).

It's also the only movie out of the 2,500 that had a disclaimer at the top to inform the viewer that the title changed. Why anyone would care or what difference it would make on your viewing of the film is beyond me, but I love that they wanted to be completely transparent about it. I get why some filmmakers would be angry about such a thing and continue to refer to the film by their preferred title (like Paul Thomas Anderson always referring to *Hard Eight* as "*Sydney*", which was the original title he wanted before the producers overruled him), but it's really bizarre to convey that info to the audience before they've even seen the movie. It's like "Hey, this movie got compromised! Enjoy!" At least they didn't make the director remove the cell charger masturbation.

MOVIE #230 – AUGUST 18th

EYE SEE YOU (aka D-TOX) (2002)
Dir: Jim Gillespie
HMAD Review Date: March 14, 2011 (DVD)
Genre: Slasher
Available from Alchemy/Millennium

Synopsis Based on Fading Memory: Sylvester Stallone (no, that's not a typo, and no, I don't mean Frank) goes to a detox center for cops, only for a slasher (!) to show up and start picking everyone off one by one.

Review excerpt:
"*Obviously the acting caliber is a lot better than your usual Jim Gillespie movie (he also directed the woeful* Venom*), and having the great Dean Semler (*Dances with Wolves*) as your DP is never a bad thing – the film looks terrific. The kills that we DO see aren't particularly memorable, but there's a good throat slashing at one point, and I like that the big budget (55 million!) and A/B+ list cast didn't stop the killer from using various implements – knives, drills, strangulation, poison... it's very "Ten Little Indians" in that respect. Too bad they didn't stick to just ten people.*"

Reflection: I wrote about this movie for Birth.Movies.Death. as well as HMAD, so I'm kind of talked out on the subject. It's not that great of a movie by any means, but Christ, it's a SLASHER MOVIE WITH SYLVESTER STALLONE. Had any one of his movies from 1996 to 2001 been a big hit, it's possible this movie would have gotten its wide theatrical release, but I much prefer it this way – those who didn't carefully follow his career might still not even know that it exists.

And Stallone is hardly the only draw here; if you count it as a slasher (which you should – it's a whodunit, albeit one that's easy to figure out, and the killer does the usual thing of killing everyone except the person he actually had the beef with) then it's got the best cast of any of them ever: Stallone, Robert Patrick, Jeffrey Wright, Tom Berenger, Kris Kristofferson, etc. Sure, most of them are wasted (the movie has too many characters; one recognizable face is killed off before you even really have time to learn his character's name), but the sheer novelty alone makes it worth a look. Sly followed it up with *Spy Kids 3D* - I DARE you to tell me that's somehow less embarrassing than showing up in a slasher from the guy who directed *I Know What You Did Last Summer*.

MOVIE #231 – AUGUST 19th

GOBLIN (2010)
Dir: Jeffery Scott Lando
HMAD Review Date: July 28, 2011 (DVD)
Genre: Supernatural
Available from Lionsgate

Synopsis Based on Fading Memory: A goblin kidnaps a baby and kills a bunch of other people.

Review excerpt:
"...something magical happens around the halfway point: our titular goblin eviscerates the ever loving shit out of one of the obligatory "cute guys in town" that have come along, distracting our heroine and her best friend away from watching the baby. Not that I was surprised he got killed – his name might as well have been Fodder – but it was so delightfully violent. The goblin is a sort of Sleepy Hollow-esque local legend and appears largely as a specter, so I wasn't expecting too much in the way of gore – it was a nice little surprise to see entrails and what not being thrown around."

Reflection: I often wonder if it's just my over-exposure to junky horror that left me hating certain clichés, or if even casual fans find them just as obnoxious as I do. One in particular that always drives me up a wall is the "heroine daughter hates her new stepmother" angle (the sexes on either side can vary, of course, but it's most commonly stepdaughter/stepmother), as well as the "teenager hates the new house" one. This movie has both, which had me rolling my eyes throughout the first 30 minutes or so, but as soon as the killing starts it picks up considerably, as the script by Raul Inglis is refreshingly mean-spirited (a bit too much so, at times), killing off many people you'd assume would be safe and allowing further generic situations to feel a bit more suspenseful than they otherwise would – you start getting the impression that NO ONE is safe, which is hard to pull off in any horror movie but certainly in one that premiered as a Syfy movie.

On that note, it's important (on a very minor and largely meaningless level) to know that some of the movies that premiere on Syfy aren't necessarily "Syfy Original Movies". Sometimes the network just picks up the premiere rights for independently made films, and those tend to be better. You can tell because they don't fade to black when it's time for the commercial breaks (meaning, they weren't made specifically for TV broadcast). I can't honestly recall if this one was a legit Syfy production or just something they premiered, but it seems it'd be the latter. If not, it's definitely one of the best movies they made themselves, as long as your definition of "best" doesn't involve how many internet jokes you can make about it (see: *Sharknado*, which I myself will hopefully never do).

MOVIE #232 – AUGUST 20th

FRANKENFISH (2004)
Dir: Mark A.Z. Dippé
HMAD Review Date: April 17, 2008 (DVD)
Genre: Monster
Available from Sony Pictures Home Entertainment

Synopsis Based on Fading Memory: Mutated fish attack some folks in/around a swamp.

Review excerpt:
"...quite simply, it's a well-made film. I hate to sound like a broken record, but it's worth re-mentioning: when the crew puts effort into the movie, it pays off, resulting in a movie that is considerably better than one might expect from the umpteenth "Terror in the Water" movie. When everyone goes through the motions, doing the bare minimum to achieve a usable piece of film footage, the movie turns out even worse. In Frankenfish's *case, it's definitely a case of the former – pacing, production value, (most of) the effects, etc. are all solid, and thus the film's weak spots are easier to overlook."*

Reflection: Just to clarify that "broken record" thing - it might actually be the first time I'm saying this in the book, but on the site, by this point, I had said it like fifty times.

Anyway, as you're probably aware if you've read the book cover to cover (or at least the earlier entry for *Suburban Sasquatch*), I am friends with this film's screenwriter, the esteemed Simon Barrett. But I didn't really know him when I saw it (though I think I had met him once), so there was no bias in my review. There's some in including it in my book of "Movies You Should Watch!", I guess, but I'm also putting it in the "these movies are stupid fun" month instead of the one with monster movies (which had no killer fish films), so it's not like I'm really trying hard to sell you on it.

Needless to say, his other movies are actually all better, and I don't think he'd disagree, but as someone who saw hundreds of these things, I assure you this one is a notch or three above average. You know how all those Syfy movies have to hold back because they're for basic cable? This is like a good one of those, but with a well-earned R rating. F-bombs, nudity, harsh gore (the body count is quite high)... it's what you WANT from those movies but can't actually get! With most of the more professionally produced films in this sub-genre being PG-13 (like the same year's *Anaconda* sequel), it was kind of refreshing to get those R rated thrills but by people who actually A. knew what they were doing and B. know to deliver what folks actually want to see when they watch something called *Frankenfish* (namely, F-bombs, nudity, and harsh gore).

MOVIE #233 – AUGUST 21st

P2 (2007)
Dir: Franck Khalfoun
HMAD Review Date: October 29, 2007 (Theatrical)
Genre: Blank From Hell, Survival
Available from Summit Entertainment

Synopsis Based on Fading Memory: The most beautiful woman in the world gets trapped in a parking garage with the plastic bag-loving psycho from *American Beauty*.

Review excerpt:
"Rachel Nichols never does anything really *stupid in the film. Most of her decisions are logical and of the "what I would do" variety, at least within the confines of the somewhat absurd premise (we have to believe that no one else who has parked there plans to come back to their car, I guess). And when the film gets to the "turn the tables" point, she kicks ass in a great mini "car chase" around the garage. Also, when she swears, it sounds natural. Maybe I am in the minority, but most of my female friends swear just as much as I do, yet whenever a film contains potty-mouthed females, it often sounds awkward and forced (the* Halloween *remake being a prime example)."*

Reflection: For a while, this movie had the record for the worst opening weekend for a movie on 2,000 or more screens (or something like that; Box Office Mojo makes up so many weird criteria that I can't keep track), which is a shame for a couple reasons. One is that it's a pretty good thriller as long as you buy into the notion that this garage only has one exit, and the other is (if you couldn't tell from my synopsis), I'd prefer to live in a world where Rachel Nichols was a big star who appeared in lots of movies, instead of starring in some Canadian Syfy TV show that I'll probably never watch. This was her first big movie as the toplined star, so that it tanked in literal record-breaking fashion probably didn't help her career any. And it certainly prevented a *P3*.

I should point out that part of my affinity for this movie stems from the time I was too late to get my car out of a garage before it closed. I went through a hole in a fence and got my car, but of course that didn't help much because I couldn't drive back out through the garage's security gate without causing some damage. So I went to the office of the garage and found a security number, and called someone to have him open the gate, at which point I had to run back outside and pretend I was never in there to begin with. Then the guard broke the gate letting me out! He also asked how I got the number in the first place, but luckily I thought quick and said that they had it at a bar across the street. Long story short: it kinda IS possible to get stuck in a garage, sort of, I think. Main difference, at least in my experience, is that the security guard is more likely to kill the gate than you.

HMAD Fun Fact: There are only ten uses of the F-word in this book, and half of them are in the excerpts. I know I use that word a bit too much, so I opted to tone it down here in honor of Tom Atkins. You see, when I hosted a Halloween III *panel at a convention, I said something like "TOM MOTHAFUCKIN' ATKINS IS HERE!", and months later when I interviewed him for* My Bloody Valentine *(where he says the word in one of its best lines), I was mortified when he said "Oh I remember you, you had the potty mouth." So I made its few appearances count, because seven years later I still feel terrible about that.*

MOVIE #234 – AUGUST 22nd

ASSAULT OF THE SASQUATCH (2009)
Dir: Andrew Gernhard
HMAD Review Date: November 8, 2010 (Streaming)
Genre: Monster
Available from Synthetic Cinema Int.

Synopsis Based on Fading Memory: A Sasquatch terrorizes the people holed up in a police station.

Review excerpt:
"...the "Assault" in its title is no accident; this is more or less Assault on Precinct 13 *with a Sasquatch, as a collection of cops, criminals, and random civilians spend a good chunk of the film "trapped" in a police station with the 'quatch outside. I've always wondered why the basic plot of* Assault *isn't ripped off more often, so I was thrilled to see it used for something as random as a Bigfoot. Even more thrilling – the kills in this movie are actually kind of awesome. I've been conditioned to expect the worst from these things, but they put the effort in here, with Sasquatch hands going through human heads, lots of general evisceration, etc. But my favorite has to be the guy who just gets pummeled by random objects – Bigfoot throws chunks of cement, a tire, even a goddamn mailbox at this poor bastard."*

Reflection: If it were up to me, each year of cinema would produce no less than ten (10) films that more or less rip off *Assault on Precinct 13*, just changing up the specifics. It's a great scenario and almost always produces a film I enjoy (if never as much as *P13* itself), but it's relatively rare that I see anything like it (even as other Carpenter films, like *Halloween* and *The Thing*, are ripped off with alarming frequency). So props to this movie for doing it with a goddamn Sasquatch, and I implore filmmakers to look to it for inspiration more often than they do. Especially if you're an independent filmmaker – what could be more enticing than a single location?

This is the month's second Sasquatch movie, and both of them are more silly than scary. This wasn't intentional on my part, it's just an unfortunate byproduct of the fact that most Sasquatch/Bigfoot movies really blow, and tend to work better when the filmmakers are just goofing around. Maybe it's because the inspiration for such fare is a faked movie so it kind of lends itself to pranksterism? Whatever the reason, if it's a "serious" Bigfoot or Sasquatch movie, chances are you're in for a bad time. The only one off the top of my head that worked (mostly) was Bobcat Goldthwait's found footage entry *Willow Creek*, which is about a hunt for the big guy but saying whether or not he appears is kind of a spoiler. Moral of the story: much like hunting for the legendary beast in reality, looking for a good Bigfoot movie is slightly dangerous and very likely to disappoint you.

MOVIE #235 – AUGUST 23rd

ROCK N' ROLL NIGHTMARE (1987)
Dir: John Fasano
HMAD Review Date: September 7, 2009 (DVD)
Genre: Supernatural
Available from Synapse Films

Synopsis Based on Fading Memory: A band is terrorized by the shittiest monster since *Dark Star*.

Review excerpt:
"Early on, we watch a van drive along for about 10 minutes, and this sort of padding is a problem that continues throughout the entire movie. Either they simply didn't have enough legitimate footage to make a full length film, or the editor suffered from whatever the exact opposite of ADD is. It never gets as bad as this part, but a shot going on longer than necessary seems to be an issue at least once per minute. And that's ignoring whether their respective scenes should be left in the movie at all - there are at least three scenes revolving around people doing dishes, with as many if not more that concern people discussing the need to do dishes. A bit of advice for any filmmaker, especially those making horror movies - NO scene in your film should revolve around making dishes, unless it is the setup for a garbage disposal and/or detergent-based kill."

Reflection: There was a *Rock N' Roll Nightmare* question at our horror trivia game recently, and I blew it. I was ashamed, but in my defense if someone would find a print (or a DCP, or even a duped VHS on EP mode) and screen this thing, my memory could have been refreshed. In looking up the key info for this entry, I discovered a sequel (titled *Intercessor: Another Rock N Roll Nightmare*), so I request, no, DEMAND that Cinefamily or Alamo LA (when it opens) program a double feature. If the sequel is half as ridiculously entertaining as the first one, it will be one of the greatest nights ever. And (for the Alamo), the alcohol sales will be enviable.

The commentary let me down though, because Fasano and John Mikl-Thor don't stick to their guns, and try to convince the listeners that a lot of the film's silliness was intentional. But I don't buy that, because they also talk about how they couldn't afford to do the FX right and stuff like that, so it doesn't add up – if they meant it to be funny, why would they want quality FX work? If the FX were good we wouldn't get the joy of seeing the star noticeably holding the bad guy's weapons (which are starfish, for some reason) against his arms and chest to make it look they were stabbing him (think Bela Lugosi waving the tentacles around in *Bride of the Monster*, or better, the *Ed Wood* recreation of that scene). No, they might have intended to add some levity to the proceedings, but the fact that it's so inept and terrible isn't on purpose, and that is precisely why it "works".

MOVIE #236 – AUGUST 24th

BACKWOODS (2008)
Dir: Marty Weiss
HMAD Review Date: February 11, 2011 (Streaming)
Genre: Cult, Survival
Available from Echo Bridge Home Entertainment

Synopsis Based on Fading Memory: A corporate paintball game gets more exciting when a cult (!) shows up and begins shooting live rounds at our heroes.

Review excerpt:
"I'm glad I watched the movie now, as opposed to maybe two months ago. See, I recently played paintball for the first time, and before then I was always under the impression that the things don't really hurt unless you've been shot point blank. Not at all – even from a distance using low caliber guns (which are harder to aim but hurt less), they can give you a pretty big welt, or even break skin if they connect with a non-protected area. My buddy got a pretty good cut on his neck from when the ball "shattered", in fact. So when our heroes arm themselves with paint guns, you might be tempted to laugh, but it's actually a pretty smart idea – a good hit to the face could blind an enemy, and you'd have to be superhuman to keep advancing on someone who was pelting you repeatedly in the chest with the damn things. Keep in mind - these guys are computer programmers on a company retreat, not survivalists."

Reflection: I seem to be the only one who doesn't hate *Child's Play 3*, but I chalk that up to the fact that it was the first R rated horror movie I saw in theaters. Not the first one I SAW, of course, thanks to VHS, but the first one I got to see on that big screen. It left an impression; in particular the scene where Chucky replaces the paint gun pellets in the army cadets' guns with real bullets... which I would later learn is complete nonsense, as loading ammo for a paint gun isn't even remotely like the way ammo is loaded into a real gun, making Chucky's switcheroo impossible. Still, it made me afraid of paint-guns for a very long time.

This movie does the whole "paintball game turned deadly" thing but with more (relative) logic, and like I said in the excerpt, I saw it not too long after I played my first, and penultimate paintball game. All due respect to the folks who play every weekend, but man, that is just not a fun "sport" at all to me. It's expensive as all hell (ammo runs out a lot quicker than you'd expect), you can get seriously injured just as easily as you might with a real gun (killed is unlikely, but considering the bruise I got on my leg – which was covered by jeans – I'd hate to see what my cheek or other exposed part of my head would look like if I took a round to it), and the only way to aim properly is to use paint pellets that hurt even more! I wasn't crazy about my first game, but I gave it another shot and liked it even less, effectively ending my career as a paintball player. To hell with that noise. I'll stay in and watch movies like this.

MOVIE #237 – AUGUST 25th

WRESTLEMANIAC (aka EL MASCARADO MASSACRE) (2006)
Dir: Jesse Baget
HMAD Review Date: February 22, 2008 (DVD)
Genre: Slasher
Available from Anchor Bay Home Entertainment

Synopsis Based on Fading Memory: A very small film crew making a porno in the desert runs afoul of the title character, who is sadly never actually referred to as "Wrestlemaniac" in the film.

Review excerpt:
"The gore in the film is pretty impressive. At first I was worried there wouldn't be any at all, as the first two victims are killed off-screen entirely. But then in the 2nd half the carnage is ramped up to 11, with generous face-ripping and impalements to enjoy. I won't deny that the film is a bit slow in parts, but there is certainly enough gore (and yes, even some nudity) to make up for it, and at 75 minutes (barely more than 65 without opening and end credits), you don't have to wait too long for it to get going. Also, while not without its share of eye-rollers, some of the attempts at humor work, which is nice."

Reflection: I made it a point to watch all of the bonus features for any DVD I reviewed for HMAD, which is why I started relying more and more on streaming sources in the last year or two of the site's run, as the same "real life" things that were causing me to quit were cutting into the time I could spend watching commentaries or whatever. But in those first four years or so, I listened to a lot of tracks and watched a lot of making of docs, and I assure you, there is no production hiccup more damaging than *Wrestlemaniac's*. As we learn on the commentary, the movie was supposed to be shot in an abandoned mental asylum, but TWO DAYS before filming that location was lost (I can't recall why, if they explained it at all), forcing them to choose between canceling the movie entirely, or relocating to whatever they could get. They went with the latter, and shot the movie in a ghost town.

So the movie has all of these bizarre issues, because scenes were written for an interior, labyrinthine building and were now being shot outside, without any time to properly rewrite them. This gives it an odd flavor, and a bit more character to what would otherwise be a routine but still fun slasher. The killer is a Mexican wrestler, which is novel, and since the characters are all kind of stupid it makes it harder to guess which one the Final Girl is, making it more suspenseful than the average slasher as well. Let's put it this way – I remember so much about the movie from that one viewing (well, two with commentary) that I was actually kind of blown away when I looked at the date of my review – I figured it had to be newer for me to remember it as well as I did. It's been almost eight years and my memory is stronger than of films I watched in the past eight weeks! That's gotta count for something, right?

MOVIE #238 – AUGUST 26th

INFESTATION (2009)
Dir: Kyle Rankin
HMAD Review Date: November 25, 2009 (DVD)
Genre: Comedic, Monster
Available from Alchemy/Millennium

Synopsis Based on Fading Memory: Chris Marquette and some other folks try to survive a giant bug invasion.

Review excerpt:
*"You know Marquette is safe, and his love interest too, but everyone else is fair game, and even in the film's final moments I was still afraid for the lives of two other characters (not to mention the fact that throughout the film they kill off people out of the order you might expect, and in at least one case, in a manner you probably won't see coming). I also liked how they pulled off the first "Guy wakes up without remembering what happened to him" opening to a horror movie that didn't annoy me in quite some time (*Saw *maybe?). Instead of taking the Roland Emmerich approach, with 60 minutes of introducing our characters before the destruction begins, the bugs attack prior to the start of the film, allowing us to learn about the survivors as they run and hide."*

Reflection: The year after I saw this I saw Marquette at Comic Con and told him how much I enjoyed the movie... and he looked at me like I had three heads. I don't know if he thought I was being a wiseass or he just hated making it or what, but dude, you're in *Freddy vs. Jason* – if a horror fan gives you props for ANYTHING you should be grateful.

Anyway, what I really liked about this one, besides the humor (Marquette's "if I turn into one of those things..." speech is incredible), is that they had a *Feast*-like approach to killing people off when you least expect them to, or letting the ones you thought were goners survive. It's something I rarely see in these movies, let alone in ones that are kind of lighthearted (there's a rom-com-y subplot, I should warn you). I get why people are afraid to kill off "safe" characters and/or let the more despicable humans live, because it'll certainly get a few rejections (even in the indie world, such chances aren't taken often), and that's why I really appreciate these occasional daredevils. Even if the overall intent of a movie is for you to laugh and have a good time, there's still no reason why you can't increase the suspense by killing off someone you would otherwise bet money on surviving. If handled with care, it won't turn the audience off – it will invest them into the scenario all the more.

I also love that there's almost no backstory on where the bugs came from, because it doesn't goddamn matter. The need to explain where everything comes from or do full blown "origin stories" (in the form of prequels) is a terrible, terrible trend in modern cinema (not just horror), so anyone that ignores this tendency is a hero.

MOVIE #239 – AUGUST 27th

ALIEN VS. NINJA (2010)
Dir: Seiji Chiba
HMAD Review Date: February 19, 2011 (DVD)
Genre: Alien
Available from Funimation

Synopsis Based on Fading Memory: Aliens fight ninjas.

Review excerpt:
"...and the splatter! At first I was sort of surprised at the movie's total lack of blood (during the opening ninja on ninja fight), but they more than make up for it once the alien arrives. Three "redshirt" ninjas are quickly torn apart by the thing, and then the fights contain plenty of grue, especially when a ninja dies. AvN must hold some sort of record for number of stomped on heads in a single film. Add in the bodily fluids and general ickiness involving the throat "controllers", and you have a perfectly "wet" affair."

Reflection: I didn't quit the site until March 31st, 2013, but you can see things starting to take a toll on me as far back as 2011, which (as I've mentioned) is when my day job got more intensive and left me with less time for doing HMAD stuff. So I began to appreciate shorter films even more than I already did, which is why this 80-minute slice of nonsense worked like a charm on me. These Funimation titles were definitely an acquired taste, and I disliked most that I saw, but this one was a most joyful exception. At least, according to my review it is; I couldn't tell you one thing about it now, almost five years later, but I can assure you that it's a little more exciting than *Law & Order* or whatever you might usually put on in the background when multitasking. It's probably one of the best "Blank vs Blank" movies ever, at any rate, and I love that they threw in a possession angle (the aliens control some of the ninjas via these neck... things) in case the titular promise wasn't enough for you.

If you need further enticing, I should note that the aliens are guys in suits instead of CGI beasties. Sure, it hampers the action a bit, because the suits hardly allow for the most graceful movement, but let's go with the "lesser of two evils" line of thinking on this one. Plus, let's face it – the days of seeing guys in suits playing monsters are decreasing, and there's a charm to it that even really good CGI monsters can't replicate. Not only does their physical presence give weight to the scenes that a computer generated version would lack, but the rampant overuse of CGI has resulted in another obnoxious problem – ugly ass monsters!

The computer wizards get so wrapped up in throwing in more "stuff" on their designs that they end up with these awful hybrid things (*Cloverfield* is a good example of a bad monster), but when they're "hampered" by something they need to make for a human to wear they end up with a much more iconic looking monster or alien. Kids will draw it, someone on Hollywood Boulevard will dress as it for tourists to take pictures with, etc. That's the sign of a memorable creation.

MOVIE #240 – AUGUST 28th

THE HITCHER (2007)
Dir: Dave Myers
HMAD Review Date: October 19, 2007 (DVD)
Genre: Breakdown, Survival
Available from Universal

Synopsis Based on Fading Memory: Platinum Dunes takes a much loved/respected thriller from 1986, focuses on the pretty girl instead of the handsome guy, adds more explosions, puts David Soul and All-American Rejects on the soundtrack, etc.

Review excerpt:
"Like McDonald's, the film is delicious even though you know it's crap, and as it gets more and more ridiculous (where the hell does that dropped car come from?), it just gets more and more hilariously fun. I don't think anyone involved thought to make any sort of realistic or thought-provoking film, so why should it be dismissed because it isn't? I don't think I need to point out again that a film simply being a remake isn't nearly enough of a reason to hate it. And come on, can anyone honestly say that The Hitcher II *had more respect for the source material?"*

Reflection: Last year, I got to host a round of Dead Right Horror Trivia (our team won so many times in a row that they said we had to either co-host or sit out of the next game to give someone else a chance!), and I did a category called "Hated Horror", which were all questions based on movies I like but are generally hated within the horror community. This was one of the movies, and I asked the players to identify the '90s alt-rock song that played over the big car chase at the film's center. I thought it was a pretty easy question, since it was one of the most ridiculed moments in the film, but even people who saw the movie got it wrong. The funny thing about the song (Nine Inch Nails' "Closer", for the record) is that director Myers fought vigorously to get the song into the movie, and in fact it was the last thing that was done before the movie was completely finished (I'm guessing the producers just added another zero to the check they had to give to Trent Reznor). And for what? People laughing at the press screening and me making a question about it for a round of trivia based on movies no one likes.

Anyway, I defend this movie not based on its amazing storytelling or anything (hell, they recycled so much of the original script that Eric Red was credited as a screenwriter even though he had nothing to do with it), but because people love to describe Platinum Dunes as simply "Michael Bay", i.e. "Michael Bay finally killed Freddy" or whatever. But the thing is, to my eyes, Bay's imprint is kind of lacking in the later Dunes films. He was involved in the first couple (*Texas Chainsaw, Amityville*, etc.) but then he got busy with making the *Transformers* movies back to back and seemingly left most of the heavy lifting to his partners, Andrew Form and Brad Fuller. So if you're a Bay fan (and I am for the most part; take out the *TF* movies and I pretty much like them all, though his first three remain his best), *The Hitcher* is the closest Platinum Dunes ever came to really aping his style, with its emphasis on action, a modern rock soundtrack, and what appears to be a permanent late afternoon sun making everything look gorgeous at all times. So I champion this enjoyably dumb movie (and kind of pity it, as it's the Dunes' only real financial dud besides *Horsemen*, which never even got a real theatrical release), and urge you to give it another chance if you've written it off. If not, well, "move along move along move along…"

MOVIE #241 – AUGUST 29th

KNOCK KNOCK (2007)
Dir: Joseph Ariola
HMAD Review Date: May 9, 2008 (DVD)
Genre: Slasher
Available from Lionsgate

Synopsis Based on Fading Memory: One of those "A prank goes wrong and the victim or someone close to him gets revenge" movies, but with ridiculous Italian stereotypes!

Review excerpt:
"The movie contains one of my favorite slasher scenes in recent history. One of our protagonists is walking down the street, singing to himself with his teeth guard (he's a football player) still in his mouth for some reason. So he's just going "mush mumble rawr flar gwar" and then all of a sudden the killer jumps out and begins stabbing the shit out of him. It's hilarious. And it's a common theme in the film, the killer coming out of nowhere. I think there were only two scenes in the film that showed the killer doing any sort of stalking; usually he just jumps out without any build up or suspense. Usually I hate this, yet it sort of worked for this particular movie."

Reflection: Like *Carver*, this one might be unbearable if you're not in the mood for its mean-spirited "charm", but it does have a couple of things undeniably going for it. One is Staten Island filming location, which should provide pleasant flashbacks of '80s indie horror (a ton of indie filmmakers were from there). The other is the wealth of graphic kills – if there's one perk to the slasher genre being more or less restricted to the indie/DTV world these days, it's that the MPAA doesn't give a crap about them and they're free to be as gory as the filmmakers like. Unfortunately, this means a lot of them just increase the slider options on their digital blood (boo), so when I see one that's practical like this, I give it an extra point or two.

It must have been a decent hit for Lionsgate, by the way – a few years later they inexplicably retitled an unrelated film to *Knock Knock 2*, even though it wasn't even a slasher, let alone one that resembled this one in any way. No, it was a found footage chore about some kids going to famous murder sites (Black Dahlia, Manson, etc.) and then they go into the house of a (fictional) murder, where the ghost traps them. You could literally pick any random slasher movie in the world (even famous ones) and it would make more sense to tie it into this movie. Hell, it didn't even take place on the same coast! This movie is most memorable for its New York/Jersey stereotypes, and the "sequel" is set in LA. Lionsgate pulled that sort of shit a lot, but usually it'd be somewhat explainable (the trio of *Dark Harvest* films – none of which are related – are at least all Midwest-set supernatural films). This was a new low for them, made even funnier when they picked up Eli Roth's film *Knock Knock*. I'm actually kind of sad they didn't retitle it *Knock Knock 3*.

MOVIE #242 – AUGUST 30th

SILENT SCREAM (2005)
Dir: Lance Kawas and Matt Cantu
HMAD Review Date: November 1, 2011 (DVD)
Genre: Slasher
Available from Lionsgate

Synopsis Based on Fading Memory: A bunch of kids go to a cabin in the woods, and most of them get killed. The next morning, more of them show up!

Review excerpt:
"...the pacing is surprisingly solid until the final 20 minutes (more on that later), with a death roughly every 5-7 minutes – even some of the Friday the 13th movies don't offer up that much carnage! The killings also start much earlier than expected, due to the fact that (spoiler) they successfully pull off the "introduce a bunch of kids, then quickly kill them all before bringing in the REAL group" approach that the Friday remake tried and most failed at. One nice thing about indies like this is that the cast of no-names (though the Final Girl is apparently from some pop band called Dream) makes it a lot easier to pull this sort of thing off, whereas the Friday remake had several known stars that weren't in that (too small) first group, making them impossible to buy as the real leads. Here, they do it the other way – like eight of them go off to the cabin first, most of them die, and then five more show up the next morning."

Reflection: I had an interesting argument with a friend a few years back; he claimed that I saw so many bad horror movies that my opinion could no longer be trusted, and I really didn't get it. The way I see it – I watched so many horrible movies that the ones that were merely just OK-ish were instantly recognizable as such. If *Silent Scream*, or pretty much any other movie this month, was the first horror movie you saw after a marathon of *Halloween*, *The Thing*, *Dawn of the Dead*, *Psycho*, and *Silence of the Lambs*, you'd probably think it was the worst movie ever made. But here's a sampling of what I watched the week I saw it: *Zombie Diaries 2*, *The Dread* (a movie I – not making this up – paused to see if it was a student film, only to discover it was the 3rd feature from a guy in his forties), *Swamp Shark*, and a dreadful bore of a film called *Ghost Month*. So no, *Silent Scream* isn't a masterpiece, but I can say with some authority that there must be SOMETHING there, because it was one of the only times that week I had anything nice to say after. My friend would probably be the type to list one of the *Underworld* sequels or something as the worst movie of the year – I'm the guy telling you that if an *Underworld* movie – or *Silent*

Scream - is truly the worst thing you saw in the past 12 months, you should consider yourself lucky. Or you should watch more movies.

Plus, it's a watchable snowbound slasher (see the *Cold Prey* entry in slasher month for my thoughts on such films), and I feel like it's my duty to give props to all of those until they put Jason Voorhees in a winter setting. IT CAN WORK, PEOPLE.

MOVIE #243 – AUGUST 31st

SUCK (2009)
Dir: Rob Stefaniuk
HMAD Review Date: October 4, 2010 (DVD)
Genre: Comedic, Vampire
Available from E1 Entertainment

Synopsis Based on Fading Memory: One by one, the members of a struggling band are turned into vampires, and they become more famous as a result.

Review excerpt:
"One thing I liked about the movie is that it doesn't waste any time. Our hero's girl is turned into a vampire pretty much in the first scene, before we really get to know any of the characters or how they relate to each other. It could have been annoying, but it fits the movie's laid back approach, and there are a number of really good laughs in the first few minutes to help you ease into it. The songs are pretty catchy as well, though there aren't as many of them as I had expected; there are two in the first few minutes but only about another four or five for the rest of the movie (performed songs, I mean – there are about 30 in the background or on the soundtrack for our benefit)."

Reflection: Jessica Paré went from starring in this movie to appearing on *Mad Men*, so hopefully, if nothing else, fans of that show have checked out this surprisingly fun vampire comedy. It's got some gore but otherwise the horror elements are lite; comedy and music are the priorities here, and happily it works. I laughed quite a bit (there's a genius running gag involving stop-motion), and the cast seems to be enjoying themselves – it's the most fun Malcolm McDowell has been in years. I also dug the songs, but that might be a red flag if you know about my musical taste.

Anyway, I think it's a perfect way to send off this month – there was a period during the site's run where too many horror films that were coming out were grim and disturbing, and I always think that sort of thing works best when it's the exception, not the norm. The horror genre has thrived, I think, because of its inherent license to do whatever its creators want and get away with it, something most other genres can't really do (if a rom-com is "hardcore" then it's probably just a porno). Because of this, the harmless and goofy movies like *Suck* can share shelf space with the likes of *A Serbian Film*, and a well-rounded horror fan should be able to appreciate both.

SEPTEMBER – VAMPIRE MOVIES

ARTIST: JACOPO TENANI

If you've read these intros for each chapter, you'll know why I picked the theme for each month (i.e. May got the weird movies because the multiplexes will be filled with all audience blockbusters), but when it came to September, I had nothing. Likewise, I knew I'd have a vampire month, but couldn't figure out any reason to tie it to any one in particular. So for no other reason than they were the odd men out, September is Vampire month. But I can still kind of justify it in a roundabout way. A lot of you are going off or returning to college this month. I met my future wife at college. Our first date was *Queen of the Damned*, a (terrible) vampire movie. So there.

That said, since I have proof that such fare can (inadvertently) lead to long-lasting relationships, and some of you will be meeting lots of folks (read: romantic interests) as you enter that crazy world of campus life, it'll be good to have a bunch of vampire movies at your disposal, right? Invite that guy or gal back to your dorm room, put a sock on the door, and hope for the best! Plus Halloween is next month and you'll probably want to start getting in the mood for the season, so why not overdose on one of our oldest movie monsters? But mostly the hooking up thing (if you're in a committed relationship already, just enjoy the movies for what they are, damn you.)

The vampire sub-genre is an interesting one, because it's so heavily driven by response to other vampire movies. The "arty" *Bram Stoker's Dracula* and *Interview with the Vampire* was the inspiration for the more down and dirty *From Dusk Till Dawn*. Likewise, the response to the *Twilights* resulted in some more counter-programming, both big budget (the *Fright Night* remake) and small-scale (*Stake Land*), both of which delivered hard-R action and far more fangs. It's Hollywood's favorite go-to as well; in the past five years there have been over twenty theatrically released vampire films, as opposed to a mere nine slashers and even fewer werewolves. Hell, there haven't even been as many zombie movies in theaters during that period, despite their seeming omnipresence.

Needless to say, it's a pretty expansive sub-genre, and also one of the oldest since there have been *Dracula* adaptations going back as far as 1921. So not only did I have a lot of material to choose from, I also had a pretty wide range of time to explore. Indeed, the oldest movie in the book is a vampire film, and that's the one I'm starting with...

MOVIE #244 – SEPTEMBER 1st

VAMPYR (1932)
Dir: Carl Theodor Dreyer
HMAD Review Date: August 5, 2008 (DVD)
Genre: Supernatural, Vampire
Available from Criterion

Synopsis Based on Fading Memory: Moody vampire movie from Germany. It's a Criterion movie so you might already own it if you're one of those weirdoes who buys everything from them for some reason.

Review excerpt:
"I really couldn't tell you what the hell was going on half the time, but the atmosphere and creepy feel the film offered made the story lapses easier to deal with. It's not like a David Lynch film where the incoherency eventually leads to just plain ol' lack of interest (Inland Empire, anyone?), but it's a very loose narrative, with little traditional structural qualities (three acts, character arcs, etc.). Lynch may have even seen the film himself; there are characters who seemingly split into two, oddball dream sequences, etc..."

Reflection: I try really hard to like David Lynch's stuff, but most of it just leaves me cold (I quite like his rare traditional narrative works, like *Elephant Man* and *Straight Story*). Yet I often quite like things that seem like they were an influence on him, which I find amusing. In turn, I usually downright HATE anything described as Lynch-esque, because most folks just assume they can throw some nice photography into a purposely incomprehensible story and it will be met with the same success. No. Lynch's movies may be hard to follow but there IS some method to his madness (at least for everything besides *Inland Empire)*, so the gibberish movies are just that, while his are simply more demanding of the viewer.

Anyway, this is the oldest movie in the book, and probably one of the most obscure. I figure if not for the Criterion release this would be nearly impossible to find in the States, and since they overprice their discs maybe you didn't take a chance on an 80-year-old weirdo German vampire movie. Well, I'm here to say you should! Go halfsies with a friend who likes to read – Criterion's release comes with "Camilla," the short story it was based on, as well as the screenplay. Speaking of which, it's a silent film (the only one of its type in the book), a type of film I could never really get into because you're basically watching it out of sync – you see someone making all these theatrical gestures while yelling, and then you have to wait to see what they're saying. The delay makes it harder to experience a big moment properly, which is why I found this one to be one of my favorites – there isn't a lot of dialogue to begin with, but that delay with what little there is kind of adds to the film's surreal nature.

MOVIE #245 – SEPTEMBER 2nd

MIDNIGHT SON (2011)
Dir: Scott Leberecht
HMAD Review Date: January 11, 2012 (Theatrical)
Genre: Vampire
Available from Image Entertainment

Synopsis Based on Fading Memory: It's one of those vampire movies that functions as a metaphor for drug addiction, but this time the vampire's lover is an actual drug addict for good measure.

Review excerpt:
"Replace the blood with any drug, and this is a fairly typical "drugs sure do ruin lives" movie – there's even a scene where Jacob shows up all "strung out" and causing a scene, which makes his dealer rough him up a bit. This plotline also goes to some interesting places though – as with a lot of the movie, it sets up things that you will probably assume will go a certain way, only for it to take a turn somewhere and make it a little more interesting and fun."

Reflection: It's a shame that Fearnet went belly-up; not only did a few good friends of mine lose their jobs, but the company was doing cool things like this – premiering indie movies that would be lost in the shuffle at IFC or whatever. As you might surmise from my "Synopsis" it's not that this is the most original movie in the world, but it's a really well done version of a common story (with a terrific ending to boot), a godsend in a sea of indie movies that are just trying to cash in on trends (you don't want to know how many awful *Underworld* wannabes I suffered through...) to increase their chances of getting picked up. This was never going to be a *Blair Witch Project*-level runaway smash, but I'm happy it got to be THE movie Fearnet focused on delivering to the masses, as opposed to one of a dozen that a more traditional company would sell as a package to Netflix Instant and never help find its audience.

It's also one of the movies that we can thank *Twilight* for. I never jumped on the anti-sparkle bandwagon, because A. they weren't aimed at my particular demographic and B. their mammoth success made it easier for ANY vampire film to get produced – such as more serious (and yes, better) ones like this. I would laugh when idiot fanboys would claim that the series was "ruining horror" or whatever – it was inadvertently helping, because as long as the studio could make the DVD cover look similar to Bella and Edward's latest adventure, they didn't care much about the content – it's not like this or many other movies were forced to *Twilight* it up to make it more appealing to 15-year-old girls. Some were, sure, but you get that sort of thing even when a legit great horror movie is a big success. Not to mention the fact that we got "Anti-*Twilight*" vampire films that wouldn't exist if there wasn't a mega-popular, polarizing vampire movie for them to counter. Basically if you saw a vampire movie released between 2010 and now, *Twilight's* billion dollar empire helped get that movie made. I'll happily put up with Taylor Lautner's acting if it means getting a couple movies like this out of the deal.

MOVIE #246 – SEPTEMBER 3rd

LIPS OF BLOOD (1975)
Dir: Jean Rollin
HMAD Review Date: March 23, 2013 (Streaming)
Genre: Vampire
Available from Kino Lorber Films

Synopsis Based on Fading Memory: A guy has a childhood memory of a castle and tries to find said castle, assisted by some mysterious vampire women.

Review excerpt:
"My favorite Jean Rollin film thus far, and the one I'd most likely revisit or recommend to pals. Everything just worked like gangbusters for me; half of his films I've wondered if I could even really count them as horror, but there's some good vampire action sprinkled throughout, all in service of his most accessible and intriguing story, and a likable male lead for a change to boot."

Reflection: I was in the final year of HMAD-ing when I finally got around to checking out some Jean Rollin films, which I regret since they kind of blend together in my head now – perhaps spacing them out over six years instead of six months would have helped. But this one definitely sticks out thanks to the more straightforward plot (and a hilarious fake head), as well as the real world setting that Rollin often ignored. Hell, there are even some light *giallo* elements. I haven't seen all of his films, but of the ones I have this is definitely where I'd encourage a newcomer to start.

Funnily enough, it was the last one I saw. My interest in Rollin was so reinvigorated that almost three years later I still haven't watched any more of his films. But it kind of works better that way, leaving myself with the memory that Rollin was a really great filmmaker instead of kind of a sloppy one, which would be my current day opinion if the last one I saw was, say, *Zombie Lake*. The familiar saying "You're only as good as your last movie!" works even when watching them out of order 35-40 years later, as it turns out.

P.S. If you're a big fan of the movie, the Redemption label (via Kino Lorber) released a ton of them, so have at it. It can be frustratingly hard to get decent/legal versions of some of these '70s Euro directors over here, but Rollin's (non-adult film) work, for the most part, is easy enough to find and often remastered to boot.

MOVIE #247 – SEPTEMBER 4th

RETURN OF COUNT YORGA (1971)
Dir: Bob Kelljan
HMAD Review Date: September 5, 2010 (Streaming)
Genre: Vampire
Available from Scream Factory

Synopsis Based on Fading Memory: Count Yorga returns, taking residence in an orphanage (?) while seeking a new bride.

Review excerpt:
"Early on, Yorga crashes the lamest costume party in history, and someone asks him "Where are your fangs?" to which he replies "Where are your manners?" And it's kind of amusing that the guy who spends the bulk of the movie trying to figure stuff out is dressed as Sherlock Holmes in this sequence. There's also a terrific bit where Yorga watches some Hammer vampire movie on TV, an early example of meta-humor. And I LOVED the scene where an old deaf dude ponders why they are asking him about "yoga" ("I tried it years ago, got stuck in a lotus position!")."

Reflection: If you haven't seen the first film, you can skip it and just watch its superior sequel. The first movie is more or less just *Dracula* with the names changed, so boom, now you're up to speed. And this one doesn't even explain how Yorga survived being killed at the end of his first adventure, so in some ways it's actually better to just watch it as a stand-alone. Robert Quarry is terrific, and unlike the first film it's actually got a couple of scary moments – but it retains that one's humor, so we have the best of both worlds. And besides, if you get the DVD it has the first one on it anyway, so you can just watch both if the idea of skipping straight to its sequel bothers you that much.

Plus: Craig T. Nelson shows up! It's his very first movie, playing a sergeant. Interestingly, his next feature (after some TV work) was *Scream, Blacula, Scream*, another superior vampire sequel – where he also played a sergeant. I like to assume it was the same character (both are set around Los Angeles), and then I like to get sad that we never got a *Blacula vs. Count Yorga* movie. Whether or not it would include Nelson's iconic sergeant character is a trivial detail.

MOVIE #248 – SEPTEMBER 5th

THE THOMPSONS (2012)
Dir: Mitchell Altieri, Phil Flores
HMAD Review Date: December 27, 2012 (Blu-ray)
Genre: Vampire
Available from Xlrator

Synopsis Based on Fading Memory: In this long-awaited (by someone, I assume, or else they wouldn't have gotten the money to make it) sequel to *The Hamiltons*, our vampire family heads to England to find other vampires and also a cure for the youngest brother, who is facing death.

Review excerpt:
"They don't need to hide anything this time, so there's a lot more action, though once again he youngest member (Lenny) is sidelined for the bulk of the film. Whereas before he was chained in the basement, this time he's seriously injured and the other members spend the movie trying to find a way to cure him. This leads them to England, where they discover another family of "vampires" who they think can help. Things don't work out, of course, and there's a fun war between the two clans. Sure, it'd be nice if all the bloodshed was practical (yep, more odd floaty digital blood on display here), but it's fun to see vamps go at it in the name of family, especially when you consider that they don't have regenerative powers or whatever."

Reflection: I don't remember much about *The Hamiltons*, only that they tried making something that was kind of obvious into a twist, hampering the narrative more than necessary. Now that we know what they are, the Butcher Brothers (ugh, please stop calling yourselves this) are free to let loose and offer stronger character development AND a more fleshed out story. It unfortunately keeps the family members apart for much of the runtime, but it makes the scenes of them together all the more compelling. I can't be 100% certain but I'm pretty sure you can follow this one if you haven't seen the original, but then again maybe watching it will make you appreciate how much better the follow-up is.

It would also help you appreciate something we rarely get in horror movies – a chance to see characters growing, and what they are like a couple years down the road. Outside of the *Scream* series, you really don't see much of that sort of thing – if anyone comes back at all (besides the killer) they usually get killed off early on, like Adrienne King in *Friday the 13th Part 2*. That or a different creative team brings a character back and they don't really seem like the same person (Laurie in *H20* is a good example – she's more just Jamie Lee Curtis than the Laurie Strode I remember). But here, the four main family members are played by the same actors, and the "Brothers" are writing/directing again, making it feel like a true sequel, the sort of thing fans of comedies and comic book movies can take for granted but in horror is fairly rare due to, you know, everyone getting killed the first time.

MOVIE #249 – SEPTEMBER 6th

LEMORA: A CHILD'S TALE OF THE SUPERNATURAL (1973)
Dir: Richard Blackburn
HMAD Review Date: March 29, 2012 (DVD)
Genre: Vampire
Available from Synapse Films

Synopsis Based on Fading Memory: A young girl searches for her father and winds up in a strange town populated with weirdoes and vampires.

Review excerpt:
"I liked that it gives viewers a variety of scary "monsters" to enjoy. Lila's encounter with an old crone is one of the most unnerving scenes I've seen in a while, as she just circles the poor girl while singing "Skin and Bones" and cackling. Then there are some creepy children, who appear to be vampires or some sort of undead given their pale/greenish skin and terrifying faces. The locals are all covered in monster makeup of various design (some are sort of Wolfman-ish), and then there's Lemora herself, a vampiress who has an eerie gaze that unsettled me every single time she was on camera."

Reflection: I was one of the editors (and talking heads!) on a documentary called *The 50 Best Horror Movies You've Never Seen*, most of which I had indeed seen, but this was one of the few exceptions. Of course, I'm kind of a special case (see: this book you're reading), as the ideal viewer of the doc would be just as curious to hear about the doc's selections like *Slumber Party Massacre* and *The Descent* for the first time, like I was to hear about this one. Indeed, that doc was partly my inspiration for this book's focus on DTV and indie titles that never got wide release, because I (and many other fans) HAD seen a lot of those movies and I wanted to dig a bit deeper to see what the reactions would be. It's like whenever I do a list of my favorite slasher movies and the first comment is inevitably "Where is (the name of THEIR favorite slasher movie)?" – I think folks just like having their tastes validated. Well to hell with those guys! If you've seen every movie in this book before picking it up, I'll eat my hat.

Lemora is one of the stranger movies in this month's selection, possibly the entire book (outside of the month devoted to such fare, obviously), as the vampires are just one of the many threats that face the title character. It plays out a lot like a fairy tale, and offers nightmare logic to boot – it's very Italian in that regard, so I couldn't help if it played a tiny part in the genesis of *Suspiria*. It gets a little TOO weird (read: needlessly confusing) in the 3rd act, but makes up for it with a killer final scene. It's a shame Blackburn never directed another feature; he did an episode of *Tales from the Darkside* (and wrote *Eating Raoul!*) but otherwise seems to have disappeared. Maybe he went to look for his dad.

HMAD Fun Fact: Despite the fact that it was a pretty standard blog with moderate at best traffic, being the "Horror Movie A Day guy" resulted in my getting to appear in a few documentaries and Chiller TV specials, and also two actual paying jobs (one of which the employer told me they Googled for someone who watches horror movies and my name kept coming up). Thanks, HMAD!

MOVIE #250 – SEPTEMBER 7th

LIFEFORCE (1985)
Dir: Tobe Hooper
HMAD Review Date: July 30, 2008 (DVD)
Genre: Vampire, Zombie
Available from Scream Factory

Synopsis Based on Fading Memory: A sexy, oft-naked space vampire comes to Earth and feeds on dudes as other dudes try to stop her. From feeding on dudes, I mean. They're probably OK with her being naked.

Review excerpt:
"...it's kind of an anomaly in Hooper's career. Not that the guy has ever had a really consistent body of work (technically or creatively), but this one REALLY sticks out. It's more like the '80s version of a Hammer film like Quatermass *or something than anything you'd expect from the usually Ameri-centric Hooper. It's also 2.35:1; he only went widescreen on a few of his films, usually opting for the smaller 1.85:1 frame. Hell, even the nudity isn't really his bag; I can't recall any real skin in any of his other movies (save* Eaten Alive*), at least not as explicit as it is here."*

Reflection: I saw this again when Scream Factory's Blu-ray came out, and liked it even more. I even wrote an article about how the two cuts of the film differed and where one improved on the other (as with most director's/extended cuts, some changes improved the film, others weakened it), because I liked it enough the 2nd time around to dive deep and spend close to a week's worth of movie-viewing time re-watching it and taking lengthy notes. I still wish Carpenter had directed it, however – the sci-fi/horror blend would have excited him, I think, and his sensibilities seem to be a good fit for the Cannon group (who he never worked with, sadly).

But it's not like Carpenter's filmography needed another good flick as much as Hooper's did. You might notice that this is his only entry in the book, and for good reason – the films that are good are the ones that are famous and you've probably seen them (i.e. *Texas Chain Saw Massacre, Poltergeist*), and the ones you haven't seen should probably stay that way. *Toolbox Murders* might be his only decent movie post-*Chainsaw 2*, actually. His most recent one is apparently unwatchable (per a close friend of his/staunch defender) but will also probably never get released from what I understand, so that's fine. I don't know what the hell happened; he was always kind of hit or miss (*Chain Saw* is a masterpiece, but his follow-up was the forgettable *Eaten Alive*) but it seems like after

Chainsaw 2 he just lost his mojo for good. His peers kept swinging and maintaining a healthy hit/miss ratio, but for whatever reason Hooper just kept striking out. Perhaps he just needs a good collaborator; it's interesting that his two best films (*TCM* and *Poltergeist*) were the result of strong partnerships with others (Kim Henkel on *TCM*, Spielberg on *Poltergeist*), with his next two best being Cannon films (*TCM 2* and this). As you know, most Cannon films are awesome (it's just science!), so even a guy on the decline couldn't screw those up. Then again, *Invaders from Mars* is pretty forgettable, so I dunno.

MOVIE #251 – SEPTEMBER 8th

GRAVE OF THE VAMPIRE (1974)
Dir: John Hayes
HMAD Review Date: April 2, 2012 (DVD)
Genre: Vampire
Public domain title, available through several DVD companies

Synopsis Based on Fading Memory: In this mellow '70s flick written by none other than David Chase (yep, that one), a vampire rapes a woman and the resulting baby, also a vampire, seeks revenge when it gets old enough.

Review excerpt:
"Making up for the lack of action is a lot of goofy dialogue, such as when a girl eats some cake and sighs "Cake is so delicious; I can't believe dead people haven't figured out a way to eat it." She's right; it seems to be that this would be the top priority for a corpse. There's also a lady that gets annoyed with a doctor and gets the final word by saying "My husband DIED from pills!", as if to explain why she wasn't listening to this poor sap who had nothing to do with her husband or his overdose. Also, being a 1970s horror movie, we are treated to out-of-nowhere dance party scenes, as well as a séance sequence. I should note that the latter is led by Michael Pataki (instead of a heroic character), which is not only unusual since he's the villain, but it also allows for more of his angry dialogue delivery."

Reflection: As I was putting this chapter together, Chase was in the news for allegedly revealing whether or not Tony died in *The Sopranos* series finale (turns out it was a misunderstanding), and I once again bemoaned why no one ever asked him to talk about the time he wrote a goofy vampire movie in the '70s. Like his more famous show, this movie also has a vague ending (with the always awesome "The end... OR IS IT?" text in its closing moments), so I guess that's just the sort of thing he liked to do. I really hope someone gets him to talk at length about this movie someday, because not only is it an anomaly on his résumé, but it's got a unique setup that establishes more about the villain than the hero.

The unusual structure of this movie is part of why I like it; it's basically two mini-films strung together, with the first depicting how our villain came to be and what led him to conceive our eventual hero. Then we spend some time with that baby, who is clearly not normal, before finally cutting ahead thirty years or whatever it was to show him, now an adult, going about getting his revenge. It's the sort of thing the '70s could get away with fairly easily and would never fly now, because everything has to be categorized and easily labeled and fit into a traditional template. It's safe to say that the '70s will probably always be my favorite decade for horror, because even though they hadn't quite gotten all of the FX stuff worked out (that's what the '80s were for), the gradual shift from arty, filmmaker driven stuff to more traditional, crowd-pleasing work allowed horror filmmakers – always operating on the fringes – to indulge in both approaches and make up a few of their own. If you haven't figured it out yet, I love variety, and the '70s offered the most of it.

MOVIE #252 – SEPTEMBER 9th

STAKE LAND (2010)
Dir: Jim Mickle
HMAD Review Date: March 23, 2011 (Theatrical)
Genre: Post-apocalyptic, Vampire
Available from Dark Sky Films

Synopsis Based on Fading Memory: A vampire hunter takes on a young charge as they make their way north to find sanctuary in a world overrun by vampires.

Review excerpt:
"I really liked how low on dialogue it could be. I think Danielle Harris has her first line (not counting her song) like 15 minutes after we've met her, and other long stretches go by with minimal or no talking at all. And that's fine by me, because then I could focus on the impressive "wasteland" look and buy into the isolation that they were feeling. Plus it's a nice looking film (a bit too dark during some action scenes however), and it seems our characters are constantly on the move – there's more change of scenery in this movie than a James Bond film. Sure, it's mostly just forests and decaying makeshift cities or back country roads, but it's not like most post-apoc movies where they settle in one particular area for a long period of time."

Reflection: Jim Mickle recently earned tons of acclaim for his revenge thriller *Cold in July*, and I wish I could add to it but I still haven't seen it! But I suspect its success means folks are checking out his earlier work, which was much-loved by the horror community but didn't branch out to the mainstream like *Cold* has. This is probably the most accessible of his three horror films, offering a standard road trip/mentor and apprentice scenario with a readily identifiable monster, not to mention a cast of recognizable actors. Danielle Harris turns in one of her best performances, and there's a fantastic long take sequence that is impressive BEFORE it turns into an action scene halfway through its runtime.

Definitely check out the bonus features on the DVD/Blu, as they include some short films that give some backstory to the film's supporting characters. Each one focuses on someone different, and they all have different directors, including Harris herself, who focused her piece on the Willie character played by Sean Nelson. Unsurprisingly, none of them focus on the anonymous extra played by someone who happens to have the name Kevin Kline – it's NOT the famous comedic actor from *A Fish Called Wanda*, and yet as of this writing it's still on HIS resumé on the IMDb. I love that neither him (well, his people), a fan, or the actual non-famous Kevin Kline have bothered to fix it, five years later.

MOVIE #253 – SEPTEMBER 10th

DAUGHTERS OF DARKNESS (1971)
Dir: Harry Kümel
HMAD Review Date: September 11, 2012 (DVD)
Genre: Vampire
Available from Blue Underground

Synopsis Based on Fading Memory: Countess Bathory tries to drive a couple apart so she can have the wife for herself.

Review excerpt:
"...the deaths are pretty nutty, so there's definitely a quality over quantity thing here as they seem like they might have inspired the Final Destination *sequences at times. For example, a girl is falling, reaching around for something to steady herself, and grabs an open razor. She screams, slips further, knocks over some stuff, her lover rushes over, he slips, etc., etc., and eventually they both tumble to the floor, where she somehow lands on the razor, impaling herself. Later there's a car accident that ends in a reverse staking - it's applause-worthy to be sure, and more than makes up for the fact that the movie can be a little slow at times."*

Reflection: I got pretty tired of Countess Bathory stories over the years (I saw at least five); much like Ed Gein, there really isn't a lot to the story that can't be summed up in ten seconds, so I remain puzzled why it was continually mined for feature film narratives. However, this one works; it may be slower than you'd like, and there's not a lot of vampire action, but I enjoyed the dismissal of many of traditional vampire rules (the only one they keep is that they can't pass through running water), and the ladies are just as lovely to look at as the Belgian scenery. Not enough Belgium-lensed horror movies, in my experience.

In retrospect, I was being kind when I said it gets "a little slow *at times*" – this is a fairly sluggish movie throughout, something even the director admits. In this case he's right, but I find it amusing how many filmmakers lose patience with their own work in hindsight, Like, whenever Carpenter does a commentary for one of his older movies he mutters about how he should have cut this or that, which is funny to me because my biggest problem with his later films is that he's constantly going too fast! Like *Vampires* – he kills off all his awesome vampire hunter dudes before we've gotten much of a chance to see them in action, and then during the finale he just fades in and out to give us the idea of a big fight before just randomly cutting to James Woods and Thomas Ian Griffith about to have their big showdown without much of a setup. Take your time, filmmakers! Not all of us have ADD! Ultimately, if the speed isn't just right, I'd rather have a movie be a little too slow than too fast – a slow movie will give you something to hold on to.

MOVIE #254 – SEPTEMBER 11th

CAPTAIN KRONOS: VAMPIRE HUNTER (1974)
Dir: Brian Clemens
HMAD Review Date: April 23, 2012 (Streaming)
Genre: Vampire
Available from Paramount

Synopsis Based on Fading Memory: Captain Kronos (a vampire hunter) is tasked with finding the monster that has been draining the blood out of locals, causing them to rapidly age.

Review excerpt:
"I quite enjoyed Kronos' partnership with John Cater as Grost, who aids him during fights and when trying to figure out the case. Grost also has a hunchback, which is pretty interesting – it's a film where Renfield assists Van Helsing instead of Dracula. There's a nice bit where some jerks at the pub are mocking him for his deformity, and Kronos doesn't miss a beat as he defends his friend's honor and then kills the shit out of all three of them in one swing of his blade. It's a great little moment; a sword-based version of a pistol duel, where you get a lot of rising tension and close-ups of handles and then BAM! It's over."

Reflection: This is one of my favorite Hammer movies, and a pretty good vampire flick in its own right. What works is that it's a sort of mystery, as we don't know the identity of the vampire that's been draining these lovely ladies of their youth. Werewolf movies often have this kind of "whodunit" flavor, but it's rare to see a vampire take on such things – I wish there were more of them. I don't recall if I figured it out before the reveal; my review says that the mystery works well so I assume not, because otherwise I'd be flaunting my oh-so-genius detective work in solving the mystery. I could be kind of a dick like that.

Hammer was developing a remake a few years back; not sure if that's still happening (save for *The Woman in Black*, they haven't really found much success with their revival, at least as of this writing) but if so I'm fine with it if it encourages more folks to go back and watch the original. The adventure/horror blend worked a lot better than I would have expected, and the addition of a mystery made it thoroughly engaging on all levels, and (don't hate me) it could work as a PG-13, even summer blockbuster kind of thing, like 1999's *The Mummy* (not the shitty sequels) but with a little more emphasis on the horror element. Plus maybe this time we can get a franchise out of it! Kronos deserves more than one film, dammit!

MOVIE #255 – SEPTEMBER 12th

THIRST [BAKJWI] (2009)
Dir: Chan-wook Park
HMAD Review Date: July 9, 2009 (Theatrical)
Genre: Vampire
Available from Focus Features

Synopsis Based on Fading Memory: A priest gets bitten by a vampire and starts to turn into one himself, which poses a giant problem for him given his particular profession.

Review excerpt:
"There have certainly been a number of horror films that revolve around priests that used to be cops (or vice versa), or priests that turn into ass-kickers, or whatever, but I think this is the first that turned the hero priest into the monster itself. Not only is he a decent guy anyway, but as a priest he is doubly against things like murder, so watching him find ways to feed his addiction and also justify his behavior later in the film when the thirst becomes stronger was quite unique and entertaining. There is nothing like the hallway fight scene in Oldboy *that will really grab your attention on a technical level, but the story itself more than makes up for it."*

Reflection: Chan-wook Park is one of the best filmmakers going right now; his US debut *Stoker* was my favorite film of 2013, and everything else I've seen from him is nothing short of great. This actually might be his WEAKEST film (it could have been tightened some), at least of the ones I've seen, and it's still something you should run out and see. I particularly loved the humor here, it's very dry (is that a pun when it concerns a movie called *Thirst*?) and some of the jokes might even take a few seconds to "get", which is always fun. Like, there's a pretty great joke about the vampire smelling a woman's menstrual blood that I recall registering at different times among my audience - some got it instantly; others took a few extra moments for what happened to dawn on them. I love audience moments like that.

Because the hero is a priest and the movie is about vampires, I am constantly referring to this movie as *Priest*, which is the name of a later, decidedly not-great vampire movie with Paul Bettany and Cam Gigandet. Even today, when looking over the list of recent vampire movies on BoxOfficeMojo (their genre sorting is far better than IMDb's, though it obviously only includes theatrical releases), I got it confused yet again. I saw a $29m gross next to *Priest* and thought that was insanely good for a foreign language film, only to realize my error a few seconds later (*Thirst* only made about $300k, sadly). Maybe I should just commit the Korean title to memory and go with that to prevent further confusion. Until then, I truly hope someone else out there makes this mistake so I feel less stupid about it.

MOVIE #256 – SEPTEMBER 13th

PLANET OF THE VAMPIRES (1965)
Dir: Mario Bava
HMAD Review Date: November 3, 2010 (Streaming)
Genre: Alien, Zombie
Available from MGM

Synopsis Based on Fading Memory: Astronauts land on a strange planet and start killing each other… but WHY?

Review excerpt:
"The stiff dubbing actually adds something to the movie, I think, because they are monotone and slightly "off", which of course would make sense if someone was being controlled by an alien vampire. Especially in the final scene, where our hero suspects one of his crewmates has been taken over by the vampires and goes to ask the heroine for her assistance. Her monotonous replies could be construed as a sign that she is infected as well, or that she simply doesn't believe him, but it could ALSO mean nothing, and was just the result of an unmotivated dubbing actress. So it allowed for a little bit of extra suspense and tension, and it also makes some of the villain's big explanation speech sound hilarious; I love when he nonchalantly explains "We arranged for several of you to kill each other."

Reflection: I keep meaning to revisit this one, post-*Prometheus*. I knew it was an influence on *Alien* (and *The Thing*, to a lesser extent) but Ridley Scott was even more direct with his sorta-prequel, as it shares this film's predilection for spending inordinate amounts of time sending our heroes back and forth between their ship and a place on the planet. Plus I genuinely really liked *Prometheus* (I'd stop short of "love" due to the two idiot pot-smoking scientists, good lord), and I figure if I can ever find the time it would make for a really fun double feature.

As with *Shock*, this isn't considered as iconic among Bava's horror films as *Black Sabbath* or *Bay of Blood*, yet I prefer it to those. I really should just sit down with his entire filmography (I own at least eleven of his films thanks to the two Anchor Bay boxed sets) and watch them all again, probably in order this time, and finally form a full opinion of the guy. He's so well regarded by my peers and every movie SOUNDS like something I'd love, but most of them I just feel kinda soft toward, without much interest about revisiting. And that can't be right, considering his reputation among horror fans and several of my genre-loving friends. Maybe it's just because I saw Lamberto's *Demons* before any of Mario's movies, and can't reconcile the fact the older Bava never gave us anything as amazing as the middle aged asshole in that movie who took his wife to a free horror movie on their anniversary.

P.S. The genre tagging isn't a mistake – the way the vampires act/operate is actually more like what you would traditionally associate with zombie behavior. Kind of fits both, but with "vampires" right there in the title it'd be a weird fit for zombie month.

MOVIE #257 – SEPTEMBER 14th

NOSFERATU: PHANTOM DER NACHT (1979)
Dir: Werner Herzog
HMAD Review Date: June 26, 2007 (DVD)
Genre: Vampire, Weird
Available from Scream Factory

Synopsis Based on Fading Memory: *Dracula,* but with (some) different names and Herzog's peculiar sensibilities. And way more rats.

Review excerpt:
"The oddball touches make the film one of my favorite Dracula *movies ever. There's the world's worst violin player, minute-long shots of clouds, etc. And in my personal favorite, there's a scene where Dracula runs past a crucifix, and Klaus Kinski (possibly the only actor who is more menacing in real life than he is playing a bloodsucking immortal) lets out this little whiny yelp that is as hilarious as it is sort of touching. For a second or two, you actually feel bad for Dracula."*

Reflection: I quite liked this one when I saw it back in 2007, but didn't get a chance to watch it again until 2014, when Scream Factory put it out on Blu-ray and I watched it a few times, thanks to the commentary and the rather unusual fact that Herzog shot the movie twice: once in English and once in German. The two versions don't differ all that much (basically just a few different camera angles/edits and slightly modified readings of the lines), but it's still fun to watch them back to back and compare. I really wish Herzog had made more horror films; I think he could make an amazing *Frankenstein* type story.

The fun thing about this one is that it's actually the rare remake that benefitted from something besides improved FX or whatever. The original *Nosferatu* was supposed to be a *Dracula* movie, but because they couldn't get the rights FW Marnau just changed the names and some details to avoid being sued – it's otherwise basically just *Dracula* (probably why he was still sued, because he didn't change it *enough*). For Herzog, almost 60 years later, obtaining the proper rights to Stoker's novel wasn't an issue, so he was able to use the name "Dracula" instead of "Orlok", "Lucy" instead of "Ellen", etc. This allowed him to set our expectations accordingly, and then he pulled the rug out from under us with his unusual take that's not quite *Nosferatu* OR *Dracula* but something in between and beyond. Enjoy!

MOVIE #258 – SEPTEMBER 15th

MR. HUSH (2010)
Dir: David Lee Madison
HMAD Review Date: September 15, 2012 (DVD)
Genre: Vampire
Available from Kino Lorber Films

Synopsis Based on Fading Memory: A guy's family is killed by a vampire. A few years later the vampire returns to do it again. Only this time... the guy still isn't ready.

Review excerpt:
"...as awful as this movie is, I recommend it wholeheartedly. I dubbed it "The Room of DTV horror" over Twitter, and while I hate repeating myself, there really isn't any better way to describe it, as it shares many of that film's strange qualities. For starters, the dialogue seems written by an alien who is approximating English; you will recognize the words, but nothing sounds like anything a human being would actually say. At one point Loree is chained up and his girlfriend's teenaged daughter helps cut him loose - his response is "Good job, sweetie, I'm so proud of you!" Huh? Who would say that in that situation? Hush's big speech about why he's so mad at them is also stunningly inept; it was like 95 degrees in the house when I was watching it and I thought for sure I was just having a heatstroke or something, because that made more sense than anything he was saying."

Reflection: The mere mention of this movie's title still sends me into giggling fits. I think it's because I recognized so many of the actors in it – usually something this incompetent and bizarre is the product of backyard productions where the cast and crew mostly have the same surname. Plus it's got a completely pointless Meat Loaf shout-out (he's referred to as an '80s icon – that's the one decade where he DIDN'T have any success), so I'm endeared to it. It's this month's bad movie "palate cleanser"... but in some ways it's also the best thing I've recommended.

Just don't expect much vampire action. The fact that the titular Mr. Hush is a vampire is actually kind of a twist, but I'm not giving anything away, really – this movie cannot be spoiled by such things! The actual plot only takes up maybe 25 minutes of the movie, and the rest is just a bunch of wacky nonsense, like a guy describing a corned beef recipe. None of the actors are cast well; nothing against their talent but the girl playing the hero's wife looks young enough to be his daughter, and then later he meets his grandmother (in a dream) and she also looks younger than him, suggesting that this family had some unusual ideas about when a woman is old enough to have a child of her own. Oh and keep watching the credits for... actually I have no words to describe it. It's like an epilogue, but concerning a minor character meeting up with one we never met at all. It'd be like staying after the credits of *Avengers* and getting a scene where a new SHIELD agent fills out his W-2 and then Maria Hill waves at him. Bless this movie.

MOVIE #259 – SEPTEMBER 16th

PERFECT CREATURE (2006)
Dir: Glenn Standring
HMAD Review Date: July 18, 2007 (DVD)
Genre: Vampire
Available from 20th Century Fox

Synopsis Based on Fading Memory: Vampires and humans get along just fine, but then a bad vampire threatens to muck it up, forcing his (still good) brother to team up with some human cops to stop him.

Review excerpt:
"It's no masterpiece, but it's certainly a cut above what you would expect for a DTV vampire movie (starring Dougray Scott no less! Stupid Ian, like you could ever compete with Mike). And it is in fact pretty damn good. Fans of films like Equilibrium *and* V for Vendetta *should certainly appreciate the production design, which looks like a combination of 19th century London, 1940's Germany, and a modern New York slum. I'm a sucker for alternate reality meshes of time and setting."*

Reflection: Before I get to the usual reflection I want to take a moment to make fun of myself here. Check out the review excerpt– it includes a reference to *Desperate Housewives* (yes, I was a fan) and then I basically endorse goddamn Steampunk. As I've said before, I'm kind of embarrassed by my older reviews (like the first 6-7 months' worth), but this one has to take the cake. In my defense, I didn't actually know what steampunk was back then (and looking back now, this movie's version of it is pretty minimalist), and my "I'm a sucker for..." comment was inspired by movies like *Payback*, where everyone had a rotary phone even though it was supposed to be the late '90s (or even Tim Burton's *Batman*, which simultaneously looked like the 1930s and the future). But still. Oof.

Anyway, this is a good flick, and I can't help but think if Dougray's career hadn't been derailed by John Woo and Tom Cruise (production delays on *Mission Impossible 2* – the worst of the series! – forced him to drop out as Wolverine in the original *X-Men*) that it woulda been one of the big draws for whatever month it had its theatrical release. Or he'd be too big to star in such things, I dunno. Either way, it seems like a movie that was probably supposed to start a franchise, with an ending suggesting darker days to come or whatever, but it doesn't leave you with movie blue balls – much like the first *Matrix*, it's a complete story with the suggestion of where it COULD go next, but not at the expense of finishing up all of the storylines it established. Unlike *Matrix*, these folks were smart enough to leave it alone.

MOVIE #260 – SEPTEMBER 17th

HABIT (1996)
Dir: Larry Fessenden
HMAD Review Date: May 24, 2009 (DVD)
Genre: Vampire
Available from Scream Factory

Synopsis Based on Fading Memory: A guy's new girlfriend turns out to be a vampire.

Review excerpt:
"I liked the non-glamorous depiction of New York; like Mulberry Street *(a film in which Fessenden appears), our characters are working class schmoes, and their apartments are hardly palaces. Most NY set films revolve around wealthy folks (or tourists), not the guys who serve your food or run the audio for your band's gig. I suck at NY geography, so I don't know which neighborhood it all takes place in, but it's much more interesting than the umpteenth Riverside Drive building-set movie where Liz Lemon and 4000 other fictional New Yorkers seem to reside. There's a great bit where they ride a Ferris wheel that is sandwiched between two buildings... there's something strange and alluring about the idea of looking out your window and seeing a carnival ride inches away."*

Reflection: I feel I got off on the wrong foot with Larry Fessenden, as far as HMAD is concerned. The first things I saw from him were a couple of the lesser films he produced (*The Off Season* and *Trigger Man*) and what is probably his weakest film as a director (*The Last Winter*), making me wonder why anyone was giving this guy any attention or praise. I've since caught up with his better films (both as director and producer) and rightfully become a fan, so it's all good. Anyway, this is his best film in my opinion – weird as it's the only one of the features he's directed where he took on a lead role as well. I usually tend to dislike this sort of thing in indies, feeling that the director is spreading himself too thin by taking the lead role as well, but it works like a charm here.

However, it's also like the 3rd or 4th "vampire and human fall in love" movie this month and there just as many to come. So I hope you aren't too big of a fan of *From Dusk Till Dawn* or *30 Days of Night* type action-heavy vampire movies, because there aren't a lot of those in this lineup. I actually can't think of too many traditional scary horror vampire movies I like – I shrug off most *Dracula* adaptations (my personal favorite is John Badham's, for what it's worth) and have zero affinity for things like the *Underworld* and *Blade* series (I still haven't even watched the 3rd *Blade* film, probably the only movie with a Marvel logo that I've skipped). But when they strip that stuff down and get more personal, I tend to enjoy them quite a bit – my favorite genre film of 2014 was probably *Only Lovers Left Alive*, which is even less of a "vampire movie" than this. In short: if you were hoping for thirty scary bloodsucker movies – sorry! There are only a few!

MOVIE #261 – SEPTEMBER 18th

LET'S SCARE JESSICA TO DEATH (1971)
Dir: John D. Hancock
HMAD Review Date: March 13, 2008 (DVD)
Genre: Psychological, Vampire
Available from Warner Archive

Synopsis Based on Fading Memory: A former mental patient seems to be going off the deep end again... or is it vampires?

Review excerpt:
"It's a good flick, definitely one to watch late at night with the lights off, instead of during the bright daylight like I did. After just watching April Fool's Day, *the title had me expecting that the movie was all just a prank (as in "Hey Guys, Let's Scare Jessica..."), so the fact that it was indeed a legit supernatural horror film (albeit a slow burn of one) was a nice surprise, and not without some well-appreciated creepiness. There's a scene late in the film where the heroine's husband walks into a general store, and then four or five of the creepy townsfolk slowly follow him in and close the door – foreboding and creepy as hell!"*

Reflection: It's a long way off since he's not even two yet, but I like to plan ahead, and one thing I will definitely try to do with my son is make sure he sees movies "in order" as much as possible, should he take an interest in horror at all. I don't mean just franchises, either – I kind of want to give him a crash course in horror history, showing him older films before the newer ones that were influenced by them (plus it's likely an older film won't have excessive nudity or gore – i.e. the things he should be older before he sees). I saw so many rip-offs of this movie that by the time I finally got around to seeing it, a lot of its impact was diluted. So if he's ever like "I want to watch *The Skeleton Key*!" or something, I'll make sure he sees this first. And then send him to bed early for asking to watch something Ehren Kruger wrote.

The original DVD was from Paramount and is now out of print. It's currently in the hands of the Warner Archive, a service I do not think too highly of since their discs are shoddy and always lack bonus features. It's a fine option for movies that never came out on the format (like *Night School*), but when a perfectly good, normally priced DVD goes away and is replaced by one that's inferior and more expensive, it's annoying. So do your best to find the Paramount one. Stick it to those Warner jerks!

MOVIE #262 – SEPTEMBER 19th

BLACULA (1972)
Dir: William Crain
HMAD Review Date: December 27, 2010 (Streaming)
Genre: Vampire
Available from MGM

Synopsis Based on Fading Memory: A former slave is turned into a vampire, and then he goes to New York to find his soul mate.

Review excerpt:
"...it's actually kind of scary at times. There's a great moment where he goes after a photographer who snapped a photo of him, because when she sees the developed picture, sans Blacula, she will expose him. So she opens the door to her darkroom and BAM! He's on the other side, ready to strike. Good stuff. Some of the other kills are kind of botched though; there's an odd moment during the climax where they suddenly just cut to a random cop getting fried on a big electric panel - it's not even clear if Manuwalde tossed him at it or if the guy was just clumsy."

Reflection: The title always had me thinking this was a goofy movie, but it's actually played straight and even has a few scares. Manuwalde is just as interesting a character as Dracula himself (Drac actually appears, surprisingly), and if you've seen *Vampire in Brooklyn* you will see where a lot of its story came from. I don't know if I ever saw a "Blaxploitation" horror movie before HMAD, and post-*30 Rock* I have trouble watching them without hearing Tracy Jordan saying *"A Blaffair To Rememblack"*, but of the ones I caught I enjoyed them all – there's at least one other one recommended in this book!

The sequel *Scream Blacula Scream* is also solid, so if you enjoy this one be sure to check that one out too. It's actually got a more interesting story and some better supporting characters (including Pam Grier as a voodoo lady who wants to help Blacula rid himself of his curse), and it's better directed as well (no surprise there, as it was helmed by Bob Kelljan of *Count Yorga* fame). But it also recycles some beats from its predecessor, giving it a typical sequel retread feel at times, which is unfortunate. Still, again, for a movie with one of the silliest looking titles ever (and in the sequel's case, one that I don't quite understand – no one is making Blacula scream in it?), you will probably be surprised how solid it is.

HMAD Fun Fact: I watched at least 32 movies with Dracula for HMAD, roughly 1/5th of all the vampire movies reviewed for the site. This includes the majority of the Universal and Hammer series as well as Dracula 3000, *which may be the absolute worst* Dracula *movie of all time.*

MOVIE #263 – SEPTEMBER 20th

VAMPIRE CIRCUS (1972)
Dir: Robert Young
HMAD Review Date: January 16, 2011 (Streaming)
Genre: Vampire
Available from Synapse Films

Synopsis Based on Fading Memory: A vampire is killed by townsfolk, so his children try to resurrect him using the blood of THEIR children. Brutal.

Review excerpt:
"...a unique and worthy entry to the Hammer canon. I liked seeing the vampire tale taking place outside of the usual castles and foggy villages, and they don't hold back on the carnage despite the plan to murder children. There are also a lot of wonderfully strange/creepy moments; I particularly liked when a would-be victim sees something watching her through some trees, but as they get closer we see it's actually a guy with shiny "eyes" glued to the shin area of his pants for some reason. And even though the animation is a bit primitive, I liked the concept behind the blood dripping onto the dead vampire and being absorbed, instead of the usual "reverse footage of someone melting" stuff."

Reflection: When you think of Hammer, you probably get images of Christopher Lee and/or Peter Cushing in the *Dracula* and *Frankenstein* movies, but while I quite liked those I was always more drawn to the one-offs, like *Captain Kronos* and this. Not that I DISLIKED the *Dracula*s and such, but the *déjà vu* was hard to ignore when watching them – I know many folks aren't crazy about *Dracula AD 1972* but I actually quite liked it, partly because it stood further from the pack than the others. That's not to say I enjoy ALL their stand-alone films (*The Reptile* sticks out as particularly rough), but if they had a boxed set of their late '60s, early '70s stuff that didn't include the two big series, I'd spare no expense to obtain it.

Anyway, this one stuck out due to the incredibly misleading PG rating, as the film contains full frontal female nudity and some very gory kills. Do NOT bring the kids! Especially since the movie is about someone trying to murder all of the youngsters – it might be a bit more frightening than they'd expect from an "old PG movie". And adults might be a bit put off too; there's a disturbing scene where the townies kill a bunch of the circus animals. RIP, cute little monkey.

MOVIE #264 – SEPTEMBER 21st

THE HUNGER (1983)
Dir: Tony Scott
HMAD Review Date: August 16, 2008 (DVD)
Genre: Vampire
Available from Warner Home Video

Synopsis Based on Fading Memory: After her lover (David Bowie) dies, a vampire seeks a new soul mate – this time a lady!

Review excerpt:
"Like Cronos or the recent Let The Right One In, The Hunger is one of those vampire movies that eschews most of the typical lore (these vampires have a reflection, which pays off quite nicely in a quick little jump scare early on) and isn't about big fangs and set pieces. It's a mood piece, very heavy on character and dialogue, and hardly the spectacle one would expect from Tony Scott if they were familiar with his recent work (though it DOES have some of his trademarks – lots of blue tinted shots, smoke and/or sunglasses in just about every shot, etc.)."

Reflection: Few celebrity deaths have bothered me as much as Tony Scott's; the manner (suicide via drowning) was upsetting enough, but the fact that he was still working regularly just really made it difficult for me to accept – this was a guy who was still releasing a film every couple years. Plus, when an actor dies early, he/she almost always has a film awaiting release, giving us one last chance to say goodbye (in Robin Williams' case, he had three or four, in fact), but Tony was in between films. When I watched *Unstoppable* – hardly a great film – I didn't realize it would be the last time I got to see a new Tony Scott movie, and that really got to me. I rarely honor a fallen entertainer so quickly, but I still recall hearing the news of his death and popping *Last Boy Scout* into my player almost instantly. That's not my favorite of his movies (*True Romance* is), but it's one of his most deliriously fun, and I wanted a drama-free evening (read: no Patricia Arquette hotel room beating) as I celebrated how many smiles the man had put on my face over the years.

One of the many things that made me particularly sad about his death is that I always hoped that he'd eventually dial things back (with *Domino* and *Man on Fire*, he had gotten excessive even by his standards) and make something else like *The Hunger*, which is more like one of his brother Ridley's films than anything else in his filmography. It's got some of his visual flair, but narratively it's unlike anything else he's ever done, and it stuck with me for a long time after seeing it, which is more than say, *Déjà Vu* or his *Pelham 123* update offered. In fact, if I had owned a copy of this I probably would have went with it that night instead of *Last Boy Scout*, and maybe even cried – like vampires, I saw bigger than life filmmakers like Scott as immortal, and his death was a sobering reminder that I was wrong.

*Late note – just weeks before this book was due to be released, David Bowie also passed away. He didn't follow his one-time director's MO when it came to leaving this world – he released a goodbye album two days before he died! So thanks for that, thanks for so many other great albums (*Ziggy Stardust *being my favorite, for the record), and thanks for inadvertently making this entry a little more prescient, Mr. Bowie. If you're not immortal, no one is. RIP.*

MOVIE #265 – SEPTEMBER 22nd

THE LIVING DEAD GIRL (1982)
Dir: Jean Rollin
HMAD Review Date: December 23, 2012 (Streaming)
Genre: Vampire
Available from Kino Lorber Films

Synopsis Based on Fading Memory: A woman sorta gets turned into a vampire by a toxic waste spill (?), so her friend helps her get the blood she needs to survive.

Review excerpt:
"Sure, the FX are cheesy as hell, but there's something quite charming about how casually vicious she is when killing folks, making up for the less than stellar prosthetic and makeup work. There's also enough fake blood being sprayed around during this and the rest of the kill scenes to make up for 3-4 CGI-heavy chores. It's a bit slow, yes, but in a way that actually works in its favor - you think it'll be talky and not much will happen, and then there will be another gory murder out of nowhere. After dispatching a couple of folks who are screwing around in her house, Catherine's childhood best friend Helene finds her, and once she realizes what her friend needs to survive, she starts helping by bringing random people from town over for Catherine to eat. It's one of the more interesting takes on the "needs blood to survive" monster that I've seen in a while, which makes sense since it's 30 years old and thus from a time when ideas took precedent over casting familiar faces and cashing in on brand name titles."

Reflection: My 2nd favorite Rollin! I think. Like I said in the entry for *Lips of Blood*, they all kind of run together in my mind now, so doing a proper ranking would probably take a dedicated re-watch of all of them. But I always like these scenarios, where one person is a monster of some sort and their human friend is helping them feed to survive, because that's just the sort of things friends do, dammit! Since it's a bit slow you can think about which friends of yours you'd help murder innocent folks to prolong their life, and which ones you'd let rot or put a bullet into. Note – if you start thinking of which ones you'd like to have a *Deadgirl* scenario with instead, please seek help.

I should note that this is not TECHNICALLY a vampire movie. She needs blood to survive but otherwise the common rules do not apply (indeed, one plot point revolves around someone taking a picture of her), so don't be looking for fangs and garlic or whatever. In fact, the movie has another wrinkle to its plot that I omitted from my excerpt above, because I can't recall if it's technically a spoiler or not. The site was pretty casual with spoilers, but now, a few years later, I have trouble remembering what I'm spoiling and what I'm just saying about the plot. It'd be like if I only saw *Empire Strikes Back* once, five years ago, and couldn't remember if Vader being Luke's father was a spoiler or just a regular plot point. Obviously that would be an example of a spoiler, and one I'd be pretty amused to be responsible for to be honest. How amazing would it be if the one person in the world who didn't already know that somehow read this book before watching one of the two *(post Force Awakens update: OK, three-ish)* good *Star Wars* movies?

MOVIE #266 – SEPTEMBER 23rd

LOVE AT FIRST BITE (1979)
Dir: Stan Dragoti
HMAD Review Date: February 11, 2012 (DVD)
Genre: Comedic, Vampire
Available from Scream Factory

Synopsis Based on Fading Memory: Dracula loses his castle, so he starts a new life in New York, where he falls in love with a fashion model.

Review excerpt:
"Of course, as with any comedy of this sort, there are as many groaners as laughs (pretty much anything revolving around Renfield is laugh-free), as well as some dated material that distracts from the fun. But again, I was surprised at how much DID still work, particularly the hilariously inept psychiatrist who is also a descendent of Van Helsing. He's a bit fuzzy on the exact ways to kill a vampire, which has some fun results: after shooting Dracula through the heart with silver bullets, he tries to get out of arrest by pointing out that he mixed him up with a werewolf and that he's actually fine. The actor is Richard Benjamin, better known for his directing these days, but he's got a fun sort of Steven Colbert-ish demeanor here, arrogant yet clueless, and ultimately well-meaning."

Reflection: As I mentioned earlier, my favorite *Dracula* movie is 1979's version directed by John Badham, with Frank Langella as the Count, and the same year produced Herzog's awesome *Nosferatu* update (which you should have watched a few days ago!) and this film. And yet of the three, this was the most successful at the box office! That's a factoid that would normally annoy me, but this is a pretty fun movie so it's all good. Besides, you can watch all three of them back to back without feeling too much repetition – it's actually interesting to see how many different ways the same basic story can be told.

Some of the humor is dated, but a lot of it still works, and while I hate to say so, it's a lot better than Mel Brooks/Leslie Nielsen's *Dracula: Dead and Loving It*. I remember Brooks (or someone from the production) specifically namechecking this as one that didn't work at the time *Dead and Loving It* was being released, but I'll take this over their lackluster 1995 effort any day of the week (the only good joke in that movie was the guy confused over the odd pronunciation of "schedule"). But it's not like Brooks is the only one to muck it up; the vampire comedy sub-genre is littered with garbage (remember *Vampires Suck*? I hope not), but this proves it can be done, more or less. Bonus points for the Sherman Hemsley cameo.

MOVIE #267 – SEPTEMBER 24th

VAMPIRE'S KISS (1989)
Dir: Robert Bierman
HMAD Review Date: June 13, 2010 (Cable)
Genre: Comedic, Vampire
Available from Scream Factory

Synopsis Based on Fading Memory: Nicolas Cage believes he is a vampire and goes to great lengths to prove it.

Review excerpt:
"...even if you're not fully satisfied with the film's climax, you cannot deny what a tour de force Cage provides here. He occasionally has an accent (part of his character's desire to be distinguished and interesting), he runs around yelling "I'm a vampire!" over and over, makes a coffin out of an overturned couch... Cage-philes will be incredibly satisfied with this film, and then some. Even the little moments killed me - I particularly loved when he talks to a woman through her window asking to be let in (not in the vampire way), and then when she gets up to open the door, he rings the doorbell anyway."

Reflection: It's been a sad couple years for Nic Cage fans like me; most of his films now go direct to video or are given such pitiful theatrical releases that you end up putting more effort into seeing them than their distributor put into promoting them. I know he's just one big hit from turning things around again (*National Treasure 3* would be the safest bet), but he is denied that chance with movies like *Stolen* or *Frozen Ground*. Thankfully, he seems to be getting at least *slightly* choosier and picking projects of actual merit (an Oliver Stone film, a new Larry Charles comedy, etc.), so hopefully a proper comeback is possible and not just the pipe dreams of his loyal fans.

Until that day comes, please go back and check out films like this that should help you understand why we love him so, especially if you're one of those bad people who think he's only worthy of internet memes and the like. I would easily put this among his best ever performances, and director Robert Bierman (working from a Joseph Minion script) is remarkably skilled at finding the balance between comedy and tragedy – the movie is essentially about a very lonely guy suffering a complete mental collapse, which should be pretty depressing, but it's endlessly entertaining, and you never feel bad for laughing. Cage is probably the only actor alive who could pull off this otherwise impossible balance, as anyone else would swing too far in one direction or the other. And he was only 23 at the time! It's an astonishing performance in a uniquely entertaining film. Pair it with *Martin* for bonus enjoyment (I assume you've seen *Martin*).

MOVIE #268 – SEPTEMBER 25th

THE VAMPIRES' NIGHT ORGY (1974)
Dir: León Klimovsky
HMAD Review Date: September 8, 2008 (DVD)
Genre: Breakdown, Vampire
Public domain title, available through several DVD companies

Synopsis Based on Fading Memory: A bus breaks down in a town full of vampires. There's no orgy.

Review excerpt:
"It sort of unfolds like a slasher movie, with our good guys constantly going off by themselves and getting killed every 10 minutes or so. Also, the vampires behave sort of like zombies; rather than just one euro-trash head vampire and a couple of lackeys, like usual, it's just a bunch of vague, hungry zombies, a la 30 Days of Night (except for the Danny Huston character), which was also a nice change of pace. It's only 79 minutes long, but it's a well-paced 79 minutes, and I could have easily enjoyed another 10-20."

Reflection: I almost put this in the slasher month since structurally it resembles a body count movie more than any vampire movie I can recall (complete with their vehicle breaking down in a town that seems oddly deserted!), but with "Vampire" right there in the title I couldn't justify it. Still, I quite like it when you get the tone of one sub-genre but the specifics of another; the (much-maligned) zombie movie *Dead Snow* also takes a slasher structure but with Nazi zombies as the villain(s) instead of a guy in a mask. Nowadays, zombies and vampires are pretty interchangeable thanks to things like *The Strain*, so movies like this, where the mashup is a bit more inspired, are twice as welcome as they were when I first saw them.

Amusingly, one of my favorite things about this had nothing to do with the movie (which I assure you is worthy of your time), but rather the fact that Mill Creek offered a 2.35:1 letterboxed presentation of it. If you're unfamiliar with the company, they're the ones who make a lot of the budget packs I used, often cramming 50 movies onto 12 discs. Unsurprisingly, these sets usually offered some of the worst transfers I've ever seen, and always full frame (making more than one movie occasionally hard to follow due to haphazard cropping), so when a few letterboxed transfers showed up on their "Tales of Terror" set, I was quite elated. This was not long after I got my Blu-ray player and was finding it even harder to train my eyes to accept the distributor's washed out, full-frame, sub-VHS looking movies, so getting something respectable probably went a long way into helping me enjoy the film. I still wonder what a Mill Creek Blu-ray set would look like...

MOVIE #269 – SEPTEMBER 26th

BLOOD OF DRACULA'S CASTLE (1969)
Dir: Al Adamson
HMAD Review Date: February 5, 2010 (DVD)
Genre: Vampire
Public domain title, available through several DVD companies

Synopsis Based on Fading Memory: *Dracula* meets *Manos*! OK that's more of a pitch than a synopsis, but that's all I got.

Review excerpt:
"...the thing I dug about the movie was that it was just so loose with both the Dracula *mythology and its own over-stuffed storyline. Johnny has no concern about the fact that his friends are vampires, and there's a wonderfully nonchalant conversation about how they hated having to bite into necks and that the new way is so much better. And the hero's wife practically has a monologue about how she can't wait to swim in the moat around the castle (again - what the?). I don't think the vampires ever actually kill anyone in the movie (though Johnny makes up for it by killing a bunch of people at random - including a hitchhiker in a surprisingly gory scene), as their butler and the aforementioned Torgo-lite guy do the bulk of the dirty work, which again, ties into the film's surprising laid back nature.*"

Reflection: The four or five budget packs I bought in the early days of HMAD were, unfortunately, mostly made up of rubbish movies that deserved to be sentenced to a life of being tossed unceremoniously onto cheapo multi-packs, but they were worth the purchase for the occasional oddball title like this. It's got some gore and (maybe?) a werewolf along with the vampires, firmly keeping it within genre territory, but the real draw of the movie is how random it was. I always meant to check out more of Al Adamson's movies to see if this was a fluke or if his movies always had this kooky "relaxed" vibe, but I never got around to it. Maybe I'll watch one in time for Volume 2 of this book!

I'm sure some feel differently, but I think the public domain status of characters like Dracula is a godsend to the horror genre. Michael Myers is always going to be a guy in a white mask killing people in the suburbs, Freddy Krueger is always going to be in your dreams, etc. – but look at how many interpretations we've gotten of Dracula over the years, because there's no owner to veto such deviations. It's a win-win situation for a filmmaker – the name brand gets eyeballs on the movie, and our familiarity with his legend gives them license to skip over the "origin" if they choose (which they should, unless they have a specific reason to include it). If *Dracula's* rights were tied up and costly, you'd see a lot of rip-offs of the character in movies that were weighed down by the need to establish who "Count Stoker" was or whatever clever name they'd use in place of the one they wanted.

MOVIE #270 – SEPTEMBER 27th

BITTEN (2008)
Dir: Harvey Glazer
HMAD Review Date: June 29, 2010 (DVD)
Genre: Vampire
Available from RHI Entertainment

Synopsis Based on Fading Memory: A late shift paramedic falls in love with a vampire, which causes problems in their dating life as he's working at the only time she can go out.

Review excerpt:
"Even though it doesn't really go into under-explored territory, it's still pretty amusing, thanks to an always entertaining Jason Mewes (as the least likely paramedic ever, but that's OK) and his frequent exchanges with his older partner, played by Richard Fitzpatrick. I sort of wish they had been a little more clever and simply let the guy know right from the start what she was, instead of hiding it from him (he finds out near the end in yet another largely standard moment), but it's still sort of charming to hear them talk about women in a "can't live with 'em, can't live without 'em" way when the woman in question is a vampire."

Reflection: I wish there were more opportunities to enjoy Jason Mewes' abilities as a performer without the constant shadow of Kevin Smith looming over him. I find that I've "outgrown" Smith these days (I recently tried to watch *Mallrats* and couldn't even get through it), but I still find Mewes amusing when he pops up in other things (his bit in *Feast* is classic). This is one of the very few times he had a lead role in a film Smith had nothing to do with, and he did a fine job if memory serves – let's hope producers continue to give him the chance to carve his own path.

Interestingly, it's sort of a reversed sexes (and funnier) version of *Midnight Son*, so maybe I should have put those closer together in the book so you could kind of double feature it. This being a 2008 release, we can't chalk up its existence to *Twilight* since that movie hadn't come out yet (and come on, no movie trend is going to be based on a book), so it's just an anomaly, since vampire movies during that period were back to being traditionally horror (or at least action) oriented, and not so much about romance. Or comedy, for that matter – 1996's *Bordello of Blood* was the last (theoretically) funny vampire movie that I can recall before this, though I've seen a few since. So whatever possessed this film's financiers to sink dough into a moribund sub-sub-genre starring a guy who hadn't really been tested as a lead, I'm glad they did. And I apologize to them for not getting around to it sooner; I think I had the screener for a year or two before I finally watched it. I assume giving it one of these precious thirty slots is acceptable penance!

MOVIE #271 – SEPTEMBER 28th

DAYBREAKERS (2009)
Dir: Michael Spierig, Peter Spierig
HMAD Review Date: December 10, 2009 (Theatrical)
Genre: Vampire
Available from Lionsgate

Synopsis Based on Fading Memory: In the future, vampires run the world and run into a problem – there are almost no humans left to feed on, which can lead to the end of their race unless a cure is found.

Review excerpt:
"The thing I liked most was that it didn't have this giant backstory and a bunch of lore and curses, like the Underworld films get bogged down in. It's actually a pretty straight forward tale told against a huge backdrop (a future where 95% of the population is comprised of vampires, who are now starving due to a lack of blood). If this movie takes off, Lionsgate can milk the property for years across a variety of mediums (it would certainly make for a good comic), because it's a pretty vast (and believable) world and this particular story only focuses on a few people living in it."

Reflection: This movie sat on the shelf for a while and didn't exactly break box office records when it was finally released, so it's been sort of forgotten it seems. And that's a shame; it's got one of the more impressive "in the future" scenarios I've seen in a genre film in quite some time, plus a terrific cast (Sam Neill AND Willem Dafoe in one movie?) and equally great Weta FX. It also made me a fan of the Spierig brothers; their low-budget zombie film *Undead* was one of the first movies I watched for HMAD and I didn't care for it. Always nice to see filmmakers improve!

Another nice thing about this movie, or at least how I saw it – it was at the Lionsgate screening room! I wasn't exactly kind to the folks at LG over the years, and for quite a long time I never got a single invite to anything they were showing. But somehow I got on the list for this one, and from then on I'd get pretty much all of their horror releases. It was a pretty far drive from me, but I'd go as often as I could just to keep the invites coming, and also because they usually served snacks. But it didn't last; the last time I got one was *Texas Chainsaw 3D*, which I didn't like very much, and I haven't heard from them since. Crybabies.

MOVIE #272 – SEPTEMBER 29th

CRAVINGS (2006)
Dir: D.J. Evans
HMAD Review Date: August 19, 2009 (DVD)
Genre: Psychological, Vampire
Available from Lionsgate

Synopsis Based on Fading Memory: A girl suffering from a disease that compels her to drink blood becomes obsessed with her psychiatrist.

Review excerpt:
"The misleading box art is a shame, because the movie is much better than I was expecting. The hero is a fascinatingly flawed character - he seemingly breaks every patient/doctor rule in the book over the course of the film - and the acting is far above what you normally get from a DTV Lionsgate movie. In fact, I'm pretty baffled why they didn't select this for one of their After Dark releases (or even Ghost House Underground), as it would give the film more exposure, instead of it being one of the dozens of undistinguished DVD cases on the shelf at Blockbuster, rented only by folks like me (indeed, even I had passed it by a couple times)."

Reflection: *Martin, Vampire's Kiss,* and now *Cravings*... there's a sub-sub-genre of horror movies where the character's vampirism is mostly in their head. And they're all good! The box art for this (which originally had the name *Daddy's Girl*) sells a generic sexy vampire movie, so I suspect many folks who rented it were mad that it was more of a drama – hopefully I can help you watch it with the right expectations. It's tough to pull off a drama/horror hybrid, so it's kind of heartbreaking when a filmmaker manages to succeed only for his distributor to sell his movie on a lie.

Oh, dead dog alert! There isn't a lot of outright horror in the movie, but a poodle owner might not feel the same way. If memory serves it's one of the more upsetting dog kills I've seen in a movie, though the family dog during most of my younger life was a poodle so I might have been a bit more sympathetic (and it's been six years so I might have exaggerated the scene in my mind). Either way, be on the lookout!

MOVIE #273 – SEPTEMBER 30th

THE REFLECTING SKIN (1990)
Dir: Phillip Ridley
HMAD Review Date: December 10, 2011 (DVD)
Genre: Vampire, Weird
Available from Echo Bridge Home Entertainment

Synopsis Based on Fading Memory: A young man comes of age, sort of, in his Midwestern town that's populated with weirdoes.

Review excerpt:
"...it's quite good, and even if you hate it you have to admit that it's hardly a "typical" movie in any way shape or form. Top billed Viggo Mortensen doesn't appear until the halfway mark, we're introduced to our hero as he kills an innocent frog (and terrorizes a woman in the process), and there's a subplot about an "angel" that is actually a discarded fetus. It FEELS like a normal movie at the outset, but it's all the little details like the above that give it such a strange, at times almost impenetrable life. Like some sort of weird Monet in movie form, I guess."

Reflection: This movie never came out on DVD prior to its Echo Bridge release, and now the stand-alone version is out of print, if the current $39.99 price on Amazon is any indication. However, the Bridge put it on some of their multi-pack sets, so you might have better luck finding it cheap and with a few random *Prophecy* sequels or *Dracula 2000* alongside it for good measure. Wal-Mart and grocery stores seem to be the main sources of these things, so keep an eye out next time you're buying bulk socks or milk.

There's a scene in the movie that really left an impression on me, where the young protagonist ponders over a couple of unrelated photographs. For as long as I can remember going to flea markets (or dirt malls, or antique fairs – whatever you want to call that giant, usually outdoor location near you that sells a bunch of old junk once a week), I've wondered why people sold boxes of random photos, and if I'd end up in a picture that someone bought 50 years after it was taken. But now that I know that person might be the lead character in a horror movie, I'm more OK with it.

As you might have guessed from the excerpt, this isn't much of a horror movie at all, let alone a vampire one. As I've said a few times, the vampire genre is one I tend to find more to like when they're going against the grain. A guy with fangs racking up a body count until someone pulls him into the sunlight just doesn't excite me – even John Carpenter himself couldn't really win me over with *Vampires,* which I put near the bottom of my obligatory ranking of his films (ironically, it was his only successful movie of the '90s). The few traditional ones I really like are the same ones EVERYONE likes, so obviously they have no place in this book – I was "forced" to broaden my horizons when it came to curating this month's selections. I hope my decision proved rewarding for you. If not... hey, we can agree *From Dusk Till Dawn* is pretty awesome, right?

OCTOBER – "ALT" HORROR

ARTIST: SEAN KASPER

For the past eight or nine years, and without fail, every October someone tweets or texts me saying "They're ripping you off!" along with a link to a blog where someone is trying to watch a horror movie every of the month. I never minded these things, of course (even if they wreaked havoc on my Google alert), as I loved seeing others attempt it, if only for a fraction of the time. If nothing else, maybe they'd appreciate my year-round dedication all the more! But when I take a look at these sites, I often find that they're merely watching their personal favorites, or the basics – *Friday the 13th*, *American Werewolf In London*, *The Shining*... the sort of movies I dubbed too obvious to put in the book, in other words. There's nothing wrong with that, but if you're gonna go to that much effort, why not dig deeper?

Also, October is when your local repertory theater (if you're lucky enough to have one) will be showing old classics (hopefully on 35mm), and the TV stations will be showing tons of standards like the *Halloween* sequels and Stephen King adaptations, and every Halloween party will have a stack of movies like *Scream* and *Evil Dead* at the ready for background noise. And that's just the viewing – the internet will be crammed with all sorts of lists and "Freddy's Best Nightmares!" type material, making the "standards" kind of inescapable, even a little overbearing. Even I'm sick of Michael Myers long before October 31st.

So I thought you might have trouble getting excited about another 30 traditional horror movies, and therefore I've opted to focus on what were mostly labeled thriller or "Horror?" movies on the site. These are movies that would be in the horror section of a video store (if those still existed), or were covered in *Fangoria* and the like, but for the most part aren't as horrific as the ones they'd be associated with - "Alternative" horror, if you will. You'll be seeing plenty of masked killers and monsters this month whether you like it or not – I want to give you some balance! Naturally, I'm kicking things off with one of the lightest in terms of horror stuff, but also the best...

MOVIE #274 – OCTOBER 1st

RESOLUTION (2012)
Dir: Justin Benson, Aaron Moorhead
HMAD Review Date: October 16, 2012 (Festival screening)
Genre: Thriller, Weird
Available from New Video Group

Synopsis Based on Fading Memory: A guy tries to detox his meth-addict best friend, and also starts seeing some weird shit in the woods.

Review excerpt:
"It's an unusual scenario for a film, but the two leads' chemistry makes it work like gangbusters, to the extent that you gotta wonder why you haven't seen it more often. One of the directors said he had heard the film described as "Lovecraftian Mumblecore", but I think of it more like True West *meets* The Shining *- whatever plot elements come into play, it never strays far from its dramatic core about two guys at a crossroads in their lives, one being high and mighty, trying to convince the other to change his ways without ever considering that the guy might be perfectly happy the way he is. Even at the end (no spoilers), they're still just chatting about their lives and the role the other plays in it - it's actually quite endearing."*

Reflection: A few months after seeing this gem for the first time, I had the pleasure of hosting a Q&A with directors Benson and Moorhead at another festival screening. And when I asked them about a particular prop we see early in the film, they told me that I was the first to notice it (or at least, point it out to them). Of course, it's the sort of thing that you'd only notice after seeing the movie two or more times, because the "payoff" comes so much later in the film that it'd be impossible to make the connection your first time watching. All of this is just a long-winded way for me to tell you that this is one of the few movies I bothered watching a second time (this screening was actually my *third*!) in the final year or so of doing the site – time would elude me and it'd be more and more rare that I'd see anything worth seeing twice even if I HAD the time. So needless to say, this one is worth tracking down.

Bonus: while the movie is somewhat obtuse at times, the directors are happy to answer questions you may have about some of its mysteries, instead of pulling the "it's what YOU think it is!" card. I really don't care for this attitude; it's one thing to debate things like "Is *Inception* still in the dream world at the end?" if that's the intent, but when filmmakers are evasive, then they're just being dicks. *Resolution's* questions have answers; some are available on its *Blair Witch*-ian website, and others might require a second viewing (due to the slightly circular nature of the story, it's the rare instance where such a thing is appealing, not obnoxious). But if you still miss something, it's nice to know the filmmakers won't take the pretentious route.

MOVIE #275 – OCTOBER 2nd

BLACK DEATH (2010)
Dir: Christopher Smith
HMAD Review Date: March 9, 2011 (DVD)
Genre: Religious
Available from Magnolia Home Entertainment

Synopsis Based on Fading Memory: It's the time of the Black Plague, and a bunch of knights (led by Sean Bean) and a priest are seeking a city that is supposedly plague-free.

Review excerpt:
"They were wise to cast an unknown in the actual lead role of Osmund and have him be act as our surrogate, instead of focusing on the big star, in this case Sean Bean. Bean is actually not in the movie all that much, but he has a presence that keeps you from noticing how often they get around showing him. It's like the old Hammer films where Cushing or Lee would get top billing but if you were to count their screen time it would be much less than their co-stars. But it's really Osmund's story, and it's remarkable how much he transforms from the beginning to the end of the film."

Reflection: As I mentioned earlier, Christopher Smith is a terrific director, and I love that he does something a bit different each time – his four genre efforts are nothing alike, unified only by the fact that they are good examples of that kind of movie. Interestingly, this one was making the rounds on the festival circuit right around the same time the bigger budgeted Nic Cage flick *Season of the Witch* was gearing up for release. The plots were pretty similar (the heroes even got their missions from beloved British actors – David Warner here, Christopher Lee in the Cage one), though that one was more full blown horror/action whereas this is more of a dark (VERY dark, by the end) drama. Needless to say, this one is also better.

Oh, the excerpt above is referencing Eddie Redmayne as the "unknown" playing Osmund, which is amusing since he's now an Oscar-winning actor. He's also part of *Jupiter Ascending*, one of the lousiest movies in recent memory and a huge box office bomb, but I note it because Sean Bean popped up in that one too. So now I worry that someone will see half the cast of *Jupiter* goddamn *Ascending* on the cover of this one and skip it – don't! It's good! It makes sense! It doesn't have tone deaf comedy bits!

MOVIE #276 – OCTOBER 3rd

DORM [DEK HOR] (2006)
Dir: Songyos Sugmakanan
HMAD Review Date: July 11, 2009 (DVD)
Genre: Ghost
Available from Tartan Video

Synopsis Based on Fading Memory: At an all-boys school, our protagonist learns to stop being such an asshole while solving the mystery of how his ghost best friend became a ghost.

Review excerpt:
"I liked that it didn't take the entire movie for us to be told that the hero's best friend, who takes an instant liking to him and never speaks to anyone else, is (spoiler) a ghost. You will probably figure it out pretty quickly, but unlike The Uninvited *or whatever, the movie gives us that information by the end of the first act or so, sparing you having to feel like an idiot in case you somehow DIDN'T figure it out. It also allows us a few scenes we don't usually get in such scenarios, like the hero asking the ghost how he became a ghost in the first place (such a conversation probably would have ruined The Sixth Sense)."*

Reflection: There's a series of movies known as the *Whispering Corridors* franchise, and they're all unrelated except for the fact that they take place at all-girls' schools. Also, they're all nigh on impenetrable (at least, the couple that I saw were; maybe I just chose poorly). So I think the reason I liked this one and continue to think of it in high regard is that it's a coherent version of one of those movies, albeit gender-swapped. This is where I'd normally make a (bad) joke about how guys just make more sense than girls, but my wife might be reading.

But what I really liked about it, and why it's in this chapter, is that the ghost isn't a scary ghost or a threat – it's just what director Sugmakanan used to tell his story. We've seen plenty of ghosts in comedies, but rarely have I seen someone use one to tell a more dramatic, largely horror-free story. I get WHY – a drama tends to only really work if it's grounded in realism, and a ghost is the furthest thing from that, but with good actors, a solid narrative, and an interesting setting, it can be done. Probably not *often* – it'd be weird to have a glut of ghost dramas – but if Hollywood suddenly got re-interested in remaking every Asian genre film they came across, I'd be kind of intrigued if this one got caught in the mix.

Also I REALLY wanted to name-drop this movie recently, because a certain well-regarded foreign horror movie (the title ends in the letter "y") had the "turns out this person was dead the whole time" twist and there's some debate over whether or not its filmmakers were even trying to hide it. My argument is that if they DID want you to know that a character was a ghost, there would be a scene like *Dorm's* where they spell it out, to make sure everyone's on the same page. But I didn't want to risk spoiling *that* movie by comparing it to *Dorm* (or any other film that used the same plot device), just in case some viewers were somehow unable to spot it right away. It's a good movie, but this approach was an unnecessary distraction. And *Dorm* is better.

MOVIE #277 – OCTOBER 4th

ALONE WITH HER (2006)
Dir: Eric Nicholas
HMAD Review Date: September 1, 2007 (DVD)
Genre: Blank from Hell, Psychological
Available from IFC Films

Synopsis Based on Fading Memory: An obsessed young man stalks the object of his affection by filming her every move.

Review excerpt:
"Story wise it's your standard "Boy meets girl, boy becomes obsessed with girl, boy forces himself into her life" movie, but that's not a concern of mine. The film is presented entirely via fixed angle cameras that the main character has placed around the girl's apartment, or from another camera he has hidden inside his shirt button or something. So while some of the plot developments are pretty standard for the psycho stalker genre (pretends to like her favorite band, her best friend distrusts him, etc.), the presentation is unique and near flawlessly implemented, which more than makes up for it."

Reflection: This hit a year or two before the new wave of POV movies, which is a shame as it would have been a standout in that glut at a time when audiences (and distributors) were excited about them. Like far too many filmmakers in this book, writer/director Eric Nicholas has yet to produce a follow-up, and I truly hope it's just because he's busy doing something else and not because the film's lack of a decent release (it had a theatrical run of exactly two screens) has producers considering it/him a failure. Rarely have I been as unnerved as I was at the ending of this movie, and I hope Colin Hanks' recent turn on the much-loved *Fargo* TV series has people tracking this down.

This one also sticks out for HMAD-y reasons, as it was my movie for the day on a weekend where I surprised my mom with a visit home to Massachusetts (amazing to think I used to have the money and time for such excursions). It was a busy weekend – I had to join my longtime *Halloween* compatriot Matt Serafini (now an author, whose books I hope you check out as well) for Rob Zombie's just-released remake, I visited friends in New York, etc. Long story short, I knew if I told my mom I'd be coming home she'd throw away her weekend plans to stay home, which would be a waste since I'd almost never actually be at the house. So I walked in to surprise her, hung out for an hour or so... and then watched the day's movie, since that was the only time all day that I had time to sit in anything besides a car or a restaurant. "Hey mom, haven't seen you in almost a year! I'm gonna watch a weirdo horror movie now." Never said HMAD-ing wasn't occasionally kind of heartbreaking.

HMAD Fun Fact: This was the first of the 80+ found footage/faux documentary horror movies I watched for HMAD. The second was The Poughkeepsie Tapes, *via screener, also in September of 2007. Despite this, the film wasn't officially released until 2013, after the site had wrapped up its daily operations.*

MOVIE #278 – OCTOBER 5th

CRAWL (2011)
Dir: Paul China
HMAD Review Date: October 15, 2011 (Festival screening)
Genre: Thriller
Available from Salient Media/Bloody Disgusting

Synopsis Based on Fading Memory: A woman is trapped in her home with a hitman who is tying up loose ends after murdering her boss.

Review excerpt:
"George Shevtsov is one of those actors that will make you wonder why he hasn't been in the spotlight sooner (he's been around for over 20 years), managing to make the guy likable even though he barely speaks and is a cold blooded murderer. His kindly face and hilarious fixation on his appearance (bleeding from a car crash, he stops to put his hat back on) are hilariously at odds with his behavior, and his methodical, two-steps ahead actions when he needs to spring into action are wholly impressive."

Reflection: There are two movies in this book that I describe as "if the Coen Brothers made a genre film". This is one of them (the other is coming up in December!), and it feels like the home invasion version of what Joel and Ethan might do. Indeed, the villain, played phenomenally by George Shevstov, has a bit of Anton Chigurh to him, and the movie has a few (not always welcome) detours into oddball comedy to boot. But rarely have I seen a first time feature so assured and entertaining, and I'm legit annoyed that four years later, Paul China's 2nd film has yet to exist.

Also, this movie has an amazing score, particularly the end credits theme. Even if the movie leaves you cold, you'll probably walk away wanting the soundtrack album. I've actually had a bunch of old Carpenter soundtracks playing while I wrote the bulk of this book (specifically *Halloween II* as I write this sentence, if you're curious), and listening to his work in particular reminded me of how rare a modern horror film has a score that really grabs me. Perhaps it's just a side effect of growing old, but I also think part of it has to do with the horror movies themselves being so referential to older material that the composers don't get much to work with. It's not really surprising that the scores I HAVE taken to (the *Maniac* remake and *It Follows*, for example) are in some of the more unique mainstream horror films in recent years (the POV aspect of the former, the unusual threat of the latter). I remember Hans Zimmer saying that he was so happy with *Team America* making fun of that certain kind of action movie and hoping it would be a huge hit so he'd stop being asked to make those kind of scores – I suspect it's similar here. What composer could possibly get the creative juices really flowing when presented with something as anonymous and hopeless as the *Poltergeist* remake?

MOVIE #279 – OCTOBER 6th

THE EXPELLED (2010)
Dir: Johannes Roberts
HMAD Review Date: August 29, 2010 (Festival screening)
Genre: Slasher, Thriller
Available from Screen Media

Synopsis Based on Fading Memory: An alcoholic teacher, his estranged daughter, and some others are trapped in their high school with a group of hooded murderers in this "almost" real time thriller.

Review excerpt:
"Since they are not trapped inside, the obvious audience questions - "Why not just leave?" and "Why doesn't so and so notice that whatshisname is missing?" - are answered simply due to the fact that it's only been a few minutes since someone disappeared anyway. And as for why they don't just leave, with the exception of the main character played (terrifically) by David Schofield, no one knows anything is up, and when he tries to warn them, he is dismissed due to the fact that he lives in fear of the students (at the top of the film we see a student attack him after he gives him a failing grade), and is also a drunk. And if you keep the real-time aspect in mind, you can assume that no one had the time to consider he might be right, since they end up dead not too long after that anyway."

Reflection: This movie was called *F* when I saw it, but even though the new title is kind of weak at least it'll be a lot easier for you to find this suspenseful flick. It's part of a sub-genre known as "hoodie horror" and more or less told in real-time once the doors get locked around our heroes – I'm a sucker for real-time AND home invasion stuff so I liked that they combined them... albeit in a school. In most countries this wouldn't set off any alarms, but in the US it's a different story, as this sort of thing tends to actually happen here (albeit with assault rifles and the like instead of knives). The idea that a survivor of Columbine or Sandy Hook might be reading this book looking for fun horror movies to watch and finds themselves reading about THIS made me kind of sick, frankly. I saw it in London where such tragedies felt far enough away to enjoy it, but still - I totally get if you want to skip this one.

Those who *do* watch will be treated to a terrific lead performance by David Schofield. There is no rarer form of hero in horror than "middle aged guy" – in any other movie his teen daughter would take the spotlight. It'd be like if Sidney's oft-mentioned, rarely seen dad in the *Scream* movies was the hero and

Neve Campbell was just in a few scenes. I'm sure an actor of Schofield's caliber was more interested in the dramatic angle of the character than the prospect of being chased by masked killers, but it doesn't matter – his work elevates the film quite a bit. I recently had to re-watch the movie for a freelance job and found it held up nicely, which is always a relief for a festival movie. During marathon viewings, your opinion can be informed by the films surrounding it (an OK movie in between two bad ones seems great when you're writing reviews of all three of them a day or two later), so take that as one of the rare extra votes of confidence I can provide in this tome.

MOVIE #280 – OCTOBER 7th

BURIED (2010)
Dir: Rodrigo Cortés
HMAD Review Date: August 29, 2010 (Festival screening)
Genre: Survival, Thriller
Available from Lionsgate

Synopsis Based on Fading Memory: An American contractor in Iraq is trapped in a coffin.

Review excerpt:
"You would think the premise/setting wouldn't be able to sustain itself for that long, but I could have even watched it longer. Ryan Reynolds has always been an appealing actor to me; he's often the best thing about lousy films (see: Amityville*), so it's great to see him in something that matches his talents. And he's personable, which keeps you from losing sympathy for the character as he begins screaming at people on the other end of the phone line (poor Donna...). At times, the film could easily lose the audience as a result of his borderline inexcusable behavior, but Reynolds makes it work and even makes it charming - rare has a "fuck you" to a woman who is actually being helpful been a crowd-pleasing moment."*

Reflection: It's weird to feel bad for a guy who is probably quite rich and has been in relationships with at least two of my celebrity crushes, but I can't help but feel kind of sad whenever a new Ryan Reynolds movie tanks. I think he's a pretty charming guy with an engaging screen presence, and I offer him the highest compliment I can bestow on any actor: I'd be OK with him playing Fletch if they ever actually get the long-threatened remake off the ground (if you are unaware – *Fletch* is one of my all-time favorite films). I don't just toss such praise around, but the likelihood of him getting such a high profile gig gets slimmer every time another dud like *The Change-Up* crashes and burns. *Deadpool* will be in theaters by the time this hits shelves, so maybe things will turn around sooner than later. *(Print version update! THEY DID.)*

Now, some of his flops are deservedly so (*RIPD, Green Lantern*), but *Buried* proved to be too apt of a title, as Lionsgate never really gave it a chance, unceremoniously dumping it on a handful of screens even though it had an easy marketing hook, not to mention a big star (at the time, his previous wide release was *The Proposal*, which was then Sandra Bullock's biggest hit, so he's gotta be given SOME credit for its fortunes). As a result, they not only denied a lot of people a chance to enjoy an impressive claustrophobic thriller that puts *Phone Booth* to shame, but also the opportunity to respond to one of the funniest deadpan responses ever with a full crowd. If you've seen the film you probably know the one; if not, I will "spoil" that it involves Sea World.

MOVIE #281 – OCTOBER 8th

THE CRIMSON RIVERS (2000)
Dir: Mathieu Kassovitz
HMAD Review Date: July 1, 2009 (DVD)
Genre: Serial Killer
Available from Sony Pictures Home Entertainment

Synopsis Based on Fading Memory: Two cops (Jean Reno and Vincent Cassell) separately investigating a serial killer eventually team up to solve the mystery before another person is killed.

Review excerpt:
"I like that it's a buddy cop movie, but only in the 2nd half. Reno and Cassell don't even meet until they've already gotten pretty much every piece of the puzzle, so when they finally meet it starts coming together for them (and us), resulting in a fast paced third act that features a terrific (if too short) car chase, a big foot chase (way better than Seven's, *if you ask me), and a finale built around an avalanche. And the killer isn't just pissed that his/her dad never went into their room."*

Reflection: After *Seven,* we had to suffer through many terrible serial killer movies (there was even a Steven Seagal movie that tried to blend his usual action stuff with a serial killer plot - it wasn't successful in any form), so when one actually worked it was like a minor miracle. Even if you know the killer's identity the movie is still exciting on repeat viewings, which is also fairly rare for this sub-genre. Not long after the *Babylon AD* debacle Kassovitz returned to France, which is fine by me – I'd hate to see him waste his time trying to work in Hollywood and see his efforts get mangled by the studios, as he's clearly talented behind AND in front of the camera (he's terrific in *Munich*, for the record).

I still haven't seen the sequel to this, and I really need to fix that. I recently had the displeasure of suffering through Roland Emmerich's *Godzilla* again, and marveled at Jean Reno's ability to shine despite working from one of the worst scripts ever written. That, dear readers, is talent, so I should be more diligent in seeing something that gives him a lead role (and a rare sequel for him as well).

P.S. The joke at the end of the excerpt is a reference to *Horsemen*, which barely manages to avoid being the worst Platinum Dunes movie (their *Elm Street* remake is their nadir). It's not worth seeing to fully enjoy the joke, I assure you.

MOVIE #282 – OCTOBER 9th

JULIA'S EYES (2010)
Dir: Guillem Morales
HMAD Review Date: February 2, 2012 (DVD)
Genre: Thriller
Available from MPI Home Video

Synopsis Based on Fading Memory: A woman (Belén Rueda from *The Orphanage*) tries to solve her twin sister's murder.

Review excerpt:
"Morales always pays off each bit with a fun scare, most of which are somewhat unexpected. For example, Rueda learns that her sister frequented a physical therapy place nearby, and when she arrives she overhears the other guests talking not too flatteringly of her sister. And since they're all blind, she is able to eavesdrop without them noticing, until one catches her scent. So you think the scene will carry out with her trying to get out before they discover her, except they DO find her after a few moments... only for one of them to realize someone else is there too. This is where the giallo elements start to come into play – our guy has the tendency to show up pretty much everywhere, and he even has black gloves for good measure. One could question the logic of it, but if you think about him/his goals as a whole (once they're revealed), it's pretty solid."

Reflection: Guillermo del Toro's productions are usually pretty good (*Don't Be Afraid of the Dark* is the only exception, that I can recall), and this is my favorite of the lot. I keep waiting for a full blown *giallo* revival, but if that never comes I'm perfectly content with movies like this, which takes influence from Argento and his peers but never feels like a rip-off, and is very much its own thing. Look, I almost *cried* at the end of the movie – that's not going to happen with *Deep Red* or whatever.

A remake was threatened a while back, but the fact that it hasn't happened isn't much of a surprise. I've lost count of how many modern foreign horror films were planned to be remade for the non-reading American audiences, only to fall apart (many of them are never mentioned again after their initial announcement). It's one thing to remake a 25-year-old movie to reflect modern sensibilities (or even to cynically cash in on a dead but not forgotten brand), but when they do it for movies that are only a few years old for no other reason than to do it in English I tend to get annoyed. Sometimes it works out perfectly well – *We Are What We Are* is not only great but complements the original film - but more often than not you're left with a "Why bother?" feeling, and since so few of them tend to become successes (*The Grudge* being the last flat out smash), it's easy to see why so many of them fizzle in the planning stages. Let the original movies stand on their own for a generation before doing them over, please.

MOVIE #283 – OCTOBER 10th

ROOM OF DEATH [LA CHAMBRE DES MORTS] (2007)
Dir: Alfred Lot
HMAD Review Date: September 6, 2009 (Cable)
Genre: Serial Killer, Thriller
Available from IFC Films

Synopsis Based on Fading Memory: A female detective attempts to find a kidnapped girl who needs medication within 48 hours or she will die.

Review excerpt:
"What really caught my attention were all the little quirks in the movie. There are not one but TWO scenes where there is music that you think is the film's soundtrack, only to find out that it's music someone in the scene is playing (and the 2nd of which, she shuts off the song and then the actual movie score kicks in!). One of the killers, attempting to perform an autopsy (or something) on a monkey, gets frustrated and tosses the poor thing's carcass across the room (all I could hear in my head was the guy on The State*: "Monkeytorture"). And my favorite has to be when a former suspect (who they had already mocked for no reason, another delight) stumbles on a major clue and informs them. If a cop ever insinuated that I had murdered a child or even stolen a goddamn candy bar, I sure as hell wouldn't bother to give them a hand in their investigation. I guess the guy is just not as stubborn and vindictive as me."*

Reflection: One of my favorite shows of recent memory was *Hannibal* (RIP), which is all the more interesting when you consider that I never found much to love in the Lecter series of films. Even *Silence of the Lambs*, while deserving of its acclaim, is not a movie I find myself wanting to revisit all that often. So your mileage may vary with films that are destined to be labeled as *"Silence of the Lambs* wannabes" – you might long for Lecter to come in and kill these people for "copying" him. This one in particular (which was released as *Room of Death* in the US) probably won't work on you if you go in expecting something as chilling as Jame Gumb, as it's more of a sad character drama that uses the language of these kinds of movies to move the plot along.

On the plus side, it stars Melanie Laurent, who I really wish had gone from *Inglourious Basterds* to become one of our biggest female stars, but alas. I don't know if she's picky with roles or if American producers are clueless, but either way I would prefer it if that changed. She is pretty great here with a bummer role, a single mom of twins who is investigating a child's death – it's impossible not to feel for her, and it's rare you can feel sorry for someone who you can also admire for their heroics. I love ass-kicking heroines as much as the next non-douche guy, but I feel with some of those roles they go overboard, making her invincible and constantly smarter than everyone else (particularly the men), to the extent that she's a lousy role model because she isn't believable in any way. It's much more interesting to see one that's capable and intelligent, but not perfect (you know, like everyone in the world). Movies like this can open a lot more doors for good female roles than *Resident Evil: Subtitle* or the next *Underworld*.

MOVIE #284 – OCTOBER 11th

CAGED [CAPTIFS] (2010)
Dir: Yann Gozlan
HMAD Review Date: October 16, 2010 (Festival screening)
Genre: Survival
Available from Mongrel Media

Synopsis Based on Fading Memory: Some doctors are kidnapped by a group looking to steal their organs.

Review excerpt:
"A solid thriller, with several nail-biter scenes (they get a lot of mileage out of the lead character's fear of dogs - justified in an opening sequence that parents may not enjoy much) and some genuinely creepy looking villains. When they kidnap our heroes, they are wearing these sort of scarecrow masks, and they come out of nowhere at a moment of the film where you're not yet expecting the bad stuff to happen (I figured we had another 5 minutes). And they hide their motive for a while, which amused me because part of their MO is to strip the victims' vehicles - for a while I thought they were just the world's most aggressive chop shop employees."

Reflection: You'd be surprised how many "They just want their organs" horror/thriller movies there are – I think I watched at least five during HMAD, of which this was my favorite. I probably could have filled up a month's worth of selections just on all the French movies I quite liked, actually (maybe in the 2nd book!), as for whatever reason they seem to have a stronger ability to create suspense and tension out of scenarios that aren't exactly unique. They also focus on adults more often than not, and that probably helps – it's easier for me to sympathize with 30-somethings now that I'm one, instead of teens who are, of course, all idiots in my eyes.

I have never again heard of Mongrel Media, who distributed the film in the US, but I guess the film is lucky to have been released here at all. This was part of a particularly troubled batch of films that showed at Screamfest, with two others taking years to come along and at least one (a wacky thing called *Hysteria*, starring Cheyenne Jackson) STILL not having a home. Others just got crap releases, like *Death & Cremation*, a film that almost made it into this book but was omitted because the existing DVD is full frame (!) and I hold out hope that it gets better treatment. I always tried to keep track of the festival films I liked so I could inform HMAD readers when they came out; 99% of the site's reviews were for films already available through normal channels, so I figured these festival ones were going to get overlooked/forgotten since I'd be reviewing them months or even years before anyone else could see them. Long story short: it was always a real bummer to check in on a solid title only to find out it was still in limbo or had gotten a half-assed release that did it no justice. If there's one good thing about all these digital platforms we have now, it's that it will hopefully allow less marketable content to find a home, as there's less of a risk to put it on a streaming service like Netflix as opposed to sending it out to hundreds of theaters.

MOVIE #285 – OCTOBER 12th

KIDNAPPED [SECUESTRADOS] (2010)
Dir: Miguel Ángel Vivas
HMAD Review Date: November 29, 2011 (Streaming)
Genre: Thriller
Available from MPI Home Video

Synopsis Based on Fading Memory: A real-time thriller concerning a trio of robbers demanding money from a family.

Review excerpt:
"The entire movie unfolds in long takes; I almost tried counting them but realized I'd be focusing on the wrong thing. This isn't an easy thing to do in ANY genre, but it's even more laudable in a violent thriller of this nature, where things (and faces) are smashed up and everyone needs to be in their exact right spots for things to go smoothly. A mistake could take quite a while to reset for a second take, and if said mistake occurred at the end of a complicated 6-7 minute shot...well, I wouldn't want to be the guy who screwed it up, that's for damn sure."

Reflection: Having watched so many movies that seemed "directed" by someone who barely knew how to turn the camera on, I grew to really, REALLY appreciate something that obviously took a lot of careful planning, skill, and patience. I'd happily watch hours of behind the scenes footage of this movie showing how it was done, not to mention go back on a future viewing and look for the tricks. And they're not doing anything unique – Hitchcock did it with *Rope*, and there was the recent *Silent House* (both the original and remake) as well. But *Rope* was stiff due to the limitations of the time, and both *Silent House*s were undone by stupid (albeit admirably so) twists, so this is the one to check out.

That said, it's a VERY grim movie, perhaps one of most upsetting I saw in all the years of HMAD-ing. Like, "Red Wedding" from *Game of Thrones* levels of "Just when you think it can't get worse it does", right up to the very end, leaving you kind of shell-shocked by how distressing it got. In fact, I suspect the way the movie was shot actually helps you get through some of its more disturbing moments, because you're partially distracted by the impressive technical aspects. If shot traditionally, watching what happens to these people might be as unbearable as *A Serbian Film* or something along those lines. Indeed, I rewatched this film a couple months ago and realized I apparently repressed the final moment from my memory because it was such a bummer. But it also cemented my belief that the film had to be included in this book.

MOVIE #286 – OCTOBER 13th

RETREAT (2011)
Dir: Carl Tibbetts
HMAD Review Date: February 20, 2012 (DVD)
Genre: Thriller
Available from Sony Pictures Home Entertainment

Synopsis Based on Fading Memory: In a remote cabin, a couple on the brink of divorce is trapped with a man claiming that there's an airborne virus that will kill them if they go outside.

Review excerpt:
"It makes good use of Jamie Bell, who hasn't gotten many opportunities to play a "villain" like this. I tend to think of him as a sort of "in over his head" nervous guy (King Kong, the recent Man On a Ledge), but he is legitimately scary here, further demonstrating his range – here's hoping his agent is looking out for him as a character actor instead of just trying to recreate Billy Elliott. On the flipside, Cillian Murphy is a guy who tends to play more villainous roles in genre films, or at least an antagonist of a sort (In Time), so it's nice to see him in the hero position again. If it was a conscious choice to reverse their "usual" roles, it was a good one."

Reflection: A lot of the movies in this chapter are thrillers that will really only work once, so I hope you're renting them or buying them from a store with a very lenient return policy. This is the poster child for such films – the entire thing rests on whether or not Jamie Bell's character is a psycho or not, and once you know, there isn't really a lot to the movie you'd need to watch over and over (beyond the fine Welsh scenery and attractive actors, of course). But man, what a fun scenario to experience the first time around; Tibbetts constantly has the heroes (and thus, you) believing/not-believing Bell's story, enough to get to a point where you can say "I knew it!" only by forgetting about all of the times you were wrong.

It's also another example of Cillian Murphy only getting to play the hero in a movie that barely gets released. When he's a villain, it's a big hit (*Batman Begins, Red Eye*), but when he's the hero the movie either tanks (*Sunshine*, and I'll never get why that one failed to connect – it's so good!) or gets a limited release. Not long after this hit DVD I saw *Red Lights*, a decent little thriller about a skeptical paranormal investigator (Murphy) who is trying to prove that a psychic is a fraud. That one even had a big cast (Robert De Niro, Sigourney Weaver, etc.) and still only got like 18 screens, which is 18 more than this one got. But the wholly stupid *In Time*, where Murphy is an antagonist (not really a villain, but certainly not the hero) makes 175 million worldwide. I don't get it. You have my axe, Mr. Murphy!

MOVIE #287 – OCTOBER 14th

THE RETURN (2006)
Dir: Asif Kapadia
HMAD Review Date: October 18, 2007 (DVD)
Genre: Horror?, Psychological
Available from Universal Studios

Synopsis Based on Fading Memory: A woman keeps having flashbacks to events that do not seem to be part of her own life.

Review excerpt:
"It's actually a character drama fused with a very basic murder mystery film, with some very light supernatural elements (sort of) thrown in for good measure. I always enjoy a film that features a character trying to put the pieces of a puzzle together (here: that would be child's artwork, an image of a barn, etc...), and watching the film a second time, it's interesting to see how well placed the necessary information is throughout the film. I do wish that the "killer" character was introduced a bit earlier, but since there are rumors of re-shoots and re-editing (otherwise non evident in the film itself), it's a surprise how well made it is at all."

Reflection: Universal recently re-released this movie out on Blu-ray, something that excited me and maybe three or four others. The movie bombed and has been completely forgotten; even the novelty of seeing Sam Shepard in a genre flick didn't entice anyone to give it a shot (that it starred Sarah Michelle Gellar and came out around the same time as her not-loved *Grudge 2* didn't help much). However, enough time has passed that I hope it gets the reevaluation it deserves; reshoots and such keep it from being a masterpiece, of course, but it's such an admirably dramatic approach to the "a ghost uses a living person to help them solve their murder" story that permeated so many '00s supernatural films. Now that most of those things have been forgotten as well (and deservedly so for the most part), I'd love to see this finally get its due for taking a less obnoxious, jump-scare filled approach to the story.

I'd also love to see Asif Kapadia direct another narrative feature. Since this (seemingly unhappy) experience he has pretty much abandoned fictional work for documentaries and short films, most recently *Amy*, the Oscar-winning look at the life of Amy Winehouse. I was not a fan of her music and was one of the ones cracking jokes every time she fell off a stage or whatever (I found a tweet from 2010 where I compared her having another bad show to me maybe watching a horror movie that day – i.e. what else is new?), but Kapadia's involvement still has me interested in seeing the movie. Even if you dislike *The Return* – and many did, probably because they were expecting a spook-a-thon – you should be able to realize that it's a risky way of tackling such fare, and that's the sort of creativity we could certainly use more of in our studio genre films.

MOVIE #288 – OCTOBER 15th

ATM (2012)
Dir: David Brooks
HMAD Review Date: April 6, 2012 (Theatrical)
Genre: Survival, Thriller
Available from MPI Home Video

Synopsis Based on Fading Memory: Three idiots are trapped in an ATM vestibule by a killer.

Review excerpt:
"The filmmakers do NOT commit to their idea; if anything the screenwriter seemingly forgot to do anything after coming up with the basic premise, more than likely after momentarily being scared to exit an ATM booth one night and thinking to himself "Hey... this might be a good idea for a movie!" on the way home. Christ, the movie burns through what little goodwill it has in the first 10-15 minutes, before they even get inside the damn thing!"

Reflection: The only reason I chose this one as this month's bad movie is because it's the same screenwriter (Chris Sparling) as *Buried*, which is one of the GOOD movies I suggested. Rarely have I seen such a difference in quality from a creative person from one film to the next, and this was so bad I considered putting him on my mental blacklist. But recently I saw the film *The Atticus Institute*, which he wrote and also directed, and it's actually pretty good! So let's just assume he either bungled this one or the director or producers did that for him.

Fun fact: I was even more annoyed by this movie because back in my hometown there's an isolated ATM booth not unlike the one here, and one night after a late movie I went to use it and actually got a bit scared because it was so far removed from the populated area. I became convinced someone was nearby and ended up driving to another one, like a wuss. So I am the TARGET AUDIENCE FOR THIS PARTICULAR, LARGELY NON-EXISTENT FEAR! And they still blew it. To this day I keep making fun of it on Twitter, reminding people that I actually went out of my way to see a movie about three people trapped in an ATM and that it managed to be even dumber than it sounded.

Be sure to stick through the credits, though! They are the "best" part, as under the names of the cast/crew we watch extra footage setting up a bunch of potential locations (in gas stations, mini-marts, etc.) that never got realized into equally stupid sequels.

MOVIE #289 – OCTOBER 16th

SUBJECT TWO (2006)
Dir: Philip Chidel
HMAD Review Date: November 27, 2009 (Cable)
Genre: Mad Scientist
Available from Alchemy/Millennium

Synopsis Based on Fading Memory: An isolated scientist repeatedly tries to create life in a Frankenstein's monster-y kind of way.

Review excerpt:
"As my buddy Mike from Icons of Fright *pointed out, this movie will appeal to Larry Fessenden fans. Indeed, I watched the film before Mike made his comment, and found myself thinking of Larry's films at different times. The snowbound locale obviously brings* Wendigo *and* Last Winter *to mind (*Wendigo *especially, during a late-film sequence revolving around an accidental shooting), and the film as a whole is sort of like* Habit*, as it's also a rather sad version of a traditional horror story, in this case* Frankenstein. *Writer/director Philip Chidel wisely chose to focus the film more on the "monster" than the doctor, but also kept the doctor from being an all-out villain, allowing you to sympathize with both men."*

Reflection: Heh, I'm reading my review and I keep mentioning a reveal at the end that I can no longer recall (it's been six years, give me a break!), so I think I need to revisit this one soon. But what I DO recall is that this is one of those rare dramatic horror films that actually works on both levels, and as I get older and less charmed by splatter comedies from wannabe Sam Raimis and things like that, I find myself gravitating toward these more dramatic, moodier genre exercises. Indeed, I recently watched one called *Spring* (from the guys behind this month's first selection, *Resolution*) which was basically a *Before Sunrise*-type movie, but where the Julie Delpy character was a monster. It made me sad in spots, which is pretty hard to believe for a movie with two tentacle scares. I'm getting to be a softie…

But as with vampires, the basic mad scientist story has been done so many times, ANY fresh approach is worth checking out, because you know that for each one of those there will be ten that do nothing new at all (or do something totally inane, like *I, Frankenstein*). I've said over and over that the genre has more license to color outside the lines than most others, so those half-assed ones that are content to just do the same old thing are even more insulting than the latest generic rom-com or *Star Wars* rip-off. Mad scientist films in particular have a pretty wide range of options – what the scientist is trying to do, what he needs to do it, etc., and if there's a human subject there's even more to explore. So, in short, don't do a straight up goddamn *Frankenstein* movie! We have plenty!

MOVIE #290 – OCTOBER 17th

NIGHT WARNING (1982)
Dir: William Asher
HMAD Review Date: October 2, 2012 (Revival screening)
Genre: Thriller, Weird
Available from Code Red DVD

Synopsis Based on Fading Memory: An aunt who REALLY loves her nephew goes to great lengths to keep him all to herself.

Review excerpt:
"...if you're up for a minor classic in the realms of WTF cinema, this will hit the spot (and then some), mainly courtesy of Susan Tyrell's unhinged turn as Aunt Cheryl. Even when she's doing something like pouring a glass of milk or giving her nephew a birthday card, she excels at making you uncomfortable in the process, and the script thankfully lets her get more and more insane as it goes. By the third act she's chopping off half her hair, making cat noises, poisoning her nephew, and murdering a few innocent folks. There's a touch of Betsy Palmer/Mrs. Voorhees in these later scenes (especially when household "weapons" come into play), but Tyrell is on a level of her own - if there were awards for playing the crazy in a horror flick, she'd even beat out the posthumous nominees."

Reflection: Recently, the Supreme Court made marriage equal for all people, a battle that took way too long. It's a fine way to realize how far we've come since this movie, where a character's rampant homophobia wasn't even frowned upon by the other characters. I mean it's *really* bad, to the point that it was kind of uncomfortable even to me (I don't offend easily; even when harsh insults are specifically about me I tend to find them funny), so it's doubly weird to see the guy saying "faggot" all casually without anyone even rolling their eyes. I unfortunately grew up during the period where saying something was "gay" was the same as saying it was stupid or lame, and felt kind of mortified as an adult when I realized how seemingly innocent it was – can't imagine how the folks writing stuff like this feel nowadays (*The Gate* is another one where the screenwriter might/should regret how their characters talk).

I want to talk a bit more about the late, great Susan Tyrell than I did in the review. It's a damn shame we don't see more performers like her; as the above excerpt describes, she can make something as simple as pouring a glass of milk look interesting – nowadays we have charisma-free piles of nothing like Jai Courtney toplining mega-budget tentpole films like *Terminator 5*. I would love a

Hollywood system where the Susan Tyrells of the world are the ones who are household names because they're so damn fun to watch. Instead, Hollywood seems to punish those who dare to go off the beaten path a bit. Look at Nic Cage – an Oscar-winning actor who chooses projects that excite him instead of doing boring stuff that will make hundreds of millions, and now his movies barely get released. Even if you think you will hate this movie (boo on you), I encourage you to watch it just to enjoy her work.

P.S. This might be a bit hard to find, as it keeps going in and out of print. It's also known as *Butcher, Baker, Nightmare Maker* and *Thrilled to Death*, so check those titles too.

MOVIE #291 – OCTOBER 18th

NINE DEAD (2010)
Dir: Chris Shadley
HMAD Review Date: March 9, 2010 (DVD)
Genre: Revenge, Thriller
Available from Image Entertainment

Synopsis Based on Fading Memory: A group of strangers are trapped somewhere and have to figure out what connects them all.

Review excerpt:
"I was engaged, and I wanted to know how they were all connected, trying to figure it out even without any information at hand. The real time aspect works really well, as do the occasional stabs at dark humor - gotta love that everyone instantly assumes that the priest is a pedophile. And it ends with a song by Course of Nature, an underrated rock band who I enjoy listening to from time to time (their "Caught in The Sun" is a great power ballad)."

Reflection: I saw some 11,000 *Saw* wannabes over the past ten years (damn, it's been over a DECADE since *Saw* came out...), and more often than not this meant a movie where people were tortured in basements or something. *Nine Dead* is not a flawless movie, but it's one of the very few that were influenced by *Saw*'s actual storyline and "sins of the past" motif, rather than its violence. Even though as presented the mystery is impossible to solve on your own (I suspect the movie was re-edited some), it's still fun getting occasional pieces of the puzzle and trying to see how they fit, instead of watching yet another person get tied to a chair and subsequently liberated of their fingers or something.

Interestingly, it sort of takes a concept from the worst *Saw* entry (that would be *Saw V*) and improves on it, primarily by not making it a twist. In *Saw V* (spoilers ahead, if that's necessary to warn about) you discover at the end that if they had just worked together from the start no one would have had to have died at all, and there was strength in numbers that would have made things easier for them as the challenges got harder (such as filling up a jar with blood to proceed – five people could have each offered a little instead of just two of them having to offer a lot). Here, the concept is that they have to figure out how they are connected or someone will die every ten minutes. Obviously, with each death the job will just be harder, so they have to communicate and work together to figure it out while they still have the majority of the pieces in play. Of course, since it's a horror movie, they don't.

MOVIE #292 – OCTOBER 19th

THE SADIST (1963)
Dir: James Landis
HMAD Review Date: April 14, 2008 (Revival screening)
Genre: Breakdown, Thriller
Public domain title, available through several DVD companies

Synopsis Based on Fading Memory: A group of schoolteachers are on their way to a baseball game when their car breaks down and they become the targets of a killer.

Review excerpt:
"Not only is it one of the few films in history to take place in real time (and pulls it off better than many of the others that have tried it, such as Nick of Time, Johnny Depp's sole attempt playing a regular guy in a normal action thriller movie*), but it's also wonderfully shot by a guy named William Zsigmond. Not familiar with the name? Well it's a pseudonym (or really bizarre misspelling) of Vilmos Zsigmond, the legendary cinematographer who has gone on to considerably classier things, such as* Close Encounters of the Third Kind *and* Deliverance *(and, for some goddamn reason,* Jersey Girl*). It's to his credit that a movie with almost nothing happening, set almost exclusively on a patch of dirt in front of a gas station, with only five people, seems as alive and exciting as it does."*

Reflection: Huh. There are a LOT of real time (or very close to it) movies in this chapter. I guess if you're a filmmaker and you want to be included in HMAD The Book: Volume 2, make sure your movie doesn't skip any significant portion of time within its narrative - your odds will be pretty good! On the other hand, there's a bit in this movie that really made me sad when I watched it, and I can't quite explain why it hit me like it did. The guy just wanted to go to a baseball game, and when Arch Hall Jr. rips up his tickets, it really bummed me out. Like, even though they had been menaced for some time at that point, it was like he was still holding out hope that he wouldn't miss the game. Filmmakers – don't do things like this in your movie! I hate feeling such pity for a fictional person!

My personal requests aside, this is a legitimately unnerving thriller, something you wouldn't expect when it stars a guy most people of my age associate with as the butt of *MST3K* jokes. I myself was expecting something kinda junky, almost the sort of movie that would BE on *MST3K*, when I went to this revival screening at the New Beverly. This is where I saw many a "so bad it's good" type, so I was happy to discover how solid a thriller it was and how much I genuinely got into it. Apparently the film was inspired by the real life crime spree engineered by Charles Starkweather and his girlfriend, which is the same one that influenced Terence Malick's *Badlands*, so there's something. I bet there weren't a lot of times where a real life guy could be portrayed by both Martin Sheen AND Arch Hall Jr.

MOVIE #293 – OCTOBER 20th

DREAD (2009)
Dir: Anthony DiBlasi
HMAD Review Date: May 5, 2009 (Theatrical)
Genre: Psychological
Available from Lionsgate

Synopsis Based on Fading Memory: A disturbed college student enlists a new friend to help him with a psychology study about fear.

Review excerpt:
"What really grabbed me is how the film accurately depicts its own title. It's not a big spectacle film with "set pieces" or anything like that - it deliberately builds at a sure and steady pace, developing the characters along with the plot as they make their way toward the horrific ending. Some may see this as "slow", but I found it refreshing. It's rare to see a horror film - especially one from a first time director, based on a work by one of the foremost names in horror - take time to really make you identify with not one but FOUR characters, to the extent that even the film's "villain" is sympathetic."

Reflection: Considering the success of *Candyman* and *Hellraiser*, you'd think any movie with Clive Barker's name on it would at least ensure a wide-ish theatrical release. Alas, *Dread* joined the previous year's *Midnight Meat Train* in the long list of movies Lionsgate never had enough faith in for whatever reason, though unlike *MMT* this is admittedly a tough sell. Still, even the full blown horror movies in this book probably didn't deliver anything as horrifying as the scene where a vegetarian is locked in a room with a raw steak – the longer she tries to hold on to her ideals, the more disgusting her only source of food becomes to eat. *Supersize Me* didn't affect my enjoyment of McDonald's one bit, but this came close to having me consider a meat-free diet.

It's also one of two films that made me reassess Jackson Rathbone's abilities as an actor. He is particularly awful in the *Twilight* movies, but in this and *Hurt* (which was in this book for a while, ultimately cut for space) he proved to be a lot better than the sparkles suggested. In fact, he's probably fared best out of all the actors playing Cullens; Robert Pattinson has proven to be a solid actor who makes primarily lousy movies (*Remember Me* being somewhat offensive on top of being bad), Nikki Reed's filmography reads like a list of war crimes (*Chain Letter, Catch .44, Murder of a Cat...* good lord) Ashley Greene... is very pretty, and poor Kellan Lutz most recently hosted a bad FOX reality show. But ol' Jasper? He stays out of the tabloids *and* pops up in solid thrillers! Score!

MOVIE #294 – OCTOBER 21st

ROADGAMES (1981)
Dir: Richard Franklin
HMAD Review Date: September 19, 2009 (Revival screening)
Genre: Serial Killer, Thriller
Available from Anchor Bay

Synopsis Based on Fading Memory: A trucker is stalked by a serial killer on the Australian Outback.

Review excerpt:
"...important to the film's success is Stacy Keach. I mainly know him from his TV work (Titus, Prison Break, and – my first awareness of the man - as the host of the short-lived Unsolved Mysteries wannabe Missing: Reward), but here he proves to be an able leading man. And I mean lead - apart from his dingo-dog, he's usually by himself. But he doesn't sit in silence; he occasionally has full blown conversations (even arguments) with himself, saying one line aloud and keeping the response in his head. Not only does it keep the film from being silent, but it also allows us to understand that the character may be suffering from a mental disorder (and in turn, that he may be the killer himself, but not in a way that prevents us from liking him)."

Reflection: One of the genre's great unsung heroes is Richard Franklin, who never really made a bad movie, and when he was at the top of his game (as he was here) he could deliver top notch thriller material like no one else. Well, no one else but Hitchcock, to whom Franklin readily acknowledged as an influence. The Australian Brian De Palma, if you will. Franklin followed this with *Psycho II*; if there was ever a definitive list of movies that were damn good when they should have been awful, that one would be near the top of the list. It's a shame he died before DVD special editions and such became the norm; it'd be wonderful to hear his long form thoughts on this one.

Sometimes this gets lumped in with *Terror Train* and such as one of Jamie Lee Curtis' post-*Halloween* slasher movies, but a. it's not a slasher and b. she's only in a supporting role at best. This is all Stacy Keach's show, and the movie is the better for it. I haven't seen too many movies where he was the lead, but I've been a fan of his character work for years, so seeing this for the first time was a real treat. It's not easy for actors to take on these sorts of roles where they're pretty much the only person on-screen, and just sitting in a car/truck to boot (at least Tom Hanks got to wander around an island in *Cast Away*). He fares better than Dennis Weaver in *Duel*, though to be fair he has a dog to talk to (and, later, Jamie Lee) whereas Weaver pretty much only had his mustache.

MOVIE #295 – OCTOBER 22ⁿᵈ

WITCHFINDER GENERAL (1968)
Dir: Michael Reeves
HMAD Review Date: October 5, 2011 (DVD)
Genre: Religious, Revenge
Available from MGM

Synopsis Based on Fading Memory: WITCH! BURN HER!

Review excerpt:
"I love when I watch a movie and have no idea what genre tags to put in - as long as the movie entertains and intrigues, I couldn't care less if it "fits" anywhere. There are no attempts to make it more like a traditional horror film (Price barely even puts up a fight at the end), and the attention to character and the ideas about the nature of violence are far more interesting than seeing Price running around yet another burning mansion. There aren't even really any scares – the concept alone provides the horror. I'm actually surprised there aren't more films about this period in history, or this character (going by IMDb's "movie connections", there doesn't seem to be a single other film about Hopkins, horror or otherwise) – this is a very loose retelling of the events; surely a more factual account would be just as if not more interesting."

Reflection: It won't be until 2020 or so that I sit down with my son during the Halloween season and watch a horror movie with him, but I like to plan ahead. So I've already started thinking of ones I might start with, and I think he'll be familiar with Vincent Price before he knows about Jason or Freddy. I won't introduce him to Price with this one, of course, since it's much more adult-leaning than his more popular titles (I think *House on Haunted Hill* would make for a good introduction), but I also think it takes knowing the icon from his lighter, campier fare to be that much more appreciative of his truly terrifying performance here. I don't think he's ever been as outright EVIL in a film as this one, which is ironic since it barely skirts the edges of a traditional horror film.

It's an oft-told story that Price did not get along with director Reeves during the making of this movie, as Reeves wanted Donald Pleasence for the role but was overruled by AIP, who demanded Price be cast instead. It's hard to choose sides really; Pleasence is just as great and no one likes to be told what to do, but on the other hand, if it was Pleasence in the role the movie might not have the legs it has. Now it lives on primarily because of Price's appeal (Reeves himself died a few months after the movie was finished and thus obviously never made another one), as it's included alongside his more traditional horror films like *Masque of the Red Death* and *Dr. Phibes* on Scream Factory's (glorious, and sadly currently out of print) Blu-ray set. And the best thing is that Price realized later it was one of his better films, and apologized to Reeves before he died. Class act, that guy.

MOVIE #296 – OCTOBER 23rd

RAW FORCE (1982)
Dir: Edward D. Murphy
HMAD Review Date: August 26, 2008 (Revival screening)
Genre: Weird, Zombie
Available from Vinegar Syndrome

Synopsis Based on Fading Memory: Uh... some folks go to an island. That much I know for sure.

Review excerpt:
"...the movie just doesn't make a lick of sense. I mean, there's a plot of some sort, but damned if I could tell you who was on whose side or what their actual objective was. It's got something to do with drugs and something called Jasper Jade, and an island where one (or maybe both) can be found. But no one seems to care about the story; the film's real focus is mainly on people doing odd things for no reason. A perfect example is a scene about midway through the film, after the boat with all of our characters is sunk. Like in Jason Takes Manhattan, *our heroes get on the lifeboat, while all the other people on the ship are left for dead. So they are floating around in the ocean, and then a plane appears, at which point Cameron Mitchell (who else?) does the only logical thing: he shoots at it. But it turns out to have our bad guys! Did Mitchell know that? The plane appears to be about 2 miles away so I doubt he could see who was flying it. But does it matter?"*

Reflection: I've seen this movie I think four times now, and I still can't tell you what is happening during a few key scenes. Its effect lessens each time, but so does the setting – this first viewing was with a packed crowd of inebriated movie fans, sometime around midnight, whereas my most recent one was with I think MAYBE a dozen people at 2pm on a Saturday. I think it's key to have a crowded room (be it a living room or a theater) for this uniquely terrible/amazing movie to really work its magic. And I wouldn't recommend too many repeat viewings, since repeated exposure to its nonsensical story will allow your brain to start actually making sense of it, and that's no good.

I should stress that it barely even qualifies as horror (hence its placement here) since the zombie guys only make fleeting appearances, and the film is more concerned with beat 'em up action and the like over anything that could be considered "scary" (even the zombie dudes engage in fisticuffs more than flesh eating or whatever). But it's also got comedy, adventure, and sci-fi elements, making it sort of every genre at once - so it certainly doesn't NOT qualify as a genre film. Disagree? Meet me at the Burbank Karate Club and we'll settle this like men.

MOVIE #297 – OCTOBER 24th

STUCK (2007)
Dir: Stuart Gordon
HMAD Review Date: April 24, 2008 (Theatrical)
Genre: Thriller
Available from Image Entertainment

Synopsis Based on Fading Memory: A drug addict hits a homeless man with her car, embedding him in the windshield. Rather than drive to the hospital, she drives home and leaves him there bleeding to death. Oh, based on a true story.

Review excerpt:
"Stephen Rea is fantastic, as always, and a scene where he attempts to remove a broken windshield wiper from his belly is a nice, bloody, cringe-worthy set piece. The scene culminates with Rea making a phone call to 911, and having to deal with none other than Jeffrey Combs (voice only) as the world's most impatient 911 operator. In fact, there are a lot of jokes at the expense of bureaucracy and "the system", which got quite a few laughs out of me. And the finale is a surprisingly bloody and violent one, with everyone more or less getting their just desserts in a crowd-pleasing fashion."

Reflection: Ask any horror fan from my generation to name the great horror directors of our lifetime, and you'll hear a lot of the same names: Carpenter, Craven, Romero... and hopefully Stuart Gordon. But unlike those other guys, Gordon has never had a big theatrical smash hit; his highest grossing film in the US is *Fortress*, at a mere 6 million. *Re-Animator*, *From Beyond*, etc. – these films are beloved by horror fans and even some mainstream critics, but they never had the big releases afforded his peers, keeping him from being a household name like they are.

On the flipside, he has never really made anything beneath him – by continuing to work with small budgets and outside of the studio system, he can continue delivering unique films like this, a rare horror film where the "based on a true story" claim is 100% accurate. The events in this movie really did happen; they pretty much only changed the city it took place and the conclusion, which offers a morally justified denouement, unlike the even more tragic version that occurred in real life. Yes, it's a horror movie based on a true story where the real life version is actually more disturbing. Only Stuart Gordon would dare do that, but that's fine - he's also the only one that could pull it off.

HMAD Fun Fact: Of the "Masters", Wes Craven was the most oft-reviewed director, with 16 separate features reviewed. Dario Argento came in 2nd with 15, plus his Masters of Horror *episode "Pelts" (so like 15.5).*

MOVIE #298 – OCTOBER 25th

STRANGE CIRCUS [KIMYÔ NA SÂKASU] (2005)
Dir: Sion Sono
HMAD Review Date: March 4, 2013 (Streaming)
Genre: Asian, Psychological
Available from TLA Releasing

Synopsis Based on Fading Memory: A young woman who is being molested by her father ultimately starts enjoying it, leading her to force her mother out of the picture permanently. And the story is being told by someone at a circus!

Review excerpt:
"As you might expect, there are a lot of head scratching plot developments, and I'm not even sure I fully understood it all by the end. To keep things from getting TOO disturbing (relatively speaking), we thankfully never see the young actress during the sex scenes - it's always played by the woman playing the mother, as we're seeing it through her head where she has taken the mother's place. But as the plot goes on, we learn just how much of an "unreliable narrator" she is, on top of the fact that there's the possibility that all of it is made up by an author looking to score a best-seller. Oh, and the entire thing is wrapped up in bookends where the story is being told at some goofy circus/stage show, so when you add in the flashback driven narrative of the third act and all the plot twists, it starts to make Tale of Two Sisters *look kids' show simple in comparison."*

Reflection: Every year for my birthday I tried to watch something kind of... well, fucked up. And as this was the last time I had to devote part of "my" special day to watching and reviewing a horror movie, I guess I went out with a bang. Rape, incest, torture, clowns... this movie has everything that can disturb a viewer, and on top of that it's a bit hard to follow at times (it's a story within a story WITHIN A STORY kind of deal), which can reduce your brain to mush. You definitely need an open mind and a high tolerance for taboo subjects to get through this one, but I guarantee it's worth the shower you might feel you'll need after seeing it.

To date it's the only Sono film I've seen; as was often the case when I saw a film from a well-regarded filmmaker, I vowed to see more of his films and then never actually got around to it. This is an issue that stretches back to my teen years, when a younger BC, high off the sublime joy of John Woo's *Hard Boiled* and *The Killer*, picked up a bootleg of *A Better Tomorrow* at a convention... and to this day I still haven't seen it. Granted, I can chalk some of this up to laziness, and some of it is due to the fact that I am a hoarder when it comes to movies I want to see (which is, all of them), but mainly it has to do with my desire to keep something "In case of emergency". Any filmmaker or actor I started admiring once their career was already well under way, I keep a couple of their films unseen, so that there's always a "new to me" one to enjoy. If Steven Spielberg dies today, I still have four movies to go through (I won't say which ones, but one of them doesn't rhyme with anything) so I can keep him "alive" for a while longer, beyond simply re-watching *Jaws* or *Jurassic Park* for the millionth time. But I should at least watch ONE other Sono, jeez.

MOVIE #299 – OCTOBER 26th

TIMECRIMES (2007)
Dir: Nacho Vigalondo
HMAD Review Date: November 25, 2008 (Theatrical)
Genre: Thriller
Available from Magnolia Home Entertainment

Synopsis Based on Fading Memory: A regular schlub is seemingly being stalked by a masked killer, and then he discovers a time travel machine.

Review excerpt:
"Unlike *Primer*, our hero isn't a genius, or even involved with the time travel experiment. Hector is more like Joe in *Idiocracy*: an average man in every way. The film's first 10-15 minutes really sell this concept, as we see that he is absent-minded, a bit lazy, and just wants to sit around and look at birds all day. How he gets involved with the time travel machine is one of the movie's most clever inventions, and writer/director (and co-star) Nacho Vigalondo wisely never bogs the movie down in explanations or special effects, keeping the entire thing from Hector's point of view."

Reflection: There's only one perfect time travel movie: *Back to the Future*. Yes, there are some minor quibbles you can make with the interior logic (like why the photograph would erase one kid at a time), but it's pretty well thought out and always engaging enough for you to not question such things anyway. So even though I know no filmmakers can ever do it as well as Zemeckis/Gale, I'm always fascinated by the different ways that the gimmick can be used for a narrative, and this one is definitely one of the most unique. It might not be too difficult to figure out why the masked man is seemingly trying to kill our hero, but it's certainly a damn fun time seeing it play out.

Interestingly, right around the same time this was made, Chris Smith was making *Triangle*, which has a similar twist, albeit in a film that's not quite as good as this (it's worth seeing, like all of Smith's films, but it's probably his least essential). The aforementioned *Primer* dips into the same territory, but explaining why would constitute a spoiler so I'll have to hope you can connect those dots yourself. It's something that I wish I saw more in time travel films, because not only is it more interesting, but it also makes for one delightful surprise when you realize what has happened. Of course, the reason you don't see too many creepy movies about time travel is because horror requires you to relax in order to get scared, and in a time travel movie you're constantly trying to keep track of things (or, for some viewers, find flaws in its mechanics), so your guard is never down long enough to get frightened. But someday someone will figure it out and I'll be pretty happy.

MOVIE #300 – OCTOBER 27th

THE TALL MAN (2012)
Dir: Pascal Laugier
HMAD Review Date: September 1, 2012 (Theatrical)
Genre: Thriller
Available from Image Entertainment

Synopsis Based on Fading Memory: A young mother loses her child to the titular killer, thought to just be an urban legend.

Review excerpt:
"Like Martyrs, *it has a polarizing twist that gets at something more human and thought-provoking than the earlier part of the movie would lead you to believe. But the great thing is, it doesn't feel like he's covering the same ground or even using the same tricks like M. Night Shyamalan. While* Martyrs *had a late-game "man behind the curtain" moment,* Tall Man's *twists come along at a steady clip, constantly having you rethink what you've seen. It's almost like an old serial, where every twenty minutes you're left with a new piece of the puzzle and most likely have an idea where you think it'll go from there, only for it to switch again at the end of the next "reel" (remember those?). It's pretty impressive."*

Reflection: I remember arguing with someone who made a particular claim about this movie that wasn't exactly false, but was inadvertently ruining something that the movie was designed to make you think was true. I won't give that away, but to clarify what I mean I'll provide another example that's similar – the nature of Teri Hatcher's character in *Tango & Cash* (yep, this is my go-to). In the movie, she is introduced vaguely, and we know only that she's close to Stallone's character. We the audience are supposed to think they are a couple, which makes us squirm when Kurt Russell hits on her and then laugh when it's revealed that she's actually Stallone's *sister*, not his girlfriend. Telling someone from the start that she's the sister is TRUE, but you're revealing something that was purposely hidden for a certain narrative effect. So if you tell someone up front that *Tall Man* is ____, you will likely kill any chance the movie has of being effective. In short, listen to no one else about this movie and just watch it ASAP.

The film is primarily known for being Laugier's follow-up to *Martyrs*, which also caused some disappointment among... people who like to see women getting tortured, I guess? To be fair *Martyrs* has some really great ideas and, while not exactly perfect, is a movie worth seeing if you can stomach the violence. But it's not like Laugier went from *Sixth Sense* to *The Happening* in terms of quality –

like his earlier film, this one likes to play on your expectations of where a narrative will go based on a particular (somewhat familiar) setup, but it seems like some audience members missed that and complained that it was "too tame". It's an obnoxious response, if you ask me – he was doing something kind of daring here and it mostly works, so we should be thanking him for trying this instead of just finding new ways to get people chained up and abused.

MOVIE #301 – OCTOBER 28th

STOKER (2013)
Dir: Chan-wook Park
HMAD Review Date: February 7, 2013 (Theatrical)
Genre: Thriller
Available from Fox Searchlight

Synopsis Based on Fading Memory: When a man dies, his creepy brother comes to live with the family he left behind. Things get weird.

Review excerpt:
"The title refers to the family name, and certainly suggests a film about vampires, but I'm not going to tell you whether or not that is actually what's going on, as that's part of the fun. Taking cues from Hitchcock's Shadow Of A Doubt, *the movie is about a mysterious uncle (also named "Charlie" just to make sure we know it's an intentional homage) who comes to live with his brother's family after he dies in a car wreck, with Mia Wasikowska in the Teresa Wright role as the suspicious niece. But the difference is, she's already seen to be a bit off, letting spiders crawl over her despite not liking to be touched, sleeping in a bed full of shoes, etc. At a certain point you'll probably start wondering if she's more dangerous than Charlie, and like the vampire thing, figuring that out is one of the movie's many joys."*

Reflection: This was my favorite movie of 2013, and I hope its relative "failure" at the box office doesn't mean we won't get another English language film from Chan-wook Park. Unlike many of his peers, he proved here that he was able to work within the American studio system (albeit an "independent" one like Fox Searchlight) and still display his knack for taking fairly typical plots (in this case, the plot of *Shadow of a Doubt*) and making something that feels unlike anything you've ever seen before.

It also contains what may be the greatest dissolve in motion picture history, so I hope you're a film geek if you're reading this or else you might say "What? Who the hell cares about a dissolve?" But seriously, you'll know it when you see it, and the film is loaded with similarly gorgeous imagery and unusual moments that will attract that far left part of the brain. There's a bit where Nicole Kidman's character is in a room that has two adjacent doors, and she has left one open – but Matthew Goode opts to open the other one to make his entrance, rather than use the one she left open for him. I love that! Ideally, the movie would be too famous for inclusion in this book, but alas it's one of those films that unfortunately not too many have seen due to its limited (and not particularly successful) release. But among that select group, you'll rarely find anyone dismissing it.

MOVIE #302 – OCTOBER 29th

ENTER NOWHERE (2011)
Dir: Jack Heller
HMAD Review Date: October 20, 2011 (Festival screening)
Genre: Horror?, Thriller
Available from Lionsgate

Synopsis Based on Fading Memory: Three people are trapped in the woods.

Review excerpt:
"What works about the film is that it totally commits to its potentially silly idea. No one questions it or tries to get ahead of the audience by pointing out a possible plot hole, something that only works in a movie like End of Days *where taking it serious would be detrimental (hence lines like "Midnight? Is that Eastern time?"). You either go with it or you don't, and as I've said a million times, I will always go with a kooky idea as long as I never get the feeling that the director is laughing at us. And any movie that uses* Pac-Man *as an example to explain part of its plot is automatically worth some respect."*

Reflection: I saw this movie with a friend who leaned over and suggested a theory as to what was going on, roughly 20 minutes into the runtime. I thought he was joking, as he often makes up outlandish things and presents them as fact for comedic effect – but it turns out he was actually being serious, and he was also 100% right. I don't know how the hell he did it, but it was really kind of extraordinary. It reminded me of that *South Park* episode where Cartman is certain Kyle and all other Jewish people have a key that unlocks their secret gold stash, which you're supposed to think is just him being a racist idiot... only for it to turn out to be true. Anyway - let me know if you figure it out as quickly as my friend did!

Heller followed this up with a slightly more traditional horror movie called *Dark Was the Night*, which had a "Stephen King short story turned into a feature" vibe to it (yes, that's a thing!) and starred the great Kevin Durand, a character actor who is often the only good part of a bad movie (*Wolverine Origins, Cosmopolis*) and rarely gets lead roles. It's clear from these two films that Heller isn't much interested in making generic genre fare – he takes these ideas that sound familiar on paper (people lost in the woods here, a small town being attacked by a monster in *Dark Was the Night*) and goes about them in a much different way than you usually see. I'd love to see what he'd do with found footage or some other tired cliché.

MOVIE #303 – OCTOBER 30th

SLEEP TIGHT (2011)
Dir: Jaume Balagueró
HMAD Review Date: September 29, 2011 (Streaming)
Genre: Blank from Hell, Thriller
Available from Dark Sky Films

Synopsis Based on Fading Memory: A building handyman/concierge becomes obsessed with one of his tenants.

Review excerpt:
"I loved how Balagueró managed to make me anxious for such an awful person. As can be expected, there's a sequence where he gets trapped in the apartment as a result of unexpected developments (namely, she doesn't fall asleep when planned), and has to sneak around to get to the door without being seen by her or her boyfriend. It's a wonderfully queasy moment when you realize that you're hoping he gets out OK, instead of being discovered and beaten to a pulp, which is what SHOULD happen. It's a testament to both Alberto Marini's script and the performance of Luis Tosar as Cesar that even when you understand how far he's been going, he's still sort of likable and sympathetic."

Reflection: By design (and this is not a complaint), the best scares in a horror movie usually come in the 3rd act, when all bets are off and the danger levels are at their highest. There are some exceptions (*Psycho*, the opening of *Scream*), but I swear, I have never seen a genre film that manages to get you completely freaked out and uncomfortable as quickly as this one does. Even knowing what the movie is about doesn't make this reveal – which occurs at maybe the five-minute mark – any less unnerving, so I can't imagine how disturbing it'd play out to someone who had no idea what kind of movie they were seeing. Balagueró made his name on the *[Rec]* films, but this is the film that convinced me to add him to the (short) list of genre filmmakers who get my ticket purchase on their name alone.

It's funny, right around the same time this came out we were cursed with *The Resident*, a very bad thriller starring Hillary Swank and Jeffrey Dean Morgan that had some very similar plot points. Normally it's annoying when two very similar movies come out practically back to back (the *Volcano/Dante's Peak* phenomenon), but here it was actually kind of fascinating, because you could see how the same basic idea could be turned into a terrific, unnerving film or a loathsome bore. I mean, sure, some folks will prefer *Volcano* to *Dante*, or vice versa, but I think we can pretty much all agree that neither of them are terrific films. It's rare you see such a vast quality difference with this sort of thing, and I am willing to bet good money that there isn't a single person in the world who would say *The Resident* was superior to this one.

MOVIE #304 – OCTOBER 31ˢᵗ

GRIMM LOVE (2006)
Dir: Martin Weisz
HMAD Review Date: September 18, 2010 (DVD)
Genre: Cannibal, Horror?
Available from Phase 4 Films

Synopsis Based on Fading Memory: A woman researches the true-life case of a man who posted an ad for a willing victim of cannibalism (and found one!).

Review excerpt:
"Both Thomas Kretschmann (as the killer) and Thomas Huber (as the guy who says, on more than one occasion, "Bite my thing off!", i.e. the "victim") won awards at Sitges for their performances, and it's easy to see why – you sympathize fully with both men and really care about them, making even the murder scene somewhat uplifting, as they both finally got what they desired most, regardless of how twisted it may seem to the rest of us. I wish they had spent a little less time on their back-stories and more on their time together (not the killing/dick-eating part, but more like the car ride to the house where they carry out their plan, things like that), but that stuff is interesting as well, depicting why these two guys have ended up in such lonely predicaments."

Reflection: A few entries back I discussed Stuart Gordon and his unusual film work – right now he's currently trying to mount a feature version of his stage production *"Taste"*, which was based on this very same story. The play found some black comedy in the situation, whereas this one's title suggests the decidedly non-hilarious tone. I also assume his version would be more focused on the two men; I'm all for Keri Russell in our movies but her (fictional) scenes aren't nearly as interesting as the ones featuring our "villain" and his "victim", and I half-wonder if Weisz had enough footage of them that he could conceivably recut the film without her and keep it at a feature length. If Gordon never gets to make his film, at least we have this one as a respectable consolation prize.

Bit of trivia: the true story was referenced during the third (and final, dammit) season of *Hannibal*, in a very delightful and sardonic way (with a would-be cannibal lamenting that they went to all that trouble and overcooked the penis). The "real world" rarely intrudes on that show, so I love that one of its very few exceptions to that rule concerns this strange and even kind of sad case. I mean, it's not like these guys were as famous as Ed Gein or whoever, and yet their story has now inspired multiple films, a play, and a pretty hilarious joke on a show not nearly enough of you were watching. Not bad!

This concludes the "alt-horror" month, and I hope you found some of the picks interesting. Again, this is the one month of the year where even non-horror fans will probably end up watching a few classics, so I really wanted to give you some unusual options. It was a tough month to put together, but I knew if I did like, "Werewolf movies" it'd make it that much harder to skip *American Werewolf* or *The Howling*, because it's the time of the year where you'll want to watch those. I'm just trying to keep it well rounded for such a celebratory month! Don't worry; next month is (mostly) full blown, hard R, traditional horror.

NOVEMBER – ZOMBIES & CANNIBALS

ARTIST: DANIEL XIII

Even once I learned what we were actually celebrating on Thanksgiving (not "one month until Christmas", which is what I thought it meant when I was a kid) I still never considered that other countries do not have this glorious holiday on the last Thursday of every November. Kind of a bummer for them; it's a great excuse to pig out, take a nap, and then burn off all that turkey and stuffing while running around a Walmart trying to beat out (or up?) 200 other people for a five dollar waffle maker.

(Wait, other countries still have Black Friday at least, right?)

Anyway, in honor of George Romero's *Dawn of the Dead*, which satirizes Black Friday-esque behavior in between scenes with lots of overeating, November's theme will be zombie and cannibal movies! By the time December hits, you may never want to eat again. Or see another blatant rip-off of Rhodes' death from *Day of the Dead*. Either or. Interestingly, watching *Dawn* on Thanksgiving morning is a long standing tradition for me, because Thanksgiving Day in 1994 was the first time I ever saw it. At 14 I didn't even get the whole "satirical jab at consumerism" angle, so it was wonderfully serendipitous timing on my part; once I realized Romero was mocking the very thing that drives the day *after* Thanksgiving, it became a tradition AND a little preview of what was to come.

But that's his take. Granted he's the creator of what modern audiences think of when they hear the word "zombie", but the rules vary even more than they do for vampires. Even shooting them in the head doesn't always work – see *Return of the Living Dead*. That's one of the things that make them such a popular option, because there's precedent to color outside the lines – some eat flesh, some just want to kill everyone in sight (*28 Days Later*-style) and some are just drones for a mad scientist or something. The flesh-eating kind tends to be the most popular and thus the most overused, and since I'll unavoidably be recommending more than a few of those, I thought I'd start off with something that shunned that particular trope...

MOVIE #305 – NOVEMBER 1st

MESSIAH OF EVIL (aka DEAD PEOPLE) (1973)
Dir: Willard Huyck, Gloria Katz (uncredited)
HMAD Review Date: July 11, 2007 (DVD)
Genre: Cult, Zombie
Public domain title, available through several DVD companies

Synopsis Based on Fading Memory: A woman looking for her father uncovers something pretty nutty instead.

Review excerpt:
"I began wondering why anyone would recommend this movie to me, as I wasn't even sure if it was a horror movie. Perhaps it was some diabolical plan to sabotage my whole "Horror Movie A Day!" streak (unbroken for nearly 5 months, that's 150 movies!!!)? But then, finally, the horror part began, and damned if the movie didn't turn out pretty dang good. It's sort of like a cross between Wicker Man *and* Body Snatchers. *But with zombies. There was still some unintentional hilarity to be had (such as the goofy sound the zombies make when they attack, which cannot possibly be described as anything but a cat howling), but some really good scenes too, like when a rather dim girl sits down to watch a Western and the theater slowly fills up with stealth zombies (patient, these guys are). And a lot of the zombies look like Herk Harvey in* Carnival of Souls, *so you know they're creepy as all hell."*

Reflection: As the excerpt says, I was only 150 movies deep into HMAD when I saw this, and it was off a lousy budget pack transfer to boot. So my review isn't as positive as it should be, because I had yet to fully develop my appreciation for the more unusual stuff. At times, this gets kooky enough to earn placement in May's chapter, because it's more like a slow burn comedy than a horror movie in its first half. Since I wrote the reviews pretty hastily back then, movies like this - the ones that kind of stick with you and get even better on repeat viewings – deserve better praise than they are offered in my quickie write-ups. Ideally I'd take solid notes and let the movie simmer in my head for a couple of days before writing down my thoughts, but alas the nature of the site (and my own terrible note-taking skills) prevented that from being feasible.

Luckily it didn't take too long to come around and see it for the gem that it is; I ended up seeing it on 35mm the following year at Cinefamily, as part of a weekly horror series that I was hosting back when I was with Bloody Disgusting. Or, I should say, SUPPOSED to be hosting, as the theater's director is kind of a spacy guy and forgot to bring me up on stage more often than not. So I watched the Q&A with Huyck and Katz from my seat instead of being the one asking them the questions I had prepared. But I didn't mind too much – I was happy to get to see the movie properly, and walk away a full-fledged fan. And now it's the lead off movie for the chapter! Take *that*, 2007 BC!

MOVIE #306 – NOVEMBER 2nd

BOY EATS GIRL (2005)
Dir: Stephen Bradley
HMAD Review Date: December 22, 2007 (DVD)
Genre: Comedic, Zombie
Available from Lionsgate

Synopsis Based on Fading Memory: A guy accidentally kills himself and returns as a zombie, hell-bent on telling his girlfriend that he loves her as his condition worsens.

Review excerpt:
"...the biggest complaint I have about it is that it is too short. Running only 80 minutes with credits, the movie could have used another set piece and maybe a tad more character time, but it works without them. It's funny when it's supposed to be, with a very good hit/miss ratio for the gags (I could do without a few of his geeky friends' quips). Almost all of the characters are likable; even the bitchy girl who you're supposed to hate is somewhat endearing (mainly for her response to "I'll eat you myself!"), and since the movie doesn't really spend a lot of time 'getting to know' them, that's high praise for the (mostly no-name) actors playing them. The lead in particular is quite good, pulling off the raging zombie version just as well as the lovesick emo kid version."

Reflection: Back in 2008, a bunch of my friends flipped their lids for a movie called *Dance of the Dead*, which was basically a "John Hughes with zombies" kinda thing – it wasn't bad, but I kept saying over and over "*Boy Eats Girl* already did this, and better!" No one listened to me though, and kept professing their love for that movie. But you guys bought this book so I assume you trust my judgment – this is the superior film. It also has a fine soundtrack of UK pop, I might add.

I should stress again that I saw this in 2007, which was about fifty zombie comedies ago. It's possible you're tired of such things by now and won't find it as novel as I did then. Luckily, if you're only interested in the zombie element (and not the humor), it's still plenty worth your while. For starters, it's a voodoo-driven zombie outbreak, a welcome change from the usual government weapon/deadly virus-type narratives. And it all actually starts with our hero – he isn't bitten by some random zombie, he's patient zero! There's also a strong mother-son relationship, something you don't usually see in horror movies unless it's a *Psycho* retread. So even though it's a comedy, there's a solid zombie horror story at its core, and you can't always say that even about the non-comedic ones.

MOVIE #307 – NOVEMBER 3rd

CANNIBAL APOCALYPSE [APOCALYPSE DOMANI] (1980)
Dir: Antonio Margheriti
HMAD Review Date: September 26, 2007 (DVD)
Genre: Cannibal, Exploitation
Available from Image Entertainment

Synopsis Based on Fading Memory: A Vietnam vet returns home, snaps, and begins eating people. John Saxon tries to stop him from doing that.

Review excerpt:
"The best surprise was how much John Morghen was in the film. Usually the poor sod is killed instantly after being introduced, but here he's got more screentime than anyone save Saxon. A film can never have too much John Morghen, so this was fantastic. His eventual death (I'm not spoiling anything. Come on, the guy NEVER lives) was amazingly well done, considering the time period. I honestly can't really figure out how it was accomplished, though I have a theory (body suspension - notice you never see the top of his head or an angled view)."

Reflection: Of the most notorious *Cannibal* ___ movies, this is the most accessible, so if you haven't seen any of them I'm glad I caught you in time! If you can stomach what's on display here, then you can try *Cannibal Ferox* if you're curious. After that, if you're STILL in the mood for this form of entertainment, head on over to *Cannibal Holocaust*, which is so messed up the director actually went on trial and had to prove that it wasn't a snuff film by bringing all of the actors into the courtroom!

The levels of violence between *Ferox* and *Holocaust* are about the same; *Ferox* might have a bit more blood spilled (it's the later film, so there might have been some one-upmanship going on), but overall it's slightly less grim and disturbing than *Holocaust*. Neither of them are likely to make you feel very good about yourself, I assure you. But this? Even with the hardcore gore and violence, it's almost like a precursor to *Falling Down* or something along those lines, as it splits its time between a crazed man (Morghen) wreaking havoc and the cop (Saxon) trying to stop him. But instead of smashing up a convenience store or trespassing on a golf course, he eats people. Fun for the whole family!

MOVIE #308 – NOVEMBER 4th

ZOMBIE APOCALYPSE (2011)
Dir: Nick Lyon
HMAD Review Date: January 15, 2012 (DVD)
Genre: Zombie
Available from The Asylum

Synopsis Based on Fading Memory: A bunch of folks try to survive the zombie, er, apocalypse.

Review excerpt:
"...it kind of reminded me of *Left 4 Dead*. The plot is similar to any level of that game, where your four characters make their way to some sort of rescue vehicle (in this case, a boat). There are different kinds of zombies (including a "tank" type), the weapons are similar, and like the game, it's remarkably straightforward. Again, no evil humans, but there aren't too many other obstacles either – it's just all run n' gun, with zombies as the only real threat. That said, they took a bit from "The Walking Dead" as well – in addition to an off-screen character named Kirkman (someone mentions Pittsburgh as well – they did their homework!), our badass black female character almost exclusively uses a sword as her weapon. But hey that means they're reading stuff instead of copying popular shows/movies like usual – Michonne hasn't appeared on the AMC show yet!"

Reflection: Four years later, I'm still kind of in shock by how genuinely fun this movie is. Most Asylum movies only offer a few fleeting moments of trash entertainment (enough to make a trailer, basically), but this one is action-packed and almost always on the move – it's like a real movie! As the *Walking Dead* show (which DOES have Michonne now, obviously) keeps finding ways to limit action in the regular episodes and save it all for the finales, it might even be more fun now than it was in 2012 – you might be conditioned to a minimum of undead action in your zombie fare.

I mentioned *Left 4 Dead* in the excerpt – I'm still baffled that the game hasn't had a new installment for the new systems. It was one of the most genuinely enjoyable online games I've ever played (I'm more into solo play, for the record – I'm terrible at things like *Call of Duty* and have no time for MMORPGs), and zombies have become far more popular in the years since the last one came out. I guess Valve (its makers) assume we have enough other zombie games to entertain us, so they can just focus on not making *Half Life 3*? At any rate, I was tickled that if they had just slapped the *L4D* title on this movie, they would have had the best video game adaptation ever.

MOVIE #309 – NOVEMBER 5th

DEAD & BURIED (1981)
Dir: Gary Sherman
HMAD Review Date: August 9, 2008 (Revival screening)
Genre: Zombie
Available from Blue Underground

Synopsis Based on Fading Memory: Murders keep happening in a seaside town and the sheriff wants to know why!

Review excerpt:
"It kind of reminds me of Messiah of Evil *at times, what with the creepy atmosphere, the non-zombie zombie town, the doomed hero, etc. It's just the type of movie you don't see quite enough, where they take a fairly silly concept and not only milk it for all its worth, but play it mostly straight (apparently it was actually written to BE a comedy, but they shot it the scary way). The result is something pretty original, always entertaining, and just plain delightful."*

Reflection: This screening was on 16mm in my buddy's backyard, and original distributor Avco Embassy seemingly never has a good print of anything (the most faded film prints I've ever seen – *Escape from New York, The Fog, Howling*, etc. – all Avco!), so while I hold out hope I can see this gem on 35mm in a proper theater, I'm OK with it if it never happens. I got a pretty decent crowd experience already, and whatever print they dig up is likely to look pretty bad. But it's just such a cool, weird little movie with a really fun (if nonsensical) twist, which is the sort of thing that I find plays great with a big crowd, one that's perfectly mixed between fans and newcomers who don't know what they're in for.

Side note – I actually recorded a commentary track for this alongside screenwriter Sean Keller for Fearnet, but it never got released before the network unexpectedly shut down. It was something they started doing right before they folded, with a variety of horror folk (Derek Mears and Ted Raimi also contributed) talking over this and other movies like *Deep Red, The Crazies*, etc. Only a few of the tracks were released, and I doubt they're a priority for whoever inherited all of Fearnet's assets. But hopefully it'll surface someday – it was the first of two that Sean and I did, and a lot better than our 2nd one (for *Zombie*), as we were kind of tired after doing *Dead & Buried* and weren't really all that peppy for Fulci's undead epic. But THAT is the one they released! Sigh.

HMAD Fun Fact: There are over two hundred zombie movies reviewed on the site, including 5/6ths of Romero's Dead *series (sorry,* Land*). That's a lot of people taking too long to realize that bullets are useless unless they go into the head.*

MOVIE #310 – NOVEMBER 6th

DYING BREED (2008)
Dir: Jody Dwyer
HMAD Review Date: April 3, 2009 (DVD)
Genre: Cannibal, Survival
Available from Lionsgate

Synopsis Based on Fading Memory: Some folks run afoul of some cannibals in the Australian forest.

Review excerpt:
"The most surprising thing about it is that, despite starring actors from Saw (Leigh Whannell) and Wolf Creek (Nathan Phillips) - the poster children for "torture porn" horror movies - it's refreshingly light on prolonged violence. A cannibal mountain man eating a girl's lip is about as brutal as it gets, and it's hardly excessive or pointless (he's hungry!). I also like that, for once, it takes place in the forest-y part of Australia. So many of these movies take place in the outback, you almost forget that Australia does in fact have trees and grass. The irony, of course, is that the setting, coupled with the seemingly permanent overcast/drizzling weather, I kept forgetting it WAS Australia, and not the usual Vancouver backdrop."

Reflection: For a time there in the late '00s, it seemed like we were witnessing the birth of Australia as THE source for foreign horror, the way Italy was in the '70s and '80s and Japan was in the '90s. Every few months there would be another solid title from Down Under, and unlike the aforementioned locales they seemed to be equally skilled at all sub-genres, instead of specializing in one or two. But for some reason it just never really took off; I don't know if the funding dried up the way it did to Italy in the late '80s, or if they just stopped finding solid distribution here in the US, but it's been a while since I've seen anything from there make a big splash, and the few that DO find their way here (such as the terrific *Crawl*, recommended last month) don't get seen nearly enough. It's a shame, really – their sensibilities match up quite well with mine, and I honestly can't think of more than one or two Aussie horror films I actively dislike.

This was also a selection from the 3rd incarnation of the After Dark Horrorfest, which has yielded two other titles for this book. As previously mentioned in one of those write-ups, the 3rd proved to be the best yet for this formerly annual event, but unfortunately the lackluster first two lineups (the 2nd one only had a single good movie, if you ask me – Jim Mickle's *Mulberry St*, ALSO accounted for in this tome) had damaged the brand too much for it to matter much. The following installment (almost as good as this one) was the last for a long time, but just recently After Dark brought the Horrorfest back. They had been focusing on their original productions for the past few years, releasing them intermittently like a regular studio, but I guess they felt the time was right to unleash a few at once. Even if the movies don't turn out to be that great (as of this writing, I haven't seen any of the new series yet), it's terrific that a few lucky films will get that extra push in an overcrowded market.

MOVIE #311 – NOVEMBER 7th

DEATHDREAM (1974)
Dir: Bob Clark
HMAD Review Date: May 22, 2007 (Revival screening)
Genre: Zombie
Available from Blue Underground

Synopsis Based on Fading Memory: A soldier returns home from Vietnam, not quite as dead as his family was led to believe.

Review excerpt:
"I urge everyone to seek out and watch this film. Some of the titles it may be listed under are The Night Andy Came Home, Dead of Night, Night Walk, The Veteran, Whispers *(???), and* Soif de Sang. *It's a shame Bob Clark focused more on comedies (and then, family films – he gave us* Baby Geniuses*) in his later years, as all three of his horror films are highly entertaining and completely unique (at the time anyway). I would have loved to have seen more from him. But alas."*

Reflection: My review of this film is entirely useless, because I spent the entire thing recounting a mangled airing of the film I had seen a few months earlier on some weird public access show, and repeatedly insulting the "singing ninja" that the show featured (they had it coming, but still). For that I apologize, because not only is the write-up not helpful in the slightest (even for the site's original, less structured version, it's remarkably light on discussion about the actual movie), but it gives the impression that the movie doesn't really offer much to talk about, which isn't remotely true. I mean sure, it's a bit dated and the central metaphor was essentially redone by Joe Dante in the "Homecoming" episode of *Masters of Horror*, but it still packs a punch, and you might even tear up at the ending (made sadder at this screening since it was a tribute for Bob Clark, who had been killed a few weeks earlier by some godless drunk driver).

Since the review is otherwise of no use, I opted to use the part where I list its alternate titles for the above excerpt. By now it's pretty much always called *Deathdream,* but non-US readers might still know it by another title, and who knows what it might be called on a budget pack release or something along those lines. Plus, whenever the planned remake comes up, *Deathdream* is what it is referred to, so that's THE title, as far as I'm concerned. Speaking of the remake, I'm not really that afraid of one – as with any war-driven narrative (not just horror), you can always update the politics surrounding the conflict of the day and give a fresh spin on the story. And it doesn't even need to be a traditional war – the hero could be killed by rampant gun violence or police brutality (today's hot button topics) and there would be plenty of material to draw from to make its point. Go for it, remake machine!

MOVIE #312 – NOVEMBER 8th

THE HORDE (2009)
Dir: Yannick Dahan, Benjamin Rocher
HMAD Review Date: May 7, 2011 (Streaming)
Genre: Zombie
Available from IFC

Synopsis Based on Fading Memory: Cops and crooks have to (sort of) band together to survive against endless waves of zombies.

Review excerpt:
"...pretty fast paced and gory, and yet not cartoonish; it's almost like the Black Hawk Down *of zombie movies – frenetic and violent (and shot SCOPE!). And it's refreshingly un-Hollywood; the enemies team up but don't become best buddies. So many of these alliance movies tend to have their characters forget about their initial issues with each other, but they're at each other's throats until the very end. Plus, the story doesn't provide any opportunities for say, one of the cops to risk his life to save one of the drug dealers or vice versa; they are basically together for a "safety in numbers" approach and nothing else. Not that I DISLIKE the other approach, but it's kind of fun to see it done without the moral ambiguity and changes of heart – these folks hate each other and always will."*

Reflection: I actually love it when a film offers an alternate to the thing that I usually admire – it's one reason why I love *Halloween* above all other slashers even though I tend to gravitate toward whodunit types. So *The Horde* worked for me because, for once, it DIDN'T have the uneasy alliance seemingly become a permanent one. Like, *Assault on Precinct 13* is awesome, but if they made a sequel it seems Napoleon and Bishop would be pals throughout the movie, which would rob it of the thing that makes the movie so memorable – seeing them become allies after their antagonistic introduction. So I dug that the guys in this movie never really got over their beef with each other; it was an entertaining alternative to what usually happens – not something I want to see over and over, but just for this one time as a change of pace.

But it's also a seriously action packed zombie movie, with one of the largest "casts" of zombie extras I've seen in years. Remember that scene in the *Dawn of the Dead* remake when their truck gets surrounded? That's the number of undead you see during a *few* key scenes here. As you can imagine, that means it's much faster paced and splatter-y than the usual French stuff. Their horror tends to be extreme, yes, but rarely "high-octane", so like the "we still hate each other" approach, this was a fun deviation from the norm.

MOVIE #313 – NOVEMBER 9th

DEADHEADS (2011)
Dir: Brett Pierce, Drew T. Pierce
HMAD Review Date: October 16, 2011 (Festival screening)
Genre: Comedic, Zombie
Available from Freestyle Digital Media

Synopsis Based on Fading Memory: A couple of zombies go on a road trip, because death won't stop one of them from telling his (still very much alive) girlfriend that he loves her.

Review excerpt:
"...it's funny as hell. The random asides, Brent's slightly stoner-esque but endlessly enthusiastic nature, and even the slapstick-y elements involving their deteriorating zombie state play great – the audience was laughing at all the right spots, with very few clunkers. The script is also careful with its movie references; this is in "our world" so they have the Transformers *movies and such (I think I even caught a* Cast Away *reference), and even go see* Evil Dead *at one point, but it never becomes too winky or even strained – they naturally feel like the sort of things an obvious slacker type like Brent would watch and reference once he found himself in the situation (as I might)."*

Reflection: Because *Night of the Living Dead* directly or indirectly inspired just about every zombie movie that came along since, you don't see a lot of scenery changes in them. Holing up somewhere and defending the chosen locale tends to be the way these things go, even in comedies (*Shaun of the Dead's* Winchester, for example). So part of what I liked about this one is that it's more of a buddy road movie than it is a zombie film, having more in common with '80s films like *The Sure Thing* and *Planes, Trains, and Automobiles* than anything from Romero.

It's also got a touch of *Starman*, so the Carpenter nut in me had to appreciate that unexpected source of inspiration, because 99/100 times that someone wants to pay homage to the master, they toss in a reference to *The Thing* or *Halloween*. I DO think modern movies get a bit too reference heavy (it always reminds me of that explanation of why *The Simpsons* started to suck: "The original writers watched films. The current writers watched *The Simpsons*."), but as long as they're inspired callbacks and just flavoring what's a fine story on its own, it's easily forgivable.

P.S. A year later the Pierce brothers made a short film called *Smush* that is set in *Deadheads'* universe, so if you enjoy this one, I encourage you to seek that out. I actually saw it with tomorrow's movie, oddly enough.

MOVIE #314 – NOVEMBER 10th

EDDIE THE SLEEPWALKING CANNIBAL (2012)
Dir: Boris Rodriguez
HMAD Review Date: October 15, 2012 (Festival screening)
Genre: Cannibal, Hero Killer
Available from Doppelganger Releasing

Synopsis Based on Fading Memory: An artist discovers he only gets inspired when his roommate kills and eats someone.

Review excerpt:
"Director/co-writer Boris Rodriguez wisely keeps the cannibalism to a minimum. Since we're supposed to sympathize with these guys to some degree, it would be pretty hard if we were constantly seeing Eddie murder innocent people (or even seeing the resulting artwork), so everything is suggested or partially obscured until the final reel. But he makes it count that way, and I was legit surprised at the amount of blood a particular character is covered in by the end of the film - you really get a sense of how dangerous things have gotten and why they need to stop. The humor is still there (and I like how his inspiration sort of dries out while he's trying to paint - it's basically treated like impotence), but the stakes are real - the escalation from "Eh, he had it coming" type kills (like the dentist in Little Shop Of Horrors) *to "OK these guys are terrible people" is handled perfectly both on the script level and in the direction - not bad for a guy making his first theatrical feature."*

Reflection: The basic plot of *Bucket of Blood* and *Little Shop of Horrors* (realizing that one can achieve success through murder) can be applied to any number of professions, which is why I'm surprised I don't see it more often. It can be disastrous, as in the largely terrible *All About Evil* (where a woman saves her dying movie theater by shooting snuff films and showing them to increasingly larger crowds), but in the right hands it can be pretty great, as is the case here. Rodriguez hasn't made another film since, and I hope that changes soon – in fact, if not for *Resolution*, this would have been my favorite selection from that year's Screamfest. When someone makes a debut that good, you should only have to wait two, MAYBE three years to see what they do next.

I mentioned the humor in the excerpt, and the title probably gives you visions of something really wacky, but it's actually (thankfully) just as much of a character drama as a comedy – the laughs are spare, and often quite dry. Not exactly Coen-esque, but closer to their territory than *Cannibal! The Musical* or something.

Basically it's exactly the sort of thing I WANT to see at a horror driven festival, in that it's different and not the sort of movie you would expect to see in a multiplex, but doesn't depress or sicken you either. I love all kinds of horror, but festivals can be kind of draining if you're going all in (as I always did, before I had a baby anyway), so I need levity, and often. More movies like this (and less rapey ones – no horror fest is complete without at least one movie with a sexual assault, apparently/sadly) and I'd be pushing harder to stay at the festival instead of going home to change a diaper!

MOVIE #315 – NOVEMBER 11th

LET SLEEPING CORPSES LIE (1974)
Dir: Jorge Grau
HMAD Review Date: June 15, 2009 (DVD)
Genre: Mad Scientist, Zombie
Available from Blue Underground

Synopsis Based on Fading Memory: A jerk cop tries to solve some murders that he believes were committed by a "hippie" cult. Spoiler: he's wrong, it's zombies.

Review excerpt:
"It's cool that there is a (movie) logical explanation for the zombies that we actually see in action. I don't mind the lack of explanation in the Romero films (or their remakes), and a lot of the films that DO explain it settle for radiation or some sort of chemical spill (zzzz). Here, it's a miscalculated formula that is intended to control the pest population. And it's delivered by a traditional farm machine that we see all the time, which makes it a bit creepier. Next time you see that TruGreen truck at your neighbors, you might want to arm yourself."

Reflection: A nearly universal tradition in zombie movies is that they end ambiguously, with the zombie masses still presenting a major threat to the surviving humans. The sheer numbers often prevent any completely definitive endings (how many have you seen where all the zombies are wiped out and things return to normal?), so I take notice when a film contains the number of undead to something that can in fact be managed. There aren't many, but this is one of those exceptions – I think there are only half a dozen or so zombies in the movie. The explanation for their existence is rather unique, and the film's emphasis on atmosphere over action makes it an unusual entry in the zombie canon.

But I guess that's not too surprising when you consider the production date. At this point, *Night of the Living Dead* was only five or six years old, so there wasn't really a glut of zombie films to rip off quite yet. Zombies as we know them (undead, flesh eating) are so common nowadays it's often hard to remember that they're a relatively new monster compared to vampires and werewolves. This has probably resulted in a number of disappointed horror fans (including myself) checking out a "zombie" movie prior to Romero's original and finding that it had nothing to do with biting humans to spread the infection. No, for those seeking out interesting stuff, look in the immediate years AFTER *Night of the Living Dead* – the "rules" were still being established, and *Dawn of the Dead* hadn't come along to change the focus to creative gore and X-rated violence. There's a lot of unique stuff like this in that era, certainly more than you'd find in the slasher films that followed *Halloween* and *Friday the 13th*. Dig in!

P.S. There are about a half dozen other titles for this one, including *The Living Dead at Manchester Morgue* and *Don't Open the Window*. The Italian title is "*Non si deve profanare il sonno dei morti*", which translates to "You must not profane the sleep of the dead." This is a lousy title, but good advice.

MOVIE #316 – NOVEMBER 12th

THE REVENANT (2009)
Dir: Kerry Prior
HMAD Review Date: October 20, 2009 (Festival screening)
Genre: Zombie
Available from Lionsgate

Synopsis Based on Fading Memory: A soldier who has become a revenant (zombie/vampire hybrid) obtains the blood he needs to survive by becoming a vigilante in Los Angeles.

Review excerpt:
"The comedy comes not from winking homage to other zombie films, but in the way that Prior presents some of the obstacles that might arise from their situation. For example, when they need blood, they try a hospital, hoping to get it in a bag instead of from some poor sod's neck. But he is thwarted by a Scientologist nurse who tries to get him to take a Thetan test, as she assumes he is a confused goth kid. And when they decide to turn to criminals to satisfy Bart's hunger, they inadvertently become vigilantes, saving would-be rape victims and liquor store owners from harm (and then grossing them out when said folks see what they were really there for). It's a unique film in that it takes a familiar premise and manages to avoid cliché (and even expectations) for the rest of its running time."

Reflection: It really aggravates me that this movie sat on the shelf for like three years before finally being released direct to DVD, without fanfare and with most of its champions (like me) having moved on to newer blood. It had an endless 3rd act (you could almost count it as a 4th act, come to think of it), but otherwise it was one of the most solid and enjoyable zombie comedies in ages, with some drama mixed in as well for good measure. This could have been a tonal disaster, but Prior kept everything almost perfectly balanced and in check.

Alas, it seems that it was just bad timing for the film. The festival screening I saw was right around the time *Zombieland* was making a mint at the box office (until *World War Z*, it was the highest grossing zombie film of all time), so I assume that either helped or hindered its chances at distribution. There are two likely scenarios: one is that the producers kept holding out for better deals than they were being offered, figuring they had a guaranteed hit on their hands now that the zom-com sub-genre was hot again, and ultimately priced themselves out of getting picked up. The other is that the distributors didn't want to touch it for fear of being labeled a rip-off. Both things happen a lot, and it's always a bummer regardless of what the reason is, because ultimately all that crap doesn't matter – horror fans getting to see it (legally) is the most important thing. I mean, the film ended up at a good home (Lionsgate), but the DVD/Blu lacked any bonus features, and Prior is only just now finally getting another film in production. And to make matters worse, there's now an unrelated (and overrated) Leonardo DiCaprio film that will forever be the one people think of when you say the title. I highly doubt being selected for my book makes up for all that aggravation.

MOVIE #317 – NOVEMBER 13th

SHRIEK OF THE MUTILATED (1974)
Dir: Michael Findlay
HMAD Review Date: April 28, 2010 (Streaming)
Genre: Cannibal, Cult, Monster
Available from Image Entertainment

Synopsis Based on Fading Memory: A bunch of folks seek a Yeti. The genre tags spoil what they actually find.

Review excerpt:
"It certainly works as a laughable "crowd" movie, and I can guarantee it would be a legendary screening at the New Beverly on par with Pieces *or* Raw Force. *We have the hero who makes out with his girlfriend at the drop of a hat, a guy singing a song about Yetis, a mute Indian slave who spends the entire movie shirtless, a Janine-from-*Ghostbusters*-esque hipster sleeping with her giant glasses on, and lots of unmotivated angry outbursts, like when the hipster offers one guy a drink and he furiously pours it out before going off to hunt so that they didn't have to eat "bear pie" (which, for the record, I would eat in a heartbeat)."*

Reflection: In 2008 and 2009, I would occasionally record commentary tracks that readers could download and watch along with their DVDs. It was a fun "bonus" thing to do for the site, but very time-consuming (and seemingly not particularly popular), so I stopped doing them. Taking their place, briefly, was @HMADLiveTweet, where I'd pick a movie (from Netflix Instant) and encourage people to tweet along with me as I watched it for my daily entry. Ultimately, I only did it two or three times; it was fun to an extent but a. clunky as hell, for obvious reasons (telling everyone to start watching a movie at the same time and hopefully follow along when dealing with rebuffering and all the other pitfalls of online viewing being a major one), and b. the experience made it hard to review the movie afterward, since I was essentially talking over the whole thing. So I'd often have to watch the movie again, and then we're back in "I don't have time for this" territory. And now I hate it when people live tweet a movie that they're watching for the first time, so I'm actually kind of embarrassed about the whole affair.

Anyway, I kind of spoiled the movie's twist in order to include it in this month's lineup, sorry about that. But (more spoilers, if you haven't pieced it together just stop reading, damn you!) I kind of like that the first big twist of *The Village* may have been inspired by this movie. There's probably a fun mini-festival to be made out of all the horror films where a monster turns out to be someone in a suit – hell, the four that I'm thinking of right now (which I otherwise won't identify so I'm not spoiling ALL of them) would include this B-movie schlock, a big Hollywood period piece, a historical epic, and a *Silence of the Lambs*-esque serial killer thriller. Such variety!

MOVIE #318 – NOVEMBER 14th

PONTYPOOL (2008)
Dir: Bruce McDonald
HMAD Review Date: October 28, 2009 (DVD)
Genre: Zombie
Available from MPI Home Video

Synopsis Based on Fading Memory: A radio DJ realizes, while on the air, that his very words are adding to the spread of a zombie-like virus.

Review excerpt:
"...a pretty terrific little thriller. The description (three people inside a radio station, merely talking about the zombie chaos occurring outside) might sound dull as dirt, but once you learn how people are being infected, it becomes pretty obvious that a radio station is the perfect setting for this particular story. See, as director Bruce Macdonald said, the "zombies" (he refers to them as "conversationists") become that way not from a bite or some sort of airborne virus, but merely infected words that they hear and understand. Terms of endearment ("honey", "sweetheart", etc.) seem to be the biggest culprits, so folks are advised to stay away from close family members and loved ones (what about truck stop waitresses?)."

Reflection: This is a bit self-indulgent, but whatever, you bought the book bearing my name. You have only yourself to blame!

Anyway, following up the previous entry (re: 'live tweeting'), I realized when I started putting this book together that my reviews used to be a lot funnier before I started using Twitter a lot. I tend to think that I was only comical when tearing a movie apart, but I really liked this movie, and that truck stop waitress line in the excerpt just made me laugh out loud. I think I used up a lot of my creative energy on jokey tweets and wouldn't have much left for the reviews, especially when you couple that with my hatred of repeating myself. I get frustrated when I click on a review from a writer I like and see that I already read a lot of the same thoughts a few days previous in their post-screening tweets, and I tried to avoid doing that. BUT, Twitter was instrumental in stopping a frequent annoyance – people asking me if I *really* watched a movie every day. Before this social media mainstay infiltrated our lives, it was basically just my say-so, but once readers had unfiltered, instant access to my thoughts and actions, it almost completely stopped the inquiries – they would just look at my Twitter feed for the proof I really was doing this to myself every goddamn day.

And this leads to my on-topic point: they really should make a sequel to this movie utilizing social media. Given the unique (and kind of genius) way the zombie virus spreads in this film, the idea of using tweets and status updates as a way of infecting hundreds of thousands of people at once seems too amazing an opportunity to pass up. Only downside: I'd turn into a zombie before I could send any good tweets out about it.

MOVIE #319 – NOVEMBER 15th

NIGHT OF THE ZOMBIES (aka HELL OF THE LIVING DEAD) (1980)
Dir: Bruno Mattei, Claudio Fragasso (uncredited)
HMAD Review Date: January 19, 2010 (Revival screening)
Genre: Zombie
Available from Blue Underground

Synopsis Based on Fading Memory: Some commandos and some other folks are attacked by zombies and stock footage of elephants.

Review excerpt:
"...as obscure as it is, it's almost a wonder it was released at all. The Wikipedia "production history" section for the film seems book-worthy, considering all of the production issues that arose (and those are just the ones that were reported - it was long before the internet, and director Bruno Mattei has been dead for over a decade). Footage that had to be junked due to not matching the other footage, rewrites that weren't reflected in the parts of the movie that were left intact, the stock footage... no wonder I didn't really understand the plot (and I was sober!). I mean, it's not exactly Southland Tales-*level baffling, but suffice to say, I learned more about the story from reading the Wiki synopsis than I did in the film itself, and others I talked to after the film seemed just as mystified by some of its plot points (such as what exactly the commando guys' mission was)."

Reflection: As you might tell from the review excerpt, the behind the scenes history of this film is far more interesting than what made it on screen. It's goofy enough to warrant a look (the tutu scene alone makes it a must-drunkenly-see), but if there was a feature-length documentary on the film's production, I'd buy it instantly, whereas I'm not sure I'd want to watch this movie again sober and/or alone. In fact, a lot of the post-Fulci *Zombie* movies have troubled productions, and I can't help but think it'd make for a fascinating book (more than this one anyway). Even if you'd have to take every single word in it with a grain of salt, as these guys' memories tend to differ (and half of the ones of note, including Mattei, are dead), it'd be a fascinating and hilarious read.

This one sticks out because of how sloppy it is. It's not as bad as many of the other "15th of the month" entries in the book, but in 1980 the Italians were still on the top of their game with this sort of stuff – you wouldn't expect something THIS incompetent until the later part of the decade, when the Italian film industry was in steep decline. That's when the really bad movies started coming (*Zombie 4*, anyone?), but the problem with those things is that they weren't just bad, they were crushingly dull. No such complaint could be levied here – it's terrible, but never boring.

MOVIE #320 – NOVEMBER 16th

GNAW (2008)
Dir: Gregory Mandry
HMAD Review Date: August 16, 2012 (DVD)
Genre: Cannibal, Survival
Available from Dark Sky Films

Synopsis Based on Fading Memory: It's *Texas Chain Saw Massacre*, basically. But from Britain!

Review excerpt:
"...they go all out with the cannibalism, which was nice since the last couple of Chainsaw sequels/remakes more or less ignored it. People find teeth and hair in their food, the chef bakes a tongue, and at the end... well, I'll leave that little surprise to you, but I will say it's kind of incredible. And unlike the insufferable Squeal, the guy takes his cannibalism seriously, trapping folks and taking care of how he cuts them instead of just hacking away like that movie's Pig-men did more often than not."

Reflection: I know this is supposed to be zombie AND cannibal movie month and I've been lacking in selections for the latter, but this should make up for it – they really dive into that angle in this somewhat shameless *Texas Chain Saw Massacre* wannabe (but they use your familiarity with that film to pull a couple twists on you). It's always kind of annoyed me how the cannibal aspects of the *Chainsaw* series were weeded out as the series went on (the remake barely even hinted at it, though the 2006 prequel film had some of that element restored), so in a way this is kind of taking it back, proudly wearing its *Chainsaw* influence on its sleeve while also subtly throwing shade at the series for abandoning its more risqué elements in favor of traditional slasher stuff.

But the imbalance between these and zombie films isn't my fault; I only saw 30 cannibal movies for HMAD and a lot of them sucked (like *Squeal*, the one I namechecked in the excerpt that also might be one of the ten worst movies I watched). Then you take out the ones that are too well known to horror fans (*Motel Hell*) or have popped up elsewhere in the book (*Don't Go Near The Park* is in May's batshit month, *Grimm Love* was horror-lite so it appeared last month, etc.), and I kind of had slim pickings. In the early days of HMAD, I had an idea of balancing the movies so that I was seeing equal amounts of everything, but that was abandoned pretty fast. Not only are there simply not as many entries in certain sub-genres, but I don't like, say, haunted house movies as much as I like slashers – so why would I choose some haunting flick over a perfectly enticing slasher? If I noticed it had been a while since I saw a particular kind of movie I'd try to correct it, but otherwise I usually just let the fates decide what I saw. But still, 30 is way too low a number; I should have looked for more cannibal movies over the years. I apologize.

MOVIE #321 – NOVEMBER 17th

WASTING AWAY (aka AAH! ZOMBIES!) (2007)
Dir: Matthew Kohnen
HMAD Review Date: January 1, 2012 (DVD)
Genre: Comedic, Zombie
Available from Level 33 Entertainment

Synopsis Based on Fading Memory: Fairly typical "army experiment goes awry and creates zombies" story, but with a fun narrative hook – it's told from the POV of both the humans *and* the zombies.

Review excerpt:
"I loved the character of Nick (Colby French), who is also a zombie but has ties with the military and may know the answers. His arc is wonderful; we know he's not exactly a level 5 clearance type but as we learn more about him he becomes more sympathetic (and thus more human, but by saying that I sound like I'm writing press notes, so let's ignore it). He's also part of the movie's best laugh, when we discover where the toxic serum was supposed to go in the first place (it's remarkably horrible). Even in some really great zombie films I don't give a shit about any of the heroes, so to be endeared to one who was actually a zombie was a pretty nice surprise."

Reflection: There are probably just as many zombie movies as vampire ones by now, and thankfully, filmmakers are still finding new ways to tackle this venerable monster. Especially in horror-comedies; in fact, most of the time I walk away from a modern zombie film impressed by its creativity, I'm usually charmed by how funny it was as well. When it's a more serious film, coming up with new kills and maybe the location itself tends to be the extent of its originality, which is why the films start to blend together for me – movie A may take place on a farm and movie B may take place in a factory, but if they're otherwise running through the same motions (Romero's motions, usually), I won't be able to tell them apart. The comedic ones, on the average, tend to try new things that, even when they fail, make them memorable years later.

But this one took the cake – rather than just have a sympathetic zombie like Bub, or make them the only major characters of note like the earlier *Deadheads*, the movie offers a traditional zombie outbreak situation from BOTH perspectives, and director Kohnen even changes the look – B&W during the zombie POV scenes, color for the ones focusing on the humans. But that's not all - the humans see zombies as traditional slow/mumbling monsters, while the zombies see humans as fast-moving, chipmunk-sounding pests who won't leave them alone. I loved the "walk a mile in a zombie's shoes" idea; it's like when a TV show shows something from a supporting characters' perspective for a week (such as the great episode of *Supernatural* that sticks with Bobby the whole time), in that you don't want to have it every time out, but as a one-off experiment, it plays like gangbusters. Good FX, too!

MOVIE #322 – NOVEMBER 18th

SUGAR HILL (1974)
Dir: Paul Maslansky
HMAD Review Date: March 27, 2011 (Streaming)
Genre: Revenge, Zombie
Available from Kino Video

Synopsis Based on Fading Memory: A woman uses voodoo and zombies to get back at the guys who killed her lover.

Review excerpt:
"The death scenes are pretty varied – one guy gets eaten by pigs (!), another gets stabbed via voodoo doll, one drowns in mud.... no lame shootings or whatever here. Plus, while I would have liked a complication or two, it's also remarkably straightforward. It's kind of like The Crow, *but without giant shootout/rooftop chase scenes coming out of nowhere and distracting away from her very specific goal of getting back at the five guys who were responsible for her man's death. Also like* The Crow, *the 5th man wasn't present at the killing but is the one who put the others up to it. And this movie's "Top Dollar" type is none other than Robert Quarry, in his final film for AIP (the plan for him to replace Vincent Price never really worked out). He's only in a few scenes, but he's as delightful as always, and also a bit admirable - at one point he admonishes his racist girlfriend for being ignorant."*

Reflection: In case you've forgotten, until 1968, zombies in movies were almost exclusively the product of voodoo, but *Night of the Living Dead* was such a giant success that its version of flesh-eating undead became the norm. So voodoo zombie movies became few and far between, which is a shame but can at least make us appreciate the rare ones that go back to the original form. This was 1973 so it's not AS novel as it might have been in the post-*Dawn/Day of the Dead* world, but it makes up for it by being part of the (also sadly limited) run of "Blaxploitation" horror films that includes *Blacula* and *Abby* (aka "Black Exorcist"). So of the Venn diagram of the above, you get this one film in its center, which means that even if it sucked it'd be worth a look.

Luckily, apart from its frustratingly un-complicated plot (Sugar's plan has exactly zero hiccups along the way) and the expected dated elements, this is a solid little gem of a film. And even if you don't enjoy it, you'll have to agree that the theme song (*"She do voodoo! Supernatural voo-doo wo-man!"*) is fantastic, and I bow to whoever made the call to make sure it was used twice so we can love it all over again. You should also enjoy the work of Sugar herself, actress Marki Bey, who is every bit as lovely and awesome as Pam Grier (who was in the similarly voodoo-charged *Blacula* sequel) yet never really had much of a career in movies. But apparently her and her husband now operate murder mystery cruises right here in LA, so if that's still the case I must check one out.

MOVIE #323 – NOVEMBER 19th

THE EARTH DIES SCREAMING (1965)
Dir: Terence Fisher
HMAD Review Date: May 31, 2008 (DVD)
Genre: Post-Apocalyptic, Zombie
Available from Fox

Synopsis Based on Fading Memory: After just about everyone on Earth is wiped out, a few survivors gather in a hotel to barricade themselves against the robot-zombie things that are trying to finish the job.

Review excerpt:
"The opening scene is fantastic, as we see the immediate results of the virus that has killed everyone. A guy driving a car dies and the car instantly beelines for a brick wall, a train conductor dies and the train smashes off the rails; a pilot dies and the plane suffers a low-budget plane crash (it goes behind some trees and then we see some smoke); etc. But just when you think that perhaps the virus is limited to killing only folks who are operating transportation vehicles, a few Brits in traditional bowler hats suddenly drop dead for good measure. If they chose to pad out the running time by just displaying an endless succession of folks dropping dead, I would fully endorse the decision."

Reflection: One thing that drove me nuts about *The Stand* is that you'd see corpses in car washes and things like that – the virus was a slow acting one, not something that killed you instantly, so why would someone in such an advanced stage of the disease think about washing their goddamn car? Another issue I have with post-apocalyptic movies (or shows, like *Walking Dead*) is that the number of zombies doesn't seem to match up; there should be way more than we see (or way more survivors). I know budgetary limitations are to blame there (not sure about the former, just a total lack of logical thinking I guess), but it always takes me out of the reality of the situation.

So what I liked about this movie – BESIDES the fact that it came before *Night of the Living Dead* and thus deserves a little more credit for its influence on the sub-genre – is that it solved both problems for me. The streets are littered with corpses, and the scene I described in the excerpt shows how an instant-acting virus can cause massive chaos, while also showing smaller scenarios where the characters' deaths don't really affect anything around them. It's just really well thought out, is what I'm saying, and I wish more movies would follow its lead – ironic considering it's one of the first of this type and thus you'd expect people to be ripping it off anyway.

MOVIE #324 – NOVEMBER 20th

DEAD MEAT (2004)
Dir: Conor McMahon
HMAD Review Date: February 22, 2010 (DVD)
Genre: Zombie
Available from Fangoria/Virgil Films

Synopsis Based on Fading Memory: Mad cow disease (remember that?) causes a zombie outbreak!

Review excerpt:
"...it's not a comedy, which was nice. I heard that the film was comparable to Evil Dead 2 and Re-Animator, *but I didn't find it particularly funny, or even really trying to be. The odd gags here and there (shoe through the eye) are of course worth a chuckle, and since the cause of the zombie virus is mad cow disease, you can probably guess what sort of non-human zombie the heroes have to eventually fight, but the tone is hardly an all-out comedy. The score is rather Carpenter-y at times (i.e. foreboding), and unlike the usual "zom-com", the human characters aren't dealing with any other crisis in their lives, thus negating most of the humor potential anyway. The funniest bit in the film has to be when they think a woman has turned, simply because she's not particularly attractive to look at. Heh. But again, a few funny moments do not make it a funny movie; it's all about the overall tone."*

Reflection: A couple years ago, I took a freelance job that had me helping to promote a series of films that Fangoria had acquired. Unfortunately, I never got to see any of the movies before signing on the dotted line; I assumed they were on the level of this and the Fangoria Frightfest series from 2009 (which offered a few titles that ended up in this book) and figured it was a safe bet. Alas, that was not the case; a couple of them were OK, but none of them truly impressed me like the films from their previous series had. Thankfully most fans agreed, and the offshoot didn't last long, sparing me from having to spend any more time making them sound good.

The thing that really appealed to me about this one over a lot of other zombie movies is that it lacked evil humans; zombies were the only real threat here for a change. I guess because *Dawn of the Dead* is such a masterpiece of the sub-genre everyone feels they need to emulate it by giving the heroes something besides zombies to worry about during the 3rd act, but while it's a perfectly logical turn of events (there WILL be opportunists in the eventual zombie outbreak, make no mistake!), I don't think it has to happen EVERY TIME. Certainly the threat of an undead flesh eater is enough to make the film terrifying, so adding another villain to the mix (particularly undeveloped ones, as they often are) is not only overkill, it's distracting. And tiresome. Such a plot point should be the exception, not the rule, and I will forever champion the zombie films made by people who trust that their snarling, drooling, undead hordes will be enough of an antagonist.

MOVIE #325 – NOVEMBER 21st

COCKNEYS VS. ZOMBIES (2012)
Dir: Matthias Hoene
HMAD Review Date: September 23, 2012 (Streaming)
Genre: Comedic, Zombie
Available from Scream Factory

Synopsis Based on Fading Memory: A group of would-be bank robbers are prevented from escaping with their loot thanks to - you guessed it - a zombie outbreak.

Review excerpt:
"The movie provides a terrific B-story: the residents of a nursing home (the main characters' granddad lives there) fending off the undead in their own way. Led by the great Alan Ford (who is backed up by the always awesome Honor Blackman), this scenario could almost be its own movie, as they have different weaponry at their disposal, some cheap but funny gags about senility and the like, and a scene 56,797 zombie movies into the making: a slow zombie "chasing" a guy with a walker. I'm sure the gag has been done elsewhere, but it doesn't make it any less funny to see all these quick cut close-ups that make it look like an exciting chase, only for a wide shot to reveal how slow and un-scary it is. It's a terrific gag. I also loved the old guy who thought they were up against *vampires*, and thus advised that they needed "garlic, sunlight, holy water, and Christopher Lee."

Reflection: This was a Fantastic Fest selection that I had to watch via online screener, because my time at FF was brief (as always) and I couldn't make any of its screenings. And that's a damn shame, because this is a terrific, crowd-pleasing movie... and I've been by myself every time I've seen it. I usually dislike criminal characters that are supposed to be our heroes (with some obvious exceptions, like *From Dusk Till Dawn's* Seth Gecko), but these guys are kind of bad at bank-robbing, not professional, career criminals – and when you find out WHY they want the money, it actually just makes them even more endearing than most regular heroes in these things. Incidentally, I saw another British zom-com with a similar plot called *Gangsters, Guns, and Zombies*, and I thoroughly disliked it, so kudos to Hoene and writer James Moran (a dependable screenwriter – he also wrote *Severance* and the solid thriller *Tower Block*) for proving that there was merit to the scenario.

It was also one of the first new movies to be released on the Scream Factory label, which usually catered to '70s/'80s fare from Carpenter, Craven, Gordon, etc. They release modern stuff a lot more often now (thanks to partnerships with IFC and Chiller), but at the time (2013) it was a great way for the film to get noticed, as Scream Factory's line is of much interest to horror fans (they are to us as Criterion is to cinema snobs) and the fact that they chose it to join so many of our childhood faves was a big deal. Due to the glut of zombie movies post-*Walking Dead* and *Zombieland*, there were probably a number of solid gems that fell through the cracks due to not having a visibility boost like that. Good on you, Scream Factory!

MOVIE #326 – NOVEMBER 22nd

WARLOCK MOON (1973)
Dir: Bill Herbert
HMAD Review Date: April 26, 2012 (DVD)
Genre: Cannibal, Cult
Available from Shriek Show

Synopsis Based on Fading Memory: A couple goes to a rundown spa in the middle of nowhere and run afoul of... well, just about everything.

Review excerpt:
"...a fun little B-movie; the sort of thing I'd be delighted to find on a budget pack but probably wouldn't want to buy on a dedicated release for more than a couple bucks. It's slowly paced and riddled with plot holes, but it's got a breezy charm that so many movies lack, and it more than makes up for its problems. You also can't dismiss a movie that combines ghosts, witchcraft, AND cannibalism, plus a random ax-wielding mute (who looks like Rob Zombie!) for good measure. Even better, it actually gels together, more or less – it doesn't seem like writer/director Bill Herbert is just making things up as he goes along, or pulling a Pieces and inserting elements into his movie at random because a producer wants it in there."

Reflection: In the last year or so of HMAD, I began to particularly enjoy the movies where the phrase "Everything but the kitchen sink" might apply. Suffering through so many anonymous slashers, zombie movies, and *Paranormal Activity* rip-offs, it would be a relief when a movie – even if it wasn't particularly great – demanded my full attention just to keep up with their labyrinthine plots and out-of-nowhere twists. This one stuck out as particularly memorable because it had like five different sub-genres, and the (relative) genius of the script is that it all has a payoff, plus successfully distracted me away from what would be an otherwise obvious twist.

Oh, if you get the DVD, I implore you to listen to the commentary for a fun theory as to who Bill Herbert actually is (since "Bill Herbert" never made another film, the possibility that the name is a fake one is strong). Or I guess just read my full review, because it explains it. It's a director whose new films I used to be excited about since he made a few I really liked in the late '90s and early '00s. Alas, he hit a slump that he has yet to recover from, and I after a couple of duds I realized his good films were probably due to him having a solid script to work from. Incidentally, if Bill Herbert IS this same man, this would be the only feature script credited to him. Maybe he should have written more often!

MOVIE #327 – NOVEMBER 23rd

BURIAL GROUND: THE NIGHTS OF TERROR (1981)
Dir: Andrea Bianchi
HMAD Review Date: July 2, 2010 (DVD)
Genre: Zombie
Available from Image Entertainment

Synopsis Based on Fading Memory: Zombies attack a big mansion. That's not me being glib, that's pretty much all there is to the movie.

Review excerpt:
"The great thing about the movie is that it has almost no discernible plot or even three-act structure. The zombies are unleashed in the first 15 minutes, and after a series of attacks in various areas on the mansion grounds, our heroes all band together and enter the mansion itself. The rest of the movie is just the zombies trying to get in, and succeeding. So it's sort of like Night of the Living Dead, *except without the escape attempt, cutaway to the "situation elsewhere" (on TV or not) or group conflict of any sort.*

It's also got some great deaths. As with most Italians, these people have no skeletons, so when a zombie hooks a sickle around the back of someone's head and pulls, the head slices off like butter. Speaking of the sickle, there's a hilarious bit where the zombies all grab tools, sort of like a scene in an old Universal monster movie with everyone grabbing a torch before heading off to "rah rah rah" their way over to the monster's hideout. We don't get to see them USE the tools all that much, but there's enough carnage to make up for it."

Reflection: In my review I claimed that this "may be the definitive batshit Italian zombie movie.", and in the nearly six years it's been since I wrote that, I can't think of anything I've seen that could challenge it. I mean, you have a mom regretting that she refused to let her son feel her up (he pouts, storms off alone, and is killed by a zombie as a result), which would be weird enough, but in this case the "kid" is played by an adult dwarf, making it even more bizarre. Furthermore, said adult dwarf playing a little kid with an Oedipal complex is dubbed by a different kid with an unusually high voice, so now we're in "holy shit" territory. AND THEN, his actual dialogue – lines like "Mommy, this cloth smells of death!" - would be ridiculous even if spoken by an average looking, totally normal guy, instead of an adult dwarf playing a little kid with an Oedipal complex and a strange high pitched voice.

So, yeah, it's the definitive batshit Italian zombie movie, and if you know of a better example, I don't know if I could handle it. I've never actually seen it theatrically or with a crowd despite several chances, and I think I am subconsciously afraid of doing so. I have a kind of obnoxious/loud laugh (several friends have told me after local screenings that they didn't realize I was there as well until they heard me laughing) and I think this one would have me guffawing far too frequently. I fear I'd ruin it for someone, and I wouldn't want to do that.

MOVIE #328 – NOVEMBER 24th

GEORGE'S INTERVENTION (2009)
Dir: J.T. Seaton
HMAD Review Date: December 10, 2012 (DVD)
Genre: Comedic, Zombie
Available from Vicious Circle Films

Synopsis Based on Fading Memory: George's friends and loved ones stage an intervention for him to get him to stop eating people. Since he's a zombie it's kind of a dick thing to ask, really.

Review excerpt:
"Interestingly, I was reminded of the early (read: watchable) films of Kevin Smith, with love triangles and heart to hearts providing the bulk of the topics of discussion. George's ex is among the folks in the intervention, and she has brought her new fella along, so there's tension there, and even the endless series of latecomers and randoms sort of provide the same narrative function that the customers at the Quick Stop did in Clerks: distractions and inadvertent insight to the problems at hand. Not only did it work for the movie (I genuinely liked just about everyone, even the dick new boyfriend had some merit), but it was nice to remember back when Smith knew/worked within his limitations and played to his strengths, instead of attempting things best left to those who know what the fuck they are doing and aren't perpetually stoned."

Reflection: When I started writing this book, Kevin Smith was said to be retiring. Now, two years later (yikes) he's not only still making movies, but they're almost all genre efforts, something I never could have predicted in the '90s when he was making little comedies. Like many people my age, I outgrew Smith a while back, and can't even really enjoy the movies I used to like with the exception of Clerks. I think that movie holds up, and even though I haven't really liked anything he's made in years, Clerks II probably came closest to enjoyable, so I'll probably still see Clerks III on opening weekend.

So it's kinda fun that we've come full circle, with this being one of a couple Kevin Smith-esque horror-comedies I saw before Smith cut out the middle man and just started making them himself. And since he's too stoned all of the time to deliver on the talent he used to display, it's nice to see people who were inspired by his early work have picked up the torch – and focused on the GOOD elements of Smith's films, instead of populating their films with Randall-esque assholes and far too many movie references. And now that Smith is making them himself, it's even easier to see how far he's fallen, as the wannabe movies actually work better than his own. Not that I think he'd care if he noticed.

MOVIE #329 – NOVEMBER 25th

SEVERED: FOREST OF THE DEAD (2005)
Dir: Carl Bessai
HMAD Review Date: February 15, 2010 (DVD)
Genre: Zombie
Available from Screen Media

Synopsis Based on Fading Memory: Loggers and tree huggers are forced to unite in order to survive a zombie outbreak that they inadvertently caused.

Review excerpt:
"...it's well paced; the zombies show up early on, and the next 50 minutes or so is pretty much a nonstop dart from one locale to another, with our core cast dropping like flies. And I liked that the inherent conflict actually made sense for once, and without clear cut villainy on one side. Basically we have environmentalists and loggers having to team up to escape, as opposed to say, a band of criminals and some cops, or just some complete asshole like Cooper in NOTLD. By leaving the guy responsible (who, again, isn't exactly a typical villain) out of the chaos, we don't automatically side with one side or the other (and, to be fair, the environmentalists are also to blame, as their tree spikes caused the injury that allowed the infected sap to enter the guy's bloodstream). It's actually kind of touching near the end when one of the enviro-folks breaks down when one of the loggers is killed, as they had realistically bonded over the course of the film."

Reflection: For some reason I distinctly remember watching a chunk of this movie at an oil change place. I had just gotten the portable DVD player for Christmas so for a while I was taking it with me when I knew I'd have to be killing time somewhere, getting a jump on HMAD-ing instead of doing something more ultimately useful, like reading a book or taking a walk. It was also great for airplanes – if I couldn't fall asleep, watching the day's movie on the redeye (once it was after midnight!) when going home to visit my family was a godsend. But using it is definitely one thing I don't miss about the site, having to watch a potentially cool movie in less than ideal settings because it was the only time I could. The player is now in my closet and hasn't been touched in years (I DO read books – on my Kindle – when I go to the oil change place or fly now, thank you very much), though I assume it'll come in handy again when my son is old enough to watch DVDs.

Anyway, I figured this would be an OK movie to watch on a portable player while waiting to decline a "radiator flush" or whatever other made-up car services the oil change guy would try to sell me, but it's actually one of the better straightforward zombie films from the period. *Shaun of the Dead*'s popularity resulted in a lot of zom-coms, and *28 Days Later's* success resulted in a lot of horrible looking zombie films shot on consumer grade cameras, but this one looks good and doesn't have any gimmicks or high concept nonsense dragging it down like the *Resident Evil* films. It's just a zombie movie, and sometimes that's all you want. Bonus points for including an enviro-message but not getting too preachy about it – this isn't Steven Seagal in *On Undeadly Ground*.

(I must admit, I would watch the shit out of that movie.)

MOVIE #330 – NOVEMBER 26th

INSANITARIUM (2008)
Dir: Jeff Buhler
HMAD Review Date: July 19, 2008 (DVD)
Genre: Cannibal, Mad Scientist
Available from Sony Pictures Home Entertainment

Synopsis Based on Fading Memory: A guy gets himself thrown into a sanitarium in order to rescue his sister, but the staff's cannibalistic ways prove to be a hurdle.

Review excerpt:
"...the gore is great. Not *Wrong Turn 2* great (the kills here are sort of standard), but there's a quantity over quality sense to it. Arms torn off, knives through the mouth, lots and lots of blood... by the end of the film, both our heroes are covered in it, as are most of the walls and floors that surround them. Keep in mind, the setting is the usual movie sanitarium, all white and sterile, so it's a nice little treat to see it all mangled and gory by the end."

Reflection: I always get this movie confused with the same year's *Asylum*, which also had some very pretty young people going up against a badass character actor (Peter Stormare here, Mark Rolston there). But THAT movie stinks (a shame, since it's from the late David R. Ellis, whose movies I usually quite liked) and THIS one's a lot of fun. There aren't many movies I would comfortably dub a "splatter flick" in the modern world; the reliance on CGI blood these days almost cancels out the sub-genre's existence – so when I saw one that did it right and kept the blood coming, I'd easily overlook its weak spots (such as a rather dull 2nd act here). The actors and set are drenched in Karo by the end, and that's something we should applaud.

Buhler also wrote *Midnight Meat Train*, but hasn't done much since (the bungled releases of these two films probably didn't help). According to the IMDb he's involved with a few remakes no one is really asking for (*The Grudge*, *Pet Sematary*, and *Jacob's Ladder*), but those are all the sort of movies that seem to be always in development, so who knows if they'll get made or if he'll still be involved with them if they are. Personally I hope he has another nutty original like this in his drawer somewhere that can get made. I'm not anti-remake, but why is a guy who wrote two splatter heavy movies wasting his time on the THIRD goddamn *Grudge* remake?

MOVIE #331 – NOVEMBER 27th

DOGHOUSE (2009)
Dir: Jake West
HMAD Review Date: November 6, 2011 (DVD)
Genre: Zombie
Available from MPI Home Video

Synopsis Based on Fading Memory: A group of pals looking to cheer up their recently divorced pal take him to a town that's rich with single females. Unfortunately, those ladies have recently become zombies.

Review excerpt:
"...just because the guys don't start getting picked off one by one until the third act doesn't mean the movie lacks action. Indeed, they're only in the town for about five minutes of screen time before the first attack, and the pace rarely lets up from that point on. It's just not body count action – the group runs, gets split up, and then each group has their own little mini-adventures as they attempt to reunite and escape. Even better, there's not a single anonymous zombie in the movie – they're all quite distinct and memorable. It goes against Darabont's philosophy regarding "hero" zombies (the one I usually agree with), but it works here, given both the fact that this is a comedy after all (unlike Walking Dead, *which uses humor so sparingly that it's almost distracting when they bother to include it), and the back-story that explains how they turned in the first place."*

Reflection: This review kind of makes me sad in retrospect, because it alludes to Frank Darabont's role on *The Walking Dead*, and made me think of some of the ideas he had for the show that were vetoed by the network. My favorite was a "spinoff" episode about a never before seen survivor, trying to make his way through the world in his own way, with his own people, and then tragically ending with him becoming one of the hundreds of random zombies we've seen Rick Grimes kill – the idea was that each of those things was a person at some point, not just some anonymous thing that came from nowhere. Alas, the network said "no way". Maybe Darabont would have run the show into the ground by now (I admit it didn't seem to be the best fit for his abilities, though the show hardly did a 180 with its new showrunners – it still suffers from the same pacing issues and invokes too much of Robert Kirkman's awful dialogue from the comic), but at least he was WORKING consistently. Since being fired he's done another quickly forgotten show (*Mob City*) and ALMOST directed a *Snow White and the Huntsman* sequel. Granted, he's only made great stuff as a director when working off of a Stephen King story, but it still seems there is a better use for him than what we're getting.

Anyway, I bring him up because he also disliked when zombies stood out too much: clown zombie, Hare Krishna zombie, etc. And I tend to agree with that idea for the most part, but the cool thing about *Doghouse* is that it goes to the extreme: each zombie we see is a former resident of this one isolated town, allowing West to make them distinct. There are no "zombie extras" in the credits, as they all have an identifying trait (and in some cases, mini arcs), and their bite doesn't turn someone into a zombie, limiting their number and adding to the other thing to make this an anomaly in zombie cinema. It's this element that made it far more memorable than I would have assumed (West's other films are of much less merit), as did the endearing camaraderie among the male heroes (swap the zombies for aliens and the movie is basically *At World's End*, but without 30 minutes of the main guy being hated by the others. Also, this movie is four years older, so in the words of the internet: FIRST!). The film's slightly chauvinistic bent might be a turn off, but if you stick with it you'll discover that the guys learn to appreciate their spouses, which is nice.

MOVIE #332 – NOVEMBER 28th

RAW MEAT (aka DEATH LINE) (1973)
Dir: Gary Sherman
HMAD Review Date: August 28, 2007 (DVD)
Genre: Cannibal
Available from MGM

Synopsis Based on Fading Memory: A scary looking dude who lives in the subway occasionally captures and eats people that ride said subway. Donald Pleasence is the cop "trying" to stop him.

Review excerpt:
"Pleasence is an absolute delight in this one. He's not as batshit insane as usual; instead he just seems sort of drunk throughout the movie. He randomly throws darts around, obsesses about tea (he IS British), makes inappropriate jokes, etc. There's a scene late in the film where he just sort of argues with a bartender while his partner plays pinball that had me in stitches. As for Christopher Lee, I am at a loss to explain his appearance here. He almost literally appears out of thin air in the middle of a scene, has a little face-off with Donald, and then is never seen or spoken of again. I suspect he happened by the set one day and they quickly threw him in there and had him just say whatever came to his head (Donald's reaction to his appearance certainly seems to support this theory)."

Reflection: The original idea for my screening series at the New Beverly was to show movies like *Raw Meat*, which I discovered thanks to writing the site and may not have seen otherwise. It was I think the 3rd or 4th one I did, and I hoped future screenings would follow suit, with screenings of movies that probably ended up in this book. Unfortunately, prints of such "discoveries" proved to be hard to come by, and eventually it was just a "Horror sequels from the '80s and '90s" screening series, as those prints were easier to find and also proved to be more popular. This meant I was occasionally hosting movies I didn't even like very much (such as *Friday the 13th part VII*, which I only wanted to do because I had seen the others thanks to revival screenings, and wanted to finish the series off), just to keep the series going while I continued to hope/pray that a print of *Cathy's Curse* or whatever would turn up in time for the next one. Alas, that never happened, and now the series is over, but at least I can cheer up by remembering that I DID get to introduce a few horror fans to this wonderful little gem.

Pointless side note – I'm Facebook friends with Gary Sherman from the time I tried to get him out to the *Raw Meat* screening. Alas, he doesn't live in LA, so it never happened, but at least I still get to be amused by seeing him pop up in my buddy list from time to time, next to random high school pals and my sister. Someday I'll have the courage to ask him about *Lisa*, his serial killer thriller that I used to watch over and over because I was smitten with the actress playing the title character. I will *not* ask about *Poltergeist III*.

HMAD Fun Fact: Both solo and with Phil Blankenship, I hosted 37 midnight screenings at the New Beverly for Horror Movie A Day. More than twenty of those had special guests from the film for Q&A, and I am proud to say HMAD presented the first legal showing of the Halloween 6 *"Producer's Cut", which played a small part in that film's eventual official release (via the boxed set from Scream Factory and Anchor Bay). It was also that version's ONLY public showing on 35mm, as far as I know.*

MOVIE #333 – NOVEMBER 29th

EXIT HUMANITY (2011)
Dir: John Geddes
HMAD Review Date: October 16, 2011 (Festival screening)
Genre: Zombie
Available from The Collective

Synopsis Based on Fading Memory: It's post-Civil War America, and a man is on a quest to spread his son's ashes while also trying to survive the cold AND a zombie outbreak.

Review excerpt:
"I liked that the movie had a sort of tragic journey built into its narrative, something that you don't often see in a zombie movie (where our heroes are usually just trying to escape to some promised safe area). Hero Mark Gibson loses his son early on, and thus commits to fulfilling the boy's promise to be taken to a waterfall that Gibson had come across during the war and had turned into his metaphorical "happy place" (my words, not theirs). Along the way he encounters the rest of the cast, but it's essentially a one man show for its first 30 minutes or so, which I also dug."

Reflection: It's not too uncommon to see zombies in a World War II setting; Nazi Zombies are of course a familiar trope, and the zombie mini-games in the *Call of Duty* franchise began with the WWII-set *World at War* entry. And we've seen a few about modern conflicts, like the terrible *Osombie*. But for some reason, the other wars are largely left out – *Deathdream* is the only major one I can recall involving Vietnam, and it barely even counts since it's not IN Vietnam and the (one) zombie displays vampire-esque tendencies. And Christ, there are barely any WWI films PERIOD, let alone something as niche as one with zombies.

As for the Civil War, there's *Grey Knight,* and this. And I've never seen *Grey Knight*, so I recommend this one if you, like me, are interested in seeing how our undead monsters fare in a war setting. Actually this is post-Civil War, but the toll it took on the nation hangs heavily over the entire thing, and the requisite human villain is a Confederate General (played by Bill Moseley!) who apparently hadn't gotten the message that the war had ended. It's a pretty bleak movie, seemingly taking cues from the more downer elements of *Walking Dead*, but it just makes those rare triumphant moments play that much better.

MOVIE #334 – NOVEMBER 30th

A CADAVER CHRISTMAS (2012)
Dir: Joe Zerull
HMAD Review Date: December 24, 2012 (DVD)
Genre: Comedic, Zombie
Available from Level 33 Entertainment

Synopsis Based on Fading Memory: A janitor and some other oddball types band together to stop a zombie outbreak at a university.

Review excerpt:
"Once it starts to click (right around the hilarious "Follow me!" gag involving a lengthy elevator wait), it's a pretty fun little flick, with lots of splatter and an admirable approach to killing people off. I honestly figured this would be one of those movies where almost none of the leads die, because if someone's dead they can't add much to the comedy, but they pull off two pretty great surprises in that department, including one around the halfway point or so. And kudos to lead actor Dan Hale (who also produced, and gives himself at least four on-screen credits for doing so, in case you miss one I guess) for playing the entire film with blood on his face. And I'm not exaggerating - the only time we see him without it is in the few pre-zombie flashbacks; he gets covered in it pretty quickly after they appear and never finds the time to wash his face throughout the rest of the narrative. I once had some of that shit on for like an hour or so and it was driving me insane - he had to do it for weeks."

Reflection: If not for the holiday setting, I would have put this in July with the other "true" indie movies. Like many of those, this had a lengthy production (three separate shooting periods over a year!), but with the added hurdle of having a narrative that plays out in one night. Maintaining continuity in ANY feature is hard (look at the list of continuity errors from any Spielberg movie – it's always pretty long, and that's in a *SPIELBERG* movie), so to have to worry about it on a very small budget indie on a movie where everything is supposed to occur over the span of a few hours is a Herculean task. Luckily, they mostly pull it off, and while the humor is hit or miss (the acting will take some getting used to), it's not hard to be won over by the sheer energy that these guys bring to the proceedings. And even though it's a comedy it's actually got a pretty cool backstory for the zombie outbreak, so points for that.

And thus ends zombie/cannibal month, so you're no doubt sick of seeing people get eaten. I did my best to avoid any zombie movies next month (I had no way to "bridge" the two themes like usual, and you'll soon see why), though a few snuck in due to lack of options. I find that unlike slashers, monster movies, etc., it's tough to watch zombie films back to back without getting overloaded with *déjà vu*. I mean, just look how many times I namechecked *NOTLD, Shaun of the Dead*, or *Walking Dead* in the above 30 entries – it's a fittingly cannibalistic sub-genre. So fear not – there's a ton of variety ahead!

DECEMBER – HORROR AROUND THE WORLD

ARTIST: JB SAPIENZA

Ah, the holiday season. I go back to Massachusetts for a week every year to visit family (not on Christmas itself – it's too expensive to travel then, plus it's too fun to be back in LA on Christmas week, as there's zero traffic), and when I was doing HMAD, it'd actually be a timely part of my packing process to find movies I could watch during those six or seven days. They had to be movies without bonus features, that were short, and that were likely to not be very good since I'd likely have to watch them in chunks in between visits to Grandma. Oh and movies that were full frame were preferable since I'd be watching them on my tiny portable or my mom's not-much-larger old-school CRT TV. This kind of narrowed down my options and went against the point of the site (to find new gems), but I refused to ever take a "break", dammit!

Don't worry - I'm not going to ask you to watch 31 such films this month, especially since I kind of already did that in August anyway. No, in the spirit of the tradition of traveling at this time of the year, I've gone around and found 31 movies from 31 different parts of the globe! No country is repeated! Some are in English, some aren't, and some were chosen simply because they were the only option (you'd be surprised how many countries seemingly produce no horror films - thanks for nothing, Uzbekistan!). For those latter ones I apologize, but hey – this site was founded on some restrictive rules, so it's only fitting that the book boxes you in, too. But so what if they're not all perfect? Get a little worldly culture via horror flicks!

That said, some are indispensable, must-see movies that would have been in the book no matter what the themes were. And luckily, if you've gotten this far I know you can read (though I *did* toy with the idea of doing an audiobook), so there's no excuse to miss...

MOVIE #335 – DECEMBER 1st

RABIES [KALEVET] (2010)
Dir: Aharon Keshales, Navot Papushado
HMAD Review Date: February 26, 2012 (DVD)
Genre: Thriller
Country: Israel
Available from Image Entertainment

Synopsis Based on Fading Memory: A group of teens enter the woods, and you'll never guess what happens next! I'm not being sarcastic; you can't possibly know where it will go from there, and I wouldn't dream of spoiling it.

Review excerpt:
"I won't go into any further plot explanation, other than to hint that it's more Fargo *than* Friday the 13th, *but still very rooted in the horror genre. The twists and turns that the movie takes are impossible to predict too far out; even when I started getting a handle on how writer/directors Aharon Keshales and Navot Papushado were planning on carrying out their film, I was still going "Oh no, shit!" every few minutes. And they deftly blend their horror with some well-placed humor (of the dark variety) and even some minor pathos near the end; they are just as good as keeping you guessing with your emotions as they are with the plot itself. No small feat, that."*

Reflection: If I had another Israeli horror movie to offer, this might have ended up in October's horror-lite lineup. But it's also a perfect candidate for the first movie for this month's theme, which celebrates terror from around the globe, as this was Israel's first ever horror film (!). It's also the debut from Keshales and Papushado, who have since become more prominent in the genre thanks to their follow-up film *Big Bad Wolves* (which got a huge boost from Quentin Tarantino) and a segment in *ABCs of Death 2*. But in my opinion this remains their finest achievement, which starts off in a manner that will have you thinking it's a slasher movie, only to - well, no. I won't go any further. I went in pretty blind, and you should, too, for maximum enjoyment.

And it's easier to go in blind to foreign films, which is another reason that I find myself more excited to watch an imported movie than a domestic one nowadays. I don't look down on the US genre market by any means, but more often than not, the new filmmakers who excite us horror fans tend to come from somewhere beyond the US, and it's important to remember that there are other sources of fright fare beyond the UK and prime Asian territories. More than any other month this year, I hope you, dear reader, are trying your best to see most, if not all, of these selections, because even if you don't walk away as engrossed as I was, at least you'll know you got to see how 31 different nations tackle our favorite genre.

MOVIE #336 – DECEMBER 2nd

THE LOVED ONES (2009)
Dir: Sean Byrne
HMAD Review Date: November 5, 2009 (DVD)
Genre: Survival
Country: Australia
Available from Paramount

Synopsis Based on Fading Memory: A teenaged girl and her father go to extreme lengths to secure a perfect prom date for the former.

Review excerpt:
"I enjoy seeing a better version of an existing story, and in that department, The Loved Ones *delivers. The tone and everything else are different, but in terms of a one-line synopsis, the film is very similar to a film called* Otis, *and at first I worried that I would feel the same way about this one (i.e. that I really wouldn't like it at all). But like I said, they only share that base plotline, and as* Loved Ones *went on I found myself thinking less and less of that other film (and others it reminded me of); it's interesting how it starts out on familiar ground and eventually finds its own voice."*

Reflection: This movie finally came out almost three years after I reviewed it, at which point my memories had mostly faded (as there had been nearly 1000 movies seen since). This was a slight issue, because I was asked to host a sold-out screening at the Mann's Chinese to promote its long-awaited release, and I was afraid that the film wouldn't be as good as I remembered. Or worse, that I'd fall asleep and not be able to conduct a very good post-movie Q&A, as my questions would be based off my vague memories or what little bit I saw before nodding off ("Tell me about that opening shot."). Luckily, it *was* as good as I remembered; it's a damn shame the movie was met with such a lackluster fate (a few midnight screenings was the extent of its theatrical release here), but Byrne's new film, *Devil's Candy*, has been met with nothing but raves after a couple of festival appearances, so he seems to be doing just fine.

Still, the long delay couldn't have been fun for anyone involved, and it's for that reason that I chose it over the other Australian films I had to choose from. As I mentioned earlier, Australia is a very reliable source of genre fare, but for whatever reason they just don't get as much attention as they deserve from US fans. And many of the others' time have come and gone, so I went with this in the hopes that some renewed interest can do some good for some of Byrne's fellow

Aussie filmmakers who might be stuck in the same boat he was, and that eventually such gems won't take three years for US distributors to pick them up and put them out.

HMAD Fun Fact: HMAD is the reason I started drinking coffee again! I had pretty much quit it when I moved to LA (no Dunkin' Donuts at the time, and I also had some stomach issues that were attributed to the drink), but I started needing a "fix" when attending (and later hosting!) midnight screenings for the site, to make sure I stayed awake (success rate: 50%). Now I'm back to having it every day. You're welcome, local coffee shops.

MOVIE #337 – DECEMBER 3rd

THE WIG [GABAL] (2005)
Dir: Shin-yeon Won
HMAD Review Date: September 11, 2008 (DVD)
Genre: Supernatural
Country: South Korea
Available from CJ Entertainment

Synopsis Based on Fading Memory: A woman gets a haunted wig.

Review excerpt:
"Wisely avoiding having a goddamn hairpiece running amok and killing folks, it's actually a borderline metaphor for a woman losing her identity. I mean, yeah, the wig IS haunted and thus there are a few scare scenes that more or less revolve around strands of hair moving around, but it's still nowhere near as schlocky or even "fun" as I thought it would be. The body count is one of the lowest in ages too, I think the total number of deaths in the film is like, three. However, those rare kill scenes are pretty damn great, particularly a car crash about halfway through that would fit right at home in one of the *Final Destination* movies."

Reflection: It's kind of funny that the easy way to mock a lot of Asian horror is to have a ghostly girl with long hair covering her face, and yet it took about a decade of consistent entries in this peculiar sub-genre for someone to just go all-out and make a movie where the hair itself is the source of the scares (in fact, on the IMDb the movie is listed under "Scary Hair"). It's actually not a goofy movie at all, but man, if I were to write up those "Fading Memory" synopses for all 2500 movies I reviewed, and then sort them by how stupid they must sound, I imagine this one would be near the top.

You might notice the date I watched the movie; I was fortunate enough not to know anyone who was hurt or killed on 9/11, but I, like anyone with a soul, still felt crushed about the events of that day, and I always felt a bit guilty watching my daily movie on those six anniversaries that occurred during the site's run. Especially when doing my daily "HMAD Today is..." Tweet, because it would almost always break up a string of poignant "Never Forget" messages. Luckily (for lack of a better word), *The Wig* is actually kind of sad and not just about killing people left and right, i.e. making death into something trivial, but my randomized selections didn't always turn out that way. Horror can be cathartic under the right conditions, but it can just as easily make you feel worse about someone or something tragic – I truly hope I haven't inadvertently drudged up any painful memories for someone who picked one of these selections at random. I've tried to avoid too many spoilers or even plot info in some cases, because I want you to go in as blind as I did for 99% of these movies, but I keep forgetting that so far I've been pretty lucky when it comes to seeing a horror movie (or any movie really) that draws uncomfortable parallels to my own personal tragedies. Knock on wood that I haven't inadvertently bummed anyone out!

MOVIE #338 – DECEMBER 4th

NIGHT DRIVE (2010)
Dir: Justin Head
HMAD Review Date: December 5, 2012 (DVD)
Genre: Survival
Country: South Africa
Available from Osiris

Synopsis Based on Fading Memory: While on a tour of the African safari, a motley group of tourists find themselves hunted by evil poachers and the mysterious Hyena Man.

Review excerpt:
"Part of what I liked was that there was a good variety to the group, and they were actually fairly interesting to boot. It would never be mistaken for a character study, but I tend to like the "motley crew" horror films more than the "group of five friends" ones, as it lends itself to natural discussion of their backstories and basic character traits (close friends don't usually tell one another what they do for a living), and also makes more sense when tensions flare. And again, they were a mixed lot; you have an elderly couple celebrating their 50th anniversary, a young couple who just met, and a late 30s-ish couple who are having some serious problems. Then you have the game warden and his estranged son (an ex-cop who is going out to spread his mother's ashes), so there are a lot of different motives for being there, and real personalities instead of "the jock, the stoner", etc."

Reflection: This was something that I watched via screener, expecting a generic movie I didn't have to give 100% of my attention, and was pleasantly surprised to discover was a legitimately solid survival thriller. Granted, it didn't have much competition for inclusion in this particular section of the book (not a lot of African horror productions, period, let alone films that I've seen and liked), but this is the sort of movie I would have highlighted in another category ("Survival horror month" or something), because it got a lot of things right. Justin Head found a terrific balance between character development and action, and stages some exciting sequences during both day and night – totally well-rounded entries aren't exactly plentiful in the survival horror sub-genre.

And the villain is truly memorable; the story is kind of a *Texas Chain Saw Massacre* kind of thing, but Hyena Man is no mere Leatherface wannabe, and part of me is kind of glad this movie is so under the radar – if it was a big hit there would be crappy Hyena Man sequels by now. But in an era where filmmakers (or distributors) try to tell *us* who the next horror icon will be, it's great to see a potential one come out of nowhere.

MOVIE #339 – DECEMBER 5th

THE SUBSTITUTE (2007)
Dir: Ole Bornedal
HMAD Review Date: November 15, 2008 (DVD)
Genre: Alien, Comedic
Country: Denmark
Available from Lionsgate

Synopsis Based on Fading Memory: The substitute teacher is an alien!!!

Review excerpt:
"...what's awesome about the movie as a whole is that there is none of the usual "reveal" shit, nor does the sub even really try to hide her non-human nature. In her first meeting with the kids, she berates them, displays superhuman intelligence, acts bizarrely... I love that writer/director Ole Bornedal just got right to the goddamn point. I don't need to "learn" that she is an alien halfway through the movie; that's a plot point that would have been spoiled by any trailer or plot synopsis anyway. And this makes the lack of violence/gore even more impressive; the movie feels fast paced despite the fact that there is no action whatsoever until the final 10 minutes (and even that is hardly a big spectacle)."

Reflection: Ghost House Underground was Sony/Lionsgate's answer to After Dark, which was also put out through Lionsgate. No theatrical releases for these, but it had the same idea: put out a bunch of indie horror flicks (once again a mix of foreign and domestic titles), give them a branding that would look nice when all the discs were next to each other on the shelf, and let horror fans' inherent collectivist nature result in them buying them all rather than just the ones they wanted.

On the whole, it was a better collection than the After Darks; there were a few stinkers in it (*Trackman* comes to mind), but in addition to this and the two or three other movies from Ghost House Underground that are in this book, they also gave us the wonderfully messed up *Last House In The Woods*, which is the only film in history to make me gag. There was a second lineup a year or so later, which only had half as many titles, and then the brand disappeared forever. A shame; on average they had better picks than in the first two years of the After Dark Horrorfest, so if they followed that company's trajectory of getting better each time out, the third and fourth incarnations of Ghost House Underground could very well have had some truly remarkable films. Oh well. It was all worth it for importing this one though; the best of the bunch and, despite the language barrier, in some ways also the most accessible.

MOVIE #340 – DECEMBER 6th

JUAN OF THE DEAD (2011)
Dir: Alejandro Brugués
HMAD Review Date: September 26, 2011 (Festival screening)
Genre: Comedic, Zombie
Country: Cuba
Available from Entertainment One

Synopsis Based on Fading Memory: A lazy man inadvertently becomes a hero (and profits!) when a zombie outbreak infects Cuba.

Review excerpt:
"The fun thing about Juan is that he's not a very noble hero. When we meet him he's banging a neighbor's wife, telling a kid that his dad is a sodomite, and can't be bothered to stop his best friend from pleasuring himself while he peeps at a couple making love through a window across the way. But nothing depicts this aspect of his character better than the first big zombie scene, as he and his equally shady pals sit and listen to a neighborhood watch group discuss a recent string of stolen car stereos (one of them is to blame). Suddenly, a single zombie attack results in pretty much the entire group being decimated/turned, but rather than help, Juan just points out that now they won't be too concerned about the stolen stereos, and shrugs off the carnage as he heads back home. Thus, he's not an unlikable asshole – he's a guy who'd rather not get involved, which is a lot easier to identify with (and like)."

Reflection: I really should have rephrased the second line of that excerpt, as I made it sound like he's doing all of those things at once. If he was it'd probably be the only movie I ever recommend to anyone, ever.

Anyway, unless I have to watch one for work or something, I try to avoid anything with a "__Of The Dead" title these days, because they tend to get on my nerves more often than not, while also going out of their way to make me think of Romero (and Wright, if it's a comedic one, which was likely the case until *Walking Dead* paved the way for zombie stories to be serious again). But this was a worthy exception; Juan was a fascinating hero for this sort of thing (see excerpt) and Brugués wisely tied the film into Cuba's own history (and current climate) rather than present an anonymous story that could have been set anywhere.

This was Cuba's first horror movie in over fifty years, which by my math means it has to be the first zombie (as flesh eater) movie they made – not bad for a first try. I haven't kept up on what Cuba has been doing since with its horror productions, but hopefully they're still trying – I want to see a Cuban slasher! Regardless, I found it fascinating that I hadn't even been born the last time they had made a genre film, and when I was putting this chapter together I realized how this isn't really that rare at all. I mean, I had to stretch to find 31 countries, when there are nearly 200 of them in the world. Now, obviously not all of them have their own version of Hollywood (not expecting to find any Antarctic directors), but the availability of quality HD cameras and the plethora of streaming services looking for content means, I hope, that more people like Brugués will wake up one day and decide to make the first ____ horror film. Ten years from now, I'd like to do another version of this chapter and have 31 different countries represented. Get on that, kids!

MOVIE #341 – DECEMBER 7th

LET THE RIGHT ONE IN (2008)
Dir: Tomas Alfredson
HMAD Review Date: June 20, 2008 (Festival screening)
Genre: Vampire
Country: Sweden
Available from Magnolia Home Entertainment

Synopsis Based on Fading Memory: A lonely boy falls in love with a mysterious girl who happens to be a vampire.

Review excerpt:
"I love how quiet the movie is (something the remake will likely replace with Fall Out Boy); entire scenes go by without dialogue, or even music (that said, the sparse score is beautiful), relying on the two young actors to sell the ideas of the scene. Both actors are terrific, which helps. This also intensifies the "horror" scenes, as they are relatively shocking in many cases. I mean, the movie's ostensibly about a little girl who happens to be a vampire aiding her friend, who is being bullied by classmates. What do you think is going to happen?"

Reflection: This might be the most well-known movie in the book, and I actually tried *not* to go down this obvious route, but I honestly had nothing better for Sweden. There's another great vampire movie from there called *Frostbitten*, but I saw it a few months before I started HMAD and thus I never actually wrote a review of it. Then there's *Blood Runs Cold*, a decent slasher from a filmmaking team that also produced one of the WORST movies I watched for the site (a terrible and nihilistic piece of crap called *Madness*), but I saw it after I retired from daily viewing, so it missed the cutoff date. And whatever Bergman films I watched were even more obvious, so here we are.

I would hope to hell every one of you had seen this by now, but just in case you (literally?) live under a rock and haven't listened to every horror site, most mainstream critics, and even John Carpenter by now: WATCH THIS MOVIE. It's damn close to perfect; everything from the score to the performances to (yes) the approach to vampire lore is wonderful and unique, and while I know it has its fans, the remake (which does not have Fall Out Boy on the soundtrack, for the record) just doesn't even come close to matching this film's singular power. I was blessed to have seen this at the LA Film Festival, knowing next to nothing about it, and I knew within thirty minutes that I was seeing something special. And, believe you me, LAFF was *not* a dependable source for anything you'd be putting at the top of your "decade's best horror films" lists. This is one of the rare horror films from the past decade that I can be certain will still be watched and talked about 100 years from now.

MOVIE #342 – DECEMBER 8th

STITCHES (2012)
Dir: Conor McMahon
HMAD Review Date: March 30, 2013 (Blu-ray)
Genre: Comedic, Slasher
Country: Ireland
Available from Dark Sky Films

Synopsis Based on Fading Memory: A clown comes back from the grave to seek revenge on the now grown kids who got him killed.

Review excerpt:
"I likened the film to Dr. Giggles *on Twitter, but I was referring more to his implements and MO, not so much his dialogue and acting. As Giggles used medical instruments for each and every kill, all of the murders here are based around familiar clown tricks - when he reaches behind your ear, he doesn't pull out a quarter, but your actual ear. A guy gets a bunny pulled out of his throat, and another is turned into a human balloon animal. And even better - they're all practical FX! You would think - especially in this day and age - that a head being expanded, with eyes bulging out and such before exploding would be created almost entirely digitally. But no - a series of fake heads were applied over the actor's, allowing him to keep moving naturally and even talking while we in the audience get to enjoy a terrific, flesh and blood creation."*

Reflection: This was the last traditional movie I watched for HMAD; I had pre-selected *Return to Horror High* as my "swan song" (as it was also the first movie I watched and I wanted to come full circle), so the day before the finale was the last time I'd sit down with something I hadn't seen and force myself to write about it. And it was such a perfect choice, because I watched a lot of bad killer clown movies over the years and was starting to wonder if it was just next to impossible to make a good one, so finally finding a successful entry at the very end was a fine way to wrap things up. The only thing better would have been a good movie set inside a movie theater (besides *Demons*, which I had already seen), but I'll take what I can get.

Funny side note to that – I could have seen this on the big screen, where it would likely even play better... but the screening was on April 1st, 2013 – my first day "off" in six years. For months (once I did the math) I had been drooling over the fact that this exact day would be the first time in over half a decade I could go 24 hours without watching a horror movie, so I had to go against everything I stand for and request a Blu-ray instead. It was hilarious and heartbreaking; I ended I don't know how many reviews with a complaint that horror fans had to stop waiting for home video and support the theatrical releases, and I wrapped things up by not only doing the opposite, but DEMANDING to do it that way! Sigh.

MOVIE #343 – DECEMBER 9th

THE COTTAGE (2008)
Dir: Paul Andrew Williams
HMAD Review Date: May 18, 2008 (DVD)
Genre: Comedic, Survival
Country: UK
Available from Sony Pictures Home Entertainment

Synopsis Based on Fading Memory: A kidnapping goes horribly wrong, and that's *before* the hulking slasher mutant shows up. But it's funny!

Review excerpt:
"It's occasionally pretty suspenseful; the film has the best "guy stupidly puts his head to the door when he knows the killer is on the other side" scene in ages, as Williams has the timing for such a clichéd sequence down perfectly, resulting in not only a jolt but a laugh as well once punchline to the bit is delivered. It should be noted that the killer doesn't make his official appearance until the end of the second act, and those seeking a nonstop gorefest will be disappointed. Structurally speaking, it's more like Hatchet *than a* Friday the 13th *movie.*

Reflection: Some of the movies this month were chosen simply because I didn't exactly have a wealth of options for that country, but that obviously wouldn't be a problem with the UK. I had nearly 100 "British" movies labeled on the site to choose from, and even if I removed all the bad or "too famous" ones I could probably make a month's worth of selections (next book!). So picking the one film to represent the area for this month's theme was difficult, to say the least.

I went with this one mainly because of the tone of the comedy, which I compared to *Severance* in my review (and even noted that it's more consistently funny). For whatever reason, the British really have a knack for this sort of thing (that or I am just easily charmed by it), and I loved seeing it applied to a *Madman*-like slasher/survival plot. Also, Edgar Wright fans should enjoy seeing Reece Shearsmith caught in the thick of the horror stuff, as he tends to show up in Wright's films but doesn't get to be part of the action (he's part of the bizarro group of survivors in *Shaun of the Dead*). Ditto for fans of Andy Serkis, who appears in tons of movies and usually gets replaced by CGI (by design, not because he was so bad) but gets to be the lead as himself here. It was the strength of this film that made me excited to see Williams' follow-up, *Cherry Tree Lane*, but alas that was a largely humor-free, rapey home invasion movie. Dammit, Williams, no! Make more like this!

MOVIE #344 – DECEMBER 10th

BAD BLOOD [COISA RUIM] (2006)
Dir: Tiago Guedes, Frederico Serra
HMAD Review Date: January 21, 2011 (DVD)
Genre: Possession, Religious
Country: Portugal
Available from Tartan Video

Synopsis Based on Fading Memory: A family moves into a big ol' creepy house and creepy things start happening.

Review excerpt:
"The performances across the board were great, and the characters came across as very real. I particularly liked when the mother looked over the older son's shoulder as he did his schoolwork, and he pointed out her feigning interest despite not understanding what it was - reminded me of my own mom, watching some god-awful horror movie with me and somehow managing to not yell "Why do you WATCH this crap?" And there's a lot of debate about superstition and faith, which I always enjoy as I myself struggle with these concepts from time to time, and it's certainly more interesting than the usual conversations I hear in horror films (which tend to be about the sexual history of its characters, or lack thereof, and/or the extent one wishes to "party")."

Reflection: I never felt surer about my need to "retire" than the night in 2012 that I watched about a half hour of this movie before realizing I had already seen it in 2011 (to be fair, I think it had a different title that second time – IMDb lists it under *Blood Curse*). It wasn't until I got to that homework scene mentioned above that I realized it wasn't just an "oh, another movie like THIS" feeling that I got from any number of slashers and found footage asylum movies. Luckily/hilariously, I started my review by saying that it was the sort of movie I enjoyed watching more or less (the ending isn't great, fair warning) but had trouble remembering much about it when it came time to write down my thoughts. So it's not like I completely forgot that I had already seen something I really loved (or hated); it was a movie that I had trouble remembering the day I saw it!

So why is it being recommended? Well A. it does have good stuff, particularly if you, like me, enjoy a good debate re: superstition vs. faith, and it's admirably more dramatic than most supernatural horror films of the past decade (plus, as mentioned above, the character work and actors' performances are solid). And

B. Portugal has a pretty lousy track record for films in general, and they barely ever make any horror at all, which I know because the one comment on the review is from a Portuguese reader who assured me as much. This film won Best Picture at their Golden Globes, in fact, which would be like your average Blumhouse movie winning the award here. Hopefully if you go in knowing that the ending fizzles you'll walk away even more satisfied than I was.

MOVIE #345 – DECEMBER 11th

APARTMENT 1303 (2007)
Dir: Ataru Oikawa
HMAD Review Date: July 27, 2009 (DVD)
Genre: Supernatural
Country: Japan
Available from Kino Lorber Films

Synopsis Based on Fading Memory: A woman with some family issues moves into a haunted apartment.

Review excerpt:
"...even though we're once again dealing with vengeful ghosts in an Asian horror movie, the actual story is a bit unique. Seems this pair of spirits is of a mother and daughter who had the least healthy relationship this side of Joan Crawford, which draws a parallel to our heroine, who has her own mother issues (exacerbated by the seeming suicide of her sister) to deal with. Unlike many of its peers, Apartment 1303 actually takes time to develop its characters, which made it easier to forgive the familiarity of the horror scenes. And Noriko Nakagoshi is terrific in the lead; there's a scene where she watches a home movie of her sister and begins wailing (good score here too) that's really sad to watch - both in a "oh that's sad that she misses her sister" way as well as a "Wow, I think this is the first time I've seen a character show an emotion besides fear in one of these movies" way."

Reflection: Heh, my review of this one starts off with my surprise that it hasn't been remade, and almost exactly four years later I found myself in a theater watching the US produced *Apartment 1303 3D*, which was also one of the worst movies I saw all year. It had more or less the same story, and Rebecca DeMornay as the mother (yay!), but man, it was a total snooze, lacking this version's rather nutty finale (not to mention stronger characters, better direction, etc.). Not that many of the remakes ever manage to live up to the original, let alone top them (the superficially similar *The Echo* is one exception), but rarely has the quality level dropped so far. And I have no idea why it was in 3D. Moral of the story: sometimes I can say "Watch *The Ring*", for instance, and you'll be fine with either version, but when it comes to *Apartment 1303*, for the love of all that is good, PLEASE make sure you're watching the Japanese original. I will come to your house and read the subtitles for you if I have to.

You might think that, like with Britain, I had a wealth of Japanese films to choose from, but that wasn't the case at all. In addition to using up a lot of good ones in

January's Asian horror theme, I tended to like Korean, Thai, Chinese, etc. films more than Japanese. I could never quite put my finger on what it was, but with those I just felt myself less engaged than the others, even when the plots were similar. Part of it might be the frequently limited character development mentioned above, but I love me some slashers and I couldn't tell you one thing about anyone in *Friday the 13th Part V* (well, Ethel makes a disgusting stew, I guess), so there must be more to it than that. Tweet me your theories!

MOVIE #346 – DECEMBER 12th

ANTIBODIES (2005)
Dir: Christian Alvart
HMAD Review Date: July 9, 2008 (DVD)
Genre: Serial Killer
Country: Germany
Available from Dark Sky Films

Synopsis Based on Fading Memory: A cop is tracking a serial killer, and it gets to his head a bit too much.

Review excerpt:
"...it's not exactly a "get drunk with buddies" movie, but it's still pretty good and worth sticking with. Some of the subplots are never really explained (why is the cop furiously cleaning a piece of valuable evidence? Why does he type up his reports outside?) but the performances, truly sick killer, and above average direction by Alvart more than make up for it. And at least it doesn't have a scene where the cop is accused of "getting too close!", so there's something."

Reflection: I don't have the stats in front of me, but I can vouch that more than a few filmmakers read my reviews of their films, which is always a scary endeavor. Say something nice, and people think you're biased because you suspected the director would read it. Say something bad, and the more thin-skinned among them will threaten to punch you or something. But I'm pretty sure that *Antibodies* director Christian Alvart is the only one to comment not only that he didn't think the film was a horror movie (and it's not, traditionally, but it *is* about a serial killer and has some *Seven/Silence of the Lambs*-y qualities, so I think it counts), but that I had the name of the movie spelled wrong! I had made a typo, and so for several months (the review went up in July, his comment was in October) I had the movie listed as *"Anitbodies"*. Typos mortify me more than anything, so to get caught on one by the film's own director was particularly upsetting to me. Luckily I had some nice things to say about the movie or I'd feel even worse. If it was a negative review he could be like "Who are you to judge my film when you can't even spell its title properly?"

I haven't researched it much, but I wouldn't be surprised if the movie had new box art that featured Norman Reedus, who appears in the film very briefly (basically only the opening sequence). Since *Walking Dead* he's become a big get for genre films (or non-genre ones; his was pretty much the only cameo in *Vacation (2015)* that wasn't shown in the trailer, and his appearance was treated like a reveal), so I'm sure a distributor would want to capitalize on his presence. Don't be swayed! He's only in it for about two minutes! And it's still good even when he exits!

MOVIE #347 – DECEMBER 13th

HELL'S GROUND [ZIBAHKHANA] (2007)
Dir: Omar Khan
HMAD Review Date: September 12, 2008 (DVD)
Genre: Slasher, Zombie
Country: Pakistan
Available from TLA Releasing

Synopsis Based on Fading Memory: A group of teens en route to a concert run afoul of... everything?

Review excerpt:
"At 75 minutes it hardly wears out its welcome, and while the pace is a bit slow at first, once it gets going it's pretty fun. The slasher has a great and unique look, and I can't recall the last slasher to use a mace as his weapon of choice. Also, one of our main characters is like the Pakistan version of me. He wakes up and has like ten DVDs around him. He looks at one as if he had no idea that it was in his possession, then watches about thirty seconds of it before laughing to himself and going outside. I myself have been surprised to discover films in my own collection, so this little bit made me smile. The actors are all pretty good too, despite the fact that none of them seemingly have any film experience (this film is the only credit on the IMDb for just about everyone in the cast). And last but not least, the gore/makeup is pretty impressive as well."

Reflection: This was the first gore film to be made in Pakistan, and as far as I can tell it's also the last. It's certainly the only one for director Khan; he has this and this alone on his IMDb which, after eight years, is depressing. His enthusiasm for the genre, not to mention resolve to make a film in a country that wasn't exactly welcoming to productions within this genre, makes me think he should have had an even better follow-up by now.

Now, I'll be honest - this is not a great movie. It's fine, but you likely won't walk away ready to declare Khan the next John Carpenter. But there's something kind of fascinating about seeing so many different sub-genres (directly inspired by classic American horror films) crammed into one narrative. In my review I compared it to *Doomsday*, where Neil Marshall was clearly just having a lot of fun (on Universal's dime) paying homage to his favorite movies, but they were all more or less post-apocalyptic ones: *Escape from New York*, *Road Warrior*, etc. Khan, on the other hand throws in homages to *Halloween* (slashers), *Mother's Day* (survival horror), *Dawn of the Dead* (zombie) and more, making it feel slightly schizophrenic at times, but as HMAD-time would go on, I'd develop more appreciation for this sort of thing. I watched so many horror movies where it seemed like the filmmakers hated the genre, or at least thought they were above it, so looking back, I realize how much more preferable it is to see a film that might lack originality, but positively oozes appreciation for the genre I, too, love so much. Here's hoping Khan makes another movie someday where we can see a little more of what he can personally add to the mix.

MOVIE #348 – DECEMBER 14th

EMBODIMENT OF EVIL (2008)
Dir: José Mojica Marins
HMAD Review Date: January 31, 2009 (DVD)
Genre: Psychological, Weird
Country: Brazil
Available from Synapse Films

Synopsis Based on Fading Memory: Coffin Joe is let out of prison and instantly resumes his quest to produce a worthy male heir.

Review excerpt:
"The movie is so gonzo (and gory!) that you might not even really notice that the script falters from time to time. Joe's re-introduction to the world is handled well (and hilariously - he is hit by a car the second he walks out of the prison), and he certainly hasn't lost his ability to cause chaos in his old age. He even gets into an epic sword fight with a monk, and has vigorous sex with a woman on the floor, as the blood from her aunts (whom he had just killed and hung from the ceiling) rains down over them. And the ending sets up a 4th film that could very well be the best movie ever made."

Reflection: Hopefully you took my advice earlier in this book and watched the previous Coffin Joe movie (*This Night I Will Possess Your Corpse*; from the May chapter), because even though this came along over forty years later, it actually counts as a direct follow-up, with Joe (aka Zé) being haunted by the ghosts of his victims from the first two movies. In this era, where five years is deemed long enough between *Spider-Man* sequels to reboot the whole thing from scratch, I love that Marins didn't seem to think forty years was enough time to even warrant a recap.

I also hope you've seen at least one of the others so you can have a better idea of what you're in for. It's got some pretty vile moments (including one involving a woman's privates, melted cheese, and a rat – you figure it out), but the blow will be softened if you've already gotten accustomed to Zé's peculiar MO and attitude toward women (not a flattering one). Then again, thanks to the color and increased production value this is actually the most accessible of the trio, so if you are a virgin to this series, or weren't enamored by the other(s), I urge you to give it a look anyway. Wikipedia can fill you in if you want a primer.

MOVIE #349 – DECEMBER 15th

CROCODILE (1981)
Dir: Sompote Sands
HMAD Review Date: June 10, 2008 (Revival screening)
Genre: Monster
Country: Thailand
Available from VCI Entertainment

Synopsis Based on Fading Memory: Some guys seek revenge on a giant crocodile that (very confusingly) killed their families.

Review excerpt:
"The film's alleged hero gets drawn into the plot when his family is presumably killed by the crocodile, but we don't really see this. Without any sort of setup, his sister goes into the water and sees his kid's floating tube, but no kid. She screams and then mimes being pulled under the water, at which point the guy's wife runs into the water and the entire process repeats again. During this entire sequence we are never even given the usual shot of the crocodile's eye blinking, which is often used in place of any actual onscreen violence. It's sort of like the opening scene of Jaws, except without even an underwater POV shot to help us out. Anyway, they're all dead, and thus he does what any man would in that situation: reads some newspapers, looks at a map he drew himself, conducts some sort of experiment that involves brightly colored fluids being mixed together, and finally assembles a team that includes his buddy and a Quint wannabe with a penchant for taking off his shirt, and heads out to the open sea to exact revenge. They are inexplicably joined by a guy who just climbs on their boat and begins taking photos, and before long the croc is carrying out a personal vendetta against them."

Reflection: I saw this in 2008, which is pretty early in the run, but I'm still going to go ahead and claim that this was the most bafflingly edited film I watched out of the 2500. Apparently it was re-cut from an earlier film called *Agowa gongpo* (or *Crocodile Fangs*), but I don't know if they made it worse or better as a result. I hope to never know. It's beautiful as is. I may have put it in the "bad movie" slot for the month, but only because I'm being technical about "bad movie". In actuality, this is probably the first one I'd want to re-watch out of the bunch.

But also I wanted to include it because I saw so few Asian monster movies over the years. *The Host* was one of the first movies I watched for the site, and then this was one of, I think, three others. I'm not counting *Godzilla* types because that's kind of its own thing (and more kid-friendly, on the average), but I can't help but wonder if the shadow that G-man cast over the sub-genre was deemed inescapable? Still, that should only be the case for Japan – the Koreans, Thai, etc. should have been delivering a lot more often than they did. Hell, they couldn't even get the *Host* sequel off the ground (yet), let alone use its success to mount many other original properties.

MOVIE #350 – DECEMBER 16th

SL8 N8 (aka SLAUGHTER NIGHT) (2006)
Dir: Frank van Geloven, Edwin Visser
HMAD Review Date: July 25, 2007 (DVD)
Genre: Slasher
Country: Belgium
Available from Kino Lorber films

Synopsis Based on Fading Memory: A young woman (and her pals, of course) travel into a mine so she can investigate something her father was researching before he died… and a killer shows up.

Review excerpt:
"All I ask of any modern slasher movie, Dutch or not, is that one character I thought would live gets killed, that the gore is sufficient, and that the lead girl is someone who I would totally love to run around in the dark with. SL8 N8 delivers on all fronts, and then some. Also I learned that "Christ!" in Dutch is "Jesus!" So there, another bonus."

Reflection: Blockbuster (RIP) had this thing where you could keep a movie you rented for a pre-determined fee that was listed on the rental receipt (instead of paying a late fee they'd charge your card on file and you'd just own it – sometimes the price was less than a rental anyway), and I only took advantage of it a couple times. One was *Marebito*, which I recommended in the January chapter, and the other was this, a solid attempt at blending supernatural/ghost stuff with a traditional slasher (one written by people who were clearly fans of the original *My Bloody Valentine*). Well, technically I did that a third time for *The Fog* remake, because it fell between the couch cushions and was forgotten, but when I realized what happened I took it back. It was too late for a refund of whatever I inadvertently paid for it, but I hated that movie so much I didn't even care, I just wanted it out of my house. So I just left it there on the counter. Wonder what they did with it.

Interestingly, this movie was at one time put out by Tartan, who usually stuck to Asian horror – it's a shame they went under, because if they were broadening their horizons to European countries, I bet they could have supplied a lot of quality HMAD entries over the years. I certainly could have used more Euro horror (specifically French, Dutch, etc. – not so much Italian and British) over the years, especially films like this that were kind of obscure. I mean, 90% of the French horror movies I watched, I had already heard about (positively) from other sources – I would have loved to have seen more films that I knew nothing about going into them. Especially if they turned out to be cool-ass *My Bloody Valentine* homages like this.

MOVIE #351 – DECEMBER 17th

AB-NORMAL BEAUTY [SEI MONG SE JUN] (2004)
Dir: Oxide Pang Chun
HMAD Review Date: September 18, 2012 (Streaming)
Genre: Psychological
Country: Hong Kong
Available from Tartan Video

Synopsis Based on Fading Memory: A girl accidentally takes a picture of someone's death, and becomes obsessed with death in art.

Review excerpt:
"...it's basically a stylish and grim drama for the first hour, something that's more or less in line with Shame *or some drug addict movie except her vice is death (and art, I guess). And not a bad one, either - Race Wong is quite good, taxed with a far more demanding role than 95% of Asian horror movies would ever require. Her real life sister Rosanne Wong is also good as her best (only) friend, who wears her kid gloves around her and does her best to keep her from going off the deep end. There's a wonderfully sad scene late in the film where she helps shower Race after one of her paint freakouts, and then helps her destroy some of her disturbing photos/art - I wish I had a friend who would help me through such a catharsis!"*

Reflection: The Pang brothers fascinate me; they've made some terrific films (*The Eye 2, Re-Cycle*), and also some dreadfully bad nonsense (their remake of *Bangkok Dangerous* – Nic Cage's worst film perhaps, and I say this as one of his constant apologists). *Ab-Normal Beauty* is closer to the terrific side; the pacing is a bit off and the final moment is botched to an almost laughable degree, but otherwise it's a surprisingly solid dramatic take on horror material (don't worry, it's an actual horror movie). As I mentioned more than once in the Asian horror chapter, these movies aren't exactly known for rich characters or strong dramatic cores, as their trend is almost always to simply scare you a lot while telling a confusing story. This film is pretty straightforward and even moving at times, which was a fine surprise.

I still need to see its sister film (*Leave Me Alone*, directed by Danny Pang – the two films are linked by a car accident); it's a full-on drama but I love the idea of two movies with different genres sharing a universe. I mean, shared universes in movies in general is a cool idea if done right (Marvel is starting to slip now, as there now always has to be a scene where the plot stops so characters can explain why Natalie Portman or someone isn't around), but they're likely always to be centered on one genre: horror films, superhero movies, etc. I'd love to see one where the characters are the only connection, spread around multiple genres. But until then, we just have this!

MOVIE #352 – DECEMBER 18th

DEAD IN 3 DAYS (2006)
Dir: Andreas Prochaska
HMAD Review Date: October 13, 2007 (Festival screening)
Genre: Slasher
Country: Austria
Available from Dimension Extreme

Synopsis Based on Fading Memory: Shortly after high school graduation, a group of teens start getting text messages saying "Dead in 3 Days", and sure enough they're killed three days later.

Review excerpt:
"The cool thing about this one was how much they played with the pace/expectations of a teen slasher. The obvious Final Girl is nearly killed a half hour in, and the requisite red herring loner character IS killed shortly thereafter, when you would assume that he would turn out to be not so bad and eventually be the Final Girl's best friend, or just get killed at the end in a (non) surprise twist."

Reflection: It's not as bad as mixing up New Zealand and Australia (which I've done more than once), but I referred to this movie as a German film in my review, when it is in fact Austrian. However, they share a border and German is Austria's official language, so I think we can let that one slide. But either way, one of the many benefits of HMAD-ing (note that this is a first year review) is that after a few years I started being able to easily spot such differences. I don't even mix up Australia and New Zealand anymore!

There's a sequel to this enjoyable slasher flick, but I recently gave the original another look and decided I don't think it needs one. Since the plot is similar to *I Know What You Did Last Summer* (sometimes to its own detriment), I don't need to see the Austrian version of "Will Benson" anytime soon. Plus the follow-up never got released in the US anyway, so I'd have to put effort into checking it out. One of the many benefits of quitting HMAD is that I'd no longer have to go out of my way to see something I wasn't particularly excited about watching, and/or that involved overseas shipping charges. Besides, the number of slasher sequels that even come close to living up to their originals is a pretty short list, so I think it's fair to assume that until it pops up on Netflix and I have nothing better to do, I'll think of this as a solid one-and-done slasher film.

MOVIE #353 – DECEMBER 19th

ROMASANTA (aka WEREWOLF HUNTER) (2004)
Dir: Paco Plaza
HMAD Review Date: May 10, 2011 (Streaming)
Genre: Werewolf
Country: Spain
Available from Lionsgate

Synopsis Based on Fading Memory: A man believes he is turning into a werewolf, and tries to pin his serial killing ways on that.

Review excerpt:
"Don't expect too much werewolf action, because it's a faithful retelling of a true story and thus that means a lack of humans turning into hairy beasts under a full moon. The brief glimpses of a wolf type creature are psychological in nature; our guy THINKS he's turning into a werewolf, and thus is treated (and sentenced) as a man with a mental disorder. It's almost kind of a shame too, because the transformation scene is actually pretty awesome, relying on practical work instead of CG and doing this interesting thing with changing the pigment of his skin – it resembles watercolor paint spilling over his body (kind of hard to explain, so just watch it! It's a good movie!)."

Reflection: I saw this as *Werewolf Hunter*, but the actual title of this movie is *Romasanta*, and for the life of me I couldn't remember it when it came up at horror trivia one time. So I answered *Werewolf Hunter*, assuming host Ryan Turek would accept it, but no, he played the "that's only the US title, it's called *Romasanta* everywhere else", which I can't even argue with much since I said the same thing in my review. It ticked me off something fierce though, because I was one of the only people in the room who actually saw the damn movie! I should have gotten points just for that!

Anyway, if you've seen *Brotherhood of the Wolf* you should enjoy this flick, as it tackles similar territory (a monster mixed with political treachery). Plus, the "based on a true story" claim isn't marketing BS – it really is based on an actual event, and a fairly interesting one. You can read up on it before you see the movie, though it might be "spoiling" something that's kind of a twist in the narrative. Of course, real life should never be considered a "spoiler" (i.e. "SPOILER for *Straight Outta Compton*: Eazy-E dies"), but given the fact that the real events occurred 200 years ago and in a different country than most of the people I'm addressing right now, the ignorance of real-life events can be forgiven.

MOVIE #354 – DECEMBER 20th

BLACK SHEEP (2006)
Dir: Jonathan King
HMAD Review Date: June 14, 2007 (Theatrical)
Genre: Comedic, Monster
Country: New Zealand
Available from Dimension Extreme

Synopsis Based on Fading Memory: Weresheep!

Review excerpt:
"While it doesn't really work as a remake of the Chris Farley movie, I really dug it. The main plot (i.e. sheep running around killing folks) begins almost immediately, after some quick setup and back-story, which is nice. Writer/Director Jonathan King knows that people are there to watch carnage, so the necessary background information is given swiftly. Our actors, none of whom I recognize, are universally appealing, especially Tucker, played by Tammy Davis (a guy named Tammy?). He reminded me of Desmond from Lost."

Reflection: Like I said a few entries ago, I used to be bad at mixing up New Zealand and Australia, something I sort of made a running gag on HMAD (playing up my ignorance but in exaggerated form, i.e. chalking up Peter Jackson's films to Australia or whatever). But like most "intentionally dumb" comedy on the internet, it didn't translate successfully, so I stopped once I got sick of comments correcting me, assuming I was serious (I even said that my confusion was due to the countries sharing a border, a joke any kid in a middle school geography class could get, but even that didn't work). In hindsight, it wasn't really the best joke, since it required reading every review to realize it was a running gag, so I apologize for it now.

Anyway, New Zealand has seen its fair share of Peter Jackson imitators over the past 10 years or so, and most are grating to me (as are actual Peter Jackson films these days), but this one really worked. King has made two films since, but neither of them are horror, so I hope he gets the itch to return to it someday – if he nailed that tricky balance between comedy and horror so well on his first time out, I can't imagine how great a follow-up would be. I mean, Christ, he pulled off WERE-SHEEP – he can do anything. This was one of the first releases for the late, lamented Dimension Extreme label, and one of the only good films they released in early days since that brand had a very rocky start (which also gave us *Broken*, one of the absolute worst films I watched for the site, and the largely terrible *Welcome to the Jungle*). Ultimately they got more selective and turned into a pretty dependable source for quality indie and foreign fare, but like all these specialty brands, it died. RIP, Dimension Extreme.

MOVIE #355 – DECEMBER 21st

HERE COMES THE DEVIL (2012)
Dir: Adrián García Bogliano
HMAD Review Date: November 5, 2012 (Festival screening)
Genre: Supernatural
Country: Mexico
Available from Magnolia Home Entertainment

Synopsis Based on Fading Memory: Some kids disappear, only to come back... slightly off.

Review excerpt:
"If you're the type that likes everything explained, you should skip this one, as Bogliano doesn't seem interested in over-explaining his plot points or filling in every blank. And to be honest, I myself tend to get frustrated with such films, but what makes this work where his similarly obtuse Penumbra *did not is that it gave me someone to care about in the lead role. Laura Caro, a singer making her feature debut, is terrific as the mother, torn between her love for her children and her fear for her own life. With each new piece of information learned, she becomes less a mother trying to avenge her children and more of a plain ol' human being trying to protect her own skin. It's a nicely paced reversal, and kudos to Caro for pulling off something that even a seasoned actress might have trouble pulling off."*

Reflection: Mr. Bogliano works more frequently than Woody Allen – this was his tenth feature in eight years. Since I didn't like the other two I saw (*Penumbra* and *Cold Sweat*), I still haven't gotten around to watching any of the others from that impressive output (some aren't available in the US, so it's not entirely my laziness to blame), but I will soon. I actually liked his newest film, *Late Phases*, even more than this one, so now I know this wasn't a fluke – he's on to something, and I really want to check out where he came from before he becomes even more well-known.

Because even if those other films leave me as cold as *Penumbra* (*Cold Sweat* is okay, just not something I'd want to watch over and over), it'll be worth my time to see this intriguing (and rather unique) talent find his voice. Like Ti West, his films demand patience, but I found the payoff here (and *Late Phases*, though that one was his English debut and had someone else writing, so it's sort of a rogue Bogliano film) to be worth the wait, which isn't always the case with West. And it legit got under my skin, which isn't something most modern horror films can ever manage. In short, this is one of the most must-see movies in this chapter.

MOVIE #356 – DECEMBER 22ⁿᵈ

CONTAMINATION .7 (1993)
Dir: Joe D'Amato, Fabrizio Laurenti
HMAD Review Date: March 30, 2011 (Streaming)
Genre: Monster
Country: Italy
Available from Scream Factory

Synopsis Based on Fading Memory: Nuclear waste dump causes the local trees to take revenge, using whatever means (read: crappy miniature effects) necessary!

Review excerpt:
"...it's a fairly bloodless movie. The plants (depicted primarily with tentacle-ish branches) just sort of drag and/or suffocate people, instead of beating them to death or tearing them apart. At one point, the greedy power plant owner (his dumping of nuclear waste is what caused the killer plants) shoots himself, but it's off-screen entirely and we don't even see his body lying on the floor. Speaking of this scene, it's another hilarious bit – he takes a good ten seconds to do it but no one makes even the slightest attempt to stop him or even yell "No!" Yet, this is the only Troll *movie that has an R rating – seems they should have just trimmed out the profanity and got themselves the same PG-13 the last one had."*

Reflection: I don't ironically worship at the altar of "worst movie of all time" candidate *Troll 2* like a lot of horror fans – as was often the case for such fare that I watched during HMAD's run, it wasn't even the worst movie I had seen that week (for the record, I saw the woeful ghost/slasher crapfest *Dark Reel* a few days before I finally took a trip to Nilbog). I found myself far more endeared by the documentary about its cult, Michael Stephenson's *Best Worst Movie*, as well as this, which is occasionally listed as *Troll 3* in some territories (it's also called *Creepers*, and it's listed on the IMDb as *The Crawlers*, for good measure). As with *Troll 2*, there's no rhyme or reason for the title, as there are no trolls here – just killer trees. Some of the locations look the same, but otherwise I have no idea why anyone would slap the title on THIS movie in particular.

But if the implied connection got a few more people to watch *Contamination*, then I guess no harm no foul. It's a laughably silly movie (the bad model work alone had me howling) and thus should be in the December 23rd "guilty pleasure" slot, but I put it a day early due to the surprise ending offered here, since it makes for a nice segue into tomorrow's movie. And it's shown up on a couple of budget packs, so you might already have it in your collection if you bought one of those for a title suggested earlier in the book.

MOVIE #357 – DECEMBER 23rd

RARE EXPORTS: A CHRISTMAS TALE (2010)
Dir: Jalmari Helander
HMAD Review Date: December 24, 2010 (Theatrical)
Genre: Monster
Country: Finland
Available from Oscilloscope Laboratories

Synopsis Based on Fading Memory: A kid and his hunter dad discover several dead reindeer on their property and set off trying to catch the culprit... Santa Claus?

Review excerpt:
"Its first hour works best, as it unfolds sort of like Jurassic Park *or something, with some guys digging up SOMETHING and we are treated to a lot of shots of "people looking" and others that slowly track in on seemingly innocuous objects. Then our heroes find a field full of slaughtered reindeer, which is quite disturbing (think the buffalo scene from* Dances With Wolves, *only with, like, Donner and Blitzen). And then the children of the town start disappearing, with only these creepy little wicker dolls left behind. Then, the Tom Jane-esque co-hero (his son is our main character) traps an old man in a wolf trap, one who says nothing, is naked, and has a penchant for gingerbread cookies. And he has a big white beard..."*

Reflection: I like this one more every time I see it. I still wish there was a little more giant ___ action (spoiler, but you'll know what I mean once you see the movie, and probably agree), but it's just so charming and weird that I've grown to forgive it. Plus it's a worthy successor to *Gremlins* in many respects, as it cherishes and bastardizes the holiday (sometimes simultaneously), and adds a layer of WTF to what seems like a G-rated yuletide romp – something tomorrow's selection can never be mistaken for, not even for a second.

Speaking of which, this is one of three Christmas movies in a row, so I hope you don't hate the holiday if you're following this book to the letter. Or prefer to limit how many Christmas movies you watch over a few days, since I'm sure you're watching your own non-horror favorites like *Home Alone* or *Christmas Vacation*, too. I didn't really plan it, it just happens that I had two ideal movies for today's and tomorrow's countries and they both happened to be set on Christmas. And then for December 25th itself... well, you'll see. At any rate, I hope you're not so burned out on seeing Christmas on-screen that it ruins your annual *Die Hard* screening. I'd feel awful.

P.S. The movie is based on a short film that's worth tracking down, but watch it after! The feature is kind of a prequel to the short.

MOVIE #358 – DECEMBER 24th

INSIDE [À L'INTÉRIEUR] (2007)
Dir: Alexandre Bustillo, Julien Maury
HMAD Review Date: October 17, 2007 (Festival screening)
Genre: Survival
Country: France
Available from Dimension Extreme

Synopsis Based on Fading Memory: A very pregnant woman is home alone on Christmas Eve... save for the crazed woman that is desperately trying to get (see title).

Review excerpt:
"Right off the bat I knew this one was going to be something memorable – we see the impact of a car accident from inside the womb, and then a truly great visual gag – a broken, bloody, mangled windshield wiper still running after the impact. Creative, horrific visuals mixed with pitch black yet understated humor? Ah, the French! The rest of the film is more or less a cat and mouse game between two women, and with the exception of an occasionally overbearing score, the film is executed as brilliantly and flawlessly as any horror film I have seen in many a moon. Or sun for that matter."

Reflection: If you've read the intro to this book, you'd know about the time I tried making my wife watch this on Christmas Eve instead of something more traditionally Christmas-y. I've since bulked up our supply of Yuletide selections so we don't run into the same issue (if memory serves, at that time all we had was *Christmas Vacation* and *Nightmare Before Christmas*, two movies we've seen way too many times), but a couple years later I began a new tradition of spending all day watching Christmas movies (including things like *Lethal Weapon* where the holiday connection is more superfluous) while building a giant Lego kit. And wouldn't you know it, the first one included *Inside* in its lineup, allowing me to finally finish my second viewing!

Yep, my main reason for picking it that time with my wife was the fact that I hadn't seen it since the original screening at Screamfest, and I wanted to know if it held up. As I've explained more than once in this book, doing HMAD left me with precious little time to re-watch anything unless I had to, so even though I loved the movie it took I think about five years for me to finally give it a complete second look. Luckily, it held up, and if not for *The Descent* I would dub it my favorite horror film of the '00s (which gave us LOTS of competition, if you recall). I love this movie, and Bustillo/Maury earned a lifetime pass on its strength – they could make movies as bad as *Beneath the Mississippi* for the next twenty years and I'd still get excited about their every project. Now to just get my wife on board so I can watch it every Christmas Eve as I would like to.

Finally, and this is the most important part of the write-up now that I think about it - there's a "rated" cut floating around out there that removes something like seven minutes from the film. For the love of all gods, PLEASE make sure you are seeing the unrated, 82 minute version!

MOVIE #359 – DECEMBER 25th

BLACK XMAS (2006)
Dir: Glen Morgan
HMAD Review Date: December 23, 2007 (DVD)
Genre: Holiday, Slasher
Country: USA
Available from Dimension Films

Synopsis Based on Fading Memory: A group of sorority girls staying behind on Christmas break are picked off one by one by a killer.

Review excerpt:
*"The DVD has some of the usual extras, though I am bummed about the lack of a commentary. It's also unrated, but I can't tell what's different from the theatrical, though I think Michelle Trachtenberg has a slightly different death, but that's about it. I should note that the scenes in the trailer that are missing from the film were in fact only shot for the trailer, without Morgan's knowledge. However, they do break the norm with a piece about, well, Morgan's hatred of the film. While technically a making-of piece, he spends most of the time he's on camera explaining why he hates these types of movies. He also points out that when he makes a movie that he likes (*Willard*), it bombs, so he has to cater to the audience just to get the opportunity to make something he DOES care about in the future. So there ya go, even the director hates the movie. I truly am the only one in its corner."*

Reflection: I was originally going to skip America, but I ran out of countries at thirty. So it was either move the theme to one of the thirty-day months or suck it up and include the good ol' US of A. And yes, it was shot in Canada, but whatever – it's an American production from an American director, so it counts. Plus, I wanted to spend just that much more of my life defending this movie – I've written positive things about it on Bloody Disgusting, Birth.Movies.Death., and (obviously) Horror Movie A Day, not to mention all the social media postings over the past nine years. No, I don't think it's a better film than the original (as some have claimed), but I really don't see what harm this movie causes. It's a gleefully mean-spirited slasher movie that combines the sensibilities of the original *Silent Night, Deadly Night* with the gonzo splatter of the *Final Destination* series, and applies it to a loose retelling of the 1973 film's basic story. It contains just enough of the original's trademark elements (the setting, the phone calls, a unicorn death, etc.) to justify its remake-ness, but spends a fair amount of time carving out its own identity as well. To me, that's exactly what a remake should be; somewhere in between a complete copy (*Psycho*) and something wholly unrelated *(Prom Night)* in terms of its narrative, but also having its own tonal identity, so that we can just enjoy it on a whole different level. You want to be scared and creeped out? Watch the original. You want gory deaths and a sick sense of humor? Go with the remake. Bob Clark gave it his blessing; I don't see why it's so hard for anyone else to do the same.

But I assume at least some of you won't see it my way, and hate this movie with a passion even if you haven't seen it. That's why the excerpt I chose bypasses the regular review part, skipping ahead to my take on the DVD's bonus features, where you learn that one of the opponents of this movie is in fact its own director. So if you're still not convinced, and/or simply don't want to risk part of the holiday on a movie you might hate, I figured I'd let you know that the director apparently is on your side. Merry Christmas! (He's wrong. Watch it!)

MOVIE #360 – DECEMBER 26th

HARPOON: WHALE WATCHING MASSACRE (2009)
Dir: Júlíus Kemp
HMAD Review Date: November 27, 2010 (Blu-ray)
Genre: Survival
Country: Iceland
Available from Image Entertainment

Synopsis Based on Fading Memory: A bunch of folks on a whale-watching tour are targeted by a deranged woman and her sons.

Review excerpt:
"I liked that they kept playing with our expectations. The seeming heroine who sleeps late and has to run through town and then jump on the boat to join the tour – you think she'd be a Ripley-esque asskicker, right? Nope, she becomes a depressed, mumbling loon over the course of the film (think Drusilla on Buffy*). The pretty blond who takes a liking to the alpha male who may ALSO be our final girl turns out to be a royal, hateful bigot; the alpha male turns out to be gay, etc. The only exception is the French asshole guy, who remains an asshole throughout the film. Perhaps there is some Icelandic/French conflict I don't know about."*

Reflection: This was the only Icelandic movie I watched for the site, so luckily it was a pretty good one. The kills aren't very memorable, but there's something just kind of off about the movie that I found very enjoyable, and like this month's earlier entry *Night Drive* (from North Africa), *Harpoon* gets a leg up by having the central group be a collection of strangers instead of the usual group of pals who seem to hate each other. This makes it harder to peg who lives and who dies, which is a godsend when those kills are underwhelming.

The movie was marketed around the presence of the late Gunnar Hansen, who is only in it for a few minutes, but if that's what it took to get more eyeballs on this odd little movie (it's the only one that I ever referred to as both "quirky" and "grim"), so be it. Normally I dislike this practice, but I can't really blame them for wanting to flaunt his appearance, as unlike many of his peers, Hansen doesn't take on too many movie roles. In fact for twenty years after *Texas Chain Saw* he only appeared in three other movies, so he didn't just do anything that meets his fee. He worked more frequently in the last five or six years of his life, but still nowhere near as often as, say, Tony Todd, who has as many credits in the past three years as Hansen has acquired in the past forty. As a result, I'm much more likely to be interested when I see Hansen in something than Todd; even if the latter man is probably a better actor, he has far too much crap on his résumé to have any faith that his presence signals a worthwhile endeavor. Be more selective, horror movie villain actors!

MOVIE #361 – DECEMBER 27th

RAAZ 3 (2012)
Dir: Vikram Bhatt
HMAD Review Date: September 8, 2012 (Theatrical)
Genre: Supernatural
Country: India
Available from Fox Star Studios

Synopsis Based on Fading Memory: Two actresses battle for dominance using supernatural means. And songs!

Review excerpt:
"...the movie is pretty fun, though the length is a major hurdle since the plot isn't very complicated and there aren't a whole lot of horror scenes, either. Basically one actress is getting older and jealous of a rising star, so she has her boyfriend (the director) cast the newcomer in his next movie so he can be close enough to put some slow-acting curse potion into her water or tea. He has to administer a dose each day for some reason, and the horror elements mostly stem from the moments where the poison takes effect, with the best being one of the first. A PA tells her she has to go to set #3, and then we see set #8, as the left side of the "8" disappears to make a "3". So she walks in there, and of course no one is around... except for a demonic killer clown! This Pennywise wannabe chases her around for a while, until she gets out, after which the clown never appears again."

Reflection: I was and still am a little disappointed that my first (and, so far, last) Bollywood horror movie only had a couple of musical numbers. For years I heard about these movies, and how they'd break into large musical/dance numbers with little instigation, so I was pretty excited to finally see one for myself. I even broke my rule about seeing sequels without having seen the originals, though I was assured beforehand that it wouldn't matter much as far as the storytelling went. But alas, there were only a handful of songs, with no dancing at all, really.

However, what it lacked in fancy footwork it made up for in really goofy but entertaining scare scenes, and at 150 minutes it was also one of the longest movies I watched for the site. I made no secret of the fact that I'd go out of my way to find movies in the 75 minute range (60 is the minimum for something to be considered a feature, but when I saw movies *that* short I felt like I was cheating), especially as the site neared its end, as my ever-shrinking amount of time to devote to the site was part of the reason for calling it a day. But when time allowed, I actually loved finding something long – it would obviously (or, at least, likely) devote time to character development and give it some weight, two things horror could always use more of, especially nowadays. Let's put it this way – of the horror films that are over two hours, the odds of them being good are a lot better than among the ones that are 70 or fewer minutes.

HMAD Fun Fact: At six hours, The Stand *is the longest movie watched for the site, and yes I watched it all in one day (albeit in two sittings; I took a break at the halfway point). The longest traditional feature was Kwaidan, at 163 minutes. Since I had a rule that it had to be over an hour to count as a movie, four or five films (such as* The Mummy's Tomb *and* Mark of the Vampire*) tie for the shortest at exactly 61 minutes.*

MOVIE #362 – DECEMBER 28th

SPLICE (2010)
Dir: Vincenzo Natali
HMAD Review Date: May 19, 2010 (Theatrical)
Genre: Mad Scientist
Country: Canada
Available from Warner Bros

Synopsis Based on Fading Memory: Two scientists create a new form of life. Bad things happen.

Review excerpt:
"Much of what makes the movie such a delightful surprise is the odd places that the story goes, and I wouldn't want to even hint at them (I was actually admonished on Twitter simply for pointing out that the 3rd act is incredible!). I will say this though - the trailers are doing a very good job at selling the concept of the movie without giving too much away. In fact, I'm pretty sure the entire trailer is comprised only of footage from the film's first act. And while the Twitter guy may feel otherwise, I think it's kind of important to let folks know that the film is much different than they might expect (while not going into details why). Based on the trailers, you might be fooled into thinking that Splice is a Species knockoff, with a monster being created by well-meaning scientists, escaping, and being tracked down by the folks who created her. But that's not what the movie is - it's much more original and interesting than that."

Reflection: Warner did pretty okay with *Orphan* in the summer of 2009, so they gave *Splice* a similar push the following summer, putting a dark horror film in the middle of all the blockbusters. Alas, it didn't work out as well, grossing a mere $17m total (less than *Orphan* did in its first week) on a $30m budget. I haven't talked about box office much in this book, but a figure like that really bums me out. You'd think an Oscar-winning star (Adrien Brody), a non-competitive market for horror films, and a budget many summer films would gross in a single day would result in a successful release, the sort of thing that could help its talented director get another movie off the ground quickly. But no, even with worldwide grosses factored in, this movie tanked.

It was kind of heartbreaking as a horror fan and as a friend to some filmmakers who had trouble getting financing for their own offbeat projects – we all need movies like this to be a success and prove they could sell tickets as easily as the next cookie cutter remake (indeed, the awful *Nightmare on Elm Street* remake –

a film no one on this planet actually likes – was still in theaters when *Splice* was released, earning the last of its $63 million). But when *Paranormal Activity 2* takes less than 24 hours to exceed *Splice's* gross, we end up with dozens of found footage and/or supernatural haunting flicks, and Natali's next film (*Haunters*) barely gets released. Sigh. Luckily, Hollywood's loss was *Hannibal*'s gain – surely if he was making big movies he wouldn't have taken the job directing episodes of that incredible show, and his were often among its best.

MOVIE #363 – DECEMBER 29th

HIDDEN [SKJULT] (2009)
Dir: Pål Øie
HMAD Review Date: June 18, 2010 (DVD)
Genre: Psychological
Country: Norway
Available from Lionsgate

Synopsis Based on Fading Memory: A guy inherits an old house, and then bad things start happening.

Review excerpt:
"Part of why I enjoyed it is that it started out like a generic haunted house movie, with a guy inheriting a big isolated house from an estranged relative. I've seen enough of those, and was about to sigh in defeat when things started happening that didn't jive with that type of movie. For example, he doesn't stay in it. Instead, he goes to a strange hotel nearby, where the walls are all decorated with backlit photos of trees and waterfalls, which offers some incredibly striking production design. And the concierge is a cute Swedish girl who speaks cryptically, giving the thing a bit of a Twin Peaks *vibe as well. And then when two teens sneak into the presumably abandoned house and get stalked by a creepy red-coat wearing slasher... let's say I was no longer feeling so "seen it!", as it was successfully blending elements of different sub-genres to create something unique (and tragic, ultimately)."*

Reflection: It's been five years and counting and I still haven't given this movie a second watch, which I planned to do when I saw it to see if it cleared up any of the mysteries I was left with after my lone viewing. Sometimes a movie will never make more sense the more you see it, but others make total sense with a second view, when seemingly superfluous details that you wouldn't think about much turn out to be the key to solving some of its puzzles. My favorite such example is in *The Usual Suspects*; about halfway through the film we learn that Kevin Pollak's character is the one who stole the truck that they were all questioned about the night they first came together. It's a reveal that doesn't mean a hell of a lot in the grand scheme of things, but it certainly makes your second viewing more fun, because only then will you appreciate that he's the only one lying down in their shared cell (proving true the whole "the guilty guy relaxes" thing). No one watched the scene where Kobayashi outed him as the thief and said "Oh right, he WAS laying down in the cell before!", because it just wouldn't stick out like that.

Now, I doubt *Hidden* is as clever as that movie, but it also seemed like the sort of film that would reveal more on a second watch. Unfortunately, it's been so long that my second viewing will be like watching it for the first time, so I'll have to actually have a THIRD to benefit from it. Luckily, re-watching movies I *like* isn't the worst thing I can do with my time. I had to sit through the *Rosemary's Baby* TV remake twice – that was soul-crushing enough the first time! And three goddamn hours long!

MOVIE #364 – DECEMBER 30th

SAUNA (2008)
Dir: Antti-Jussi Annila
HMAD Review Date: April 16, 2010 (DVD)
Genre: Psychological
Country: Czech Republic
Available from MPI Home Video

Synopsis Based on Fading Memory: A team of mapmakers stumble on a mysterious sauna on the border between Sweden and Russia.

Review excerpt:
"A word of advice to any potential viewers - you might be tempted to ignore the subtitles because it's such a gorgeous film, but do NOT take your eyes off of them for even a single moment. Part of the reason that I had to watch it again is because some of the stuff that WAS explained was a bit confusing to me, such as the fact that the "girl" in a pivotal plot scene early on was left to die by the more violent brother. It's somewhat of a difficult movie to get a handle on already due to certain period concepts not being common knowledge (at least to me - it seems understanding a bit about the war would help at least get a sense of where the characters had gone through), it will be even doubly so if you miss a line or two of crucial dialogue."

Reflection: My only Czech film! Actually it's a Finnish/Czech co-production, but close enough. Besides, I would have found a spot for this movie somewhere else in this book even if I did have a better or solo Czech entry, simply because I want to once again profess my love for the end credits theme music by Timo Hänninen (not Panu Aaltio as originally listed – this movie had a couple of composers I guess). It is one of my favorite bits of film score in the past twenty years, and I let it loop for a solid hour after watching the film. I even ripped the music from the DVD to have an mp3 of it. It didn't come out so good, but it's better than popping the DVD in every time I wanted to listen to it, which is often. Luckily someone put a high quality version on YouTube a few months later, so I didn't have to settle for my crappy copy anymore. Thank you, YouTube user Kanał użytkownika Inaegram! If you're reading this, email me, I'll refund your money for this book as my way of saying thanks.

Oh, the movie's good, too! If you watched *Black Death* (recommended in October) and enjoyed that one, you'll probably find just as much to like here – it shares some of that film's themes and much of its overall look (i.e. it's the very definition of "dreary"). And it has plot points that take a bit of thinking to track (the specific number of people in the village outside the sauna, for example), rather than beat you over the head with them like most movies would. This is part of why I stress paying close attention to the subtitles – there isn't a lot of fat on this one; just about everything is important in some way or other. There aren't a lot of sophisticated horror movies that I really like, so I hope my singling out this title stresses how worthwhile it is (unlike, say, whatever random slasher movies I may have championed, because I'm not exactly discerning when it comes to those).

MOVIE #365 – DECEMBER 31st

MACABRE [DARAH] (2009)
Dir: Kimo Stamboel, Timo Tjahjanto
HMAD Review Date: October 17, 2009 (Festival screening)
Genre: Cannibal
Country: Indonesia
Available from Bloody Disgusting Selects

Synopsis Based on Fading Memory: A group of friends bring a girl to her home and are invited to a feast for their trouble. Then the fun starts.

Review excerpt:
"I enjoyed the mild dark humor, something almost NEVER seen in an Asian horror film (y'all too serious!). They get a lot of mileage out of one guy's decapitated head sliding around the floor, and there's a great sight gag of our heroes, chained up in a room, trying to avoid being covered in blood that is pooling toward the drain (the killer in the next room is tidying up after a kill). And there are a few cops who show up halfway through (this would be one of the few instances where I felt they were padding it a bit prior to the ending) that are oblivious to what is going on, which of course is always a delight to the audience who knows better."

Reflection: Nowadays, thanks to Kickstarter and the like, you often see horror shorts that are made in order to get funding for the feature version (sometimes people even crowd-fund the short as well, which is silly to me – shouldn't I know what your skill is with a short before giving you money for a damn feature?), and 99 times out of 100 that feature never actually gets made. On the other hand, there are a lot of films that were expanded from shorts, but in those cases I usually didn't know about the short until the feature was out (last week's suggestion *Rare Exports* is one such example). But this, I believe, is the first time I saw a feature based on a short (*Dara*) that I previously saw and enjoyed, so it was nice to see that progression sans any bias about being asked to pay for it myself.

I wish I could have had a New Year's-themed Asian movie to recommend today; I wanted to make the book a circular loop, so the usual "last movie of the month ties into the next month's theme" rule still works from December going into January. But if there is an Asian horror movie about New Year's I didn't see it (or couldn't remember it), so I went with this, because it's the rare "fun" Asian horror movie. Most of them are pretty grim or at least humor-free, but this has some terrific black humor and a lot more action than such films usually offer, *and* it's about cannibalism, so I figured it'd be a good film to watch on a day where you might be having people over with some form of (traditional New Year's choice) Asian food on the menu. Bon appetit!

THE END

And that's it! I have nothing else to recommend... for now (if you want another book, I certainly have enough movies to fill up another one!). For those of you who were inexplicably watching every movie for the past year – how do you feel? Pretty worn out, I'd imagine. Now try to picture doing it for six years, without a road map, and with over 2,000 movies that weren't as good as these. NOW do you see why I was so eager to "retire" and find something else to do with my time?

But like I said in the intro, I highly doubt anyone will ever follow this book to the letter for a year, and the bulk of you are just using it as a guide to find some offbeat, obscure, or just plain under-the-radar gems. For those folks, I truly hope it's been helpful in that regard. There's a lot of clutter on the site, and without any sort of grading system in place I realized it'd be tough for a new reader to find those needles in the giant HMAD haystack – this book was the solution.

At any rate, I hope you enjoyed the book however you used it (for this printed version, my dream is that it's by your toilet. Seriously.). It was fun to revisit all those reviews (even when I cringed at the bad writing on the old ones), especially when I'd read my thoughts on a film that I longer feel as strongly (or as ambivalent) about. It's amazing how a few years of perspective – plus a thousand movies or more in between – can make me realize that some movie I originally considered awful wasn't really that bad, or that something that seemed like one of the better movies of the year would fall apart on a second viewing. Hell, it took me so long to finish this goddamn thing that my opinion changed on some of the movies that I was going to include (or had deemed unworthy) by the time I actually got to the point of finalizing their respective chapters.

On that note, thumb through this book again in a few years and see if you've softened on some of the titles you thought I was insane to recommend! It'd be weird if your opinions didn't change on certain films; you'll always love your favorites, but time and maturity can do wonders for your tastes. If you asked me in 1994 which was the better film: *The Crow* or *Pulp Fiction*, guess which one I would have said (hint: I was only fourteen then). Hell, twenty years ago I hated *Halloween III* – now I'm on the film's definitive Blu-ray release singing its praises. That wouldn't happen – and I'd have a giant Stonehenge-sized hole in my genre appreciation – if I didn't give it the benefit of the doubt and a fresh pair of eyes after a few years had passed. So if you hated something in here, I heartily encourage giving it another chance down the road.

Except for *Beneath The Mississippi*. Fuck that movie.

- BC, August 2013- December 2015

INDEX

100 FEET (2008)	165
100 TEARS (2007)	304
666: THE CHILD (2006)	139
A CADAVER CHRISTMAS (2012)	534
A NIGHT TO DISMEMBER (1983)	243
A REAL FRIEND (2006)	208
AB-NORMAL BEAUTY [SEI MONG SE JUN] (2004)	563
ABSENTIA (2011)	341
ALIEN RAIDERS (2008)	356
ALIEN VS. NINJA (2010)	386
ALIVE OR DEAD (2008)	372
ALONE IN THE DARK (1982)	080
ALONE WITH HER (2006)	449
AMER (2009)	084
ANTIBODIES (2005)	557
ANTICHRIST, THE [L'ANTICRISTO] (1974)	229
APARTMENT 1303 (2007)	555
ASSAULT OF THE SASQUATCH (2009)	378
ATM (2012)	465
AWAKENING, THE (2011)	184
BABY BLUES (2008)	133
BABY, THE (1973)	219
BABY'S ROOM (2006)	164
BABYSITTER WANTED (2008)	192
BACKWOODS (2008)	380
BAD BLOOD [COISA RUIM] (2006)	553
BARRENS, THE (2012)	265
BAY, THE (2012)	284
BEDEVILLED (2010)	029
BENEATH THE MISSISSIPPI (2008)	321
BEREAVEMENT (2010)	113
BEYOND DREAM'S DOOR (1989)	340
BIG BAD WOLF (2006)	371
BIKINI GIRLS ON ICE (2009)	354
BITTEN (2008)	435
BLACK DEATH (2010)	446
BLACK HOUSE [GEOMEUN JIP] (2007)	051

INDEX (cont'd)

BLACK SHEEP (2006)	566
BLACK XMAS (2006)	572
BLACULA (1972)	425
BLOOD OF DRACULA'S CASTLE (1969)	434
BLOOD ON SATAN'S CLAW, THE (1971)	134
BLOOD RAGE (1987)	095
BLOODLINES (2007)	335
BLOODY BIRTHDAY (1981)	147
BLOODY MOON (1981)	091
BLOODY REUNION [SEUSEUNG-UI EUNHYE] (2006)	074
BOOGEY MAN, THE (1980)	102
BORN (2007)	227
BOY EATS GIRL (2005)	492
BROKEN, THE (2008)	179
BURIAL GROUND: THE NIGHTS OF TERROR (1981)	523
BURIED (2010)	455
BURNING BRIGHT (2010)	280
BURROWERS, THE (2008)	289
BUTCHER, THE (2007)	054
CAGED [CAPTIFS] (2010)	460
CANNIBAL APOCALYPSE [APOCALYPSE DOMANI] (1980)	493
CAPTAIN KRONOS: VAMPIRE HUNTER (1974)	414
CAR, THE (1977)	270
CARVED [KUCHISAKE-ONNA] (2007)	046
CARVER (2008)	090
CATHY'S CURSE (1977)	121
CAVED IN: PREHISTORIC TERROR (2006)	282
CHAWZ (2009)	043
CHILDREN, THE (1980)	125
CHILDREN, THE (2008)	148
CHILDREN OF THE CORN (2009)	145
CINDERELLA [SIN-DE-REL-LA] (2006)	031
CITADEL (2012)	151
CLINIC, THE (2010)	124
COCKNEYS VS. ZOMBIES (2012)	520
COLD PREY (2006)	079
COLIN (2008)	314

INDEX (cont'd)

COMBAT SHOCK (1984)	303
CONTAMINATION .7 (1993)	568
COTTAGE, THE (2008)	552
CRAVINGS (2006)	438
CRAWL (2011)	451
CRIMSON RIVERS, THE (2000)	456
CROCODILE (1981)	561
DARK FLOORS (2008)	237
DARK SKIES (2013)	188
DAUGHTERS OF DARKNESS (1971)	413
DAY OF THE ANIMALS (1977)	258
DAYBREAKERS (2009)	437
DEAD & BURIED (1981)	495
DEAD IN 3 DAYS (2006)	564
DEAD MEAT (2004)	518
DEAD NEXT DOOR, THE (1989)	328
DEAD SILENCE (2007)	170
DEAD SUSHI [DEDDO SUSHI] (2012)	218
DEADHEADS (2011)	500
DEADLY SPAWN, THE (1983)	332
DEATH TUBE (2010)	034
DEATHDREAM (1974)	498
DESCENT: PART 2, THE (2009)	358
DETENTION (2011)	224
DEVIL TIMES FIVE (1974)	135
DEVIL WITHIN HER, THE (aka SHARON'S BABY) (1975)	157
DEVIL'S ROCK, THE (2011)	193
DIE YOU ZOMBIE BASTARDS! (2005)	299
DOGHOUSE (2009)	529
DON'T GO NEAR THE PARK (1979)	217
DORM [DEK HOR] (2006)	447
DR. JEKYLL'S DUNGEON OF DEATH (1979)	209
DREAD (2009)	471
DREAM HOME [WAI DOR LEI AH YUT HO] (2010)	057
DUMPLINGS [JIAO ZI] (2004)	065
DYING BREED (2008)	496
EARTH DIES SCREAMING, THE (1965)	517

INDEX (cont'd)

ECHO, THE (2008)	191
ECLIPSE, THE (2009)	163
EDDIE THE SLEEPWALKING CANNIBAL (2012)	501
EDEN LAKE (2008)	141
EMBODIMENT OF EVIL (2008)	560
ENTER NOWHERE (2011)	482
ENTRANCE (2011)	312
EPITAPH [GIDAM] (2007)	067
ESCAPE FROM VAMPIRE ISLAND [HIGANJIMA] (2009)	062
EVIL THINGS (2009)	297
EXIT HUMANITY (2011)	533
EXPELLED, THE (2010)	453
EYE 2, THE (2004)	070
EYE SEE YOU (aka D-TOX) (2002)	373
FACE [PEISEU] (2004)	052
FINAL EXAM (1981)	105
FORGET ME NOT (2009)	100
FRANKENFISH (2004)	375
FRAYED (2007)	085
GEORGE'S INTERVENTION (2009)	525
GHOST SON (2007)	137
GNAW (2008)	512
GOBLIN (2010)	374
GOKE, BODY SNATCHER FROM HELL (1968)	055
GRACE (2009)	144
GRAVE MISTAKE (2008)	306
GRAVE OF THE VAMPIRE (1974)	410
GRIMM LOVE (2006)	485
GRIZZLY PARK (2008)	271
GUARD POST [GP506], THE (2008)	071
HABIT (1996)	422
HALLOWED (2005)	336
HARDWARE (1990)	279
HARPOON: WHALE WATCHING MASSACRE (2009)	574
HAUNTING, THE (2009)	189
HELL'S GROUND [ZIBAHKHANA] (2007)	558
HERE COMES THE DEVIL (2012)	567

INDEX (cont'd)

HIDDEN [SKJULT] (2009)	579
HITCHER, THE (2007)	388
HOLLOW (2011)	174
HOME MOVIE (2008)	123
HOME SWEET HOME (1981)	115
HORDE, THE (2009)	499
HORRIBLE (1981)	093
HOUSE [HAUSU] (1977)	239
HOUSE OF THE DEAD II (2005)	353
HOUSE THAT SCREAMED, THE (1969)	106
HUNGER, THE (1983)	427
HYPOTHERMIA (2010)	260
I SAW THE DEVIL (2010)	038
INCREDIBLE MELTING MAN, THE (1977)	370
INFECTION [KANSEN] (2004)	032
INFESTATION (2009)	384
INSANITARIUM (2008)	528
INSIDE [À L'INTÉRIEUR] (2007)	570
ISOLATION (2005)	268
IT'S ALIVE (1974)	138
IT'S ALIVE 2: IT LIVES AGAIN (1978)	152
IT'S MY PARTY AND I'LL DIE IF I WANT TO (2007)	338
JAWS OF SATAN (1981)	257
JOHN DIES AT THE END (2012)	244
JOSHUA (2007)	132
JUAN OF THE DEAD (2011)	548
JULIA'S EYES (2010)	457
JULIE DARLING (1983)	128
JU-REI: THE UNCANNY (2004)	073
KAW (2007)	274
KIDNAPPED [SECUESTRADOS] (2010)	462
KILL HOUSE (2006)	334
KILLER MOVIE (2008)	103
KILLER'S MOON (1978)	230
KILLING SPREE (1987)	301
KNOCK KNOCK (2007)	390
LAKE MUNGO (2008)	167

INDEX (cont'd)

LEGACY, THE (1978)	199
LEMORA: A CHILD'S TALE OF THE SUPERNATURAL (1973)	406
LET SLEEPING CORPSES LIE (1974)	503
LET THE RIGHT ONE IN (2008)	550
LET'S SCARE JESSICA TO DEATH (1971)	424
LIFEFORCE (1985)	408
LIPS OF BLOOD (1975)	402
LITTLE DEATHS (2011)	231
LIVING DEAD GIRL, THE (1982)	429
LO (2009)	343
LOVE AT FIRST BITE (1979)	431
LOVED ONES, THE (2009)	542
MACABRE [DARAH] (2009)	583
MADHOUSE (1981)	108
MAFU CAGE, THE (1978)	222
MANITOU, THE (1978)	207
MANSQUITO (aka MOSQUITOMAN) (2004)	357
MAREBITO (2004)	060
MASK MAKER (2010)	087
MESSIAH OF EVIL (aka DEAD PEOPLE) (1973)	491
MIDNIGHT SON (2011)	400
MOLEMAN OF BELMONT AVENUE, THE (2010)	310
MR. HUSH (2010)	419
MULBERRY ST. (2006)	308
MURDER OBSESSION (1981)	110
MY SOUL TO TAKE (2010)	214
MY SUPER PSYCHO SWEET 16 (2009)	092
NATURE'S GRAVE (2008)	269
NEW DAUGHTER, THE (2009)	256
NIGHT DRIVE (2010)	546
NIGHT EVELYN CAME OUT OF THE GRAVE, THE (1971)	242
NIGHT OF DEATH [LA NUIT DE LA MORT!] (1980)	235
NIGHT OF THE ZOMBIES (1980)	511
NIGHT TRAIN TO TERROR (1985)	225
NIGHT WARNING (1982)	467
NIGHTMARE (1981)	082
NIGHTMARE DETECTIVE [AKUMU TANTEI] (2006)	036

INDEX (cont'd)

NINE DEAD (2010)	469
NINJAS VS. ZOMBIES (2008)	315
NOSFERATU: PHANTOM DER NACHT (1979)	418
OF UNKNOWN ORIGIN (1983)	255
OGROFF: THE MAD MUTILATOR (1983)	211
ONE-EYED MONSTER (2008)	248
ORCA (1977)	288
ORPHAN (2009)	129
OTHER, THE (1972)	158
OTHER HELL, THE (1981)	245
OUTCAST (2010)	197
OUTPOST (2007)	172
P2 (2007)	376
PACT, THE (2012)	180
PELT (2010)	352
PERFECT CREATURE (2006)	421
PETER ROTTENTAIL (2004)	327
PIG HUNT (2008)	291
PIT , THE (1981)	127
PLAGUE, THE (2006)	143
PLAGUE TOWN (2008)	146
PLANET OF THE VAMPIRES (1965)	416
PONTYPOOL (2008)	509
POULTRYGEIST: NIGHT OF THE CHICKEN DEAD (2006)	345
PRESENCE, THE (2010)	176
PSYCHOMANIA (1973)	216
Q: THE WINGED SERPENT (1982)	259
RAAZ 3 (2012)	575
RABIES [KALEVET] (2010)	541
RARE EXPORTS: A CHRISTMAS TALE (2010)	569
RAW FORCE (1982)	474
RAW MEAT (aka DEATH LINE) (1973)	531
RAZORBACK (1984)	278
RE-CYCLE [GWAI WIK] (2006)	035
RED VELVET (2008)	101
REFLECTING SKIN, THE (1990)	439
RESOLUTION (2012)	445

INDEX (cont'd)

RETREAT (2011)	463
RETRIBUTION [SAKEBI] (2006)	047
RETURN, THE (2006)	464
RETURN IN RED (2007)	344
RETURN OF COUNT YORGA (1971)	403
REVENANT, THE (2009)	505
RISE OF THE DEAD (2007)	140
ROADGAMES (1981)	472
ROCK N' ROLL NIGHTMARE (1987)	379
ROGUE (2007)	276
ROMASANTA: THE WEREWOLF HUNT (2004)	565
ROOM OF DEATH [LA CHAMBRE DES MORTS] (2007)	458
ROOT OF EVIL [AKASIA] (2003)	063
ROT: REUNION OF TERROR (2008)	323
RUINS, THE (2008)	261
SADIST, THE (1963)	470
SATAN'S LITTLE HELPER (2004)	221
SAUNA (2008)	581
SCREAMERS: THE HUNTING (2009)	366
SEA BEAST (2008)	364
SECONDS APART (2011)	185
SENTINEL, THE (1977)	234
SEVERANCE (2006)	112
SEVERED: FOREST OF THE DEAD (2005)	526
SHADOW WITHIN, THE (2007)	195
SHADOWS RUN BLACK (1984)	099
SHATTERED LIVES (2009)	109
SHRIEK OF THE MUTILATED (1974)	507
SHUTTER (2004)	059
SHUTTERED ROOM, THE (1967)	187
SIDE SHO (2007)	363
SIGNAL, THE (2007)	320
SILENT SCREAM (2005)	392
SILK [GUI SI] (2006)	040
SL8 N8 (aka SLAUGHTER NIGHT) (2006)	562
SLEDGEHAMMER (1983)	330
SLEEP TIGHT (2011)	483

INDEX (cont'd)

SLEEPER, THE (2012)	337
SLUGS (1988)	283
SOFT FOR DIGGING (2004)	319
SOLITARY (2009)	177
SPECTRE (2006)	194
SPLICE (2010)	242
SPLINTER (2008)	273
STAKE LAND (2010)	412
STITCHES (2012)	551
STOKER (2013)	481
STRANGE CIRCUS [KIMYÔ NA SÂKASU] (2005)	476
STUCK (2007)	475
SUBJECT TWO (2006)	466
SUBSTITUTE, THE (2007)	547
SUBURBAN SASQUATCH (2004)	351
SUCK (2009)	394
SUGAR HILL (1974)	515
SWAMP DEVIL (2008)	266
SWEATSHOP (2009)	317
SWEET INSANITY (2006)	107
TALE OF THE MUMMY (1998)	362
TALL MAN, THE (2012)	479
TENTACLES (1977)	286
TERROR (1978)	213
TERROR CIRCUS (1974)	240
THALE (2012)	272
THAW, THE (2009)	168
THEM [ILS] (2006)	196
THINGS (1989)	205
THIRST [BAKJWI] (2009)	415
THIS NIGHT I WILL POSSESS YOUR CORPSE (1967)	247
THOMPSONS, THE (2012)	404
TIMECRIMES (2007)	478
TO LET (2006)	178
TONY (2009)	325
TORSO (1973)	097
TORTURE CHAMBER OF DR. SADISM, THE (1967)	166

INDEX (cont'd)

TOURIST TRAP (1979)	088
TRILOQUIST (2008)	360
UNINVITED (1988)	262
UNSEEN, THE (1980)	233
URBAN EXPLORER (aka THE DEPRAVED) (2011)	186
URBAN LEGENDS: FINAL CUT (2000)	368
VALENTINE (2001)	098
VAMPIRE CIRCUS (1972)	426
VAMPIRE'S KISS (1989)	432
VAMPIRES' NIGHT ORGY, THE (1974)	433
VAMPYR (1932)	399
VICTIM [PHII KHON PEN], THE (2006)	041
VINYAN (2008)	131
VOICES [DU SARAM-YIDA] (2007)	068
WAKE WOOD (2011)	155
WARLOCK MOON (1973)	522
WASTING AWAY (aka AAH! ZOMBIES!) (2007)	513
WE NEED TO TALK ABOUT KEVIN (2011)	153
WEREWOLF: THE BEAST AMONG US (2012)	365
WHISPER (2007)	142
WHO CAN KILL A CHILD? (1976)	150
WIG [GABAL], THE (2005)	544
WIND CHILL (2007)	181
WITCHFINDER GENERAL (1968)	473
WOLF TOWN (2011)	287
WRECKAGE (2010)	104
WRESTLEMANIAC (aka EL MASCARADO MASSACRE) (2006)	382
X-CROSS (2007)	042
YELLOW WALLPAPER, THE (2012)	182
YETI: CURSE OF THE SNOW DEMON (2008)	264
YOGA [YOGA HAKWON] (2009)	044
ZOMBIE APOCALYPSE (2011)	494
ZOMBIE STRIPPER APOCALYPSE (2010)	049